# 721 Rapid Recipes For Busy Cooks

THE TRADITION of fast food full of "from scratch" flavor continues in this fifth edition of the cookbook based on the recipes from *Quick Cooking* magazine.

This *2003 Quick Cooking Annual Recipes* cookbook includes every fast-to-fix recipe published in *Quick Cooking* during 2002—that's 721 recipes in all—and combines them in one reader-friendly collection. This recipe-packed volume is filled with hundreds of mouth-watering photos so you can see what many of the dishes look like before you prepare them.

Here's what else you'll find inside:

**Chapters That Meet Your Needs.** With 21 chapters that correspond to popular features in Quick Cooking magazine, it's a snap to find a recipe that matches your family's taste and timetable. (See page 3 for a complete list of chapters.)

For example, when your family is eyeing the table and you're eyeing the clock, see the "30 Minutes to Mealtime" chapter for 12 complete meals that go from start to finish in less than half an hour.

Or when you'd prefer a delicious dish made from a mere five ingredients or fewer, check out Pork Chop Casserole, Maple Barbecued Chicken, Saucy Spareribs, Blueberry Pear Cobbler or any of the 39 other tiny-yet-tempting recipes in the "Give Me Five or Fewer" chapter.

**Award-Winning Recipes.** You'll get all the palate-pleasing, quick-to-prepare foods that earned top honors in the six national recipe contests we held last year: Speedy Skillet Suppers, Easy Breakfasts, Quick Microwave Dishes, Tasty in 10 Minutes, Mighty Quick Muffins and Dessert Fixes with Mixes.

**Easy-to-Use Indexes.** To make all 721 recipes easy to find, we've listed them in two indexes. (See page 332.) The general index lists every recipe by category and/or major food ingredient. The alphabetical listing is great for folks who are looking for a specific family favorite. In both indexes, you'll find a bold red checkmark (✓) in front of all recipes that use less fat, sugar or salt and include Nutritional Analysis and Diabetic Exchanges.

**What's on the Menu?** To make meal planning simple, our food editors grouped several recipes from various chapters to create a host of around-the-clock suggested menus. (This time-saving tool appears on page 4.)

Every rapid recipe and helpful hint in this *2003 Quick Cooking Annual Recipes* cookbook was specifically selected with the busy cook in mind. You're sure to enjoy this timeless treasury for years to come...and you'll be able to treat your loved ones to comforting, wholesome home cooking without spending all of your precious time in the kitchen.

# 2003 Quick Cooking Annual Recipes

**Editor:** Faithann Stoner

**Art Director:** Lori Arndt

**Food Editor:** Janaan Cunningham

**Associate Editors:** Heidi Reuter Lloyd, Julie Schnittka, Jean Steiner

**Graphic Art Associates:** Ellen Lloyd, Catherine Fletcher

**Cover Photography:** Dan Roberts, Rob Hagen

**Senior Food Photography Artist:** Stephanie Marchese

**Food Photography Artists:** Julie Ferron, Vicky Marie Moseley

*Taste of Home* Books
©2003 Reiman Media Group, Inc.
5400 S. 60th St., Greendale WI 53129

International Standard Book Number:
0-89821-356-8
International Standard Serial Number:
1522-6603

**PICTURED ON THE COVER:** New Year's Surf 'n' Turf (p. 47), Midnight Mashed Potatoes (p. 47) and No-Bake Chocolate Cheesecake (p. 201).

To order additional copies of this book or any other Reiman Publications books, write: *Taste of Home* Books, P.O. Box 908, Greendale WI 53129; call toll-free 1-800/344-2560 to order with a credit card or visit our Web site at **www.reimanpub.com**.

## *Taste of Home's* QUICK COOKING

**Executive Editor:** Kathy Pohl
**Editor:** Julie Kastello
**Food Editor:** Janaan Cunningham
**Associate Editor:** Mark Hagen
**Art Director:** Brian Sienko
**Associate Food Editor:** Coleen Martin
**Senior Recipe Editor:** Sue A. Jurack
**Copy Editor:** Kristine Krueger
**Test Kitchen Editor:** Karen Johnson
**Test Kitchen Home Economists:** Karen Wright, Julie Herzfeldt, Sue Draheim, Peggy Fleming, Joylyn Jans, Kristin Koepnick, Mark Morgan, Patricia Schmeling, Wendy Stenman
**Test Kitchen Assistants:** Rita Krajcir, Megan Taylor
**Editorial Assistants:** Ursula Maurer, Mary Ann Koebernik
**Food Photographers:** Rob Hagen, Dan Roberts
**Senior Food Photography Artist:** Stephanie Marchese
**Food Photography Artist:** Julie Ferron
**Photo Studio Manager:** Anne Schimmel
**Graphic Art Associates:** Ellen Lloyd, Catherine Fletcher
**Chairman and Founder:** Roy Reiman
**President:** Tom Curl

# ⏱ Contents

**What's on the Menu?** .....................4
Using the recipes in this book, we've put together 55 menus that make meal planning a snap.

**Chapter 1: The Busiest Cooks in the Country** .....................6
Fellow cooks share fast-to-fix meals and timely tips.

**Chapter 2: 30 Minutes to Mealtime**..........20
Each of this chapter's 12 full menus can be prepared in 30 minutes or less.

**Chapter 3: Thinking Up a Theme**..............34
Host a festive get-together with a theme-related meal.

**Chapter 4: Give Me 5 or Fewer** .................48
Although each of these recipes has a mere five ingredients or fewer, they're all long on flavor.

**Chapter 5: 10 Minutes to the Table**..........62
Next time you're hungry, hurried and truly "down to the wire" on feeding your family, take a deep breath, count to 10 and turn to this chapter.

**Chapter 6: Handy Mix Tricks**.......................74
Rely on a variety of packaged convenience foods for fast fixes to your dining dilemmas. Or save shopping time—and money—by making your own.

**Chapter 7: Look Ahead for Lively Leftovers** .....................98
On the weekend, cook up a hearty dish and then use the "planned leftovers" in a whole different dish or two during the week.

**Chapter 8: Freezer Pleasers**.......................112
When time allows, create appetizing dishes you can pop into the freezer for fast, no-fuss later meals.

**Chapter 9: Easy Morning Eye-Openers** ......126
You don't need to scramble in order to serve your family a rise-and-shine breakfast.

**Chapter 10: Casseroles and Skillet Suppers** .....................142
Comforting casseroles and timeless skillet suppers always satisfy.

**Chapter 11: Breads in a Jiffy** ....................160
Quick breads and bread machines let you enjoy home-baked goodness with minimal kitchen time.

**Chapter 12: Snappy Soups, Salads & Sandwiches** .................182
Taste-tempting trio is a classic mealtime mainstay.

**Chapter 13: Delectable Desserts**.............196
You can soon have treats to share with time to spare!

**Chapter 14: Bake Sale Sprint**...................208
These time-saving and taste-tempting goodies are sure to sell out in seconds at your next bake sale.

**Chapter 15: Fast, Delicious...and Nutritious** .....................216
If you're trying to reduce fat, sugar or salt in your diet, these good-for-you dishes fit right in.

**Chapter 16: Centsible Foods—Fast and Frugal**.....................230
When you're counting pennies as well as minutes, look here for easy, economical and appetizing foods.

**Chapter 17: Kids in the Kitchen**..............238
Kids of all ages will jump at the chance to lend a helping hand with these fast, fun foods.

**Chapter 18: Timeless Recipes with Kitchen Tools** ..............................254
Put your slow cooker, grill and microwave to work making effortless, flavorful meals.

**Chapter 19: On-the-Go Odds & Ends** ......284
Here's a collection of reliable theme-related recipes that are tops for taste.

**Chapter 20: Company's Coming!** ............298
When you rely on these step-saving recipes and inexpensive table decorating ideas, you'll see how fun and easy entertaining can be.

**Chapter 21: Back to the Basics**................318
On leisurely weekend days when you have a few minutes on hand, why not take some time out to cook using these special recipes and tips?

**Indexes** .....................332
Two handy indexes make it easy to locate any of the 721 recipes in this book.

# What's on The Menu?

GRAB A MENU from the best "fast food" place in town—your kitchen! The price is right, the atmosphere is relaxing, and the service couldn't be friendlier nor the guests more appreciative. And with the *2003 Quick Cooking Annual Recipes* book in your hands, you've already given yourself a generous tip!

Here's how to use the menu ideas featured here: Our food editors screened all the recipes that appear in this book, then "grouped" several from various chapters to make up menus for everyday and special-occasion family meals. Plus, you can mix and match recipes to make up menus of your own.

For even more complete meals, turn to the following chapters: The Busiest Cooks in the Country (p. 6), 30 Minutes to Mealtime (p. 20), Thinking Up a Theme (p. 34) and Company's Coming! (p. 298).

## Six Breakfast Choices

| | |
|---|---|
| Asparagus Omelet | p. 134 |
| Coconut Loaf | p. 164 |
| Frozen Banana Pineapple Cups | p. 141 |
| Meaty Apple Skillet | p. 141 |
| Cheesy Egg Puffs | p. 135 |
| Frosty Mocha Drink | p. 140 |
| Baked Eggs with Basil Sauce | p. 130 |
| Cran-Apple Ham Slice | p. 281 |
| Fruit Yogurt Medley | p. 66 |
| Sausage Egg Puff | p. 224 |
| Granola Peach Bread | p. 169 |
| Creamy Orange Drink | p. 133 |
| Bacon Cheddar Quiche | p. 276 |
| Honey Oat Muffins | p. 169 |
| Frozen Fruit Fluff | p. 121 |
| Crispy Baked Oatmeal | p. 139 |
| Walnut Cinnamon Rolls | p. 170 |
| Hot Drink Mix | p. 97 |

## Eighteen Lunch Choices

| | |
|---|---|
| Four-Bean Taco Chili | p. 100 |
| Bacon Cheese Biscuits | p. 162 |
| Caramel Pecan Bars | p. 51 |
| Ribs for Kids | p. 240 |
| Cheddar Vegetable Soup | p. 100 |
| Red-Hot Candy Fluff | p. 51 |
| Open-Faced Sandwich Supreme | p. 76 |
| Chicken Wild Rice Soup | p. 76 |
| Glazed Mint Brownies | p. 198 |
| Italian Subs | p. 184 |
| Corn Pasta Salad | p. 218 |
| Pretzel-Topped Sugar Cookies | p. 210 |
| Bandito Chili Dogs | p. 259 |
| Mallow Fruit Salad | p. 79 |
| Surprise Cupcakes | p. 294 |
| Turkey Sloppy Joes | p. 220 |
| Brown Rice Slaw | p. 220 |
| Orange Crispy Cookies | p. 211 |
| Chicken Salad in Melon Rings | p. 188 |
| Apricot Muffins | p. 166 |
| Double Frosted Brownies | p. 80 |
| Eggplant Pockets | p. 223 |
| Tropical Fruit Salad | p. 130 |
| Rhubarb Dream Bars | p. 202 |
| Triple-Decker Salmon Club | p. 188 |
| Cucumber Shell Salad | p. 54 |
| Chocolate Oatmeal Bars | p. 212 |
| Celery Potato Chowder | p. 105 |
| Savory Sausage Bread | p. 166 |
| Frosted Orange Cookies | p. 202 |
| BBQ Chicken Sandwiches | p. 235 |
| Stovetop Baked Beans | p. 106 |
| S'more Parfaits | p. 57 |
| Two-Cheese Quesadillas | p. 72 |
| Colorful Black Bean Salad | p. 191 |
| Lime Cooler Bars | p. 205 |
| Reuben Burgers | p. 272 |
| German Potato Salad | p. 291 |
| Crispy Kiss Squares | p. 214 |
| Chicken Salad Clubs | p. 71 |
| Fruity Gelatin Salad | p. 59 |
| Cheerio Treats | p. 250 |
| Salmon Chowder | p. 72 |
| Jumbo Onion Cheese Muffins | p. 172 |
| Cranberry Crispies | p. 206 |
| Ham 'n' Egg Salad Subs | p. 195 |
| Creamy Waldorf Salad | p. 73 |
| Mint Sandwich Cookies | p. 89 |
| Sausage Tomato Soup | p. 195 |
| Pizza Bread | p. 181 |
| Fruity Sherbet | p. 125 |
| Italian Chicken Pockets | p. 195 |
| Cheesy Vegetable Soup | p. 125 |
| Apple Spice Snack Cake | p. 237 |

# Thirty-One Dinner Choices

Round Steak Roll-Ups .................................... p. 256
Green Beans with a Twist ............................. p. 50
No-Knead Casserole Bread ......................... p. 163
Heart's Delight Torte .................................... p. 293

Black-Eyed Pea Sausage Stew ................... p. 159
Monterey Ranch Bread ............................... p. 51
Glazed Lemon Cake ..................................... p. 232

Hearty Burritos ............................................. p. 115
Mexican Rice Mix ......................................... p. 92
Caramel Brownies ........................................ p. 210

Ham and Rice Bake ...................................... p. 56
Shoepeg Corn Salad .................................... p. 191
Poppy Seed Lemonade Muffins ................. p. 168

Herbed Salmon Steaks ................................ p. 321
Spinach Mushroom Salad ........................... p. 184
Chocolate Berry Pound Cake ..................... p. 198

Chicken in Sour Cream Sauce ..................... p. 257
Broccoli Corn Casserole .............................. p. 51
Spiced Peaches ............................................ p. 219

Pork Chops in Tomato Sauce ...................... p. 228
Potato Bean Skillet ...................................... p. 228
Cherry Dream Cake ...................................... p. 87

Maple Barbecued Chicken ........................... p. 53
Cheddar Stuffing Puff .................................. p. 79
Tangy Cauliflower Salad .............................. p. 68
Banana Macaroon Trifle .............................. p. 201

Pizza Rigatoni .............................................. p. 259
Herbed Bread ............................................... p. 323
Frosty Pineapple Salad ................................ p. 233

Crab-Stuffed Chicken ................................... p. 276
Marinated Artichoke Salad .......................... p. 52
Cornmeal Muffins ........................................ p. 93

Baked Haddock ............................................ p. 103
Potato Rosettes ............................................ p. 117
Honey Mustard Dressing (over greens) ...... p. 187
Peach-Glazed Cake ...................................... p. 52

Three-Cheese Pasta Shells .......................... p. 220
Antipasto Salad ............................................ p. 187
Fruit Cup with Citrus Sauce ........................ p. 221

Barbecued Beef Brisket ............................... p. 261
Catalina Rice Salad ...................................... p. 188
Banana Cream Pie ........................................ p. 279

Hearty Fajitas ............................................... p. 151
California Avocado Salsa .............................. p. 288
Tex-Mex Rice ................................................ p. 234
Pineapple Ice Cream .................................... p. 119

Crabby Alfredo ............................................. p. 67
French Bean Salad ........................................ p. 66
Parmesan Herb Bread .................................. p. 179

Raspberry Chicken ....................................... p. 290
Twice-Baked Ranch Potatoes ...................... p. 121
Mock Caesar Salad ...................................... p. 56
Chocolate Caramel Fondue ......................... p. 66

Garden Squash Ravioli .................................. p. 65
Smoky Corn Muffins ..................................... p. 82
Blackberry Cake ............................................ p. 224

Grilled Rib Eye Steaks .................................. p. 106
Lime-Thyme Potato Wedges ........................ p. 235
Cheesy Vegetable Medley ........................... p. 147
Peanut Ice Cream Squares .......................... p. 121

Hurry-Up Ham Carbonara ........................... p. 232
Family Favorite Bread .................................. p. 176
Hungarian Salad ........................................... p. 64
Orange-Swirl Yogurt Pie .............................. p. 115

Flavorful Beef in Gravy ................................ p. 262
Pineapple Lime Molds .................................. p. 83
Hawaiian Dinner Rolls .................................. p. 178
Fresh Raspberry Pie ..................................... p. 290

Warm Shrimp Salad ..................................... p. 70
Chive Cheese Biscuits .................................. p. 169
Mandarin Orange Cream Pie ....................... p. 205

Savory Pork Roast ........................................ p. 108
Golden Corn Casserole ................................ p. 85
Red Cabbage Slaw ........................................ p. 286
Frost-on-the-Pumpkin Pie ........................... p. 206

Angel Hair Tuna ........................................... p. 153
Cauliflower Romaine Salad .......................... p. 192
Coconut Peach Pie ....................................... p. 59

Chicken Supreme .......................................... p. 226
Vibrant Veggie Stir-Fry ................................ p. 226
Wild Rice Bread ............................................ p. 108
Fudgy Peanut Butter Cake ........................... p. 265

Taco Chicken Rolls ....................................... p. 58
Salsa Rice ..................................................... p. 58
Cinnamon Apple Pizza ................................. p. 85

Thanksgiving in a Pan .................................. p. 87
Sweet Potato Bread ...................................... p. 170
Creamy Cranberry Gelatin ........................... p. 86
Caramel Ship Bars ....................................... p. 91

Unstuffed Cabbage ...................................... p. 149
Gingered White Bread .................................. p. 181
Peachy Cream Pie ........................................ p. 90

Zippy Pork Chops ......................................... p. 269
Blue Cheese Potatoes .................................. p. 52
Mixed Vegetable Bake .................................. p. 145
No-Bake Chocolate Cheesecake .................. p. 210

Christmas Meatballs ..................................... p. 278
Cornish Hens with Potatoes ........................ p. 267
Hollandaise Sauce (over broccoli) .............. p. 278
Gingerbread Trifle ........................................ p. 111

Quick 'n' Easy Lasagna ................................ p. 61
Herbed Onion Salad Dressing (over greens) .......... p. 195
Garlic-Cheese Flat Bread ............................. p. 170
Mocha Pie ..................................................... p. 88

Smothered Chicken ...................................... p. 73
Almond Rice Seasoning Mix ........................ p. 97
Raspberry Icebox Dessert ............................ p. 89

# Chapter 1

THE DAY BEGINS early in the morning and ends late in the evening for many folks. Between work, school and a slew of other activities, you probably pack as much as possible into a typical day.

It's no wonder you think there's little extra time to prepare a wholesome, hearty dinner for your famished family. But this chapter pleasantly proves that speedy yet memorable meals are within reach.

Six fellow frenzied cooks from across the country share their reliable rapid recipes, time-saving tips and menu-planning pointers, all of which are guaranteed to put you on the meal-making fast track in no time.

**SUPER SUPPER.** Clockwise from upper left: Sweet Sesame Salad, Mayonnaise Chocolate Cake and Pepper Steak with Potatoes (all recipes on pp. 10 and 11).

# Simple Meal Has Twice The Appeal

TWO SEEMS to be Debra Hartze's lucky number. You see, Debra and her husband, Andrew, have two daughters—Gabrielle and Jessica. The couple owns two businesses and lives in Zeeland, North Dakota, which has a population of about 200.

Debra also raises two types of livestock, chickens and calves, and volunteers reading stories to preschoolers two times a month.

"Between caring for our daughters, running the businesses and keeping up with other obligations, there are days I feel like I have 22 jobs!" she says.

"My husband and I own a welding business, and I handle all of the bookwork," Debra explains. "But because I love to bake, I started a career in cake decorating as well."

Several regular clients and some 200 cake pans later, Debra turned her creative cakes into a bustling business she runs out of her home.

When she's not in the kitchen, you might find the busy baker tending to her large vegetable garden, which encourages a healthy menu—something that's important to Debra.

"Andrew and Gabrielle must follow special diets," she shares. "This makes cooking challenging. While their needs have to be met, I want to prepare foods that are tasty enough to keep everyone satisfied and simple enough to throw together when time is short.

"But no matter how busy I get, I'm sure to make time to spend with my family," Debra says.

For a simple but sensational dinner, try Debra's Pepper Jack Meat Loaf. "This is a quick way to put a zesty twist on a traditional main dish," she says.

And if you're looking to bring a new side dish to the table, consider golden Potato Chip Potatoes. "I hate to throw out the crushed chips at the bottom of potato chip bags," says Debra. "I put the crumbs in a resealable bag I keep in the freezer. They make a savory crunchy topping for this hearty favorite."

While the potatoes and meat loaf are baking, Debra whips up refreshing Creamy Pea Salad. "You can also prepare it ahead of time, so it's ideal when you're having company for dinner," she notes.

It should come as no surprise that Debra ends her meals with a baked treat. A cake mix keeps Chocolate Cherry Angel Cake simple, but cherries and a rich chocolate glaze make it extraordinary.

"Friends and family will think you spent hours preparing this pretty dessert," promises Debra.

## Pepper Jack Meat Loaf

✓ Uses less fat, sugar or salt. Includes Nutritional Analysis and Diabetic Exchanges.

1 egg *or* 1/4 cup egg substitute
1 cup seasoned bread crumbs
1/4 cup chopped onion
1/2 to 1 teaspoon salt
1/2 teaspoon pepper
1-1/2 pounds lean ground beef
1 cup (4 ounces) shredded pepper Jack *or* Monterey Jack cheese, *divided*

In a large bowl, combine the egg, bread crumbs, onion, salt and pepper. Crumble beef over mixture and mix well. Press half of the beef mixture onto the bottom and halfway up the sides of a greased 8-in. x 4-in. x 2-in. loaf pan. Sprinkle 3/4 cup cheese over meat to within 1/2 in. of sides. Pat remaining beef mixture over cheese.

Bake, uncovered, at 350° for 50-55 minutes until meat is no longer pink and a meat thermometer reads 160°. Sprinkle with remaining cheese. Bake 5 minutes longer or until cheese is melted. Let stand for 10 minutes before slicing. **Yield:** 6 servings.

**Nutritional Analysis:** One serving (prepared with egg substitute, 1/2 teaspoon salt and reduced-fat cheese) equals 339 calories, 15 g fat (7 g saturated fat), 55 mg cholesterol, 976 mg sodium, 16 g carbohydrate, 1 g fiber, 33 g protein. **Diabetic Exchanges:** 3 lean meat, 2 fat, 1 starch.

## Potato Chip Potatoes

**Ready in 1 hour or less**

6 medium potatoes, peeled and cut into 1/2-inch cubes
3/4 cup crushed potato chips, *divided*
1/2 cup chopped onion

## Debra's Irresistible Ideas

- To make quick salad croutons on the stovetop, lightly brown bite-size pieces of bread heels in a skillet in a little butter mixed with your favorite herbs. Remove with a slotted spoon to paper towels and cool.
- Want to make ordinary finger food more attractive in a short amount of time? Use a pastry bag and star tip to fill items like stuffed celery or deviled eggs. Or spoon the filling into a sandwich bag, snip off a corner of the bag and pipe the filling into the appetizer. This also makes cleanup a snap. —*Debra Hartze*

2 tablespoons butter *or* margarine,
  melted
3/4 teaspoon salt
1/4 teaspoon pepper

In a bowl, combine the potatoes, 1/2 cup of potato chips, onion, butter, salt and pepper; toss to combine. Transfer to a greased shallow 2-qt. baking dish. Sprinkle with remaining potato chips. Bake, uncovered, at 350° for 40-50 minutes or until potatoes are tender. **Yield:** 6-8 servings.

## Creamy Pea Salad

**Ready in 15 minutes or less**

2 packages (16 ounces *each*) frozen
  peas, thawed
1/2 cup diced cheddar cheese
1/2 cup diced mozzarella cheese
1 medium onion, chopped
1 cup mayonnaise *or* salad dressing
Salt and pepper to taste
4 bacon strips, cooked and crumbled

In a bowl, combine the peas, cheeses, onion, mayonnaise, salt and pepper; mix well. Refrigerate until serving. Sprinkle with bacon. **Yield:** 6-8 servings.

## Chocolate Cherry Angel Cake

1 package (16 ounces) angel food
  cake mix
1/3 cup finely chopped maraschino
  cherries, well drained
1 square (1 ounce) semisweet
  chocolate, grated
GLAZE:
2 tablespoons butter (no substitutes)
1 square (1 ounce) semisweet
  chocolate
1 tablespoon light corn syrup
1 cup confectioners' sugar
3 to 5 teaspoons maraschino
  cherry juice
Maraschino cherries and fresh mint,
  optional

In a large mixing bowl, prepare cake mix according to package directions. Fold cherries and chocolate into the batter. Pour into an ungreased 10-in. tube pan. Bake at 350° for 40-45 minutes or until cake springs back when lightly touched. Immediately invert pan; cool completely. Run a knife around sides of cake and remove from pan.

In a saucepan, combine butter, chocolate and corn syrup. Cook and stir over low heat until chocolate is melted. Stir in confectioners' sugar and cherry juice until glaze reaches desired consistency. Drizzle over cake. Garnish with cherries and mint if desired. **Yield:** 12 servings.

# She Plans Sit-Down Family Dinners

LATE AFTERNOONS and early evenings are busy times in Kristine Marra's home. "Even though things can get pretty hectic, I'm committed to having sit-down family dinners nearly every night of the week," she says.

Located in Clifton Park, New York, just about 150 miles outside of New York City, the Marra family home is always bustling and full of energy.

"My husband, Frank, and I have six children—Bryan, Stephen, Kyle, Brendan and twins Colin and Taryn," shares Kristine.

"Getting meals on the table can be a challenge when you're trying to cook around homework needs and extracurricular activities," she explains. "But I come from a family with five children and my mother always had sit-down dinners. I'm determined to do the same.

"To help free up weekday evenings, I spend Sunday cooking several meals," Kristine notes. "I prepare skillet dinners and roasts for later in the week, then make a lighter meal, such as homemade pizza or soup and sandwiches, for that evening's supper.

"I also assemble school and work lunches that will keep in the refrigerator throughout the week."

In addition to raising the children, Kristine works as a health-care consultant. "After the twins were born, I decided to work from home," she says. "As a registered nurse, I code patient charts and offer guidance on medical legalities."

Frank's job as a merchandise manager with a nationwide retailer keeps him on the go, and both he and Kristine volunteer in their children's classrooms. "I'm also on the membership committee of our local parent-teacher association," she adds.

In her free time, Kristine enjoys walking, reading and clipping coupons. (For a few of her time- and money-saving tips, see the box titled "Coupon-Clipping Clues" at far right.)

In order to accommodate her lively schedule, the busy cook does as much preparation as possible before mealtime. "I wash and chop ingredients for side dishes the night before or early in the day," she comments. "Then I simply assemble and cook the dish while reheating an entree I made on Sunday."

Like many busy cooks, Kristine depends on recipes that are fast and delicious, and Pepper Steak with Potatoes fits the bill nicely.

"I added potatoes to an Oriental favorite to create this well-rounded skillet dish," she says. "It's a snap to prepare because the potatoes are cooked in the microwave, plus it's hearty enough to satisfy all the men in our house."

To complement the main dish, Kristine tosses together Sweet Sesame Salad. She jazzes up salad greens with tomato, mandarin oranges and sesame seeds, then tops it off with a honey vinaigrette for a sweet and fruity sensation the whole family loves.

An old-fashioned favorite—Mayonnaise Chocolate Cake—often ends meals at the Marra home. "My aunt has made this moist, rich sheet cake for as long as I can remember," Kristine says.

"Not only is it a cake I can quickly make from scratch, but it calls for ingredients I usually have in the pantry. It's great dusted with confectioners' sugar, but I keep prepared frosting on hand so I can always whip up a last-minute dessert that's guaranteed to get rave reviews."

## Pepper Steak with Potatoes

### Ready in 30 minutes or less

✓ Uses less fat, sugar or salt. Includes Nutritional Analysis and Diabetic Exchanges.

        5 medium red potatoes, cut into 1/4-inch slices
    1/2 cup water
        1 pound boneless beef sirloin steak, thinly sliced
        1 garlic clove, minced
        2 tablespoons olive *or* canola oil
        1 medium green pepper, julienned
        1 small onion, chopped
Pepper to taste
        4 teaspoons cornstarch
        1 cup beef broth

Place the potatoes and water in a microwave-safe bowl; cover and microwave on high for 8-10 minutes or until tender. Meanwhile, in a skillet, saute beef and garlic in oil until meat is no longer pink. Remove and keep warm; drain drippings. In the same skillet, saute green pepper and onion until crisp-tender. Return beef to the pan. Add potatoes and pepper; heat through.

In a small saucepan, combine cornstarch and broth until smooth. Bring to a boil; cook and stir for 2 minutes or until thickened. Drizzle over meat mixture; toss to coat. **Yield:** 6 servings.

**Nutritional Analysis:** One serving (1 cup) equals 277 calories, 10 g fat (2 g saturated fat), 55 mg cholesterol, 179 mg sodium, 27 g carbohydrate, 3 g fiber, 23 g protein. **Diabetic Exchanges:** 2 meat, 2 vegetable, 1 starch.

## Sweet Sesame Salad

**Ready in 30 minutes or less**

1 package (10 ounces) ready-to-serve
   salad greens
1 medium tomato, cut into thin wedges
2/3 cup balsamic vinaigrette salad dressing
2 teaspoons honey
1 can (11 ounces) mandarin oranges, drained
1 teaspoon sesame seeds, toasted

In a salad bowl, combine the greens and tomato; set aside. In a jar with a tight-fitting lid, combine salad dressing and honey; shake well. Drizzle over greens. Sprinkle with oranges and sesame seeds; toss to coat. **Yield:** 6 servings.

## Mayonnaise Chocolate Cake

1 cup all-purpose flour
3/4 cup sugar
1/4 cup baking cocoa
1 teaspoon baking powder
1 teaspoon baking soda
1 cup mayonnaise*
1 cup water
1 can (16 ounces) French vanilla *or* vanilla
   frosting

In a large mixing bowl, combine the flour, sugar, cocoa, baking powder and baking soda. Add the mayonnaise and water; mix well. Pour into a greased 13-in. x 9-in. x 2-in. baking pan. Bake at 350° for 20-25 minutes or until a toothpick inserted near the center comes out clean. Cool on a wire rack. Spread with frosting. **Yield:** 12-15 servings.

   ***Editor's Note:** Reduced-fat or fat-free mayonnaise may not be substituted for regular mayonnaise in this recipe.

## Coupon-Clipping Clues

- My sons use sheets of clear plastic pockets to hold their baseball cards. I use the same sheets to organize and store my coupons. The sheets fit into a three-ring binder that I take along to the grocery store with me.
- I keep a basket on my kitchen counter specifically for coupons that are attached to cans and packages. If anyone in the house opens a package and finds a coupon, they place it in the basket for me to file.
- To save time and confusion at the cash register, be sure to check the expiration date on the coupons you plan to use. It helps to constantly review your coupons, tossing those that have expired.

*—Kristine Marra*

# Easy Satisfying Menu Fits Into Busy Schedule

ANNE WEGENER rarely gets a break in her day. When her children start school each morning, she follows them right into the classroom!

"My husband, Tim, and I are lucky enough to have eight children—Andrew, Kara, Kristen, Jonathan, Peter, Amanda, Faith and Paul," says the Springville, Indiana cook. "Several years ago, we decided to home-school them.

"Due to the differences in their ages, I teach them everything from the alphabet and basic arithmetic to Spanish and precalculus," says Anne.

"While I'm busy at home, Tim works as a building contractor and grows corn and soybeans on our farm. We both teach Sunday school classes at our church, and I'm very involved in a support group for families that home-school. Plus, our children are active in 4-H and church activities," she adds.

Anne is always looking for ways to save time, particularly in the kitchen. Since the kids are home for breakfast and lunch as well as dinner, she serves sit-down meals for all 10 family members about 20 times a week.

"With so many hungry mouths to feed, menu planning and preparation can be a lengthy task," notes Anne. "However, I've learned a few tricks to streamline the process yet still fix quality low-cost meals that are nutritious, too.

"My biggest time-saver comes in knowing what we'll have for each meal, so I'm not wasting time trying to decide what to make," she says.

"I plan menus using a 4-week rotation chart. It gives me several entree options for each meal of every day. For example, on one night, the chart lists traditional pizza, rice-crust pizza or calzones for dinner," she explains. "It also offers blank spaces for new recipes.

"At the beginning of the week, I select all of our meals from the chart, make a corresponding grocery list, grab my coupons and head to the store."

It comes as no surprise that Anne favors foods that she can throw together in a snap, and tender Sesame Chicken is a prime example.

"I triple the recipe when chicken is on sale, freezing it with the marinade in resealable bags," she says. "The night before I need it, I place a bag in the refrigerator and the chicken marinates as it thaws."

The juicy entree broils quickly and makes a popular main dish when served over rice.

One of Anne's specialties is a combination of fresh greens, tangy oranges, savory bacon and crunchy almonds. Topped with a pleasantly sweet dressing, Tossed Salad with Oranges brings a splash of color to any table.

For dessert, consider a Wegener family favorite— Peanut Butter Chip Cookies. "These cookies are so yummy that we bake them a few times a month," says Anne. "For a fun change of pace, use vanilla or butterscotch chips or mix several different chips together."

Thanks to this speedy meal, Anne gets a little free time to do some of the things she enjoys. "I like quilting and exploring the trails through our woods and fields," she shares. "I also love being outdoors with my favorite people...my family."

## Sesame Chicken

**Plan ahead...needs to marinate**

✓ Uses less fat, sugar or salt. Includes Nutritional Analysis and Diabetic Exchanges.

1/4 cup lemon juice
1/4 cup soy sauce
  2 tablespoons canola oil
  3 garlic cloves, minced
1/2 teaspoon ground ginger
  6 boneless skinless chicken breast halves (4 ounces *each*)
  4 teaspoons cornstarch
1/2 cup water
1/4 cup chicken broth
Hot cooked rice
1/4 cup sesame seeds, toasted

In a large resealable plastic bag, combine the lemon juice, soy sauce, oil, garlic and ginger. Add chicken; seal bag and turn to coat. Refrigerate for 8 hours or overnight.

Remove chicken from marinade and place on a greased broiler pan; set marinade aside. Broil chicken 4 in. from the heat for 12-14 minutes or until juices run clear, turning once. Meanwhile, strain the marinade. In a saucepan, com-

## Family Finds Time to Help

- Our kids pitch in when it comes to kitchen chores. Each of the older children is paired with a younger sibling. The younger child clears the plates and wipes the table, and the older one washes the dishes.
- When measuring dry ingredients for cookies or muffins, ask a child to repeat the same steps, dumping the ingredients into a resealable storage bag for future use. Label the bag with the wet ingredients that need to be added and the baking directions.

—Anne Wegener

bine cornstarch, water, broth and marinade until smooth. Bring to a rolling boil; cook and stir
for 2 minutes or until thickened. Serve chicken
and sauce over rice. Sprinkle with sesame seeds.
**Yield:** 6 servings.

**Nutritional Analysis:** One serving (prepared
with reduced-sodium soy sauce; calculated without rice) equals 242 calories, 8 g fat (1 g saturated fat), 73 mg cholesterol, 506 mg sodium,
4 g carbohydrate, trace fiber, 27 g protein.
**Diabetic Exchanges:** 4 very lean meat, 1 vegetable, 1 fat.

## Tossed Salad with Oranges

### Ready in 30 minutes or less

POPPY SEED DRESSING:
- 1/2 cup vegetable oil
- 6 tablespoons cider vinegar
- 3/4 cup sugar
- 1 small onion, quartered
- 1/2 teaspoon ground mustard
- 1/4 teaspoon salt
- 1 teaspoon poppy seeds

SALAD:
- 10 cups torn salad greens
- 1 can (11 ounces) mandarin oranges, drained
- 6 bacon strips, cooked and crumbled
- 2 to 4 tablespoons slivered almonds

In a food processor or blender, combine oil, vinegar, sugar, onion, mustard and salt. Cover and
process until smooth. Stir in the poppy seeds.

In a salad bowl, combine the greens, oranges,
bacon and almonds. Drizzle with dressing and
toss to coat. Serve immediately. **Yield:** 10
servings (1-1/2 cups dressing).

## Peanut Butter Chip Cookies

- 1/2 cup butter *or* margarine, softened
- 1/2 cup peanut butter
- 3/4 cup packed brown sugar
- 1/4 cup sugar
- 1 egg
- 2 tablespoons milk
- 1 teaspoon vanilla extract
- 1-3/4 cups all-purpose flour
- 1 teaspoon baking soda
- 1/2 teaspoon salt
- 3/4 cup semisweet chocolate chips

Additional sugar

In a mixing bowl, cream butter, peanut butter and sugars. Beat in egg, milk and vanilla.
Combine the flour, baking soda and salt; add
to creamed mixture and mix well. Stir in
chocolate chips.

Roll into 1-in. balls; roll in additional sugar.
Place 2 in. apart on ungreased baking sheets.
Flatten if desired. Bake at 375° for 7-9 minutes
or until golden brown. Remove to wire racks to
cool. **Yield:** 4 dozen.

# Super Summer Supper Comes From Experience

CHRISTI ROSS owes her culinary skills to a bunch of hungry, hard-working cowboys...well, sort of.

"My family has been in the cattle ranching business for a long time," shares the Guthrie, Texas cook.

"The cowboys working on my parents' ranch enjoy hearty servings of beef, garden-fresh side dishes, home-baked rolls and fantastic desserts...all prepared by my mother. I grew up watching her cook these huge meals, and I was eager to lend a helping hand."

Christi's father is also quite a chef. "He often cooks delicious campfire meals for the ranch hands when it's too far or too late to go home for a meal. My mother taught me about recipes and kitchen skills, and my dad explained grilling techniques and the importance of simplicity," she says.

Christi continues to enjoy her passion for cooking, but now she's able to share it with her own family.

"My husband, Ryan, and I have a daughter, Kate, who fills my days with activities, as well as a baby on the way," Christi reports.

"When I'm not tending to Kate, I'm busy running my own machine-quilting business. Customers from all over the country ship their quilts to me for custom stitching," she says.

"I also teach quilting classes, contribute to a quilting Web site, write a weekly newspaper column and tutor high school students in writing."

Ryan works as a stallion manager, looking after performance and race horses. He also helps feed, doctor and care for the cattle on Christi's parents' ranch. In addition, Christi's father and Ryan raise and train Border collies to assist on cattle ranches.

Even though the couple's jobs demand a lot of time, Christi insists on serving a homemade sit-down supper 7 nights a week. "I'm still a 'from-scratch' cook. But to streamline preparation, I create meal plans and rely on recipes that come together without much fuss," she says.

One of the entrees she likes to cook is Summer Steak Kabobs. The meaty skewers not only satisfy her love of outdoor cooking, but feature a mouth-watering marinade.

You might want to add Christi's beyond-compare Veggie Pull-Apart Bread to your menu, particularly if you have bacon left over from breakfast.

A bread machine hurries along the dough-making process, but chopped vegetables, bacon and cheese make the buttery wreath unforgettable.

And if you're baking the bread, why not throw together creamy Crustless Pineapple Pie, too? "Both items call for the same oven time and temperature," Christi notes. "I took a favorite pie recipe and substituted canned pineapple for the coconut it called for. The results were delicious.

"I sometimes bake the pie a day early to really help me beat the clock," she concludes. "After all, having more family time is important to everyone."

## Summer Steak Kabobs

**Plan ahead...needs to marinate**

1/2 cup vegetable oil
1/4 cup soy sauce
3 tablespoons honey
2 tablespoons white vinegar
1/2 teaspoon ground ginger
1/2 teaspoon garlic powder
1-1/2 pounds boneless beef sirloin steak, cut into 1-inch cubes
1/2 pound fresh mushrooms
2 medium onions, cut into wedges
1 medium sweet red pepper, cut into 1-inch chunks
1 medium green pepper, cut into 1-inch chunks
1 medium yellow summer squash, cut into 1/2-inch slices
Hot cooked rice

In a large resealable plastic bag, combine the first six ingredients; add the steak. Seal bag and turn to coat; refrigerate for 8 hours or overnight.

Drain and discard marinade. On 12 metal or soaked

## Advantageous Organizing

- I turned a few of my kitchen cabinets into "stations". The cabinet above my bread machine, for example, is the baking station as it contains the ingredients and supplies for breads, cookies and pies. I even reserve one cupboard for cookbooks.

- Try organizing recipes by dividing them into separate boxes. Purchase a few inexpensive recipe boxes and designate each one for a specific type of dish. I have one box each for entrees, side dishes, breads and desserts.

- My mother shared a great trick with me to keep recipe cards in good condition—laminate them. I buy packs of laminating sheets at department or discount stores and use the sheets to help protect my favorite recipes.
                                                    —*Christi Ross*

wooden skewers, alternately thread steak, mushrooms, onions, peppers and squash. Grill, uncovered, over medium heat for 12-14 minutes or until meat reaches desired doneness, turning occasionally. Serve with rice. **Yield:** 6 servings.

## Veggie Pull-Apart Bread

**Plan ahead...uses bread machine**

4-1/2 teaspoons butter *or* margarine
  1/2 cup water
  1/2 cup sour cream
    3 tablespoons sugar
1-1/2 teaspoons salt
    3 cups all-purpose flour
1-1/2 teaspoons active dry yeast
**VEGETABLE MIXTURE:**
    1 cup chopped celery
    1 cup chopped green pepper
    1 cup chopped green onions
  1/2 cup butter *or* margarine
    6 bacon strips, cooked and crumbled
    1 cup (4 ounces) shredded cheddar cheese

In bread machine pan, place butter, water, sour cream, sugar, salt, flour and yeast in order suggested by manufacturer. Select dough setting (check dough after 5 minutes of mixing; add 1 to 2 tablespoons water or flour if needed). Meanwhile, in a skillet, saute celery, green pepper and onions in butter. Remove from the heat; stir in bacon and cheese.

When the cycle is complete, turn dough onto a lightly floured surface. Punch down; cover and let rest for 10 minutes. Divide dough into 24 balls; dip into the vegetable mixture. Place in a greased 9-in. fluted tube pan. Cover and let rise in a warm place until doubled, about 45 minutes. Bake at 350° for 40-45 minutes or until golden brown. **Yield:** 8-10 servings.

## Crustless Pineapple Pie

    2 cups milk
  2/3 cup sugar
  1/2 cup biscuit/baking mix
  1/4 cup butter *or* margarine, melted
    2 eggs
1-1/2 teaspoons vanilla extract
Yellow food coloring, optional
    2 cans (8 ounces *each*) crushed pineapple, well drained
Whipped topping, optional

In a blender, combine the milk, sugar, biscuit mix, butter, eggs, vanilla and food coloring if desired; cover and process until smooth. Sprinkle the pineapple into a greased deep-dish 9-in. pie plate. Pour batter over pineapple. Bake at 350° for 40-45 minutes or until a knife inserted near the center comes out clean. Garnish with whipped topping if desired. **Yield:** 6-8 servings.

# Fast Recipes Still Make Fine Dinner

FAMILY FOODS need to be as fast as they are flavorful at Susan Lasken's home. "I enjoy cooking and would love nothing more than spending the entire day in the kitchen," she says. "However, the reality is that time is of the essence."

Susan and her husband, Douglas, live in Woodland Hills, California—a quiet suburb of Los Angeles—with their two sons, Connor and Andrew. Their daughter, Hilary, is a Web designer living in New York.

"When I come home from work, Connor usually needs a ride to soccer practice, and Andrew is rushing off to a night class. Everyone is hungry, and I have to get dinner on the table as quickly as possible," Susan explains.

"Plus, Douglas and I have professional commitments to keep. I'm a fifth-grade teacher and Douglas teaches high school English, so we often bring home papers to grade," she says. "I also coordinate a schoolwide arts program and am working toward a master's degree in school administration.

"My work is very fulfilling, but it doesn't leave much time for other interests, including cooking, painting furniture, participating in a monthly book club and attending Connor's school, sporting and Scouting activities," she adds. "That's why I rely on recipes that streamline preparation without sacrificing taste."

Susan's curiosity with culinary crafts began at a young age. "I was born in Visuel de Sus, Romania, and my family immigrated to the United States when I was 7," she says. "At the time, Mother never let my siblings or me help with cooking. She kept a kosher kitchen and simply did not want anyone interfering with her well-organized system.

"Like most children, I was intrigued by what I couldn't be a part of, so I watched my mother work in the kitchen whenever possible," Susan recalls.

"My mother is a great cook, but back then, there wasn't much variety in her menus. She influenced my cooking in that I was determined to explore new flavors while becoming just as good a cook as she is.

"After Douglas and I were married, I taught myself how to cook, and before I knew it, I was preparing sit-down suppers nearly every night of the week.

"As I began to feel comfortable in the kitchen, I started making more elaborate meals on Saturdays and Sundays. While these foods required a little more time, their leftovers gave me a jump-start on dinners during the rest of the week. I found this to be a great time-saver in the long run," Susan says.

"When preparing weeknight meals, I do most of the cooking on the stovetop because it's usually quicker than baking in the oven. That's why I adapted my mother's recipe for cabbage rolls into thick and hearty Turkey Cabbage Stew."

Chock-full of ground turkey, cabbage, carrots and tomatoes, Susan's speedy stew delivers delicious down-home comfort on cool days.

"If you don't like cabbage, replace it with chopped green peppers," she suggests. "Simply saute the peppers with the turkey, onion and garlic."

Serve steaming bowls of this stew alongside wedges of Herbed Focaccia. A handful of ingredients is all you'll need to turn frozen bread dough into this full-flavored favorite.

"Not only is the bread easy, but it's delicious," Susan attests. "Plus, you can add shredded cheese or adjust the herbs to suit your taste."

And there's no better way to end dinner than with Raisin-Nut Baked Apples, an autumn-inspired treat. "We like the stuffed apples for dessert. But because they cook so quickly in the microwave, I make them for snacks, too," Susan adds.

"It's always a delight when I find recipes that everyone likes," says the busy cook. "And this terrific meal gives me time to sit down and enjoy the company of my family."

## Turkey Cabbage Stew

### Ready in 30 minutes or less

✓ Uses less fat, sugar or salt. Includes Nutritional Analysis and Diabetic Exchanges.

- 1 pound ground turkey
- 1 medium onion, chopped
- 3 garlic cloves, minced
- 4 cups chopped cabbage
- 2 medium carrots, sliced
- 1 can (28 ounces) diced tomatoes, undrained
- 3/4 cup water
- 1 tablespoon brown sugar
- 1 tablespoon white vinegar
- 1 teaspoon salt
- 1 teaspoon dried oregano
- 1/4 teaspoon dried thyme
- 1/4 teaspoon pepper

In a large saucepan, cook turkey, onion and garlic over medium heat until meat is no longer pink; drain. Add the remaining ingredients. Bring to a boil; cover and simmer for 6-8 minutes or until the vegetables are tender. **Yield:** 6 servings.

**Nutritional Analysis:** One 1-cup serving (prepared with lean ground turkey) equals 268 calories, 10 g fat (3 g saturated fat), 90 mg cholesterol, 1,014 mg sodium, 23 g carbohydrate, 6 g fiber, 24 g protein. **Diabetic Exchanges:** 3 lean meat, 1 starch, 1 vegetable.

## Herbed Focaccia

### Ready in 45 minutes or less

1 loaf (1 pound) frozen bread dough, thawed
2 teaspoons dried basil
2 teaspoons dried oregano
2 teaspoons rubbed sage
Salt and pepper to taste
2 tablespoons olive *or* vegetable oil, *divided*

Place dough in a bowl. Combine the basil, oregano and sage; sprinkle 4-1/2 teaspoons over dough. Sprinkle with salt and pepper; knead into dough. Let rest for 10 minutes. Press onto a greased 12-in. pizza pan. Let rest for 10 minutes.

Brush with 1 tablespoon oil. With a wooden spoon handle, make indentations at 1-in. intervals. Bake at 425° for 10 minutes. Brush with remaining oil; sprinkle with the remaining herb mixture. Bake 5 minutes longer or until golden brown. Cut into wedges; serve warm. **Yield:** 6 servings.

## Raisin-Nut Baked Apples

### Ready in 15 minutes or less

6 medium Rome *or* Golden Delicious apples
6 tablespoons chopped walnuts
6 tablespoons raisins
1/4 cup honey
1-1/2 teaspoons ground cinnamon

Core apples; place in a greased 11-in. x 7-in. x 2-in. microwave-safe dish. Fill the center of each apple with walnuts and raisins. Drizzle with honey; sprinkle with cinnamon. Microwave, uncovered, on high for 6 minutes or until apples are tender. **Yield:** 6 servings.

**Editor's Note:** This recipe was tested in an 850-watt microwave.

## Quick Kitchen Cleanup

- I like to use my kitchen scissors for cutting green onions and herbs because I can often cut the items directly into the skillet or pot. This means there's no cutting board to clean.
- When I must use a cutting board to chop vegetables, I wrap the board in waxed paper before I begin. There isn't much of mess on the board when I'm done, saving a little cleanup time.
- If a salad dressing recipe calls for mustard, vinegar or oil, and I only have a bit of one ingredient left in the bottle, I simply add the other ingredients to this bottle. I replace the cap tightly and shake everything together in the container before pouring it over greens. It uses the last bit of the product and eliminates a dirty dish.
—*Susan Lasken*

# Quick Cooking Leaves Time For Dreaming

NANCY BROWN is a dream builder...literally! The Dahinda, Illinois cook always wanted to live in a log home, so she built one herself. "The only part of our home we did not do ourselves was the foundation," explains Nancy. "Once that was complete, I spent the next 9 months building the house.

"I enjoyed the process so much that I began building and selling log homes for a living. That was 8 years ago, and I've built homes all over the Midwest since then."

Nancy uses her house as a model to show prospective customers. "About 5,000 people walk through my home each year," she says. "That's a lot of company, so I'm always cleaning up and baking homemade treats to share.

"Between us, my husband, Marc, and I have five children—Laura, Jesse, Aimee and twins Matthew and Luke," Nancy notes.

"With Marc's job as a physical therapist, my meetings with customers and the children's many extracurricular activities, family time can be tough to come by.

"But my family's health and happiness are my top priorities, so I strive to prepare good food for them, no matter how little time I have."

Despite her hectic schedule, Nancy serves sit-down dinners nearly every night. "I'd be lost without my weekly meal plan," she acknowledges. "It takes the guesswork out of deciding what to have for dinner. It also eliminates extra trips to the grocery store because I make my shopping list as I create our meal plan.

"I keep convenience items on hand for nights when I'm not able to follow the plan," she adds.

"I keep fish fillets in the freezer and canned salmon in the pantry for easy main courses," Nancy elaborates. "To round out meals, I can steam some veggies, make seasoned rice or pasta from a boxed mix and bake a pan of refrigerated crescent rolls."

When planning menus, Nancy looks for recipes that allow her to do some of the prep work ahead of time. Perhaps that's why Moist Ham Loaf is a savory entree she turns to often.

"Not only is this main dish special enough for entertaining, but I can assemble it early in the day and pop it in the oven before dinnertime," she says.

"It seems so much fancier than meat loaf, but it's just as easy to make. Plus, the cherry sauce really dresses it up, so guests think I fussed."

Plan-ahead convenience is apparent in colorful Winter Vegetable Medley as well. "I peel and cut the veggies early, then refrigerate them in a resealable storage bag," she says. "The dish bakes at the same temperature as the ham loaf, so serving is a snap."

And if you're looking for a simple sensation to wrap up your meal, why not give Easy Tiramisu a try?

"This no-bake treat comes together quickly and can even be made the night before," Nancy notes. "Sometimes I drizzle additional chocolate syrup over the coffee and pound cake. Other times, I add sliced almonds to the topping.

"Cooking is a wonderful way to express love for friends and family," she concludes, "and this meal is guaranteed to generate appreciation, smiles and hugs in return."

## Moist Ham Loaf

✓ Uses less fat, sugar or salt. Includes Nutritional Analysis and Diabetic Exchanges.

    1 egg, lightly beaten
1/2 cup milk
1/3 cup dry bread crumbs
1/2 teaspoon onion powder
1/4 teaspoon pepper
    1 pound ground fully cooked ham
1/2 pound ground turkey
CHERRY SAUCE:
1/2 cup cherry preserves
    1 tablespoon cider vinegar
1/8 teaspoon ground cloves

In a bowl, combine the first five ingredients. Crumble ham and turkey over mixture and mix well. Press into a

## Cooperation Clues

- Get the whole family into the act. Involving kids in meal preparation is a good chance to talk about nutrition. It's also a good time to talk about what happened at school. You never know what interesting stories your teen may have to tell you while you're working together in the kitchen.

- Keep things organized so everyone knows where to find ingredients. I alphabetize my spices so we don't have to hunt for a certain seasoning. And I group similar canned items together. For instance, the soups are grouped together, and Mexican items such as refried beans and enchilada sauce are next to one another.

—Nancy Brown

greased 9-in. x 5-in. x 3-in. loaf pan. Bake, uncovered, at 375° for 50-55 minutes or until a meat thermometer reads 160°. In a saucepan, combine sauce ingredients. Cook and stir over medium heat for 5 minutes or until heated through. Serve with ham loaf. **Yield:** 6 servings.

**Nutritional Analysis:** One serving with 1 tablespoon sauce (prepared with egg substitute, fat-free milk and lean ham) equals 269 calories, 7 g fat (2 g saturated fat), 53 mg cholesterol, 980 mg sodium, 25 g carbohydrate, trace fiber, 25 g protein. **Diabetic Exchanges:** 3 lean meat, 1 starch, 1/2 fruit.

## Winter Vegetable Medley

### Ready in 1 hour or less

- 1/2 pound fresh brussels sprouts, halved
- 1/2 pound parsnips, peeled and cut into 1/2-inch cubes
- 1/2 pound fresh baby carrots
- 1 medium sweet potato, peeled and cut into 1/2-inch cubes
- 2 medium red potatoes, cut into 1/2-inch cubes
- 2 medium white potatoes, peeled and cut into 1/2-inch cubes
- 1/2 cup butter *or* margarine, melted
- 1-1/2 teaspoons rubbed sage
- 2 garlic cloves, minced

Place vegetables in a greased 13-in. x 9-in. x 2-in. baking dish. In a small bowl, combine the butter, sage and garlic; drizzle over vegetables. Cover and bake at 375° for 40-50 minutes or until tender. **Yield:** 8 servings.

## Easy Tiramisu

### Ready in 30 minutes or less

- 1 package (10-3/4 ounces) frozen pound cake, thawed
- 3/4 cup strong brewed coffee
- 1 package (8 ounces) cream cheese, softened
- 1 cup sugar
- 1/2 cup chocolate syrup
- 1 cup whipping cream, whipped
- 2 Heath candy bars (1.4 ounces *each*), crushed

Cut cake into nine slices. Arrange in an ungreased 11-in. x 7-in. x 2-in. dish, cutting to fit if needed. Drizzle with coffee. In a small mixing bowl, beat the cream cheese and sugar until smooth. Add the chocolate syrup. Fold in whipped cream. Spread over cake. Sprinkle with crushed candy bars. Refrigerate until serving. **Yield:** 8 servings.

# Chapter 2

ON BUSY DAYS, wouldn't it be great to have an appealing assortment of menus that can go from start to finish in a mere half hour?

When your hectic schedule doesn't allow you to spend hours in the kitchen, rely on these 12 complete meals that you can put together in 30 minutes or less.

Each and every fast-to-fix favorite comes from the recipe file of a fellow busy cook. So your family is sure to give each delicious dish rave reviews.

**GOOD FOOD FAST.** Greek Tossed Salad and Bacon-Feta Stuffed Chicken (p. 30).

# Spicy Supper Is Swift to Fix

PATIENCE and patients are two things Tracy Golder has in abundant supply. The Bloomsburg, Pennsylvania wife and mother of two works part-time as a registered nurse in the pediatric intensive care unit at a medical center.

"Sometimes it seems as if there is never enough time in the day, especially when I'm keeping up with my husband Rob's and my work schedules, juggling household duties, and caring for daughters Taylor and Meghan," Tracy remarks.

"When planning menus, I look for dishes that are quick to prepare as well as those that can be reheated," she says. "Rob works 12-hour rotating shifts as a security officer at the power company, so he needs meals that can easily be rewarmed in the microwave at work."

Tracy shares one of her favorite fast-to-fix dinners here. "I start backward and prepare light fluffy Rocky Road Pudding first so it has time to chill while I finish the rest of the supper," she explains.

Next, Tracy stirs together the ingredients for Green Chili Corn Bread. "I serve it with honey butter to help tone down the bread's spiciness," she says.

Speedy stovetop preparation makes flavorful zippy Chili Mac Skillet a winner at Tracy's table.

## Rocky Road Pudding

1-1/2 cups cold milk
1 package (3.9 ounces) instant chocolate pudding mix
1 carton (8 ounces) frozen whipped topping, thawed
1 cup (6 ounces) semisweet chocolate chips
1 cup miniature marshmallows, *divided*
1/2 cup salted peanuts
1/4 cup chocolate syrup, optional

In a mixing bowl, beat milk and pudding mix on low speed for 2 minutes. Fold in the whipped topping, chocolate chips, 3/4 cup marshmallows and peanuts. Pour into dessert dishes. Refrigerate until serving. Sprinkle with remaining marshmallows; drizzle with chocolate syrup if desired. **Yield:** 8 servings.

## Green Chili Corn Bread

1 package (8-1/2 ounces) corn bread/muffin mix
1 egg
2 tablespoons butter *or* margarine, melted
1 can (11 ounces) Mexicorn, drained
1 can (4 ounces) chopped green chilies, drained
1-1/2 cups (6 ounces) shredded pepper Jack cheese
1/4 teaspoon hot pepper sauce
HONEY BUTTER:
1/2 cup butter (no substitutes), softened
2 tablespoons honey

In a large bowl, combine the corn bread mix, egg and butter. Stir in the corn, chilies, cheese and hot pepper sauce. Pour into a greased 11-in. x 7-in. x 2-in. baking dish. Bake at 400° for 20-22 minutes or until a toothpick inserted near the center comes out clean. In a small bowl, combine the butter and honey. Serve with warm bread. **Yield:** 8 servings.

## Chili Mac Skillet

1 pound ground beef
1 medium onion, chopped
1 medium green pepper, chopped
2 garlic cloves, minced
2 cans (14-1/2 ounces *each*) diced tomatoes, undrained
1 can (16 ounces) kidney beans, rinsed and drained
1 package (10 ounces) frozen corn, thawed
2 tablespoons chili powder
1/2 to 1 teaspoon salt
1/2 teaspoon ground cumin
1-1/4 cups uncooked macaroni
1/2 cup shredded pepper Jack cheese

In a large skillet, cook beef, onion, green pepper and garlic over medium heat until meat is no longer pink; drain. Stir in the tomatoes, beans, corn, chili powder, salt and cumin. Bring to a boil. Reduce heat; cover and simmer for 15 minutes or until heated through. Meanwhile, cook the macaroni according to package directions. Drain and add to skillet; stir to coat. Garnish with cheese. **Yield:** 8 servings.

sent in by Barbara Nowakowski. These soft and chewy treats have a hint of orange marmalade, so they're a fun change of pace from typical granola bars.

"They're so easy to put together and so delicious, you'll find yourself making them all the time," notes the North Tonawanda, New York cook.

## Ham and Egg Pizza

1 cup cubed fully cooked ham
1 can (8 ounces) water chestnuts, drained and finely chopped
1 can (2-1/4 ounces) sliced ripe olives, drained
3 green onions, chopped
2 tablespoons butter *or* margarine
6 eggs
1/4 cup water
Salt and pepper to taste
1 prebaked Italian bread shell crust
1 medium tomato, seeded and diced
1/3 cup shredded mozzarella cheese
1/3 cup shredded cheddar cheese

In a large skillet, saute the ham, water chestnuts, olives and onions in butter until heated through. In a bowl, beat the eggs, water, salt and pepper; add to skillet. Cook over medium heat until eggs begin to set, stirring occasionally.

Place crust on a pizza pan or baking sheet; top with egg mixture. Sprinkle with tomato and cheeses. Bake at 425° for 7-10 minutes or until cheese is melted. **Yield:** 6-8 servings.

## Strawberry Yogurt Shakes

1 carton (16 ounces) plain yogurt
1 cup milk
1/2 cup honey
1-1/2 cups frozen unsweetened strawberries
1/4 cup toasted wheat germ
1/4 teaspoon almond extract
Dash salt

In two batches, process all ingredients in a blender until smooth. Pour into chilled glasses; serve immediately. **Yield:** 6 servings.

## Oatmeal Breakfast Bars

4 cups quick-cooking oats
1 cup packed brown sugar
1 teaspoon salt
1-1/2 cups chopped walnuts
1 cup flaked coconut
3/4 cup butter *or* margarine, melted
3/4 cup orange marmalade

In a mixing bowl, combine the oats, brown sugar and salt. Stir in remaining ingredients and mix well. Press into a greased 15-in. x 10-in. x 1-in. baking pan. Bake at 425° for 15-17 minutes or until golden brown. Cool on a wire rack. **Yield:** about 2-1/2 dozen.

# Quick Morning Meal Satisfies

WHEN time is tight, busy cooks look for complete meals they can put on the table in a jiffy. Here, our food editors pulled together three rapid recipes from readers for this brisk breakfast.

But the mouth-watering morning menu is so versatile, you can prepare these daybreak dishes for brunch, lunch or even supper.

In Wichita, Kansas, Carol Smith makes the most of a convenient prebaked pizza crust to create Ham and Egg Pizza.

Tasty toppings such as scrambled eggs, diced ham, crunchy water chestnuts, fresh tomatoes, ripe olives and shredded cheese provide plenty of pizzazz and a pretty presentation.

"For variety, try crumbled bacon, cooked sausage or diced leftover turkey instead of the ham, or substitute celery or diced cooked potatoes for the water chestnuts," Carol suggests.

To complement the main dish, whip up a thick batch of Strawberry Yogurt Shakes from Laurel Adams of Dryden, Ontario. Toasted wheat germ adds good-for-you flavor to her fruity shakes. Honey sweetens this beverage while yogurt gives it a bit of tanginess.

"Years ago, I was a cook at the local day care," Laurel recalls. "I'd prepare this creamy pink concoction for a mid-morning snack. It was always a favorite."

Round out the meal with Oatmeal Breakfast Bars

## Chicken Spaghetti Toss

5 green onions, chopped
2 garlic cloves, minced
2 tablespoons butter *or* margarine
2 tablespoons olive *or* vegetable oil
1-1/2 pounds boneless skinless chicken breasts, cubed
3 tablespoons lemon juice
3 tablespoons minced fresh parsley
1 teaspoon seasoned salt
1/2 teaspoon lemon-pepper seasoning
1 package (7 ounces) thin spaghetti

In a large skillet, saute onions and garlic in butter and oil until tender. Stir in the chicken, lemon juice, parsley, seasoned salt and lemon-pepper. Saute for 15-20 minutes or until chicken juices run clear. Meanwhile, cook spaghetti according to package directions; drain. Add to chicken mixture and toss. **Yield:** 4 servings.

## Roasted Tarragon Asparagus

✓ Uses less fat, sugar or salt. Includes Nutritional Analysis and Diabetic Exchanges.

1-1/2 pounds fresh asparagus, trimmed
2 to 3 tablespoons olive *or* canola oil
1/2 teaspoon coarsely ground pepper
1/8 teaspoon salt
1-1/2 teaspoons minced fresh tarragon *or* 1/2 teaspoon dried tarragon

Place asparagus in a shallow baking dish coated with nonstick cooking spray. Drizzle with oil; sprinkle with pepper and salt. Toss to coat. Bake, uncovered, at 450° for 13-15 minutes or until crisp-tender, turning occasionally. Sprinkle with tarragon. **Yield:** 6 servings.
**Nutritional Analysis:** One serving (prepared with 2 tablespoons oil) equals 71 calories, 5 g fat (1 g saturated fat), 0 cholesterol, 49 mg sodium, 5 g carbohydrate, 2 g fiber, 2 g protein. **Diabetic Exchanges:** 1 vegetable, 1 fat.

## Chocolate Peanut Sundaes

1 package (3.4 ounces) cook-and-serve chocolate pudding mix
3/4 cup water
3/4 cup corn syrup
1/4 teaspoon salt
1/3 cup peanut butter
1 tablespoon butter *or* margarine
1/2 teaspoon vanilla extract
Vanilla ice cream
Chopped peanuts, optional

In a saucepan, combine the pudding mix, water, corn syrup and salt. Cook and stir until mixture comes to a boil. Remove from the heat; stir in the peanut butter, butter and vanilla until smooth. Serve warm over ice cream. Sprinkle with peanuts if desired. **Yield:** about 1-2/3 cups sauce.

# Dressy Dinner In a Dash

ARE YOU searching for a quick-to-fix meal that's nice enough for guests? Consider this made-in-minutes menu compiled by our food editors.

The three rapid recipes shared by readers are a little more special than everyday fare, yet can be table-ready in a half hour or less.

Chicken Spaghetti Toss is a tempting entree from Cindy Dorband of Monument, Colorado. She says this family favorite can easily be increased for larger get-togethers.

"When my brother graduated from high school, the church had a banquet and my mom was in charge of the meal," Cindy recalls.

"My brother, who is the pickiest eater, requested this mildly flavored main dish. It was a success, and many people asked for the recipe."

While the chicken is cooking on the stovetop, make Roasted Tarragon Asparagus from Joyce Speckman of Holt, California. Her simple seasoning turns fresh asparagus spears into a special spring side dish that's speedy, too.

Then top off the meal with individual Chocolate Peanut Sundaes. "I stumbled upon the recipe for this sauce in an old farm cookbook years ago and have been using it ever since," says Karen Ellinwood from her home in Liberty Center, Ohio.

Scoops of ice cream are irresistible when covered with the warm thick topping and garnished with peanuts.

"I've shared the recipe many times with friends," Karen notes.

# Menu Features Fast-to-Fix Fare

A COLLECTION of rapid recipes has simplified mealtime at Jerraine Barlow's home in the small rural community of Colorado City, Arizona. She relies on these fast favorites when planning meals for husband Howard and their three children—Chantell, Monica and Owen.

While the stay-at-home mother enjoys taking walks with her family, roller skating, sewing, oil painting and landscaping their yard, she's always sure to save time to make a sit-down dinner no matter how pressed for time.

"Howard started a small computer store a few years ago," Jerraine explains. "Running a new business makes for a lot of hurried meals. Many times Howard would come home and want something fast to eat so he could get back to work."

On those occasions when her family needs a quick "byte", Jerraine turns to her cache of tried-and-true time-savers to fix a family-pleasing menu like the one featured here.

"I start by preparing dessert first because it needs to chill," Jerraine says. "Coconut Cream Pie is a favorite since it takes only a few minutes to prepare. It's so simple, yet it's so good!"

Then she assembles Beef Stroganoff Melt, a recipe that's been in her collection for a long time. Piled with ground beef, mushrooms, green peppers and tomatoes, the open-faced sandwich can feed a crowd. Once she pops the loaf in the oven to heat it through, she has more than enough time to stir together Cottage Cheese Veggie Salad.

## Coconut Cream Pie

1-1/2 cups cold milk
    1 package (3.4 ounces) instant coconut cream pudding mix
    1 package (8 ounces) cream cheese, softened
    1 carton (8 ounces) frozen whipped topping, thawed
    2 graham cracker crusts (9 inches *each*)
  1/2 cup flaked coconut, toasted

In a mixing bowl, beat milk and pudding mix on low speed for 2 minutes or until thickened. In another bowl, beat cream cheese. Add to pudding and mix well. Fold in whipped topping. Spoon into the crusts; sprinkle with coconut. Refrigerate until serving. **Yield:** 2 pies (6-8 servings each).

## Beef Stroganoff Melt

    2 pounds ground beef
    1 cup sliced fresh mushrooms
    1 medium onion, chopped
    1 teaspoon salt
  1/2 teaspoon garlic powder
  1/2 teaspoon pepper
    2 cups (16 ounces) sour cream
    1 loaf (1 pound) French bread
    3 tablespoons butter *or* margarine, softened
    3 cups (12 ounces) shredded Swiss cheese
    1 medium green pepper, thinly sliced
    2 medium tomatoes, thinly sliced

In a large skillet, cook the beef, mushrooms and onion over medium heat until meat is no longer pink; drain. Stir in the salt, garlic powder and pepper. Remove from the heat; stir in sour cream.

Cut French bread in half lengthwise. Place on a baking sheet. Spread butter over cut halves; top with meat mixture and half of the cheese. Arrange green pepper and tomatoes on top. Sprinkle with remaining cheese. Bake at 375° for 15 minutes or until cheese is melted. **Yield:** 8 servings.

## Cottage Cheese Veggie Salad

    3 cups (24 ounces) small-curd cottage cheese
    1 large ripe avocado, peeled, pitted and chopped
    1 medium tomato, chopped
  1/4 cup sliced stuffed olives
    2 tablespoons sliced green onions

In a serving bowl, combine the first four ingredients. Sprinkle with onions. **Yield:** 8 servings.

# Fix Special Meal On a Weeknight

BUSY COOKS need complete meals they can put on the table fast. That's why our food editors pulled together these three tempting recipes that feature speed as the key ingredient.

With this time-saving trio of dishes, you can have a "nice enough for company" meal ready in less than a half hour—even on a hectic weeknight.

For an effortless entree that tastes as good as it looks, try Herbed Pork Medallions shared by Jodie Arkin of Waconia, Minnesota. The pork slices have a nice blend of seasonings and broil in just minutes.

"I like to serve this tender pork for special occasions. My husband thinks I spend hours preparing it, but it's really easy to fix," she says.

An attractive accompaniment is Vinaigrette Vegetables from Mary Buhl of Duluth, Georgia.

Top off the meal with dishes of tasty Toasted Coconut Pudding.

"I decided to jazz up homemade vanilla pudding to make it taste like a Mounds candy bar," says JoAnn Moseman of Altus Air Force Base, Oklahoma.

"When the miniature chips are topped with the warm pudding, they melt into a rich creamy chocolate that's great with the chewy coconut."

## Herbed Pork Medallions

✓ Uses less fat, sugar or salt. Includes Nutritional Analysis and Diabetic Exchanges.

1-1/2 pounds pork tenderloin
   2 tablespoons butter *or* stick margarine, melted
1/4 teaspoon garlic powder
1/2 teaspoon salt
1/2 teaspoon dried tarragon
1/2 teaspoon dried thyme
1/2 teaspoon paprika
1/8 teaspoon pepper
1/8 teaspoon cayenne pepper
   1 tablespoon honey

Cut pork into 1/2-in. slices and pound to flatten. Combine butter and garlic powder; brush over pork. Combine the seasonings; sprinkle over pork. Place in two greased 15-in. x 10-in. x 1-in. baking pans. Broil 4-6 in. from the heat for 5 minutes; turn and broil 3 minutes longer. Brush with honey; broil for 1 minute or until meat juices run clear. **Yield:** 6 servings.
   **Nutritional Analysis:** One serving (3 ounces of cooked pork) equals 182 calories, 8 g fat (4 g saturated fat), 84 mg cholesterol, 292 mg sodium, 3 g carbohydrate, trace fiber, 24 g protein. **Diabetic Exchanges:** 3 lean meat, 1/2 fat.

## Vinaigrette Vegetables

✓ Uses less fat, sugar or salt. Includes Nutritional Analysis and Diabetic Exchanges.

   4 cups fresh broccoli florets
   1 medium zucchini, cut into 1/4-inch slices
1/3 cup julienned sweet yellow *or* red pepper
   3 tablespoons olive *or* canola oil
   4 to 5 teaspoons red wine vinegar
     *or* cider vinegar
   1 garlic clove, minced
1/2 teaspoon salt
1/4 to 1/2 teaspoon dried thyme

Place broccoli in a steamer basket. Place in a saucepan over 1 in. of water. Bring to a boil; cover and steam for 5 minutes. Add zucchini and yellow pepper; cover and steam for 2 minutes or until vegetables are crisp-tender. In a jar with a tight-fitting lid, combine the oil, vinegar, garlic, salt and thyme; shake well. Transfer vegetables to a serving bowl; add dressing and toss to coat. **Yield:** 6 servings.
   **Nutritional Analysis:** One 3/4-cup serving equals 81 calories, 7 g fat (1 g saturated fat), 0 cholesterol, 210 mg sodium, 4 g carbohydrate, 2 g fiber, 2 g protein. **Diabetic Exchanges:** 1 vegetable, 1 fat.

## Toasted Coconut Pudding

1/2 cup sugar
   3 tablespoons cornstarch
   3 cups milk
   3 egg yolks, beaten
   3 teaspoons butter *or* margarine
1-1/2 teaspoons vanilla extract
   3/4 cup flaked coconut, toasted
   3/4 cup miniature chocolate chips

In a large saucepan, combine the sugar and cornstarch. Stir in milk and egg yolks until smooth. Bring to a boil over medium heat; cook and stir for 2 minutes or until thickened. Remove from the heat; add butter and vanilla.
   Sprinkle 2 teaspoons each of coconut and chips into dessert dishes. Top with pudding mixture and remaining coconut and chips. Serve warm or refrigerate until serving. **Yield:** 6 servings.

# Comforting Fare Suits Busy Family

WHEN Julie Jahnke plans meals, she does it with style. "I like to prepare meals that are fun," says the wife, mother of two and full-time cosmetologist.

"For instance, I might make seasonal shapes out of bread dough or hide fruit under a scoop of cottage cheese.

"A big hit for a quick dinner is 'make-your-own' night. By putting all the ingredients on the table for sub sandwiches or hamburgers, each family member can assemble his own creation to his specific tastes."

Julie's husband, Michael, is a travel consultant who specializes in hunting and fishing trips and works out of the family's Green Lake, Wisconsin home.

"Once a week, he cooks a wonderful dinner for me and our sons, Dustin and Christopher," she says. "He's a terrific cook, so it's a real treat."

In her free time, Julie enjoys watching football with her family, donating baked goods to local churches and volunteering to help area hospice patients with their hair and nail care needs.

Despite an activity-packed calendar, nightly dinners are a priority at the Jahnke house.

For the made-in-minutes menu she shares here, Julie works backward and starts by preparing Heavenly Strawberry Tarts first. Convenient graham cracker tart shells are filled with a rich cream cheese layer and covered with gorgeous glazed strawberries.

While the tarts chill, Julie assembles Green Beans with Bacon. "I enjoy dishes that are salty and sweet, so I changed a recipe to create this version," she says.

With the beans cooking in the microwave, Julie busies herself with Breaded Turkey Slices. Seasoned bread crumbs—or finely crushed saltine crackers for a change of pace—coat the tender turkey that's fried in butter to a golden brown.

"The main dish calls for only a few ingredients and tastes so comforting," Julie assures. "My family loves it, so I fix this entree at least once a month."

## Heavenly Strawberry Tarts

✓ Uses less fat, sugar or salt. Includes Nutritional Analysis and Diabetic Exchanges.

    4 ounces cream cheese, softened
  1/4 cup sugar
2-1/4 teaspoons milk
1-1/2 teaspoons sour cream
  1/2 teaspoon vanilla extract
    1 package (6 count) individual graham cracker tart shells

1-1/2 cups sliced unsweetened strawberries
    1 cup strawberry glaze

In a small mixing bowl, beat the cream cheese, sugar, milk, sour cream and vanilla. Spoon into crusts. Combine the strawberries and glaze; spoon over cream cheese. Refrigerate until serving. **Yield:** 6 servings.

**Nutritional Analysis:** One tart (prepared with reduced-fat cream cheese, fat-free milk and reduced-fat sour cream) equals 264 calories, 10 g fat (3 g saturated fat), 11 mg cholesterol, 248 mg sodium, 40 g carbohydrate, 2 g fiber, 3 g protein. **Diabetic Exchanges:** 2 fat, 1-1/2 fruit, 1 starch.

## Green Beans with Bacon

    1 package (16 ounces) frozen cut green beans
    3 tablespoons water
    2 tablespoons butter *or* margarine
    7 teaspoons brown sugar
  1/2 teaspoon salt
  1/2 teaspoon chicken bouillon granules
    6 bacon slices, cooked and crumbled

In a microwave-safe bowl, combine the first six ingredients. Cover and microwave on high for 6 minutes or until the beans are crisp-tender. Sprinkle with bacon. **Yield:** 6 servings.

**Editor's Note:** This recipe was tested in an 850-watt microwave.

## Breaded Turkey Slices

    2 eggs
    3 tablespoons milk
    2 cups seasoned bread crumbs
  1/2 teaspoon salt
1-1/2 pounds boneless skinless turkey breast slices
  1/2 cup butter *or* margarine

In a shallow bowl, beat the eggs and milk. In another shallow bowl, combine bread crumbs and salt. Dip turkey slices in egg mixture, then coat with crumb mixture. In a large skillet, melt butter; brown turkey for about 2 minutes on each side or until juices run clear. **Yield:** 6 servings.

# Grill Streamlines Summery Supper

NOTHING saves time and rouses taste buds quite like grilled goods. That's why our food editors compiled a few of these summertime specialties into a made-in-minutes menu. The three rapid recipes offered here will help keep your kitchen cool...and cut down on cleanup, too.

Start with Bacon-Wrapped Corn. "After one bite of this grilled corn on the cob, you'll never go back to your old ways of preparing it," says Lori Bramble from Omaha, Nebraska.

"The incredible flavor of roasted corn combined with bacon and chili powder is sure to please your palate and bring rave reviews at your next backyard barbecue."

Next, throw together mouth-watering Beef 'n' Pork Burgers, which cook on the grill alongside the corn.

"The combination of ground beef and pork is the secret behind these juicy burgers," shares Sharon Adamczyk of Wind Lake, Wisconsin. "The never-fail burgers are ideal for summer grilling, so I depend on them time and again. Everyone loves them. Plus, you can easily double or triple the recipe for large get-togethers."

Cap off the meal with glasses of Lemonade Slush sent in by Tracy Brousseau of Orem, Utah. "I used to make a similar beverage with orange juice concentrate, but I enjoy lemonade so much I use that," she says.

"My family loved the results and now I fix this lemon version all the time. Not only is the drink fast and refreshing, but it's perfect at breakfast, after school or any time of the day."

## Bacon-Wrapped Corn

8 large ears sweet corn, husks removed
8 bacon strips
2 tablespoons chili powder

Wrap each ear of corn with a bacon strip; place each on a piece of heavy-duty aluminum foil. Sprinkle with chili powder. Wrap securely, twisting ends to make handles for turning. Grill, uncovered, over medium-hot heat for 20 minutes or until corn is tender and bacon is cooked, turning once. **Yield:** 8 servings.

## Beef 'n' Pork Burgers

4 bacon strips, diced
1 large onion, finely chopped
1 garlic clove, minced
1-1/2 cups soft bread crumbs
1 egg, beaten
1/2 cup water
1 tablespoon dried parsley flakes
2 to 3 teaspoons salt
1/4 teaspoon dried marjoram
1/4 teaspoon paprika
1/4 teaspoon pepper
1 pound ground beef
1 pound ground pork
8 hamburger buns, split and toasted
Mayonnaise, lettuce leaves and tomato slices

In a skillet, cook bacon, onion and garlic over medium heat until the bacon is crisp; drain and place in a bowl. Stir in the bread crumbs, egg, water, parsley, salt, marjoram, paprika and pepper. Crumble beef and pork over the mixture and mix well. Shape into eight 3/4-in.-thick patties.

Grill, uncovered, over medium-hot heat for 9-12 minutes or until juices run clear, turning occasionally. Serve on buns with mayonnaise, lettuce and tomato. **Yield:** 8 servings.

## Lemonade Slush

✓ Uses less fat, sugar or salt. Includes Nutritional Analysis and Diabetic Exchanges.

2/3 cup lemonade concentrate, partially thawed
1 cup milk
2/3 cup water
1 teaspoon vanilla extract
Yellow food coloring, optional
12 ice cubes, crushed

In a blender, combine lemonade concentrate, milk, water, vanilla and food coloring if desired; cover and process until blended. While processing, slowly add crushed ice. Process until slushy. Serve immediately. **Yield:** 8 servings.

**Nutritional Analysis:** One 3/4-cup serving (prepared with fat-free milk) equals 56 calories, trace fat (trace saturated fat), 1 mg cholesterol, 17 mg sodium, 13 g carbohydrate, trace fiber, 1 g protein. **Diabetic Exchange:** 1 fruit.

# Fabulous Fare's Ready in No Time

SITTING DOWN to a home-cooked supper is important to Becky Lohmiller of Monticello, Indiana. "My husband, John, and I make it a priority to sit down to an evening meal 6 nights a week," she shares.

"We both have hectic schedules, so mealtime is a good time to reconnect and talk about our day," says Becky. "Any day is better when you are with the ones you love and good food!"

Becky likes to have dinner ready soon after she gets home from her job as a public health nurse and John returns from the car dealership where he works. This tight timeline makes fuss-free recipes a necessity.

"Picking up fast food would be an easy solution, but it doesn't feed the soul like serving something you prepared yourself," Becky notes.

"When our daughter, Stacey, and her husband, Jon, visit us at our lake home, I look forward to relaxing with them over a homemade meal. However, I turn to recipes that come together quickly as I'd rather spend less time in the kitchen and more time with my family," she explains.

One of the menus Becky relies on most includes Italian Pineapple Chicken. "I created this one night when I was in a particular hurry," she recalls. "There is hardly any preparation involved, and everyone who tries it asks for the recipe."

The tender five-ingredient entree features skillet-browned chicken breasts and pineapple slices seasoned with bottled salad dressing.

"I make it a few times a month and often serve Feta-Topped Asparagus alongside it," she notes.

For a unique take on the versatile veggie, Becky jazzes up steamed asparagus with crumbed feta cheese and red onion. The colorful side dish is an ideal accompaniment to chicken and also a welcome addition to any summertime supper.

And if you're looking for something to tickle your sweet tooth, consider Becky's cheery Cherry Mousse. She promises that the three-item treat is a cinch to whip up no matter how busy you are.

"The fluffy dessert is a wonderful way to end a meal," she concludes. "I just know your family will find it as tasty as mine does."

## Italian Pineapple Chicken

- 4 boneless skinless chicken breast halves
- 1/2 cup Italian salad dressing
- 2 tablespoons olive *or* vegetable oil
- 1 can (8 ounces) sliced pineapple, drained
- 1/3 cup shredded Swiss cheese, optional

Flatten chicken to 1/2-in. thickness. Pour salad dressing into a shallow bowl; dip chicken in dressing. In a large skillet, heat oil. Add chicken; cook over medium-high heat for 5-7 minutes on each side or until juices run clear. Remove and keep warm.

Add pineapple slices to the skillet; cook for 30 seconds on each side or until lightly browned. Place a slice on each chicken breast half. Sprinkle with cheese if desired. **Yield:** 4 servings.

## Feta-Topped Asparagus

- 1-1/2 pounds fresh asparagus
- 1 medium red onion, sliced and separated into rings
- 2 tablespoons olive *or* vegetable oil
- Salt and pepper to taste
- 1/4 cup crumbled feta cheese

Place 1/2 in. of water and the asparagus in a large skillet; bring to a boil. Reduce heat; cover and simmer for 3-5 minutes or until crisp-tender; drain. Remove asparagus and keep warm. Saute onion in oil until crisp-tender. Return asparagus to the pan. Sprinkle with salt, pepper and cheese. **Yield:** 4 servings.

## Cherry Mousse

- 1 tablespoon cherry gelatin powder
- 1 can (14-1/2 ounces) tart cherries, drained
- 1 carton (8 ounces) frozen whipped topping, thawed

In a bowl, combine the gelatin powder and the cherries; fold in the whipped topping. Serve immediately. **Yield:** 4 servings.

'easy', 'good', 'easy and good', etc. My son liked it so much, he requested that I write 'easy, good, quick and make three times a week' on this recipe!"

Convenience items, including packaged greens and bottled dressing, speed along preparation of Greek Tossed Salad. The pretty medley gets great Greek flavor from more feta cheese, sliced cucumber and ripe olives.

"I like to serve this meal with some crusty bread," Vicki says. "I simply warm a loaf of French bread in the oven for about 10 minutes, then slice it.

"I add a tablespoon of Italian seasoning to 1/3 cup extra-virgin olive oil, then I serve the bread with individual bowls of the seasoned oil for dipping," she says. "We love this treatment with all types of bread.

"Guests always ask for the secrets behind this special and speedy dinner," Vicki states. "And I'm more than happy to share them."

# Marvelous Menu Has Greek Flair

VISIT Vicki Smith's home in the small farming and ranching community of Okeechobee, Florida, and you might be treated to a dinner featuring feta cheese and other ingredients common in Greek cooking.

Vicki is a full-time secretary in a busy office with Okeechobee County government. "In my free time, I enjoy gardening, bowling, racquetball and traveling," she shares.

"I also love cooking for my son, Josh, my mom, Elouise, and my friend Dean.

"It's fun to experiment in the kitchen," she says. "But my cooking time is limited, so I'm always looking for meals like this one that can be made in 30 minutes or less.

"Josh and I love feta cheese, so we tucked some into quick-cooking chicken breasts to create Bacon-Feta Stuffed Chicken," Vicki explains.

"Chicken breasts are incredibly versatile, and I think feta cheese is so underrated," she notes. "You can buy feta in so many different flavors...basil and tomato is our favorite."

While the chicken tastes especially good when browned in bacon drippings, using precooked bacon instead keeps this dish under a half hour.

"When we first tried it, we knew it was a keeper," Vicki says. "I label my recipes with notes such as

## Bacon-Feta Stuffed Chicken

    4 boneless skinless chicken breasts
1/4 cup crumbled cooked bacon
1/4 cup crumbled feta cheese
1/2 teaspoon salt
1/4 teaspoon pepper
    1 tablespoon vegetable oil
    2 cans (14-1/2 ounces *each*) diced tomatoes
    1 tablespoon dried basil

Carefully cut a pocket in each chicken breast. Fill with bacon and cheese; secure with toothpicks. Sprinkle with salt and pepper. In a large skillet, brown chicken in oil.

Drain one can of tomatoes, discarding juice; add to the skillet with the undrained can of tomatoes. Sprinkle with basil. Cover and simmer for 10 minutes. Uncover; simmer 5 minutes longer or until the chicken is no longer pink and the tomato mixture is thickened. **Yield:** 4 servings.

## Greek Tossed Salad

    5 cups ready-to-serve salad greens
3/4 cup sliced cucumber
    1 medium tomato, cut into wedges
    2 tablespoons crumbled feta cheese
    2 tablespoons sliced ripe olives
2/3 cup Greek vinaigrette *or* salad dressing of your choice

In a salad bowl, toss the greens, cucumber, tomato, cheese and olives. Drizzle with dressing; toss to coat. **Yield:** 4 servings.

# Down-Home Dishes Are Fast

SEARCHING for quick-to-fix fare with old-fashioned family appeal? Look no further than this time-saving trio of dishes.

Our food editors pulled together this comforting menu that takes advantage of both the microwave and the stove. So you can have a home-cooked dinner on the table in half an hour.

Start by preparing this meaty main dish shared by Karen Kurtz. "When my daughters were little, the only meats they ate were hot dogs and hamburger," recalls the Muskegon, Michigan cook. "But when I served Microwave Stroganoff, they loved it!"

To complement the effortless entree, toss together Wilted Lettuce Salad from Cheryl Newendorp of Pella, Iowa.

Cap off the meal by serving dishes of ice cream topped with warm Apricot Pecan Sauce. In Rosenort, Manitoba, Eleanor Martens needs just six ingredients to make this speedy sauce, "I enjoy fixing this simple dessert for all of our grandchildren," Eleanor says.

## Microwave Stroganoff

✓ Uses less fat, sugar or salt. Includes Nutritional Analysis and Diabetic Exchanges.

    2 tablespoons butter *or* stick margarine
1-1/2 pounds boneless beef sirloin steak, cut
       into thin strips
  1/4 cup all-purpose flour
    1 envelope onion soup mix
2-1/4 cups hot water
    1 can (4 ounces) mushroom stems and
       pieces, drained
  1/2 cup sour cream
Hot cooked noodles

Melt butter in a 2-qt. microwave-safe dish; arrange meat evenly in dish. Microwave, uncovered, on high for 6-8 minutes, stirring once. Remove meat with a slotted spoon and keep warm.

Stir flour and soup mix into drippings until blended. Gradually add water, stirring until smooth. Add mushrooms and beef. Cover and microwave on high for 18-20 minutes or until meat is tender and sauce is thickened, stirring several times and rotating a half turn once. Stir in sour cream. Serve over noodles. **Yield:** 6-8 servings.

**Nutritional Analysis:** One 1/2-cup serving (prepared with fat-free sour cream; calculated without noodles) equals 231 calories, 9 g fat (4 g saturated fat), 83 mg cholesterol, 304 mg sodium, 10 g carbohydrate, 1 g fiber, 26 g protein. **Diabetic Exchanges:** 3 lean meat, 1/2 starch, 1/2 fat.

**Editor's Note:** This recipe was tested in an 850-watt microwave.

## Wilted Lettuce Salad

    6 cups torn leaf lettuce
    3 tablespoons finely chopped onion
    3 bacon strips, diced
    2 tablespoons red wine vinegar *or*
       cider vinegar
2-1/4 teaspoons sugar
1-1/2 teaspoons water
Salt and pepper to taste
    1 hard-cooked egg, sliced

In a salad bowl, combine the lettuce and onion; set aside.

Place the bacon in a microwave-safe dish; cover with a microwave-safe paper towel. Cook on high for 5 minutes or until crisp, stirring every 30 seconds. Using a slotted spoon, remove bacon to paper towels.

In a 1-cup microwave-safe dish, combine 1-1/2 teaspoons bacon drippings, vinegar, sugar and water. Cook, uncovered, on high for 1 minute. Pour over lettuce; sprinkle with salt and pepper. Add bacon and egg; toss to coat. **Yield:** 6 servings.

**Editor's Note:** This recipe was tested in an 850-watt microwave.

## Apricot Pecan Sauce

  1/2 cup apricot spreadable fruit
  1/2 cup whipping cream
    2 tablespoons butter *or* margarine
  1/2 cup chopped pecans
  1/2 teaspoon vanilla extract
  1/4 to 1 teaspoon rum extract, optional
Vanilla ice cream

In a saucepan, bring spreadable fruit, cream and butter to a boil. Reduce heat; simmer, uncovered, for 3-5 minutes. Stir in pecans, vanilla and rum extract if desired. Remove from the heat. Serve over ice cream. **Yield:** 1 cup.

this flavorful meal is sure to be a hit with the whole family.

## Raspberry Yogurt Pie

✓ Uses less fat, sugar or salt. Includes Nutritional Analysis and Diabetic Exchanges.

- 2 cartons (8 ounces *each*) raspberry yogurt
- 1 carton (8 ounces) frozen whipped topping, thawed
- 1 graham cracker crust (9 inches)

Fresh raspberries, optional

Place yogurt in a bowl; fold in whipped topping. Spoon into crust. Garnish with raspberries if desired. Refrigerate until serving. **Yield:** 8 servings.

**Nutritional Analysis:** One piece (prepared with fat-free yogurt, reduced-fat whipped topping and a reduced-fat graham cracker crust) equals 200 calories, 6 g fat (4 g saturated fat), 2 mg cholesterol, 137 mg sodium, 28 g carbohydrate, 0 fiber, 4 g protein. **Diabetic Exchanges:** 1-1/2 starch, 1 fat, 1/2 fat-free milk.

## Seasoned Green Beans

- 3-1/2 cups fresh *or* frozen green beans (about 1 pound)
- 2 tablespoons butter *or* margarine, melted
- 1/4 to 1/2 teaspoon seasoned salt
- 1/4 to 1/2 teaspoon chili powder
- 1/8 teaspoon garlic powder
- 1/8 teaspoon onion powder

Place beans in a steamer basket; place in a saucepan over 1 in. of water. Bring to a boil; cover and steam for 7-8 minutes or until crisp-tender. In a small bowl, combine the butter and seasonings. Drain beans; add butter mixture and toss to coat. **Yield:** 4 servings.

## Chicken with Peach Stuffing

- 1 can (15-1/4 ounces) sliced peaches
- 4 boneless skinless chicken breast halves
- 2 tablespoons vegetable oil
- 2 tablespoons butter *or* margarine
- 1 tablespoon brown sugar
- 1 tablespoon cider vinegar
- 1/8 teaspoon ground allspice
- 1 package (6 ounces) chicken stuffing mix

Drain peaches, reserving syrup. Set aside eight peach slices for garnish; dice the remaining peaches. Add enough water to the syrup to measure 1 cup. Set peaches and syrup aside.

In a large skillet, brown chicken in oil. Add the butter, brown sugar, vinegar, allspice and reserved syrup. Bring to a boil. Reduce heat; cover and simmer for 5 minutes. Add the dry stuffing mix and diced peaches. Remove from the heat; cover and let stand for 5 minutes. Garnish with peach slices. **Yield:** 4 servings.

# Tasty Trio Is Quick, Delicious

FIXING a cozy family meal can be simple when you follow this fuss-free menu. By combining a few streamlined specialties, our food editors were able to create a heartwarming dinner that comes together in half an hour.

Since the dessert needs time to chill, start by preparing refreshing Raspberry Yogurt Pie first. A handful of ingredients is all you'll need to assemble the delightful no-bake treat from Margaret Schneider of Utica, Michigan. Try it with your favorite yogurt flavor and corresponding berries or fruit slices.

After placing the pie in the refrigerator, stir up a side dish of buttery Seasoned Green Beans.

"I like to add a little extra flavor to my green beans," says Katherine Firth of Oro Ballay, Arizona. "And this mouth-watering recipe is one of the quickest and most delicious I have."

While the beans steam, you'll have just enough time to fix Chicken with Peach Stuffing. "I turn to this main course over and over again," states Theresa Stewart from New Oxford, Pennsylvania.

Tender chicken breasts are simmered with brown sugar, cider vinegar and a hint of allspice, then dressed up with packaged stuffing mix and convenient canned peaches.

With its comforting flavor and quick prep time,

# Soup Makes Speedy Supper

DEEP in the heart of Texas City, Texas, Jennifer Villarreal knows how to cook filling fare with time to spare.

She works as a social worker and her husband, Steve, is a salesman. "While our jobs don't affect our cooking habits, our lifestyle does," says Jennifer.

"We like to eat healthy, and that means bypassing restaurants and cooking at home. However, we'd rather spend time with Steve's son, Cameron, than spend hours in the kitchen," she explains.

"In the winter, I stock up on turkey. Once a month, I cook a whole bird. Then I freeze the meat to use in everything from soups to sandwiches."

Jennifer loves to sew and go dancing, so she's always looking for meals that free up her schedule. And this south-of-the-border supper is no exception.

"When I serve Taco Soup at parties, everyone asks for the recipe," she says. "It makes a lot, so if I'm not feeding a crowd, I freeze the leftovers."

While the soup is simmering, toss together Jalapeno Avocado Salad. "This salad's tangy dressing will have everyone asking for seconds," she promises. "Guests like it because it's different, and I enjoy it because I can add whatever vegetables I have."

For a swift sweet dessert, try Cinnamon Graham Sundaes. "Many Mexican restaurants serve ice cream in deep-fried shells," says Jennifer. "I use cinnamon graham crackers and honey to get a similar taste.

## Taco Soup

1-1/2 pounds ground beef
   1 envelope taco seasoning
   2 cans (15-1/4 ounces *each*) whole kernel corn, undrained
   2 cans (15 ounces *each*) ranch-style *or* chili beans, undrained
   2 cans (14-1/2 ounces *each*) diced tomatoes, undrained
Crushed tortilla chips and shredded cheddar cheese
Flour tortillas, warmed

In a Dutch oven or large saucepan, cook beef over medium heat until no longer pink; drain. Stir in taco seasoning, corn, beans and tomatoes. Cover and simmer for 15 minutes or until heated through, stirring occasionally. Place tortilla chips in soup bowls; ladle soup over chips. Sprinkle with cheese. Serve with warmed tortillas. **Yield:** 8-10 servings (about 2 quarts).

## Jalapeno Avocado Salad

✓ Uses less fat, sugar or salt. Includes Nutritional Analysis and Diabetic Exchanges.

   2 medium ripe avocados, peeled and cubed
   2 medium tomatoes, chopped
   1 medium onion, chopped
   2 jalapeno peppers, seeded and chopped*
   1 cup lime juice
1-1/2 teaspoons sugar
   8 cups torn salad greens

In a bowl, combine the avocados, tomatoes, onion, jalapenos and lime juice; let stand for 5 minutes. Drain, reserving 1/3 cup juice.

Stir sugar into reserved juice; add to avocado mixture. Place greens in a salad bowl; add avocado mixture and toss to coat. **Yield:** 10 servings.

**Nutritional Analysis:** One serving (3/4 cup) equals 93 calories, 6 g fat (1 g saturated fat), 0 cholesterol, 18 mg so-dium, 10 g carbohydrate, 4 g fiber, 2 g protein. **Diabetic Exchanges:** 2 vegetable, 1 fat.

**\*Editor's Note:** When cutting or seeding hot peppers, use rubber or plastic gloves to protect your hands. Avoid touching your face.

## Cinnamon Graham Sundaes

20 cinnamon graham cracker squares
1/2 gallon vanilla ice cream
   3 tablespoons honey
   2 teaspoons ground cinnamon

For each serving, place two graham cracker squares on a plate. Top with ice cream and drizzle with honey. Sprinkle with cinnamon. **Yield:** 10 servings.

# Chapter 3

THE NEXT TIME you're hosting a party for family and friends, why not make your ordinary get-together extraordinary?

Our Quick Cooking kitchen staff has done the planning for you by creating six easy menus so you can have a fun, festive and fuss-free theme party.

From a fanciful fairy-tale feast, race car cuisine and a cute-as-a-bug buffet to an "apple-tizing" harvest menu, a memorable New Year's Eve meal and a lovely luau, you can easily create long-remembered occasions for your relatives and friends with just a short time spent in the kitchen.

**ALOHA!** Clockwise from top right: Sunset Cooler, Cookie Lei, Luau Chicken Sandwiches and Hawaiian Fruit Salad (all recipes on p. 39).

# Enchanting Edibles Make A Fairy-Tale Feast

TREAT YOUR FAMILY like royalty with this fuss-free feast created by our Test Kitchen. It's a merry meal that ensures you'll all live happily ever after.

## King-Size Drumsticks

### Plan ahead...uses slow cooker

*Let your slow cooker do the work when these tangy tender turkey legs make an appearance at your stately supper.*

- 1 can (10 ounces) enchilada sauce
- 1 can (4 ounces) chopped green chilies, drained
- 1 teaspoon dried oregano
- 1/2 teaspoon garlic salt
- 1/2 teaspoon ground cumin
- 6 turkey drumsticks
- 3 tablespoons cornstarch
- 3 tablespoons cold water

In a bowl, combine the enchilada sauce, chilies, oregano, garlic salt and cumin. Place the drumsticks in a 5-qt. slow cooker; top with sauce. Cover and cook on low for 8-10 hours or until a meat thermometer reads 180°. Remove turkey and keep warm. Strain sauce into a saucepan. Combine cornstarch and water until smooth; stir into pan. Bring to a boil; cook and stir for 2 minutes or until thickened. Serve with turkey. **Yield:** 6 servings.

## Dragon Dippers

### Ready in 30 minutes or less

*Once you taste these crispy chips, you may never buy store-bought tortilla chips again. The homemade snacks are a snap to prepare.*

- 2 tablespoons butter *or* margarine, melted
- 10 flour tortillas (7 inches)
- 3/4 teaspoon garlic salt
- 3/4 teaspoon ground cumin
- 3/4 teaspoon chili powder

Brush butter on one side of each tortilla. Combine the seasonings; sprinkle over tortillas. Cut each into eight wedges. Place on ungreased baking sheets. Bake at 400° for 6-8 minutes or until crisp. **Yield:** 6-1/2 dozen.

## Taco Dip Dragon

*Brave knights and lovely maidens are sure to clamor for this mythical monster. Refried beans are spread into a dragon shape and sprinkled with tempting toppings.*

- 1 can (16 ounces) refried beans
- 2 tablespoons taco seasoning
- 1 cup (8 ounces) sour cream
- 1 cup (4 ounces) shredded cheddar cheese
- 1 cup chopped fresh tomatoes
- 1/2 cup sliced ripe olives
- 1 cup guacamole
- 2 cups torn lettuce
- 1 whole ripe olive

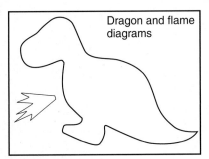

Dragon and flame diagrams

Dragon Dippers (recipe on this page) *or* purchased tortilla chips
1/2 medium sweet red pepper

In a bowl, combine beans and taco seasoning. Cut a large hole in the corner of a pastry or plastic bag; fill with bean mixture. Trace a dragon shape (about 16 in. x 10 in.) onto waxed paper (see diagram below); cut out. Place pattern on an 18-in. x 12-in. covered board. Pipe bean mixture around pattern. Remove pattern. Pipe remaining mixture within dragon outline; spread to fill.

Set aside 1 tablespoon sour cream. Spread remaining sour cream over bean mixture. Top with cheese, tomatoes, olives, guacamole and lettuce. For the eye, spoon reserved sour cream onto head; top with the olive.

Place Dragon Dippers along back and top of head. With a sharp knife, cut red pepper into a flame (see diagram); position below mouth. **Yield:** 6-8 servings.

## Miniature Castle Cakes

*You can easily make several of these pretty palaces with a cake mix, canned frosting and common confections.*

- 1 package (18-1/4 ounces) white cake mix
- 2-1/2 cups vanilla frosting
- 2 milk chocolate candy bars (1.55 ounces *each*)
- 21 chocolate nonpareil candies
- 12 pretzel sticks
- 1/2 cup flaked coconut
- 1 drop blue food coloring
- 3 sticks Fruit Stripe gum
- 6 small ice cream sugar cones
- 6 round wooden toothpicks

Prepare cake mix according to package directions. Pour batter into a greased 11-in. x 7-in. x 2-in. baking pan and six greased muffin cups. Bake at 350° for 20-30 minutes for cake and 15-18 minutes for cupcakes or until a toothpick comes out clean. Cool cupcakes for 5 minutes and cake for 10 minutes before removing from pans to wire racks. Cut the cake into six square pieces; place on serving plates. Frost cake top and sides. Position a cupcake on top of each; frost cupcakes.

For drawbridge, divide each candy bar into four three-piece sections. Center one section on one side of each cake; gently press into cake. Divide the two remaining chocolate sections into three pieces; place one piece above each drawbridge for door. Cut three nonpareil candies in half; arrange a half circle above each door. Press pretzels into cake on each side of bridge.

In a resealable plastic bag, shake coconut and food coloring until coconut is evenly colored. Sprinkle around bases of castles to represent water in the moat. Cut each stick of gum in half widthwise; cut one end to form a flag. Insert toothpick into gum. Trim sugar cone tips; insert flags into cones.

Place a nonpareil candy on two sides of each cupcake for windows. Frost backs of remaining candies; place one on the front of each cone. Position cones on cupcakes. **Yield:** 6 cakes.

# Lovely Luau Offers
# Flavor of the Islands

ALOHA! Do the sparkling white beaches, gentle ocean breezes, swaying palm trees and fragrant flowers of Hawaii sound appealing?

You don't have to fly there to enjoy a taste of this tropical paradise. For your next get-together, grab a grass skirt and greet guests with this mouth-watering menu compiled by our Test Kitchen.

Since Hawaii is one of the world's leading producers of pineapples, we feature the sweet and tangy fruit in two recipes. The fast flavorful chicken and pineapple sandwiches are low on fuss.

A pineapple cut into a boat makes a snappy serving dish for a fruit salad coated with coconut dressing.

Use convenience items to hurry along the three-ingredient beverage and colorful cookie lei. Both are sure to satisfy your appetite for the Aloha State.

## Luau Chicken Sandwiches

*(Also pictured on page 34)*

**Plan ahead...needs to marinate**

*A friend at work gave me the recipe for this marinade. After grilling the tender chicken a few times for company, I decided to turn it into a sandwich. It's complemented by a pineapple ring and a mild dill and mustard sauce.*
—Denise Pope, Mishawaka, Indiana

   1 can (20 ounces) sliced pineapple
   1 tablespoon brown sugar
   1 teaspoon ground mustard
   1 teaspoon garlic salt
1/2 teaspoon pepper
   6 boneless skinless chicken breast halves
1/4 cup mayonnaise
   1 tablespoon Dijon mustard
1/4 teaspoon dill weed
   6 kaiser rolls, split and toasted
   6 lettuce leaves, optional

Drain pineapple, reserving 1 cup juice and six pineapple slices (save remaining juice and pineapple for another use). In a large resealable plastic bag, combine the brown sugar, ground mustard, garlic salt, pepper and reserved pineapple juice; add chicken. Seal bag and turn to coat; refrigerate for at least 2 hours, turning occasionally. In a small bowl, combine the mayonnaise, Dijon mustard and dill. Refrigerate until serving.

Drain and discard marinade. Grill chicken, covered, over medium heat for 5-6 minutes on each side or until juices run clear. Grill pineapple slices for 1 minute on each side. Spread mayonnaise mixture on rolls. Top with lettuce if desired, chicken and pineapple. **Yield:** 6 servings.

## Hawaiian Fruit Salad

*(Also pictured on page 34)*

**Ready in 45 minutes or less**

*A simple dressing made with flavored yogurt coats this refreshing combination of fresh and canned fruit. It looks spectacular when presented in a pineapple boat and sprinkled with toasted coconut.*

   1 whole fresh pineapple
   1 can (15 ounces) mandarin oranges, drained
1-1/2 cups sliced fresh strawberries
1-1/2 cups green grapes, halved
1-1/4 cups pina colada-flavored *or* vanilla yogurt
1/2 cup flaked coconut, toasted, *divided*
1/4 to 1/2 teaspoon coconut *or* vanilla extract

Stand the pineapple upright and vertically cut a third from one side, leaving the leaves attached. Set cut piece aside. Using a paring or grapefruit knife, remove strips of pineapple from the large section, leaving a 1/2-in. shell; discard core. Cut strips into bite-size chunks. Invert shell onto paper towels to drain. Remove fruit from the small pineapple piece and cut into chunks; discard peel. Place shell in a serving basket or bowl.

In another bowl, combine the pineapple chunks, oranges, strawberries and grapes. Combine the yogurt, 1/4 cup coconut and extract; spoon over fruit and stir gently. Spoon into pineapple shell. Sprinkle with remaining coconut. **Yield:** 6 servings.

## Sunset Cooler

*(Also pictured on page 35)*

**Ready in 15 minutes or less**

*You don't have to reserve store-bought strawberry syrup just for making malts and shakes. Stirred into orange juice, it gives festive flair to this tropical-tasting beverage.*

   6 cups crushed ice
   6 cups orange juice
1/2 to 3/4 cup strawberry syrup*

In a pitcher, combine all ingredients; mix well. **Yield:** 6 servings.

  **\*Editor's Note:** This recipe was tested with Hershey's strawberry syrup.

## Cookie Lei

*(Also pictured on page 35)*

*Capture the spirit of Hawaiian hospitality with this sweet make-ahead lei that even kids can help assemble. Frost packaged butter cookies to create brilliant blooms, then thread them on shoestring licorice.*

1-2/3 cups confectioners' sugar
4-1/2 to 6 teaspoons water
  3/4 teaspoon light corn syrup
  1/4 teaspoon vanilla extract
Purple and deep pink gel *or* paste food coloring
   21 butter cookies with cutout centers
Yellow colored sugar
   1 piece shoestring licorice (30 inches)

In a mixing bowl, beat the confectioners' sugar, water, corn syrup and vanilla until smooth. Evenly divide frosting between three bowls. Tint one purple and one pink; leave the remaining frosting white. Frost cookie tops. Immediately dip the white frosted cookies in colored sugar. Let stand, uncovered, until dry, about 6 hours.

String cookies onto licorice piece, forming a lei. Store in an airtight container. **Yield:** 21 cookies (1 lei).

# Race Car Cuisine Puts Fun on Fast Track

ON YOUR MARK, get set, go! Race fans in your home will rush to the table in record time when this fast-paced fare cruises into the party.

The home economists in our Test Kitchen relied on pantry staples to shift this meal into high gear.

## Hot Dog Race Cars

*The members of your pit crew won't believe their eyes when these clever cars pull up to supper's starting line. Cheese, olives and ketchup help green-onion drivers feel at home in the rapid racers.*

      8 green onions with roots
Mustard and ketchup
    40 toothpicks
      8 hot dog buns
    32 large pitted ripe olives, halved
    16 slices process American cheese
      8 hot dogs
      8 radish slices

Cut root end of onions into 2-1/2-in. lengths; dip roots in mustard. Insert a toothpick into opposite end; set aside. Place buns on plates. To fasten wheels, insert four toothpicks in each bun, two on each side. Place an olive half, cut side out, on each toothpick. Cut cheese slices into 3-1/4-in. triangles; set aside.

Cook hot dogs according to package directions; place in buns. Insert green onion, using the toothpick, into the center of hot dog for driver. Cut a small widthwise slit in hot dog in front of driver; insert a radish slice for the steering wheel.

Place one cheese triangle in front of steering wheel and one behind the driver. Cut a hole in the corner of a pastry or plastic bag; fill with ketchup. Pipe numbers on front cheese slices and sides of buns. Pipe eyes and mouth on driver. **Yield:** 8 servings.

## Start-Your-Engine Salad

**Ready in 30 minutes or less**

*This sensational salad has a sweet-and-sour carrot dressing that perfectly complements its combination of lettuce, tomatoes and peppers.* —Darlis Wilfer
Phelps, Wisconsin

    1/3 cup chopped carrot
    1/3 cup chopped celery
      2 tablespoons chopped onion
      6 tablespoons sugar
      6 tablespoons vegetable oil
    1/4 cup cider vinegar
    1/4 teaspoon salt
      8 cups torn salad greens
      1 medium sweet yellow pepper, chopped
      1 medium green pepper, chopped
    3/4 cup shredded Parmesan cheese
    3/4 cup cherry tomatoes, halved

For dressing, combine the first seven ingredients in a blender. Cover and process until smooth. In a salad bowl, combine the greens, peppers, Parmesan cheese and tomatoes. Drizzle with dressing and toss to coat. Serve immediately. **Yield:** 8-10 servings.

## Checkered Flag Cookies

*Signal the end of dinner by waving these crunchy cookies. Boxed mixes speed along preparation of the dough.*

      1 cup butter (no substitutes), *divided*
    1/2 cup semisweet chocolate chips
      2 packages (17-1/2 ounces *each*) sugar cookie mix
      2 eggs
      4 tablespoons all-purpose flour, *divided*
    36 wooden skewers (5 inches)

In a large microwave-safe bowl, combine 1/2 cup butter and chocolate chips. Cover and microwave on high for 1-2 minutes or until melted; stir until blended. Add the contents of one cookie mix package, 1 egg and 2 tablespoons flour; stir until combined. Cover and refrigerate for 1-2 hours or until dough is firm.

Meanwhile, place the remaining butter in a microwave-safe bowl. Cover and heat on high for 1 minute or until melted. Add the remaining cookie mix, egg and flour; mix well. Cover and refrigerate for 1-2 hours or until firm.

On waxed paper, roll out the plain and chocolate dough into separate 9-in. x 5-in. rectangles. Cut each rectangle into nine 1-in. strips. Stack the strips in groups of three, alternating plain and chocolate strips, and forming six separate stacks. Form two blocks by placing one plain-topped stack on each side of a chocolate-topped stack and one chocolate-topped stack on each side of a plain-topped stack; press together gently.

Cut both stacks into 1/4-in. slices. Place 3 in. apart on ungreased baking sheets. Bake at 375° for 10-12 minutes or until edges are golden brown. Immediately insert a skewer into each cookie. Remove from pans to wire racks to cool. **Yield:** about 3 dozen.

## Winner's Trophy Dessert

**Plan ahead...needs to chill**

*Lemon and orange gelatin make these tangy trophies simple, but vanilla ice cream and mandarin oranges are what really get the crowd cheering.*

      1 package (3 ounces) lemon gelatin
      2 cups boiling water, *divided*
      2 cups vanilla ice cream,* softened
      1 package (3 ounces) orange gelatin
      1 cup cold water
      1 can (11 ounces) mandarin oranges, drained

In a bowl, dissolve lemon gelatin in 1 cup boiling water. Whisk in ice cream until blended. Pour into 4-oz. stemmed glasses. Chill for 2 hours or until set. Dissolve orange gelatin in remaining boiling water. Stir in cold water and oranges. Chill for 2 hours or until partially set. Pour over the lemon layer. Chill for 2 hours or until set. **Yield:** 8-10 servings.

**\*Editor's Note:** Reduced-fat ice cream or frozen yogurt may not be used in this recipe.

# Cute-as-a-Bug Buffet Gets Guests Buzzing

BUSY as a bee? Then you'll love this irresistible insect-themed menu compiled by the home economists in our Test Kitchen.

## Beetle Juice

**Ready in 15 minutes or less**

*The fruity combination in this refreshing beverage is a nice switch from plain orange juice.* —Mary Herron
Meshoppen, Pennsylvania

1 cup sugar
1 cup water
2-1/2 cups white grape juice
1-1/2 cups orange juice
1 cup lemon juice

In a large saucepan over medium heat, dissolve sugar in water. Remove from the heat. Stir in the juices; strain to remove pulp. Add enough water or ice to measure 1 gallon; stir well. **Yield:** 16 servings (4 quarts).

## Ladybug Appetizers

**Ready in 30 minutes or less**

*Cherry tomato quarters form the wings of these adorable little ladybugs dreamed up by our Test Kitchen. The delightful creatures sit on crunchy crackers spread with a seasoned cream cheese mixture.*

2 ounces cream cheese, softened
2 tablespoons sour cream
1/2 teaspoon snipped chives
1/8 teaspoon minced parsley
1/8 teaspoon garlic salt
Black paste food coloring
36 butter-flavored crackers
18 cherry tomatoes, quartered
18 large pitted ripe olives
72 fresh chive pieces (about 1-1/2 inches long)

In a small mixing bowl, beat the cream cheese until smooth. Add sour cream, chives, parsley and garlic salt; mix well. Place 1 tablespoon in a small plastic bag and tint black; set aside.

Spread remaining cream cheese mixture on crackers. Arrange two tomato quarters on each for the ladybug wings. For heads, halve the olives widthwise; place one half on each cracker. Insert two chives into olives for antennae. Use tinted cream cheese mixture to pipe spots onto wings. **Yield:** 3 dozen.

## Butterfly Sandwiches

*I never have any trouble getting my grandchildren to eat lunch when these cute butterfly sandwiches are on their perched plates. You can use chives or little pieces of celery for the antennae.* —Maggie Lanksbury
Seattle, Washington

1 pound boneless skinless chicken breasts
3 green onions, chopped
1/4 cup shredded carrot
1/4 cup shredded cheddar cheese
1 envelope (1 ounce) ranch salad dressing mix
3/4 cup mayonnaise
18 slices white bread
18 fresh baby carrots
36 fresh chive pieces (about 1-1/2 inches long)
36 carrot strips (about 1-1/2 inches long)
Sliced stuffed olives

Place chicken in a large skillet; add enough water to cover. Bring to a boil. Reduce heat; cover and simmer for 12-14 minutes or until chicken is tender and juices run clear. Drain and cool.

Shred chicken; place in a bowl. Add onions, carrot and cheese. Combine the salad dressing mix and mayonnaise; add to the chicken mixture. Spread over half of the bread slices; top with remaining bread. Diagonally cut each sandwich in half, creating four triangles.

To form wings, arrange two triangles with points toward each other and crust facing out. For each butterfly body, place one baby carrot between triangles; insert two chives into filling for antennae. Place one carrot strip in the center of each triangle. Place olive slices on wings. **Yield:** 9 servings.

## Caterpillar Cake

*This colorful creeping caterpillar is easy to make with a boxed cake mix and prepared frosting. To save a step, tint the frosting and omit the coconut.* —Lee Dean
Boaz, Alabama

1 package (18-1/4 ounces) yellow cake mix
1 can (16 ounces) vanilla frosting
2-1/2 cups flaked coconut, *divided*
2 small purple gumdrops
1 small red gumdrop
2 small orange gumdrops
2 pretzel sticks
Yellow, red and green liquid food coloring

Prepare cake batter according to package directions. Fill a greased 8-oz. custard cup three-fourths full. Pour remaining batter into a greased 10-in. fluted tube pan. Bake the custard cup at 350° for 20-25 minutes and the tube cake for 40-45 minutes or until a toothpick inserted near the center comes out clean. Cool for 10 minutes before removing cakes to wire racks; cool completely.

Cut large cake in half widthwise. To form caterpillar, place one half on a 15-in. x 10-in. covered board. Place the remaining portion next to the first to form an "S". With a serrated knife, level top and bottom of small cake; place on one end of caterpillar for head.

Frost the small cake with vanilla frosting; gently press 1/4 cup coconut into frosting. Add purple gumdrops for eyes. For mouth, flatten red gumdrop with a rolling pin between waxed paper; place below eyes. For antennae, press orange gumdrops onto pretzels; insert into head.

Place 3/4 cup coconut each in three small resealable plastic bags. Tint one orange with yellow and red food coloring; tint one green and one yellow. Frost the caterpillar with the remaining vanilla frosting. Press alternate colors of coconut into the frosting. **Yield:** 8-10 servings.

# Harvest Menu Has Real Appeal

WELCOME AUTUMN with an apple-inspired menu guaranteed to warm spirits on the coolest of fall days. Our Test Kitchen staff selected a few "apple-tizing" recipes to create a fruit-filled dinner that's as simple as it is sensational.

## Harvest Apple Cider

**Plan ahead...uses slow cooker**

*I simmer this comforting cider in my slow cooker every fall. It's a fruity blend with just the right spice. You'll enjoy this heartwarming beverage at any gathering. It's a nice alternative to hot chocolate on cold days.* —Lesley Geisel
Severna Park, Maryland

```
   8 whole cloves
   4 cups apple cider
   4 cups pineapple juice
1/2 cup water
   1 cinnamon stick (3 inches)
   1 individual tea bag
```

Place cloves on a double thickness of cheesecloth; bring up corners of cloth and tie with kitchen string to form a bag. Place the remaining ingredients in a slow cooker; add spice bag. Cover and cook on low for 2 hours or until cider reaches desired temperature. Discard spice bag, cinnamon stick and tea bag before serving. **Yield:** about 2 quarts.

## Apple-Glazed Pork Chops

**Ready in 30 minutes or less**

*Simple enough for weeknights yet impressive enough to serve to guests, these juicy chops are topped with a glaze of herbs, apple cider and brown sugar. The cooked apple slices and onions will make this pork dish a fast favorite in your home.*

```
   4 bone-in pork chops (3/4 inch thick)
   2 tablespoons vegetable oil
   1 cup apple cider or apple juice
   2 tablespoons brown sugar, divided
   1 teaspoon salt
1/4 teaspoon dried rosemary, crushed
1/4 teaspoon dried thyme
   1 tablespoon cornstarch
   1 tablespoon cold water
   2 large tart apples, sliced
1/2 cup sliced onion
   2 tablespoons butter or margarine
```

In a large skillet, brown pork chops in oil. Add the cider, 1 tablespoon brown sugar, salt, rosemary and thyme. Cover and cook for 7-8 minutes or until meat juices run clear. Combine the cornstarch and water until smooth; add to the skillet. Bring to a boil; cook and stir for 1-2 minutes or until thickened.

Meanwhile, in another skillet, cook the apples, onion, butter and remaining brown sugar over medium heat for 3-4 minutes or until apples are softened. Serve over pork chops. **Yield:** 4 servings.

## Fruity Apple Salad

**Ready in 30 minutes or less**

*Green and red apples add a nice crunch to this pretty medley of blueberries, grapes, pineapple and mandarin oranges.*

✓ Uses less fat, sugar or salt. Includes Nutritional Analysis and Diabetic Exchanges.

```
   1 large green apple, chopped
   1 medium red apple, chopped
1/2 cup seedless red grapes, halved
1/2 cup seedless green grapes, halved
   1 can (8 ounces) unsweetened pineapple
     tidbits, drained
1/2 cup fresh or frozen blueberries
3/4 cup mandarin oranges
1/4 cup sugar
1/4 cup lemon juice
1/4 cup water
```

In a serving bowl, combine the apples, grapes, pineapple, blueberries and oranges. In a small bowl, combine the sugar, lemon juice and water; stir until sugar is dissolved. Pour over fruit and toss gently. Serve with a slotted spoon. **Yield:** 6 servings.
**Nutritional Analysis:** One serving (3/4 cup) equals 109 calories, trace fat (trace saturated fat), 0 cholesterol, 2 mg sodium, 29 g carbohydrate, 3 g fiber, 1 g protein. **Diabetic Exchange:** 2 fruit.

## Apple Spice Cupcakes

*A spice cake mix makes these moist treats a snap to stir up. A fast frosting helps them stand out from an orchard of goodies.*

```
      1 package (18-1/4 ounces) spice cake mix
1-1/4 cups water
      3 eggs
   1/3 cup applesauce
FROSTING:
      1 package (8 ounces) cream cheese, softened
   1/4 cup butter or margarine, softened
      1 teaspoon vanilla extract
      4 cups confectioners' sugar
Red paste or liquid food coloring
     24 pieces black licorice (3/4 inch)
     12 green spice gumdrops
```

In a large mixing bowl, beat the cake mix, water, eggs and applesauce on low speed for 30 seconds or just until moistened. Beat on medium for 2 minutes or until smooth. Pour into 24 red paper-lined muffin cups. Bake at 350° for 18-20 minutes or until a toothpick comes out clean. Cool for 5 minutes before removing from pans to wire racks.

In a small mixing bowl, beat the cream cheese, butter and vanilla. Gradually add sugar, beating until smooth. Stir in food coloring. Frost tops of cupcakes. Insert licorice into centers for apple stems. Cut gumdrops in half; flatten and pinch to form leaves. Place one leaf next to each stem. **Yield:** 2 dozen.

# Memorable Meal Marks New Year

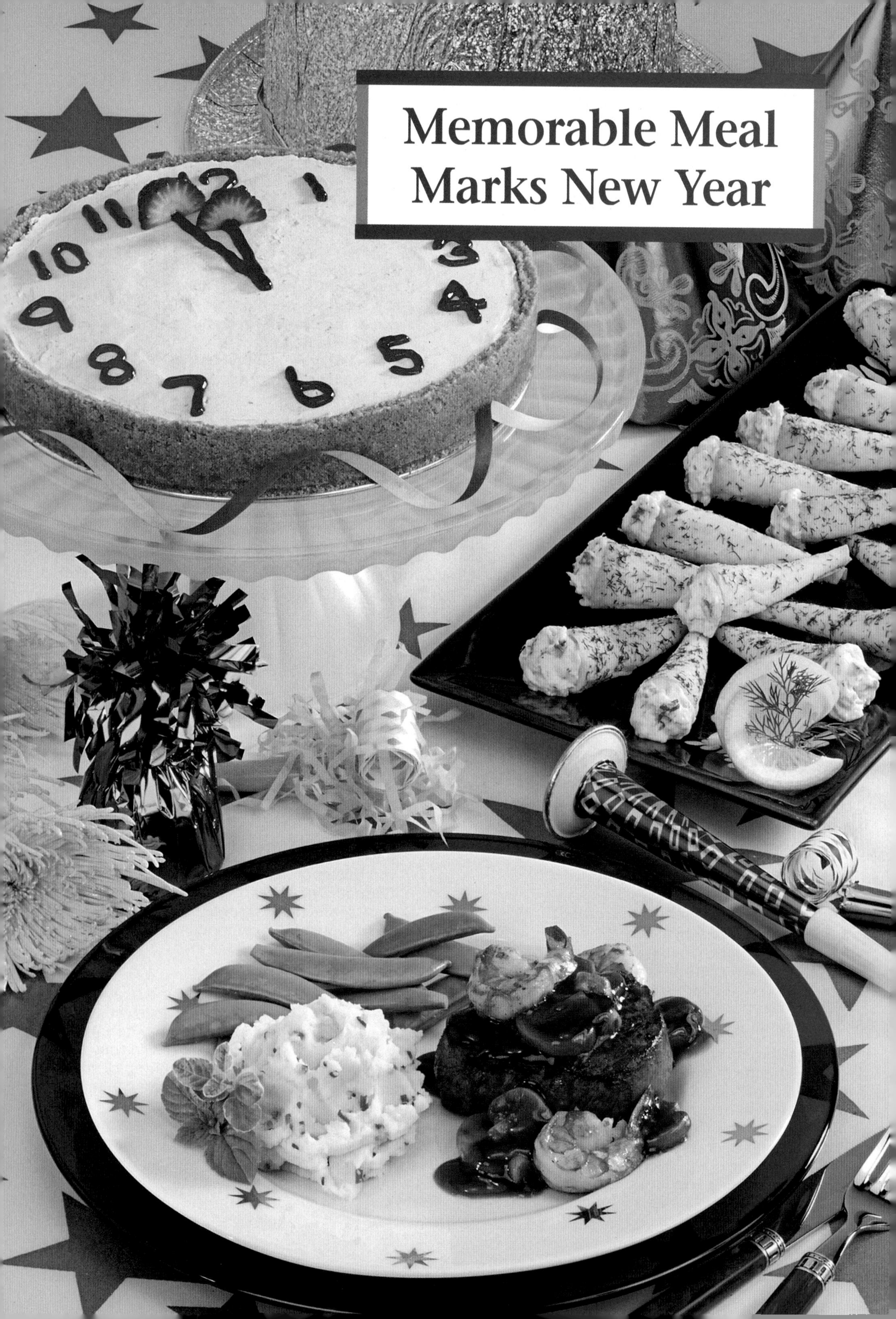

CREATE restaurant-quality New Year's Eve cuisine in your kitchen with help from our home economists.

## Noisemaker Appetizers

*Wonton wrappers form crunchy little horns filled with a creamy mixture of crab and dill in these savory sensations.*

24 wonton wrappers
1/4 cup butter *or* margarine, melted
1 teaspoon dill weed, *divided*
1/4 teaspoon garlic salt
1 package (8 ounces) cream cheese, softened
1 tablespoon sour cream
1/2 teaspoon lemon juice
1 can (6 ounces) crabmeat, drained, flaked and cartilage removed *or* 1 cup chopped imitation crabmeat

Place a wonton wrapper on a work surface with one corner facing you; roll into a cone. Cut the open end with a sharp scissors until edge is even. Place a 1-in. foil ball in opening. Place seam side down on a greased baking sheet. Repeat with remaining wonton wrappers.

Bake at 375° for 10 minutes or until golden brown. In a small bowl, combine the butter, 1/2 teaspoon dill and garlic salt. Brush over horns. Remove to a wire rack to cool completely. Remove foil balls.

In a mixing bowl, beat cream cheese until smooth. Add the sour cream, lemon juice and remaining dill; mix well. Fold in the crab. Transfer to a pastry or plastic bag; cut a hole in the corner. Pipe into cooled horns. **Yield:** 2 dozen.

## New Year's Surf 'n' Turf

*(Also pictured on front cover)*

*A mild mushroom sauce pulls together this pleasing pairing of tender steaks and firm shrimp.*

2 cups sliced fresh mushrooms
2 tablespoons finely chopped green onion
1-1/2 teaspoons minced garlic, *divided*
5 tablespoons olive *or* vegetable oil, *divided*
5 tablespoons butter *or* margarine, *divided*
1/2 cup red wine *or* beef broth
2 tablespoons minced fresh parsley
2 tablespoons minced fresh basil
1/2 teaspoon browning sauce, optional
8 beef tenderloin steaks (1 to 1-1/2 inches thick)
24 uncooked medium shrimp, peeled and deveined

In a large skillet, saute the mushrooms, onion and 1 teaspoon garlic in 2 tablespoons oil and 2 tablespoons butter until tender. Add wine or broth; cook and stir for 1 minute. Stir in the parsley, basil and browning sauce if desired. Remove from the skillet; keep warm.

In the same skillet, heat 2 tablespoons oil and 2 tablespoons butter over medium-high heat. Add the steaks; cook for 5-8 minutes on each side or until meat reaches desired doneness (for rare, a meat thermometer should read 140°; medium, 160°; well-done, 170°). Return mushroom mixture to the pan; heat through.

In another skillet, combine remaining butter and oil. Add shrimp and remaining garlic; cook and stir until shrimp turn pink. Serve with steaks. **Yield:** 8 servings.

## Midnight Mashed Potatoes

*(Also pictured on front cover)*

*Garlic, onion salt and Parmesan cheese season these mashed potatoes that get richness from sour cream.*

6 medium russet potatoes, peeled and cubed
2 garlic cloves, minced
1 tablespoon butter *or* margarine
1/2 cup milk
1/2 cup sour cream
2 tablespoons grated Parmesan cheese
2 tablespoons snipped chives
1 teaspoon salt
3/4 teaspoon onion salt
1/2 teaspoon garlic powder
1/4 teaspoon pepper

Place potatoes in a saucepan and cover with water. Bring to a boil. Reduce heat; cover and cook for 15-20 minutes or until tender. Meanwhile, in a small skillet, saute the garlic in butter.

Drain potatoes and place in a large mixing bowl; add the garlic. Beat until smooth. Add the remaining ingredients; mix well. Transfer to a greased 2-qt. baking dish. Bake, uncovered, at 350° for 35-40 minutes or until heated through. **Yield:** 8 servings.

## Countdown Cheesecake

**Plan ahead...needs to chill**

*Guests will surely count down the minutes until they can dig into this creamy strawberry cheesecake.*

1-1/2 cups graham cracker crumbs (about 24 squares)
3 tablespoons sugar
1/3 cup butter *or* margarine, melted
FILLING:
2 cartons (8 ounces *each*) strawberry cream cheese
1/2 cup sugar
1 carton (8 ounces) frozen whipped topping, thawed
1-1/2 cups sliced fresh strawberries
Red decorating gel
1 fresh strawberry, halved

In a bowl, combine the cracker crumbs, sugar and butter. Press onto the bottom and 1 in. up the sides of a greased 9-in. springform pan. Bake at 325° for 10 minutes; cool.

In a mixing bowl, beat the cream cheese and sugar until smooth. Fold in the whipped topping. Gently spread a third of the filling over crust. Arrange strawberries on top. Spoon remaining filling over berries; smooth top. Refrigerate overnight. With decorating gel, pipe numerals and the minute and hour hands for a clock dial on the cheesecake. Place strawberry halves at the tips of the clock hands. **Yield:** 8-10 servings.

# Chapter 4

LESS IS MORE. That's especially true for today's time-pressed cooks. Recipes that call for fewer ingredients usually take less time to prepare.

So it's no wonder that busy cooks who steer clear of long lists of ingredients will turn to this chapter frequently.

With just five ingredients—or fewer—per recipe, each delicious dish is so simple to assemble.

But while these tasty entrees, side dishes, soups, salads and desserts are short on ingredients, they're long on flavor. So you can offer wholesome foods your whole family will favor.

**SIMPLE YET SENSATIONAL.** Clockwise from top: Coconut Peach Pie, Taco Chicken Rolls and Salsa Rice (all recipes on pp. 58 and 59).

## Green Beans with a Twist

*(Pictured below)*

**Ready in 15 minutes or less**

*Green beans get a makeover in this side dish with help from fresh mushrooms, ranch salad dressing mix and crumbled bacon. For added convenience, I sometimes use canned mushrooms.* —Nicole Orr, Columbus, Ohio

> 1 package (16 ounces) frozen French-style green beans
> 1 cup sliced fresh mushrooms
> 2 tablespoons butter *or* margarine
> 1 envelope ranch salad dressing mix
> 4 bacon strips, cooked and crumbled

In a skillet, saute the beans and mushrooms in butter. Sprinkle with dressing mix; toss to coat. Just before serving, sprinkle with bacon. **Yield:** 4-6 servings.

## Sausage Spaghetti Spirals

*(Pictured below)*

**Ready in 45 minutes or less**

*My family loves this flavorful Italian-style casserole with hearty chunks of sausage, green pepper and a melted mozzarella cheese on top. The recipe makes a big pan, so it's nicely sized to share at a potluck.* —Carol Carlton, Wheaton, Illinois

✓ Uses less fat, sugar or salt. Includes Nutritional Analysis and Diabetic Exchanges.

> 1 pound bulk Italian sausage
> 1 medium green pepper, chopped
> 5 cups spiral pasta, cooked and drained
> 1 jar (28 ounces) meatless spaghetti sauce
> 1-1/2 cups (6 ounces) shredded mozzarella cheese

In a skillet, cook sausage and green pepper over medium heat until meat is no longer pink; drain. Stir in pasta and spaghetti sauce; mix well. Transfer to a greased 13-in. x 9-in. x 2-in. baking dish. Cover and bake at 350° for 25 minutes. Uncover; sprinkle with cheese. Bake 5-10 minutes longer or until the cheese is melted. **Yield:** 10 servings.

**Nutritional Analysis:** One 1-cup serving (prepared with turkey Italian sausage and reduced-fat mozzarella) equals 249 calories, 8 g fat (3 g saturated fat), 34 mg cholesterol, 710 mg sodium, 28 g carbohydrate, 2 g fiber, 16 g protein. **Diabetic Exchanges:** 2 starch, 1-1/2 lean meat.

**Sausage Spaghetti Spirals**
**Monterey Ranch Bread**
**Green Beans with a Twist**

# Monterey Ranch Bread

*(Pictured below left)*

**Ready in 30 minutes or less**

*This rich, cheesy loaf is a quick-and-easy addition to any meal. Or serve it as an appealing appetizer for a casual get-together.* —Shirley Privratsky, Dickinson, North Dakota

```
    2 cups (8 ounces) shredded Monterey
      Jack cheese
  3/4 cup ranch salad dressing with bacon
    1 loaf (1 pound) unsliced French bread
    2 tablespoons butter or margarine, melted
Minced fresh parsley
```

In a bowl, combine the cheese and salad dressing; set aside. Cut bread in half lengthwise; brush with butter. Place on baking sheets. Broil 4 in. from the heat until golden brown. Spread with cheese mixture. Bake at 350° for 10-15 minutes or until cheese is melted. Sprinkle with parsley. Cut into 1-1/2-in. slices. **Yield:** 6-8 servings.

# Broccoli Corn Casserole

**Ready in 45 minutes or less**

*I had a hard time getting my three sons to eat vegetables when they were young. So I fooled them with this casserole that looks just like stuffing when it comes out of the oven. Now that they're grown, they still ask for "broccoli stuffing" when they come for dinner.* —Lucille Wermes Camp, Arkansas

```
    1 package (10 ounces) frozen chopped
      broccoli, thawed
    1 can (14-3/4 ounces) cream-style corn
    1 egg
1-1/2 cups stuffing mix
  1/2 cup butter or margarine, melted
```

In a bowl, combine broccoli, corn and egg. Transfer to a greased 1-qt. baking dish. Sprinkle with stuffing mix and drizzle with butter. Bake, uncovered, at 350° for 30-35 minutes or until golden brown and bubbly. **Yield:** 6 servings.

# Red-Hot Candy Fluff

**Plan ahead...start the night before**

*A friend at work gave me the recipe for this fluffy pink pineapple salad a few years ago, and I've been preparing it ever since. My two young children really enjoy it.* —Shelley Vickrey, Strafford, Missouri

```
    1 can (20 ounces) crushed pineapple, drained
  1/4 cup red-hot candies
    2 cups miniature marshmallows
    1 carton (8 ounces) frozen whipped topping,
      thawed
```

In a bowl, combine the pineapple and candies. Cover and refrigerate for 8 hours or overnight. Stir in the marshmallows and whipped topping. Cover and refrigerate until serving. **Yield:** 6-8 servings.

# Caramel Pecan Bars

**Ready in 45 minutes or less**

*These bars are so simple to fix, yet so delicious. You'll want to cut them small because the combination of caramel, chocolate and pecans makes them rich and sweet.* —Rebecca Wyke, Morganton, North Carolina

```
1-1/2 cups crushed vanilla wafers (about 50 wafers)
  1/4 cup butter or margarine, melted
    2 cups (12 ounces) semisweet chocolate chips
    1 cup chopped pecans
    1 jar (12 ounces) caramel ice cream topping
```

In a bowl, combine the wafer crumbs and butter. Press into a greased 13-in. x 9-in. x 2-in. baking pan. Sprinkle with chocolate chips and pecans. In a microwave, heat caramel topping on high for 1-2 minutes or until warm. Drizzle over the top. Bake at 350° for 10 minutes or until chips are melted. Cool on a wire rack. **Yield:** 6 dozen.

# Cheesy Crab Burritos

**Ready in 30 minutes or less**

*Everyone who tries this elegant variation on the standard burrito loves it. Serve with a green salad for a lighter lunch or with traditional rice and beans for supper.* —Karen Dye, Tempe, Arizona

```
    1 package (8 ounces) cream cheese, softened
    2 cups (8 ounces) shredded cheddar cheese
    1 package (8 ounces) imitation crabmeat,
      flaked
    8 flour tortillas (10 inches)
Salsa
```

In a mixing bowl, combine the cream cheese and cheddar cheese. Stir in the crab. Spoon down the center of each tortilla; roll up tightly and place on an ungreased baking sheet. Bake at 350° for 20 minutes or until heated through. Serve with salsa. **Yield:** 4 servings.

# Pork Chop Casserole

**Ready in 1 hour or less**

*I rely on orange juice and canned soup to boost the flavor of this tender pork chop and rice bake. It's very good...and a little different from your usual fare.* —Wanda Plinsky Wichita, Kansas

```
    4 bone-in pork loin chops (1/2 inch thick)
    1 tablespoon vegetable oil
1-1/3 cups uncooked long grain rice
    1 cup orange juice
    1 can (10-1/2 ounces) condensed chicken
      with rice soup, undiluted
```

In a large skillet, brown pork chops in oil; drain. Place the rice in an ungreased shallow 3-qt. baking dish; pour orange juice over rice. Top with pork chops and soup. Cover and bake at 350° for 40-45 minutes or until pork juices run clear and rice is tender. **Yield:** 4 servings.

## Hamburger Skillet Supper

**Ready in 15 minutes or less**

*When time is tight, this one-dish wonder is a surefire way to beat the clock. I created this recipe while looking for a new stovetop meal. You can easily double the ingredients for a larger group.* —Donna Gardner, Ottumwa, Iowa

✓ Uses less fat, sugar or salt. Includes Nutritional Analysis and Diabetic Exchanges.

 1 pound ground beef
 1 package (3 ounces) ramen noodles
 2 cups water
 2 cups frozen mixed vegetables, thawed

In a skillet, cook beef until no longer pink; drain. Add noodles with contents of seasoning packet and water. Bring to a boil; cook for 3 minutes or until noodles are tender. Add the vegetables and cook until tender, about 3 minutes. **Yield:** 4 servings.
 **Nutritional Analysis:** One 1-cup serving (prepared with lean ground beef) equals 342 calories, 14 g fat (6 g saturated fat), 41 mg cholesterol, 361 mg sodium, 26 g carbohydrate, 4 g fiber, 28 g protein. **Diabetic Exchanges:** 3 lean meat, 2 vegetable, 1 starch, 1 fat.


## Blue Cheese Potatoes

**Ready in 30 minutes or less**

*I serve this warm creamy potato salad to the blue cheese lovers in my home. It's quick to fix because you don't need to peel the potatoes.* —Brandi Rook, Salina, Kansas

 2 pounds red potatoes, cut into chunks
 1/4 cup whipping cream, whipped
 1/4 cup crumbled blue cheese
 1 cup mayonnaise
 1/2 pound sliced bacon, cooked and crumbled

Place potatoes in a saucepan and cover with water. Bring to a boil over medium-high heat; cover and cook until tender, about 15-20 minutes. Meanwhile, in a small bowl, fold whipped cream and blue cheese into mayonnaise. Drain potatoes; gently stir in blue cheese mixture. Sprinkle with bacon. Serve warm. **Yield:** 6-8 servings.


## Buttery Almond Cookies

*My husband loves these cookies. They have an old-fashioned flavor that goes well with a cup of tea.*
 —Elaine Anderson, Aliquippa, Pennsylvania

 1 cup butter (no substitutes), softened
 1 cup confectioners' sugar, *divided*
 2 cups all-purpose flour
 1 teaspoon vanilla extract
 3/4 cup chopped almonds

In a mixing bowl, cream butter and 1/2 cup confectioners' sugar. Add flour and vanilla; mix well. Stir in almonds. Shape into 1-in. balls. Place 2 in. apart on ungreased baking sheets.
 Bake at 350° for 13-16 minutes or until the bottoms

are golden brown and cookies are set. Cool for 1-2 minutes before removing cookies to wire racks to cool completely. Roll in remaining confectioners' sugar. **Yield:** about 4 dozen.


## Creamy Corn

**Ready in 30 minutes or less**

*A packet of seasoned noodles is jazzed up with just two ingredients—cream-style corn and process cheese—in this comforting side dish. I make this recipe often.*
 —Carol White, Verona, Illinois

 1 package (4.3 ounces) quick-cooking noodles and butter herb sauce mix
 1 can (14-3/4 ounces) cream-style corn
 2 ounces process cheese (Velveeta), cubed

Prepare noodles and sauce mix according to package directions. When the noodles are tender, stir in corn and cheese; cook and stir until cheese is melted. Let stand for 5 minutes. **Yield:** 6-8 servings.


## Marinated Artichoke Salad

*(Pictured at right)*

**Plan ahead...needs to chill**

*Artichoke hearts, fresh vegetables and Italian salad dressing combine to make this no-fuss favorite. I always take this salad to get-togethers. A special event wouldn't be the same without it.* —Ann Marie Petri, Barron, Wisconsin

✓ Uses less fat, sugar or salt. Includes Nutritional Analysis and Diabetic Exchanges.

 1 can (14 ounces) water-packed artichoke hearts, drained and quartered
 1 medium tomato, cut into wedges
 1/2 cup chopped green pepper
 1/3 cup chopped red onion
 1/4 cup prepared Italian salad dressing

In a bowl, combine artichokes, tomato, green pepper and onion. Drizzle with salad dressing; toss to coat. Cover and refrigerate for at least 1 hour. **Yield:** 4 servings.
 **Nutritional Analysis:** One 3/4-cup serving (prepared with fat-free salad dressing) equals 80 calories, trace fat (trace saturated fat), 1 mg cholesterol, 821 mg sodium, 16 g carbohydrate, 5 g fiber, 4 g protein. **Diabetic Exchange:** 3 vegetable.


## Peach-Glazed Cake

*(Pictured above right)*

*After tasting this cake, guests always ask for a second slice...and the recipe. Everyone is surprised when they learn this dessert is so easy to make. I often garnish servings with pear slices instead of peaches.*
 —Samantha Jones, Morgantown, West Virginia

 1 can (15 ounces) pear halves, drained
 1 package (18-1/4 ounces) white cake mix

Marinated Artichoke Salad
Peach-Glazed Cake
Maple Barbecued Chicken

**3 eggs**
**1 jar (12 ounces) peach preserves,** *divided*
**Fresh** *or* **frozen sliced peaches, thawed**

In a blender or food processor, cover and process pears until pureed. Transfer to a mixing bowl; add the cake mix and eggs. Beat on medium speed for 2 minutes. Pour into a greased and floured 10-in. fluted tube pan. Bake at 350° for 30-35 minutes or until a toothpick inserted near the center comes out clean. Cool for 10 minutes before removing from pan to a wire rack.

In a microwave-safe bowl, heat 1/2 cup of peach preserves, uncovered, on high for 60-90 seconds or until melted. Slowly brush over warm cake. Cool completely. Slice cake; top with peaches. Melt remaining preserves; drizzle over top. **Yield:** 10-12 servings.

## Maple Barbecued Chicken

*(Pictured above)*

### Ready in 30 minutes or less

*This tender glazed chicken is so delicious, it will disappear very quickly. The sweet maple sauce is used to baste the* chicken while grilling, with additional sauce served alongside for dipping. —Ruth Lowen, Hythe, Alberta

✓ Uses less fat, sugar or salt. Includes Nutritional Analysis and Diabetic Exchanges.

**3/4 cup barbecue sauce**
**3/4 cup maple pancake syrup**
**1/2 teaspoon salt**
**1/2 teaspoon maple flavoring**
**8 boneless skinless chicken breast halves**
**(2 pounds)**

In a bowl, combine the first four ingredients; mix well. Remove 3/4 cup to a small bowl for serving; cover and refrigerate. Grill chicken, uncovered, over medium heat for 3 minutes on each side. Grill 6-8 minutes longer or until juices run clear, basting with remaining sauce and turning occasionally. Serve with reserved sauce. **Yield:** 8 servings.

**Nutritional Analysis:** One serving (one chicken breast with 1-1/2 tablespoons sauce) equals 228 calories, 2 g fat (trace saturated fat), 66 mg cholesterol, 436 mg sodium, 26 g carbohydrate, trace fiber, 27 g protein. **Diabetic Exchanges:** 3 lean meat, 1-1/2 fruit.

Oven-Baked Burgers
Cucumber Shell Salad
Easy Cherry Tarts

## Oven-Baked Burgers

*(Pictured above)*

**Ready in 30 minutes or less**

*A seasoned coating mix and steak sauce dress up these hamburgers that cook in the oven rather than on the grill. I like to use a sweet and spicy steak sauce for the best flavor. It's a unique way to serve burgers.*
—Mike Goldman
Arden Hills, Minnesota

1/4 cup steak sauce
2 tablespoons plus 1/3 cup Shake'n Bake seasoned coating mix, *divided*
1 pound ground beef
4 hamburger buns, split
4 lettuce leaves

In a bowl, combine the steak sauce and 2 tablespoons of coating mix. Crumble beef over mixture and mix until combined. Shape into four 3-1/2-in. patties. Dip both sides of patties in remaining coating. Place on an ungreased baking sheet. Bake at 350° for 20 minutes or until no longer pink, turning once. Serve on buns with lettuce. **Yield:** 4 servings.

## Cucumber Shell Salad

*(Pictured above)*

**Plan ahead...needs to chill**

*Ranch dressing is the mild coating for this pleasant pasta salad chock-full of crunchy cucumber, onion and peas.*
—Paula Ishii, Ralston, Nebraska

✓ Uses less fat, sugar or salt. Includes Nutritional Analysis and Diabetic Exchanges.

1 package (16 ounces) medium shell pasta
1 package (16 ounces) frozen peas, thawed
1 medium cucumber, halved and sliced
1 small red onion, chopped
1 cup ranch salad dressing

Cook pasta according to package directions; drain and rinse in cold water. In a large bowl, combine the pasta, peas, cucumber and onion. Add dressing; toss to coat. Cover and chill at least 2 hours. **Yield:** 16 servings.

**Nutritional Analysis:** One 3/4-cup serving (prepared with fat-free ranch dressing) equals 165 calories, 1 g fat (trace saturated fat), trace cholesterol, 210 mg sodium, 33 g carbohydrate, 3 g fiber, 6 g protein. **Diabetic Exchange:** 2 starch.

## Easy Cherry Tarts

*(Pictured at left)*

**Plan ahead...needs to chill**

*Refrigerated crescent rolls simplify preparation of these delightful cherry bites. They're an elegant treat. I cut the dough into circles with a small juice glass. —Frances Poste*
*Wall, South Dakota*

> 1 tube (8 ounces) refrigerated crescent rolls
> 1 package (3 ounces) cream cheese, softened
> 1/4 cup confectioners' sugar
> 1 cup canned cherry pie filling
> 1/4 teaspoon almond extract

Place crescent dough on a lightly floured surface; seal seams and perforations. Cut into 2-in. circles. Place in greased miniature muffin cups. In a small mixing bowl, beat cream cheese and confectioners' sugar until smooth. Place about 1/2 teaspoon in each cup. Combine pie filling and extract; place about 2 teaspoons in each cup.

Bake at 375° for 12-14 minutes or until edges are lightly browned. Remove to wire racks to cool. Refrigerate until serving. **Yield:** 2 dozen.

## Cheesy Carrots

**Ready in 30 minutes or less**

*When I am looking for a streamlined side dish, I turn to this comforting recipe. Convenient frozen carrots are baked in a smooth creamy sauce and topped with bread crumbs for a golden appearance.*
*—Lois Harbold*
*Elizabethtown, Pennsylvania*

> 1 package (16 ounces) frozen sliced carrots, thawed
> 1 can (10-3/4 ounces) condensed cream of celery soup, undiluted
> 8 ounces process cheese (Velveeta), cubed
> 1/3 cup dry bread crumbs
> 2 tablespoons butter *or* margarine, melted

In a bowl, combine the carrots, soup and cheese. Transfer to a greased 1-1/2-qt. baking dish. Bake, uncovered, at 350° for 10 minutes; stir. Toss bread crumbs and butter; sprinkle over the top. Bake 10-15 minutes longer or until carrots are tender and mixture is bubbly. **Yield:** 4-6 servings.

## Fried Chicken Nuggets

**Ready in 30 minutes or less**

*I stir together pancake mix and lemon-lime soda to create the quick coating for these tender chicken chunks.*
*—Dorothy Smith, El Dorado, Arkansas*

> 2-1/2 pounds boneless skinless chicken breasts, cut into 1-inch cubes
> 2-2/3 cups pancake mix
> 1-1/2 cups lemon-lime soda

> 1/4 cup butter *or* margarine, melted
> Vegetable oil for deep-fat frying

Place chicken in a 2-qt. microwave-safe bowl. Cover and microwave on high for 8-10 minutes or until juices run clear, stirring every 2 minutes; drain. In a shallow bowl, combine the pancake mix, soda and butter.

Heat oil in an electric skillet or deep-fat fryer to 375°. Dip chicken cubes into batter; fry in oil until golden on both sides, about 2 minutes. Drain on paper towels. **Yield:** 8-10 servings.

## Strawberry Dip

**Ready in 15 minutes or less**

*After a card game one evening, our hostess served graham crackers spread with prepared strawberry cream cheese. The flavor combination was delicious. So I decided to make a similar blend using fresh berries. Guests appreciate this simple snack.* —Carol Gaus, Itasca, Illinois

✓ Uses less fat, sugar or salt. Includes Nutritional Analysis and Diabetic Exchanges.

> 1 package (8 ounces) cream cheese, softened
> 2 tablespoons honey
> 1 teaspoon vanilla extract
> 1 pint fresh strawberries, sliced
> Graham crackers

In a mixing bowl, beat cream cheese, honey and vanilla until smooth. Add strawberries; beat for 1 minute. Serve with graham crackers. **Yield:** 2 cups.

**Nutritional Analysis:** 2 tablespoons dip (prepared with reduced-fat cream cheese) equals 82 calories, 5 g fat (3 g saturated fat), 16 mg cholesterol, 84 mg sodium, 6 g carbohydrate, trace fiber, 3 g protein. **Diabetic Exchanges:** 1 fat, 1/2 fruit.

## Fiesta Macaroni

**Ready in 45 minutes or less**

*This family-pleasing main dish is so easy to fix, and everyone loves the zesty flavor that the salsa and chili beans provide. It's a hearty warming dish on a cool day.*
*—Sandra Castillo, Sun Prairie, Wisconsin*

> 1 package (16 ounces) elbow macaroni
> 1 pound ground beef
> 1 jar (16 ounces) salsa
> 10 ounces process cheese (Velveeta), cubed
> 1 can (15 ounces) chili-style beans

Cook macaroni according to package directions. Meanwhile, in a skillet, cook beef over medium heat until no longer pink; drain. Drain macaroni; set aside.

In a microwave-safe bowl, combine salsa and cheese. Microwave, uncovered, on high for 3-4 minutes or until cheese is melted. Stir into the skillet; add the macaroni and beans. Transfer to a greased 13-in. x 9-in. x 2-in. baking dish. Bake, uncovered, at 350° for 30-35 minutes or until heated through. **Yield:** 6-8 servings.

## Ham and Rice Bake

**Ready in 45 minutes or less**

*You can put this satisfying meal on your supper table in a jiffy. Add a can of soup, rice and a few convenience items to leftover ham for a flavorful no-fuss casserole.*
—Sharol Binger, Tulare, South Dakota

> 1 can (10-3/4 ounces) condensed cream of chicken soup, undiluted
> 1 cup (4 ounces) shredded cheddar cheese, *divided*
> 1 package (16 ounces) frozen California-blend vegetables, thawed
> 1 cup cooked rice
> 1 cup cubed fully cooked ham

In a large saucepan, combine the soup and 1/2 cup cheese; cook and stir until cheese is melted. Stir in the vegetables, rice and ham. Transfer to a greased 1-1/2-qt. baking dish. Sprinkle with remaining cheese. Bake, uncovered, at 350° for 25-30 minutes or until heated through. **Yield:** 4 servings.

## Artichoke Chicken

**Ready in 45 minutes or less**

*A friend agreed to repair some plumbing in exchange for a home-cooked dinner, but he showed up before I could shop for groceries. A can of artichokes in the pantry inspired me to combine a favorite hot dip recipe with a chicken bake. The results were so delicious, he said he'd rush over anytime.*
—Lisa Robisch, Cincinnati, Ohio

> 1 can (14 ounces) water-packed artichoke hearts, well drained and chopped
> 3/4 cup grated Parmesan cheese
> 3/4 cup mayonnaise*
> Dash garlic powder
> 4 boneless skinless chicken breast halves

In a bowl, combine the artichokes, cheese, mayonnaise and garlic powder. Place chicken in a greased 11-in. x 7-in. x 2-in. baking dish. Spread with artichoke mixture. Bake, uncovered, at 375° for 30-35 minutes or until chicken juices run clear. **Yield:** 4 servings.
**\*Editor's Note:** Reduced-fat or fat-free mayonnaise may not be substituted for regular mayonnaise in this recipe.

## Blueberry Pear Cobbler

**Ready in 30 minutes or less**

*Mom used her home-canned pears in this warm dessert, but the store-bought variety works just as well. People are always amazed that something that comes together in a cinch tastes this wonderful.*
—Susan Pumphrey, Hot Springs, Arkansas

> 2 cans (15-1/4 ounces *each*) sliced pears
> 1 package (7 ounces) blueberry muffin mix
> 3 tablespoons butter *or* margarine, cubed

Drain pears, reserving 3/4 cup juice (discard remaining juice or save for another use). Pour pears and reserved juice into a greased 2-qt. baking dish. Sprinkle with muffin mix; dot with butter. Bake, uncovered, at 400° for 20-25 minutes or until bubbly and top is lightly browned. **Yield:** 8 servings.

## Zippy Sausage Spread

**Ready in 30 minutes or less**

*I always keep the three ingredients for this zesty appetizer on hand. This spread is quick, hearty and delicious on crackers. I serve it from my slow cooker so it stays warm during parties.*
—Bridget Miller, Colorado Springs, Colorado

> 1 pound bulk Italian sausage
> 1 can (10 ounces) diced tomatoes and green chilies, drained
> 1 package (8 ounces) cream cheese, cubed
> Assorted crackers

In a skillet, cook sausage over medium heat until no longer pink; drain. Stir in the tomatoes and cream cheese; cook until cheese is melted. Serve warm with crackers. Store leftovers in the refrigerator. **Yield:** 3 cups.

## Mock Caesar Salad

*(Pictured at right)*

**Ready in 15 minutes or less**

*I first tried this simple salad at a dinner party. The hostess wouldn't part with her secret recipe, so I experimented until I perfected the thick Parmesan-and-garlic dressing myself.*
—Carol Bland, Banning, California

> 3 tablespoons cider vinegar
> 1/2 cup shredded Parmesan cheese
> 1/2 teaspoon garlic powder
> 1/3 cup olive *or* vegetable oil
> 7 cups torn romaine

In a blender or food processor, combine the vinegar, cheese and garlic powder; cover and process until combined. While processing, gradually add oil in a steady stream. Place romaine in a salad bowl; drizzle with dressing and toss to coat. Serve immediately. **Yield:** 6-8 servings.

## Tomato Bacon Pie

*(Pictured at right)*

**Ready in 1 hour or less**

*This simple but savory pie makes a tasty addition to brunch buffets and leisurely luncheons. I rely on a cheesy mixture for the pie's golden topping and a refrigerated pastry shell for easy preparation.*
—Gladys Gibson, Hodgenville, Kentucky

> 1 unbaked deep-dish pastry shell (9 inches)
> 3 medium tomatoes, cut into 1/4-inch slices
> 10 bacon strips, cooked and crumbled
> 1 cup (4 ounces) shredded cheddar cheese
> 1 cup mayonnaise*

Bake pastry shell according to package directions; cool. Place tomatoes in the crust; sprinkle with bacon. In a bowl, combine the cheese and mayonnaise. Spoon over bacon in the center of pie, leaving 1 in. around edge. Bake at 350° for 30-40 minutes or until golden brown (cover edges with foil if necessary to prevent overbrowning). **Yield:** 6 servings.

   ***Editor's Note:** Reduced-fat or fat-free mayonnaise may not be substituted for regular mayonnaise in this recipe.

## S'more Parfaits

*(Pictured below)*

### Plan ahead...needs to chill

*Our son Jason loves s'mores and parfait desserts, so we combined them to create these treats. Crushed graham crackers, chocolate pudding, mini marshmallows and chips are layered into tall glasses for a pretty presentation and that classic s'more flavor.*   —Vonnie Oyer
*Hubbard, Oregon*

✓ Uses less fat, sugar or salt. Includes Nutritional Analysis and Diabetic Exchanges.

   **2 cups cold milk**
   **1 package (3.9 ounces) instant chocolate fudge *or* chocolate pudding mix**
   **2 cups coarsely crushed graham crackers (about 24 squares)**
   **1 cup miniature marshmallows**
   **4 tablespoons miniature chocolate chips**

In a bowl, whisk milk and pudding mix for 2 minutes. Spoon 3 tablespoons each into four parfait glasses. Layer each with 1/4 cup cracker crumbs, 3 tablespoons pudding, 1/4 cup marshmallows and 1 tablespoon chocolate chips. Top with the remaining pudding and crumbs. Refrigerate for 1 hour before serving. **Yield:** 4 servings.

   **Nutritional Analysis:** One parfait (prepared with fat-free milk and sugar-free chocolate pudding) equals 218 calories, 5 g fat (2 g saturated fat), 3 mg cholesterol, 361 mg sodium, 40 g carbohydrate, 2 g fiber, 6 g protein. **Diabetic Exchanges:** 2-1/2 starch, 1/2 fat.

Mock Caesar Salad
S'more Parfaits
Tomato Bacon Pie

Coconut Peach Pie
Taco Chicken Rolls
Salsa Rice

## Taco Chicken Rolls

*(Pictured above and on page 49)*

*I always keep the ingredients for this tender flavorful chicken on hand for a mouth-watering meal in no time. The cheese-stuffed rolls are nice with a green salad or plate of fresh vegetables and Spanish rice.*
—Kara De la vega, Suisun City, California

1 cup finely crushed cheese-flavored crackers
1 envelope taco seasoning
6 boneless skinless chicken breast halves
    (about 2 pounds)
2 ounces Monterey Jack cheese, cut into
    six 2-inch x 1/2-inch sticks
1 can (4 ounces) chopped green chilies

In a shallow dish, combine the cracker crumbs and taco seasoning; set aside. Flatten chicken between two sheets of waxed paper to 1/4-in. thickness. Place a cheese stick and about 1 tablespoon of chilies on each piece of chicken. Tuck ends of chicken in and roll up; secure with a toothpick.

Coat chicken with crumb mixture. Place in a greased 13-in. x 9-in. x 2-in. baking dish. Bake, uncovered, at 350° for 35-40 minutes or until chicken juices run clear. Remove toothpicks. **Yield:** 6 servings.

## Salsa Rice

*(Pictured above and on page 48)*

**Ready in 15 minutes or less**

*It's a snap to change the spice level in this popular rice side dish by choosing a milder or hotter salsa. It's an easy accompaniment to burritos or tacos.*          —Molly Ingle
Canton, North Carolina

✓ Uses less fat, sugar or salt. Includes Nutritional Analysis and Diabetic Exchanges.

1-1/2 cups water
1-1/2 cups chunky salsa
    2 cups uncooked instant rice
    1 to 1-1/2 cups shredded Colby-Monterey
    Jack cheese

In a saucepan, bring water and salsa to a boil. Stir in rice. Remove from the heat; cover and let stand for 5 minutes. Stir in cheese; cover and let stand for 30 seconds or until cheese is melted. **Yield:** 5 servings.

**Nutritional Analysis:** One 1-cup serving (prepared with 1 cup reduced-fat cheese) equals 215 calories, 4 g fat (3 g saturated fat), 12 mg cholesterol, 491 mg sodium, 32 g carbohydrate, 1 g fiber, 9 g protein. **Diabetic Exchanges:** 2 starch, 1 lean meat.

## Coconut Peach Pie

*(Pictured at left and on page 49)*

**Plan ahead...needs to chill**

*I usually prepare desserts for potluck luncheons at our office. My co-workers really enjoy this delightful combination of coconut pudding and fresh peaches.* —Betsy Furin
Rockville, Maryland

    4 cups sliced fresh *or* frozen peaches,
       thawed, *divided*
1-3/4 cups cold milk
    1 package (3.4 ounces) instant coconut
       cream pudding mix
    1 graham cracker crust (9 inches)
    1 cup whipped topping
Additional sliced peaches, optional

If using frozen peaches, pat dry with paper towels. In a mixing bowl, beat milk and pudding mix on low speed for 2 minutes. Arrange a third of the peaches in crust; top with half of the pudding. Repeat layers once. Refrigerate for at least 3 hours or until serving.

Top with remaining peaches. Garnish with whipped topping and additional peaches if desired. **Yield:** 8 servings.

## Pineapple Ham Spread

**Ready in 15 minutes or less**

*This is a recipe I served my kids when time was short ...and so was leftover ham. Spread the sweet ham mixture on rye bread or crunchy crackers for an effortless appetizer.* —Delia Kennedy, Deer Park, Washington

    4 ounces cream cheese, softened
    1 can (8 ounces) crushed pineapple, drained
1/2 cup ground fully cooked ham
Crackers *or* snack rye bread

In a bowl, combine the cream cheese, pineapple and ham. Serve with crackers or bread. **Yield:** 1-1/3 cups.

## Bacon Tater Bake

*I make the most of convenient Tater Tots in this down-home dish. A ham dinner would not be complete without this creamy casserole. It always gets compliments.* —Nita Cinquina, Surprise, Arizona

    2 cans (10-3/4 ounces *each*) condensed
       cream of mushroom soup, undiluted
1-1/3 cups sour cream

    1 large onion, chopped
    1 pound sliced bacon, cooked and crumbled
    1 package (32 ounces) frozen Tater Tots

In a large bowl, combine the soup, sour cream and onion. Add the bacon and Tater Tots; stir until combined. Transfer to a greased 13-in. x 9-in. x 2-in. baking dish. Cover and bake at 350° for 50 minutes. Uncover and bake 8-10 minutes longer or until golden brown. **Yield:** 10 servings.

## Banana Nut Bread

*A yellow cake mix streamlines assembly of this moist golden bread. I searched a long while for a banana bread that was easy to make. This one takes no time at all, and makes two loaves, so one can be frozen to enjoy later.* —Marie Davis
Pendleton, South Carolina

    1 package (18-1/4 ounces) yellow cake mix
    1 egg
1/2 cup milk
    1 cup mashed ripe bananas (about 2 medium)
1/2 cup chopped pecans

In a mixing bowl, combine cake mix, egg and milk. Add bananas; beat on medium speed for 2 minutes. Stir in pecans. Pour into two greased 8-in. x 4-in. x 2-in. loaf pans. Bake at 350° for 40-45 minutes or until a toothpick inserted near the center comes out clean. Cool for 10 minutes before removing from pans to wire racks to cool completely. **Yield:** 2 loaves.

## Fruity Gelatin Salad

**Plan ahead...needs to chill**

*For a refreshing addition to a potluck or other gathering, jazz up gelatin with crushed pineapple, bananas and strawberries. This salad can be made quickly and is a favorite of my friends.* —Pat Whitten
St. Albans, West Virginia

✓ Uses less fat, sugar or salt. Includes Nutritional Analysis and Diabetic Exchanges.

    1 package (6 ounces) strawberry gelatin
    1 cup boiling water
    2 packages (10 ounces *each*) sweetened
       frozen strawberries, thawed
    2 cans (8 ounces *each*) unsweetened
       crushed pineapple, undrained
    3 medium firm bananas, mashed

In a bowl, dissolve gelatin in boiling water. Stir in strawberries, pineapple and bananas; mix well. Transfer to a 2-qt. serving bowl. Refrigerate until firm. **Yield:** 9 servings.

**Nutritional Analysis:** One 3/4-cup serving (prepared with sugar-free gelatin and unsweetened strawberries) equals 82 calories, trace fat (trace saturated fat), 0 cholesterol, 55 mg sodium, 19 g carbohydrate, 3 g fiber, 2 g protein. **Diabetic Exchange:** 1 fruit.

Pineapple Strawberry Punch
Fudge Berry Pie
Peppermint Pretzel Dippers

## Fudge Berry Pie

*(Pictured above)*

**Plan ahead...needs to freeze**

*I've made this pie several times and it always gets great reviews. With its refreshing berry flavor and chocolate crust, the no-bake delight is sure to receive thumbs-up approval from your gang, too.* —Sharlene Cullen
Robbinsdale, Minnesota

  2 packages (10 ounces *each*) frozen sweetened raspberries *or* sliced strawberries, thawed and drained
1/4 cup corn syrup
  1 carton (12 ounces) frozen whipped topping, thawed, *divided*
  1 chocolate crumb crust (9 inches)
  1 cup (6 ounces) semisweet chocolate chips

In a blender, process the berries until pureed. Pour into a large bowl. Add the corn syrup; mix well. Fold in 2 cups of whipped topping. Spoon into the crust. Freeze for 2 hours or until firm.

In a saucepan, combine 1 cup of whipped topping and chocolate chips; cook and stir over low heat until smooth. Spread over filling. Cover and freeze for 4 hours or until firm. Remove from the freezer 30 minutes before serving. Garnish with remaining whipped topping. **Yield:** 6-8 servings.

## Pineapple Strawberry Punch

*(Pictured above)*

**Ready in 15 minutes or less**

*We enjoyed this delicious drink at my wedding reception. Since then, it's been a must at Christmas gatherings and other special occasions.* —Heather Dollins
Poplar Bluff, Missouri

✓ Uses less fat, sugar or salt. Includes Nutritional Analysis and Diabetic Exchanges.

2 packages (10 ounces *each*) frozen sweetened
   sliced strawberries, thawed
1 can (46 ounces) pineapple juice, chilled
4 cups lemon-lime soda, chilled

In a food processor or blender, puree the strawberries. Pour into a large punch bowl. Stir in the pineapple juice and soda. Serve immediately. **Yield:** 12 servings (3 quarts).

   **Nutritional Analysis:** One 1-cup serving (prepared with sugar-free soda) equals 99 calories, trace fat (trace saturated fat), 0 cholesterol, 9 mg sodium, 25 g carbohydrate, 1 g fiber, 1 g protein. **Diabetic Exchange:** 1-1/2 fruit.

## Peppermint Pretzel Dippers

### *(Pictured at left)*

### Plan ahead...needs to chill

*A friend fixed these treats and gave them away in pretty canning jars. The combination of sweet, salty and peppermint is just right. Try dipping them in white candy coating and rolling them in crushed candy canes for variety.*
   *—Michelle Krzmarzick, Redondo Beach, California*

2 cups (12 ounces) semisweet chocolate chips
1 tablespoon shortening
1 package (10 ounces) pretzel rods
40 red *and/or* green hard mint candies, crushed

Place chocolate chips and shortening in a 2-cup microwave-safe measuring cup; heat until melted. Stir until smooth. Break each pretzel rod in half. Dip the broken end about halfway into melted chocolate; roll in crushed candies. Place on a waxed paper-lined baking sheet. Chill until set. **Yield:** about 4 dozen.

## Gumdrop Fudge

### Plan ahead...needs to chill

*Making candy is one of my favorite things to do during the holidays. This sweet white fudge is as easy to put together as it is beautiful to serve.* *—Jennifer Short, Omaha, Nebraska*

1-1/2 pounds white candy coating
   1 can (14 ounces) sweetened condensed milk
1/8 teaspoon salt
1-1/2 teaspoons vanilla extract
1-1/2 cups chopped gumdrops

Line a 9-in. square pan with foil; set aside. In a saucepan, heat the candy coating, milk and salt over low heat until melted. Remove from the heat; stir in vanilla and gumdrops. Spread into prepared pan. Cover and refrigerate until firm. Using foil, remove fudge from the pan; cut into 1-in. squares. Store at room temperature. **Yield:** about 3 pounds.

## Pork Chops with Pears

### Ready in 1 hour or less

*Pear slices make a satisfying alternative to apples in this delicious down-home dish. I dress up this incredibly easy entree even further by adding a hint of brown sugar for a bit of sweetness.*    *—Kathy Stooksbury*
*Aiken, South Carolina*

1 can (15 ounces) pear halves
6 bone-in pork chops (3/4 inch thick)
3 tablespoons butter *or* margarine
1/3 cup packed brown sugar
1 teaspoon prepared mustard

Drain pears, reserving the juice; cut pears into slices and set aside. In a large skillet, brown the pork chops in butter. Transfer to a greased 13-in. x 9-in. x 2-in. baking dish.

   In a small bowl, combine the brown sugar, mustard and reserved pear juice. Pour over chops; top with pear slices. Bake, uncovered, at 350° for 40-45 minutes or until a meat thermometer reads 160°. **Yield:** 6 servings.

## Saucy Spareribs

*My husband likes spareribs, so when my mom gave me this stovetop recipe, I knew I had to try it. He loves the tender ribs and barbecue sauce.*    *—Melanie Sanders*
*Kaysville, Utah*

2 pounds bone-in pork spareribs
2 cans (12 ounces *each*) cola
1 cup ketchup
2 tablespoons cornstarch
2 tablespoons cold water

In a large nonstick skillet, brown the ribs; drain. Add the cola and ketchup; cover and simmer for 1 hour or until the meat is tender.

   Remove ribs and keep warm. Transfer 2 cups of sauce to a saucepan. Bring to a boil. In a small bowl, combine the cornstarch and cold water; stir into sauce. Bring to a boil; cook for 1-2 minutes or until thickened. Serve over the ribs. **Yield:** 2 servings.

## Quick 'n' Easy Lasagna

### Ready in 1 hour or less

*I never have leftovers when I prepare this hearty crowd-pleasing casserole. It's my son's favorite meal, and my husband and I like to make it on nights when we have some friends over to play cards.*    *—Brenda Richardson*
*Rison, Arkansas*

16 lasagna noodles
2 pounds ground beef
1 jar (28 ounces) spaghetti sauce
1 pound process cheese (Velveeta), cubed

Cook noodles according to package directions. Meanwhile, in a large skillet, cook beef over medium heat until no longer pink; drain. Add the spaghetti sauce; heat through. Rinse and drain the noodles.

   In a greased 13-in. x 9-in. x 2-in. baking dish, layer a third of the meat sauce and half of the noodles and cheese. Repeat layers. Top with remaining meat sauce. Cover and bake at 350° for 35 minutes or until bubbly. **Yield:** 6-8 servings.

# Chapter 5

SOME DAYS when you're running behind, 10 minutes may actually be all the time you have to prepare something delicious and satisfying.

So the next time you're hungry and truly "down to the wire" on putting a homemade meal on the table, take a deep breath and count to 10.

Then turn to this time-saving chapter to quickly uncover a flavorful assortment of main dishes, sandwiches, side dishes, snacks, desserts and more. Each fantastic dish goes from start to finish in just about 10 minutes...but tastes like you were in the kitchen all day.

**ON-THE-RUN RECIPE.** Almond Sole Fillets (p. 67).

# Hungarian Salad

*(Pictured below)*

*My whole family enjoys this change-of-pace salad. I add a fast-to-fix dressing to make the colorful crunchy medley a hit.*
—David Wasson, Tulsa, Oklahoma

✓ Uses less fat, sugar or salt. Includes Nutritional Analysis and Diabetic Exchanges.

   1 package (10 ounces) frozen mixed vegetables, thawed
   1 cup fresh cauliflowerets
1/4 to 1/2 cup sliced stuffed olives
1/2 cup sliced green onions
1/4 cup canola oil
   3 tablespoons white vinegar
   1 teaspoon garlic salt
1/4 teaspoon pepper

In a bowl, combine the first four ingredients. In a small bowl, whisk together the oil, vinegar, garlic salt and pepper. Pour over vegetable mixture and toss to coat. Serve with a slotted spoon. **Yield:** 8 servings.

**Nutritional Analysis:** One 1/2-cup serving (prepared with 1/4 cup olives) equals 94 calories, 8 g fat (1 g saturated fat), 0 cholesterol, 350 mg sodium, 6 g carbohydrate, 2 g fiber, 2 g protein. **Diabetic Exchanges:** 1-1/2 fat, 1 vegetable.

# Zippy Chicken Soup

*Give canned soup a zesty touch with spicy diced tomatoes, canned corn and shredded cheese. This warming mixture really hits the spot on cool days.* —Rose Mary Corbett
Johnson City, Tennessee

   1 can (10-3/4 ounces) condensed chicken noodle soup, undiluted

   1 can (10-3/4 ounces) condensed cream of chicken soup, undiluted
   1 can (10 ounces) diced tomatoes and green chilies
   1 can (7 ounces) white *or* shoepeg corn, drained
   1 cup (4 ounces) shredded Monterey Jack cheese
1/2 cup water

In a large saucepan, combine all ingredients. Cook and stir for 5 minutes or until the cheese is melted. **Yield:** 5 servings.

# Sweet Pineapple Sauce

*I simmer up a yummy pineapple sauce that's sensational whether served warm or cold. It's delicious drizzled over ice cream for a simple dessert. Or try it with ham for a dressed-up dinner.* —Mary Herron
Meshoppen, Pennsylvania

   1 can (20 ounces) pineapple tidbits
1/2 cup sugar
   1 tablespoon cornstarch
   2 teaspoons butter *or* margarine
   1 teaspoon white vinegar
Pinch salt
Vanilla ice cream
Chopped walnuts

Drain pineapple, reserving juice; set pineapple aside. In a saucepan, combine sugar and cornstarch; stir in pineapple juice until smooth. Bring to a boil over medium heat; cook and stir for 2 minutes or until thickened and bubbly.

Remove from the heat; stir in the butter, vinegar, salt and pineapple. Serve over ice cream; sprinkle with walnuts. **Yield:** 4 servings.

Hungarian Salad

Garden Squash Ravioli

In a large saucepan, cook ravioli according to package directions. Meanwhile, in a 1-1/2-qt. microwave-safe dish, combine the squash, zucchini, tomato sauce and seasonings. Cover and cook on high for 6-7 minutes or until vegetables are tender. Drain ravioli; top with sauce. **Yield:** 6 servings.

**Editor's Note:** This recipe was tested in an 850-watt microwave.

## Rosemary Chicken

*(Pictured below)*

*This is a terrific recipe for anyone who cooks for one or two people. Plus, it can easily be doubled to feed more. It is perfect for fast-paced weekdays and makes a complete meal when served with buttered beans and rolls.* —Luke Armstead
Oregon City, Oregon

 Uses less fat, sugar or salt. Includes Nutritional Analysis and Diabetic Exchanges.

- **2 boneless skinless chicken breast halves**
- **2 teaspoons canola oil**
- **1 tablespoon lemon juice**
- **1 teaspoon dried rosemary, crushed**
- **1/2 teaspoon dried oregano**
- **1/4 teaspoon pepper**

Flatten chicken to 1/4-in. thickness. In a nonstick skillet, cook chicken in oil over medium-high heat for 3-4 minutes on each side or until juices run clear. Sprinkle with lemon juice, rosemary, oregano and pepper. **Yield:** 2 servings.

**Nutritional Analysis:** One serving equals 172 calories, 6 g fat (1 g saturated fat), 66 mg cholesterol, 74 mg sodium, 1 g carbohydrate, 1 g fiber, 26 g protein. **Diabetic Exchanges:** 3-1/2 very lean meat, 1 fat.

## Garden Squash Ravioli

*(Pictured above)*

*I created this dish to make the most of an overabundance of yellow squash and zucchini from our garden. It was a hit with the whole family. It's so easy to ladle the homemade sauce over quick-cooking frozen ravioli for a satisfying pasta dinner.* —Teri Christensen
West Jordan, Utah

- **1 package (24 ounces) frozen miniature cheese ravioli**
- **1 medium yellow summer squash, cut into 1/2-inch pieces**
- **1 medium zucchini, cut into 1/2-inch pieces**
- **2 cans (one 15 ounces, one 8 ounces) tomato sauce**
- **1 teaspoon garlic salt**
- **1 teaspoon dried minced onion**
- **1 teaspoon dried oregano**
- **1 teaspoon dried basil**
- **1/2 teaspoon sugar**
- **1/2 teaspoon chili powder**
- **1/4 teaspoon pepper**

## Easy Chopped Pickles

I like to add chopped sweet pickles to my tuna, chicken and egg salads. But cutting up those pickles each time gets tiresome, so I use my food processor to mince an entire jar at once.

I process the pickles in batches, adding a few tablespoons of pickle juice to each batch. I return the minced pickles to the jar with just enough juice to cover them.

When I need chopped pickles, I just spoon out a bit and drain the juice by pressing the spoon against the inside of the jar. —*Shirl Turner*
*Memphis, Tennessee*

Rosemary Chicken

Speedy Southwest Salad

In a serving bowl, combine the beans, onion and bacon; stir in dressing. Refrigerate until serving. **Yield:** 3 servings.

## Fruit Yogurt Medley

*When I'm out of fresh vegetables and greens for a salad, I grab some fruit and toss together this refreshing medley instead. Try it with your favorite yogurt flavor.*
—Corbin Detgen
Buchanan, Michigan

☑ Uses less fat, sugar or salt. Includes Nutritional Analysis and Diabetic Exchanges.

 1 medium red apple, chopped
 1 medium firm banana, sliced
 1/3 cup halved seedless green grapes
 3 tablespoons chopped walnuts
 2 tablespoons chopped dates
 1 carton (6 ounces) peach yogurt

In a bowl, combine the apple, banana, grapes, walnuts and dates. Fold in yogurt. **Yield:** 4 servings.
**Nutritional Analysis:** One 3/4-cup serving (prepared with reduced-fat yogurt) equals 148 calories, 4 g fat (1 g saturated fat), 3 mg cholesterol, 21 mg sodium, 27 g carbohydrate, 2 g fiber, 3 g protein. **Diabetic Exchanges:** 1-1/2 fruit, 1 fat.

## Chocolate Caramel Fondue

*It's easy to keep the ingredients for this wonderfully rich fondue on hand in case unexpected company drops by. I serve the thick sauce in punch cups, so guests can carry it on a dessert plate alongside their choice of fruit, pretzels and other dippers.* —Cheryl Arnold, Lake Zurich, Illinois

## Speedy Southwest Salad

*(Pictured above)*

*I used leftover corn and black beans I had in the fridge to throw together this simple Southwestern layered salad. It's a big time-saver because it requires little chopping and features a quick dressing. The crunchy combination is always in demand at our house.*
—Kara Ann Goff
Loveland, Colorado

 1 package (10 ounces) ready-to-serve
    salad greens
 1 can (15 ounces) whole kernel corn, drained
 1 can (15 ounces) black beans, rinsed and
    drained
 1/2 cup ranch salad dressing
 1/2 cup picante sauce
 1 cup broken tortilla chips
 1/2 cup shredded cheddar cheese
 1/2 cup diced tomatoes

Place the greens in a large salad bowl. Top with corn and beans. In a small bowl, combine the salad dressing and picante sauce; spoon over vegetables. Sprinkle with tortilla chips, cheese and tomatoes. Serve immediately. **Yield:** 6 servings.

## French Bean Salad

*(Pictured at right)*

*I jazz up frozen green beans with onion, bacon and bottled salad dressing for a cool dish that's as big on flavor as it is on convenience. I created this recipe after trying a similar salad at a restaurant.*
—Penni Barringer, Rosalia, Washington

 2 cups frozen French-style green beans, thawed
 2 tablespoons chopped onion
 3 bacon strips, cooked and crumbled
 1/4 cup ranch salad dressing

French Bean Salad

Almond Sole Fillets

## Tuna Delight

*A handful of ingredients is all it takes to put a meal on the table. This makes a speedy dinner on busy weeknights or a tasty lunch when unexpected guests drop by.*
—Marie Green
Belle Fourche, South Dakota

✓ Uses less fat, sugar or salt. Includes Nutritional Analysis and Diabetic Exchanges.

1-3/4 cups frozen mixed vegetables, thawed
1 can (12 ounces) tuna, drained and flaked
1 can (10-3/4 ounces) condensed cream of chicken *or* celery soup, undiluted
Hot cooked rice *or* noodles

In a large saucepan, combine the vegetables, tuna and soup. Cook and stir until heated through. Serve over rice or noodles. **Yield:** 3 servings.

**Nutritional Analysis:** One 1-cup serving (prepared with water-packed tuna and reduced-fat cream of chicken soup; calculated without rice) equals 260 calories, 4 g fat (1 g saturated fat), 42 mg cholesterol, 1,166 mg sodium, 21 g carbohydrate, 5 g fiber, 34 g protein. **Diabetic Exchanges:** 3 lean meat, 1 starch, 1 vegetable.

## Almond Sole Fillets

*(Pictured above left and on page 62)*

*My husband is a real fish lover. This buttery treatment is his favorite way to prepare sole, perch or halibut. It cooks quickly in the microwave oven, so it's perfect for a busy weekday meal.* —Erna Farnham, Marengo, Illinois

1/3 cup butter *or* margarine
1/4 cup slivered almonds
1 pound sole fillets
2 tablespoons lemon juice
1/2 teaspoon dill weed
1/4 teaspoon salt
1/4 teaspoon pepper
1/4 teaspoon paprika

In a microwave-safe bowl, combine the butter and almonds. Heat, uncovered, on high for 2 minutes or until almonds are golden brown. Place the fillets in a greased microwave-safe 11-in. x 7-in. x 2-in. dish. Top with almond mixture.

Combine the lemon juice, dill, salt and pepper; drizzle over fish. Sprinkle with paprika. Cover and microwave on high for 4 minutes or until fish flakes easily with a fork. **Yield:** 4 servings.

**Editor's Note:** This recipe was tested in an 850-watt microwave.

1 can (14 ounces) sweetened condensed milk
1 jar (12 ounces) caramel ice cream topping
3 squares (1 ounce *each*) unsweetened chocolate
Assorted fresh fruit *and/or* pretzels

In a saucepan, combine the milk, caramel topping and chocolate. Cook over low heat until chocolate is melted. Serve with fruit and/or pretzels. **Yield:** 2-1/2 cups.

## Crabby Alfredo

*Supper couldn't be easier when you put this quick creamy entree on the menu. My mother-in-law gave me this wonderful recipe. The whole family loves it and everyone asks for more.* —Tara Kampman, Manchester, Iowa

4 cups cooked egg noodles
1 package (16 ounces) imitation crabmeat, chopped
1 jar (16 ounces) Alfredo sauce
Seafood seasoning *or* minced chives

In a large saucepan, combine the noodles, crab and Alfredo sauce. Cook and stir until heated through. Sprinkle with seafood seasoning or chives. **Yield:** 4 servings.

## Tangy Cauliflower Salad

*Grapes are the surprising ingredient in this crunchy vegetable salad. Sweet honey and prepared mustard give the dressing just the right amount of flavor.*
*—Sharon Skildum, Maple Grove, Minnesota*

    1 large head cauliflower, broken into florets
      (about 6 cups)
    1 cup halved green grapes
    1 cup coarsely chopped walnuts
    1 cup mayonnaise *or* salad dressing
  1/3 cup honey
    1 tablespoon prepared mustard

In a large bowl, toss cauliflower, grapes and walnuts. Combine the mayonnaise, honey and mustard; pour over cauliflower mixture and stir to coat. Serve immediately. **Yield:** 10 servings.

## Dilly Pork Chops

*(Pictured below)*

*Everyone who tastes these tender chops loves them. In fact, they're so good that I often cook extra and freeze them for another busy night. The savory mixture of butter, mustard and dill is wonderful on chicken or fish, too.*
*—Robin Hightower Parker, Church Hill, Tennessee*

    6 boneless pork loin chops (1/2 inch thick)
  1/4 cup butter *or* margarine, melted
    1 tablespoon Dijon mustard
    1 to 1-1/2 teaspoons dill weed
    1 teaspoon Worcestershire sauce
  1/8 teaspoon garlic powder

Prick pork chops with a fork. In a small bowl, combine the remaining ingredients; spoon over both sides of chops. Place on a broiler pan; broil 4-6 in. from the heat for 4 minutes on each side or until juices run clear. **Yield:** 6 servings.

Italian Steak Sandwiches

## Italian Steak Sandwiches

*(Pictured above)*

*My sister came up with these quick sandwiches that use minced garlic and other seasonings to bring pizzazz to deli roast beef. Add some carrot sticks or a tomato salad for a fantastic lunch in no time.*
*—Maria Regakis*
*Somerville, Massachusetts*

    2 garlic cloves, minced
  1/8 teaspoon crushed red pepper flakes
    2 tablespoons olive *or* vegetable oil
   16 slices deli roast beef
  1/2 cup beef broth
    2 tablespoons red wine *or* additional beef broth
    2 teaspoons dried parsley flakes
    2 teaspoons dried basil
  1/4 teaspoon salt
  1/4 teaspoon dried oregano
  1/8 teaspoon pepper
    4 sandwich rolls, split
    4 slices provolone cheese

In a large skillet, saute garlic and pepper flakes in oil. Add the roast beef, broth, wine or additional broth and seasonings; heat through. Place beef slices on rolls; drizzle with the broth mixture. Top with cheese. **Yield:** 4 servings.

## Enchilada Chicken Soup

*(Pictured at right)*

*Canned soups, bottled enchilada sauce and a few other convenience items make this recipe one of my fast-to-fix favorites. Use mild green chilies if they suit your tastes, or try a spicier variety to give the soup more kick.*
*—Cristin Fischer, Bellevue, Nebraska*

    1 can (11 ounces) condensed fiesta nacho
      cheese soup, undiluted

Dilly Pork Chops

1 can (10-3/4 ounces) condensed cream
   of chicken soup, undiluted
2-2/3 cups milk
1 can (10 ounces) chunk white chicken, drained
1 can (10 ounces) enchilada sauce
1 can (4 ounces) chopped green chilies
Sour cream

In a large saucepan, combine the soups, milk, chicken, enchilada sauce and chilies; mix well. Cook until heated through. Garnish with sour cream. **Yield:** 7 servings.

## Pesto Pasta

*Add crusty bread and a salad to this easy pasta dish to make a complete meal in mere minutes. The creamy sauce with fresh tomatoes and basil is a pleasant change from traditional tomato-based sauces.* —Irene Smoliga
      Harrisburg, Pennsylvania

 8 ounces uncooked angel hair pasta
 6 tablespoons olive oil
 2 packages (3 ounces *each*) cream cheese, cubed
 2 garlic cloves, minced
16 fresh basil leaves
 2 plum tomatoes, chopped

3 tablespoons shredded mozzarella cheese
2 tablespoons grated Parmesan cheese

Cook pasta according to package directions. Meanwhile, for pesto, combine the oil, cream cheese, garlic and basil in a blender or food processor; cover and process until smooth.

Drain the pasta and place in a serving bowl. Top with tomatoes and pesto; sprinkle with mozzarella and Parmesan cheeses. **Yield:** 4 servings.

## Simple Guacamole

*This homemade guacamole is pretty basic, but it always gets compliments. A jar of salsa makes it a breeze to stir up and serve with crunchy tortilla chips for an effortless appetizer.* —Heidi Main, Anchorage, Alaska

2 medium ripe avocados
1 tablespoon lemon juice
1/4 cup chunky salsa
1/8 to 1/4 teaspoon salt

Peel and chop avocados; place in a small bowl. Sprinkle with lemon juice. Add salsa and salt; mash coarsely with a fork. Refrigerate until serving. **Yield:** 1-1/2 cups.

**Enchilada Chicken Soup**

Warm Shrimp Salad

4 cups cubed cooked peeled potatoes
2 cups diced fully cooked ham
1/2 cup mayonnaise *or* salad dressing
1/4 teaspoon salt
1/8 teaspoon pepper
2 cups (8 ounces) shredded mozzarella cheese

In a large skillet, combine the potatoes, ham, mayonnaise, salt and pepper. Cook and stir over medium-low heat until heated through. Stir in cheese until melted. **Yield:** 4 servings.

## Cinnamon 'n' Spice Dip

*Cinnamon, nutmeg and brown sugar dress up whipped topping in this extremely easy party pleaser. My gang especially likes the dip with apples and pears, but feel free to try it with pineapple slices, strawberries and other fresh fruit.*
—Julie Bertha, Pittsburgh, Pennsylvania

✓ Uses less fat, sugar or salt. Includes Nutritional Analysis and Diabetic Exchanges.

2 cups whipped topping
1/4 cup packed brown sugar
1/8 to 1/4 teaspoon ground cinnamon
Dash ground nutmeg
Assorted fresh fruit

In a small bowl, combine the whipped topping, brown sugar, cinnamon and nutmeg. Serve with fruit. **Yield:** about 2 cups.

**Nutritional Analysis:** 2 tablespoons dip (prepared with reduced-fat whipped topping; calculated without fruit) equals 66 calories, 2 g fat (2 g saturated fat), 0 cholesterol, 3 mg sodium, 11 g carbohydrate, trace fiber, 0 protein. **Diabetic Exchange:** 1/2 starch.

## Warm Shrimp Salad

*(Pictured above)*

*For a delicious change of pace, try this zesty shrimp mixture spooned over fresh salad greens. The blend of herbs provides plenty of zippy flavor. Serve it with thick slices of Italian or garlic bread for an easy supper.*
—Judith LaBrozzi, Canton, Ohio

1/4 cup chopped onion
1 garlic clove, minced
1 tablespoon butter *or* margarine
1 pound cooked medium shrimp, peeled and deveined
1/2 cup chicken broth
1 teaspoon dried oregano
1 teaspoon dried basil
1/2 teaspoon dried thyme
1/8 to 1/4 teaspoon crushed red pepper flakes
4 cups torn salad greens

In a large skillet, saute the onion and garlic in butter until onion is tender. Add shrimp; cook and stir for 2 minutes. Stir in the broth and seasonings. Bring to a boil. Reduce heat; simmer, uncovered, for 4 minutes or until heated through. Place salad greens on four plates; top with shrimp mixture. **Yield:** 4 servings.

## Potato Ham Skillet

*(Pictured at right)*

*My mother prepared this cheesy stovetop dish when I was young. Now I make it for my family. It's a great way to use ham and potatoes left over from last night's meal. Or buy cubed cooked ham to fix it anytime.*
—Sharon Price, Urbana, Ohio

Potato Ham Skillet

Chicken Salad Clubs

## Chicken Salad Clubs

(Pictured above)

*Mondays have always been soup and sandwich night at our house. One evening, I embellished a regular chicken salad sandwich with some not-so-usual ingredients, like rye bread and honey-mustard dressing. The results were delicious.*
—*Sarah Smith, Edgewood, Kentucky*

    8 bacon strips
    4 lettuce leaves
    8 slices rye *or* pumpernickel bread
    1 pound deli chicken salad
    4 slices Swiss cheese
    8 slices tomato
1/3 cup honey-mustard salad dressing

In a skillet or microwave, cook bacon until crisp; drain on paper towels. Place lettuce on four slices of bread; top each with chicken salad, two bacon strips, one cheese slice and two tomato slices. Spread salad dressing on remaining bread; place over tomatoes. **Yield: 4 servings.**

## Pepperoni Angel Hair

*This noodle side dish is so versatile that it can accompany steak, pork chops, chicken or hamburgers. Chill leftovers to serve as a cool main-dish salad on a warm summer night. When time allows, I like to replace the pepperoni with sliced cooked chicken.* —*Julie Mosher, Coldwater, Michigan*

    8 ounces uncooked angel hair pasta,
      broken into thirds
    1 small cucumber, peeled and chopped
    1 medium green pepper, chopped
    1 package (8 ounces) sliced pepperoni,
      quartered
    2 cans (2-1/4 ounces *each*) sliced ripe
      olives, drained
  1/2 cup Italian salad dressing
1-1/4 cups shredded Parmesan cheese

Cook the pasta according to package directions. Meanwhile, combine the cucumber, green pepper, pepperoni and olives in a large bowl. Drain pasta and add to pepperoni mixture. Top with salad dressing and Parmesan cheese; toss to coat. **Yield: 4-6 servings.**

## Two-Cheese Quesadillas

*(Pictured below)*

*When we have to eat on the run, I turn to this tasty recipe because it comes together in a snap. Best of all, I can customize the ingredients to satisfy each member of my family.* —Sharron Kemp, High Point, North Carolina

4 flour tortillas (8 inches)
1 cup (4 ounces) shredded cheddar cheese
1 cup (4 ounces) shredded mozzarella cheese
2 small tomatoes, diced
1/2 cup finely chopped green pepper
1/4 cup chopped onion
Salsa and sour cream

Sprinkle each tortilla with cheeses, tomatoes, green pepper and onion. Fold in half and press edges lightly to seal. On a griddle, cook quesadillas over low heat for 1-2 minutes on each side or until cheese is melted. Cut into wedges. Serve with salsa and sour cream. **Yield: 2-4 servings.**

### Keep Cheese on Hand

Shredded cheese always spoiled before I had a chance to use it all. My dad taught me to buy a 5-pound bag of shredded cheddar, put small amounts in resealable freezer bags and freeze individually. Now when I need cheese, I just thaw a bag. It tastes the same and I no longer worry about wasting it. —Rose McNatt, Plano, Texas

Two-Cheese Quesadillas

## Salmon Chowder

*I made up this quick creamy chowder one winter afternoon. I like to use a can of red sockeye salmon for best flavor. The soup also can be seasoned with tarragon instead of dill.* —Tom Bailey, Golden Valley, Minnesota

3 cans (10-3/4 ounces *each*) condensed cream of potato soup, undiluted
2-2/3 cups half-and-half cream
1 can (14-3/4 ounces) salmon, drained, bones and skin removed
1 teaspoon dill weed
1/2 teaspoon salt
1/4 teaspoon white pepper
1/4 teaspoon crushed red pepper flakes

In a large saucepan, combine all of the ingredients. Cook and stir over medium heat until chowder is heated through. **Yield: 7 servings.**

## Mushroom Rice Pilaf

*Sliced fresh mushrooms and green onions sauteed in a bit of wine dress up instant rice in this recipe. The speedy side dish is an effortless accompaniment to chicken, pork or beef. This elegant pilaf is even nice enough to serve to company.* —Genny Monchamp, Redding, California

✓ Uses less fat, sugar or salt. Includes Nutritional Analysis and Diabetic Exchanges.

1 cup water
1 teaspoon chicken bouillon granules
1 cup uncooked instant rice
2 cups sliced fresh mushrooms
3 green onions, thinly sliced
1 to 2 tablespoons butter *or* stick margarine
1/4 cup white wine *or* chicken broth

In a saucepan, bring water and bouillon to a boil. Stir in rice. Remove from the heat; cover and let stand for 5 minutes. Meanwhile, in a skillet, saute mushrooms and onions in butter and wine or broth until mushrooms are tender and liquid is absorbed, about 6 minutes. Fluff rice with a fork; stir in mushroom mixture. **Yield: 4 servings.**

**Nutritional Analysis:** One 1/2-cup serving (prepared with wine and 1 tablespoon butter) equals 132 calories, 3 g fat (2 g saturated fat), 8 mg cholesterol, 324 mg sodium, 20 g carbohydrate, 1 g fiber, 3 g protein. **Diabetic Exchanges:** 1 starch, 1 vegetable, 1/2 fat.

## Mushroom Meatball Soup

*After a busy day, I wanted something fast but hearty for dinner. I combined prepared meatballs with canned soup, mushrooms and seasonings. My husband loved my creation and thought I spent hours preparing it.* —Sue Fuller, Quincy, Michigan

2 cans (10-3/4 ounces *each*) condensed cream
   of mushroom soup, undiluted
2-2/3 cups milk
1/2 teaspoon dried oregano
1/8 to 1/4 teaspoon pepper
1 package (12 ounces) frozen cooked Italian
   meatballs, thawed
1 jar (4-1/2 ounces) sliced mushrooms, drained

In a large saucepan, whisk the soup, milk, oregano and
pepper until blended. Add the meatballs and mushrooms. Cover and cook until heated through. **Yield: 6**
servings.

## Creamy Waldorf Salad

*Things don't get much easier than preparing this pleas-
antly dressed fruit salad. Crunchy apples and nuts con-
trast nicely with juicy grapes and chewy raisins.*
—*Linda Stateler, Ottumwa, Iowa*

✓ Uses less fat, sugar or salt. Includes Nutritional Analysis
   and Diabetic Exchanges.

1 large red apple, chopped
1/2 cup halved seedless red grapes
1/2 cup whipped topping
1/4 cup raisins
1/4 cup mayonnaise *or* salad dressing
3 tablespoons coarsely chopped walnuts

In a bowl, combine all ingredients. Refrigerate until serving. **Yield: 3 servings.**

**Nutritional Analysis:** One 3/4-cup serving (prepared
with reduced-fat whipped topping and fat-free mayonnaise) equals 177 calories, 7 g fat (2 g saturated fat), 0
cholesterol, 142 mg sodium, 31 g carbohydrate, 3 g
fiber, 2 g protein. **Diabetic Exchanges:** 1-1/2 fruit, 1 fat,
1/2 starch.

## Smothered Chicken

(Pictured above)

*You can't go wrong when serving this speedy skillet spe-
cialty. I top tender chicken breasts with mushrooms, bacon, green onions and cheese for a swift and savory sensation that's sure to become a family favorite.*
—*Penny Walton, Westerville, Ohio*

4 boneless skinless chicken breast halves
Garlic powder and seasoned salt to taste
1 tablespoon vegetable oil
1 jar (4-1/2 ounces) sliced mushrooms, drained
1 cup (4 ounces) shredded Mexican
   cheese blend
1/2 cup chopped green onions
1/2 cup bacon bits

Flatten chicken to 1/4-in. thickness. Sprinkle with garlic
powder and seasoned salt. In a large nonstick skillet over
medium heat, brown chicken in oil for 4 minutes; turn.
Top with the mushrooms, cheese, green onions and
bacon. Cover and cook until chicken juices run clear and
cheese is melted, about 4 minutes. **Yield: 4 servings.**

# Chapter 6

A PEEK into your pantry may be all that's needed to put together a mouth-watering meal pronto!

A wide range of packaged convenience foods can help you find fast fixes to your dinner dilemmas.

It can be as simple as beefing up canned goods to make a comforting casserole, jazzing up frozen potatoes to fix an effortless entree or using a cake mix to create quick bars.

Or save even more time—and money, too—by making your own homemade mixes. The awesome assortment in this chapter is easy to assemble in advance and will provide a super head start on menu planning.

**MIX MARVELS.** Clockwise from top: Hawaiian Sunset Cake, Peanut Butter Chocolate Dessert, Mocha Pie and Raspberry Icebox Dessert (all recipes on pp. 88 and 89).

# Fast Fixes With Mixes

THE WORD IS OUT! Packaged convenience foods are a surefire way to save time in the kitchen. Big on flavor and low on fuss, today's boxed cake mixes, canned pie fillings, bottled sauces and other items give fast-to-fix dishes a down-home flavor the whole family enjoys.

So the next time you need a shortcut snack, easy entree or dessert in a dash, check your cupboard and whip up one of these speedy specialties.

## Chicken Wild Rice Soup

### (Pictured below)

### Ready in 30 minutes or less

*Because this warming soup takes advantage of several convenience items, it's very quick to make. It's perfect for casual entertaining because you can keep it warm in the slow cooker. The pot is always scraped clean.*
—Gayle Holdman
Highland, Utah

5-2/3 cups water
1 package (4.3 ounces) long grain and
    wild rice mix
1 envelope chicken noodle soup mix

1 celery rib, chopped
1 medium carrot, chopped
1/3 cup chopped onion
2 cans (10-3/4 ounces *each*) condensed
    cream of chicken soup, undiluted
1 cup cubed cooked chicken

In a large saucepan, combine water, rice with contents of seasoning packet and soup mix. Bring to a boil. Reduce heat; cover and simmer for 10 minutes. Stir in the celery, carrot and onion. Cover and simmer for 10 minutes. Stir in chicken soup and chicken. Cook 8 minutes longer or until the rice and vegetables are tender. **Yield:** 5 servings.

## Open-Faced Sandwich Supreme

### (Pictured below left)

### Ready in 15 minutes or less

*My husband and I first sampled this delicious open-faced sandwich at a restaurant. It seemed so easy, I duplicated it at home. It's also tasty with cheese sauce in place of the hollandaise sauce or asparagus instead of broccoli.* —Phyllis Smith, Mariposa, California

3 cups small broccoli florets
1 package (.9 ounce) hollandaise sauce mix
8 ounces sliced deli turkey
8 ounces sliced deli ham
4 slices sourdough bread, toasted

In a saucepan, cook broccoli in a small amount of water until tender; drain. Prepare the hollandaise sauce according to package directions. Warm turkey and ham if desired; layer over toast. Top with broccoli and sauce. **Yield:** 4 servings.

Chicken Wild Rice Soup
Open-Faced Sandwich Supreme

## Creamy Chicken Spread

### Plan ahead...needs to chill

*I used three different recipes to come up with this simple spread that my family loves. With its mild taste, it's a popular party appetizer when accompanied by assorted crackers, toast points or raw vegetables.* —Joann Hensley
McGaheysville, Virginia

1 package (8 ounces) cream cheese, softened
1/2 cup sour cream
1 teaspoon dried minced onion
1/2 teaspoon onion salt
1/2 teaspoon Worcestershire sauce
1/4 teaspoon cayenne pepper
2 cans (10 ounces *each*) chunk white chicken,
    drained
Paprika, optional
Assorted crackers

In a mixing bowl, combine the first six ingredients. Fold in chicken. Cover and refrigerate for at least 1 hour. Sprinkle with paprika if desired. Serve with crackers. **Yield:** about 3 cups.

## Butterscotch Muffins

*(Pictured above)*

**Ready in 45 minutes or less**

*Butterscotch pudding gives a distinctive flavor to these muffins topped with brown sugar and nuts. My son made them for a 4-H competition and they won first-place purple ribbons.* —Jill Hazelton, Hamlet, Indiana

    2 cups all-purpose flour
    1 cup sugar
    1 package (3.4 ounces) instant butterscotch
      pudding mix
    1 package (3.4 ounces) instant vanilla
      pudding mix
    2 teaspoons baking powder
    1 teaspoon salt
    1 cup water
    4 eggs
  3/4 cup vegetable oil
    1 teaspoon vanilla extract
TOPPING:
  2/3 cup packed brown sugar
  1/2 cup chopped pecans
    2 teaspoons ground cinnamon

In a bowl, combine the flour, sugar, pudding mixes, baking powder and salt. Combine the water, eggs, oil and vanilla; stir into the dry ingredients just until moistened. Fill greased or paper-lined muffin cups two-thirds full.

Combine the topping ingredients; sprinkle over batter. Bake at 350° for 15-20 minutes or until a toothpick comes out clean. Cool for 5 minutes before removing from pans to wire racks. **Yield:** about 1-1/2 dozen.

## Speedy Beef Hash

**Ready in 30 minutes or less**

*I rely on frozen hash browns and prepared salsa to hurry along this stovetop specialty. I'm a registered nurse who likes to spend my free time with my family, so this time-saving twist on ground beef hash is a favorite.* —Sara McCoy
Goshen, Kentucky

    1 pound ground beef
    1 medium onion, chopped
    3 cups frozen O'Brien hash brown potatoes,
      thawed
  1/2 teaspoon salt
  1/4 teaspoon pepper
    1 cup salsa
  1/2 cup shredded Colby-Monterey Jack
      cheese
Sliced green onions and ripe olives, optional

In a skillet, cook beef and onion over medium heat until the meat is no longer pink; drain. Stir in the potatoes, salt and pepper.

Cook and stir over medium-high heat for 7-9 minutes or until potatoes are lightly browned. Stir in salsa. Sprinkle with cheese; cook until melted. Sprinkle with onions and olives if desired. **Yield:** 4 servings.

## Tortellini Alfredo

*(Pictured below)*

**Ready in 30 minutes or less**

*Refrigerated tortellini, ham, mushrooms and peas are treated to a mild homemade Alfredo sauce in this fast fix. When we're having company, I prepare this dinner shortly before guests arrive, put it in a casserole dish and keep it warm in the oven.*  —Chris Snyder, Boulder, Colorado

   2 packages (9 ounces *each*) refrigerated cheese tortellini
1/2 cup chopped onion
1/3 cup butter *or* margarine
1-1/2 cups frozen peas, thawed
   1 cup thinly sliced fresh mushrooms
   1 cup cubed fully cooked ham
1-3/4 cups whipping cream
1/4 teaspoon coarsely ground pepper
3/4 cup grated Parmesan cheese
Shredded Parmesan cheese, optional

Cook tortellini according to package directions. Meanwhile, in a skillet, saute the onion in butter until tender. Add the peas, mushrooms and ham; cook until mushrooms are tender. Stir in cream and pepper; heat through. Stir in grated Parmesan cheese until melted.

Drain tortellini and place in a serving dish; add the sauce and toss to coat. Sprinkle with the shredded Parmesan cheese if desired. **Yield:** 4-6 servings.

## Walnut-Rippled Coffee Cake

*(Pictured below)*

*An ideal treat any time of the day, this moist yellow cake offers a delightful surprise of cinnamon, nuts and brown sugar in every slice. I rely on a boxed mix to make preparation easier.*  —Nanetta Larson, Canton, South Dakota

   1 package (18-1/4 ounces) yellow cake mix
   2 tablespoons sugar
   4 eggs
   1 cup (8 ounces) sour cream

Tortellini Alfredo
Walnut-Rippled Coffee Cake

1/3 cup vegetable oil
1/4 cup water
1 cup chopped walnuts
2 tablespoons brown sugar
2 teaspoons ground cinnamon

Set aside 2 tablespoons cake mix. Place the remaining cake mix in a mixing bowl. Add sugar, eggs, sour cream, oil and water; beat on low speed for 2 minutes. Pour half into a greased fluted 10-in. tube pan. Combine the walnuts, brown sugar, cinnamon and reserved cake mix; sprinkle over batter. Top with the remaining batter.

Bake at 350° for 40-45 minutes or until a toothpick inserted near the center comes out clean. Cool for 10 minutes before removing from pan to a wire rack. **Yield:** 12-14 servings.

## Orange Chicken Supper

*(Pictured at right)*

**Ready in 30 minutes or less**

*We're an American military family stationed in Germany. Since we're just as busy as stateside families, this meal really fits our lifestyle. Because it uses a rice mix, orange juice and other items I keep on hand, it's both satisfying and swift.* —Lynda Muller, Germany

Orange Chicken Supper

1 package (6.9 ounces) chicken-flavored rice mix
2 tablespoons butter *or* margarine
1-1/2 cups hot water
1 cup orange juice
1/4 teaspoon garlic powder
1/4 teaspoon ground ginger
1/8 teaspoon cayenne pepper, optional
2 cups cubed cooked chicken
1-1/2 cups frozen sliced carrots, thawed

Set aside seasoning packet from rice mix. In a large skillet, cook rice mix in butter over medium heat until golden brown. Stir in the water, orange juice, garlic powder, ginger, cayenne if desired and contents of seasoning packet; bring to a boil. Reduce heat; cover and simmer for 10 minutes.

Add chicken and carrots. Cover and simmer for 5-10 minutes or until heated through and liquid is absorbed. **Yield:** 4 servings.

## Mallow Fruit Salad

**Plan ahead...needs to chill**

*A handful of ingredients is all you'll need for this sweet and fluffy salad. Your gang will love the combination of canned fruit, mini marshmallows and whipped topping, and you'll love how simple it is to assemble.* —Sandy Ward, Madisonville, Texas

1-1/3 cups buttermilk
1 package (5.1 ounces) instant vanilla pudding mix

1 can (30 ounces) fruit cocktail, drained
2 cans (11 ounces *each*) mandarin oranges, drained
1 cup pastel miniature marshmallows
1 carton (8 ounces) frozen whipped topping, thawed

In a mixing bowl, beat the buttermilk and pudding mix on medium speed for 1 minute. Let stand for 5 minutes. Fold in fruit cocktail, oranges, marshmallows and whipped topping. Refrigerate until serving. **Yield:** 8-10 servings.

## Cheddar Stuffing Puff

**Ready in 1 hour or less**

*This full-flavored side dish is always a hit with guests. Stuffing mix hurries along preparation of the moist golden brown puff that's a wonderful complement to most meats.* —Geneva Clouser, Springfield, Ohio

1 package (8 ounces) crushed stuffing mix
3 tablespoons all-purpose flour
4 eggs, lightly beaten
3 cups milk
2 tablespoons butter *or* margarine, melted
2 cups (8 ounces) shredded cheddar cheese

In a bowl, combine stuffing mix and flour. Add eggs, milk, butter and cheese; mix well. Pour into a greased 2-qt. baking dish. Bake, uncovered, at 350° for 35-40 minutes or until a knife comes out clean. **Yield:** 8 servings.

Kielbasa Pasta Salad
Double Frosted Brownies

## Kielbasa Pasta Salad

*(Pictured above)*

**Ready in 30 minutes or less**

*The sausage adds wonderful flavor and heartiness to this main-dish salad. But the secret to its appeal is the crunchy croutons. It's a deliciously different dish to share at a potluck.* —Jean Dantinne, Chehalis, Washington

   1 package (16 ounces) spiral pasta
1-1/2 cups thinly sliced fully cooked kielbasa *or*
     Polish sausage
   1 can (2-1/4 ounces) sliced ripe olives, drained
1/4 cup shredded Parmesan cheese
   1 cup mayonnaise
   3 tablespoons cider vinegar
   1 envelope Italian salad dressing mix
   1 cup salad croutons

Cook pasta according to package directions; drain and rinse in cold water. Place pasta in a large bowl; add the sausage, olives and Parmesan cheese. In a small bowl, combine the mayonnaise, vinegar and salad dressing mix. Stir into the pasta mixture. Add croutons and toss to coat. Serve immediately. **Yield:** 12 servings.

## Double Frosted Brownies

*(Pictured above)*

*I stir up fudgy brownies from a boxed mix, then dress them up with two kinds of frosting. The two-toned treats have a luscious look and sweet taste.* —Jean Kolessar
Orland Park, Illinois

   1 package fudge brownie mix (13-inch x
     9-inch pan size)
1/2 cup butter *or* margarine, softened
1-1/2 cups confectioners' sugar
   2 tablespoons instant vanilla pudding mix
   2 to 3 tablespoons milk
   1 can (16 ounces) chocolate fudge frosting

Prepare brownie mix according to package directions. Spread the batter into a greased 13-in. x 9-in. x 2-in. baking pan. Bake at 350° for 25-30 minutes or until a toothpick inserted 2 in. from side of pan comes out clean. Cool completely on a wire rack.

In a mixing bowl, beat butter, sugar and pudding mix until blended. Add enough milk to achieve spreading consistency. Frost brownies. Cover and refrigerate for 30 minutes. Spread with fudge frosting. Cut into bars. Store in the refrigerator. **Yield:** 3 dozen.

## Chicken Asparagus Bake

**Ready in 1 hour or less**

*Layers of crunchy Triscuits sandwich a chicken and vegetable filling in this down-home casserole. A friend served this delicious dish for an evening meal and I couldn't resist asking for the recipe.* —Margaret Carlson
Amery, Wisconsin

   1 package (9-1/2 ounces) Triscuit crackers
   2 cups cubed cooked chicken
   2 cans (10-3/4 ounces *each*) condensed cream
     of chicken soup, undiluted

1 package (10 ounces) frozen chopped asparagus, thawed and drained
1 can (8 ounces) sliced water chestnuts, drained
1 can (4 ounces) mushroom stems and pieces, drained
1/2 cup mayonnaise*

Break two-thirds of the crackers into bite-size pieces; place in a greased 2-1/2-qt. baking dish. Top with chicken; spread soup over chicken. Combine the asparagus, water chestnuts, mushrooms and mayonnaise; spoon over soup. Crush remaining crackers; sprinkle over the top.

Bake, uncovered, at 350° for 30-40 minutes or until heated through. **Yield:** 4 servings.

**\*Editor's Note:** Reduced-fat or fat-free mayonnaise may not be substituted for regular mayonnaise in this recipe.

## Tater Taco Casserole

*(Pictured below)*

### Ready in 1 hour or less

*Our family lives and works on a ranch. I like to fix this nicely seasoned casserole ahead of time and freeze it for use on especially busy days. Its Southwestern flavors go great with a tossed salad or nacho chips and dip.* —Ronna Lewis Plains, Kansas

2 pounds ground beef
1/4 cup chopped onion
1 envelope taco seasoning
2/3 cup water
1 can (11 ounces) whole kernel corn, drained
1 can (11 ounces) condensed fiesta nacho cheese soup, undiluted
1 package (32 ounces) frozen Tater Tots

In a skillet, cook beef and onion over medium heat until meat is no longer pink; drain. Stir in taco seasoning and water. Simmer, uncovered, for 5 minutes. Add corn and soup; mix well.

Transfer to a greased 13-in. x 9-in. x 2-in. baking dish. Arrange Tater Tots in a single layer over the top. Bake, uncovered, at 350° for 30-35 minutes or until potatoes are crispy and golden brown. **Yield:** 8 servings.

## Orange Banana Tapioca

### Plan ahead...needs to chill

*Tapioca lovers will enjoy the fruity twist that mandarin oranges and banana slices give this old-fashioned favorite. For variety, use any type of juice concentrate instead of orange.* —Penny Patras, Sargent, Nebraska

1-1/2 cups water
1 can (6 ounces) orange juice concentrate, thawed
1/4 cup quick-cooking tapioca
3 tablespoons sugar
Dash salt
1 can (11 ounces) mandarin oranges, drained
1 medium banana, sliced

In a large saucepan, combine the water, orange juice concentrate, tapioca, sugar and salt; mix well. Let stand for 15 minutes. Bring to a boil; cook and stir until thickened. Fold in the oranges. Pour into serving dishes. Cover and refrigerate for 1 hour or until set. Garnish with banana slices. **Yield:** 3 servings.

Tater Taco Casserole

# Strawberry Cheesecake Trifle

*(Pictured below)*

**Ready in 30 minutes or less**

*The only drawback to this lovely dessert is that there's never any left over. Folks just can't stop going back for more. For a patriotic look, replace one of the layers of strawberry pie filling with blueberry...or use whatever filling you prefer.*
—Lori Thorp, Frazee, Minnesota

1 package (8 ounces) cream cheese, softened
1 cup (8 ounces) sour cream
1/2 cup cold milk
1 package (3.4 ounces) instant vanilla pudding mix
1 carton (12 ounces) frozen whipped topping, thawed
1-1/2 cups crushed butter-flavored crackers (about 38 crackers)
1/4 cup butter *or* margarine, melted
2 cans (21 ounces *each*) strawberry pie filling

In a large mixing bowl, beat the cream cheese until smooth. Add the sour cream; mix well. In a small mixing bowl, beat milk and pudding mix on low speed for 2 minutes. Stir into cream cheese mixture. Fold in whipped topping.

Toss the cracker crumbs and butter. In a 2-1/2-qt. trifle bowl, layer half of the cream cheese mixture, crumbs and pie filling. Repeat layers. Refrigerate until serving. **Yield:** 12-16 servings.

**Strawberry Cheesecake Trifle**

# Smoky Corn Muffins

**Ready in 45 minutes or less**

*I jazz up corn bread mix with salsa, corn, cheese and liquid smoke to create these spicy muffins. The moist morsels are an ideal accompaniment to chili or a Southwestern supper.*
—Marg Ogden, Palmerton, Pennsylvania

✓ Uses less fat, sugar or salt. Includes Nutritional Analysis and Diabetic Exchanges.

1 egg
1/2 cup chunky salsa
1/3 cup milk
1 drop liquid smoke
1 package (8-1/2 ounces) corn bread/muffin mix
1 can (8-3/4 ounces) whole kernel corn, drained
1/2 cup shredded sharp cheddar cheese

In a bowl, beat egg. Add salsa, milk and liquid smoke; mix well. Stir in corn bread mix just until moistened. Fold in corn and cheese. Fill greased muffin cups three-fourths full. Bake at 400° for 20-23 minutes or until golden brown. Cool for 5 minutes before removing from pan to a wire rack. **Yield:** 1 dozen.

**Nutritional Analysis:** One muffin (prepared with fat-free milk and reduced-fat cheddar cheese) equals 121 calories, 4 g fat (1 g saturated fat), 26 mg cholesterol, 278 mg sodium, 18 g carbohydrate, 1 g fiber, 4 g protein. **Diabetic Exchanges:** 1 starch, 1 fat.

# Chili Macaroni Soup

**Ready in 30 minutes or less**

*Turn a boxed macaroni dinner into a thick zesty soup with this recipe. It ladles out hearty helpings, which are chock-full of ground beef, tomatoes, corn, seasonings and more. I often rely on this tried-and-true soup.*
—Flo Burtnett Gage, Oklahoma

1 pound ground beef
1 medium onion, chopped
1/4 cup chopped green pepper
5 cups water
1 can (14-1/2 ounces) diced tomatoes, undrained
1 package (7-1/2 ounces) chili macaroni dinner mix
1 teaspoon chili powder
1/2 teaspoon garlic salt
1/4 teaspoon salt
1 can (8-3/4 ounces) whole kernel corn, drained
2 tablespoons sliced ripe olives

In a large saucepan or soup kettle, cook beef, onion and green pepper over medium heat until meat is no longer pink; drain. Add water, tomatoes, contents of sauce mix from the dinner mix, chili powder, garlic salt and salt. Simmer, uncovered, for 10 minutes.

Pineapple Lime Molds
Chicken Broccoli Shells

Add macaroni from dinner mix, corn and olives. Cover and simmer for 10 minutes or until macaroni is tender, stirring occasionally. **Yield:** 9 servings (about 2 quarts).

## Chicken Broccoli Shells

*(Pictured above)*

**Ready in 45 minutes or less**

*This cheesy entree can be assembled ahead of time and popped in the oven when company arrives. I suggest rounding out the meal with a tossed salad and warm bread.*
—Karen Jagger, Columbia City, Indiana

- 1 jar (16 ounces) Alfredo sauce
- 2 cups frozen chopped broccoli, thawed
- 2 cups diced cooked chicken
- 1 cup (4 ounces) shredded cheddar cheese
- 1/4 cup shredded Parmesan cheese
- 21 jumbo pasta shells, cooked and drained

In a large bowl, combine the Alfredo sauce, broccoli, chicken and cheeses. Spoon into pasta shells. Place in a greased 13-in. x 9-in. x 2-in. baking dish. Cover and bake at 350° for 30-35 minutes or until heated through. **Yield:** 7 servings.

## Pineapple Lime Molds

*(Pictured above)*

**Plan ahead...needs to chill**

*This five-ingredient gelatin salad is big on flavor and convenience. It's a family favorite on special occasions. Mold the refreshing combination into individual salads or double the recipe to form one large ring.* —Meredith Bell
Glendale, New York

- 1 can (8 ounces) unsweetened crushed pineapple
- 1 package (3 ounces) lime gelatin
- 1 package (8 ounces) cream cheese, softened
- 3/4 cup lemon-lime soda
- 1 teaspoon vanilla extract

Drain pineapple, reserving juice; set the pineapple aside. Add enough water to the juice to measure 1 cup; transfer to a saucepan. Bring to a boil; stir in gelatin until dissolved. In a small mixing bowl, beat cream cheese until smooth. Add gelatin mixture; beat on medium speed for 2 minutes. Add soda and vanilla; beat for 1 minute. Add reserved pineapple; beat on low for 1 minute. Pour into six individual molds or dessert dishes. Refrigerate for 4 hours or until set. **Yield:** 6 servings.

Pizza Macaroni Bake
Poppy Seed Biscuit Ring

## Pizza Macaroni Bake

*(Pictured above)*

**Ready in 1 hour or less**

*What do you get when you combine macaroni and cheese with pizza fixings? This family-pleasing casserole. It's easy and tasty, and my grandchildren really like it. The wonderful aroma calls people to the table.*
                                   —Nancy Porterfield
                                   Gap Mills, West Virginia

1 package (7-1/4 ounces) macaroni
  and cheese dinner mix
6 cups water
1 pound ground beef
1 medium onion, chopped
1 small green pepper, chopped
1 cup (4 ounces) shredded cheddar cheese
1 jar (14 ounces) pizza sauce
1 package (3-1/2 ounces) sliced pepperoni
1 cup (4 ounces) shredded mozzarella cheese

Set the cheese packet from dinner mix aside. In a saucepan, bring water to a boil. Add macaroni; cook for 8-10 minutes or until tender. Meanwhile, in a large skillet, cook the beef, onion and green pepper over medium heat until meat is no longer pink; drain.

Drain macaroni; stir in the contents of cheese packet. Transfer to a greased 13-in. x 9-in. x 2-in. baking dish. Sprinkle with cheddar cheese. Top with beef mixture, pizza sauce, pepperoni and mozzarella cheese. Bake, uncovered, at 350° for 20-25 minutes or until heated through. **Yield:** 6-8 servings.

## Poppy Seed Biscuit Ring

*(Pictured above)*

**Ready in 30 minutes or less**

*It takes just a few simple ingredients to dress up refrigerated biscuits and form this pretty ring. My daughter Robin first brought these rolls to a family celebration. Now they're a must at special occasions and family get-togethers.*
                      —Elnora Willhite, Ontario, California

1/3 cup butter *or* margarine, melted
  1 teaspoon dried minced onion
  1 teaspoon poppy seeds
1/2 teaspoon dried minced garlic
  2 tubes (12 ounces *each*) refrigerated
    buttermilk biscuits

In a bowl, combine butter, onion, poppy seeds and garlic. Separate each tube of biscuits into 10 biscuits; dip in butter mixture and stand up on end in a lightly greased 10-in. fluted tube pan.

Bake at 400° for 14-16 minutes or until golden brown. Immediately invert onto a serving plate. Serve warm. **Yield:** 10-15 servings.

## Golden Corn Casserole

**Ready in 1 hour or less**

*I stir together corn bread mix, French onion dip and canned corn to make this super-moist side dish. It went over so well at Thanksgiving one year that it's now served at all our holiday gatherings.* —Marcia Braun Scott City, Kansas

3 eggs
1 carton (8 ounces) French onion sour cream dip
1/4 cup butter *or* margarine, softened
1 package (8-1/2 ounces) corn bread/ muffin mix
1/2 teaspoon salt
1/2 teaspoon pepper
1 can (15-1/4 ounces) whole kernel corn, drained
1 can (14-3/4 ounces) cream-style corn

In a mixing bowl, beat eggs, dip, butter, corn bread mix, salt and pepper until combined. Stir in the corn. Pour into a greased 11-in. x 7-in. x 2-in. baking dish. Bake, uncovered, at 350° for 35-40 minutes or until edges are lightly browned and pull away from sides of dish. **Yield:** 8-10 servings.

## Cinnamon Apple Pizza

*(Pictured below)*

*My son asked me to make something the night before a bake sale. He was pleased with this pizza that I created using on-hand ingredients.* —Cherron Walker, Columbus, Ohio

1 tube (12.4 ounces) refrigerated cinnamon roll dough

1 can (21 ounces) apple pie filling
1/4 cup packed brown sugar
1 tablespoon butter *or* margarine, melted

Set cinnamon roll icing aside. Separate dough into individual rolls; roll out each into a 4-in. circle. Arrange on a greased 12-in. pizza pan, overlapping edges. Bake at 400° for 8 minutes.

Spoon the apple pie filling over rolls to within 1/2 in. of edge. Combine the brown sugar and butter; sprinkle over pie filling. Bake 6-8 minutes longer or until the crust is golden brown. Cool. Drizzle with the reserved icing. **Yield:** 10-12 servings.

## Coconut Oat Cookies

*Instant coconut cream pudding mix is the key to these crunchy cookies that are perfect for dunking. For variety, use chocolate or lemon pudding instead.*
—Susan Putkonen, Gilbert, Minnesota

1/2 cup shortening
1/2 cup sugar
1 egg
1 cup quick-cooking oats
1 cup all-purpose flour
1 package (3.4 ounces) instant coconut cream pudding mix
1/2 teaspoon baking soda
1/2 teaspoon cream of tartar
1/4 teaspoon salt

In a mixing bowl, cream shortening and sugar. Add the egg; mix well. Combine the remaining ingredients; add to the creamed mixture and mix well. Roll into 1-in. balls. Place on greased baking sheets. Flatten with a fork. Bake at 350° for 10-12 minutes or until edges begin to brown. Remove to wire racks to cool. **Yield:** 2-1/2 dozen.

**Cinnamon Apple Pizza**

## Turkey Crescents

*(Pictured below)*

**Ready in 30 minutes or less**

*Refrigerated crescent rolls and mushroom soup make the golden bites simple, and a filling of turkey, onion and celery makes them delicious.*
—*Marye Jo Timmons, Alexandria, Virginia*

✓ Uses less fat, sugar or salt. Includes Nutritional Analysis and Diabetic Exchanges.

    1/2 cup finely chopped celery
    1/4 cup finely chopped onion
      1 teaspoon butter *or* stick margarine
      2 cups chopped cooked turkey
      1 can (10-3/4 ounces) condensed cream
        of mushroom soup, undiluted
      3 packages (8 ounces *each*) refrigerated
        crescent rolls
Dill weed

In a nonstick skillet, saute celery and onion in butter for 3-4 minutes or until tender. Add turkey and soup; mix well. Remove from the heat.

Separate crescent dough into 24 triangles. Place 1 tablespoon turkey mixture on the wide end of each triangle; roll up from wide end. Place pointed side down 2 in. apart on greased baking sheets. Curve ends to form crescent shape. Sprinkle with dill. Bake at 350° for 8-9 minutes or until golden brown. Serve immediately. **Yield:** 2 dozen.

**Nutritional Analysis:** One crescent (prepared with turkey breast, reduced-fat soup and reduced-fat crescent rolls) equals 117 calories, 5 g fat (1 g saturated fat), 5 mg cholesterol, 324 mg sodium, 13 g carbohydrate, trace fiber, 4 g protein. **Diabetic Exchanges:** 1 starch, 1 fat.

## Fish with Florentine Rice

**Ready in 30 minutes or less**

*A handful of ingredients is all you'll need to prepare this speedy skillet supper. The entire dinner cooks in one pan and eliminates the hassle of breading and frying the fish.*
—*Margrit Eagen, Crestwood, Missouri*

      1 package (6.9 ounces) chicken-flavored rice mix
      2 tablespoons butter *or* margarine
  2-3/4 cups water
      1 package (10 ounces) frozen chopped spinach
      1 pound orange roughy *or* tilapia fillets
    1/4 cup slivered almonds, toasted

Set rice seasoning packet aside. In a large skillet, saute rice mix in butter. Add the water, spinach and contents of seasoning packet. Bring to a boil. Reduce heat; cover and simmer for 10 minutes. Top with the fish fillets. Cover and simmer for 5-10 minutes or until fish flakes easily with a fork. Sprinkle with almonds. **Yield:** 4 servings.

## Creamy Cranberry Gelatin

**Plan ahead...needs to chill**

*Looking for a tasty take-along for holiday potlucks? Consider this colorful contribution. The sweet-tart salad can be started the day before your event.*
—*Collette Burch, Edinburg, Texas*

✓ Uses less fat, sugar or salt. Includes Nutritional Analysis and Diabetic Exchanges.

      1 package (12 ounces) fresh *or*
        frozen cranberries, chopped
      1 to 1-1/4 cups sugar
      2 packages (3 ounces *each*) cherry
        gelatin
      1 carton (16 ounces) plain yogurt
      1 carton (8 ounces) frozen whipped
        topping, thawed
    1/3 cup chopped pecans

In a bowl, combine the cranberries and sugar; cover and refrigerate for 8 hours or overnight. In a large saucepan, combine the cranberry mixture and gelatin. Cook and stir until gelatin is completely dissolved; cool. Fold in the yogurt and whipped topping. Pour into a 2-qt. serving bowl. Sprinkle with pecans. Refrigerate for 2 hours or until firm. **Yield:** 10 servings.

**Nutritional Analysis:** One serving (prepared with 1 cup sugar, sugar-free gelatin, fat-free yogurt and reduced-fat whipped topping) equals 204 calories, 6 g fat (3 g saturated fat), 1 mg cholesterol, 83 mg sodium, 33 g carbohydrate, 2 g fiber, 4 g protein. **Diabetic Exchanges:** 2 fruit, 1 fat.

**Turkey Crescents**

Cherry Dream Cake
Thanksgiving in a Pan

## Cherry Dream Cake

*(Pictured above)*

**Plan ahead...needs to chill**

*I serve this at Christmas because it's so festive. I use cherry gelatin to give a boxed cake mix a neat marbled effect.* —Margaret McNeil, Germantown, Tennessee

✓ Uses less fat, sugar or salt. Includes Nutritional Analysis and Diabetic Exchanges.

> 1 package (18-1/4 ounces) white cake mix
> 1 package (3 ounces) cherry gelatin
> 1-1/2 cups boiling water
> 1 package (8 ounces) cream cheese, softened
> 2 cups whipped topping
> 1 can (21 ounces) cherry pie filling

Prepare cake mix according to package directions, using a greased 13-in. x 9-in. x 2-in. baking pan. Bake at 350° for 30-35 minutes or until a toothpick comes out clean. Dissolve gelatin in boiling water. Cool cake on a wire rack for 3-5 minutes. Poke holes in cake with a meat fork; gradually pour gelatin over cake. Cool for 15 minutes. Cover and refrigerate for 30 minutes.

In a mixing bowl, beat cream cheese until light. Fold in whipped topping. Carefully spread over cake. Top with the pie filling. Refrigerate for at least 2 hours before serving. **Yield:** 20 servings.

**Nutritional Analysis:** One serving (prepared with sugar-free gelatin, fat-free cream cheese, reduced-fat whipped topping and light cherry pie filling) equals 164 calories, 4 g fat (1 g saturated fat), 1 mg cholesterol, 251 mg sodium, 28 g carbohydrate, trace fiber, 3 g protein. **Diabetic Exchanges:** 1-1/2 starch, 1 fat, 1/2 fruit.

## Thanksgiving in a Pan

*(Pictured above)*

**Ready in 45 minutes or less**

*This meal-in-one tastes like a big holiday dinner without the work. It's a great way to use up leftover turkey, but I often use thick slices of deli turkey instead.*
—Lynne Hahn, Winchester, California

✓ Uses less fat, sugar or salt. Includes Nutritional Analysis and Diabetic Exchanges.

> 1 package (6 ounces) stuffing mix
> 2-1/2 cups cubed cooked turkey
> 2 cups frozen cut green beans, thawed
> 1 jar (12 ounces) turkey gravy

Pepper to taste

Prepare stuffing mix according to package directions. Transfer to a greased 11-in. x 7-in. x 2-in. baking dish. Top with turkey, beans, gravy and pepper. Cover and bake at 350° for 30-35 minutes or until heated through. **Yield:** 6 servings.

**Nutritional Analysis:** One serving (prepared with fat-free gravy) equals 251 calories, 4 g fat (1 g saturated fat), 49 mg cholesterol, 848 mg sodium, 31 g carbohydrate, 2 g fiber, 22 g protein. **Diabetic Exchanges:** 2 lean meat, 1-1/2 starch, 1 vegetable.

**Peanut Butter Chocolate Dessert**

## Peanut Butter Chocolate Dessert

*(Pictured above and on page 75)*

**Plan ahead...needs to chill**

*For me, the ideal dessert combines the flavors of chocolate and peanut butter. So when I came up with this rich treat, it quickly became my all-time favorite. It's a cinch to whip together because it doesn't require any baking.*

—Debbie Price, LaRue, Ohio

  20 chocolate cream-filled chocolate sandwich cookies, *divided*
   2 tablespoons butter *or* margarine, melted
   1 package (8 ounces) cream cheese, softened
 1/2 cup peanut butter
1-1/2 cups confectioners' sugar, *divided*
   1 carton (16 ounces) frozen whipped topping, thawed, *divided*
  15 miniature peanut butter cups, chopped
   1 cup cold milk
   1 package (3.9 ounces) instant chocolate fudge pudding mix

Crush 16 cookies; toss with the butter. Press onto the bottom of an ungreased 9-in. square dish. In a mixing bowl, beat the cream cheese, peanut butter and 1 cup confectioners' sugar until smooth. Fold in half of the whipped topping. Spread over crust. Sprinkle with peanut butter cups.

In another mixing bowl, beat the milk, pudding mix and remaining confectioners' sugar on low speed for 2 minutes. Fold in remaining whipped topping. Spread over peanut butter cups. Crush remaining cookies; sprinkle over the top. Cover and chill for at least 3 hours. **Yield:** 12-16 servings.

## Mocha Pie

*(Pictured on page 75)*

**Plan ahead...needs to chill**

*A friend gave me this divine recipe after I asked how she managed to put together such an elegant pie after a long day at work. Prepared cookie dough, marshmallow creme and a little instant coffee make it a breeze to assemble.*

—Barbara Keller, Highlands Ranch, Colorado

  1 tube (18 ounces) refrigerated chocolate chip cookie dough
  1 package (3 ounces) cream cheese, softened
  2 tablespoons milk
  1 jar (7 ounces) marshmallow creme
  1 tablespoon instant coffee granules
  1 tablespoon hot water
  1 carton (8 ounces) frozen whipped topping, thawed
  2 tablespoons chocolate syrup, *divided*
  3 tablespoons chopped walnuts

Cut cookie dough in half widthwise; let one half stand at room temperature for 5-10 minutes to soften (save the other half for another use). Press dough onto the bottom and up the sides of an ungreased 9-in. pie plate. Bake, uncovered, at 375° for 11-12 minutes or until lightly browned. Cool on a wire rack.

In a large mixing bowl, beat cream cheese and milk until smooth. Add the marshmallow creme; beat until blended. Dissolve coffee granules in water. Fold the coffee, whipped topping and 1 tablespoon chocolate syrup into the cream cheese mixture. Pour into cooled crust. Chill for 1 hour. Just before serving, sprinkle with nuts and drizzle with remaining chocolate syrup. **Yield:** 6-8 servings.

## Hawaiian Sunset Cake

*(Pictured on page 74)*

*This three-layer orange cake is pretty enough for company, but it's so simple to fix that you'll find yourself making it all the time. A boxed mix keeps it convenient while the pineapple-coconut filling makes it a crowd-pleaser at all kinds of gatherings.*

—Kara De la vega
Suisun City, California

  1 package (18-1/4 ounces) white *or* orange cake mix
  1 package (3.4 ounces) instant vanilla pudding mix
  1 package (3 ounces) orange gelatin
  4 eggs
1-1/2 cups milk
 1/2 cup vegetable oil
**FILLING:**
  1 can (20 ounces) crushed pineapple, drained
  2 cups sugar
  1 package (10 ounces) flaked coconut
  1 cup (8 ounces) sour cream

1 carton (8 ounces) frozen whipped
    topping, thawed
Toasted coconut, optional

In a large mixing bowl, combine the first six ingredients; mix well. Pour into three greased and floured 9-in. round baking pans. Bake at 350° for 25-30 minutes or until a toothpick inserted near the center comes out clean. Cool for 10 minutes before removing from pans to wire racks to cool completely.

In a bowl, combine the pineapple, sugar, coconut and sour cream. Remove 1 cup to another bowl; set aside. Place one cake on a serving plate; top with a third of the remaining pineapple mixture. Repeat layers twice. Fold whipped topping into the reserved pineapple mixture. Spread over top and sides of cake. Sprinkle with toasted coconut if desired. Refrigerate. **Yield:** 12-16 servings.

## Mint Sandwich Cookies

*Canned frosting, peppermint extract and chocolate candy coating quickly turn crackers into these wonderful little no-bake cookies. My children and I like to assemble them for parties and holidays. I hope you and your family enjoy them as much as we do.* —Melissa Thompson
Anderson, Ohio

     1 can (16 ounces) vanilla frosting
 1/2 teaspoon peppermint extract
     3 to 5 drops green food coloring, optional
  72 butter-flavored crackers
     1 pound dark chocolate candy coating,
        coarsely chopped

In a bowl, combine the frosting, extract and food coloring if desired. Spread over half of the crackers; top with remaining crackers. Place candy coating in a microwave-safe bowl. Microwave on high for 1-2 minutes or until smooth. Dip the cookies in coating. Place on waxed paper until chocolate is completely set. Store in an airtight container at room temperature. **Yield:** 3 dozen.

## Coconut Angel Squares

### Plan ahead...needs to chill

*I have so many speedy dessert recipes, but this one is truly special. A friend shared it with me, and it immediately became the one I prefer because it tastes like a coconut cream pie with only a fraction of the work.*
—Betty Claycomb, Alverton, Pennsylvania

     1 prepared angel food cake (8 inches), cut
        into 1/2-inch cubes
 1-1/2 cups cold milk
     2 packages (3.4 ounces *each*) instant
        coconut cream pudding mix
     1 quart vanilla ice cream, softened
     1 carton (8 ounces) frozen whipped topping,
        thawed
 1/4 cup flaked coconut, toasted

Place cake cubes in a greased 13-in. x 9-in. x 2-in. dish. In a mixing bowl, beat milk and pudding mixes on low speed for 2 minutes. Add ice cream; beat on low just until

combined. Spoon over cake cubes. Spread with whipped topping; sprinkle with coconut. Cover and chill for at least 1 hour. Refrigerate leftovers. **Yield:** 12-15 servings.

## Raspberry Icebox Dessert

### *(Pictured below and on page 74)*

### Plan ahead...needs to chill

*After tasting this dessert at a church social, I just had to track down the recipe. I was thrilled to learn how easy it is to make. With its smooth pudding layer and colorful berry topping, it's a hit with everyone who tries it.*
—Magdalene Dyck, Burns Lake, British Columbia

     2 packages (3 ounces *each*) raspberry gelatin
     2 cups boiling water
     3 cups fresh *or* frozen raspberries
     2 cups graham cracker crumbs (about
        32 squares)
 1/4 cup packed brown sugar
 1/2 cup butter *or* margarine, melted
 1-1/2 cups cold milk
     1 package (3.4 ounces) instant vanilla
        pudding mix
     1 package (8 ounces) cream cheese, softened

In a bowl, combine the gelatin and water; stir until gelatin is dissolved. Fold in the raspberries. Refrigerate for 1 hour or until syrupy.

In a small bowl, combine the cracker crumbs, brown sugar and butter. Press into a greased 13-in. x 9-in. x 2-in. dish. In a mixing bowl, beat the milk and pudding mix on low speed for 2 minutes. In another mixing bowl, beat cream cheese until smooth. Gradually add pudding. Spread over crust. Spoon gelatin mixture over the top. Chill until set. Refrigerate leftovers. **Yield:** 12-15 servings.

Raspberry Icebox Dessert

## Peanut Mallow Bars

*(Pictured below)*

*Big and little kids alike look forward to eating these snacks that have all the flavor of Payday candy bars. Not only do they beat the clock when time is tight, but they make great contributions to bake sales.* —Janice Huelsmann
Trenton, Illinois

    1 package (18-1/4 ounces) yellow cake mix
    2 tablespoons water
1/3 cup butter *or* margarine, softened
    1 egg
    4 cups miniature marshmallows
PEANUT TOPPING:
    1 package (10 ounces) peanut butter chips
2/3 cup light corn syrup
1/4 cup butter *or* margarine
    2 teaspoons vanilla extract
    2 cups crisp rice cereal
    2 cups salted peanuts

In a mixing bowl, beat the cake mix, water, butter and egg until blended (batter will be thick). Spread into a greased 13-in. x 9-in. x 2-in. baking pan. Bake at 350° for 22-25 minutes or until a toothpick inserted near the center comes out clean. Sprinkle with marshmallows. Bake 2 minutes longer. Place on a wire rack while preparing topping.

In a large saucepan, combine the peanut butter chips, corn syrup and butter; cook and stir over medium-low heat until melted and smooth. Remove from the heat; stir in vanilla, cereal and peanuts. Spread over marshmallows. Cool completely. Cut with a sharp knife. **Yield:** 2-1/2 dozen.

Peanut Mallow Bars

## Toffee Brownie Trifle

*This decadent combination of pantry items is a terrific way to dress up a brownie mix. Try it with other flavors of pudding or substitute your favorite candy bar. It tastes great with low-fat and sugar-free products, too.*
—Wendy Bennett, Sioux Falls, South Dakota

    1 package brownie mix (13-inch x 9-inch pan size)
2-1/2 cups cold milk
    1 package (3.4 ounces) instant cheesecake *or* vanilla pudding mix
    1 package (3.3 ounces) instant white chocolate pudding mix
    1 carton (8 ounces) frozen whipped topping, thawed
    2 to 3 Heath candy bars (1.4 ounces *each*), chopped

Prepare and bake brownies according to package directions for cake-like brownies, using a greased 13-in. x 9-in. x 2-in. baking pan. Cool completely on a wire rack.

In a mixing bowl, beat the milk and pudding mixes on low speed for 2 minutes. Fold in whipped topping. Cut the brownies into 1-in. cubes; place half in a 3-qt. glass trifle bowl or serving dish. Cover with half of the pudding. Repeat layers. Sprinkle with chopped candy bars. Refrigerate leftovers. **Yield:** 16 servings.

## Peachy Cream Pie

**Plan ahead...needs to chill**

*Turn a store-bought graham cracker crust, frozen peaches and whipped topping into this pretty pie. Fruit-flavored gelatin provides a refreshing topping for the delightful cream cheese filling.* —Gina Glassford, Provo, Utah

3/4 cup sugar
    5 teaspoons cornstarch
1-1/2 cups cold water
    1 package (3 ounces) peach, apricot *or* orange gelatin
    2 cups frozen unsweetened sliced peaches
    1 package (3 ounces) cream cheese, softened
    3 tablespoons confectioners' sugar
    1 tablespoon milk
1-1/2 cups whipped topping
    1 extra-servings-size graham cracker crust (9 ounces)*

In a large saucepan, combine the sugar and cornstarch. Stir in water until smooth. Bring to a boil; cook and stir for 1-2 minutes or until thickened. Remove from the heat; whisk in gelatin until dissolved. Add peaches. Refrigerate until slightly thickened, about 20 minutes.

In a mixing bowl, beat cream cheese, confectioners' sugar and milk until smooth. Fold in whipped topping. Spoon into pie crust. Spoon gelatin mixture over cream cheese layer. Refrigerate until set, about 3 hours. **Yield:** 8 servings.

**\*Editor's Note:** This recipe was tested with a Keebler extra-servings-size graham cracker crust. This pie crust size is needed for the large amount of filling.

## Banana Cream Brownie Dessert

(Pictured at right)

*I always keep the ingredients for this extremely delicious dessert on hand because I make it quite often for potlucks and family gatherings. I'm frequently asked for the recipe. After one bite, you'll understand why.*  —Julie Nowakowski
Geneseo, Illinois

Banana Cream Brownie Dessert

1 package fudge brownie mix (13-inch x 9-inch pan size)
1 cup (6 ounces) semisweet chocolate chips, *divided*
3/4 cup dry-roasted peanuts, chopped, *divided*
3 medium firm bananas
1-2/3 cups cold milk
2 packages (5.1 ounces *each*) instant vanilla pudding mix
1 carton (8 ounces) frozen whipped topping, thawed

Prepare brownie batter according to package directions for fudge-like brownies. Stir in 1/2 cup chocolate chips and 1/4 cup peanuts. Spread into a greased 13-in. x 9-in. x 2-in. baking pan. Bake at 350° for 28-30 minutes or until a toothpick inserted near the center comes out clean. Cool on a wire rack.

Slice bananas; arrange in a single layer over brownies. Chop the remaining chocolate chips. Sprinkle 1/4 cup chopped chips and 1/4 cup peanuts over bananas. In a mixing bowl, beat the milk and pudding mixes on low speed for 2 minutes. Fold in whipped topping. Spread over the top. Sprinkle with remaining chips and peanuts. Refrigerate leftovers. **Yield:** 12-15 servings.

## Caramel Chip Bars

**Plan ahead...needs to chill**

*It's fun to take a yellow cake mix and create something that is this rich and wonderful. We like eating the bars when they are cold, right out of the refrigerator. They're ideal with a tall glass of milk.*
—LaDonna Reed, Ponca City, Oklahoma

1/2 cup butter (no substitutes)
32 caramels*
1 can (14 ounces) sweetened condensed milk
1 package (18-1/4 ounces) yellow cake mix
1/2 cup vegetable oil
2 eggs
2 cups miniature semisweet chocolate chips
1 cup vanilla *or* white chips
1 Heath candy bar (1.4 ounces), chopped

In a large saucepan, combine the butter, caramels and milk; cook and stir over medium-low heat until smooth. Cool. In a mixing bowl, combine the cake mix, oil and eggs; mix well. Stir in chips and chopped candy bar (dough will be stiff).

Press three-fourths into a greased 13-in. x 9-in. x 2-in. baking pan. Bake at 350° for 15 minutes. Place on a wire rack for 10 minutes.

Pour caramel mixture over the crust. Drop remaining dough by spoonfuls onto caramel layer. Bake for 25-30 minutes or until edges are golden brown. Cool for 10 minutes; run a knife around edges of pan. Cool 40 minutes longer; cover and refrigerate for at least 1 hour or until serving. **Yield:** 2 dozen.

***Editor's Note:*** This recipe was tested with Hershey caramels.

## Pecan Chip Tube Cake

*This is a fun recipe you can make with kids. They will love sprinkling the pecans, chocolate chips and marshmallows over the batter, and they'll be so proud of the final result. Plus, the cake comes together in minutes and feeds a crowd.*
—Janet Keppinger, Salem, Oregon

1 package (18-1/4 ounces) yellow cake mix
1 package (3.4 ounces) instant vanilla pudding mix
4 eggs
1 cup vegetable oil
1 cup (8 ounces) sour cream
1 cup chopped pecans
1 cup (6 ounces) semisweet chocolate chips
1 cup miniature marshmallows

In a large mixing bowl, combine the first five ingredients. Beat on low speed for 2 minutes or until combined. Pour half of the batter into a greased and floured 10-in. tube pan. Combine pecans and chocolate chips; sprinkle half over batter. Top with marshmallows and remaining batter; sprinkle with remaining pecan mixture.

Bake at 350° for 55-60 minutes or until a toothpick inserted near the center comes out clean. Cool for 10 minutes; invert cake to remove from pan and immediately invert again onto a serving plate. **Yield:** 12-16 servings.

# Homemade Mixes

Coffee Cake Mix

BY KEEPING these homemade mixes on hand, you'll have made-in-minutes meals and time-saving treats at your fingertips whenever you need a quick fix.

And because these family-tested mixes are as economical as they are simple, you can put that boxed mix back on your grocer's shelf and put the money you save back in your wallet!

**Editor's Note:** The contents of mixes may settle during storage. When preparing the recipe, spoon the mix into a measuring cup.

## Coffee Cake Mix
### (Pictured above)

*Keep this handy mix in your pantry and you can whip up a last-minute coffee cake in no time. Cinnamon and nutmeg provide a delicious homemade taste that's better than any boxed mix. It makes a wonderful gift.*
—Linnea Rein, Topeka, Kansas

    4 cups all-purpose flour
    2 cups packed brown sugar
    2/3 cup quick-cooking oats
    1/3 cup buttermilk blend powder
    2 teaspoons baking powder
    2 teaspoons ground cinnamon
    1 teaspoon salt
    1/2 teaspoon ground nutmeg
    1 cup shortening
TOPPING MIX:
    1/2 cup graham cracker crumbs (about 8 squares)
    1/2 cup chopped pecans
    1/4 cup packed brown sugar
    1/2 teaspoon ground cinnamon
ADDITIONAL INGREDIENTS:
    2 eggs
    1 cup water

In a large bowl, combine the first eight ingredients. Cut in shortening until mixture is crumbly. In a small bowl, combine the topping mix ingredients. Store both mixes in separate airtight containers in a cool dry place for up to 6

months. **Yield:** 2 batches (9 cups cake mix, 1-1/3 cups topping).

**To prepare coffee cake:** In a mixing bowl, combine eggs, water and 4-1/2 cups cake mix just until blended. Transfer to a greased 9-in. square baking pan. Sprinkle with 2/3 cup topping mix. Bake at 350° for 30-35 minutes or until a toothpick comes out clean. **Yield:** 1 cake (9 servings per batch).

## Mexican Rice Mix

*Cumin and garlic powder season long grain rice in this simple side dish. The mild mixture would be a great complement to a spicy Mexican entree.*
—Sonya Dueck, Cartwright, Manitoba

    2 tablespoons chicken bouillon granules
    1 tablespoon salt
    2 teaspoons garlic powder
    2 teaspoons ground cumin
ADDITIONAL INGREDIENTS:
    1 cup uncooked long grain rice
    1/2 cup chopped onion
    1/2 cup chopped green pepper
    2 tablespoons butter *or* margarine
2-1/2 cups water

In a bowl, combine the bouillon, salt, garlic powder and cumin. Store in an airtight container in a cool dry place for up to 1 year. **Yield:** about 5 tablespoons.

**To prepare rice:** In a saucepan, saute rice, onion and green pepper in butter until rice is lightly browned. Stir in water and 5 teaspoons seasoning mix. Bring to a boil. Reduce heat; cover and simmer for 15 minutes or until rice is tender. **Yield:** 4-6 servings.

## Cajun Seasoning Mix

*Use this fiery blend to add spark to baked sweet potato wedges. Or try the spicy mixture on pork, chicken or beef for a boost of zippy flavor.*
—Joy Rackham
Yuma, Arizona

    2 tablespoons salt
    1 to 2 teaspoons cayenne pepper
    1 teaspoon garlic powder
    1 teaspoon onion powder
    1 teaspoon paprika
    1 teaspoon white pepper
    1 teaspoon pepper
ADDITIONAL INGREDIENTS FOR CAJUN POTATO WEDGES:
    4 medium sweet potatoes *or* baking potatoes (about 3 pounds)
    3 tablespoons vegetable oil
    1/2 to 1 teaspoon hot pepper sauce

In a bowl, combine the first seven ingredients. Store in an airtight container in a cool dry place for up to 6 months. **Yield:** about 1/4 cup.

**To prepare Cajun Potato Wedges:** Cut each potato into eight wedges. In a large bowl, combine oil, hot pepper sauce and 2 tablespoons seasoning mix.

Add potatoes; stir to coat evenly. Place in a greased 15-in. x 10-in. x 1-in. baking pan. Bake, uncovered, at 450° for 15 minutes; turn. Bake 8-10 minutes longer or until the potatoes are tender. **Yield:** 8 servings.

## Basic Cake Mix

*After preparing this simple mix, you'll have enough to make three moist cakes. So you can try my white cake for an after-dinner delight or the spice cake for a short-on-time snack.*            —Fredrica Hanson, Neosho, Missouri

    1-3/4 cups shortening
    3-1/2 cups sugar
    5-1/2 cups all-purpose flour
        2 tablespoons baking powder
    4-1/2 teaspoons salt
**ADDITIONAL INGREDIENTS FOR WHITE CAKE:**
        3 egg whites
        3/4 cup milk
        1 teaspoon vanilla extract
Frosting of your choice
**ADDITIONAL INGREDIENTS FOR SPICE CAKE:**
        2 eggs
        3/4 cup milk
        1 teaspoon ground cinnamon
        1/2 teaspoon ground allspice
        1/2 teaspoon ground cloves
Frosting of your choice

In a mixing bowl, cream shortening and sugar. Combine flour, baking powder and salt; gradually add to creamed mixture until blended and crumbly. Store in an airtight container in a cool dry place for up to 3 months. **Yield:** about 11 cups (enough for three cakes).

**To prepare white cake:** In a mixing bowl, combine 3-1/2 cups cake mix, egg whites, milk and vanilla. Beat on medium speed for 2 minutes. Pour into a greased 9-in. square baking pan. Bake at 350° for 35-40 minutes or until a toothpick inserted near the center comes out clean. Cool completely on a wire rack before frosting. **Yield:** 9 servings.

**To prepare spice cake:** In a mixing bowl, combine 3-1/2 cups cake mix, eggs, milk and spices. Beat on medium speed for 2 minutes. Pour into a greased 9-in. square baking pan. Bake at 350° for 35-40 minutes or until a toothpick inserted near the center comes out clean. Cool completely on a wire rack before frosting. **Yield:** 9 servings.

## Fried Chicken Coating

*(Pictured at right)*

*I rely on this made-in-minutes mixture to cook up a down-home chicken dinner. We think this flavorful coating tastes a lot like the one at a well-known chicken restaurant chain.*
            —Eileen Frank, Castor, Alberta

        2 cups all-purpose flour
        1/4 cup paprika
        2 tablespoons salt
        2 tablespoons pepper
        1 tablespoon ground mustard
        1 tablespoon dried thyme

        1 teaspoon ground ginger
        1/2 teaspoon dried oregano
**ADDITIONAL INGREDIENTS:**
        2 eggs
        1/2 cup milk
        1 broiler/fryer chicken (3 to 3-1/2 pounds),
            cut up
Vegetable oil

In a bowl, combine the first eight ingredients; mix well. Store in an airtight container in a cool dry place for up to 1 year. **Yield:** 3 batches (2-1/2 cups total).

**To prepare chicken:** Place about 3/4 cup of coating in a large resealable plastic bag. In a shallow dish, beat eggs and milk. Dip chicken pieces into egg mixture, then place in the bag; seal and shake until coated.

In a large skillet, heat 1/2 in. of oil over medium-high heat. Brown chicken on all sides; remove to a greased 13-in. x 9-in. x 2-in. baking pan. Bake, uncovered, at 350° for 50-60 minutes or until juices run clear. **Yield:** 4 servings.

## Cornmeal Muffins

*(Pictured below)*

*I can throw together these tender treats in no time. I just add egg and milk to the blend to bake these golden cornmeal muffins that are a nice accompaniment to most entrees.*
            —Dorothy Smith, El Dorado, Arkansas

    4-1/2 cups cornmeal
        4 cups all-purpose flour
        1 cup sugar
        1/4 cup baking powder
        4 teaspoons salt
        1 cup butter-flavored shortening
**ADDITIONAL INGREDIENTS:**
        1 egg
    1-1/4 cups milk

In a large bowl, combine the cornmeal, flour, sugar, baking powder and salt. Cut in shortening until crumbly. Store in an airtight container in a cool dry place for up to 6 months. **Yield:** about 4 batches (about 11 cups total).

**To prepare muffins:** In a bowl, combine egg and milk. Stir in 2-1/2 cups of cornmeal mix just until blended (batter will be thin). Fill greased muffin cups two-thirds full. Bake at 425° for 15-20 minutes or until a toothpick comes out clean. Cool for 5 minutes before removing from pan to a wire rack. **Yield:** 1 dozen.

Cornmeal Muffins
Fried Chicken Coating

## Whole-Grain Waffle Mix

(Pictured below)

*My mother-in-law shared the recipe for these golden waffles our daughter, Kayla, loves. Just add a few ingredients to the mix and you'll be enjoying their homemade taste in minutes.* —Michelle Sheldon, Edmond, Oklahoma

    4 cups whole wheat flour
    2 cups all-purpose flour
    1 cup toasted wheat germ
    1 cup toasted oat bran
    1 cup buttermilk blend powder*
    3 tablespoons baking powder
    2 teaspoons baking soda
    1 teaspoon salt
ADDITIONAL INGREDIENTS:
    2 eggs
    1 cup water
    2 tablespoons vegetable oil
    2 tablespoons honey

In a large bowl, combine the first eight ingredients. Store in an airtight container in the refrigerator for up to 6 months. **Yield:** 8-1/2 cups mix (about 4 batches).

    **To prepare waffles:** Place 2 cups waffle mix in a bowl. Combine eggs, water, oil and honey; stir into waffle mix just until moistened. Bake in a preheated waffle iron according to manufacturer's directions until golden brown. **Yield:** 5 waffles (about 6 inches) per batch.

    **\*Editor's Note:** Look for buttermilk blend powder next to the powdered milk in your grocery store.

Whole-Grain Waffle Mix

## Herb Muffin Mix

*I stir together a dried herb mix to add savory flavor to whole wheat muffins. But the blend also can be used to season chicken, pork, fried potatoes or vegetable side dishes. Use your imagination.* —Tina Gyles, Barnesville, Ohio

    1 tablespoon dried basil
    1 tablespoon ground coriander
    1 tablespoon dried thyme
    2 teaspoons ground cumin
    2 teaspoons dried minced onion
    1 teaspoon garlic powder
    1 teaspoon dried parsley flakes
    1 teaspoon paprika
ADDITIONAL INGREDIENTS:
    1 cup all-purpose flour
    1/2 cup whole wheat flour
    1/2 teaspoon baking soda
    1/2 teaspoon salt
    2 eggs
    3/4 cup milk
    1/4 cup honey
    2 tablespoons vegetable oil
    1 tablespoon lemon juice

In a bowl, combine the first eight ingredients; mix well. Store in a cool dry place for up to 1 year. **Yield:** 2 batches (about 1/4 cup total).

    **To prepare muffins:** In a bowl, combine the flours, baking soda, salt and 2 tablespoons herb mix. In another bowl, beat the eggs, milk, honey, oil and lemon juice; stir into dry ingredients just until moistened.

    Fill greased muffin cups half full. Bake at 350° for 16-20 minutes or until a toothpick comes out clean. Cool for 5 minutes before removing from pan to a wire rack. Serve warm. **Yield:** 1 dozen.

## Caramel Oat Bar Mix

*I keep a big batch of this oat mixture on hand so I can bake these rich treats in a hurry. The moist bars get extra sweetness from caramel ice cream topping and chocolate chips.* —Jennifer Jensen, Boise, Idaho

    3 cups all-purpose flour
    3 cups quick-cooking oats
    1 cup packed brown sugar
    1/2 cup sugar
3-1/2 teaspoons baking powder
1-1/2 teaspoons salt
1-1/2 cups shortening
ADDITIONAL INGREDIENTS:
    1/2 cup butter *or* margarine, softened
    1/3 cup sugar
    1 cup (6 ounces) semisweet chocolate chips
    1 jar (12 ounces) hot caramel ice cream topping

In a large bowl, combine the first six ingredients. Cut in shortening until crumbly. Store in an airtight container in a cool dry place for up to 6 months. **Yield:** 3 batches (about 8-1/3 cups total).

    **To prepare bars:** In a mixing bowl, cream butter and sugar. Gradually add 2-3/4 cups oat mix, beating until combined. Press 1-1/2 cups into a greased 13-in. x 9-in. x 2-in. baking pan. Bake at 350° for 10 minutes.

Sprinkle with the chips. Drizzle with caramel topping and carefully spread evenly to within 1/4 in. of edges. Crumble remaining oat mixture over the top. Bake 15-18 minutes longer or until bubbly and lightly browned. Cool before cutting. **Yield:** 2-1/2 to 3 dozen per batch.

**Walnut Brownies**
**Fudge Sauce**
**Brownie Crinkles**

## Brownie Mix

*My grandmother discovered this recipe over 50 years ago. When I began baking for weekly church dinners, my mother shared it. Stir up a big batch and you'll have more than enough for the chocolaty sweets that follow.* —Teresa Jarnot, Monroe, Washington

    8 cups sugar
    4 cups all-purpose flour
2-1/2 cups baking cocoa
    4 teaspoons baking powder
    4 teaspoons salt
    2 cups shortening

In a large bowl, combine sugar, flour, cocoa, baking powder and salt. Cut in shortening until mixture resembles coarse crumbs. Store in an airtight container in a cool dry place for up to 6 months. **Yield:** 18 cups.

## Fudge Sauce

### (Pictured above right)

*With a little help from Teresa's Brownie Mix and your stovetop, you can stir up this homemade sauce in no time. The warm topping is wonderful over ice cream.*

    1 cup Brownie Mix (recipe on this page)
    2/3 cup water
Ice cream
Maraschino cherries, optional

In a saucepan, bring the brownie mix and water to a boil. Reduce heat; simmer for 1-2 minutes or until thickened. Serve over ice cream. Garnish with cherries if desired. **Yield:** about 1 cup.

## Walnut Brownies

### (Pictured above right)

*Teresa's family loves these moist brownies. The recipe makes a big pan, so you have lots of treats to share.*

    4 cups Brownie Mix (recipe on this page)
    4 eggs
    2 teaspoons vanilla extract
1-1/3 cups chopped walnuts
    1 cup (6 ounces) semisweet chocolate chips

In a mixing bowl, combine the brownie mix, eggs and vanilla; mix well. Fold in the walnuts and chocolate chips. Pour into a greased 13-in. x 9-in. x 2-in. baking pan. Bake at 350° for 35 minutes or until a toothpick

inserted near the center comes out clean. Cool on a wire rack. **Yield:** 2 dozen.

## Brownie Crinkles

### (Pictured above)

*Throw together these delightful morsels in a snap by adding two ingredients to Teresa's Brownie Mix. The crinkle-topped cookies are crunchy outside and chewy inside.*

    4 cups Brownie Mix (recipe on this page)
    2 eggs
    2 teaspoons vanilla extract

In a mixing bowl, combine the brownie mix, eggs and vanilla; mix well. Drop by tablespoonfuls 2 in. apart onto ungreased baking sheets. Bake at 375° for 8-10 minutes or until the tops are cracked. Cool for 2 minutes before removing from pans to wire racks to cool completely. **Yield:** about 3 dozen.

## Brownie Snack Cake

*Theresa uses a few cups of her homemade mix to create a snack that's ideal for those who prefer their cake with mild chocolate flavor.*

    2 cups Brownie Mix (recipe on this page)
    3 eggs, *separated*
    3 tablespoons milk
    1 teaspoon vanilla extract

In a mixing bowl, combine the brownie mix, egg yolks, milk and vanilla; mix well. In a small mixing bowl, beat egg whites until stiff peaks form; fold into the batter. Pour into a greased 8-in. square baking pan. Bake at 350° for 25-30 minutes or until a toothpick inserted near the center comes out clean. Cool on a wire rack. **Yield:** 9 servings.

2-1/4 cups Quick Baking Mix (recipe on this page)
1/3 cup sugar
1 egg
1/3 cup milk
TOPPING:
1/2 cup packed brown sugar
1 tablespoons all-purpose flour
1/2 teaspoon ground cinnamon
3 tablespoons cold butter *or* margarine

In a bowl, combine mix and sugar. Beat the egg and milk; stir into dry ingredients just until moistened. Spread into a greased 9-in. square baking pan.

For topping, combine the brown sugar, flour and cinnamon in a bowl. Cut in butter until mixture is crumbly. Sprinkle over batter. Bake at 400° for 18-20 minutes or until a toothpick inserted near the center comes out clean. Cool on a wire rack. **Yield:** 9 servings.

## Golden Biscuits

*(Pictured at left)*

*All you need is milk and Quick Baking Mix to make these flaky biscuits. They're wonderful served warm with butter and honey...or use as a base for creamed dishes.*

3 cups Quick Baking Mix (recipe on this page)
2/3 cup milk

Place mix in a bowl. Add milk; stir just until combined. Turn onto a lightly floured surface; knead 10-15 times. Pat or roll out to 1/2-in. thickness; cut with a 2-1/2-in. biscuit cutter. Place 2 in. apart on ungreased baking sheets. Bake at 425° for 12-14 minutes or until golden brown. Serve warm. **Yield:** 9 biscuits.

## Country Corn Bread

*(Pictured above left)*

*A few cups of Alice's mix streamlines preparation of this corn bread that bakes up nice and high. The squares have a lovely golden color and light texture.*

1-1/2 cups Quick Baking Mix (recipe on this page)
3/4 cup cornmeal
2 tablespoons sugar
1/2 teaspoon salt
1 egg
1 cup milk

In a bowl, combine the mix, cornmeal, sugar and salt. Beat egg and milk; stir into dry ingredients just until moistened. Pour into a greased 8-in. square baking pan. Bake at 400° for 20-22 minutes or until a toothpick inserted near the center comes out clean (corn bread will not brown). Cool for 10 minutes on a wire rack before cutting. **Yield:** 6-8 servings.

Cinnamon Coffee Cake
Golden Biscuits
Country Corn Bread

## Quick Baking Mix

*A fast-to-fix bread is one of the best ways to dress up a meal any time of day. With this versatile mix, you can make all of the items on this page. It's a great helper in the kitchen.* —*Alice Wrisley, Mohawk, New York*

9 cups all-purpose flour
1/3 cup baking powder
1/4 cup sugar
3 teaspoons salt
1 teaspoon cream of tartar
2 cups butter-flavored shortening

In a large bowl, combine the dry ingredients. Cut in shortening until the mixture resembles coarse crumbs. Store in an airtight container in a cool dry place or in the freezer for up to 6 months. **Yield:** 12 cups.

## Cinnamon Coffee Cake

*(Pictured above)*

*Tempt taste buds in the morning by stirring up this sweet and cinnamony breakfast treat. It calls for Alice's mix and just a few additional ingredients.*

## Hot Drink Mix

### (Pictured below right)

*This is a great mix to have in the cupboard for cold wintry days. Using strawberry drink mix instead of chocolate makes it fun for kids of all ages. For gifts, put it in a pretty jar and attach directions to fix one serving.*
*—Nancy Zimmerman, Cape May Court House, New Jersey*

2-1/2 cups nonfat dry milk powder
    2 cups white *or* pastel miniature marshmallows
    1 cup instant chocolate *or* strawberry
      drink mix
  1/2 cup confectioners' sugar
  1/3 cup buttermilk blend powder
  1/3 cup powdered nondairy creamer
**ADDITIONAL INGREDIENT (for each batch):**
  3/4 cup boiling water

In a bowl, combine the first six ingredients; mix well. Store in an airtight container in a cool dry place for up to 6 months. **Yield:** 15 batches (5 cups total).

    **To prepare hot drink:** Dissolve 1/3 cup mix in boiling water; stir well. **Yield:** 1 serving.

## Currant Scone Mix

### (Pictured at right)

*You can make a wonderful present of this mix. I pack it in a decorative container along with the recipe for making the scones. I also include a few tea towels.*     *—Delores Hill, Helena, Montana*

    4 cups all-purpose flour
  2/3 cup sugar
  1/2 cup nonfat dry milk powder
    4 teaspoons baking powder
    1 teaspoon ground cinnamon
  1/2 teaspoon salt
  2/3 cup shortening
1-1/2 cups dried currants *or* raisins
**ADDITIONAL INGREDIENTS (for each batch):**
    1 egg, lightly beaten
  1/2 cup water

In a large bowl, combine the flour, sugar, milk powder, baking powder, cinnamon and salt. Cut in shortening until mixture resembles coarse crumbs. Add currants. Store in an airtight container in a cool dry place for up to 6 months. **Yield:** 2 batches (6 cups total).

    **To prepare scones:** In a large bowl, combine 3 cups mix, egg and water until moistened. Turn onto a lightly floured surface; knead 5-6 times. Transfer to a greased baking sheet and pat into a 9-in. circle. Cut into eight wedges (do not separate). Bake at 400° for 20-25 minutes or until golden brown. Serve warm. **Yield:** 8 scones.

## Almond Rice Seasoning Mix

*With its lemon and dill flavors, this side dish is ideal alongside any entree. I've been making it for*

*more than 10 years and my family still loves it. Add cubes of leftover cooked chicken for a fast main course.*
*—Linda Emery, Tuckerman, Arkansas*

    1 cup slivered almonds, toasted
    2 tablespoons dried parsley flakes
4-1/2 teaspoons dill weed
    1 tablespoon dried minced onion
    1 teaspoon salt
  3/4 teaspoon celery seed
  3/4 teaspoon garlic powder
  1/2 teaspoon pepper
**ADDITIONAL INGREDIENTS (for each batch):**
    2 cups chicken broth
    1 cup long grain rice
    1 tablespoon butter *or* margarine
  1/2 teaspoon grated lemon peel

Combine the first eight ingredients. Store in an airtight container in a cool dry place for up to 3 months. **Yield:** 7 batches (1-1/3 cups total).

    **To prepare rice:** In a saucepan, bring broth and 3 tablespoons mix to a boil. Add the rice, butter and lemon peel. Reduce heat; cover and simmer for 15-20 minutes or until broth is absorbed. **Yield:** 3-4 servings per batch.

**Hot Drink Mix**
**Currant Scone Mix**

# Chapter 7

# Look Ahead for Lively Leftovers

SPENDING a little more time in the kitchen on the weekend can reap big rewards in the middle of the week when you turn the leftovers into sensational second-day dishes.

For example, start by offering your family Grilled Rib Eye Steaks pictured at left and featured on page 106. (Like all the weekend dishes that supply the main ingredient for the weekday recipes, its title is highlighted in a colored box.) Later, surprise them with such lively leftovers as Steak Tortillas and Pepper Steak Salad.

The results taste so good that no one will realize they're eating leftovers!

**TWICE AS TASTY.** Clockwise from top: Grilled Rib Eye Steaks, Steak Tortillas and Pepper Steak Salad (all recipes on pp. 106-107).

## Cheddar Cheese Sauce

**Ready in 15 minutes or less**

*Our Test Kitchen shares the recipe for this speedy sauce that's perfect over vegetables, omelets or any items made tastier with melted cheddar. Surprise your family tonight by drizzling some on baked potatoes. Then use up the extra sauce in the two dishes that follow.*

    1/2 cup butter *or* margarine
    1/2 cup all-purpose flour
      1 teaspoon salt
    1/2 teaspoon pepper
      4 cups milk
      2 cups (8 ounces) shredded cheddar cheese
      6 hot baked potatoes

In a saucepan over medium heat, melt butter. Stir in the flour, salt and pepper until smooth. Gradually add milk. Bring to a boil; cook and stir for 2 minutes or until thickened. Reduce heat; add the cheese. Cook and stir until cheese is melted.

Serve 1-1/2 cups of cheese sauce with the baked potatoes. Refrigerate remaining sauce. **Yield:** 5-1/2 cups.

## Home-Style Mac 'n' Cheese

*Take advantage of the leftover Cheddar Cheese Sauce to prepare this comforting casserole. I coat macaroni, ham and chopped onion with the creamy mixture before popping the much-loved combination into the oven to bake.*
*—Phyllis Schmalz, Kansas City, Kansas*

      2 cups uncooked elbow macaroni
      1 small onion, chopped
      1 tablespoon butter *or* margarine
      2 cups cubed fully cooked ham
      2 cups Cheddar Cheese Sauce (recipe on
        this page)
Salt and pepper to taste
    1/2 cup shredded cheddar cheese

Cook macaroni according to package directions; drain. In a large saucepan, saute onion in butter until tender. Add the macaroni, ham, cheese sauce, salt and pepper. Pour into a greased 2-qt. baking dish. Sprinkle with cheese. Cover and bake at 350° for 20-25 minutes or until heated through. **Yield:** 4-6 servings.

## Cheddar Vegetable Soup

*After one taste, this cozy soup is bound to become a family favorite. It's a snap to stir up with leftover Cheddar Cheese Sauce and frozen vegetables.* —*Lisa Welch*
*Germantown, Tennessee*

      3 cups chicken broth
      1 package (16 ounces) frozen cauliflower,
        broccoli and carrot blend
    1/2 cup chopped celery
    1/2 cup chopped onion
      2 cups Cheddar Cheese Sauce (recipe on
        this page)
    1/2 teaspoon salt

    1/2 teaspoon Italian seasoning
      1 cup (4 ounces) shredded cheddar cheese,
        optional

In a large saucepan, bring broth, frozen vegetables, celery and onion to a boil. Reduce heat; cover and simmer for 10-15 minutes or until vegetables are tender. Stir in cheese sauce, salt and Italian seasoning. Cook on low heat until heated through. Sprinkle with cheese if desired. **Yield:** 6 servings.

## Four-Bean Taco Chili
*(Pictured at right)*

**Ready in 45 minutes or less**

*This zesty chili is chock-full of ground beef, beans and south-of-the-border flair. Whip up the stovetop sensation when you're feeding a crowd, or make sure to save leftovers for the following two recipes.* —*Amy Martell*
*Canton, Pennsylvania*

      2 pounds ground beef
      3 cups tomato juice
      1 jar (16 ounces) salsa
      1 can (16 ounces) kidney beans, rinsed
        and drained
      1 can (15-1/2 ounces) great northern
        beans, rinsed and drained
      1 can (15 ounces) butter beans, rinsed
        and drained
      1 can (15 ounces) black beans, rinsed
        and drained
      1 can (8 ounces) tomato sauce
      1 can (6 ounces) tomato paste
      1 can (4 ounces) chopped green chilies
      1 envelope taco seasoning

In a soup kettle or Dutch oven, cook beef over medium heat until no longer pink; drain. Stir in the remaining ingredients. Bring to a boil. Reduce heat; simmer, uncovered, for 15 minutes, stirring occasionally. **Yield:** 12 cups.

## Cheesy Chili Dip
*(Pictured above right)*

*Three ingredients are all Amy adds to a few cups of chili to create this fast-to-fix snack. Simply zap the lip-smacking appetizer in the microwave, serve it with tortilla chips and stand back as the zesty party-pleaser disappears.*

      2 cups Four-Bean Taco Chili (recipe on this page)
      1 jar (8 ounces) salsa
      1 can (4 ounces) chopped green chilies
      1 package (16 ounces) process cheese
        (Velveeta), cubed
Tortilla chips

In a microwave-safe bowl, combine the chili, salsa, chilies and cheese. Cover and microwave on high for 4-5 minutes or until cheese is melted, stirring occasionally. Serve with tortilla chips. **Yield:** 5 cups.

**Editor's Note:** This recipe was tested in an 850-watt microwave.

## Chili Manicotti

*(Pictured above)*

*No one will guess that the secret to this taste-tempting entree is yesterday's chili. A jar of spaghetti sauce combined with Amy's specialty creates the ideal sauce for this cheese-filled manicotti. Topped with mozzarella, the mouth-watering meal will receive rave reviews...and requests for seconds.*

      10 uncooked manicotti shells
       2 cups (8 ounces) shredded mozzarella cheese,
         *divided*
       1 carton (15 ounces) ricotta cheese
    1/4 cup shredded Parmesan cheese
       1 egg, beaten
       3 cups Four-Bean Taco Chili (recipe on
         opposite page)
       1 jar (14 ounces) meatless spaghetti sauce
Minced fresh parsley, optional

Cook manicotti according to package directions. Meanwhile, in a bowl, combine 1 cup mozzarella cheese, ricotta cheese, Parmesan cheese and egg; set aside. Combine the chili and spaghetti sauce; pour half into a greased 13-in. x 9-in. x 2-in. baking dish.

Rinse and drain manicotti shells; stuff with cheese mixture. Place over sauce. Top with remaining sauce; sprinkle with remaining cheese. Bake, uncovered, at 350° for 40-45 minutes or until heated through. Sprinkle with parsley if desired. **Yield:** 5 servings.

## Fresh-Baked Bowls

For a novel way to serve soup, I make my own bread bowls. I prepare the dough in my bread machine, shape it into large round buns, let them rise until doubled in size, then bake until crispy. When the buns have cooled, I cut the top off each one, scoop out the center, fill it with any cream soup and replace the top. Since you can eat the bread bowl, no crackers are required. It's attractive and delicious. —*Kathleen Sadler*
*Souris, Manitoba*

## Creamy Egg Salad

*(Pictured below)*

**Ready in 15 minutes or less**

*I like to prepare this rich classic filling when fixing a soup-and-sandwich meal. It's hearty and nicely seasoned. It's great spread on toast for a quick breakfast bite, too.*
—Linda Potter, Sioux Falls, South Dakota

2 packages (8 ounces *each*) cream cheese, softened
1/2 cup mayonnaise
1 teaspoon ground mustard
1/2 teaspoon paprika
1/2 teaspoon salt
8 hard-cooked eggs, chopped
1 medium onion, chopped
Croissants *or* sandwich rolls, optional
Lettuce leaves, optional

In a mixing bowl, beat cream cheese, mayonnaise, mustard, paprika and salt. Stir in eggs and onion. Serve on croissants with lettuce if desired. **Yield:** about 5 cups.

## Pasta Crab Egg Salad

*(Pictured below)*

*Your family will never guess that the flavorful coating for this pasta and crab combination starts with yesterday's egg salad. This delicious second-day dish supplied by our Test Kitchen is simple to assemble and pretty, too.*

4 cups cooked tricolor spiral pasta
1 cup imitation crabmeat, chopped
1 cup Creamy Egg Salad (recipe on this page)
1 cup mayonnaise
1/2 cup shredded carrot
1 teaspoon dill weed
1/4 teaspoon salt

In a bowl, combine all ingredients; mix well. Refrigerate until serving. **Yield:** 4 servings.

Layered Veggie Egg Salad
Creamy Egg Salad
Pasta Crab Egg Salad

# Layered Veggie Egg Salad

*(Pictured below left)*

*For a tasty twist on a traditional layered vegetable salad, our Test Kitchen added leftover egg salad to the mayonnaise in this version. Fresh spinach as well as lettuce adds interest to the colorful and crowd-pleasing variation.*

    1 cup Creamy Egg Salad (recipe on opposite
       page)
  1/2 cup mayonnaise
    2 tablespoons chopped green onion
    4 cups torn spinach
    1 cup shredded carrot
    8 cups torn lettuce
    1 medium red onion, chopped
    1 cup frozen peas, thawed
    2 medium tomatoes, seeded and chopped
1-1/2 cups (6 ounces) shredded cheddar cheese
    8 bacon strips, cooked and crumbled

In a bowl, combine the egg salad, mayonnaise and green onion. In a 2-1/2-qt. glass serving bowl, layer the spinach, carrot, lettuce, red onion, peas and tomatoes (do not toss). Spread the egg salad mixture over the top; sprinkle with cheddar cheese and bacon. **Yield:** 10-12 servings.

## Baked Haddock

**Ready in 45 minutes or less**

*Our Test Kitchen shares this recipe for tender haddock fillets mildly seasoned with lemon and dill. They're accompanied by a thick and creamy homemade tartar sauce. Use up the extra fish in the two dishes that follow.*

    6 haddock fillets (5 pounds)
    1 teaspoon dill weed
    3 medium lemons, sliced
TARTAR SAUCE:
    1 cup mayonnaise
  1/4 cup dill pickle relish
    1 tablespoon sugar
    1 tablespoon finely chopped onion
    1 tablespoon diced pimientos
    1 teaspoon lemon juice
  1/2 teaspoon dill weed

Place fillets in a greased 15-in. x 10-in. x 1-in. baking pan. Sprinkle with dill. Arrange lemon slices over fillets. Cover and bake at 350° for 30 minutes or until fish flakes easily with a fork. In a small bowl, combine the tartar sauce ingredients. Serve with fish. **Yield:** 6-8 servings (3 fillets) plus 6 cups cooked fish.

## Mushroom Haddock Loaf

*I have a creative way to use up cooked fish. I stir together this savory loaf that tastes much like a tuna casserole. I've made it often for family and friends, and they all enjoy it.*
*—Craig Brown, Sioux City, Iowa*

1-1/2 cups crushed saltines (about 45 crackers)

    1 can (10-3/4 ounces) condensed cream of
       mushroom soup, undiluted
    2 eggs, lightly beaten
  1/3 cup milk
    2 tablespoons chopped green onion
    1 tablespoon lemon juice
    2 drops hot pepper sauce
    2 cups flaked cooked haddock

In a bowl, combine the cracker crumbs, soup, eggs, milk, onion, lemon juice and pepper sauce; mix well. Add the haddock. Press into a greased 8-in. x 4-in. x 2-in. loaf pan. Bake at 350° for 55-60 minutes or until a knife inserted near the center comes out clean. **Yield:** 6 servings.

## Haddock Clam Chowder

*Using a recipe shared by Doris Bergquist of Fort Mohave, Arizona, our Test Kitchen made modifications to take advantage of leftover cooked fish. The seafood soup is wonderful served with warm homemade bread.*

    4 bacon strips, diced
    3 tablespoons sliced green onions
    2 celery ribs, chopped
    2 cups diced peeled potatoes
    1 can (14-1/2 ounces) chicken broth
    1 teaspoon dill weed
    1 teaspoon celery seed, crushed
1-1/4 teaspoons salt
  1/4 teaspoon pepper
    3 cups milk, *divided*
    3 tablespoons all-purpose flour
2-1/2 cups cubed cooked haddock
    1 cup whipping cream
    1 package (10 ounces) frozen chopped
       spinach, thawed
    1 can (6-1/2 ounces) minced clams

In a Dutch oven or large saucepan, cook bacon until crisp. Remove to paper towels. In the drippings, saute onions and celery for 5 minutes or until crisp-tender. Add the potatoes, broth, dill, celery seed, salt and pepper. Bring to a boil. Reduce heat; cover and simmer for 15 minutes or until potatoes are tender. Add 2-1/2 cups of milk.

Combine flour and remaining milk; stir into soup. Bring to a boil; cook and stir for 2 minutes or until thickened. Add the haddock, cream, spinach and clams. Cook and stir until heated through. Garnish with bacon. **Yield:** 8 servings.

## "Egg-Cellent" Appetizers

If you're looking for the secret to swift deviled eggs come Easter, consider this idea. I simply add ranch salad dressing to the cooked egg yolks until I get the consistency I want. Then I spoon it into the egg whites. I'm always asked to bring these deviled eggs to gatherings. People cannot believe how easy they are to make.
—*Terri Chapman*
*Kewanee, Illinois*

## Seasoned Taco Meat

*(Pictured above)*

**Ready in 45 minutes or less**

*I'm happy to share the recipe for this tongue-tingling combination of savory ground beef and zippy seasonings. Turn a big batch of this mixture into a taco supper when serving plenty of hungry guests. Or use a portion to feed your family, saving the extra meat for the following dishes.* —Margaret Peterson, Forest City, Iowa

4 pounds ground beef
3 tablespoons chopped onion
1 can (14-1/2 ounces) beef broth
1 can (8 ounces) tomato sauce
1/4 cup chili powder
2 tablespoons paprika
1 tablespoon beef bouillon granules
1 tablespoon ground cumin
1 teaspoon chicken bouillon granules
1 teaspoon garlic powder
1 teaspoon cayenne pepper
1/2 teaspoon pepper
1/2 teaspoon lime juice
1/4 teaspoon onion powder
1/4 teaspoon sugar
1/4 teaspoon salt
1/4 teaspoon garlic salt
Taco shells *or* flour tortillas
Shredded cheese and salsa

In a Dutch oven, cook the beef and onion over medium heat until meat is no longer pink; drain. Stir in the next 15 ingredients. Bring to a boil. Reduce heat; cover and simmer for 10 minutes. Serve in taco shells with shredded cheese and salsa. **Yield:** 8 cups.

**Seasoned Taco Meat**
**Taco Pizza Squares**
**Taco Pinwheels**

## Taco Pizza Squares

*(Pictured at left)*

*Your gang will come running the minute you take this zesty pizza out of the oven. I top convenient refrigerated pizza dough with leftover taco meat, tomatoes and cheese, bringing a full-flavored fiesta to the table.* —Sarah Vovos
Middleton, Wisconsin

2 tubes (10 ounces *each*) refrigerated
    pizza dough
1 can (8 ounces) pizza sauce
2 cups Seasoned Taco Meat (recipe on
    opposite page)
2 medium tomatoes, seeded and chopped
2 cups (8 ounces) shredded mozzarella cheese
Shredded lettuce and sour cream, optional

Unroll pizza dough and place in a 15-in. x 10-in. x 1-in. baking pan. Spread with pizza sauce; sprinkle with the taco meat, tomatoes and cheese. Bake at 400° for 15-20 minutes or until crust is golden brown. Top with shredded lettuce and sour cream if desired. **Yield:** 8-10 servings.

## Taco Pinwheels

*(Pictured at left)*

*Extra taco meat makes these appealing appetizers easy to assemble. I add the seasoned meat to a cream cheese mixture.* —Cindy Reams, Philipsburg, Pennsylvania

4 ounces cream cheese, softened
3/4 cup Seasoned Taco Meat (recipe on opposite
    page)
1/4 cup finely shredded cheddar cheese
1/4 cup salsa
2 tablespoons mayonnaise
2 tablespoons chopped ripe olives
2 tablespoons finely chopped onion
5 flour tortillas (7 inches)
1/2 cup shredded lettuce
Additional salsa

In a small mixing bowl, beat the cream cheese. Stir in the taco meat, cheese, salsa, mayonnaise, olives and onion. Spread over tortillas. Sprinkle with lettuce; roll up tightly. Wrap in plastic wrap and refrigerate for at least 1 hour.
    Unwrap and cut into 1-in. pieces. Serve with additional salsa. **Yield:** about 3 dozen appetizers.

## Mashed Potatoes

### Ready in 30 minutes or less

*Mayonnaise is the secret behind these comforting spuds. Not only are they special enough for company, but they're a cinch to whip up on weeknights. Try a batch tonight and use what's left in other recipes.* —Brenda Pulley
Waynesboro, Tennessee

3 large potatoes, peeled and cubed
1/2 cup mayonnaise

1/2 cup butter *or* margarine, cubed
3/4 to 1 teaspoon salt
1/4 teaspoon pepper

Place the potatoes in a large saucepan and cover with water. Bring to a boil. Reduce heat; cover and cook for 15-20 minutes or until very tender. Drain. Place potatoes in a mixing bowl; beat until smooth. Add the mayonnaise, butter, salt and pepper; mix well. Refrigerate any leftovers. **Yield:** 5 cups.

## Celery Potato Chowder

*I discovered this thick no-fuss soup more than 20 years ago. Our family loves it and now our daughters prepare it themselves. It's a delicious way to finish off last night's potatoes.* —Deborah Johnson, Calgary, Alberta

1 medium onion, chopped
2 celery ribs, chopped
1/2 cup sliced fresh mushrooms
1 tablespoon butter *or* margarine
2 cups frozen corn, thawed
1 can (10-3/4 ounces) condensed cream
    of celery soup, undiluted
1 can (10-3/4 ounces) condensed cream
    of mushroom soup, undiluted
1-1/2 cups milk
1 cup mashed potatoes
5 bacon strips, cooked and crumbled

In a large saucepan, saute onion, celery and mushrooms in butter until tender. Add corn, soups, milk and potatoes. Cook and stir over medium heat until heated through. Garnish with bacon. **Yield:** 5 servings.

## Potato Chocolate Cake

*When I have mashed potatoes for dinner, I always use the leftovers for this moist chocolate cake the next day. The lightly colored treat freezes well, too, but don't frost it until serving.* —J.P. DeGagne, Kaneohe, Hawaii

3/4 cup butter *or* margarine, softened
2 cups sugar
4 eggs, *separated*
1 cup mashed potatoes
1/2 cup water
1 teaspoon vanilla extract
2 cups all-purpose flour
3 tablespoons baking cocoa
2 teaspoons baking powder
1 cup chopped walnuts
1 can (16 ounces) chocolate frosting

In a large mixing bowl, cream the butter and sugar. Add the egg yolks, potatoes, water and vanilla; mix well. Combine the flour, cocoa and baking powder; add to the creamed mixture. In a small mixing bowl, beat egg whites until stiff peaks form; fold into batter along with walnuts.
    Pour into a greased 13-in. x 9-in. x 2-in. baking pan. Bake at 350° for 30-35 minutes or until a toothpick inserted near the center comes out clean. Cool on a wire rack. Frost with frosting. **Yield:** 12-15 servings.

## Stovetop Baked Beans

**Ready in 30 minutes or less**

*Molasses flavor really comes through in this big batch of sweet baked beans shared by our Test Kitchen. The recipe cooks quickly on the stove and makes enough for a barbecue. Or save the leftovers to use in the next two recipes.*

- 1 large onion, chopped
- 1 tablespoon vegetable oil
- 6 cans (15-1/2 ounces *each*) great northern beans, rinsed and drained
- 3 cans (8 ounces *each*) tomato sauce
- 1/2 pound sliced bacon, cooked and crumbled
- 2/3 cup packed brown sugar
- 1/3 cup molasses
- 2 tablespoons cider vinegar
- 1 to 1-1/2 teaspoons ground mustard
- 1 teaspoon Worcestershire sauce
- 1/4 teaspoon pepper

In a large saucepan, saute the onion in oil. Stir in the remaining ingredients. Simmer, uncovered, for 15 minutes or until heated through. **Yield: 8-1/2 cups.**

## Pork Chops with Baked Beans

*I enjoy making this hearty meal-in-one. I place tender pork chops on a bed of baked beans, then top them with lemon and onion slices before baking. Use leftover baked beans or try the canned variety for anytime convenience.*
—*Kris Wenner, Shoreview, Minnesota*

- 3 cups Stovetop Baked Beans (recipe on this page)
- 1 can (8 ounces) tomato sauce
- 8 boneless pork loin chops (1/2 inch thick)
- 1 tablespoon vegetable oil
- 4-1/2 teaspoons brown sugar
- 4-1/2 teaspoons ketchup
- 2 teaspoons prepared mustard
- 1 medium onion, cut into 8 slices
- 1 medium lemon, cut into 8 slices

In a greased 13-in. x 9-in. x 2-in. baking dish, combine the beans and tomato sauce. In a skillet, brown pork chops on both sides in oil; place over the beans. In a bowl, combine the brown sugar, ketchup and mustard; pour over chops. Top each with an onion and lemon slice. Cover and bake at 350° for 40-45 minutes or until meat juices run clear. **Yield: 8 servings.**

## Baked Bean Chili

*Leftover baked beans are the key to this thick and hearty chili. I simmer them with just a few ingredients and a generous amount of chili powder to create this sweet and spicy mixture.* —*Marcy Cella, L'Anse, Michigan*

- 2 cups water
- 1 medium onion, chopped
- 2 celery ribs, chopped
- 1 medium carrot, chopped
- 3 cups Stovetop Baked Beans (recipe on this page)
- 2 cans (14-1/2 ounces *each*) diced tomatoes, undrained
- 4 teaspoons chili powder
- Salt and pepper to taste

In a large saucepan, combine the water, onion, celery and carrot. Bring to a boil. Reduce heat; simmer, uncovered, for 8-10 minutes or until vegetables are crisp-tender. Stir in the remaining ingredients; heat through. **Yield: 8 servings.**

## Grilled Rib Eye Steaks

*(Pictured below right and on page 99)*

**Plan ahead...needs to marinate**

*In summer, I love to marinate these steaks overnight, then grill them for family and friends. When the weather is not as nice, they can be cooked under the broiler. The recipe makes a lot, so you can use the extra steak to make other dishes.*
—*Tim Hanchon, Muncie, Indiana*

- 1/2 cup soy sauce
- 1/2 cup sliced green onions
- 1/4 cup packed brown sugar
- 2 garlic cloves, minced
- 1/4 teaspoon ground ginger
- 1/4 teaspoon pepper
- 2-1/2 pounds beef rib eye steaks

In a large resealable plastic bag, combine the soy sauce, onions, brown sugar, garlic, ginger and pepper. Add the steaks. Seal bag and turn to coat; refrigerate for 8 hours or overnight.

Drain and discard marinade. Grill steaks, uncovered, over medium-hot heat for 8-10 minutes or until the meat reaches desired doneness (for rare, a meat thermometer should read 140°; medium, 160°; well-done, 170°). **Yield: 2-4 servings and about 1-1/4 pounds leftover steak.**

## Pepper Steak Salad

*(Pictured at right and on page 98)*

*This hearty luncheon salad is a great way to use up leftover steak. Pepper strips give the chilled medley color while store-bought Italian dressing makes assembly a breeze.*
—*Amanda Prestigiacomo, Seabrook, Texas*

- 1-1/2 cups thinly sliced cooked beef rib eye steak (1/2 pound)
- 1 small green pepper, julienned
- 1 small sweet yellow pepper, julienned
- 1 small sweet orange pepper, julienned
- 1 small sweet red pepper, julienned
- 1 can (6 ounces) pitted ripe olives, drained
- 1/3 cup Italian salad dressing

In a bowl, combine the steak, peppers and olives. Add the salad dressing and toss to coat. **Yield: 7 servings.**

## Steak Tortillas

*(Pictured below and on page 99)*

*When I fix steak, I always grill one extra so I have leftovers to make these delicious filled tortillas. The steak strips are seasoned with salsa, chili powder and cumin, then tucked inside soft flour tortillas with tasty toppings.*
—Kris Wells, Hereford, Arizona

    2 cups thinly sliced cooked beef rib eye steak
      (about 3/4 pound)
    1 small onion, chopped
  1/4 cup salsa *or* picante sauce
  1/2 teaspoon ground cumin
  1/2 teaspoon chili powder
  1/4 teaspoon garlic powder
1-1/2 teaspoons all-purpose flour
  1/2 cup cold water
    6 flour tortillas (8 inches), warmed
Shredded cheese, chopped lettuce and tomatoes
    and additional salsa, optional

In a nonstick skillet, saute the steak and onion. Stir in the salsa, cumin, chili powder and garlic powder. In a small bowl, combine the flour and water until smooth; add to the skillet. Bring to a boil; cook and stir for 1-2 minutes or until thickened. Serve on tortillas with cheese, lettuce, tomatoes and additional salsa if desired. **Yield:** 6 servings.

### Storage Savvy

- To maintain freshness, place rib eye steaks and other larger cuts of beef in the refrigerator as soon as you return from the grocery store. In their original packaging, they'll keep in the fridge for 3-4 days or in the freezer for up to 2 weeks.

- For longer freezer storage, remove meat from the store package and wrap tightly in freezer paper or heavy-duty foil or place in a freezer bag for up to 1 year. To defrost, place on a tray to thaw overnight in the refrigerator.

- Extra cooked steak can be refrigerated for 3-4 days. Leftovers can also be frozen in foil or freezer bags for up to 3 months.

Grilled Rib Eye Steaks
Steak Tortillas
Pepper Steak Salad

## Vegetable Wild Rice

*Chock-full of mushrooms, celery and green onions, this hearty side dish is an ideal accompaniment to cool-weather meals. Our Test Kitchen staff seasoned it with garlic, thyme and rosemary so it complements nearly any entree. Plus, it makes a big batch, so you can use the extra in the next two dishes.*

```
3-1/2  cups chicken broth
2-1/2  cups water
    2  cups uncooked wild rice
  1/2  teaspoon salt
  1/2  teaspoon dried thyme
  1/2  teaspoon pepper
  1/4 to 1/2 teaspoon dried rosemary, crushed
    1  pound fresh mushrooms, sliced
  3/4  cup diced celery
  1/2  cup sliced green onions
    2  garlic cloves, minced
    4  teaspoons vegetable oil
```

In a large saucepan, bring broth and water to a boil. Add the rice, salt, thyme, pepper and rosemary. Reduce heat; cover and simmer for 60-65 minutes or until rice is tender; drain.

In a large skillet, saute the mushrooms, celery, green onions and garlic in oil. Add the rice; heat through. **Yield:** 8-10 servings (7 cups).

## Wild Rice Bread

### Plan ahead...uses bread machine

*Cooked wild rice and molasses steal the show in this old-fashioned loaf. My family really enjoys this bread, especially when used for egg salad sandwiches. Try adding some caraway and fennel seeds with the rosemary.*
—*Diane Nord*
*Wolverton, Minnesota*

```
    1  cup water (70° to 80°)
4-1/2  teaspoons vegetable oil
4-1/2  teaspoons molasses
1-1/2  teaspoons salt
2-3/4  cups bread flour
    1  teaspoon dried rosemary, crushed
1-3/4  teaspoons active dry yeast
  3/4  cup Vegetable Wild Rice (recipe on this
       page) or cooked wild rice
```

In bread machine pan, place the first seven ingredients in order suggested by manufacturer. Select basic bread setting. Choose crust color and loaf size if available. Bake according to bread machine directions (check dough after 5 minutes of mixing; add 1 to 2 tablespoons of water or flour if needed).

Just before the final kneading (your machine may audibly signal this), add the rice. **Yield:** 1 loaf (1-1/2 pounds).

## Spinach Wild Rice Quiche

*I turn to this recipe when entertaining a small group or looking for a quick Sunday meal. Swiss cheese and spinach make this quiche tasty, but a store-bought pastry shell and last night's wild rice make it easy to assemble.*
—*Leah Zimmerman, Ephrata, Pennsylvania*

```
    1  unbaked pastry shell (9 inches)
    3  eggs
    1  cup half-and-half cream
    1  cup Vegetable Wild Rice (recipe on
       this page) or cooked wild rice
    1  cup (4 ounces) shredded Swiss cheese
    3  bacon strips, cooked and crumbled
  1/2  cup frozen chopped spinach, thawed
```

Line unpricked pastry shell with a double thickness of heavy-duty foil. Bake at 450° for 5 minutes. Remove foil; bake 5 minutes longer. Remove from the oven; reduce heat to 350°.

In a bowl, beat the eggs and cream. Add rice, cheese, bacon and spinach; mix well. Pour into prepared crust. Cover edges of pastry with foil. Bake for 30-35 minutes or until a knife inserted near the center comes out clean. **Yield:** 6-8 servings.

## Savory Pork Roast

### (Pictured at right)

*I love this herbed roast so much that I make it as often as I can. It's wonderful for special occasions, particularly when served with sweet potatoes and corn muffins. It makes a lot, so you'll have leftover pork for other recipes.*
—*Edie DeSpain, Logan, Utah*

```
    1  garlic clove, minced
    2  teaspoons dried marjoram
    1  teaspoon salt
    1  teaspoon rubbed sage
    1  boneless pork loin roast (4 pounds)
```

Combine the seasonings; rub over roast. Place on a rack in a shallow roasting pan. Bake, uncovered, at 350° for 1 hour and 20 minutes or until a meat thermometer reads 160°. Let stand for 10-15 minutes before slicing. **Yield:** 9-12 servings (or 3-4 servings plus leftovers).

## Pork Fried Rice

### (Pictured at right)

### Ready in 30 minutes or less

*My husband anxiously awaits the nights we have pork because he knows I'll use the leftovers in this recipe. Add a few fortune cookies to make the meal special.*
—*Norma Reynolds, Overland Park, Kansas*

```
  1/2  cup diced carrots
  1/2  cup diced celery
  1/2  cup diced sweet red pepper
  1/2  cup sliced green onions
    2  tablespoons vegetable oil, divided
    3  eggs, beaten
    2  cups cubed cooked pork (about 1 pound)
    2  cups cold cooked rice
    4 to 5 teaspoons soy sauce
```
**Salt and pepper to taste**

Savory Pork Roast
Pork Fried Rice
Italian Pork Hoagies

In a large skillet, saute the vegetables in 1 tablespoon of oil; remove and keep warm. Heat remaining oil over medium heat. Add eggs; cook and stir until set. Add the pork, rice, soy sauce, salt, pepper and vegetables; cook and stir until heated through. **Yield:** 5 servings.

## Italian Pork Hoagies

*(Pictured above)*

**Ready in 30 minutes or less**

*I like to prepare these quick toasted sandwiches whenever I have extra pork. I spread pizza sauce over hoagie buns before adding sliced pork, Italian salad dressing and mozzarella cheese.    —Jackie Hannahs, Fountain, Michigan*

    6 hoagie buns, split
1/2 cup pizza sauce
  12 slices cooked pork (1/4 inch thick)
1/2 cup Italian salad dressing
1/2 cup shredded mozzarella cheese

Open hoagie buns and place cut side up on a baking sheet. Spread pizza sauce on the bottom half of each bun. Top with pork; drizzle with salad dressing. Sprinkle with cheese. Bake at 350° for 5-10 minutes or until cheese is melted and tops of buns are lightly toasted. Replace bun tops. **Yield:** 6 servings.

## Gingerbread Cake
*(Pictured below)*

*I drizzle an easy orange sauce over homemade gingerbread for an old-fashioned holiday dessert. Cut just the number of squares needed, so you can use the extra cake to make additional gingerbread treats.*
—Shannon Sides
Selma, Alabama

  1/2 **cup butter-flavored shortening**
  1/3 **cup sugar**
    1 **cup molasses**
  3/4 **cup water**
    1 **egg**
2-1/3 **cups all-purpose flour**
    1 **teaspoon baking soda**
    1 **teaspoon ground ginger**
    1 **teaspoon ground cinnamon**
  3/4 **teaspoon salt**
**ORANGE SAUCE:**
    1 **cup confectioners' sugar**
    2 **tablespoons orange juice**
  1/2 **teaspoon grated orange peel**

In a large mixing bowl, cream shortening and sugar. Add the molasses, water and egg. Combine the flour, baking soda, ginger, cinnamon and salt; add to creamed mixture and beat until combined. Pour into a greased 15-in. x 10-in. x 1-in. baking pan.

Bake at 350° for 18-22 minutes or until a toothpick inserted near the center comes out clean. Cool on a wire rack.

In a bowl, combine the sauce ingredients. Serve with cake. **Yield:** 4 servings with sauce plus leftovers.

## Gingerbread Men
*(Pictured below)*

*Cookie cutters work well to form these fun and festive fellows from our Test Kitchen. Kids of all ages will enjoy spreading the cutouts with soft, sweet white chocolate frosting, then giving them character by decorating with colorful store-bought candies.*

Gingerbread Trifle
Gingerbread Men
Gingerbread Cake

1 piece (10 inches x 7 inches) Gingerbread
  Cake (recipe on opposite page)
1/4 cup butter (no substitutes), softened
1-1/2 squares (1-1/2 ounces) white baking
  chocolate, melted
1/2 cup confectioners' sugar
Assorted candies

Using a 3-1/2-in. gingerbread man cookie cutter, cut out six men from the gingerbread cake. In a small mixing bowl, combine the butter, chocolate and confectioners' sugar; beat for 2 minutes or until light and fluffy. Frost gingerbread men and decorate with candies as desired. **Yield:** 6 gingerbread men.

## Gingerbread Trifle

*(Pictured at left)*

*This tasty dessert was a hit when I served it to our Bible study group. It's a wonderful blend of flavors and a great ending to holiday meals. If you don't have leftover gingerbread, bake some from a boxed mix to assemble this trifle. —Betty Kleberger*
*Florissant, Missouri*

2 cups cold milk
1 package (3.4 ounces) instant French vanilla
  pudding mix
7 cups cubed Gingerbread Cake (recipe on
  opposite page)
3/4 cup English toffee bits *or* almond
  brickle chips
1 carton (8 ounces) frozen whipped
  topping, thawed
1 maraschino cherry

In a mixing bowl, beat milk and pudding mix on low speed for 2 minutes. In a 2-qt. serving bowl, layer half of the cake cubes and pudding. Sprinkle with 1/2 cup toffee bits. Top with remaining cake and pudding. Spread whipped topping over the top; sprinkle with remaining toffee bits. Garnish with the cherry. **Yield:** 8-10 servings.

## Cranberry Beef Brisket

*My mother-in-law gave me the recipe for this tender flavorful brisket. It yields a lot, so the leftover beef can be used in other recipes.*
*—Annette Bartle*
*Lees Summit, Missouri*

1 beef brisket* (4 to 5 pounds)
2 tablespoons vegetable oil
1 can (16 ounces) whole-berry cranberry sauce
1/2 cup beef broth
1/2 cup red wine *or* additional beef broth
1 envelope onion soup mix

In a large skillet, brown beef in oil on both sides. Transfer to a greased roasting pan. In a bowl, combine the remaining ingredients; pour over beef. Cover and bake at 350° for 3-4 hours or until meat is tender. Strain cooking juices if desired to serve with meat. **Yield:** 10-12 servings.

**\*Editor's Note:** This is a fresh beef brisket, not corned beef.

## Mushroom Beef Skillet

*I simmer fresh mushrooms, onions and tender hearty chunks of leftover beef in a seasoned tomato sauce. This is a tasty and satisfying main dish when served over rice. It's even nice enough to serve to company.*
*—Dorothy Pritchett, Wills Point, Texas*

1 pound fresh mushrooms, quartered
1 cup sliced green onions
2 garlic cloves, minced
3 tablespoons butter *or* margarine
1 can (15 ounces) tomato puree
1 can (14-1/2 ounces) beef broth
2 tablespoons tomato paste
1/2 to 1 teaspoon dried thyme
1/2 teaspoon pepper
3 bay leaves
Salt to taste
3 cups cubed cooked beef
Hot cooked rice *or* noodles

In a large skillet, saute the mushrooms, onions and garlic in butter until tender. Add the tomato puree, broth, tomato paste and seasonings. Cover and simmer for 30 minutes, stirring occasionally. Add beef; heat through. Discard the bay leaves. Serve over rice or noodles. **Yield:** 6 servings.

## Tomato and Beef Soup

*On a cool night, your family will be thrilled to warm up with bowls of this steaming soup shared by our home economists. It's brimming with good-tasting ingredients, including carrots, celery, tomatoes, pasta shells and leftover beef.*

2 cans (14-1/2 ounces *each*) beef broth
2 celery ribs, chopped
2 large carrots, sliced
1 medium onion, chopped
2 garlic cloves, minced
1 can (46 ounces) V8 juice
1 can (14-1/2 ounces) Italian diced
  tomatoes, undrained
1 can (6 ounces) Italian tomato paste
2 tablespoons sugar
1 tablespoon dried oregano
1-1/2 teaspoons beef bouillon granules
1 to 1-1/2 teaspoons pepper
1/2 teaspoon dried basil
1/4 teaspoon garlic powder
2 cups cubed cooked beef
2 cups small shell pasta, cooked and drained

In a Dutch oven, combine the broth, celery, carrots, onion and garlic; bring to a boil. Reduce heat; cover and simmer for 5-7 minutes or until the vegetables are crisp-tender. Stir in the next nine ingredients. Cover and simmer for 10 minutes. Add beef and pasta; heat through. **Yield:** 15 servings (3-3/4 quarts).

# Chapter 8

# Freezer Pleasers

WHEN your schedule heats up, cool down the dinnertime rush.

By doing a lot of the prep work on more leisurely days, it's easy to pop an already assembled entree in the oven after a long day. Soon you have a hot and homemade dinner on the table without a lot of fuss—and all the while keeping your cool in the kitchen.

In addition to main dishes, this chapter features time-easing and appetite-appeasing recipes for soups, salads and desserts you can freeze to make mealtime a breeze.

**FANTASTIC FROZEN FARE.** Peanut Ice Cream Squares and Jalapeno Chicken Enchiladas (pp. 120-121).

## Beef 'n' Bean Starter

**Plan ahead...uses slow cooker**

*I use my slow cooker to prepare this hearty beef and bean mixture, then divide it into two freezer bags. When I'm racing against the clock, I pull a bag of starter from the freezer to fix a savory soup or quick chili. —Nancy Ware Enon, Ohio*

2-1/2 pounds beef stew meat, cut into 1-inch cubes
2 cans (14-1/2 ounces *each*) diced tomatoes with garlic and onions, undrained
1 can (16 ounces) kidney beans, rinsed and drained
1 can (15-1/2 ounces) great northern beans, rinsed and drained
1 teaspoon salt
1/2 teaspoon pepper

In a slow cooker, combine all ingredients; mix well. Cover and cook on low for 8-9 hours or until beef is tender. Cool. Transfer to two freezer bags or containers, 4 cups in each. May be frozen for up to 3 months. **Yield:** 8 cups.

## Beef 'n' Bean Tortellini Soup

*(Pictured below)*

*Full of vegetables, beans and tortellini, this sensational soup from our Test Kitchen is a fast fix with Nancy's starter mix on hand. Simply stir in four ingredients and simmer. Then dinner is served.*

Orange-Swirl Yogurt Pie
Beef 'n' Bean Tortellini Soup

4 cups Beef 'n' Bean Starter, thawed (recipe
    on opposite page)
2 cans (14-1/2 ounces *each*) beef broth
2 cups frozen broccoli stir-fry
1 cup frozen cheese tortellini
3/4 teaspoon Italian seasoning
Shredded Parmesan cheese, optional

In a large saucepan, combine the first five ingredients. Bring to a boil. Reduce heat; cook and stir for 6-8 minutes or until vegetables and tortellini are tender. Garnish with Parmesan cheese if desired. **Yield:** 8 servings.

## Beef 'n' Bean Chili

*Picante sauce, green onions and a little seasoning go a long way when combined with Nancy's beef and bean mixture. Warm up a winter night with this tangy change-of-pace chili from our home economists. Your family will enjoy the flavor, and you'll appreciate the time you saved.*

4 cups Beef 'n' Bean Starter, thawed (recipe
    on opposite page)
1 jar (16 ounces) picante sauce
1/2 cup sliced green onions
2 teaspoons chili powder
Sour cream, optional

In a large saucepan, combine the first four ingredients. Cook, uncovered, over medium heat until heated through. Serve with sour cream if desired. **Yield:** 5 servings.

## Orange-Swirl Yogurt Pie

(Pictured at left)

*This refreshing frozen pie is an excellent grand finale to any meal. The gingersnap crust complements the frozen yogurt and citrus sauce nicely. It's great for entertaining because you make it a day early.* —Nancy Zimmerman
Cape May Court House, New Jersey

1/4 cup sugar
4 teaspoons cornstarch
1 can (6 ounces) frozen orange juice
    concentrate, thawed
1/3 cup water
2 tablespoons butter *or* margarine
1 tablespoon grated orange peel
6 cups frozen vanilla yogurt, *divided*
CRUST:
1-1/4 cups crushed gingersnaps (about 20 cookies)
1/3 cup butter *or* margarine, melted

In a small saucepan, combine the sugar and cornstarch. Stir in orange juice concentrate and water until smooth. Bring to a boil; cook and stir for 1-2 minutes or until thickened. Remove from the heat; stir in butter and orange peel. Cool to room temperature, stirring several times.

Soften 4 cups of frozen yogurt. Combine gingersnaps and butter; press onto bottom and up sides of a greased

9-in. pie plate. Spoon softened yogurt into crust. Top with half of the orange sauce; cut through with a knife to swirl. Place scoops of remaining frozen yogurt over filling. Drizzle with remaining orange sauce.

Cover and freeze for at least 8 hours before cutting. May be frozen for up to 3 months. **Yield:** 6-8 servings.

## Hearty Burritos

*Looking for a fast family meal or single-serving supper? Try these beyond-compare burritos. They're chock-full of tasty ingredients and frozen individually, so you can bake only as many as needed.* —Janelle McEachern
Riverside, California

1/2 pound ground beef
1 large green pepper, chopped
1 medium onion, chopped
1 package (16 ounces) frozen cubed hash
    brown potatoes, thawed
1 can (15 ounces) black beans, rinsed and
    drained
1 can (14-1/2 ounces) Mexican diced
    tomatoes, undrained
1 cup frozen corn, thawed
1/2 cup salsa
1/2 cup cooked rice
2 teaspoons chili powder
1/2 teaspoon salt
2 cups (8 ounces) shredded cheddar cheese
8 flour tortillas (10 inches)
Sour cream, chopped tomatoes, guacamole,
    additional cheddar cheese and salsa, optional

In a large skillet, cook the beef, green pepper and onion over medium heat until meat is no longer pink; drain. Add the next eight ingredients; mix well. Sprinkle about 1/4 cup cheese off-center on each tortilla; top with about 1 cup beef mixture. Fold sides and ends over filling.

Wrap burritos individually in foil and freeze for up to 3 months. Or place burritos seam side down on a baking sheet; bake at 350° for 25 minutes or until heated through. Serve with sour cream, tomatoes, guacamole, cheese and salsa if desired.

**To use frozen burritos:** Thaw in the refrigerator overnight. Bake and serve as directed. **Yield:** 8 burritos.

## Cook Ahead Then Freeze

My husband and I take advantage of sales at the grocery store by buying in large quantities. We purchase cube steaks, flour and fry them, then freeze on a waxed paper-lined baking sheet. When they're frozen, we transfer them to a heavy-duty resealable plastic bag.

Before work, I put a few thawed steaks in the slow cooker, along with cream of mushroom soup, prepared brown gravy and a dash of browning sauce. When I get home, I warm up leftover mashed potatoes, cook green beans and have dinner ready in no time.

—Nancy Mckee, The Plains, Ohio

## Beef Barley Soup

*This satisfying soup loaded with beef, barley and vegetables is wonderful for a busy day when you want something hot in a hurry. It makes a hearty meal with warm bread and a green salad.* —Lisa Otis, Drain, Oregon

2 pounds ground beef
2 medium onions, chopped
1/2 cup chopped celery
3 cups water
2 cans (14-1/2 ounces *each*) beef broth
1 cup quick-cooking barley
2 cans (14-1/2 ounces *each*) diced tomatoes with garlic and onion, undrained
2 teaspoons Worcestershire sauce
1 teaspoon salt
1 teaspoon dried basil

In a Dutch oven, cook beef, onions and celery until meat is no longer pink and vegetables are tender; drain. Stir in the water and broth; bring to a boil. Reduce heat. Add barley; cover and simmer for 10-20 minutes or until barley is tender. Stir in the remaining ingredients; heat through. Transfer to three 1-qt. freezer containers; cover and freeze for up to 3 months.

**To use frozen soup:** Thaw in the refrigerator; place in a saucepan and heat through. **Yield:** 3 batches (3 quarts total).

## Creamy Fruit Fluff

*For a refreshing ending to a meal, serve this cool and creamy fruit dessert. I make this sweet treat all year. It's just as good prepared with fat-free cream cheese and whipped topping.*

—Kristy Joy Nieuwenhuis
Grand Rapids, Michigan

1 package (8 ounces) cream cheese, softened
2/3 cup sugar
1 can (20 ounces) crushed pineapple, drained
1 package (10 ounces) frozen sweetened sliced strawberries, thawed
2 medium firm bananas, cut into 1/4-inch slices
1 carton (12 ounces) frozen whipped topping, thawed

In a mixing bowl, beat cream cheese and sugar. Stir in pineapple, strawberries and bananas. Fold in whipped topping. Transfer to a 13-in. x 9-in. x 2-in. dish coated with nonstick cooking spray. Cover and freeze for up to 1 month. Remove from the freezer 20 minutes before serving. **Yield:** 12-15 servings.

## Spaghetti Ham Bake

*My sister passed along the recipe for this saucy convenient casserole. I appreciate being able to freeze an extra pan for a hectic day. The generous portions are bound to feed a hungry family or an extra mouth or two that happen to show up at your table.* —Mary Killion
Hermiston, Oregon

2 packages (7 ounces *each*) thin spaghetti, broken into 2-inch pieces
4 cups cubed fully cooked ham
2 cans (10-3/4 ounces *each*) condensed cream of chicken soup, undiluted
2 cups (16 ounces) sour cream
1/2 pound fresh mushrooms, sliced
1/2 cup chopped onion
1/2 cup sliced ripe olives, optional
1-1/2 teaspoons ground mustard
1 teaspoon seasoned salt
2 teaspoons Worcestershire sauce
TOPPING:
2 cups soft bread crumbs
1/4 cup butter *or* margarine, melted
2 cups (8 ounces) shredded cheddar cheese

Cook spaghetti according to package directions; drain and place in a large bowl. Add the ham, soup, sour cream, mushrooms, onion, olives if desired, mustard, seasoned salt and Worcestershire sauce. Transfer to two greased 11-in. x 7-in. x 2-in. baking dishes.

In a bowl, toss bread crumbs and butter; add cheese. Sprinkle over casseroles. Cover and freeze one for up to 2 months. Bake the second casserole, uncovered, at 325° for 30 minutes or until heated through.

**To use frozen casserole:** Thaw in the refrigerator overnight. Bake, uncovered, at 325° for 50-55 minutes or until heated through. **Yield:** 2 casseroles (6 servings each).

## Mini Meat Loaves

*(Pictured at right)*

*This main dish is a favorite to prepare for church suppers. The tasty individual meat loaves get spark from a topping made of chili sauce, ketchup and horseradish. I like to keep extras on hand in the freezer for a fast meal.* —Janet Hyson
Pasadena, Maryland

2 eggs, lightly beaten
1/2 cup dry bread crumbs
1/4 cup chopped onion
1/4 cup prepared horseradish
2 tablespoons dried parsley flakes
2 teaspoons salt
1/4 teaspoon pepper
2 pounds ground beef
SAUCE:
1 cup chili sauce
1/3 cup ketchup
2 teaspoons Worcestershire sauce
1 teaspoon ground mustard
Dash hot pepper sauce

In a bowl, combine the first seven ingredients. Crumble beef over mixture and mix well. Shape into six loaves, about 5 in. x 2 in. x 1-1/2 in. Place in a greased 13-in. x 9-in. x 2-in. baking dish.

In a bowl, combine the sauce ingredients. Spoon half over the top and sides of loaves. Bake, uncovered, at 350° for 20 minutes. Spread with remaining sauce.

Bake 20-30 minutes longer or until meat is no longer pink and a meat thermometer reads 160°. Serve immediately; or cool, wrap individually and freeze for up to 3 months.

**To use frozen meat loaves:** Thaw in the refrigerator. Unwrap loaves and place in a greased baking dish. Cover and bake at 350° for 30-35 minutes or until heated through. **Yield:** 6 meat loaves (1-2 servings each).

## Potato Rosettes

*(Pictured above)*

*When I make these attractive mashed potato rosettes, I usually double or triple the recipe so I have more to freeze. It's easy to pull out only as many portions as I need for myself or for company.* —Florence Arbes, Courtland, Minnesota

**2 medium potatoes, peeled and quartered
1/2 cup shredded cheddar cheese**
**1 egg, beaten
2 tablespoons chopped green onion
3 tablespoons sour cream
1 teaspoon salt
1/4 to 1/2 teaspoon white pepper**

Place potatoes in a large saucepan and cover with water; bring to a boil over medium-high heat. Cover and cook for 15-20 minutes or until tender; drain. Transfer to a mixing bowl; mash. Beat in the cheese, egg, onion, sour cream, salt and pepper.

Cut a hole in the corner of a pastry bag or heavy-duty plastic bag. Insert large star tip #409. Fill bag with potato mixture. Pipe potatoes into eight mounds on a greased baking sheet. Cover and freeze for up to 1 month.

**To use frozen potatoes:** Place on a microwave-safe plate. Cover with waxed paper; microwave on high for 6 minutes or until heated through. **Yield:** 8 servings.

Beef-Stuffed Peppers
Pineapple Ice Cream

## Basic Beef Starter

*I prepare this savory combination of ground beef, onions and garlic, then store it in my freezer. This meaty mixture has saved me many hours in the kitchen. It gives me a convenient head start on a wide variety of easy entrees.*
—Amie Wollgast
*Florissant, Missouri*

5 pounds ground beef
4 medium onions, chopped
3 garlic cloves, minced
1 bottle (12 ounces) chili sauce
1 envelope brown gravy mix
1 envelope onion soup mix
1 teaspoon salt

In a Dutch oven, cook the beef, onions and garlic over medium heat until meat is no longer pink; drain. Stir in the remaining ingredients. Cook for 10 minutes or until heated through. Cool. Place about 2-3/4 cups each in four freezer containers. May be frozen for up to 3 months. **Yield:** 4 portions (11-1/2 cups).

## Beef-Stuffed Peppers

*(Pictured above)*

*Use a container of Amie's beef mix and your microwave oven to make this main dish from our Test Kitchen in minutes. Green peppers are stuffed with the ground beef blend, tomato sauce, rice and seasonings.*

1 portion Basic Beef Starter (recipe on this page), thawed
1-1/4 cups cooked rice
1 can (8 ounces) tomato sauce
1/2 teaspoon dried basil
1/8 teaspoon pepper

4 medium green peppers
1/3 cup shredded cheddar cheese

In a bowl, combine the beef starter, rice, tomato sauce, basil and pepper. Cut tops off green peppers and remove seeds. Spoon 1 cup of beef mixture into each pepper. Place in a 10-in. round microwave-safe dish. Cover loosely; cook on high for 10-12 minutes or until peppers are tender, rotating a half turn once. Let stand, covered, for 3 minutes. Sprinkle with cheese. **Yield:** 4 servings.

**Editor's Note:** This recipe was tested in an 850-watt microwave.

## Pineapple Ice Cream

*(Pictured at left)*

*I rely on my ice cream maker when whipping up this five-ingredient frozen treat. The creamy concoction has just the right amount of pineapple to keep my guests asking for more. It's so easy yet has all the goodness of homemade ice cream.* —Phyllis Schmalz, Kansas City, Kansas

    3 eggs, beaten
    2 cups milk
    1 cup sugar
1-3/4 cups whipping cream
    1 can (8 ounces) crushed pineapple, undrained

In a saucepan, cook the eggs and milk over medium heat for 8 minutes or until a thermometer reads 160° and mixture coats a metal spoon. Stir in sugar until dissolved. Cool. Stir in the cream and pineapple.

Fill cylinder of ice cream freezer two-thirds full; freeze according to manufacturer's directions. Refrigerate remaining mixture until ready to freeze. Allow ice cream to ripen in refrigerator freezer for 2-4 hours before serving. May be frozen for up to 2 months. **Yield:** 6 servings.

## Homemade Ladyfingers

*Having a difficult time finding ladyfingers in the grocery store? Try baking your own! I keep a few dozen of these light sponge cookies in my freezer to serve with fresh fruit or to use in trifles and other desserts.* —Peggy Bailey
Covington, Kentucky

    3 eggs, *separated*
1/4 teaspoon cream of tartar
1/4 cup plus 1/3 cup sugar, *divided*
    3 tablespoons water
1/2 teaspoon vanilla extract
1/4 teaspoon lemon extract
3/4 cup all-purpose flour
1/4 teaspoon baking powder
1/8 teaspoon salt
**Confectioners' sugar**

Grease and flour a baking sheet; set aside. In a small mixing bowl, beat egg whites and cream of tartar until foamy. Gradually add 1/4 cup sugar, beating until stiff peaks form; set aside. In another bowl, beat egg yolks with remaining sugar for 3 minutes; add water and extracts. Combine the flour, baking powder and salt; stir into yolk mixture. Fold in egg white mixture.

Cut a small hole in the corner of a pastry or plastic bag; insert round tip #12. Spoon batter into bag. Pipe 3-1/2-in.-long lines 2 in. apart onto prepared baking sheet. Bake at 350° for 10-12 minutes or until lightly browned. Remove to a wire rack; cool completely. Cover and freeze for up 1 month.

**To use ladyfingers:** Thaw in the refrigerator; dust with confectioners' sugar. Serve as a cookie or use in desserts. **Yield:** about 2-1/2 dozen.

## Baked Ham Sandwiches

 *Minced onion and prepared mustard put a flavorful spin on these ham and cheese sandwiches. I simply take a few foil-wrapped favorites from the freezer and warm them in the oven for effortless lunches.* —Charlotte Rowe
Alto, New Mexico

1/3 cup butter *or* margarine, softened
1/2 cup dried minced onion
1/3 to 1/2 cup prepared mustard
    2 tablespoons poppy seeds
    8 hamburger buns, split
   16 slices deli ham
    8 slices Swiss cheese

In a bowl, combine butter, onion, mustard and poppy seeds. Spread about 1 tablespoon over both halves of buns. Layer ham and cheese on the bottom halves; replace tops. Wrap each sandwich in foil. Bake at 350° for 6-10 minutes or until cheese is melted, or freeze for up to 2 months.

**To use frozen sandwiches:** Bake at 350° for 30-35 minutes or until cheese is melted. **Yield:** 8 servings.

## Start-Ahead Stroganoff

*It takes only a few moments to stir up our home economists' hearty Stroganoff when you have a portion of Amie's basic beef mix on hand in the freezer. Simply combine it with canned mushrooms and a few other items, and simmer gently. Then ladle servings over cooked noodles for a sensational supper in no time.*

    1 portion Basic Beef Starter (recipe on opposite page), thawed
    1 can (4 ounces) mushroom stems and pieces, drained
    1 teaspoon beef bouillon granules
    1 teaspoon Worcestershire sauce
    3 tablespoons all-purpose flour
1/2 cup cold water
    1 package (8 ounces) cream cheese, cubed
**Hot cooked noodles**

In a large skillet over medium heat, combine the beef starter and mushrooms. Add the bouillon and Worcestershire sauce. Combine flour and water until smooth; stir into the beef mixture. Bring to a boil. Reduce heat; simmer, uncovered, for 5 minutes. Stir in cream cheese until melted. Serve over noodles. **Yield:** 4 servings.

## Jalapeno Chicken Enchiladas

*(Pictured below and on page 112)*

*These zippy creamy enchiladas are likely to be as popular at your house as they are at my home. I have many requests for this delicious recipe. For weddings, I place a copy of the recipe in a nice casserole dish to give as a gift.*
  —Kaylin DeVries, Magna, Utah

2 cans (15 ounces *each*) tomato sauce, *divided*
4 cans (10-3/4 ounces *each*) condensed
  cream of chicken soup, undiluted
4 cups (32 ounces) sour cream
4 jalapeno peppers, seeded and chopped*
1 teaspoon onion salt
1/4 teaspoon pepper
4 cups cubed cooked chicken
3 cups (12 ounces) shredded cheddar
  cheese, *divided*
20 flour tortillas (8 inches)

In each of two greased 13-in. x 9-in. x 2-in. baking dishes, spread 1/2 cup of tomato sauce; set aside. In a large bowl, combine the soup, sour cream, jalapenos, onion salt and pepper. Stir in chicken and 2 cups cheese.

Spread about 1/2 cup of the chicken mixture down the center of each tortilla. Roll up the tortillas and place seam side down in prepared dishes. Top with the remaining tomato sauce and sprinkle with the remaining cheese. Cover and bake one casserole at 350° for 35-45 minutes or until the edges are bubbly. Cover

Peanut Ice Cream Squares
Jalapeno Chicken Enchiladas

and freeze the remaining casserole for up to 1 month.

**To use frozen casserole:** Thaw in the refrigerator overnight. Bake, covered, at 350° for 40-45 minutes or until edges are bubbly. **Yield:** 2 casseroles (5 servings each).

***Editor's Note:*** When cutting or seeding hot peppers, use rubber or plastic gloves to protect your hands. Avoid touching your face.

## Peanut Ice Cream Squares

*(Pictured at left and on page 113)*

*With its thick peanut and fudge topping, this ice cream cake is always a hit with our family. It's a handy dessert because it can be prepared well in advance. It's a scrumptious treat that appeals to both children and adults.*
—Kathy Pahl
*Medicine Hat, Alberta*

2 cups confectioners' sugar
1 can (12 ounces) evaporated milk
2/3 cup chocolate chips
1 cup butter (no substitutes), *divided*
1 teaspoon vanilla extract
3 cups finely crushed chocolate wafers
   (about 48 wafers)
1/2 gallon vanilla ice cream*
2 cups salted dry roasted peanuts, crushed

In a large saucepan, bring the sugar, milk, chocolate chips and 1/2 cup butter to a boil. Reduce heat; simmer, uncovered, for 8 minutes. Remove from the heat; stir in vanilla. Cool completely.

Melt the remaining butter; toss with wafer crumbs. Press onto the bottom of a 13-in. x 9-in. x 2-in. pan. Cut ice cream into 1-1/2-in. slices; arrange over crust. Sprinkle with nuts. Freeze for 30 minutes. Spread cooled sauce over nuts. Cover and freeze for 1 hour or until firm. May be frozen for up to 2 months. Remove from the freezer 15 minutes before serving. **Yield:** 20 servings.

***Editor's Note:*** Purchase a rectangular-shaped carton of ice cream for easiest cutting.

## Twice-Baked Ranch Potatoes

*I make the most of leftover mashed potatoes to create these creamy stuffed potatoes. You can enjoy two and store the other two in the freezer for an easy elegant side dish later. They warm up nicely in the microwave.*
—Janice Arnold, Gansevoort, New York

4 large baking potatoes (about 2-1/4 pounds)
1 package (3 ounces) cream cheese, softened
2 tablespoons milk
1 envelope (1 ounce) ranch salad dressing mix
1-1/2 cups mashed potatoes
1/4 cup shredded cheddar cheese

Scrub and pierce potatoes; place on a microwave-safe plate. Microwave, uncovered, on high for 18-20 minutes or until tender, turning several times. Let stand for 10 minutes.

Meanwhile, in a small mixing bowl, combine cream cheese and milk; beat in salad dressing mix. Add mashed

potatoes; mix well. Cut a thin slice from the top of each potato; scoop out pulp, leaving a thin shell. Add pulp to the cream cheese mixture and mash. Spoon into potato shells. Top with cheese.

Place two potatoes on a microwave-safe plate. Microwave, uncovered, on high for 3-1/2 to 4-1/2 minutes or until heated through. Place remaining potatoes on a baking sheet. Freeze overnight or until thoroughly frozen; transfer to a freezer bag. May be frozen for up to 3 months.

**To use frozen potatoes:** Place potatoes on a microwave-safe plate. Microwave, uncovered, at 50% power for 8-9 minutes or until heated through. **Yield:** 4 servings.

**Editor's Note:** This recipe was tested in an 850-watt microwave.

## Mini Sausage Pizzas

*I dress up English muffins with sausage and cheese to make these tasty handheld breakfast pizzas. It's so convenient to have them waiting in the freezer for busy mornings. My husband and son really gobble them up.*   —Janice Garvert
*Plainville, Kansas*

1 pound bulk pork sausage
2 jars (5 ounces *each*) sharp American
   cheese spread
1/4 cup butter *or* margarine, softened
1/8 to 1/4 teaspoon cayenne pepper
12 English muffins, split

In a large skillet, cook sausage over medium heat until no longer pink; drain well. In a small mixing bowl, beat the cheese, butter and pepper. Stir in the sausage. Spread on cut sides of muffins.

Wrap individually and freeze for up to 2 months. Or place on a baking sheet and bake at 425° for 8-10 minutes or until golden brown.

**To use frozen pizzas:** Unwrap and place on a baking sheet. Bake at 425° for 10-15 minutes or until golden brown. **Yield:** 2 dozen.

## Frozen Fruit Fluff

*I think this sweet and refreshing dessert is the best. It's so simple to prepare ahead of time...and people rave about its yummy flavor.*   —Deb Palmer, Verona, Wisconsin

3 medium firm bananas, sliced
1 can (29 ounces) peach halves, drained and
   diced
1 can (21 ounces) cherry pie filling
1 can (14 ounces) sweetened condensed milk
1 carton (8 ounces) frozen whipped topping,
   thawed

In a large bowl, combine the bananas, peaches, pie filling and milk; mix well. Fold in whipped topping. Pour into a 13-in. x 9-in. x 2-in. dish. Cover and freeze for 8 hours or overnight. May be frozen for up to 1 month. **Yield:** 12-16 servings.

# Breakfast Burritos

*I steer clear of hunger without hitting the brakes—I simply zap one of these frozen morning morsels in the microwave. These handheld breakfast sandwiches have my family's favorite combination of flavors, but you could try replacing the bacon with cooked breakfast sausage.*
—*Audra Niederman, Aberdeen, South Dakota*

      12 bacon strips, diced
      12 eggs, lightly beaten
Salt and pepper to taste
      10 flour tortillas (7 inches)
1-1/2 cups (6 ounces) shredded cheddar cheese
   1/2 cup thinly sliced green onions

In a skillet, cook bacon until crisp; remove to paper towels. Drain, reserving 1-2 tablespoons drippings. Add eggs, salt and pepper to drippings; cook and stir over medium heat until the eggs are completely set.

Spoon about 1/4 cup of egg mixture down the center of each tortilla; sprinkle with cheese, onions and bacon. Fold bottom and sides of tortilla over filling. Wrap each in waxed paper and aluminum foil. Freeze for up to 1 month.

**To use frozen burritos:** Remove foil. Place waxed paper-wrapped burritos on a microwave-safe plate. Microwave at 60% power for 1-1/2 to 2 minutes or until heated through. Let stand for 20 seconds. **Yield:** 10 burritos.

**Editor's Note:** This recipe was tested in an 850-watt microwave.

# Cranberry Cream Delight

*Loaded with goodies like walnuts, cranberries and pineapple, this fruity frozen dessert also can be served on lettuce leaves as a refreshing side salad.* —*Judy Heiser, Uvalde, Texas*

✓ Uses less fat, sugar or salt. Includes Nutritional Analysis and Diabetic Exchanges.

   2 packages (3 ounces *each*) cream cheese, softened
   1/2 cup confectioners' sugar
   2 tablespoons sugar
   2 tablespoons mayonnaise
   1 teaspoon vanilla extract
   1 can (16 ounces) whole-berry cranberry sauce
   1 can (8 ounces) unsweetened crushed pineapple, undrained
   1 cup whipped topping
   1/3 to 1/2 cup chopped walnuts

In a mixing bowl, combine the first five ingredients. Beat in cranberry sauce and pineapple. Fold in whipped topping and nuts. Pour into a freezer-proof serving bowl. Cover and freeze for up to 3 months. Remove from the freezer 10-15 minutes before serving. **Yield:** 10 servings.

**Nutritional Analysis:** One serving (prepared with reduced-fat cream cheese, fat-free mayonnaise, reduced-fat whipped topping and 1/3 cup nuts) equals 190 calories, 6 g fat (3 g saturated fat), 10 mg cholesterol, 83 mg sodium, 31 g carbohydrate, 1 g fiber, 2 g protein.
**Diabetic Exchanges:** 1 starch, 1 fruit, 1 fat.

# Potato Pancakes

*I enjoy these crispy pancakes with steak, asparagus and a Caesar salad. With flavored cream cheese, Swiss cheese and a hint of cayenne pepper, they're sure to be popular at your house, too.* —*Otto Woltersdorf Jr. Chalfont, Pennsylvania*

   4 medium uncooked baking potatoes
   1/2 cup softened chive and onion cream cheese
   1 tablespoon all-purpose flour
   1 egg
   1/4 cup whipping cream
   1/2 to 1 teaspoon onion salt
   1/8 teaspoon cayenne pepper
   3/4 cup shredded Swiss cheese
   1/4 to 1/3 cup vegetable oil

Peel and grate potatoes; drain on paper towels. Squeeze dry and set aside. In a bowl, combine cream cheese and flour until blended. Stir in the egg, cream, onion salt and cayenne until smooth. Stir in potatoes and cheese.

In an electric skillet, heat 1/8 in. of oil to 375°. Drop batter by 1/3 cupfuls into skillet; press lightly to flatten. Fry for about 5 minutes on each side or until the potatoes are tender and golden brown. Drain on paper towels.

Arrange the patties in a single layer on a baking sheet. Freeze overnight or until thoroughly frozen. Place in a resealable plastic bag. May be frozen for up to 2 months.

**To use frozen potato pancakes:** Place frozen pancakes on a lightly greased baking sheet. Bake at 400° for 10-12 minutes or until heated through. **Yield:** 16 pancakes.

# Meat Sauce for Pasta

(Pictured at right)

*I freeze a batch of this chunky sauce when I know I'll be entertaining weekend guests. The classic flavors make this sauce very popular. It easily defrosts and reheats for a hearty meal in no time.*
—*Alberta McKay, Bartlesville, Oklahoma*

   2 pounds bulk Italian sausage *or* ground beef
   1 large onion, chopped
   2 cans (15 ounces *each*) tomato sauce
   2 cans (14-1/2 ounces *each*) diced tomatoes, undrained
   2 cans (4 ounces *each*) mushroom stems and pieces, drained
   1/2 cup minced fresh parsley
   2 teaspoons garlic salt
   1 teaspoon dried oregano
   1/2 teaspoon *each* dried basil, chili powder and pepper
   2 bay leaves
Hot cooked pasta

In a Dutch oven, cook meat and onion over medium heat until meat is no longer pink; drain. Add the tomato sauce, tomatoes, mushrooms, parsley and seasonings. Bring to a boil. Reduce heat; cover and simmer for 45 minutes,

stirring occasionally. Uncover; simmer 15 minutes longer or until sauce reaches desired consistency. Discard bay leaves. Freeze in meal-size portions.

**To use frozen meat sauce:** Thaw in the refrigerator overnight. Place in a saucepan; heat through. Serve over pasta. **Yield:** about 14 (3/4-cup) servings.

## Frosty Chocolate Pie

*(Pictured above)*

*This chilled treat takes me back to my childhood because it tastes like a Fudgsicle. I turn sandwich cookies, chocolate pudding and vanilla ice cream into a dessert guaranteed to satisfy the kid in everyone.*
—Maria Regakis
Somerville, Massachusetts

  15 cream-filled chocolate sandwich cookies, crushed
1/4 cup butter *or* margarine, melted
   1 cup cold milk
   1 package (3.9 ounces) instant chocolate pudding mix

   2 cups vanilla ice cream, softened
Whipped topping and grated chocolate, optional

In a bowl, combine the cookie crumbs and butter; mix well. Press into a greased 9-in. pie plate. In a mixing bowl, beat the milk and pudding mix on low speed for 2 minutes. Fold in ice cream. Spoon into the prepared crust. Cover and freeze for 4 hours or until firm.

Remove pie from the freezer 15 minutes before serving. Garnish with whipped topping and grated chocolate if desired. **Yield:** 6-8 servings.

### Packing Particulars

When bagging your own groceries at the supermarket, the National Frozen & Refrigerated Foods Association suggests packing all of the frozen foods together to help maintain their cold temperature on the drive home. When placing the items in your freezer, leave space around them for cold air to circulate properly.

## Make-Ahead Burritos

*(Pictured above)*

*With two active children, I love meals I can pull out of the freezer. The burritos are wrapped individually so it's easy to take out only the number you need.*

*—Jennifer Shafer*
*Durham, North Carolina*

✓ Uses less fat, sugar or salt. Includes Nutritional Analysis and Diabetic Exchanges.

**3 cups shredded cooked chicken *or* beef**
**1 jar (16 ounces) salsa**

**1 can (16 ounces) refried beans**
**1 can (4 ounces) chopped green chilies, drained**
**1 envelope burrito *or* taco seasoning**
**1/2 cup water**
**16 flour tortillas (8 inches), warmed**
**1 pound Monterey Jack *or* cheddar cheese, cut into 5-inch x 1/2-inch strips**

In a large skillet or saucepan, combine meat, salsa, beans, chilies, seasoning and water. Bring to a boil. Reduce heat; simmer, uncovered, for 5 minutes or until heated through.

Spoon about 1/3 cup off-center on each tortilla; top

with a cheese strip. Fold edge of tortilla nearest filling over to cover. Fold ends of tortilla over filling and roll up. Wrap individually in aluminum foil. Freeze for up to 2 months. **Yield:** 16 burritos.

**To use frozen burritos:** Place the frozen foil packets on a baking sheet. Bake at 350° for 50 minutes or until heated through. If thawed, bake at 350° for 25-30 minutes.

**Nutritional Analysis:** One burrito (prepared with chicken breast, fat-free refried beans and reduced-fat cheddar cheese) equals 270 calories, 10 g fat (5 g saturated fat), 42 mg cholesterol, 754 mg sodium, 25 g carbohydrate, 4 g fiber, 22 g protein. **Diabetic Exchanges:** 2 lean meat, 1-1/2 starch, 1 fat.

## Pizza Meat Loaf Cups
### (Pictured at left)

*I fix and freeze these moist little meat loaves that are packed with pizza flavor. They're great to reheat for an after-school snack or quick dinner on soccer night. My family likes to drizzle extra pizza sauce on top. Treat your gang to a few tonight.* —Susan Wollin
*Marshall, Wisconsin*

> 1 egg, beaten
> 1/2 cup pizza sauce
> 1/4 cup seasoned bread crumbs
> 1/2 teaspoon Italian seasoning
> 1-1/2 pounds ground beef
> 1-1/2 cups (6 ounces) shredded mozzarella cheese
> Additional pizza sauce, optional

In a bowl, combine the egg, pizza sauce, bread crumbs and Italian seasoning. Crumble beef over mixture and mix well. Divide between 12 greased muffin cups; press onto the bottom and up the sides. Fill center with cheese.

Bake at 375° for 15-18 minutes or until meat is no longer pink. Serve immediately with additional pizza sauce if desired. Or cool, place in freezer bags and freeze for up to 3 months. **Yield:** 1 dozen.

**To use frozen pizza cups:** Thaw in the refrigerator for 24 hours. Heat on a microwave-safe plate on high for 2-3 minutes or until heated through.

## Ground Beef Baked Beans

*I serve this hearty ground beef and bean bake with a tossed salad and some crusty bread for a balanced one-pot meal. It's nice to have this casserole in the freezer for those nights when there's no time to cook.* —Louann Sherbach
*Wantagh, New York*

> 3 pounds ground beef
> 4 cans (16 ounces each) pork and beans
> 2 cups ketchup
> 1 cup water
> 2 envelopes onion soup mix
> 1/4 cup packed brown sugar
> 1/4 cup ground mustard
> 1/4 cup molasses

> 1 tablespoon white vinegar
> 1 teaspoon garlic powder
> 1/2 teaspoon ground cloves

In a Dutch oven, cook beef over medium heat until no longer pink; drain. Stir in the remaining ingredients; heat through. Transfer to two greased 2-qt. baking dishes. Cover and freeze one dish for up to 3 months.

Cover and bake the second dish at 400° for 30 minutes. Uncover; bake 10-15 minutes longer or until bubbly. **Yield:** 2 casseroles (10-12 servings each).

**To use frozen casserole:** Thaw in the refrigerator. Cover and bake at 400° for 40 minutes. Uncover; bake 15-20 minutes longer or until bubbly.

## Cheesy Vegetable Soup

*My sister brought this soup to a New Year's Eve get-together. After one taste, I was hooked. It makes a large batch, so I freeze leftovers in single-serving containers.*
*—Sandra Goetzinger-Andrews, Hiawatha, Iowa*

> 6 cups water
> 1 package (30 ounces) frozen shredded hash brown potatoes
> 1 package (16 ounces) frozen California-blend vegetables
> 4 teaspoons chicken bouillon granules
> 1 pound process cheese (Velveeta), cubed
> 2 cans (10-3/4 ounces each) condensed cream of mushroom soup, undiluted
> 1 cup milk

In a large kettle, bring water to a boil. Add hash browns, vegetables and bouillon. Reduce heat; cover and simmer for 10 minutes or until vegetables are tender. Stir in the cheese, soup and milk; cook and stir until cheese is melted. Serve immediately, or cool and freeze for up to 3 months. **Yield:** 14 servings.

**To use frozen soup:** Thaw in the refrigerator. Heat in a saucepan, adding additional milk if desired to achieve desired thickness.

## Fruity Sherbet

*Icy chunks of fruit add color and interest to this pretty pink alternative to ice cream. My family and I love this cool dessert because it's not overly sweet and it's so refreshing.* —Robyn Jessop
*North Ogden, Utah*

> 4 pints pineapple or lemon sherbet, softened
> 2 medium firm bananas, quartered lengthwise and thinly sliced
> 1 package (10 ounces) frozen sweetened raspberries, thawed
> 1 cup blueberries

In a large bowl, combine all ingredients. Cover and freeze for up to 1 month. **Yield:** about 5 pints (16-20 servings).

# Chapter 9

RUSHING to get to work, school and other activities leaves little time to prepare and enjoy a satisfying breakfast.

Too many times, folks either head to their nearest fast-food drive-thru or, even worse, forgo a morning meal altogether.

This chapter steers you to quick and tasty recipes that will help get your family's day off to a delicious, nutritious start in short order. You can even serve them as a beautiful brunch for weekend guests.

Families on the go will make time for these fast-to-fix egg dishes, beverages, pancakes, fruit salads and more.

**SUNRISE SENSATIONS.** Clockwise from center top: Ham 'n' Egg Sandwich, Asparagus Omelet, Carrot Pancakes and Southwest Sausage Bake (all recipes on pp. 134 and 135).

Sausage Hash Brown Bake
Apple Walnut Crescent
Cream-Topped Grape

# Cream-Topped Grapes

## (Pictured at left)

### Ready in 15 minutes or less

*I dress up brunches with a decadent dressing that I can make in a dash. I dollop the heavenly four-ingredient sauce over refreshing red and green grapes. It's a delisiously different way to serve fruit salad.*
—*Vioda Geyer, Uhrichsville, Ohio*

✓ Uses less fat, sugar or salt. Includes Nutritional Analysis and Diabetic Exchanges.

    4 ounces cream cheese, softened
1/4 cup sugar
1/2 teaspoon vanilla extract
1/2 cup sour cream
    3 cups seedless green grapes
    3 cups seedless red grapes

In a small mixing bowl, beat the cream cheese, sugar and vanilla. Add the sour cream; mix well. Divide grapes among individual serving bowls; dollop with topping. **Yield:** 8 servings.
**Nutritional Analysis:** One serving (3/4 cup grapes plus 2 tablespoons topping, prepared with reduced-fat cream cheese and fat-free sour cream) equals 120 calories, 3 g fat (2 g saturated fat), 8 mg cholesterol, 55 mg sodium, 22 g carbohydrate, 1 g fiber, 3 g protein. **Diabetic Exchanges:** 1-1/2 fruit, 1/2 fat.

# Apple Walnut Crescents

## (Pictured at left)

### Ready in 45 minutes or less

*A local apple orchard had a cook-off I wanted to enter, so I created these golden cinnamon treats. They're a snap to assemble with convenient crescent roll dough. They taste like pastries with baked apple filling.* —*Karen Petzold Vassar, Michigan*

    2 packages (8 ounces *each*) refrigerated crescent rolls
1/4 cup sugar
    1 tablespoon ground cinnamon
    4 medium tart apples, peeled, cored and quartered
1/4 cup chopped walnuts
1/4 cup raisins, optional
1/4 cup butter *or* margarine, melted

Unroll crescent roll dough and separate into 16 triangles. Combine sugar and cinnamon; sprinkle about 1/2 teaspoon on each triangle. Place an apple quarter near the short side and roll up. Place in a lightly greased 15-in. x 10-in. x 1-in. baking pan.
Press walnuts and raisins if desired into top of dough. Drizzle with butter. Sprinkle with the remaining cinnamon-sugar. Bake at 375° for 20-24 minutes or until golden brown. Serve warm. **Yield:** 16 servings.

# Sausage Hash Brown Bake

## (Pictured at left)

*Pork sausage is sandwiched between layers of creamy hash browns. Cheddar cheese tops the all-in-one breakfast casserole.* —*Esther Wrinkles, Vanzant, Missouri*

    2 pounds bulk pork sausage
    2 cups (8 ounces) shredded cheddar cheese, *divided*
    1 can (10-3/4 ounces) condensed cream of chicken soup, undiluted
    1 cup (8 ounces) sour cream
    1 carton (8 ounces) French onion dip
    1 cup chopped onion
1/4 cup chopped green pepper
1/4 cup chopped sweet red pepper
1/8 teaspoon pepper
    1 package (30 ounces) frozen shredded hash brown potatoes, thawed

In a large skillet, cook sausage over medium heat until no longer pink; drain on paper towels. In a large bowl, combine 1-3/4 cups cheese and the next seven ingredients; fold in potatoes.
Spread half into a greased shallow 3-qt. baking dish. Top with sausage and remaining potato mixture. Sprinkle with remaining cheese. Cover and bake at 350° for 45 minutes. Uncover; bake 10 minutes longer or until heated through. **Yield:** 10-12 servings.

# Omelet with Cheese Sauce

### Read in 15 minutes or less

*In this effortless egg dish, the cheesy sauce is easy to make and the green chilies really jazz up the omelet.*
—*Joan Enerson, Waupaca, Wisconsin*

    1 can (10-3/4 ounces) condensed cheddar cheese soup, undiluted
1/2 cup half-and-half cream
    6 eggs
1/2 teaspoon salt
1/4 teaspoon pepper
    2 tablespoons chopped green chilies
    1 tablespoon butter *or* margarine

In a small saucepan, cook soup and cream over low heat until warm, stirring occasionally. In a small bowl, beat the eggs, salt and pepper; stir in chilies. Melt butter in a 10-in. skillet over medium heat; add egg mixture. As the eggs set, lift edges, letting uncooked portion flow underneath.
When eggs are completely set, remove from the heat. Fold omelet in half; cut into three wedges. Serve with sauce. Refrigerate any leftover sauce. **Yield:** 3 servings.

## No Morning Mess

I transfer jelly to a plastic squeeze bottle. It's easy to squeeze onto toast or bagels, and there are no jars or knives to clean up. —*Jacci Gunther, Maine, New York*

## Baked Eggs with Basil Sauce

*(Pictured at right)*

**Ready in 45 minutes or less**

*A creamy sauce adds great basil flavor to these eggs baked in individual custard cups. You can even pop the eggs out of the cups and place them between toasted English muffin halves for on-the-go sandwiches.* —Maria Regakis
Somerville, Massachusetts

>     3 tablespoons butter *or* margarine
>     2 tablespoons all-purpose flour
>     1/4 teaspoon salt
>     1/8 teaspoon pepper
>     1 cup milk
>     1/4 cup shredded Muenster *or* mozzarella
>         cheese
>     3 tablespoons minced fresh basil
>         *or* 1 teaspoon dried basil
>     4 eggs
> Basil sprigs, optional

In a small saucepan, melt butter over medium heat. Stir in the flour, salt and pepper until smooth. Gradually add milk. Bring to a boil; cook and stir for 1 minute or until thickened. Remove from the heat; stir in cheese and basil.

Spoon 3 tablespoons of sauce into four greased 6-oz. custard cups. Gently break an egg into the center of each cup. Spoon the remaining sauce over eggs. Bake at 350° for 20-25 minutes or until the eggs are completely set. Garnish with basil sprigs if desired. **Yield:** 4 servings.

## Ham 'n' Cheese Egg Loaf

*(Pictured at right)*

*My family has enjoyed attractive slices of this moist brunch loaf for many years. Whenever I serve it at gatherings, there are lots of recipe requests but never any leftovers.* —Connie Bair
East Wenatchee, Washington

>     6 eggs
>     3/4 cup milk
>     1 teaspoon prepared mustard
> 1-1/2 cups all-purpose flour
> 2-1/2 teaspoons baking powder
>     1/4 teaspoon salt
>     6 bacon strips, cooked and crumbled
>     1 cup cubed fully cooked ham
>     4 ounces cheddar cheese, cut into
>         1/2-inch cubes
>     4 ounces Monterey Jack cheese, cut
>         into 1/2-inch cubes

In a mixing bowl, beat eggs until frothy, about 1 minute. Add milk and mustard. Combine the flour, baking powder and salt. Add to the egg mixture and beat until smooth. Stir in bacon, ham and cheeses. Transfer to a greased and floured 9-in. x 5-in. x 3-in. loaf pan.

Bake, uncovered, at 350° for 55-60 minutes or until golden brown and a toothpick inserted near the center comes out clean. Cool for 10-15 minutes. Run a knife around edge of pan to remove. Slice and serve warm. Refrigerate leftovers. **Yield:** 6-8 servings.

## Tropical Fruit Salad

*(Pictured at right)*

**Ready in 15 minutes or less**

*You don't need a long list of ingredients to toss together this refreshing medley. A wonderful light dressing made with pineapple yogurt nicely coats the appealing assortment of fresh and canned fruit.* —Nancy Stinson
Texarkana, Texas

✓ Uses less fat, sugar or salt. Includes Nutritional Analysis and Diabetic Exchanges.

>     2 cans (8-1/4 ounces *each*) tropical fruit salad
>     1/2 cup pineapple *or* vanilla yogurt
>     1 teaspoon honey
>     1 small apple, chopped
>     1/2 cup halved fresh strawberries
>     1/2 cup halved green grapes

Drain fruit salad, reserving 1/4 cup juice (discard remaining juice or save for another use). In a bowl, combine yogurt, honey and reserved juice. Fold in fruit salad, apple, strawberries and grapes. Serve immediately. **Yield:** 4 servings.

**Nutritional Analysis:** One 3/4-cup serving (prepared with reduced-fat yogurt) equals 143 calories, trace fat (trace saturated fat), 1 mg cholesterol, 23 mg sodium, 35 g carbohydrate, 2 g fiber, 1 g protein. **Diabetic Exchange:** 2-1/2 fruit.

## Amish Breakfast Casserole

**Ready in 1 hour or less**

*We enjoyed a hearty breakfast bake during a visit to an Amish inn. When I asked for the recipe, one of the ladies told me the ingredients right off the top of her head. I modified it to create this version my family loves. Try breakfast sausage in place of bacon.* —Beth Notaro
Kokomo, Indiana

>     1 pound sliced bacon, diced
>     1 medium sweet onion, chopped
>     6 eggs, lightly beaten
>     4 cups frozen shredded hash brown potatoes,
>         thawed
>     2 cups (8 ounces) shredded cheddar cheese
> 1-1/2 cups (12 ounces) small-curd cottage cheese
> 1-1/4 cups shredded Swiss cheese

In a large skillet, cook bacon and onion until bacon is crisp; drain. In a bowl, combine the remaining ingredients; stir in bacon mixture. Transfer to a greased 13-in. x 9-in. x 2-in. baking dish.

Bake, uncovered, at 350° for 35-40 minutes or until set and bubbly. Let stand for 10 minutes before cutting. **Yield:** 12 servings.

**Tropical Fruit Salad**
**Baked Eggs with Basil Sauce**
**Ham 'n' Cheese Egg Loaf**

Creamy Orange Drink
Bacon Quiche Tarts
French Toast Bake

# Creamy Orange Drink

*(Pictured at left)*

**Ready in 15 minutes or less**

*Few beverages are as simple and refreshing as this one. Bring this swift slushy specialty to your breakfast table and watch how quickly glasses are raised for seconds.*
*—Sybil Brown, Highland, California*

✓ Uses less fat, sugar or salt. Includes Nutritional Analysis and Diabetic Exchanges.

      2 cups orange juice
  1/2 cup water
  1/2 cup milk
  1/4 cup sugar
  1/2 teaspoon vanilla extract
      1 tablespoon instant vanilla pudding mix
      1 tablespoon whipped topping mix
      1 tablespoon powdered nondairy creamer
      6 to 8 ice cubes

In a blender, combine all ingredients; cover and process until slushy. Serve immediately. **Yield:** 5 servings.

**Nutritional Analysis:** One 1-cup serving (prepared with fat-free milk and sugar-free pudding) equals 107 calories, 1 g fat (1 g saturated fat), 1 mg cholesterol, 98 mg sodium, 24 g carbohydrate, trace fiber, 1 g protein. **Diabetic Exchange:** 1-1/2 fruit.

# Bacon Quiche Tarts

*(Pictured at left)*

**Ready in 45 minutes or less**

*Flavored with vegetables, cheese and bacon, these memorable morsels are an impressive addition to brunch, but they're quite easy to make.* *—Kendra Schertz, Nappanee, Indiana*

      2 packages (3 ounces *each*) cream cheese,
        softened
      5 teaspoons milk
      2 eggs
  1/2 cup shredded Colby cheese
      2 tablespoons chopped green pepper
      1 tablespoon finely chopped onion
      1 tube (8 ounces) refrigerated crescent rolls
      5 bacon strips, cooked and crumbled

In a small mixing bowl, beat cream cheese and milk until smooth. Add eggs, Colby cheese, green pepper and onion; mix well. Separate dough into eight triangles; press onto the bottom and up the sides of greased muffin cups. Sprinkle half of the bacon into cups. Pour egg mixture over bacon; top with remaining bacon. Bake at 375° for 18-22 minutes or until a knife comes out clean. Serve warm. **Yield:** 8 servings.

# French Toast Bake

*(Pictured at left)*

**Plan ahead...start the night before**

*If you like blueberries and pecans, you'll love this take on a breakfast favorite. I assemble it the night before. Then*

*I bake it in the morning to surprise my roommates, who finish it in one sitting.* *—Melissa Winona*
*Salt Lake City, Utah*

    12 slices day-old French bread
        (1 inch thick)
      5 eggs
2-1/2 cups milk
      1 cup packed brown sugar, *divided*
      1 teaspoon vanilla extract
  1/2 teaspoon ground nutmeg
      1 cup chopped pecans
  1/4 cup butter *or* margarine, melted
      2 cups fresh *or* frozen blueberries

Arrange bread in a greased 13-in. x 9-in. x 2-in. baking dish. In a bowl, combine the eggs, milk, 3/4 cup brown sugar, vanilla and nutmeg; pour over bread. Cover and refrigerate for 8 hours or overnight.

Remove from the refrigerator 30 minutes before baking. Sprinkle pecans over egg mixture. Combine butter and remaining sugar; drizzle over the top. Bake, uncovered, at 400° for 25 minutes. Sprinkle with blueberries. Bake 10 minutes longer or until a knife inserted near the center comes out clean. **Yield:** 6-8 servings.

# Ranch Eggs 'n' Biscuits

**Ready in 45 minutes or less**

*I rely on these tender homemade biscuits topped with poached eggs and a slightly spicy sauce to wake up my family's taste buds. My teenage son would eat the whole batch if I'd let him.* *—Melinda Kimlinger*
*Jefferson City, Missouri*

      2 cups all-purpose flour
      5 teaspoons baking powder
      2 teaspoons sugar
      1 teaspoon salt
  1/2 teaspoon cream of tartar
  1/2 cup cold butter *or* margarine
  3/4 cup milk
  1/2 pound bacon, diced
  1/3 cup chopped onion
      1 teaspoon chili powder
      2 cups picante sauce
      2 tablespoons minced fresh cilantro
        *or* parsley
      6 eggs

In a bowl, combine the first five ingredients. Cut in butter until mixture resembles coarse crumbs. With a fork, stir in milk until the mixture forms a ball. Turn onto a floured surface; knead 8-10 times. Roll to 1/2-in. thickness; cut out 12 biscuits with a 2-in. biscuit cutter. Place on an ungreased baking sheet. Bake at 450° for 10-12 minutes or until golden brown.

Meanwhile, in a large skillet, cook bacon until almost crisp; drain. Add onion and chili powder; cook until onion is tender. Stir in picante sauce and cilantro. Make six wells in picante mixture; break an egg into each. Cover and cook over medium heat until eggs are completely set. Serve over warm biscuits. **Yield:** 6 servings (12 biscuits).

**Blintz Pancakes**

greased hot griddle. Turn when edges are set; cook until the second side is golden brown. Serve with syrup and strawberries if desired. **Yield:** 12 pancakes.

**Nutritional Analysis:** Two pancakes (prepared with reduced-fat sour cream, fat-free cottage cheese and 1 cup egg substitute; calculated without syrup or strawberries) equals 184 calories, 4 g fat (3 g saturated fat), 17 mg cholesterol, 429 mg sodium, 23 g carbohydrate, 1 g fiber, 14 g protein. **Diabetic Exchanges:** 1-1/2 starch, 1 lean meat.

## Asparagus Omelet

*(Pictured on page 127)*

### Ready in 1 hour or less

*My fiance and I created this recipe when trying to use up leftover asparagus and hollandaise sauce. The vegetable-filled omelet gets its irresistible flavor from the creamy sauce and a nice crunch from crumbled bacon. We think this is special enough for company.* —Becky Roth, Kawkawlin, Michigan

  1 envelope hollandaise sauce mix
  1 cup milk
1/4 cup butter *or* margarine
  8 bacon strips, diced
1/2 pound fresh mushrooms, sliced
  1 pound fresh asparagus, trimmed and cut into 1-inch pieces
  3 tablespoons water
12 eggs, lightly beaten
  1 cup (4 ounces) shredded mozzarella cheese

In a saucepan, prepare the hollandaise sauce mix with milk and butter according to package directions; keep warm. In a skillet, cook bacon over medium heat until crisp; remove to paper towels. In the drippings, saute mushrooms until tender; set aside.

Place asparagus and water in a microwave-safe bowl. Cover and microwave on high for 4-5 minutes or until crisp-tender; drain and keep warm.

Heat an 8-in. skillet coated with nonstick cooking spray over medium-low heat; add 3/4 cup beaten eggs (3 eggs). As eggs set, lift edges, letting uncooked portion flow underneath. Sprinkle with a fourth of the asparagus, 1/4 cup cheese and a fourth of the mushrooms. Fold omelet in half. Cover for 1-2 minutes or until the cheese is melted. Repeat for remaining omelets. Top with hollandaise sauce and bacon. **Yield:** 4 omelets.

## Blintz Pancakes

*(Pictured above)*

### Ready in 30 minutes or less

*Blending sour cream and cottage cheese—ingredients traditionally associated with blintzes—into the batter of these pancakes provides them with their old-fashioned flavor. Top the family favorites with berry syrup to turn an ordinary morning into an extraordinary day.*
—Dianna Digoy, San Diego, California

✓ Uses less fat, sugar or salt. Includes Nutritional Analysis and Diabetic Exchanges.

  1 cup all-purpose flour
  1 tablespoon sugar
1/2 teaspoon salt
  1 cup (8 ounces) sour cream
  1 cup (8 ounces) small-curd cottage cheese
  4 eggs, lightly beaten
Strawberry *or* blueberry syrup
Sliced fresh strawberries, optional

In a bowl, combine the flour, sugar and salt; mix well. Add the sour cream, cottage cheese and eggs; mix just until combined. Spoon 1/4 cupfuls of batter onto a

## Carrot Pancakes

*(Pictured on page 126)*

### Ready in 30 minutes or less

*When I fix this quick breakfast for overnight guests, they always ask for the recipe. Everyone enjoys the sweet carrot cake flavor and rich cream cheese topping. The pancakes are a snap to make, but you can save even more time by grating the carrots in a food processor.*
—Denise Rushing, Greenwood, Arkansas

---

### Great Glaze

When visiting my mother-in-law, I learned a quick foolproof way to make glaze. Simply spoon out the amount of store-bought vanilla frosting from its can and place it in a microwave-safe measuring cup. Warm it in the microwave, stirring frequently until it reaches the right consistency. Then drizzle it over cinnamon buns, raisin bread or coffee cake.
—Rachel Love
Wilmore, Kentucky

1-1/4 cups all-purpose flour
2 tablespoons finely chopped pecans
2 teaspoons baking powder
1 teaspoon ground cinnamon
1/4 teaspoon salt
1/4 teaspoon ground ginger
1 egg, lightly beaten
1/3 cup packed brown sugar
1 cup milk
1 cup grated carrots
1 teaspoon vanilla extract
CREAM CHEESE SPREAD:
4 ounces cream cheese, softened
1/4 cup confectioners' sugar
2 tablespoons milk
1/2 teaspoon vanilla extract
Dash ground cinnamon

In a bowl, combine the first six ingredients. Combine the egg, brown sugar, milk, carrots and vanilla; mix well. Stir into the dry ingredients just until moistened. Pour batter by 1/4 cupfuls onto a greased hot griddle. Turn when bubbles form on top of pancake; cook until second side is golden brown.

Place the cream cheese, confectioners' sugar, milk and vanilla in a blender or food processor; cover and process until smooth. Transfer to a bowl; sprinkle with cinnamon. Serve with pancakes. **Yield:** 4 servings.

## Southwest Sausage Bake

*(Pictured on page 126)*

**Plan ahead…start the night before**

*This layered tortilla dish is not only delicious, but it's a real time-saver because it's put together the night before. The tomato slices provide a nice touch of color.*
—Barbara Waddel, Lincoln, Nebraska

6 flour tortillas (10 inches), cut into 1/2-inch strips
4 cans (4 ounces *each*) chopped green chilies, drained
1 pound bulk pork sausage, cooked and drained
2 cups (8 ounces) shredded Monterey Jack cheese
10 eggs
1/2 cup milk
1/2 teaspoon *each* salt, garlic salt, onion salt, pepper and ground cumin
Paprika
2 medium tomatoes, sliced
Sour cream and salsa

In a greased 13-in. x 9-in. x 2-in. baking dish, layer half of the tortilla strips, chilies, sausage and cheese. Repeat layers. In a bowl, beat the eggs, milk and seasonings; pour over cheese. Sprinkle with paprika. Cover and refrigerate overnight.

Remove from the refrigerator 30 minutes before baking. Bake, uncovered, at 350° for 50 minutes. Arrange tomato slices over the top. Bake 10-15 minutes longer or until a knife inserted near the center comes out clean. Let stand for 10 minutes before cutting. Serve with sour cream and salsa. **Yield:** 12 servings.

## Cheesy Egg Puffs

**Ready in 1 hour or less**

*My father loves to entertain, and these buttery egg delights are one of his favorite items to serve at brunch.*
—Amy Soto, Winfield, Kansas

1/2 pound fresh mushrooms, sliced
4 green onions, chopped
1 tablespoon plus 1/2 cup butter *or* margarine, *divided*
1/2 cup all-purpose flour
1 teaspoon baking powder
1/2 teaspoon salt
10 eggs, lightly beaten
4 cups (16 ounces) shredded Monterey Jack cheese
2 cups (16 ounces) small-curd cottage cheese

In a skillet, saute the mushrooms and onions in 1 tablespoon butter until tender. In a large bowl, combine the flour, baking powder and salt. In another bowl, combine eggs and cheeses. Melt remaining butter; add to egg mixture. Stir into dry ingredients along with mushroom mixture.

Fill greased muffin cups three-fourths full. Bake at 350° for 35-40 minutes or until a knife inserted near center comes out clean. Carefully run the knife around edge of muffin cups before removing. **Yield:** 2-1/2 dozen.

## Ham 'n' Egg Sandwich

*(Pictured on page 126)*

**Ready in 45 minutes or less**

*Whenever the whole family gets together for a holiday or long weekend, they request this all-in-one breakfast sandwich.*         —DeeDee Newton, Toronto, Ontario

1 unsliced loaf (1 pound) French bread
4 tablespoons butter *or* margarine, softened, *divided*
2 tablespoons mayonnaise
8 thin slices deli ham
1 large tomato, sliced
1 small onion, thinly sliced
8 eggs, lightly beaten
8 slices cheddar cheese

Cut bread in half lengthwise; carefully hollow out top and bottom, leaving 1/2-in. shells (discard removed bread or save for another use). Spread 3 tablespoons of butter and all of the mayonnaise inside bread shells. Line bottom bread shell with ham; top with tomato and onion.

In a skillet, melt remaining butter; add eggs. Cook over medium heat, stirring occasionally until eggs are almost set. Spoon into bottom bread shell; top with cheese. Cover with bread top. Wrap in greased foil. Bake at 375° for 15-20 minutes or until heated through. Cut into serving-size pieces. **Yield:** 6-8 servings.

## Warm Fruit Compote

*(Pictured at right)*

**Ready in 15 minutes or less**

*This sunny-colored medley smells so good while it cooks. The cream cheese topping adds a touch of elegance to individual servings of the not-too-sweet fruit.*
—Page Alexander, Baldwin City, Kansas

  1/4 cup packed brown sugar
    1 teaspoon cornstarch
  1/4 cup water
  1/4 cup orange juice concentrate
    2 tablespoons butter *or* margarine
    1 can (20 ounces) pineapple chunks, drained
    1 can (15-1/4 ounces) sliced pears, drained and halved
    1 can (15 ounces) mandarin oranges, drained
TOPPING:
    1 package (3 ounces) cream cheese, softened
    1 tablespoon sugar
    1 tablespoon orange juice concentrate

In a large saucepan, combine the brown sugar and cornstarch. Stir in the water, orange juice concentrate and butter. Bring to a boil; cook and stir for 2 minutes or until thickened. Reduce heat. Add the fruit; heat through. In a small mixing bowl, beat the topping ingredients until smooth. Dollop over fruit. **Yield:** 6 servings.

## Jam Biscuits

*(Pictured at right)*

**Ready in 1 hour or less**

*My teenage granddaughter, Holly, and I have enjoyed cooking together since she was 4 years old. We like to make these golden biscuits for holiday gatherings. Fill the centers with homemade jam, orange marmalade or cheese.*
—Mary Lindsay, Durango, Colorado

    4 teaspoons active dry yeast
    5 tablespoons warm water (110° to 115°)
    5 cups all-purpose flour
  1/4 cup sugar
    4 teaspoons baking powder
    1 teaspoon salt
  1/4 teaspoon baking soda
    1 cup shortening
1-1/2 cups warm buttermilk* (110° to 115°)
Raspberry *or* plum jelly *or* jam

In a small bowl, dissolve yeast in warm water; set aside. In a large bowl, combine the flour, sugar, baking powder, salt and baking soda; cut in shortening until mixture resembles coarse crumbs. Add yeast mixture to buttermilk; stir into dry ingredients until combined.

Turn dough onto a lightly floured surface. Knead 5-6 times. Roll or pat to 1/2-in. thickness. Cut with a 2-1/2-in. biscuit cutter. Cut a 1-in. slit at an angle halfway through center of each biscuit. Separate dough at cut;

fill with 1/4 to 1/2 teaspoon of jelly or jam. Place on ungreased baking sheets (do not let rise). Bake at 400° for 16-20 minutes or until golden brown. **Yield:** about 2-1/2 dozen.

  **\*Editor's Note:** Warmed buttermilk will appear curdled.

## Denver Omelet Pie

*(Pictured at right)*

**Ready in 1 hour or less**

*My family requests this hearty satisfying breakfast pie quite often. It's very easy to make with frozen hash browns, looks pretty garnished with tomato slices and tastes absolutely delicious.* —Barbara Nowakowski
North Tonawanda, New York

    6 eggs
  1/2 teaspoon onion powder
  1/2 teaspoon dried thyme
  1/2 teaspoon salt
  1/8 teaspoon pepper
    3 cups frozen shredded hash brown potatoes
    1 cup (4 ounces) shredded Swiss cheese
  1/2 cup diced fully cooked ham
  1/2 cup chopped green pepper
    1 medium tomato, thinly sliced

In a large bowl, beat the eggs, onion powder, thyme, salt and pepper. Stir in the potatoes, cheese, ham and green pepper. Pour into a greased 9-in. pie plate. Bake at 350° for 40-45 minutes or until a knife inserted near the center comes out clean. Garnish with tomato slices. **Yield:** 6 servings.

## Eggs Bravo

**Ready in 45 minutes or less**

*I stir leftover ham and hard-cooked eggs into a creamy cheese sauce, then drape the savory mixture over toasted English muffins. This simple stovetop dish is nice for breakfast, brunch or a light lunch.* —Erika Anderson
Wausau, Wisconsin

  1/3 cup all-purpose flour
  1/8 to 1/4 teaspoon salt
Dash pepper
1-3/4 cups milk
    4 ounces process cheese (Velveeta), cubed
1-1/2 cups cubed fully cooked ham
    4 hard-cooked eggs, chopped
  1/2 cup mayonnaise
  1/4 cup sliced green onions
  1/4 cup chopped pimientos
    6 to 8 English muffins, split and toasted

In a saucepan, combine the flour, salt, pepper and milk until smooth. Bring to a boil; cook and stir for 2 minutes or until thickened. Add the cheese; cook and stir until melted. Stir in the ham, eggs, mayonnaise, onions and pimientos; heat through. Serve over English muffins. **Yield:** 6-8 servings.

Jam Biscuits
Warm Fruit Compote
Denver Omelet Pie

Cherry Berry Smoothies
Pumpkin Pancakes
Glazed Apples and Sausage

## Pumpkin Pancakes

### (Pictured at left)

**Ready in 30 minutes or less**

*We have pancakes a lot at our house, so I like to look for variations on traditional recipes. Our daughter just loves the great taste of these moist pumpkin pancakes.*
*—Elizabeth Montgomery, Taylorville, Illinois*

2 cups biscuit/baking mix
2 tablespoons brown sugar
2 teaspoons ground cinnamon
2 eggs
1 can (12 ounces) evaporated milk
1/2 cup cooked *or* canned pumpkin
2 tablespoons vegetable oil
1 teaspoon vanilla extract
Maple syrup

In a bowl, combine baking mix, brown sugar and cinnamon. In another bowl, combine eggs, milk, pumpkin, oil and vanilla. Stir into dry ingredients; mix well.

Pour batter by 1/3 cupfuls onto a lightly greased hot griddle; turn when bubbles form on top of pancakes. Cook until second side is golden brown. Serve with syrup. **Yield:** 1 dozen.

## Cherry Berry Smoothies

### (Pictured at left)

**Ready in 10 minutes or less**

*We have three young children, so we always have fruit juices on hand to experiment with when making smoothies. I turn cherry juice, fruit and yogurt into this colorful family favorite.* *—Shonna Thibodeau, Fort Huachuca, Arizona*

1 cup cherry juice
1 carton (8 ounces) vanilla yogurt
1 cup frozen unsweetened raspberries
1/2 cup seedless red grapes
3 to 4 teaspoons sugar

In a blender, combine all ingredients. Cover and process until well blended. Pour into glasses; serve immediately. **Yield:** 3 servings.

## Glazed Apples and Sausage

### (Pictured at left)

**Ready in 30 minutes or less**

*I dress up hearty pork sausage links with sliced tart apples, chopped onion and brown sugar to make this morning mainstay. I fix the full-flavored side dish when hosting brunch.* *—Jennie Wible, Hamilton Square, New Jersey*

2 pounds uncooked pork sausage links
2 large tart apples, peeled and sliced
1 large onion, chopped
1/3 cup water
1/4 cup packed brown sugar

Cook the sausage according to package directions. Meanwhile, in a large saucepan, combine the apples, onion, water and brown sugar. Cook over medium heat for 5-8 minutes, stirring occasionally. Add the sausage; heat through. **Yield:** 8 servings.

## Crispy Baked Oatmeal

**Ready in 1 hour or less**

*This change-of-pace cereal is a hit with my family. With cinnamon and chocolate chips, the mixture is sure to be popular with yours, too.* *—Shirley Martin*
*Ephrata, Pennsylvania*

2 eggs
1/2 cup vegetable oil
1/3 cup packed brown sugar
3 cups old-fashioned oats
3 teaspoons baking powder
1 teaspoon salt
3/4 teaspoon ground cinnamon
1/3 cup flaked coconut
1/3 cup raisins
1/3 cup semisweet chocolate chips
Milk, optional

In a bowl, combine eggs, oil and brown sugar. Combine the oats, baking powder, salt and cinnamon; add to egg mixture, stirring just until moistened. Stir in the coconut, raisins and chocolate chips.

Spoon into a greased 13-in. x 9-in. x 2-in. baking dish. Bake, uncovered, at 350° for 20-25 minutes or until edges are golden brown. Serve warm with milk if desired. **Yield:** 4 servings.

## Breakfast Pie

**Plan ahead...start the night before**

*This crustless pie is wonderful to serve to overnight guests, because you assemble it the night before.* *—Pam Botine*
*Goldsboro, North Carolina*

8 bacon strips, diced
1/4 cup crushed cornflakes
5 eggs, lightly beaten
1/2 cup milk
1/2 cup small-curd cottage cheese
1-1/2 cups (6 ounces) shredded cheddar cheese
1 green onion, sliced
1/2 teaspoon salt
1/8 teaspoon pepper
2-1/2 cups frozen cubed hash brown potatoes

In a large skillet, cook bacon over medium heat until crisp. Remove to paper towels. Drain, reserving 2 teaspoons drippings. Stir reserved drippings into cornflakes; set aside. In a bowl, combine the eggs, milk, cottage cheese, cheddar cheese, onion, salt and pepper until blended. Stir in hash browns. Pour into a greased 9-in. pie plate. Sprinkle with bacon and the cornflake mixture. Cover and refrigerate overnight.

Remove from the refrigerator 30 minutes before baking. Bake, uncovered, at 325° for 45-50 minutes or until a knife inserted near the center comes out clean. Let stand for 5-10 minutes before cutting into slices. **Yield:** 6 servings.

**Frosty Mocha Drink**

ples are tender. Stir in nuts. Serve over waffles or pancakes. **Yield:** 8 servings.

## Bacon Swiss Squares

*(Pictured below)*

### Ready in 30 minutes or less

*Not only does this savory breakfast pizza come together easily, but it's a cinch to double the ingredients when I'm hosting a large event. Biscuit mix makes it convenient, and the combination of eggs, bacon and Swiss cheese keeps guests coming back for more.*
—*Agarita Vaughan*
*Fairbury, Illinois*

   2 cups biscuit/baking mix
1/2 cup cold water
   8 ounces sliced Swiss cheese
   1 pound sliced bacon, cooked and crumbled
   4 eggs, lightly beaten
1/4 cup milk
1/2 teaspoon onion powder

In a bowl, combine the biscuit mix and water; stir 20 strokes. Turn onto a floured surface; knead 10 times. Roll into a 14-in. x 10-in. rectangle. Place on the bottom and 1/2 in. up the sides of a greased 13-in. x 9-in. x 2-in. baking dish. Arrange cheese over dough. Sprinkle with bacon. In a bowl, whisk eggs, milk and onion powder; pour over bacon.

Bake at 425° for 15-18 minutes or until a knife inserted near the center comes out clean. Cut into squares; serve immediately. **Yield:** 12 servings.

## Frosty Mocha Drink

*(Pictured above)*

### Ready in 15 minutes or less

*I like to make this chilly chocolate-flavored coffee drink when friends stop by for a visit. I always double the recipe, however, because I know they'll come back for seconds. For a richer and creamier version, replace the milk with half-and-half cream.* —*Lauren Nance, San Diego, California*

  1 cup milk
  3 tablespoons instant chocolate drink mix
  2 tablespoons instant coffee granules
  2 tablespoons honey
  1 teaspoon vanilla extract
14 to 16 ice cubes

In a blender, combine all ingredients; cover and process until smooth. Pour into chilled glasses; serve immediately. **Yield:** 4 servings.

## Maple Apple Topping

### Ready in 30 minutes or less

*I discovered this sweet topping when I had an abundance of apples to use up. It's a great alternative to bottled syrup. My family enjoys the tender apples and crunchy nuts over waffles, but the topping is also wonderful over slices of pound cake or scoops of vanilla ice cream.*
—*Ruth Harrow, Alexandria, New Hampshire*

1/2 cup butter *or* margarine
   3 large tart apples, peeled and sliced
1-1/2 cups maple syrup
   1 teaspoon ground cinnamon
1/2 cup chopped nuts

In a large skillet, melt butter. Add the apples, syrup and cinnamon. Cook and stir over medium-low heat until ap-

**Bacon Swiss Squares**

# Breakfast Upside-Down Cake

*(Pictured at right)*

*This moist golden morning treat quickly became my husband's favorite. And because it calls for a boxed blueberry muffin mix and canned pineapple, I never have a problem finding the time to make it for him. Plus, it looks pretty enough to serve company.        —Stacy Walker*
*Windsor Heights, Iowa*

- 1 package (18.9 ounces) blueberry muffin mix*
- 1 package (1/4 ounce) quick-rise yeast
- 1 can (8 ounces) pineapple slices
- 1 egg, beaten
- 1/3 cup packed brown sugar
- 1/4 cup butter *or* margarine, melted
- 4 maraschino cherries, halved
- Fresh blueberries, optional

Rinse and drain blueberries from muffin mix; set aside. Place muffin mix and yeast in a bowl. Drain pineapple, reserving the juice in a measuring cup. Set pineapple aside. Add enough water to juice to measure 2/3 cup. Pour into a saucepan; heat to 120°-130°. Add to muffin mix; stir just until moistened. Beat in the egg. Cover and let rest for 10 minutes.

Combine brown sugar and butter; pour into a greased 9-in. round baking pan. Cut each pineapple slice in half; arrange over brown sugar mixture. Tuck cherries into pineapple. Spoon half of batter over pineapple. Sprinkle with reserved blueberries. Spread with remaining batter. Bake at 350° for 40-45 minutes or until a toothpick inserted into cake comes out clean. Immediately invert onto a serving plate. Cool completely. Garnish with fresh blueberries if desired. **Yield:** 8 servings.

*Editor's Note: This recipe was tested with Duncan Hines muffin mix.

Breakfast Upside-Down Cake

# Frozen Banana Pineapple Cups

**Plan ahead...needs to freeze**

*You can stir together this sweet tangy fruit mixture with just five ingredients, then pop it in the freezer overnight. The frosty results are a refreshing addition to a brunch. In summer, our kids prefer this snack to store-bought frozen treats.        —Alice Miller, Middlebury, Indiana*

- 3 cups water
- 2-2/3 cups mashed ripe bananas (5 to 6 medium)
- 1-1/2 cups sugar
- 1 can (20 ounces) crushed pineapple, undrained
- 1 can (6 ounces) frozen orange juice concentrate, thawed

In a 2-qt. freezer container, combine all ingredients; mix well. Cover and freeze for 5 hours or overnight. Remove from the freezer 15 minutes before serving. **Yield:** 9-12 servings.

# Meaty Apple Skillet

**Ready in 30 minutes or less**

*I love having family over for breakfast, and they all look forward to this down-home specialty. Cinnamon, nutmeg and apple slices help combine the flavors of the four different meats in this robust dish. I slice and cook the meat the day before to save time in the morning.*
*—Sharon Berry, Henderson, Nevada*

- 1 large tart apple, peeled and thinly sliced
- 2 tablespoons butter *or* margarine
- 1 teaspoon ground cinnamon
- 1/8 teaspoon ground nutmeg
- 2 teaspoons cornstarch
- 2/3 cup cranberry-apple juice
- 1 pound fully cooked kielbasa *or* Polish sausage, cubed
- 3/4 pound bulk pork sausage, cooked and drained
- 3/4 pound pork sausage links, cooked and sliced
- 1-1/2 cups cubed fully cooked ham

In a skillet, saute apple slices in butter; sprinkle with cinnamon and nutmeg. Cover and cook for 5 minutes or until apples are tender. Combine cornstarch and juice until smooth; stir into apple mixture. Bring to a boil; cook and stir for 2 minutes or until thickened. Add the sausage and ham; heat through. **Yield:** 12-16 servings.

# Chapter 10

# ⊙ *Casseroles and Skillet Suppers*

FOR COOKS who don't have much time on their hands, convenience is often the key to success in the kitchen.

That's what makes all-in-one casseroles so appealing. This "comfort food" is packed with a blend of meat, vegetables, pasta, rice and sauces, and can be tossed together while you wait for the oven to preheat. In no time at all, you'll be dishing out hearty helpings of a tempting main course or side dish.

For even faster preparation, turn to this chapter's assortment of skillet suppers that require just a single pan and only a few minutes to make. You'll surely file these in-a-dash dinners under "F" for filling, flavorful...and flat-out fast!

**SUPER SKILLETS.** Clockwise from top right: Taco Skillet (p. 156), Pineapple Chicken Lo Mein (p. 157), Savory Sausage and Peppers (p. 156) and Broccoli Shrimp Alfredo (p. 155).

# Catchall Casseroles

WHETHER you call them casseroles, bakes or hot dishes, these comforting oven-baked standbys satisfy hunger in a hurry. And they don't take hours to put together. Most can be assembled while you wait for the oven to preheat.

## Golden Tuna Casserole

*(Pictured below)*

**Ready in 45 minutes or less**

*Mushrooms, green pepper and onion are added to a package of macaroni and cheese in this comforting take on the classic tuna bake. It is a delicious, hearty and quick-to-fix main dish. I serve it with a tossed salad and hot rolls.*
—Helen Suter
Golconda, Illinois

  1 package (7-1/4 ounces) macaroni and cheese mix
1/2 cup chopped onion
1/4 cup chopped green pepper
1/3 cup butter *or* margarine
3/4 cup milk
  1 can (10-3/4 ounces) condensed cream of celery soup, undiluted
  1 can (6 ounces) tuna, drained
  1 jar (4-1/2 ounces) sliced mushrooms, drained
  1 jar (2 ounces) diced pimientos, drained

Golden Tuna Casserole

Set aside the cheese sauce packet. In a saucepan, cook macaroni according to package directions; drain and set aside. In the same pan, saute onion and green pepper in butter. Return macaroni to the pan. Add milk and contents of cheese sauce packet; stir until smooth. Stir in the soup, tuna, mushrooms and pimientos.

Pour into a greased 2-qt. baking dish. Cover and bake at 350° for 25-30 minutes or until bubbly. **Yield:** 4-6 servings.

## Hawaiian Ham Bake

**Ready in 45 minutes or less**

*Take this sweet-and-sour specialty to your next potluck and get ready to hand out the recipe. When I buy a ham, I choose a large one so I'll have leftovers to use in this dish. It's special enough for Sunday dinners yet simple enough for busy weeknights.*
—Judy Reist, Bloomingdale, Ontario

  3 cups cubed fully cooked ham
  1 medium onion, thinly sliced
  1 small green pepper, cut into rings
2/3 cup raisins
  1 can (8 ounces) pineapple tidbits, drained
3/4 cup packed brown sugar
  3 tablespoons cornstarch
  3 teaspoons ground mustard
1/4 teaspoon salt
1-1/2 cups pineapple juice
1/2 cup cider vinegar
4-1/2 teaspoons soy sauce
Hot cooked rice

In a greased 2-qt. baking dish, layer ham, onion, green pepper, raisins and pineapple. In a saucepan, combine the brown sugar, cornstarch, mustard and salt. Stir in pineapple juice and vinegar until smooth. Bring to a boil; cook and stir for 2 minutes or until thickened.

Remove from the heat; stir in soy sauce. Pour over pineapple. Cover and bake at 350° for 30 minutes or until heated through. Serve over rice. **Yield:** 4-6 servings.

## Cheesy Beef Macaroni

**Ready 45 minutes or less**

*Little ones will light up the room with smiles when you bring this five-ingredient supper to the table. Crunchy canned corn is an appealing addition to the mild and cheesy combination of ground beef and pasta.*
—Dena Evetts, Sentinel, Oklahoma

  1 pound ground beef
  1 can (15-1/4 ounces) whole kernel corn, drained
  1 can (10-3/4 ounces) condensed cream of chicken soup, undiluted
  8 ounces process cheese (Velveeta), shredded
2-1/2 cups cooked elbow macaroni

In a large skillet, cook beef over medium heat until no longer pink; drain. Add the corn and soup. Set aside 1/2 cup cheese for topping; stir remaining cheese into meat mixture until melted. Gently stir in macaroni until coated. Transfer to a greased 8-in. square baking dish. Top with reserved cheese. Bake, uncovered, at 350° for 20-25 minutes or until heated through. **Yield:** 4-6 servings.

## Cheddar Chicken Pie

*(Pictured at right)*

**Ready in 1 hour or less**

*This speedy main dish pie uses handy biscuit mix, so there's no need to fuss with a complicated crust. It goes together in a flash. Just add fruit salad and crusty hot bread for a delicious meal.*
—*Betty Pierce*
*Slaterville Springs, New York*

3 cups (12 ounces) shredded cheddar cheese, *divided*
1 package (10 ounces) frozen chopped broccoli, thawed and drained
1-1/2 cups cubed cooked chicken
2/3 cup finely chopped onion
1-1/3 cups milk
3 eggs
3/4 cup biscuit/baking mix
3/4 teaspoon salt
1/4 teaspoon pepper

In a bowl, combine 2 cups cheese, broccoli, chicken and onion; spread into a greased 10-in. pie plate. In a small mixing bowl, beat the milk, eggs, biscuit mix, salt and pepper until smooth. Pour over broccoli mixture (do not stir).

Bake at 400° for 30-35 minutes or until a knife inserted near the center comes out clean. Sprinkle with the remaining cheese. Let stand for 5 minutes or until cheese is melted. **Yield:** 6 servings.

## Mixed Vegetable Bake

**Ready in 1 hour or less**

*I combine convenient frozen veggies with crunchy water chestnuts and chopped celery in this cheesy side dish topped with golden cracker crumbs. It tastes special for so little effort.* —*Carolyn Woodall*
*Roxboro, North Carolina*

2 cups frozen mixed vegetables, thawed
1 can (8 ounces) sliced water chestnuts, drained and halved
1 celery rib, chopped
1/4 cup chopped onion
1/2 cup mayonnaise*
1 cup (4 ounces) shredded cheddar cheese
1/2 cup crushed butter-flavored crackers (about 13 crackers)
1 tablespoon butter *or* margarine, melted

In a bowl, combine the mixed vegetables, water chestnuts, celery, onion and mayonnaise. Stir in cheese. Transfer to

Cheddar Chicken Pie

a greased shallow 1-qt. baking dish. Toss cracker crumbs and butter; sprinkle over vegetables. Bake, uncovered, at 350° for 30-35 minutes or until golden brown. **Yield:** 4-6 servings.

**\*Editor's Note:** Reduced-fat or fat-free mayonnaise may not be substituted for regular mayonnaise.

## Popular Potluck Casserole

**Ready in 1 hour or less**

*Spice up suppertime with this hearty main dish. With plenty of Tex-Mex taste, this crowd-pleasing ground beef and pasta bake is sure to disappear in a hurry at potlucks.*
—*Debbi Smith, Crossett, Arkansas*

1 package (7 ounces) shell macaroni
2 pounds ground beef
1 medium onion, chopped
1/4 cup chopped green pepper
1/4 cup thinly sliced celery
1 can (10-3/4 ounces) condensed cream of mushroom soup, undiluted
1 can (10 ounces) diced tomatoes with green chilies
1 can (8 ounces) tomato sauce
1 to 2 tablespoons chili powder
1 can (15-1/4 ounces) whole kernel corn, drained
2 cups (8 ounces) shredded cheddar cheese, *divided*

Cook macaroni according to package directions. Meanwhile, in a large skillet, cook the beef, onion, green pepper and celery until meat is no longer pink and vegetables are tender; drain. Stir in the soup, tomatoes, tomato sauce and chili powder; mix well.

Drain the macaroni; stir into beef mixture. Add the corn and 1-1/2 cups of cheese. Transfer to a greased 13-in. x 9-in. x 2-in. baking dish. Sprinkle with remaining cheese. Bake, uncovered, at 350° for 25-30 minutes or until heated through. **Yield:** 10-12 servings.

Colorful Pasta with Ham

## Ground Beef 'n' Rice Pie

### Ready in 1 hour or less

*I press seasoned ground beef into a pie plate to form the crust of this comforting dish. It's a terrific time-saver because you don't brown the beef separately.*
—Rhonda Van Gelderen
Menomonee Falls, Wisconsin

   1 pound uncooked lean ground beef
   1 can (15 ounces) tomato sauce, *divided*
1/2 cup dry bread crumbs
1/4 cup chopped onion
1/4 cup chopped green pepper, optional
1/2 teaspoon salt
1/2 teaspoon Italian seasoning
1/8 teaspoon dried oregano
1/8 teaspoon pepper
   1 can (6 ounces) tomato paste
2-1/2 cups cooked rice
   1 cup (4 ounces) shredded cheddar
      cheese, *divided*

In a bowl, combine beef, 3/4 cup tomato sauce, bread crumbs, onion, green pepper if desired and seasonings. Press evenly onto the bottom and up the sides of an ungreased 9-in. pie plate, forming a crust.

In a bowl, combine the tomato paste and remaining tomato sauce. Stir in the rice and 3/4 cup cheese; pour into crust. Place pie plate on a baking sheet. Cover and bake at 350° for 25 minutes or until the meat is no longer pink. Uncover; drain. Sprinkle with remaining cheese. Bake 10-15 minutes longer or until the cheese is melted. Let stand for 5 minutes before cutting. **Yield:** 6-8 servings.

## Colorful Pasta with Ham

### (Pictured above)

### Ready in 1 hour or less

*I made up this hearty noodle casserole as I went along, and my family was pleased with the end result. I now double the rapid recipe and store the extra casserole in the freezer for a night when time is at a premium.*
—Heather Rowan, Richmond, Missouri

   1 package (16 ounces) tricolor spiral pasta
1-1/2 cups cubed fully cooked ham
   1 can (15-1/4 ounces) whole kernel corn,
      drained
1-1/2 cups (6 ounces) shredded cheddar
      cheese, *divided*
   1 can (2.8 ounces) french-fried onions,
      *divided*
   1 can (14-1/2 ounces) chicken broth
   1 can (10-3/4 ounces) condensed cream of
      chicken soup, undiluted
1/2 cup milk
1/2 teaspoon *each* celery salt, garlic powder
      and pepper

Cook pasta according to package directions; drain. In a greased shallow 3-qt. baking dish, combine the pasta, ham, corn, 1 cup cheese and 3/4 cup onions. In a bowl, combine the broth, soup, milk and seasonings. Pour over pasta mixture; mix well.

Bake, uncovered, at 350° for 30 minutes. Sprinkle with remaining cheese and onions. Bake 5 minutes longer or until heated through. **Yield:** 8 servings.

## Onion-Chicken Stuffing Bake

### Ready in 1 hour or less

*A friend shared this savory meal-in-one with me, and it has since become my favorite dinner to serve guests. It's sure to be a hit at your home, too.* —Audrey Aldrich
Berlin Heights, Ohio

   1 package (6 ounces) seasoned stuffing mix
   3 cups cubed cooked chicken
   1 can (10-3/4 ounces) condensed cream of
      chicken soup, undiluted
   1 cup (8 ounces) sour cream
   2 tablespoons onion soup mix
   1 can (4 ounces) mushroom stems and pieces,
      drained
   1 can (8 ounces) sliced water chestnuts,
      drained
1/4 cup grated Parmesan cheese

Prepare stuffing mix according to package directions; set aside. Place chicken in a greased 2-qt. baking dish. Combine the soup, sour cream and soup mix; spread over the chicken.

Sprinkle with mushrooms and water chestnuts. Spread stuffing over top. Sprinkle with Parmesan cheese. Bake, uncovered, at 350° for 30-35 minutes or until bubbly. **Yield:** 6-8 servings.

## Comforting Chicken

*When you don't need to cook for a whole crew, try this smaller sized casserole that feeds just four. The delicious saucy combination of chicken and rice is one of our favorite suppers. It may serve fewer people, but it still has lots of flavor.*
—Edna Thomas, Warsaw, Indiana

        1 tablespoon vegetable oil
        1 tablespoon butter *or* margarine
        1 pound boneless skinless chicken breasts, cut into cubes
    1/2 cup finely chopped onion
    1/2 cup finely chopped green pepper
        1 can (10-3/4 ounces) condensed cream of mushroom soup, undiluted
        1 cup water
    3/4 cup uncooked long grain rice
    1/2 teaspoon salt
    1/2 teaspoon chili powder
    1/4 teaspoon pepper
    1/4 teaspoon paprika

In a large skillet, heat oil and butter. Add chicken, onion and green pepper; cook and stir until the chicken is lightly browned and vegetables are tender. Stir in the remaining ingredients. Transfer to a lightly greased 1-1/2-qt. baking dish. Cover and bake at 375° for 55-60 minutes or until the rice is tender. **Yield:** 4 servings.

## Baked Spaghetti

*(Pictured at right)*

**Ready in 1 hour or less**

*This satisfying pasta bake is quick to make and pleases young and old alike. The classic flavors in this dish prompt folks to come back for more. Add a salad and breadsticks, and you're ready for company.* —Betty Rabe
Mahtomedi, Minnesota

        8 ounces uncooked spaghetti, broken into thirds
        1 egg
    1/2 cup milk
    1/2 teaspoon salt
    1/2 pound ground beef
    1/2 pound bulk Italian sausage
        1 small onion, chopped
    1/4 cup chopped green pepper
        1 jar (14 ounces) meatless spaghetti sauce
        1 can (8 ounces) tomato sauce
        1 to 2 cups (4 to 8 ounces) shredded mozzarella cheese

Cook spaghetti according to package directions; drain. In a large bowl, beat the egg, milk and salt. Add spaghetti; toss to coat. Transfer to a greased 13-in. x 9-in. x 2-in. baking dish.

In a large skillet, cook the beef, sausage, onion and green pepper over medium heat until meat is no longer pink; drain. Add spaghetti sauce and tomato sauce; mix well. Spoon over the spaghetti mixture. Bake, uncovered, at 350° for 20 minutes. Sprinkle with the cheese. Bake 10 minutes longer or until cheese is melted. Let stand for 10 minutes before cutting. **Yield:** 6-8 servings.

## Cheesy Vegetable Medley

**Ready in 30 minutes or less**

*This dish is great using garden tomatoes and zucchini. And it cooks in the microwave to keep your kitchen cool.*
—Suzanne Priest, Attleboro, Massachusetts

        2 medium zucchini, quartered and sliced
        2 medium tomatoes, cut into wedges
        1 small onion, quartered and sliced
        1 teaspoon Italian seasoning
        1 teaspoon salt
    1/2 teaspoon pepper
    1-1/2 cups (6 ounces) shredded mozzarella cheese

In a greased 2-qt. microwave-safe dish, combine the zucchini, tomatoes and onion. Cover and microwave on high for 13 minutes or until vegetables are tender, stirring three times; drain. Sprinkle with Italian seasoning, salt, pepper and cheese. Cover and let stand for 2-3 minutes or until the cheese is melted. **Yield:** 4-6 servings.

**Editor's Note:** This recipe was tested in an 850-watt microwave.

Baked Spaghetti

# Turkey Broccoli Hollandaise

## (Pictured below)

**Ready in 1 hour or less**

*This delectable dish is a great way to use extra turkey. The original recipe called for Thanksgiving leftovers, but my family loves it so much that I prepare this version all year long.* —Pamela Yoder, Elkhart, Indiana

- 1 cup fresh broccoli florets
- 1 package (6 ounces) stuffing mix
- 1 envelope hollandaise sauce mix
- 2 cups cubed cooked turkey *or* chicken
- 1 can (2.8 ounces) french-fried onions

Place 1 in. of water and broccoli in a saucepan. Bring to a boil. Reduce heat; cover and simmer for 5-8 minutes or until crisp-tender. Meanwhile, prepare stuffing and sauce mixes according to package directions.

Spoon stuffing into a greased 11-in. x 7-in. x 2-in. baking dish. Top with turkey. Drain broccoli; arrange over turkey. Spoon sauce over the top; sprinkle with onions. Bake, uncovered, at 325° for 25-30 minutes or until heated through. **Yield:** 6 servings.

# Swiss Macaroni

**Ready in 1 hour or less**

*It's easy to bring smiles to the faces of family and friends with this comforting and special combination of macaroni, onion and Swiss cheese. I enjoy sharing this casserole with neighbors.* —Carolyn Steele Marathon Shores, Florida

- 1 package (7 ounces) elbow macaroni
- 1 jar (2 ounces) diced pimientos, drained
- 2 eggs, lightly beaten
- 1 cup half-and-half cream
- 1 small onion, chopped
- 2 tablespoons minced fresh parsley
- 1-1/2 teaspoons salt
- 1/8 teaspoon pepper
- 1 cup soft bread crumbs
- 1 cup (4 ounces) shredded Swiss cheese
- 1/4 cup butter *or* margarine, melted

Cook macaroni according to package directions; drain and place in a greased 11-in. x 7-in. x 2-in. baking dish. Stir in the pimientos. In a bowl, combine the eggs, cream, onion, parsley, salt and pepper. Pour over macaroni mixture. Sprinkle with bread crumbs and cheese; drizzle with butter. Bake, uncovered, at 350° for 30 minutes or until golden brown. **Yield:** 6-8 servings.

# Tuna Noodle Supreme

**Ready in 1 hour or less**

*This tangy tuna bake is well received at potluck suppers. I've made it with reduced-fat sour cream and mayonnaise with equally good results. It is a quick tasty dinner.* —Ellen Proctor Great Barrington, Massachusetts

- 1-1/2 cups (12 ounces) sour cream
- 1/2 cup mayonnaise
- 1/2 cup milk
- 1/4 cup grated Parmesan cheese
- 1 teaspoon Dijon mustard
- 1/4 teaspoon salt
- 1/4 teaspoon pepper
- 4 cups cooked small shell pasta
- 2 cups fresh broccoli florets
- 1 can (12 ounces) tuna, drained and flaked
- 1/2 cup chopped sweet red pepper
- 1/2 cup sliced green onions

In a large bowl, combine the first seven ingredients; stir until smooth. Stir in the pasta, broccoli, tuna, red pepper and onions. Transfer to a greased 2-qt. baking dish. Cover and bake at 350° for 40-45 minutes or until hot and bubbly. **Yield:** 4-6 servings.

Turkey Broccoli Hollandaise

## Sausage with Corn Stuffing

*(Pictured at right)*

**Ready in 1 hour or less**

*This is a quick-and-easy main dish that my family enjoys. Cooked ham, chicken or turkey make an excellent alternative to the breakfast sausages.* —Del Mason
Martensville, Saskatchewan

✓ Uses less fat, sugar or salt. Includes Nutritional Analysis and Diabetic Exchanges.

  3/4 pound pork sausage links
1-1/4 cups water
    1 tablespoon butter *or* stick margarine
    1 package (6 ounces) corn bread stuffing mix
    1 tablespoon minced fresh parsley
    1 medium carrot, shredded
  1/2 cup frozen corn, thawed
  1/4 cup chopped onion
  1/4 cup chopped celery
  1/2 cup shredded cheddar cheese

In a skillet, cook sausage over medium heat until browned and juices run clear. Meanwhile, in a large saucepan, heat water. Stir in butter until melted; remove from the heat. Add stuffing mix and parsley; stir just until moistened.

Drain sausage; cut into 1/4-in. slices. Stir the sausage, carrot, corn, onion and celery into stuffing mixture. Add cheese; toss to combine. Spoon into a greased 2-qt. baking dish. Cover and bake at 350° for 25-30 minutes or until heated through. **Yield:** 6 servings.

**Nutritional Analysis:** One serving (prepared with turkey sausage and reduced-fat cheese) equals 277 calories, 12 g fat (5 g saturated fat), 59 mg cholesterol, 824 mg sodium, 28 g carbohydrate, 5 g fiber, 16 g protein. **Diabetic Exchanges:** 2 lean meat, 1-1/2 starch, 1 vegetable, 1/2 fat.

## Unstuffed Cabbage

*I received the recipe for this hearty ground beef and cabbage casserole from a teacher at the preschool where I work. It's like stuffed cabbage without the fuss. It's a nutritious and economical meal for busy families.*
—Judy Thorn, Mars, Pennsylvania

✓ Uses less fat, sugar or salt. Includes Nutritional Analysis and Diabetic Exchanges.

    6 cups chopped cabbage
  1/2 pound ground beef
    1 small onion, chopped
    1 cup uncooked instant rice
  1/2 teaspoon salt, optional
  1/4 teaspoon pepper
    2 cans (10-3/4 ounces *each*) condensed
      tomato soup, undiluted
    1 cup water
  1/3 cup shredded cheddar cheese

Place the cabbage in a greased 2-1/2-qt. baking dish. In a skillet, cook beef and onion over medium heat until meat

Sausage with Corn Stuffing

is no longer pink; drain. Stir in the rice, salt if desired and pepper; spoon over cabbage. Combine soup and water; pour over beef mixture.

Cover and bake at 350° for 40-50 minutes or until rice and cabbage are tender. Uncover; sprinkle with cheese. Bake 5-10 minutes longer or until the cheese is melted. **Yield:** 4 servings.

**Nutritional Analysis:** One serving (prepared with lean ground beef, reduced-fat reduced-sodium tomato soup and reduced-fat cheese and without salt) equals 342 calories, 8 g fat (3 g saturated fat), 23 mg cholesterol, 690 mg sodium, 48 g carbohydrate, 5 g fiber, 19 g protein. **Diabetic Exchanges:** 2-1/2 starch, 2 lean meat, 2 vegetable.

## Ground Beef Shepherd's Pie

**Ready in 45 minutes or less**

*This hearty supper-in-one uses ground beef, frozen veggies and canned gravy to hurry along the down-home dinner. It's also a great use for leftover mashed potatoes.*
—Elaine Williams
Surrey, British Columbia

1-1/2 pounds ground beef
    1 small onion, chopped
    2 garlic cloves, minced
    1 can (10-1/2 ounces) beef gravy
    1 cup frozen mixed vegetables
  1/4 teaspoon Worcestershire sauce
Salt and pepper to taste
2-1/2 cups mashed potatoes

In a large skillet, cook the beef, onion and garlic over medium heat until meat is no longer pink; drain. Stir in the gravy, vegetables, Worcestershire sauce, salt and pepper. Transfer to a greased 1-1/2-qt. baking dish. Spread potatoes over the top. Bake, uncovered, at 350° for 30 minutes or until heated through. **Yield:** 4 servings.

Chicken Pasta Primavera

## Dash in the Pan

YOU'VE COME to the right place if "going steady" with your stove doesn't fit your active lifestyle. The mouth-watering recipes on this page take a half hour or less to put on the table. That's not all—afterward, cleanup's quick, too!

### Chicken Pasta Primavera

**(Pictured above)**

**Ready in 30 minutes or less**

*This colorful combination of chicken, pasta and vegetables is very popular at my house. Coated in a creamy sauce, the made-in-minutes meal is sure to be well-received at your house, too.* —Raelynn Bulkley, Pleasant Grove, Utah

- 2 cups uncooked spiral pasta
- 1 pound boneless skinless chicken breasts, cubed
- 2 garlic cloves, minced
- 2 tablespoons butter *or* margarine
- 1 package (16 ounces) frozen broccoli, cauliflower and carrots, thawed
- 3/4 cup whipping cream
- 3/4 cup grated Parmesan cheese
- 1 teaspoon salt
- 1/4 teaspoon pepper

Cook pasta according to package directions. Meanwhile, in a large skillet, saute chicken and garlic in butter until chicken is no longer pink. Add the vegetables and cream; cook until vegetables are tender. Drain pasta. Add the pasta, Parmesan cheese, salt and pepper to the skillet; cook and stir until heated through. **Yield:** 4 servings.

### Veggies and Ham

**Ready in 30 minutes or less**

*Canned soup and frozen vegetables streamline this fast-to-fix fare. Our son has loved this cheesy ham skillet since he was a little boy. Now he requests it when he and his college roommate come home to visit.* —Barb Sears
Falconer, New York

- 3 cups frozen cut green beans, thawed
- 2 cups frozen corn, thawed
- 2 tablespoons butter *or* margarine
- 1 tablespoon all-purpose flour
- 1 can (10-3/4 ounces) condensed cream of chicken soup, undiluted
- 1/2 cup sour cream
- 2 cups cubed cooked ham
- 1 cup (4 ounces) shredded cheddar cheese

In a large skillet, saute the green beans and corn in butter. Sprinkle with flour; mix well. In a bowl, combine the soup, sour cream and ham. Stir into vegetable mixture. Cook over medium heat until heated through. Remove from the heat. Sprinkle with the cheese; cover and let stand for 3 minutes or until cheese is melted. **Yield:** 4 servings.

### Sausage Rice Skillet

**Ready in 30 minutes or less**

*Flavorful pork sausage, fresh zucchini and instant rice make this stovetop sensation a favorite with family and friends. Everyone I have shared this recipe with tells me how delicious it is.* —Connie Putnam
Clayton, North Carolina

✓ Uses less fat, sugar or salt. Includes Nutritional Analysis and Diabetic Exchanges.

- 1 pound bulk pork sausage
- 2 medium zucchini, chopped
- 1 small onion, chopped
- 1/2 cup chopped green pepper
- 1 teaspoon dried oregano
- 1/2 teaspoon garlic salt *or* garlic powder
- 1 can (11-1/2 ounces) V8 juice
- 2/3 cup uncooked instant rice

In a large skillet, cook the sausage until no longer pink; drain. Add the zucchini, onion, green pepper, oregano and garlic salt; cook and stir until onion is tender, about 5 minutes. Stir in V8 juice; bring to a boil. Reduce heat; cover and simmer for 10-14 minutes or until the vegetables are tender.

Return to a boil. Stir in rice; cover and remove from the heat. Let stand for 5-7 minutes or until rice is tender. Fluff with a fork. **Yield:** 6 servings.

**Nutritional Analysis:** One 1-cup serving (prepared with turkey sausage, reduced-sodium V8 and garlic powder) equals 240 calories, 8 g fat (2 g saturated fat), 41 mg cholesterol, 503 mg sodium, 26 g carbohydrate, 2 g fiber, 16 g protein. **Diabetic Exchanges:** 2 lean meat, 1-1/2 starch.

## Pasta Carbonara

**Ready in 30 minutes or less**

*This rich-tasting pasta toss is great for everyday dinners or special occasions. I can come home from work and throw this dish together in a half hour. Wherever I take it, I'm constantly asked for the recipe.* —Cathy Lorenzini
St. Charles, Missouri

    3 cups uncooked tube pasta
    6 bacon strips, diced
    2 garlic cloves, minced
1-1/4 cups milk
    1 package (8 ounces) cream cheese, cubed
1/2 cup butter *or* margarine, cubed
1/2 cup grated Parmesan cheese

Cook pasta according to package directions. Meanwhile, in a large skillet, cook bacon until crisp. Remove to paper towels. In the drippings, saute garlic until tender. Add the milk, cream cheese and butter; stir until smooth. Stir in the Parmesan cheese and bacon; heat through. Drain pasta; toss with sauce. **Yield:** 4 servings.

## Hearty Fajitas

*(Pictured below right)*

**Ready in 30 minutes or less**

*When I need to get dinner on the table fast for my husband and three children, I fix these filling fajitas. With beef, chicken and shrimp, they satisfy everyone's tastes. They're wonderful with Spanish rice.* —Elaine Keith
Mineral Wells, West Virginia

✓ Uses less fat, sugar or salt. Includes Nutritional Analysis and Diabetic Exchanges.

1/2 pound boneless beef round steak, cut into strips
1/4 pound boneless skinless chicken breast, cut into strips
    2 to 3 tablespoons vegetable *or* canola oil
1/2 pound uncooked medium shrimp, peeled and deveined
    1 medium green pepper, thinly sliced
    1 medium sweet red pepper, thinly sliced
    2 small onions, thinly sliced
    2 to 3 medium tomatoes, cut into wedges
    2 teaspoons chili powder
    1 teaspoon salt
    1 can (16 ounces) refried beans
1/2 cup shredded mozzarella cheese
    14 flour tortillas (7 inches), warmed

In a skillet, stir-fry steak and chicken in oil. Add the shrimp, peppers, onions, tomatoes, chili powder and salt; cook until chicken juices run clear and vegetables are crisp-tender. Meanwhile, in a saucepan, heat the refried beans and cheese until cheese is melted. Spoon over tortillas; top with meat mixture. **Yield:** 14 fajitas.
**Nutritional Analysis:** One fajita (prepared with 2 tablespoons oil, fat-free refried beans and part-skim mozzarella cheese) equals 409 calories, 10 g fat (2 g saturated fat), 82 mg cholesterol, 788 mg sodium, 49 g

carbohydrate, 7 g fiber, 31 g protein. **Diabetic Exchanges:** 3 starch, 3 lean meat, 1 vegetable.

## Pork Chops and Kraut

**Ready in 45 minutes or less**

*I love sauerkraut, so this is one of my favorite dinners. I brown pork chops in a skillet, simmer them with a nicely seasoned sauerkraut mixture, then stir in sour cream for a fast finishing touch.* —Myra Innes, Auburn, Kansas

    4 bone-in pork loin chops (1 inch thick)
1/4 teaspoon salt
1/8 teaspoon pepper
    1 tablespoon vegetable oil
    1 small onion, sliced and separated into rings
    1 garlic clove, minced
    1 can (14 ounces) sauerkraut, rinsed and drained
1/4 cup chicken broth
1/2 teaspoon caraway seeds
1/2 teaspoon paprika
    3 to 4 tablespoons all-purpose flour
1/2 cup sour cream

Sprinkle pork chops with salt and pepper. In a large skillet, brown chops on both sides in oil. Add onion and garlic. Combine the sauerkraut, broth, caraway and paprika; spoon over chops. Bring to a boil. Reduce heat; cover and simmer for 20-25 minutes or until a meat thermometer reads 160°.

Remove pork and keep warm. Sprinkle flour over sauerkraut; cook and stir for 2 minutes. Remove from the heat; stir in sour cream. Serve with pork. **Yield:** 4 servings.

Hearty Fajitas

# Bean and Ham Pasta

*(Pictured below)*

**Ready in 30 minutes or less**

*This pleasant pasta medley is brimming with ham, corn and black beans. If you'd like, you can thicken the juices with cornstarch to make a sauce.* —Maureen De Garmo
Martinez, California

    1 can (14-1/2 ounces) chicken broth
1-1/2 cups uncooked spiral pasta
    1 can (15 ounces) black beans, rinsed and
       drained
1-1/2 cups frozen corn
    1 cup cubed fully cooked ham
  1/4 teaspoon dried thyme
Salt and pepper to taste
Dash ground cumin
  1/4 cup shredded Parmesan cheese

In a large saucepan, bring broth to a boil. Add the pasta; cook, uncovered, for 10 minutes or until tender. Do not drain. Stir in the beans, corn, ham and seasonings; heat through. Sprinkle with cheese. **Yield:** 4 servings.

**Bean and Ham Pasta**

# Creamy Shrimp Linguine

**Ready in 30 minutes or less**

*My husband loves shrimp, so I'm always looking for different ways to fix it. This easy recipe, nicely seasoned with fresh garlic, tastes so good.* —Jackie Hannahs
Cadillac, Michigan

    8 ounces uncooked linguine
  3/4 cup chopped onion
    2 garlic cloves, minced
1-1/2 teaspoons dried oregano
    3 tablespoons butter *or* margarine
  3/4 cup whipping cream
  3/4 cup shredded Swiss cheese
  3/4 cup shredded Parmesan cheese
    1 pound cooked small shrimp, peeled
       and deveined

Cook linguine according to package directions. Meanwhile, in a saucepan, saute the onion, garlic and oregano in butter until onion is crisp-tender. Gradually add the cream and cheeses; cook and stir over low heat until cheese is melted. Add the shrimp; heat through. Drain linguine; top with shrimp mixture. **Yield:** 4 servings.

# Turkey Pea Skillet

**Ready in 30 minutes or less**

*This dish is an all-time favorite. It's a snap to make for a group when time is short. Plus, the recipe is very flexible—you can substitute chicken and use whatever vegetables your family prefers.*
—Barbara Sonsteby, Mesa, Arizona

    1 small onion, chopped
    2 tablespoons butter *or* margarine
1-1/4 cups sliced celery
    1 can (4 ounces) mushroom stems
       and pieces, drained
    1 can (10-1/2 ounces) condensed
       chicken broth, undiluted
    1 cup water, *divided*
    3 tablespoons soy sauce
    2 teaspoons chicken bouillon granules
  1/4 cup cornstarch
    3 cups cubed cooked turkey
    2 cups frozen peas
    1 can (8 ounces) pineapple chunks,
       drained
    1 can (8 ounces) sliced water
       chestnuts, drained
Hot cooked rice *or* chow mein noodles

In a skillet, saute onion in butter until tender. Stir in celery and mushrooms; cook and stir for 2 minutes. Combine the broth, 3/4 cup water, soy sauce and bouillon; stir into skillet. Bring to a boil. Reduce heat; cover and simmer for 3 minutes.

    Combine cornstarch and remaining water until smooth; stir into skillet. Return to a boil. Cook and stir for 1-2 minutes or until thickened and bubbly. Stir in the turkey, peas, pineapple and water chestnuts; heat through. Serve over rice or chow mein noodles. **Yield:** 6 servings.

## Orange Cashew Chicken

*(Pictured at right)*

### Ready in 30 minutes or less

*This delicious stir-fry is quick to fix yet tasty enough to serve to company. The tender chicken, crunchy cashews and sweet citrus sauce are always a hit. It tastes so special people assume I went to a lot of trouble.*
—Andrea Bolden
*Unionville, Tennessee*

✓ Uses less fat, sugar or salt. Includes Nutritional Analysis and Diabetic Exchanges.

```
1 pound boneless skinless chicken breasts, cut
   into 1-inch cubes
2 medium carrots, sliced
1/2 cup chopped celery
2 tablespoons vegetable or canola oil
2 tablespoons cornstarch
1/4 teaspoon ground ginger
3/4 cup orange juice
1/4 cup honey
3 tablespoons soy sauce
1/4 to 1/2 cup salted cashews
Hot cooked rice
```

In a large skillet or wok, stir-fry chicken, carrots and celery in oil for 8-10 minutes or until juices run clear. Reduce heat. In a bowl, combine the cornstarch, ginger, orange juice, honey and soy sauce until blended. Stir into chicken mixture. Bring to a boil; cook and stir for 2 minutes or until thickened. Stir in cashews. Serve over rice. **Yield:** 4 servings.

**Nutritional Analysis:** One 3/4-cup serving (prepared with reduced-sodium soy sauce and 1/4 cup cashews; calculated without rice) equals 375 calories, 13 g fat (2 g saturated fat), 66 mg cholesterol, 625 mg sodium, 34 g carbohydrate, 2 g fiber, 29 g protein. **Diabetic Exchanges:** 3-1/2 lean meat, 2 vegetable, 1-1/2 starch.

## Angel Hair Tuna

### Ready in 15 minutes or less

*This wonderful stovetop recipe came from a dear friend, and it quickly became a favorite standby. It comes together in a snap. Simply toss together a green salad and toast some garlic bread for a complete meal.* —Collette Burch
*Edinburg, Texas*

```
2 packages (5.1 ounces each) angel hair pasta
   with Parmesan cheese dinner mix
1 can (12 ounces) tuna, drained and flaked
1/2 teaspoon Italian seasoning
3/4 cup crushed butter-flavored crackers
   (about 15)
1/4 cup butter or margarine, melted
```

Prepare pasta dinner mixes according to package directions. Stir in the tuna and Italian seasoning. Transfer

**Orange Cashew Chicken**

to a serving bowl; cover and let stand for 5 minutes to thicken. Toss cracker crumbs and butter; sprinkle over the top. Serve immediately. **Yield:** 4 servings.

## One-Pot Ham Dinner

### Ready in 1 hour or less

*I add potato slices and frozen green beans to ham steak before topping off the down-home dinner with a comforting mushroom sauce. It's great to serve a satisfying supper and have only one pan to clean.*
—Jody Cohen
*Mackeyville, Pennsylvania*

```
1 fully cooked ham slice (1 to 1-1/2 pounds)
4 medium potatoes, peeled and sliced
1/4 to 1/2 teaspoon salt
1/4 teaspoon pepper
2 cups frozen cut green beans
1 medium onion, thinly sliced
1 can (10-3/4 ounces) condensed cream of
   mushroom soup, undiluted
1/2 cup water
```

In a large skillet over medium heat, brown the ham slice. Arrange potatoes over ham; sprinkle with salt and pepper. Top with beans and onion. Combine soup and water; pour over all. Cook for 2 minutes. Reduce heat; cover and simmer for 45-50 minutes or until potatoes are tender. **Yield:** 4 servings.

Southwestern Spaghetti

to a boil. Stir in spaghetti; return to a boil. Boil for 6 minutes.

Add the zucchini. Cook 4-5 minutes longer or until spaghetti and zucchini are tender, stirring several times. Stir in the beef; sprinkle with cheese. Serve immediately. **Yield:** 5 servings.

**Nutritional Analysis:** One serving (prepared with lean ground beef and reduced-fat cheese and without salt) equals 340 calories, 10 g fat (4 g saturated fat), 33 mg cholesterol, 676 mg sodium, 39 g carbohydrate, 3 g fiber, 24 g protein. **Diabetic Exchanges:** 2 starch, 2 lean meat, 2 vegetable, 1/2 fat.

## Curried Shrimp

### Ready in 15 minutes or less

*If you like curry, you'll enjoy the rich flavor of this creamy shrimp mixture that is delicious served over rice. I like to garnish it with bacon bits and chopped hard-cooked eggs.* —Sue Friend
*Lynden, Washington*

- 1 small onion, chopped
- 1 tablespoon vegetable oil
- 1 can (10-3/4 ounces) condensed cream of shrimp soup, undiluted
- 1 teaspoon curry powder
- 1 package (1 pound) frozen uncooked small shrimp, thawed, peeled and deveined
- 1 cup (8 ounces) sour cream

Hot cooked rice

In a large saucepan, saute onion in oil until tender. Stir in soup and curry powder; bring to a boil. Add the shrimp; cook and stir until shrimp turn pink. Reduce heat. Stir in sour cream; heat through. Serve over rice. **Yield:** 4 servings.

## Cajun Hot Dish

### Ready in 30 minutes or less

*I invented this dish to satisfy my cravings for something zesty. It's a great standby for busy nights. It takes only minutes, and I'm always sure to keep the ingredients on hand.* —RoxAnne Wienckowski, Smithtown, New York

- 1 pound fully cooked smoked sausage, cut into 1/4-inch slices
- 1/4 cup chopped onion
- 1 cup frozen corn
- 1 can (15-1/2 ounces) hot chili beans
- 1 cup V8 juice
- 1 tablespoon paprika
- 2 to 3 teaspoons ground cumin
- 1/4 teaspoon cayenne pepper, optional
- 1 cup uncooked instant rice
- 1/2 cup shredded cheddar cheese

In a large skillet, saute sausage and onion until sausage is lightly browned. Add corn; cook and stir for 1 minute. Stir in the beans, V8 juice, paprika, cumin and cayenne if desired. Bring to a boil. Reduce heat; simmer, uncovered, for

## Southwestern Spaghetti

### (Pictured above)

### Ready in 30 minutes or less

*Chili powder and cumin give a mild Mexican flavor to this colorful one-skillet supper. With chunks of fresh zucchini, it's a nice change of pace from typical spaghetti dishes.*
—*Beth Coffee, Hartford City, Indiana*

✓ Uses less fat, sugar or salt. Includes Nutritional Analysis and Diabetic Exchanges.

- 3/4 pound ground beef
- 2-1/4 cups water
- 1 can (15 ounces) tomato sauce
- 2 teaspoons chili powder
- 1/2 teaspoon garlic powder
- 1/2 teaspoon salt, optional
- 1/2 teaspoon ground cumin
- 1 package (7 ounces) thin spaghetti, broken into thirds
- 6 small zucchini (about 1 pound), cut into chunks
- 1/2 cup shredded cheddar cheese

In a large skillet, cook beef over medium heat until no longer pink; drain. Remove beef and keep warm. In the same skillet, combine the water, tomato sauce, chili powder, garlic powder, salt if desired and cumin; bring

3 minutes. Stir in the rice. Remove from the heat; cover and let stand for 5 minutes. Sprinkle with cheese. **Yield:** 4 servings.

## Ginger Pork Stir-Fry

*(Pictured at right)*

**Ready in 30 minutes or less**

*My recipe box is full of delicious pork recipes, but this fast-to-fix stir-fry really stands out from the rest. My family loves the citrus glaze that coats the tender pork and vegetables.* —Jackie Hannahs, Fountain, Michigan

✓ Uses less fat, sugar or salt. Includes Nutritional Analysis and Diabetic Exchanges.

    1 tablespoon cornstarch
    1 cup orange juice
    2 tablespoons soy sauce
    2 garlic cloves, minced
  1/4 teaspoon ground ginger
    1 pound pork tenderloin, cut into thin strips
    1 tablespoon canola oil
    1 small onion, chopped
  1/4 pound pea pods *or* snow peas
  1/4 cup chopped sweet red pepper
Hot cooked rice

In a small bowl, combine cornstarch, orange juice, soy sauce, garlic and ginger until smooth; set aside. In a large skillet or wok, stir-fry pork in oil for 5 minutes or until lightly browned; drain. Add the onion, peas and red pepper; cook and stir for 3-5 minutes or until crisp-tender.

Stir orange juice mixture; add to the skillet. Bring to a boil; cook and stir for 2 minutes or until thickened. Serve over rice. **Yield:** 4 servings.

**Nutritional Analysis:** One 3/4-cup serving (prepared with reduced-sodium soy sauce; calculated without rice) equals 230 calories, 7 g fat (2 g saturated fat), 74 mg

Ginger Pork Stir-Fry

cholesterol, 361 mg sodium, 14 g carbohydrate, 1 g fiber, 26 g protein. **Diabetic Exchanges:** 3 lean meat, 1 vegetable, 1/2 fruit.

## Broccoli Shrimp Alfredo

*(Pictured below left and on page 142)*

**Ready in 30 minutes or less**

*After tasting fettuccine Alfredo at a restaurant, I tried to duplicate the recipe at home. You can't imagine how pleased I was when I came up with this delicious version. Not only does my family love the creamy dish, but my husband prefers it to the one at the restaurant.*
—Rae Natoli, Kingston, New York

    1 package (16 ounces) fettuccine
    1 pound uncooked medium shrimp, peeled and deveined
    3 garlic cloves, minced
  1/2 cup butter *or* margarine
    1 package (8 ounces) cream cheese, cubed
    1 cup milk
  1/2 cup shredded Parmesan cheese
    1 package (10 ounces) frozen broccoli florets
  1/2 teaspoon salt
Dash pepper

Cook fettuccine according to package directions. Meanwhile, in a large skillet, saute the shrimp and garlic in butter until shrimp turn pink. Remove and keep warm. In the same skillet, combine the cream cheese, milk and Parmesan cheese; cook until cheeses are melted and smooth.

Place broccoli in a saucepan with 1 in. of water. Bring to a boil. Reduce heat; cover and simmer for 6-8 minutes or until tender. Drain. Stir broccoli, shrimp, salt and pepper into cheese sauce; heat through. Drain fettuccine; top with shrimp mixture. **Yield:** 4 servings.

Broccoli Shrimp Alfredo

## Taco Skillet

*(Pictured below and on page 143)*

**Ready in 30 minutes or less**

*I enjoy preparing one-dish dinners, and this is one of my favorites because it's so easy and attractive. Served with tortilla chips or taco shells, it's a fun meal for everyone. And because it's so festive looking, I put the skillet right on the table when we have company.*
—Tina Schaubroeck, Greencastle, Pennsylvania

   1 **pound ground beef**
   1 **medium onion, chopped**
   1 **can (16 ounces) refried beans**
   1 **can (4 ounces) chopped green chilies**
1/4 to 1/2 **teaspoon garlic powder**
3/4 **cup sour cream**
1/2 to 1 **teaspoon ground cumin**
1/2 to 1 **teaspoon chili powder**
   1 **medium tomato, seeded and chopped**
   1 **can (2-1/4 ounces) sliced ripe olives, drained**
   1 **small green pepper, chopped**
   1 **cup (4 ounces) shredded Mexican cheese blend**
**Tortilla chips *or* taco shells, shredded lettuce and salsa**

In a large skillet, cook beef and onion over medium heat until meat is no longer pink; drain. Stir in the beans, chilies and garlic powder; heat through.

Combine the sour cream, cumin and chili powder; spread over beef mixture. Top with tomato, olives and green pepper. Sprinkle with cheese. Serve with tortilla chips or taco shells, lettuce and salsa. **Yield:** 4-6 servings.

**Taco Skillet**

**Savory Sausage and Peppers**

## Savory Sausage and Peppers

*(Pictured above and on page 142)*

**Ready in 30 minutes or less**

*My mother gave me the recipe for this tasty kielbasa meal that's loaded with colorful pepper chunks. I like to use a soup mix that adds a hint of garlic, but you can substitute other varieties to suit your family's tastes.*
—Rickey Madden, Americus, Georgia

1/2 **pound fully cooked kielbasa *or* Polish sausage, cut into 1/2-inch slices**
   3 **tablespoons olive *or* vegetable oil**
   1 **medium sweet red pepper, cut into 1-inch chunks**
   1 **medium sweet yellow pepper, cut into 1-inch chunks**
   1 **medium green pepper, cut into 1-inch chunks**
   1 **medium onion, cut into small wedges**
   1 **cup water**
   1 **package (1.2 ounces) herb and garlic soup mix**
1/8 **teaspoon hot pepper sauce**
**Hot cooked rice**

In a large skillet, brown the sausage in oil over medium-high heat. Remove with a slotted spoon and keep warm. In the drippings, saute the peppers and onion until crisp-tender.

In a bowl, combine the water and contents of one soup mix envelope (save the second envelope for another use). Add soup mixture, hot pepper sauce and sausage to the vegetables. Reduce heat; cover and simmer for 5 minutes or until thickened. Serve over rice. **Yield:** 2-3 servings.

## Shrimp Jambalaya

*(Pictured at right)*

**Ready in 45 minutes or less**

*This delightfully different jambalaya is lighter than many of the traditional sausage varieties. Plus, it's a great way to use up leftover ham. I appreciate how easy it is to prepare, and I love the aroma while it's cooking.* —Marguerite Shaeffer
Sewell, New Jersey

**Shrimp Jambalaya**

1 cup cubed fully cooked ham
3/4 cup chopped onion
1 garlic clove, minced
2 tablespoons vegetable oil
2 cups chicken broth
1 can (14-1/2 ounces) stewed tomatoes
2 tablespoons minced fresh parsley
1/2 teaspoon salt
1/4 teaspoon dried thyme
1/8 teaspoon *each* cayenne pepper, chili
    powder and pepper
1 bay leaf
1 cup uncooked long grain rice
1 pound uncooked medium shrimp, peeled
    and deveined

In a large skillet, cook the ham, onion and garlic in oil until onion is tender. Stir in the broth, tomatoes, parsley and seasonings. Bring to a boil. Stir in rice. Reduce heat; cover and simmer for 15-20 minutes or until rice is tender. Add shrimp; cook 5 minutes longer or until shrimp turn pink. Discard bay leaf before serving. **Yield:** 4 servings.

## Pineapple Chicken Lo Mein

*(Pictured on page 143)*

*The perfect supper to serve on busy weeknights, this speedy lo mein combines tender chicken and colorful veggies with a tangy sauce. Quick-cooking spaghetti and canned pineapple make it a cinch to throw together when time is short.* —Linda Stevens, Madison, Alabama

✓ Uses less fat, sugar or salt. Includes Nutritional Analysis and Diabetic Exchanges.

1 can (20 ounces) unsweetened pineapple
    chunks
1 pound boneless skinless chicken breasts, cut
    into 1-inch cubes
2 garlic cloves, minced
3/4 teaspoon ground ginger *or* 1 tablespoon
    minced fresh gingerroot
3 tablespoons vegetable *or* canola oil, *divided*
2 medium carrots, julienned
1 medium green pepper, julienned
4 ounces spaghetti, cooked and drained
3 green onions, sliced
1 tablespoon cornstarch
1/3 cup soy sauce

Drain pineapple, reserving 1/3 cup juice (discard remaining juice or save for another use); set pineapple aside. In a large skillet over medium heat, cook the chicken, garlic and ginger in 2 tablespoons oil for 6 minutes. Add the carrots, green pepper and pineapple. Cover and cook for 2-3 minutes or until vegetables are crisp-tender and chicken juices run clear. Stir in spaghetti and onions.

In a small bowl, combine the cornstarch, soy sauce, reserved pineapple juice and remaining oil until smooth. Stir into chicken mixture. Bring to a boil; cook and stir for 2 minutes or until thickened. **Yield:** 4 servings.

**Nutritional Analysis:** One 1-1/2-cup serving (prepared with reduced-sodium soy sauce) equals 379 calories, 12 g fat (1 g saturated fat), 66 mg cholesterol, 895 mg sodium, 35 g carbohydrate, 5 g fiber, 31 g protein. **Diabetic Exchanges:** 4 lean meat, 1 starch, 1 fruit, 1 fat.

## Pork Chops with Apples

**Ready in 30 minutes or less**

*These moist tender chops get delicious flavor from Dijon mustard, onions and apple slices. Or try replacing the apples with pineapple rings for an appealing variation. I like to serve mashed sweet potatoes with this main course, along with a simple salad.* —Marilou Robinson
Portland, Oregon

4 bone-in pork loin chops (3/4 inch thick)
2 tablespoons vegetable oil
1/2 teaspoon salt
1/4 teaspoon pepper
2 medium onions, thinly sliced
1 large green apple, cut into thin wedges
1 large red apple, cut into thin wedges
2 tablespoons Dijon mustard
1 tablespoon brown sugar

In a large skillet, brown pork chops in oil on each side. Season with salt and pepper; remove and keep warm. In the same skillet, saute onions and apple wedges until crisp-tender. Combine mustard and brown sugar; brush over chops. Return to the skillet; cook for 4 minutes or until meat juices run clear. **Yield:** 4 servings.

**Santa Fe Supper**

## Santa Fe Supper

*(Pictured at left)*

**Ready in 30 minutes or less**

*This zesty skillet meal is a great way to bring a little variety to your dinnertime lineup. Green chilies spice up the rice, while salsa, zucchini, onion and cheddar cheese dress up the ground beef mixture.*
—*Valerie Collier, Charleston, South Carolina*

  1 cup uncooked long grain rice
  1 pound ground beef
  2 small zucchini, cut into 1/4-inch slices
  1 large onion, halved and sliced
1-1/2 cups chunky salsa, *divided*
  1/4 teaspoon salt
  1/4 teaspoon pepper
  1 cup (4 ounces) shredded pepper Jack cheese
  1 can (4 ounces) chopped green chilies, drained
  1 cup (4 ounces) shredded cheddar cheese

Cook rice according to package directions. Meanwhile, in a large skillet, cook the beef over medium heat until no longer pink; drain. Stir in the zucchini, onion, 1 cup salsa, salt and pepper; cook until vegetables are crisp-tender.

Add pepper Jack cheese and chilies to the rice. Sprinkle cheddar cheese over beef mixture; serve with rice and remaining salsa. **Yield:** 4 servings.

## Vegetarian Linguine

**Ready in 30 minutes or less**

*Looking for a tasty alternative to meat-and-potatoes meals? Try this colorful pasta dish, which is the brainchild of my oldest son. It's a stick-to-the-ribs supper that takes advantage of fresh mushrooms, zucchini and other vegetables as well as basil and provolone cheese.*
—*Jane Bone, Cape Coral, Florida*

✓ Uses less fat, sugar or salt. Includes Nutritional Analysis and Diabetic Exchanges.

  6 ounces uncooked linguine
  2 medium zucchini, thinly sliced
1/2 pound fresh mushrooms, sliced
  2 green onions, chopped
  1 garlic clove, minced
  2 tablespoons butter
  1 tablespoon olive *or* canola oil
  1 large tomato, chopped
  2 teaspoons minced fresh basil
1/2 teaspoon salt
1/4 teaspoon pepper
  4 ounces provolone cheese, shredded
  3 tablespoons shredded Parmesan cheese

Cook linguine according to package directions. Meanwhile, in a large skillet, saute the zucchini, mushrooms, onions and garlic in butter and oil for 3-5 minutes. Add the tomato, basil, salt and pepper; cover and simmer for 3 minutes. Drain linguine; add to vegetable mixture. Sprinkle with cheeses and toss to coat. **Yield:** 6 servings.

**Nutritional Analysis:** One 1-cup serving (prepared with reduced-fat provolone) equals 216 calories, 11 g fat (5 g saturated fat), 22 mg cholesterol, 416 mg sodium, 22 g carbohydrate, 3 g fiber, 12 g protein. **Diabetic Exchanges:** 1 starch, 1 lean meat, 1 vegetable, 1 fat.

## Creamy Chicken and Broccoli

**Ready in 30 minutes or less**

*My gang likes the taste of chicken cordon bleu, but I don't like the time required to make it. This skillet sensation, with the addition of broccoli, gives my family the flavors they crave with only a fraction of the work.*
—*Tamara Kalsbeek, Grand Rapids, Michigan*

  1 pound boneless skinless chicken breasts, cut into 1-inch cubes
  1 small onion, chopped
  2 tablespoons butter *or* margarine
  1 can (10-3/4 ounces) condensed cream of mushroom soup, undiluted
2/3 cup mayonnaise*
1/2 cup sour cream
  2 tablespoons white wine *or* chicken broth
1/8 teaspoon garlic powder
Salt and pepper to taste
  1 cup cubed fully cooked ham
  1 package (10 ounces) frozen broccoli florets, thawed
  3 bacon strips, cooked and crumbled
Hot cooked pasta *or* rice
  1 cup (4 ounces) shredded Swiss cheese, optional

In a large skillet, saute chicken and onion in butter until meat is no longer pink. In a bowl, combine the soup, mayonnaise, sour cream, wine or broth, garlic powder, salt and pepper. Add to the chicken mixture. Stir in the ham, broccoli and bacon; cover and cook until heated through. Serve over pasta; sprinkle with cheese if desired. **Yield:** 4 servings.

**\*Editor's Note:** Reduced-fat or fat-free mayonnaise may not be substituted for regular mayonnaise.

## Black-Eyed Pea Sausage Stew

*(Pictured below)*

**Ready in 45 minutes or less**

*I've always wanted to try black-eyed peas, and I happened to have smoked sausage on hand one night, so I invented this full-flavored stew. It's the perfect way to heat up a cold night without spending a lot of time in the kitchen. I usually double the seasonings because we like our food spicier.     —Laura Wimbrow, Bridgeville, Delaware*

    1 package (16 ounces) smoked sausage links,
       halved lengthwise and sliced
    1 small onion, chopped
    2 cans (15 ounces *each*) black-eyed peas,
       rinsed and drained
    1 can (14-1/2 ounces) diced tomatoes, drained
    1 can (8 ounces) tomato sauce
    1 cup beef broth
  1/4 teaspoon garlic powder
  1/4 teaspoon Cajun seasoning
  1/4 teaspoon pepper
  1/8 teaspoon salt
  1/8 teaspoon cayenne pepper
  1/8 teaspoon hot pepper sauce
1-1/2 cups frozen corn, thawed

Black-Eyed Pea Sausage Stew

Fruited Chicken Curry

In a large skillet, cook sausage and onion over medium heat until meat is lightly browned; drain. Stir in the peas, tomatoes, tomato sauce, broth and seasonings. Cook and stir for 10-12 minutes or until hot and bubbly. Stir in the corn; cook 5 minutes longer or until heated through. **Yield:** 6 servings.

## Fruited Chicken Curry

*(Pictured above)*

**Ready in 1 hour or less**

*The curry lovers in your house will certainly take to this juicy chicken that's served over a bed of hot rice. Dried fruits and toasted almonds make it a wonderful change-of-pace entree for any occasion.     —Bernadine Dirmeyer Harpster, Ohio*

    4 bone-in chicken breast halves
    1 tablespoon butter *or* margarine
  1/4 cup chopped onion
    2 teaspoons curry powder
  1/2 teaspoon salt
  1/8 teaspoon pepper
    1 cup dried mixed fruit (such as apples,
       apricots and prunes)
  3/4 cup hot water
    1 tablespoon sugar
    1 teaspoon lemon juice
Hot cooked rice
  1/4 cup slivered almonds, toasted

In a large skillet, brown the chicken in butter on each side; remove and keep warm. In the drippings, cook the onion, curry, salt and pepper until onion is tender. Stir in the fruit, water, sugar and lemon juice.

Return chicken to the pan. Bring to a boil. Reduce heat; cover and simmer for 25-30 minutes or until meat juices run clear. Serve over rice; sprinkle with almonds. **Yield:** 4 servings.

# Chapter 11

# ⏱ *Breads in a Jiffy*

BUTTERY BREADS...fruity muffins...sweet coffee cakes...and savory biscuits. Cooks agree breads make great accompaniments to a delicious breakfast, hearty lunch or speedy supper.

You can enjoy home-baked items such as these without spending hours in the kitchen.

The quick breads featured here promise oven-fresh flavor without the work traditional yeast breads require. Just mix the batter, fill the pan and pop it in the oven.

Don't think you have the time to make old-fashioned homemade bread from scratch? Think again!

Thanks to today's bread machines, yummy yeast breads can be quick and easy, too.

**FUSS-FREE AND FANTASTIC.** Top to bottom: Pineapple Date Bread and Blueberry Cream Muffins (recipes on pp. 170 and 171).

# Oven-Fresh Quick Breads

YOU DON'T "knead" to spend hours in the kitchen to enjoy the old-fashioned taste of freshly baked goodies. The quick breads, muffins, biscuits and other items we share here promise homemade flavor without all the work of traditional yeast breads. Most can be assembled while your oven preheats, then just pop them in to bake.

## Chunky Apple Bread

*These rugged loaves are chock-full of goodies, including tender apple chunks, nuts and chewy raisins. They freeze well and are wonderful to have on hand for drop-in company. The slices are also super for breakfast.*
—Joan Hallford, North Richland Hills, Texas

      4 eggs
      2 cups sugar
  1/2 cup buttermilk
  1/2 cup mayonnaise*
      1 teaspoon vanilla extract
3-1/2 cups all-purpose flour
      1 teaspoon baking powder
      1 teaspoon ground cinnamon
  1/2 teaspoon baking soda
  1/4 teaspoon salt
      2 medium tart apples, peeled and chopped
      1 cup raisins
      1 cup chopped walnuts

In a mixing bowl, combine the eggs, sugar, buttermilk, mayonnaise and vanilla. Combine the flour, baking powder, cinnamon, baking soda and salt; add to egg mixture and beat just until combined. Fold in the apples, raisins and walnuts. Spoon into two greased 8-in. x 4-in. x 2-in. loaf pans.

Bake at 375° for 1 hour or until a toothpick inserted near the center comes out clean. Cool for 10 minutes before removing from pans to wire racks to cool completely. **Yield:** 2 loaves.

**\*Editor's Note:** Reduced-fat or fat-free mayonnaise may not be substituted for regular mayonnaise.

## Brown Sugar Muffins

### Ready in 30 minutes or less

*This is one of my favorite muffin recipes because it goes with anything. The sweet treats have a crusty top and tender cake-like interior, so they're good for breakfast or as a snack.* —Marian Smith, Sandy, Utah

  1/2 cup shortening
      1 cup packed brown sugar
      1 egg

      1 cup milk
      2 teaspoons vanilla extract
      2 cups all-purpose flour
      1 teaspoon baking soda
  1/2 teaspoon salt

In a mixing bowl, cream shortening and brown sugar. Add egg, milk and vanilla. Combine the dry ingredients; add to creamed mixture just until combined. Fill greased or paper-lined muffin cups three-fourths full. Bake at 400° for 16-20 minutes or until a toothpick comes out clean. Cool for 5 minutes before removing from pan to a wire rack. **Yield:** 1 dozen.

## Bacon Cheese Biscuits

### Ready in 30 minutes or less

*I can stir up a golden batch of these simple savory biscuits in no time. With bacon and cheese throughout, they make a nice accompaniment to soup or chili. They also make an ordinary morning meal special served alongside eggs.*
—Kimberly Harrell, Douglas, Georgia

      2 cups self-rising flour*
      1 tablespoon sugar
  1/2 teaspoon baking soda
  1/2 cup shortening
      1 cup buttermilk
    12 ounces sliced bacon, cooked and crumbled
      1 cup (4 ounces) shredded cheddar cheese

In a large bowl, combine the flour, sugar and baking soda. Cut in shortening until mixture resembles coarse crumbs. Stir in buttermilk just until combined. Fold in the bacon and cheese.

Turn onto a lightly floured surface; knead 4-5 times. Roll to 1/2-in. thickness; cut with a 2-1/2-in. biscuit cutter. Place on a greased baking sheet. Bake at 425° for 12-15 minutes or until golden brown. **Yield:** 9 biscuits.

**\*Editor's Note:** As a substitute for each cup of self-rising flour, place 1-1/2 teaspoons baking powder and 1/2 teaspoon salt in a measuring cup. Add all-purpose flour to measure 1 cup.

## Coconut Pecan Rolls

### Ready in 45 minutes or less

*Your family will enjoy the old-fashioned appeal of these nutty rolls. Convenient refrigerated breadsticks are dressed up with a coconut coating that's oh-so-good. No one will believe how easy they are to prepare.* —Theresa Gingery
Holmesville, Nebraska

      1 tablespoon sugar
  1/2 teaspoon ground cinnamon
      1 tube (11 ounces) refrigerated breadsticks
  2/3 cup coconut pecan frosting
  1/3 cup chopped pecans

In a small bowl, combine sugar and cinnamon. Remove breadstick dough from tube (do not unroll); cut into eight slices with a serrated knife. Dip both sides of each slice in cinnamon-sugar. Place in a greased 9-in. round baking pan. Spread with frosting; sprinkle with pecans.

Bake at 350° for 25-30 minutes or until golden brown. Serve warm. **Yield:** 8 rolls.

## Banana Chip Muffins

*(Pictured below)*

**Ready in 45 minutes or less**

*I combined a few recipes to come up with these banana muffins. The chocolate chips often surprise people who try them. Our four boys make these disappear in a hurry, so I usually double the recipe.* —Colleen Johnson
Elbridge, New York

✓ Uses less fat, sugar or salt. Includes Nutritional Analysis and Diabetic Exchanges.

1-3/4 cups all-purpose flour
1/4 cup sugar
2-1/2 teaspoons baking powder
3/4 teaspoon salt
1 egg
1/2 cup milk
1/3 cup vegetable oil
1/2 cup mashed ripe banana
1/2 cup unsweetened applesauce
1 cup miniature semisweet chocolate chips

In a large bowl, combine the flour, sugar, baking powder and salt. Combine the egg, milk, oil, banana and applesauce; stir into dry ingredients just until moistened. Fold in the chocolate chips. Fill greased muffin cups two-thirds full. Bake at 400° for 20 minutes or until a toothpick comes out clean. Cool for 5 minutes before removing from pan to a wire rack. **Yield:** 1 dozen.
**Nutritional Analysis:** One muffin (prepared with fat-free milk) equals 232 calories, 11 g fat (3 g saturated fat), 18 mg cholesterol, 206 mg sodium, 32 g carbohydrate, 1 g fiber, 3 g protein. **Diabetic Exchanges:** 2 fat, 1 starch, 1 fruit.

## No-Knead Casserole Bread

*(Pictured below)*

*You'll love this cheddar bread. It is an easy yeast bread to make. Since it calls for quick-rise yeast, you don't have to wait long to enjoy it!* —Peggy Key, Grant, Alabama

5-1/2 cups all-purpose flour, *divided*
2 tablespoons sugar
2 packages (1/4 ounce *each*) quick-rise yeast
1-1/2 teaspoons salt
1/2 teaspoon pepper
2 cups water
2 tablespoons butter *or* margarine
3/4 cup plus 2 tablespoons shredded cheddar cheese, *divided*
1/4 cup finely chopped onion

In a mixing bowl, combine 2-1/2 cups flour, sugar, yeast, salt and pepper. In a saucepan, heat water and butter to 120°-130°. Add to dry ingredients; beat just until moistened. Stir in 3/4 cup of cheese, onion and remaining flour; beat until smooth. Turn onto a lightly floured surface; shape into a ball. Place in a greased 2-qt. round baking dish. Cover and let rise in a warm place until doubled, about 20 minutes.

Bake at 350° for 40-45 minutes or until golden brown. Sprinkle with remaining cheese. Bake 5 minutes longer or until cheese is melted. Remove from dish to a wire rack. **Yield:** 1 loaf.

No-Knead Casserole Bread
Banana Chip Muffins

Cinnamon Fruit Biscuits
Coconut Loaf

## Cinnamon Fruit Biscuits

*(Pictured above)*

### Ready in 45 minutes or less

*Because these sweet treats are so easy, I'm almost embarrassed when people ask me for the recipe. They're fancy but are a snap to make with refrigerated buttermilk biscuits, sugar, cinnamon and your favorite fruit preserves.* —Ione Burham
Washington, Iowa

    1/2 cup sugar
    1/2 teaspoon ground cinnamon
      1 tube (12 ounces) refrigerated buttermilk
        biscuits, separated into 10 biscuits
    1/4 cup butter *or* margarine, melted
     10 teaspoons strawberry preserves

In a small bowl, combine the sugar and cinnamon. Dip top and sides of biscuits in butter, then in cinnamon-sugar. Place on ungreased baking sheets. With the end of a wooden spoon handle, make a deep indentation in the center of each biscuit; fill with 1 teaspoon preserves.

Bake at 375° for 15-18 minutes or until golden brown. Cool for 15 minutes before serving (preserves will be hot). **Yield:** 10 servings.

## Coconut Loaf

*(Pictured above)*

*Sit down with a hot cup of coffe or tea when enjoying a slice of this cake-like quick bread. It does well at bake sales and is a wonderful gift—particularly for coconut lovers.* —Mary Ann Dudek
Cleveland, Ohio

    1/2 cup butter *or* margarine, softened
      1 cup sugar
      2 eggs
      1 teaspoon vanilla extract
      2 cups all-purpose flour
      2 teaspoons baking powder

1/2 teaspoon salt
3/4 cup milk
1-1/4 cups flaked coconut

In a mixing bowl, cream butter and sugar. Add eggs, one at a time, beating well after each addition. Beat in vanilla. Combine the flour, baking powder and salt; add to creamed mixture alternately with milk. Stir in coconut.

Pour into a greased 9-in. x 5-in. x 3-in. loaf pan. Bake at 350° for 1 hour or until a toothpick inserted near the center comes out clean. Cool for 10 minutes before removing from the pan to a wire rack to cool completely. **Yield:** 1 loaf.

## Tropical Muffins

### Ready in 1 hour or less

*Let pineapple and coconut bring a refreshing twist to muffins with this delicious recipe. Topped with sliced almonds, the moist morsels include sour cream and cream cheese. They're super for breakfast or a snack.*
—Vicki Schrupp, Saint Cloud, Minnesota

1 package (3 ounces) cream cheese, softened
1 cup sugar
1 teaspoon vanilla extract
1/2 teaspoon almond extract
1 egg
2 cups all-purpose flour
1 teaspoon baking soda
1/2 teaspoon salt
1/4 cup sour cream
2 cans (8 ounces *each*) crushed pineapple, drained
1/4 cup flaked coconut
1/2 cup sliced almonds

In a mixing bowl, beat cream cheese, sugar and extracts until smooth; stir in egg. Combine flour, baking soda and salt; add to the creamed mixture alternately with sour cream just until moistened. Fold in pineapple and coconut.

Fill greased or paper-lined muffin cups three-fourths full. Sprinkle with almonds. Bake at 350° for 25 minutes or until muffins test done. Cool for 10 minutes before removing from pans to wire racks. **Yield:** 1-1/2 dozen.

## Pepperoni Drop Biscuits

### Ready in 30 minutes or less

*I use garlic powder, Italian seasoning, sliced pepperoni and cheddar cheese to whip up a savory sensation my family loves. These yummy biscuits go great with spaghetti, macaroni and cheese or breaded fish.* —Sandra Buchanan, Bath, New York

2 cups biscuit/baking mix
3/4 cup milk
3 tablespoons butter *or* margarine, melted

1/2 teaspoon garlic powder
1/2 teaspoon Italian seasoning
1 package (3-1/2 ounces) sliced pepperoni, finely chopped
2/3 cup shredded cheddar cheese

In a bowl, combine biscuit mix, milk, butter, garlic powder and Italian seasoning. Stir in pepperoni and cheese just until combined. Drop by heaping tablespoonfuls 2 in. apart onto ungreased baking sheets. Bake at 400° for 16-18 minutes or until golden brown. Serve warm. **Yield:** 2 dozen.

## Quick Onion Bread

### Ready in 45 minutes or less

*I'm always looking for nifty ingredients like hot pepper sauce to jazz up biscuit mix. Warm wedges of this low-fuss round loaf are an ideal match with most any entree.*
—Faith Siegrist, Lititz, Pennsylvania

1-1/2 cups biscuit/baking mix
2 tablespoons dried minced onion
1/2 cup milk
1/3 cup water
1 egg, lightly beaten
1/2 to 1 teaspoon hot pepper sauce
2 tablespoons butter *or* margarine, melted

In a bowl, combine the first six ingredients (mixture will be lumpy). Transfer to a greased 9-in. pie plate. Drizzle butter over top. Bake at 400° for 18-22 minutes or until a toothpick inserted near the center comes out clean. Cool for 10 minutes before cutting. Serve warm. **Yield:** 8 servings.

## Apple-Nut Coffee Cake

### Ready in 1 hour or less

*My great-grandmother created this recipe, and it has been passed down through our family. Cinnamon nicely spices the moist snack cake that's made with tart apples, crunchy nuts and other everyday ingredients.*
—Cyndi Martin, Montgomery, Illinois

1/2 cup butter *or* margarine, softened
1 cup sugar
1 egg
1 teaspoon vanilla extract
1 cup plus 2 tablespoons all-purpose flour
1/2 teaspoon baking powder
1/2 teaspoon baking soda
1/2 teaspoon ground cinnamon
1/4 teaspoon salt
2 medium tart apples, peeled and chopped
1/2 cup chopped walnuts

In a mixing bowl, cream butter and sugar. Beat in egg and vanilla; mix well. Combine the dry ingredients; gradually add to creamed mixture. Stir in apples and walnuts. Transfer to an ungreased 8-in. square baking dish. Bake at 350° for 35-40 minutes or until a toothpick inserted near the center comes out clean. Cool on a wire rack. **Yield:** 9 servings.

## Pineapple Biscuits

**Ready in 30 minutes or less**

*Refrigerated biscuits hurry along the preparation of these sweet breakfast buns. The tempting pineapple topping has just four ingredients and is a snap to stir together. Guests are always impressed with these easy special biscuits.* —Carol Henderson
Stephenville, Texas

1/2 cup packed brown sugar
1/4 cup butter *or* margarine, softened
1 can (8 ounces) crushed pineapple, drained
1 teaspoon ground cinnamon
1 tube (12 ounces) refrigerated biscuits

In a bowl, combine the brown sugar and butter; stir in the pineapple and cinnamon. Spoon into 10 greased muffin cups. Place one biscuit in each prepared cup. Bake at 425° for 10 minutes or until golden brown. Let stand for 5 minutes before inverting onto a serving platter. **Yield:** 10 servings.

## Savory Sausage Bread

**Ready in 45 minutes or less**

*A pound of sausage adds zip to these flavorful round loaves of bread. Sprinkled with shredded cheddar cheese, warm wedges are delicious at brunch, as a snack or as an appetizer. They're also great alongside soup or a salad.*
—Fritzie Edwards, Bunnlevel, North Carolina

2 eggs
1 cup milk
1 pound bulk pork sausage, cooked and drained
3 cups biscuit/baking mix
2 cups (8 ounces) shredded cheddar cheese, *divided*
2 tablespoons finely chopped onion
2 tablespoons butter *or* margarine, melted

In a large bowl, combine the eggs and milk. Add the sausage, biscuit mix, 1 cup cheese and onion; stir just until blended. Spoon into two greased 9-in. round baking pans. Sprinkle with the remaining cheese. Drizzle with butter. Bake at 350° for 25-30 minutes or until golden brown. Cut into wedges; serve warm. **Yield:** 2 round loaves.

## Lemon Coffee Cake

*This quick coffee cake was one of the first recipes I tried after I got married more than 30 years ago. Since then, I have received many compliments and requests for the recipe.* —Darlene Markel, Salem, Oregon

1-1/4 cups sugar, *divided*
3/4 cup vegetable oil
4 eggs
2 cups all-purpose flour
1 teaspoon baking powder
1/2 teaspoon salt

1 can (15-3/4 ounces) lemon pie filling
1-1/2 teaspoons ground cinnamon

In a mixing bowl, combine 1 cup sugar and oil; mix well. Add eggs; beat until light and lemon-colored. Combine flour, baking powder and salt; add to the egg mixture and mix well. Pour half into a greased 13-in. x 9-in. x 2-in. baking dish. Spread pie filling over batter. Top with remaining batter.

Combine the cinnamon and remaining sugar; sprinkle over the top. Bake at 350° for 30 minutes or until a toothpick comes out clean. Cool on a wire rack. **Yield:** 12-16 servings.

## Apricot Muffins

**Ready in 30 minutes or less**

*Orange zest enhances the apricot flavor of these muffins. Sometimes, I substitute raisins or chopped dates for the apricots.* —Lois Gelzer, Cape Elizabeth, Maine

2 cups all-purpose flour
1/2 cup sugar
2 teaspoons baking powder
1/2 teaspoon salt
2 eggs
1 cup milk
1/4 cup vegetable oil
1/2 to 3/4 cup chopped dried apricots
2 teaspoons grated orange peel

In a large bowl, combine the flour, sugar, baking powder and salt. In another bowl, combine the eggs, milk and oil; mix well. Stir into the dry ingredients just until combined. Fold in apricots and orange peel. Fill paper-lined muffin cups two-thirds full.

Bake at 400° for 15-20 minutes or until a toothpick comes out clean. Cool for 5 minutes before removing from pan to a wire rack. Serve warm. **Yield:** 1 dozen.

## Coconut Muffins

*(Pictured at right)*

**Ready in 30 minutes or less**

*I dress up a muffin recipe with flaked coconut, coconut extract and a streusel topping to create these tender treats. We like them so much, they're a regular at Saturday morning breakfast.* —Sue Gronholz, Beaver Dam, Wisconsin

2 cups all-purpose flour
1/2 cup sugar
3 teaspoons baking powder
1/2 teaspoon salt
1 egg
2/3 cup milk
1/3 cup vegetable oil
1/2 teaspoon coconut extract
1/4 cup flaked coconut
TOPPING:
1/4 cup sugar
1/4 cup flaked coconut
1 tablespoon butter *or* margarine, softened
1/2 teaspoon ground cinnamon

In a large bowl, combine the flour, sugar, baking powder and salt. In another bowl, combine the egg, milk, oil and extract; mix well. Stir into dry ingredients just until combined. Stir in coconut. Fill greased or paper-lined muffin cups two-thirds full.

Combine the topping ingredients; sprinkle over batter. Bake at 400° for 18-20 minutes or until a toothpick comes out clean. Cool for 5 minutes before removing from pan to a wire rack. **Yield:** 8 muffins.

## Honey Spice Bread

*(Pictured below)*

*The texture of this moist spice bread is almost like a cake, so I usually serve yummy slices of it for dessert. Plus, the loaf looks so festive with the pretty glaze drizzled on top. It's also nice on a holiday morning.*
—*Gaye O'Dell
Binghamton, New York*

2/3 cup packed brown sugar
1/3 cup milk
  2 cups all-purpose flour

1-1/2 teaspoons baking powder
  1/2 teaspoon ground cinnamon
  1/2 teaspoon ground nutmeg
  1/8 teaspoon ground cloves
    2 eggs
  1/2 cup honey
  1/3 cup vegetable oil
**GLAZE:**
  1/3 cup confectioners' sugar
    2 teaspoons milk

In a saucepan over low heat, cook and stir brown sugar and milk for 5 minutes or until sugar is dissolved. Remove from the heat. In a large bowl, combine dry ingredients. In another bowl, combine the eggs, honey, oil and brown sugar mixture; mix well. Stir into dry ingredients just until moistened. Pour into a greased 8-in. x 4-in. x 2-in. loaf pan.

Bake at 350° for 55-60 minutes or until a toothpick inserted near the center comes out clean (cover with foil if top browns too quickly). Cool for 10 minutes before removing from pan to a wire rack to cool completely. Combine glaze ingredients until smooth; drizzle over bread. **Yield:** 1 loaf.

Coconut Muffins
Honey Spice Bread

Poppy Seed Lemonade Muffins
Blueberry Scones

## Blueberry Scones

*(Pictured above)*

**Ready in 45 minutes or less**

*Stash a few of these homemade morsels in the freezer to serve to visitors who drop in unexpectedly. Pop a frozen scone in the microwave for 20 seconds or so for a warm treat.*
            —*Joan Francis, Spring Lake, New Jersey*

    4 cups all-purpose flour
    6 tablespoons sugar
4-1/2 teaspoons baking powder
  1/2 teaspoon salt
  1/2 cup plus 2 tablespoons cold butter
        *or margarine*
    2 eggs
  3/4 cup plus 2 tablespoons milk, *divided*
1-1/2 cups fresh *or* frozen blueberries*

In a bowl, combine the flour, sugar, baking powder and salt; cut in butter until mixture resembles coarse crumbs. In a bowl, whisk eggs and 3/4 cup milk; add to dry ingredients just until moistened. Turn onto a lightly floured surface; gently knead in the blueberries.

Divide the dough in half. Pat each portion into an 8-in. circle; cut each into eight wedges. Place on greased baking sheets. Brush with remaining milk. Bake at 375° for 15-20 minutes or until tops are golden brown. Serve warm. **Yield:** 16 scones.

**\*Editor's Note:** If using frozen blueberries, do not thaw before adding to dough.

## Poppy Seed Lemonade Muffins

*(Pictured above)*

**Ready in 45 minutes or less**

*It's hard to beat the delicious combination of flavors baked into these lemony muffins. The lightly glazed gems are so tasty that our family looks forward to them for dessert.*
            —*Karen Ann Bland, Gove, Kansas*

    2 cups all-purpose flour
    9 tablespoons sugar, *divided*
    4 teaspoons poppy seeds
    3 teaspoons baking powder
  1/2 teaspoon salt
  3/4 cup lemonade concentrate, *divided*
  1/2 cup milk
  1/3 cup butter *or* margarine, melted
    1 egg

In a large bowl, combine the flour, 5 tablespoons sugar, poppy seeds, baking powder and salt. In another bowl, combine 1/2 cup lemonade concentrate, milk, butter and egg until blended. Stir into dry ingredients just until combined. Fill greased or paper-lined muffin cups three-fourths full.

Bake at 400° for 15-20 minutes or until a toothpick comes out clean. Cool for 5 minutes before removing from pan to a wire rack. In a small bowl, combine the remaining sugar and lemonade concentrate. Pierce muffin tops several times with a fork; drizzle with lemonade mixture. **Yield:** 1 dozen.

## Bacon Cheddar Pinwheels

### Ready in 30 minutes or less

*These fast flaky rolls are perfect any time of the day. Try them with scrambled eggs at breakfast or with potato soup at lunch. Our family also enjoys them with a little butter as a snack.   —Marlene Wyatt, New Franklin, Missouri*

      2 cups all-purpose flour
      3 teaspoons baking powder
   1/4 teaspoon salt
   1/3 cup shortening
   3/4 cup milk
   1/2 pound sliced bacon, cooked and crumbled
   3/4 cup shredded cheddar cheese

In a bowl, combine the flour, baking powder and salt; cut in shortening. Add milk and mix well. Turn onto a floured surface; knead 6-8 times. Roll into a 16-in. x 10-in. rectangle. Sprinkle with bacon and cheese.

Roll up from a long side. Cut into 15 slices; place cut side down in greased muffin cups. Bake at 450° for 12-15 minutes or until golden brown. Serve warm. Refrigerate leftovers. **Yield:** 15 rolls.

## Honey Oat Muffins

### Ready in 45 minutes or less

*I've made these muffins many times because they taste so good. Not only are they extremely easy to throw together, but they're well received whenever I serve them.*
*—Audrey Carr, Powell, Ohio*

1-1/2 cups quick-cooking oats
      1 cup all-purpose flour
   1/3 cup packed brown sugar
      3 teaspoons baking powder
   3/4 teaspoon salt
      1 egg
   2/3 cup milk
   1/3 cup vegetable oil
   1/4 cup honey
   1/2 cup raisins, optional
   1/2 cup chopped walnuts, optional

In a bowl, combine the oats, flour, brown sugar, baking powder and salt. In another bowl, combine egg, milk, oil and honey. Stir into dry ingredients just until moistened. Fold in raisins and walnuts if desired.

Fill greased or paper-lined muffin cups two-thirds full. Bake at 400° for 15-18 minutes or until a toothpick comes out clean. Cool for 5 minutes before removing from pan to a wire rack. **Yield:** 1 dozen.

## Granola Peach Bread

*Ground cloves, sweet peaches and hearty granola share the stage in this flavorful loaf. Brunch guests are often treated to moist tender slices when they visit.*
*—Regina Albright, Clinton, Michigan*

✓ Uses less fat, sugar or salt. Includes Nutritional Analysis and Diabetic Exchanges.

      1 can (16 ounces) sliced peaches
      2 cups all-purpose flour
   2/3 cup sugar
      2 teaspoons baking powder
   1/4 to 1/2 teaspoon ground cloves
   1/4 teaspoon salt
      2 tablespoons cold butter *or* stick margarine
      2 eggs, beaten
      1 cup granola without raisins

Drain peaches, reserving 1/2 cup syrup (discard remaining syrup or save for another use). Chop peaches; set aside. In a bowl, combine the flour, sugar, baking powder, cloves and salt. Cut in butter until the mixture resembles coarse crumbs. Stir in eggs and reserved syrup. Fold in granola and peaches.

Pour into a greased 9-in. x 5-in. x 3-in. loaf pan. Bake at 350° for 60-65 minutes or until a toothpick inserted near the center comes out clean. Cool for 10 minutes before removing from pan to a wire rack. **Yield:** 1 loaf (16 slices).
   **Nutritional Analysis:** One slice (prepared with reduced-fat granola) equals 155 calories, 3 g fat (1 g saturated fat), 30 mg cholesterol, 110 mg sodium, 30 g carbohydrate, 1 g fiber, 3 g protein. **Diabetic Exchanges:** 1 starch, 1 fruit.

## Chive Cheese Biscuits

### Ready in 45 minutes or less

*These are the lightest biscuits I've ever baked. My husband loves them with a meal of macaroni and cheese and coleslaw. They're very versatile and go with any entree. Flecks of fresh chives and golden bits of cheddar cheese make the biscuits a savory standout.   —Joan Baskin*
*Black Creek, British Columbia*

      2 cups all-purpose flour
      3 teaspoons baking powder
   1/2 teaspoon cream of tartar
   1/2 teaspoon salt
   3/4 cup shredded cheddar cheese
   1/2 cup shortening
   3/4 cup milk
   1/3 cup snipped chives

In a bowl, combine the flour, baking powder, cream of tartar and salt. Cut in cheese and shortening until mixture resembles coarse crumbs. Stir in milk and chives until moistened.

Turn onto a lightly floured surface; gently knead 8-10 times. Roll to 3/4-in. thickness; cut with a 2-1/2-in. biscuit cutter. Place on an ungreased baking sheet. Bake at 400° for 13-15 minutes or until golden brown. Serve warm. **Yield:** about 1 dozen.

## Turkey Dinner Muffins

**Ready in 30 minutes or less**

*I love experimenting in the kitchen. That's how I created these muffins that use up leftovers from a turkey dinner. Team them with a bowl of soup and some fresh fruit for a satisfying lunch.* —Margaret Berardi
Bridgeport, Connecticut

```
1-3/4 cups all-purpose flour
    3 tablespoons sugar
    3 teaspoons baking powder
  1/2 teaspoon salt
  1/4 teaspoon poultry seasoning
    1 egg
  3/4 cup turkey gravy
  1/3 cup vegetable oil
  3/4 cup diced cooked turkey
    2 tablespoons jellied cranberry sauce
```

In a bowl, combine the flour, sugar, baking powder, salt and poultry seasoning. In another bowl, combine the egg, gravy and oil; mix well. Stir into dry ingredients just until combined. Fold in the turkey.

Fill greased muffin cups two-thirds full. Top each with 1/2 teaspoon cranberry sauce. Bake at 400° for 15-18 minutes or until a toothpick inserted near the center comes out clean. Cool for 5 minutes before removing from pans to wire racks. Serve warm. **Yield:** 10 muffins.

## Walnut Cinnamon Rolls

*It's impossible to resist these ooey-gooey cinnamon rolls. They're fast to assemble using hardy frozen bread dough, and they get their great flavor from cinnamon, brown sugar and chopped walnuts.* —Jill Defries
Windom, Minnesota

```
    1 loaf (1 pound) frozen bread dough, thawed
    2 tablespoons butter or margarine, melted
  2/3 cup packed brown sugar
  1/2 cup chopped walnuts
    1 teaspoon ground cinnamon
  1/2 cup whipping cream
  2/3 cup confectioners' sugar
    1 tablespoon milk
```

Roll dough into a 20-in. x 6-in. rectangle. Brush with butter. Combine the brown sugar, walnuts and cinnamon; sprinkle over dough. Roll up jelly-roll style, starting with a long side. Cut into 20 slices, 1 in. thick. Place in a greased 13-in. x 9-in. x 2-in. baking pan. Cover and let rise in a warm place until doubled, about 45 minutes.

Drizzle with cream. Bake at 350° for 25-30 minutes or until golden brown. Invert onto a serving platter. In a small bowl, combine the confectioners' sugar and milk; drizzle over rolls. Serve warm. **Yield:** 20 rolls.

## Garlic-Cheese Flat Bread

**Ready in 30 minutes or less**

*I use convenient refrigerated pizza dough to create these savory squares with Italian flair. They're perfect alongside a salad or soup, or try them as a snack with spaghetti sauce for dipping.* —Tom Hilliker
Lake Havasu City, Arizona

```
    1 tube (10 ounces) refrigerated pizza dough
  1/4 cup butter or margarine, melted
    4 garlic cloves, minced
    1 tablespoon minced fresh basil
    1 cup (4 ounces) shredded cheddar cheese
  1/2 cup grated Romano cheese
  1/4 cup grated Parmesan cheese
```

Press dough onto a greased 15-in. x 10-in. x 1-in. baking pan. In a small bowl, combine butter, garlic and basil; drizzle over dough. Sprinkle with the cheeses. Bake at 400° for 10-12 minutes or until crisp. Cut into squares. Serve warm. **Yield:** 12-15 servings.

## Sweet Potato Bread

*This quick recipe makes two pleasantly spiced loaves—one to eat and one to share. Sweet potatoes lend nice color and moistness to the easy bread.* —Dixie Burnham
Hernando, Florida

```
    3 eggs
  1/2 cup vegetable oil
  1/2 cup applesauce
    1 teaspoon vanilla extract
    1 cup mashed sweet potatoes
    2 teaspoons grated orange peel
    3 cups all-purpose flour
    1 cup sugar
    1 cup packed brown sugar
    1 teaspoon salt
    1 teaspoon baking soda
    1 teaspoon ground cinnamon
    1 teaspoon ground nutmeg
  1/4 teaspoon baking powder
    1 cup chopped pecans or walnuts
```

In a large mixing bowl, combine eggs, oil, applesauce and vanilla. Stir in sweet potatoes and orange peel; mix well. Combine the flour, sugars, salt, baking soda, cinnamon, nutmeg and baking powder; stir into sweet potato mixture just until combined. Stir in nuts.

Pour into two greased 9-in. x 5-in. x 3-in. loaf pans. Bake at 350° for 50-60 minutes or until a toothpick inserted near the center comes out clean. Cool for 10 minutes before removing from pans to wire racks. **Yield:** 2 loaves.

## Pineapple Date Bread

*(Pictured at right and on page 160)*

*My family asked for a pineapple upside-down cake, but I didn't have all of the ingredients. Since I had a quick bread mix in the house, I came up with this easy version. It even won a blue ribbon at our county fair.* —Phy Bresse
Lumberton, North Carolina

```
  1/3 cup packed brown sugar
    1 can (8 ounces) sliced pineapple, drained
    4 maraschino cherries
```

2 tablespoons butter *or* margarine
1 package (16.6 ounces) date quick
 bread/muffin mix
1/3 cup chopped walnuts
1 cup water
2 eggs
1 tablespoon applesauce
1 tablespoon vegetable oil

Sprinkle brown sugar into a greased 9-in. square baking dish. Top with pineapple slices; place a cherry in the center of each pineapple slice. Dot with butter.

In a bowl, combine quick bread mix and nuts. In another bowl, combine the water, eggs, applesauce and oil; stir into mix just until combined. Spoon over pineapple slices. Bake at 350° for 35-40 minutes or until a toothpick inserted near the center comes out clean. Immediately invert onto a serving plate. Cool for 15 minutes before cutting. Serve warm. **Yield:** 9 servings.

## Blueberry Cream Muffins

*(Pictured below and on page 161)*

**Ready in 1 hour or less**

*I combined two recipes to create these delicious berry muffins. The creamy filling makes them a real delight for breakfast or a snack.* —Shari Zimmerman
Orfordville, Wisconsin

4 cups all-purpose flour
1 cup sugar
6 teaspoons baking powder
1 teaspoon salt
2 eggs
2 cups milk
1/2 cup butter *or* margarine, melted
2 cups fresh *or* frozen blueberries*
FILLING:
1 package (8 ounces) cream cheese,
 softened
1 egg
1/3 cup sugar
Dash salt

In a large bowl, combine the flour, sugar, baking powder and salt. In another bowl, beat the eggs, milk and butter; stir into dry ingredients just until moistened. Fold in the blueberries. Spoon about 2 rounded tablespoonfuls into greased muffin cups.

In a small mixing bowl, beat cream cheese, egg, sugar and salt; place about 1 tablespoon in the center of each muffin cup (do not spread). Top with remaining batter. Bake at 375° for 18-20 minutes or until a toothpick inserted in muffin comes out clean. Cool for 10 minutes before removing from pans to wire racks. **Yield:** 2 dozen.

**\*Editor's Note:** If using frozen blueberries, do not thaw before adding to batter.

Pineapple Date Bread
Blueberry Cream Muffins

Cranberry Cream Cheese Muffins

## Cranberry Cream Cheese Muffins

(Pictured at left)

**Ready in 45 minutes or less**

*The sweet creamy filling in these cranberry muffins makes them popular at my house. The tender treats also have a crispy sugar topping that is bound to be a hit.* —Sharon Hartman, Twin Falls, Idaho

      1 package (3 ounces) cream cheese, softened
      4 tablespoons sugar, *divided*
      1 package (15.6 ounces) cranberry-orange quick bread mix
      1 cup milk
    1/3 cup vegetable oil
      1 egg

In a small mixing bowl, beat the cream cheese and 2 tablespoons sugar until smooth; set aside. Place the bread mix in another bowl. Combine the milk, oil and egg; stir into bread mix just until moistened. Fill paper-lined muffin cups one-fourth full with batter. Place 2 teaspoons cream cheese mixture in the center of each; top with remaining batter. Sprinkle with remaining sugar.

Bake at 400° for 18-20 minutes or until a toothpick comes out clean. Cool for 5 minutes before removing from pan to a wire rack. **Yield:** 1 dozen.

## Apple Streusel Muffins

**Ready in 45 minutes or less**

*I was looking for something warm to make for my daughter before school on a rainy morning. So I jazzed up a boxed muffin mix with a chopped apple, walnuts, brown sugar and a fast-to-fix vanilla glaze. The tasty results really hit the spot.* —Elizabeth Calabrese
Yucaipa, California

      1 package (6-1/2 ounces) apple cinnamon muffin mix*
      1 large tart apple, peeled and diced
    1/3 cup chopped walnuts
      3 tablespoons brown sugar
  4-1/2 teaspoons all-purpose flour
      1 tablespoon butter *or* margarine, melted
GLAZE:
    3/4 cup confectioners' sugar
    1/2 teaspoon vanilla extract
      1 to 2 tablespoons milk

Prepare muffin mix according to package directions; fold in apple. Fill greased muffin cups three-fourths full. In a small bowl, combine the walnuts, brown sugar, flour and butter; sprinkle over batter.

Bake at 400° for 15-20 minutes or until a toothpick comes out clean. Cool for 5 minutes before removing from pan to a wire rack. Combine the glaze ingredients; drizzle over warm muffins. **Yield:** 6 muffins.

**\*Editor's Note:** This recipe was tested with Betty Crocker apple cinnamon muffin mix.

## Jumbo Onion Cheese Muffins

**Ready in 45 minutes or less**

*Chopped green onions, along with mozzarella, Romano and Parmesan cheese, perk up these favorite suppertime specialties. The large light-textured muffins have a lovely golden look and tempting savory flavor that's ideal with any entree.* —Valerie Collier
Charleston, South Carolina

      2 cups all-purpose flour
      3 teaspoons baking powder
    1/4 teaspoon pepper
Dash ground nutmeg
  1-1/4 cups milk
    1/4 cup butter *or* margarine, melted
      1 egg
    1/4 cup chopped green onions
    1/4 cup shredded mozzarella cheese
    1/4 cup grated Romano cheese
    1/4 cup shredded Parmesan cheese

In a bowl, combine the flour, baking powder, pepper and nutmeg. In another bowl, combine the milk, butter and egg; stir into dry ingredients just until moistened. Fold in the onions and cheeses. Fill greased jumbo muffin cups two-thirds full.

Bake at 400° for 20-25 minutes or until a toothpick comes out clean. Cool for 5 minutes before removing from pan to a wire rack. **Yield:** 6 muffins.

**Editor's Note:** Muffins may be baked in regular-size muffin cups for 16-18 minutes; recipe makes 1 dozen.

## Triple Berry Muffins

**Ready in 45 minutes or less**

*Fresh blueberries, raspberries and strawberries bring eye-catching color and fruity taste to these moist muffins.*
—Michelle Turnis, Hopkinton, Iowa

    3 cups all-purpose flour
1-1/2 cups sugar
4-1/2 teaspoons ground cinnamon
    3 teaspoons baking powder
    1/2 teaspoon salt
    1/2 teaspoon baking soda
    2 eggs
1-1/4 cups milk
    1 cup butter *or* margarine, melted
    1 cup fresh blueberries
    1/2 cup fresh raspberries
    1/2 cup chopped fresh strawberries

In a large bowl, combine the dry ingredients. In another bowl, beat the eggs, milk and butter; stir into dry ingredients just until moistened. Fold in berries. Fill greased or paper-lined muffin cups three-fourths full.

Bake at 375° for 18-20 minutes or until a toothpick comes out clean. Cool for 5 minutes before removing from pans to wire racks. **Yield:** about 1-1/2 dozen.

## Cheeseburger Mini Muffins

*(Pictured below right)*

*I came up with the recipe for these cute little muffins so I could enjoy the flavor of cheeseburgers without resorting to fast food. I often freeze a batch and reheat however many I want to serve. They're also great as appetizers.*
—Teresa Kraus, Cortez, Colorado

    1/2 pound ground beef
    1 small onion, finely chopped
2-1/2 cups all-purpose flour
    1 tablespoon sugar
    2 teaspoons baking powder
    1 teaspoon salt
    3/4 cup ketchup
    3/4 cup milk
    1/2 cup butter *or* margarine, melted
    2 eggs
    1 teaspoon prepared mustard
    2 cups (8 ounces) shredded cheddar cheese

In a skillet, cook beef and onion over medium heat until meat is no longer pink; drain. In a bowl, combine the flour, sugar, baking powder and salt. In another bowl, combine the ketchup, milk, butter, eggs and mustard; stir into the dry ingredients just until moistened. Fold in the beef mixture and cheese. Fill greased miniature muffin cups three-fourths full.

Bake at 425° for 15-18 minutes or until a toothpick comes out clean. Cool for 5 minutes before removing from pans to wire racks. Refrigerate leftovers. **Yield:** 5 dozen.

**Editor's Note:** Muffins may be baked in regular-size muffin cups for 20-25 minutes; recipe makes 2 dozen.

## Raspberry Corn Bread Muffins

**Ready in 1 hour or less**

*These are my son's favorites. He calls them "surprise muffins" because I pipe raspberry preserves into their centers. He likes them so much that sometimes I bake them in jumbo muffin tins, adding more preserves than I do for the regular size.*
—Sue Santulli
Sea Girt, New Jersey

    3 cups all-purpose flour
    1 cup cornmeal
    1 cup sugar
    6 teaspoons baking powder
1-1/2 teaspoons salt
    2 eggs
1-1/2 cups milk
    1 cup butter *or* margarine, melted
    1/2 cup raspberry preserves

In a large mixing bowl, combine the flour, cornmeal, sugar, baking powder and salt. In another bowl, combine the eggs, milk and butter; add to dry ingredients and beat on low speed just until blended. Fill paper-lined muffin cups two-thirds full.

Bake at 350° for 17-19 minutes or until a toothpick comes out clean. Cool for 5 minutes before removing from pans to wire racks to cool completely.

Using the end of a 3/8-in.-wide wooden spoon handle, make a hole in the center of each muffin. Place preserves in a resealable plastic bag; cut a small hole in a corner of bag. Fill the hole in each muffin with preserves. **Yield:** about 2 dozen.

**Cheeseburger Mini Muffins**

## Coffee Cake Muffins

### Ready in 45 minutes or less

*I combine the dry ingredients for these muffins the night before baking. In the morning, I add the remaining items, fill the muffin cups and pop them in the oven. Brown sugar, cinnamon and pecans give them coffee cake-like flavor.* —Margaret McNeil, Germantown, Tennessee

    1/4 cup packed brown sugar
    1/4 cup chopped pecans
      1 teaspoon ground cinnamon
  1-1/2 cups all-purpose flour
    1/2 cup sugar
      2 teaspoons baking powder
    1/4 teaspoon baking soda
    1/4 teaspoon salt
      1 egg
    3/4 cup milk
    1/3 cup vegetable oil
GLAZE:
    1/2 cup confectioners' sugar
      1 tablespoon milk
      1 teaspoon vanilla extract

Combine the brown sugar, pecans and cinnamon; set aside. In a large bowl, combine the flour, sugar, baking powder, baking soda and salt. In another bowl, beat the egg, milk and oil; stir into dry ingredients just until moistened. Spoon 1 tablespoon of batter into paper-lined muffin cups. Top each with 1 teaspoon nut mixture and about 2 tablespoons batter. Sprinkle with the remaining nut mixture.

Bake at 400° for 22-24 minutes or until a toothpick comes out clean. Cool for 5 minutes before removing from pan to a wire rack. Combine glaze ingredients; spoon over muffins. **Yield:** 1 dozen.

**Pecan Pear Muffins**

## Pecan Pear Muffins

### (Pictured below left)

### Ready in 1 hour or less

*These muffins are delicious! Chock-full of pears, pecans and down-home goodness, the moist sweet treats are terrific with a glass of cold milk or a steaming cup of coffee.* —Laura Ward, Las Vegas, Nevada

      3 cups all-purpose flour
      2 cups sugar
      2 teaspoons baking soda
      1 teaspoon ground cinnamon
    1/2 teaspoon salt
      2 eggs
      1 cup vegetable oil
      1 teaspoon vanilla extract
      4 cups chopped peeled ripe pears (about 6
        medium)
      1 cup chopped pecans

In a large bowl, combine the flour, sugar, baking soda, cinnamon and salt. In another bowl, combine the eggs, oil and vanilla; stir into dry ingredients just until moistened. Fold in the pears and pecans. Fill paper-lined muffin cups two-thirds full.

Bake at 350° for 25-30 minutes or until a toothpick comes out clean. Cool for 5 minutes before removing from pans to wire racks. **Yield:** about 2 dozen.

## Sausage Swiss Muffins

### Ready in 45 minutes or less

*Sage and thyme really perk up these mouth-watering muffins made with handy baking mix. I like to keep a few in the refrigerator because the pork sausage and Swiss cheese make them perfect for breakfast in a hurry.* —Patsy Spires, Cheshire, Ohio

      8 ounces pork sausage
  1-3/4 cups biscuit/baking mix
    3/4 teaspoon rubbed sage
    1/4 teaspoon dried thyme
      1 egg
    1/2 cup milk
    1/2 cup shredded Swiss cheese

In a small skillet, cook sausage over medium heat until no longer pink; drain. In a bowl, combine the baking mix, sage and thyme. In another bowl, combine the egg and milk; stir into dry ingredients just until moistened. Fold in the cheese and sausage. Fill greased muffin cups two-thirds full.

Bake at 375° for 15-18 minutes or until a toothpick comes out clean. Cool for 5 minutes before removing from pan to a wire rack. Serve warm. Refrigerate leftovers. **Yield:** 9 muffins.

## Peanut Butter 'n' Jelly Mini Muffins

### Ready in 45 minutes or less

*Kids love these mini jelly-filled treats...and so do adults. Packed with peanut butter flavor, they're a fun and easy*

way to start off the day...or to share as an after-school snack.

—Vickie Barrow
Edenton, North Carolina

1 cup all-purpose flour
1/3 cup packed brown sugar
1 teaspoon baking powder
1/2 teaspoon baking soda
1/4 teaspoon salt
2 eggs
1/2 cup vanilla yogurt
3 tablespoons creamy peanut butter
2 tablespoons vegetable oil
3 tablespoons strawberry *or* grape jelly

In a large bowl, combine the flour, brown sugar, baking powder, baking soda and salt. In a small mixing bowl, beat the eggs, yogurt, peanut butter and oil on low speed until smooth; stir into the dry ingredients just until moistened. Fill greased or paper-lined miniature muffin cups half full. Top each with 1/4 teaspoon jelly and the remaining batter.

Bake at 400° for 10-12 minutes or until golden brown. Cool for 5 minutes before removing from pans to wire racks. **Yield:** 2-1/2 dozen.

**Editor's Note:** Muffins may be baked in regular-size muffin cups for 16-18 minutes; use 3/4 teaspoon jelly for each instead of 1/4 teaspoon. Recipe makes 10 muffins.

**Berry Pleasing Muffins**

## Berry Pleasing Muffins

*(Pictured above right)*

**Ready in 45 minutes or less**

*These are scrumptious with sausage and scrambled eggs for breakfast or with cottage cheese and a sliced apple for a light lunch. The handheld snacks also make a coffee break special and afternoon tea a real treat.*

—Julie Wood, Vancouver, Washington

1 cup fresh *or* frozen blueberries
1/2 cup chopped fresh *or* frozen cranberries
1 cup sugar, *divided*
1 package (8 ounces) cream cheese, softened
2 eggs
1 teaspoon vanilla extract
1 cup all-purpose flour
1 teaspoon baking soda
1/2 teaspoon salt
1/4 teaspoon ground nutmeg
TOPPING:
1/4 cup finely chopped walnuts *or* hazelnuts
1/4 cup flaked coconut
2 tablespoons brown sugar
1/4 teaspoon ground cinnamon

In a bowl, combine the blueberries, cranberries and 1/4 cup sugar; set aside. In a large mixing bowl, beat cream cheese and remaining sugar until smooth. Add eggs, one at a time, beating well after each addition. Beat in vanilla. Combine the flour, baking soda, salt and nutmeg; add to the creamed mixture. Fold in the berry mixture. Fill greased or paper-lined muffin cups two-thirds full.

Combine topping ingredients; sprinkle over batter. Bake at 400° for 18-20 minutes or until a toothpick comes out clean. Cool for 5 minutes before removing to a wire rack. **Yield:** 1 dozen.

**Editor's Note:** Muffins may be baked in miniature muffin cups for 10-12 minutes; recipe makes 4 dozen. If using frozen berries, do not thaw.

## Banana Bran Muffins

**Ready in 1 hour or less**

*Several years ago, I experimented with a banana muffin recipe by adding bran cereal. I loved the results and have been making this flavorful version ever since. Try replacing the chocolate chips and nuts with chopped dates for a delicious change of pace.*

—Alyce Wyman
Pembina, North Dakota

1/2 cup butter *or* margarine, softened
1 cup sugar
2 eggs
3 medium ripe bananas, mashed
1/2 cup buttermilk
1-1/2 cups all-purpose flour
1-1/2 teaspoons baking soda
1/2 teaspoon salt
4 cups Raisin Bran
1 cup miniature semisweet chocolate chips
1/2 cup chopped pecans

In a mixing bowl, cream butter and sugar. Add the eggs, bananas and buttermilk. Combine the flour, baking soda and salt; stir into creamed mixture just until moistened. Fold in the cereal, chocolate chips and pecans. Fill greased or paper-lined muffin cups two-thirds full.

Bake at 350° for 23-25 minutes or until a toothpick comes out clean. Cool for 5 minutes before removing from pans to wire racks. **Yield:** 2 dozen.

# Bread at The Touch Of a Button

NOTHING BEATS the mouth-watering aroma and old-fashioned flavor of homemade yeast bread, rolls and other baked goods. But preparing them from scratch can be taxing when time is tight.

That's why savvy cooks keep their bread machines close at hand. It's a snap to toss the ingredients in the pan, turn on the switch and make a simple check. The step-saving appliance does the kneading for you, so your family can be enjoying fresh bread in no time.

**Editor's Note:** Recipes were tested in a Regal brand bread machine and in a West Bend or Black & Decker bread machine.

## Carrot Raisin Bread

### (Pictured below)

*Grated carrot adds color and interest to this wheat bread that's good when spread with butter and served with a hearty soup.* —Dolores Tommer, Frankfort, Kansas

        1 cup water (70° to 80°)
        2 tablespoons butter *or* margarine, softened
    1/2 cup grated carrot
        2 tablespoons nonfat dry milk powder
    1-1/2 teaspoons salt
        3 tablespoons brown sugar
        2 cups whole wheat flour

Carrot Raisin Bread

        1 cup bread flour
        2 teaspoons active dry yeast
    1/3 cup chopped walnuts
    1/2 cup raisins

In bread machine pan, place the first nine ingredients in order suggested by manufacturer. Select basic bread setting. Choose crust color and loaf size if available. Bake according to bread machine directions (check dough after 5 minutes of mixing; add 1 to 2 tablespoons of water or flour if needed). Just before final kneading (your machine may audibly signal this), add walnuts and raisins. **Yield:** 1 loaf (2 pounds).

## Family-Favorite Bread

*I received this wonderful recipe from a friend and now make it more than any other loaf in my bread machine.*
—Dawn Glynn, Twin Bridges, Montana

    2/3 cup water (70° to 80°)
        2 tablespoons white vinegar
    1/2 cup sour cream
        1 tablespoon sugar
    1-1/2 teaspoons salt
        3 cups bread flour
    2-1/4 teaspoons active dry yeast

In bread machine pan, place all ingredients in order suggested by manufacturer. Select basic bread setting. Choose crust color and loaf size if available. Bake according to bread machine directions (check dough after 5 minutes of mixing; add 1 to 2 tablespoons of water or flour if needed). **Yield:** 1 loaf (about 1-1/2 pounds).

**Editor's Note:** If your bread machine has a time-delay feature, we recommend you do not use it for this recipe.

## Pineapple Bread

*This light loaf gets its subtle sweetness from pineapple juice. My daughter loves this bread. I frequently bake it after we've enjoyed a ham dinner, so we can use it for ham sandwiches.* —Marion Shelton, Nicholville, New York

        1 cup warm pineapple juice (70° to 80°)
        2 tablespoons water (70° to 80°)
        1 egg
        1 tablespoon butter *or* margarine, softened
        3 tablespoons sugar
        1 teaspoon salt
    3-1/4 cups bread flour
    2-1/4 teaspoons active dry yeast
        2 tablespoons finely chopped candied
            pineapple, optional

In bread machine pan, place the first eight ingredients in order suggested by manufacturer. Select basic bread setting. Choose crust color and loaf size if available. Bake according to bread machine directions (check dough after 5 minutes of mixing; add 1 to 2 tablespoons of water or flour if needed). Just before final kneading (your machine may audibly signal this), add the pineapple if desired. **Yield:** 1 loaf (1-1/2 pounds).

**Editor's Note:** If your bread machine has a time-delay feature, we recommend you do not use it for this recipe.

**Poppy Seed Lemon Bread**

Picture caption: Poppy Seed Lemon Bread

## Poppy Seed Lemon Bread

*(Pictured above)*

*A mild lemon flavor comes through in this tall loaf flecked with poppy seeds. Slices are good spread with nutmeg butter or cream cheese.*
—Claudine Moffatt
Manchester, Missouri

3/4 cup water (70° to 80°)
1 egg
3 tablespoons lemon juice
3 tablespoons butter (no substitutes), softened
3 tablespoons sugar
1 tablespoon grated lemon peel
3/4 teaspoon salt
3 cups bread flour
2 tablespoons poppy seeds
1/4 teaspoon ground nutmeg
2-1/4 teaspoons active dry yeast
NUTMEG BUTTER:
1/2 cup butter, softened
1/2 cup confectioners' sugar
1/4 teaspoon ground nutmeg

In bread machine pan, place the first 11 ingredients in order suggested by manufacturer. Select basic bread setting. Choose crust color and loaf size if available. Bake according to bread machine directions (check dough after 5 minutes of mixing; add 1 to 2 tablespoons of water or flour if needed).

In a small mixing bowl, combine nutmeg butter ingredients; beat until blended. Refrigerate until serving. **Yield:** 1 loaf (1-1/2 pounds).

**Editor's Note:** If your bread machine has a time-delay feature, we recommend you do not use it for this recipe.

Hawaiian Dinner Rolls

## Hawaiian Dinner Rolls

*(Pictured above)*

*Sunny pineapple and chewy coconut give a subtle sweetness to these golden rolls. They're super with a ham dinner. If there are any leftovers, they're also great for sandwiches.*
—*Kathy Kurtz*
*Glendora, California*

1 can (8 ounces) crushed pineapple, undrained
1/4 cup warm pineapple juice (70° to 80°)
1/4 cup water (70° to 80°)
1 egg
1/4 cup butter *or* margarine, cubed
1/4 cup nonfat dry milk powder
1 tablespoon sugar
1-1/2 teaspoons salt
3-1/4 cups bread flour
2-1/4 teaspoons active dry yeast
3/4 cup flaked coconut

In bread machine pan, place the first 10 ingredients in order suggested by manufacturer. Select dough setting (check dough after 5 minutes of mixing; add 1 to 2 tablespoons of water or flour if needed). Just before final kneading (your machine may audibly signal this), add coconut.

When cycle is complete, turn dough onto a lightly floured surface. Cover with plastic wrap; let rest for 10 minutes. Divide into 15 portions; roll each into a ball. Place in a greased 13-in. x 9-in. x 2-in. baking pan. Cover and let rise in a warm place for 45 minutes or until doubled. Bake at 375° for 15-20 minutes or until golden brown. **Yield:** 15 rolls.

**Editor's Note:** If your bread machine has a time-delay feature, we recommend you do not use it for this recipe.

## Parmesan Herb Bread

*I modified a recipe to come up with this savory bread that my family loves. A loaf does not last long. In fact, they begin cutting it while it's still hot!* —Dolores Bell
Belleview, Florida

    1 cup water (70° to 80°)
    3 tablespoons butter *or* margarine
    1 egg, beaten
    2 tablespoons sugar
    1 teaspoon salt
    1 teaspoon garlic powder
    1 teaspoon dried oregano
  1/2 teaspoon dried basil
  1/4 teaspoon dried marjoram
  1/4 teaspoon dried tarragon
  1/4 teaspoon dill weed
  1/8 teaspoon dried thyme
  2/3 cup grated Parmesan cheese
    3 cups bread flour
2-1/4 teaspoons active dry yeast

In bread machine pan, place all ingredients in order suggested by manufacturer. Select basic bread setting. Choose crust color and loaf size if available. Bake according to bread machine directions (check dough after 5 minutes of mixing; add 1 to 2 tablespoons of water or flour if needed). **Yield:** 1 loaf (1-1/2 pounds).

**Editor's Note:** If your bread machine has a time-delay feature, we recommend you do not use it for this recipe.

## Date-Nut Yeast Bread

*For a special breakfast treat, try this bread toasted, buttered and topped with cinnamon-sugar. It's delicious!*
—Roseanne Farulli, Burgettstown, Pennsylvania

    1 cup plus 2 tablespoons water (70° to 80°)
    2 tablespoons brown sugar
    1 tablespoon butter *or* margarine
1-1/2 teaspoons salt
3-1/4 cups bread flour
2-1/4 teaspoons active dry yeast
  1/2 cup chopped dates
  1/4 cup chopped walnuts

In bread machine pan, place the first six ingredients in order suggested by manufacturer. Select basic bread setting. Choose crust color and loaf size if available. Bake according to bread machine directions (check dough after 5 minutes of mixing; add 1 to 2 tablespoons of water or flour if needed).

Just before the final kneading (your machine may audibly signal this), add dates and walnuts. **Yield:** 1 loaf (1-1/2 pounds).

## Nutty Wheat Bread

*We prefer whole wheat bread, but sometimes it can taste a bit plain. I added pecans and walnuts to give this loaf wonderful flavor.* —Amy Pennington, San Antonio, Texas

✔ Uses less fat, sugar or salt. Includes Nutritional Analysis and Diabetic Exchanges.

    1 cup water (70° to 80°)
    2 tablespoons honey
    2 tablespoons molasses
    2 tablespoons olive *or* canola oil
1-1/2 teaspoons salt
    1 cup whole wheat flour
    2 cups bread flour
2-1/4 teaspoons active dry yeast
  1/3 cup chopped pecans
  1/3 cup chopped walnuts

In bread machine pan, place the first eight ingredients in order suggested by manufacturer. Select basic bread setting. Choose crust color and loaf size if available. Bake according to bread machine directions (check dough after 5 minutes of mixing; add 1 to 2 tablespoons of water or flour if needed).

Just before the final kneading (your machine may audibly signal this), add the pecans and walnuts. **Yield:** 1 loaf (1-1/2 pounds, 12 slices).

**Nutritional Analysis:** One slice equals 187 calories, 7 g fat (1 g saturated fat), 0 cholesterol, 296 mg sodium, 28 g carbohydrate, 2 g fiber, 5 g protein. **Diabetic Exchanges:** 2 starch, 1/2 fat.

## White Rice Bread

*If you like potato bread, you're sure to enjoy this soft moist specialty.* —Lorraine Dallmann
Thief River Falls, Minnesota

    1 cup water (70° to 80°)
    1 tablespoon sugar
4-1/2 teaspoons butter *or* margarine
    1 teaspoon salt
    3 cups bread flour
2-1/4 teaspoons active dry yeast
    1 cup cooked white rice, cooled

In bread machine pan, place the first six ingredients in order suggested by manufacturer. Select basic bread setting. Choose crust color and loaf size if available. Bake according to bread machine directions (check dough after 5 minutes of mixing; add 1 to 2 tablespoons of water or flour if needed).

Pat rice with paper towels until dry. Just before the final kneading (your machine may audibly signal this), add rice. **Yield:** 1 loaf (about 1-1/2 pounds).

## Great Garlic Bread

To save time and avoid leftovers, I prepare several half loaves of garlic bread at a time and freeze them.

I slice two loaves of French bread lengthwise and then widthwise. I spread a mixture of garlic, butter and cheese on the cut sides and place the tops and bottoms together.

I wrap these four small loaves individually in heavy-duty foil and freezer bags or place them in an airtight freezer container. When I want to serve garlic bread, I just pull one out to thaw and broil it.

—Shelli Deckard, Glendale, Arizona

Raisin Bran Bread

## Raisin Bran Bread

*(Pictured above)*

*You won't even realize you're getting bran cereal in your diet when you sample this fantastic bread. It is moist and slightly sweet from raisins. Grab a few yummy slices when you need to have breakfast on the run.*
—Jean Daviau
*San Jacinto, California*

  1 cup plus 1 tablespoon water (70° to 80°)
1/4 cup packed brown sugar
  2 tablespoons butter *or* margarine, softened
1/2 teaspoon salt
1/4 teaspoon baking soda
1-1/2 cups Raisin Bran
2-1/4 cups bread flour
2-1/4 teaspoons active dry yeast
1/2 cup raisins

In bread machine pan, place the first eight ingredients in order suggested by manufacturer. Select basic bread setting. Choose crust color and loaf size if available. Bake according to bread machine directions (check dough after 5 minutes of mixing; add 1 to 2 tablespoons of water or flour if needed).

Just before the final kneading (your machine may audibly signal this), add the raisins. **Yield:** 1 loaf (1-1/2 pounds).

## Cornmeal Molasses Bread

*You're sure to appreciate the nice texture and mild molasses flavor in this golden loaf.* —Elizabeth Betterman
*Long Prairie, Minnesota*

  1 cup water (70° to 80°)
1/4 cup molasses
  1 tablespoon vegetable oil
1/4 cup cornmeal
1/2 teaspoon salt
  3 cups bread flour
2-1/4 teaspoons active dry yeast

In bread machine pan, place all ingredients in order suggested by manufacturer. Select basic bread setting. Choose crust color and loaf size if available. Bake according to bread machine directions (check dough after 5 minutes of mixing; add 1 to 2 tablespoons of water or flour if needed). **Yield:** 1 loaf (1-1/2 pounds).

## Bread Bowls

*I never thought it could be this easy to make bread bowls at home. While the dough is mixing and rising, you have time to stir up a thick soup or chili to fill the bowls.*
—Renee Keller, Dodgeville, Wisconsin

  1 cup plus 3 tablespoons water (70° to 80°)
  2 tablespoons olive *or* vegetable oil
1/4 cup grated Parmesan cheese
  1 teaspoon sugar

1 teaspoon salt
3 cups bread flour
2-1/2 teaspoons active dry yeast

In bread machine pan, place all ingredients in order suggested by manufacturer. Select dough setting (check after 5 minutes of mixing; add 1 to 2 tablespoons of water or flour if needed).

When the cycle is completed, turn dough onto a lightly floured surface. Divide into fourths; shape each into a ball. Place on a greased baking sheet. Cover and let rise in a warm place until doubled, about 30 minutes.

Bake at 400° for 15-20 minutes or until golden brown. Cool. Cut the top fourth off each roll; carefully hollow out bottom, leaving a 1/4-in. shell (discard removed bread or save for another use). Fill with chili, chowder or stew. **Yield:** 4 servings.

## Granola Wheat Bread

*Whole wheat flour and granola add wholesome goodness to this moist bread. With its not-too-sweet taste, it's nice topped with jam, jelly, cream cheese or honey butter for breakfast.* —Star Pooley, Paradise, California

1 cup water (70° to 80°)
2/3 cup unsweetened applesauce
1 tablespoon butter *or* margarine, softened
3/4 teaspoon salt
2-1/4 cups whole wheat flour
1-1/4 cups all-purpose flour
3/4 cup granola cereal without raisins
1/3 cup nonfat dry milk powder
4 teaspoons brown sugar
3/4 teaspoon ground cinnamon
1-1/2 teaspoons active dry yeast

In bread machine pan, place all ingredients in order suggested by manufacturer. Select basic bread setting. Choose crust color and loaf size if available. Bake according to bread machine directions (check dough after 5 minutes of mixing; add 1 to 2 tablespoons of water or flour if needed). **Yield:** 1 loaf (2 pounds).

## Gingered White Bread

*My bread machine makes a 1-pound loaf, which is just the right size for me since I live alone. This compact loaf has a hint of ginger.* —Lois Lovejoy, Waupun, Wisconsin

3/4 cup water (70° to 80°)
2 tablespoons vegetable oil
2 tablespoons honey
1 teaspoon salt
2-1/2 cups bread flour
2 tablespoons nonfat dry milk powder
1/4 teaspoon ground ginger
1-1/2 teaspoons active dry yeast

In bread machine pan, place all ingredients in order suggested by manufacturer. Select basic bread setting. Choose crust color and loaf size if available. Bake according to bread machine directions (check dough after 5 minutes of mixing; add 1 to 2 tablespoons water or flour if needed). **Yield:** 1 loaf (1 pound).

## Pizza Bread

*(Pictured below)*

*This flavorful bread is delicious by itself. But my husband likes to spoon a little pizza sauce on a slice, sprinkle it with mozzarella cheese and microwave it until the cheese melts.*
—Rena Malek, Dubuque, Iowa

3/4 cup water (70° to 80°)
2 tablespoons dried minced onion
1 tablespoon nonfat dry milk powder
1 tablespoon sugar
1 tablespoon butter *or* margarine, softened
1 teaspoon salt
1/2 teaspoon garlic powder
1/2 teaspoon dried oregano
2 cups bread flour
2 teaspoons active dry yeast
1/3 cup chopped pepperoni
1/4 cup chopped canned mushrooms
1/4 cup shredded mozzarella cheese
2 teaspoons grated Parmesan cheese

In bread machine pan, place the first 10 ingredients in order suggested by manufacturer. Select basic bread setting. Choose crust color and loaf size if available. Bake according to bread machine directions (check dough after 5 minutes of mixing; add 1 to 2 tablespoons of water or flour if needed).

Just before the final kneading (your machine may audibly signal this), add the pepperoni, mushrooms and cheeses. **Yield:** 1 loaf (1 pound).

Pizza Bread

# Chapter 12

# Snappy Soups, Salads & Sandwiches

LIP-SMACKING LUNCHES and super suppers are mere minutes away when you start with fast-to-fix soups, salads and sandwiches. When time is at a premium, these mouth-watering mainstays are ideal for lunch, dinner or snacks in between.

Meal planning is a snap when you add one or more of the rapid recipes here to your menu.

All of these simple-to-make soups, speedy salads and shortcut sandwiches are family favorites, undeniably delicious and surprisingly filling.

**SPEED EATING.** Clockwise from upper left: Herbed Onion Salad Dressing, Sausage Tomato Soup and Italian Chicken Pockets (all recipes on p. 195).

## Italian Subs

*(Pictured at right)*

**Plan ahead...needs to chill**

*Olive lovers will certainly rejoice over this hearty stacked sandwich! Marinate stuffed and ripe olives in white wine vinegar and garlic before using them to flavor these speedy salami, ham and provolone subs.*
*—Delores Christner Spooner, Wisconsin*

  1/3 cup olive *or* vegetable oil
4-1/2 teaspoons white wine vinegar
     *or* cider vinegar
    1 tablespoon dried parsley flakes
    2 to 3 garlic cloves, minced
    1 can (2-1/4 ounces) sliced ripe olives, drained
  1/2 cup chopped stuffed olives
    6 submarine sandwich buns (10 inches), split
  24 thin slices hard salami
  24 slices provolone *or* mozzarella cheese
  24 thin slices fully cooked ham
Lettuce leaves, optional

In a bowl, combine the oil, vinegar, parsley and garlic. Stir in olives. Cover and refrigerate for 8 hours or overnight.

    Place about 2 tablespoons olive mixture on the bottom of each bun. Top each with four slices of salami, cheese and ham; add lettuce if desired. Replace tops. **Yield:** 6 servings.

## Spinach Mushroom Salad

*(Pictured at right)*

**Plan ahead...needs to chill**

*It takes only minutes to put together this salad's tangy citrus and herb dressing. A vinaigrette of basil, oregano and sage complements the crisp spinach and fresh mushrooms.*
*—Lynn Larkin, Sterling Heights, Michigan*

    5 tablespoons olive *or* vegetable oil
    1 tablespoon lemon juice
    1 tablespoon lime juice
1-1/2 teaspoons white wine vinegar *or* cider
     vinegar
    1 garlic clove, minced
  3/4 teaspoon minced fresh parsley
  1/4 teaspoon salt
  1/4 teaspoon ground mustard
  1/8 teaspoon dried basil
  1/8 teaspoon dried oregano
  1/8 teaspoon rubbed sage
Dash to 1/8 teaspoon coarsely ground pepper
    8 medium fresh mushrooms, sliced
    7 cups torn fresh spinach

In a small bowl, combine the first 12 ingredients; mix well. Add mushrooms and toss to coat. Cover and refrigerate for at least 30 minutes. Just before serving, toss the spinach and mushroom mixture in a salad bowl. **Yield:** 6 servings.

## Black-Eyed Pea Soup

*(Pictured at right)*

**Ready in 45 minutes or less**

*Even people who generally don't care for black-eyed peas will enjoy them in this chunky meatless soup. It's deliciously different. With a crusty loaf of bread, it makes a heartwarming meal for those cold winter days.*
*—Donna Ambrose, Mt. Wolf, Pennsylvania*

    4 bacon strips, diced
    1 medium green pepper, chopped
    1 small onion, chopped
    2 garlic cloves, minced
    2 cans (15-1/2 ounces *each*) black-eyed peas, undrained
    2 cans (14-1/2 ounces *each*) diced tomatoes, undrained
    1 cup water
1-1/2 teaspoons salt
    1 to 1-1/4 teaspoons ground cumin
    1 to 1-1/4 teaspoons ground mustard
    1 teaspoon chili powder
  1/2 teaspoon curry powder
  1/2 teaspoon pepper
  1/4 to 1/2 teaspoon sugar, optional
Shredded Colby-Monterey Jack cheese and
  minced fresh parsley

In a large saucepan, cook bacon over medium heat until crisp; remove to paper towels. Drain, reserving 1 tablespoon drippings. In the drippings, saute the green pepper, onion and garlic until tender.

    Add peas, tomatoes, water and seasonings. Bring to a boil. Reduce heat; cover and simmer for 15-20 minutes. Sprinkle with cheese, parsley and bacon. **Yield:** 8 servings (2 quarts).

## Hot Ham 'n' Egg Sandwiches

**Ready in 30 minutes or less**

*Hard-cooked eggs and chopped ham take center stage in these warm sandwiches. I have relied on this rapid recipe since my mother-in-law shared it with me. It fits my busy schedule perfectly.*
*—Barbara Adams North Andover, Massachusetts*

    1 cup finely chopped fully cooked ham
    2 cups (8 ounces) shredded cheddar cheese
    1 small onion, chopped
  1/3 cup chopped stuffed olives
    2 hard-cooked eggs, chopped
  1/2 cup chili sauce
    3 tablespoons mayonnaise
    8 hot dog buns

In a bowl, combine the ham, cheese, onion, olives and eggs. Stir in chili sauce and mayonnaise. Place about 1/3 cupful in each bun; wrap individually in foil. Place on a baking sheet. Bake at 400° for 10 minutes or until heated through. **Yield:** 8 servings.

**Black-Eyed Pea Soup**
**Italian Subs**
**Spinach Mushroom Salad**

Hot Ham and Pineapple Sub
Antipasto Salad
Beefy Tomato Pasta Soup

## Antipasto Salad

*(Pictured at left)*

**Ready in 30 minutes or less**

*This salad is packed with pizza ingredients. It's always a hit at gatherings. And it's so flexible. I've used spinach instead of lettuce and pepperoni in place of salami.*
*—Crystal Ranft, Forestville, New York*

- 6 cups torn leaf lettuce
- 8 ounces hard salami, julienned
- 6 ounces provolone cheese, julienned
- 1 cup (4 ounces) shredded mozzarella cheese
- 2 medium tomatoes, chopped
- 1 can (6 ounces) pitted ripe olives, drained and halved
- 1 tablespoon minced chives
- 1 can (8 ounces) tomato sauce
- 1/2 cup vegetable oil
- 1/4 cup red wine vinegar *or* cider vinegar
- 1 teaspoon sugar
- 1 teaspoon salt
- 1 teaspoon dried oregano
- 1/2 teaspoon garlic powder
- 1/4 teaspoon pepper

Place the lettuce on a large serving platter. Arrange the salami, cheeses, tomatoes and olives over top. Sprinkle with chives. In a blender, combine the remaining ingredients; cover and process until smooth. Drizzle over salad. **Yield:** 8-10 servings.

## Beefy Tomato Pasta Soup

*(Pictured at left)*

**Ready in 1 hour or less**

*If you're a fan of Italian fare, you'll like this chunky satisfying soup, and it's easier to fix than lasagna.*
*—Nancy Rollag, Kewaskum, Wisconsin*

✓ Uses less fat, sugar or salt. Includes Nutritional Analysis and Diabetic Exchanges.

- 1 pound ground beef
- 2 medium green peppers, cut into 1-inch chunks
- 1 medium onion, cut into chunks
- 2 garlic cloves, minced
- 5 to 6 cups water
- 2 cans (14-1/2 ounces *each*) Italian diced tomatoes, undrained
- 1 can (6 ounces) tomato paste
- 1 tablespoon brown sugar
- 2 to 3 teaspoons Italian seasoning
- 1 teaspoon salt
- 1/4 teaspoon pepper
- 2 cups uncooked spiral pasta
- Croutons, optional

In a Dutch oven or soup kettle, cook the beef, green peppers, onion and garlic over medium heat until meat is no longer pink; drain. Add the water, tomatoes, tomato paste, brown sugar, Italian seasoning, salt and pepper. Bring to a boil. Add pasta. Cook for 10-14 minutes or until pasta is tender, stirring occasionally. Serve with croutons if desired. **Yield:** 10 servings (about 2-1/2 quarts).

**Nutritional Analysis:** One 1-cup serving (prepared with lean ground beef; calculated without croutons) equals 207 calories, 5 g fat (2 g saturated fat), 17 mg cholesterol, 718 mg sodium, 28 g carbohydrate, 3 g fiber, 13 g protein. **Diabetic Exchanges:** 2 starch, 1 meat.

## Hot Ham and Pineapple Sub

*(Pictured at left)*

**Ready in 1 hour or less**

*I love homemade ham and pineapple pizza, but I don't care to make the pizza crust. So I came up with this sub sandwich that has the same flavors but is a snap to put together.*
*—Julie Valdez, Walnut Hill, Florida*

- 1 tube (11 ounces) refrigerated crusty French loaf
- 2 tablespoons vegetable oil
- 1 teaspoon Italian seasoning
- 1/4 teaspoon garlic salt
- 1 can (8 ounces) pizza sauce, *divided*
- 1/3 pound sliced deli ham
- 1 can (8 ounces) crushed pineapple, drained
- 1 cup (4 ounces) shredded mozzarella cheese

Place the French loaf dough seam side down on a lightly greased baking sheet. With a sharp knife, cut six slashes, about 1/2 in. deep, on top of dough. Bake at 350° for 25-30 minutes or until golden brown. Combine the oil, Italian seasoning and garlic salt; brush over hot bread. Cool on a wire rack for 8 minutes.

Split bread in half lengthwise. Hollow out bottom half, leaving a 1/4-in. shell (discard removed bread or save for another use). Spread 2-3 tablespoons of pizza sauce over shell; top with the ham, pineapple and cheese. Replace bread top. Bake for 6-8 minutes or until cheese is melted. Heat the remaining pizza sauce; serve with the sandwich. **Yield:** 4-6 servings.

## Honey Mustard Dressing

**Ready in 15 minutes or less**

*With only six ingredients, his creamy dressing is so easy to whip up. It's a great way to top off a green salad tossed with grapes or grapefruit segments. Dijon mustard provides the lively taste. We enjoy the homemade goodness.* *—Carol Severson Shelton, Washington*

- 1/3 cup honey
- 1/4 cup Dijon mustard
- 1/4 cup white wine vinegar *or* cider vinegar
- 2 tablespoons lemon juice
- 1 garlic clove, minced
- 1 cup vegetable oil

In a blender, combine the first five ingredients. While processing, gradually add oil in a steady stream until smooth and creamy. Store in the refrigerator. **Yield:** 2 cups.

## Triple-Decker Salmon Club

*(Pictured at right)*

**Ready in 15 minutes or less**

*You're in for a tasty treat with these deliciously different triple-deckers. My guests love it when I serve these tall short-on-time sandwiches. Even those who don't ordinarily like salmon or cottage cheese seem to enjoy them.* —Jane Bone
Cape Coral, Florida

3/4 cup small-curd cottage cheese
1/4 cup dill pickle relish
1 can (6 ounces) salmon, drained, bones and skin removed
1 celery rib, chopped
6 slices bread, toasted
2 lettuce leaves, optional

In a small bowl, combine cottage cheese and pickle relish. In another bowl, combine salmon and celery. For each sandwich, top one piece of toast with lettuce if desired and half of the cottage cheese mixture. Top with a second piece of toast; spread with half of the salmon mixture. Top with a third piece of toast. Serve immediately. **Yield:** 2 servings.

## Chicken Salad in Melon Rings

*(Pictured at right)*

**Ready in 30 minutes or less**

*This refreshing salad is sure to please everyone at your next luncheon. It's eye-catching and easy to prepare, requiring less time in the kitchen so you have more time to spend with your friends.* —Kim Ozak, Winnipeg, Manitoba

✓ Uses less fat, sugar or salt. Includes Nutritional Analysis and Diabetic Exchanges.

4 cups cubed cooked chicken
3 tablespoons lemon juice
1 cup sliced celery
1 cup halved seedless grapes
1/3 cup chopped onion
1/3 to 1/2 cup vinaigrette *or* salad dressing of your choice
1/4 cup sliced almonds, toasted
1 tablespoon diced pimientos
1/4 teaspoon salt
1/8 teaspoon pepper
Lettuce leaves
6 cantaloupe rings (1-1/2 inches thick), peeled

In a bowl, toss the chicken and lemon juice. Add the celery, grapes, onion, dressing, almonds, pimientos, salt and pepper; mix well. Cover and refrigerate. Just before serving, arrange lettuce on salad plates; top each with a melon ring. Fill center with chicken salad. **Yield:** 6 servings.

**Nutritional Analysis:** One serving (1 melon ring with 1 cup chicken salad, prepared with 1/3 cup fat-free salad dressing) equals 278 calories, 10 g fat (2 g saturated fat), 79 mg cholesterol, 346 mg sodium, 18 g carbohydrate, 2 g fiber, 30 g protein. **Diabetic Exchanges:** 4 lean meat, 1 fruit, 1 fat.

## Asparagus Soup

*(Pictured at right)*

**Ready in 30 minutes or less**

*My kids wouldn't eat asparagus when they were young. But after trying this smooth creamy soup, they all wanted seconds. To hurry along preparation I rely on frozen asparagus.* —Lois McAtee, Oceanside, California

1 package (10 ounces) frozen asparagus cuts
1 large onion, chopped
1 cup water
1 teaspoon salt
1 teaspoon chicken bouillon granules
1/2 teaspoon dried basil
1/8 teaspoon white pepper
1-1/2 cups milk
1/2 cup whipping cream
Seasoned salad croutons

In a saucepan, combine the asparagus, onion, water, salt, bouillon, basil and pepper. Bring to a boil. Reduce heat; cover and simmer for 10-12 minutes or until vegetables are tender. Cool for 5 minutes; stir in milk.

In a blender or food processor, process the soup in batches until smooth; return to the pan. Stir in cream; heat through. Garnish with croutons. **Yield:** 4-6 servings.

## Catalina Rice Salad

**Plan ahead...needs to chill**

*Crisp peppers, chunks of ham and kidney beans make this one of the heartiest rice salads you'll ever sample. I top off the colorful combination with a bottle of Catalina dressing that I add zip to with cayenne pepper.*
—Sharon McClatchey, Muskogee, Oklahoma

✓ Uses less fat, sugar or salt. Includes Nutritional Analysis and Diabetic Exchanges.

2-1/2 cups cooked long grain rice
1 can (16 ounces) kidney beans, rinsed and drained
1 cup cubed fully cooked ham
1/2 cup *each* chopped sweet red, green and yellow pepper
1/2 cup chopped red onion
1 bottle (8 ounces) Catalina salad dressing
1/4 teaspoon cayenne pepper

In a bowl, combine the rice, beans, ham, peppers and onion. Combine the salad dressing and cayenne; pour over rice mixture and toss to coat. Cover and refrigerate for 1 hour before serving. **Yield:** 8 servings.

**Nutritional Analysis:** One 3/4-cup serving (prepared with fat-free Catalina dressing) equals 182 calories, 1 g fat (trace saturated fat), 5 mg cholesterol, 688 mg sodium, 34 g carbohydrate, 3 g fiber, 8 g protein. **Diabetic Exchanges:** 2 starch, 1/2 lean meat.

Chicken Salad in Melon Rings
Asparagus Soup
Triple-Decker Salmon Club

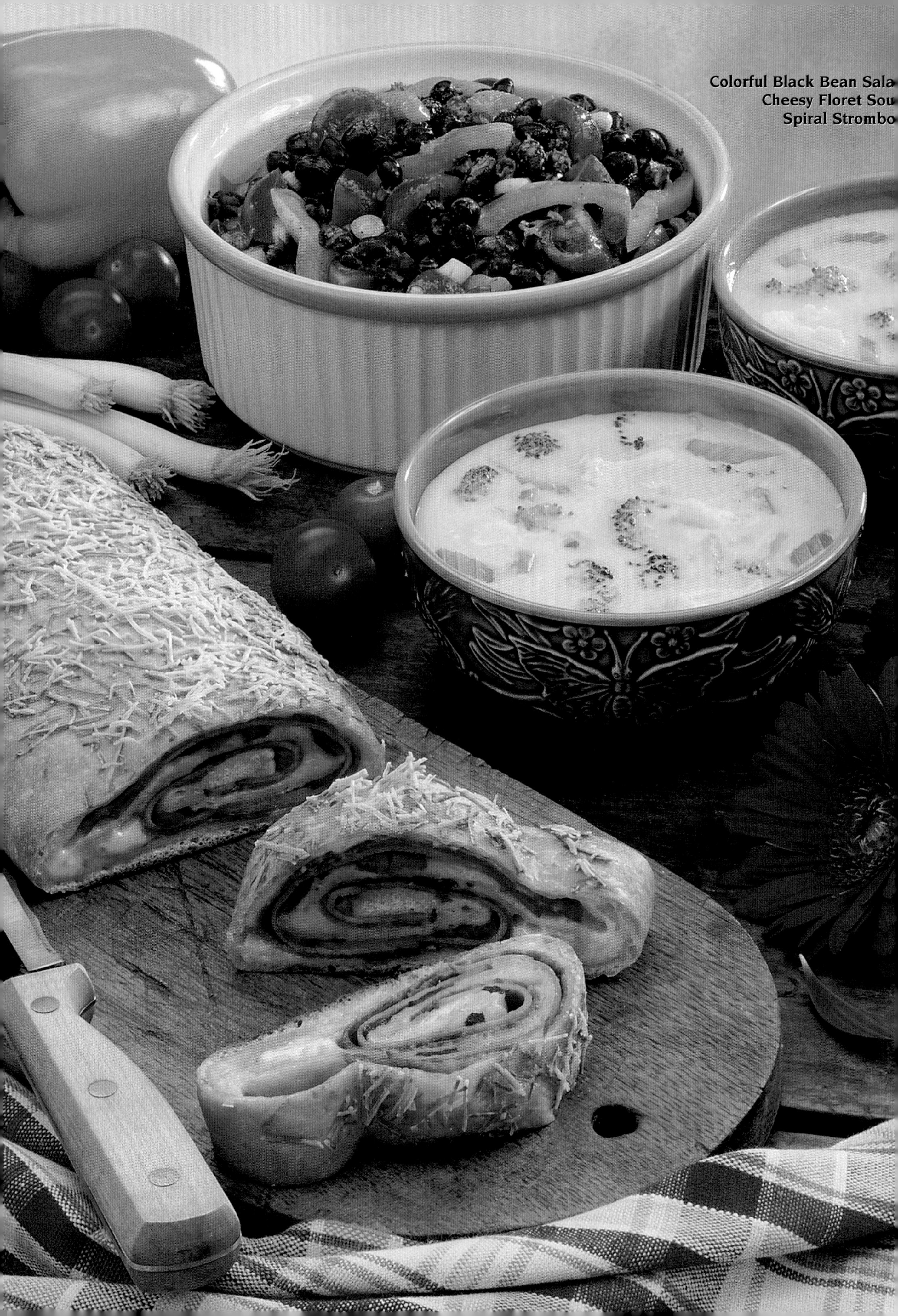

Colorful Black Bean Sala
Cheesy Floret Sou
Spiral Strombo

## Colorful Black Bean Salad

*(Pictured at left)*

**Ready in 15 minutes or less**

*Cherry tomatoes and yellow pepper add brilliant splashes of color to this wonderful black bean salad. I like to let the mixture stand for at least 15 minutes before serving to allow the flavors to blend. It's a fun salad for a picnic or potluck.*
—*Laurie Mace, Los Osos, California*

✓ Uses less fat, sugar or salt. Includes Nutritional Analysis and Diabetic Exchanges.

    2 cans (15 ounces *each*) black beans, rinsed
      and drained
    1 pint cherry tomatoes, quartered
    1 medium sweet yellow *or* green pepper,
      julienned
    4 green onions, chopped
    3 tablespoons minced fresh cilantro *or* parsley
DRESSING:
    3 tablespoons lemon juice
    2 tablespoons olive *or* canola oil
    1 garlic clove, minced
  3/4 teaspoon ground cumin
  1/2 teaspoon salt
  1/4 teaspoon pepper

In a salad bowl, combine the beans, tomatoes, yellow pepper, onions and cilantro. In a jar with a tight-fitting lid, combine dressing ingredients; shake well. Drizzle over vegetables and toss to coat. Chill until serving. **Yield:** 8 servings.
**Nutritional Analysis:** One serving (3/4 cup) equals 137 calories, 4 g fat (trace saturated fat), 0 cholesterol, 480 mg sodium, 18 g carbohydrate, 7 g fiber, 6 g protein. **Diabetic Exchanges:** 1 starch, 1 lean meat.

## Cheesy Floret Soup

*(Pictured at left)*

**Ready in 45 minutes or less**

*I received the recipe for this creamy comforting soup from my mom, and my family requests it often. I like that it includes both broccoli and cauliflower. This cheesy blend is especially good with crusty French bread.* —*Janice Russell Kingfisher, Oklahoma*

    3 cups fresh broccoli florets
    3 cups fresh cauliflowerets
    3 celery ribs, sliced
    1 small onion, chopped
    2 cups water
  1/2 teaspoon celery salt
    3 tablespoons butter *or* margarine
    3 tablespoons all-purpose flour
2-1/3 cups milk
    1 pound process cheese (Velveeta), cubed

In a large saucepan, combine the first six ingredients. Bring to a boil. Reduce heat; cover and simmer for 12-15 minutes or until vegetables are tender.
Meanwhile, in a small saucepan, melt butter; stir in flour until smooth. Gradually stir in milk. Bring to a boil; cook and stir for 2 minutes or until thickened. Reduce heat; add cheese. Cook and stir until cheese is melted. Drain vegetables; add cheese sauce and heat through. **Yield:** 4-6 servings.

## Spiral Stromboli

*(Pictured at left)*

**Ready in 45 minutes or less**

*I frequently fix this speedy sandwich on days we return from our cabin and it's suppertime when we get home. The stuffed loaf takes advantage of refrigerated dough, so it's easy to assemble for a meal, appetizer or late-night snack.*
—*Jean Gruenert, Burlington, Wisconsin*

    1 tube (11 ounces) refrigerated crusty
      French loaf
  3/4 to 1 cup shredded mozzarella cheese
  3/4 to 1 cup shredded cheddar cheese
  1/4 pound *each* thinly sliced deli salami
      and ham
  1/4 cup chopped roasted red peppers
      *or* 1 jar (2 ounces) pimientos, drained
    1 tablespoon butter *or* margarine, melted
2 to 3 tablespoons shredded Parmesan cheese

Unroll the dough and pat into a 14-in. x 12-in. rectangle. Sprinkle with mozzarella and cheddar cheeses to within 1/2 in. of edges; top with meat and red peppers. Roll up jelly-roll style, starting with a short side; seal seam and tuck ends under.
Place seam side down on an ungreased baking sheet. Brush with butter; sprinkle with Parmesan cheese. Bake at 375° for 25-30 minutes or until golden brown. Slice with a serrated knife. **Yield:** 4 servings.

## Shoepeg Corn Salad

**Plan ahead...needs to chill**

*I toss crunchy corn, red pepper, green onions and tomatoes with mayonnaise to make this simple yet special salad. This is a favorite in our household. It's also a big hit at church dinners. I never bring any home.* —*April Ingram Sweetwater, Tennessee*

    3 cans (11 ounces *each*) shoepeg corn, drained
    3 plum tomatoes, seeded and chopped
  1/2 cup thinly sliced green onions
  1/2 cup chopped sweet red pepper
  1/2 cup mayonnaise
  1/2 teaspoon salt
  1/8 teaspoon pepper

In a bowl, combine all ingredients. Cover and refrigerate for at least 1 hour. **Yield:** 6-8 servings.

## Antipasto Pasta Salad

*(Pictured at right)*

**Ready in 30 minutes or less**

*I received the recipe for this cool pasta salad from friends. A pleasant dressing complements the meats, veggies and cheese, making this colorful combination popular any time of year.* —Brenda Novak, New Holland, Pennsylvania

  3 cups uncooked tricolor spiral pasta
  4 ounces provolone cheese, cubed
  4 ounces sliced pepperoni, quartered
  4 ounces hard salami, cubed
  1 medium green pepper, diced
  2 celery ribs, chopped
  1 small onion, chopped
  1/2 cup cherry tomatoes, halved
  1/3 cup olive *or* vegetable oil
  1/4 cup cider vinegar
  1-1/2 teaspoons dried oregano
  3/4 teaspoon salt
  1/2 teaspoon pepper

Cook pasta according to package directions; drain and rinse in cold water. In a bowl, combine the pasta, cheese, pepperoni, salami, green pepper, celery, onion and tomatoes. In a jar with a tight-fitting lid, combine the remaining ingredients; shake well. Pour over pasta mixture and toss to coat. **Yield:** 10 servings.

## Parmesan Corn Chowder

*(Pictured at right)*

**Ready in 45 minutes or less**

*My mom made this thick soup when I was young. She passed the recipe on to me with a "Favorite Recipes Box" she created when I started college. That was 10 years ago, and the dish remains one of my favorites.*
—Michelle Kaiser, Bozeman, Montana

  2 cups water
  2 cups diced peeled potatoes
  1/2 cup sliced carrots
  1/2 cup sliced celery
  1/4 cup chopped onion
  1/4 cup butter *or* margarine
  1/4 cup all-purpose flour
  1 teaspoon salt
  1/2 teaspoon pepper
  2 cups milk
  1 can (14-3/4 ounces) cream-style corn
1-1/2 cups (6 ounces) shredded Parmesan cheese

In a large saucepan, combine the first five ingredients; bring to a boil. Reduce heat; cover and simmer for 12-15 minutes or until vegetables are tender (do not drain). Meanwhile, in a small saucepan, melt butter. Stir in flour, salt and pepper until smooth; gradually stir in milk. Bring to a boil; cook and stir for 2 minutes or until thickened. Stir into the vegetable mixture. Add corn and Parmesan cheese. Cook 10 minutes longer or until heated through. **Yield:** 7 servings.

## Pepper Steak Sandwiches

*(Pictured at right)*

**Ready in 30 minutes or less**

*My family loves these warm sandwiches that dress up deli roast beef with sauteed peppers, cheese and Italian salad dressing. Include a salad or soup and your meal is set.*
—Hosanna Miller, Dundee, Ohio

  1 medium onion, thinly sliced
  1 medium green pepper, thinly sliced
  1 medium sweet red pepper, thinly sliced
  1/2 cup mayonnaise, *divided*
  1/4 cup Italian salad dressing
  3/4 pound thinly sliced deli roast beef
  5 sandwich rolls, split
  3/4 cup shredded mozzarella cheese

In a large skillet, saute the onion and peppers in 2 tablespoons of mayonnaise until crisp-tender. Remove vegetables and keep warm.
  Reduce heat. Add the Italian dressing, roast beef and remaining mayonnaise to the skillet. Cook and stir until heated through, about 5 minutes. Place beef and vegetables on rolls; top with mozzarella cheese. **Yield:** 5 servings.

## Cauliflower Romaine Salad

**Ready in 30 minutes or less**

*I brown bread crumbs and grate fresh cauliflower for the top layer of this sensational salad that features a fast-to-fix Parmesan dressing. I make this unique salad for everything from potlucks to special occasions.*
—Eileen Blick, Andale, Kansas

  1 cup dry bread crumbs
  3 tablespoons butter *or* margarine
 10 cups torn romaine
  1 cup mayonnaise
  2 tablespoons grated Parmesan cheese
  1 tablespoon lemon juice
  1 garlic clove, minced
  1/4 teaspoon salt
  1/8 teaspoon pepper
1-3/4 cups coarsely grated cauliflower

In a small skillet, brown bread crumbs in butter; set aside. Place the romaine in a large salad bowl. In a small bowl, combine mayonnaise, Parmesan cheese, lemon juice, garlic, salt and pepper. Pour over romaine and toss to coat. Top with cauliflower and reserved crumbs. Serve immediately. **Yield:** 8-10 servings.

### Simple Salad

I save the liquid from bread and butter pickles to use in my three-bean salad. Just add the beans of your choice along with some chopped onion and green pepper to the juice. Then refrigerate to allow the flavors to blend. —Alice Komic, Warren, Michigan

Parmesan Corn Chowder
Antipasto Pasta Salad
Pepper Steak Sandwiches

Herbed Onion Salad Dressing
Sausage Tomato Soup
Italian Chicken Pocket

## Sausage Tomato Soup

*(Pictured at left and on page 183)*

**Ready in 45 minutes or less**

*We tasted soup a lot like this at a local restaurant. When I came across a recipe that sounded similar, I made a few changes to create this version.* —Marilyn Lee
Manhattan, Kansas

✓ Uses less fat, sugar or salt. Includes Nutritional Analysis and Diabetic Exchanges.

    1/2 pound bulk Italian sausage
      1 medium onion, chopped
      1 small green pepper, chopped
      1 can (28 ounces) diced tomatoes, undrained
      1 can (14-1/2 ounces) beef broth
      1 can (8 ounces) tomato sauce
    1/2 cup picante sauce
  1-1/2 teaspoons sugar
      1 teaspoon dried basil
    1/2 teaspoon dried oregano
    1/2 to 3/4 cup shredded mozzarella cheese

In a large saucepan, cook the sausage, onion and green pepper over medium heat until meat is no longer pink; drain. Stir in tomatoes, broth, tomato sauce, picante sauce, sugar, basil and oregano. Bring to a boil. Reduce heat; cover and simmer for 10 minutes. Sprinkle with cheese. **Yield:** 6 servings.
   **Nutritional Analysis:** One 1-cup serving (prepared with turkey sausage, reduced-sodium broth and 1/2 cup part-skim mozzarella) equals 161 calories, 6 g fat (2 g saturated fat), 26 mg cholesterol, 870 mg sodium, 16 g carbohydrate, 4 g fiber, 12 g protein. **Diabetic Exchanges:** 3 vegetable, 1 lean meat, 1/2 fat.

## Italian Chicken Pockets

*(Pictured at left and on page 182)*

**Ready in 15 minutes or less**

*At a gthering we attended, my sister-in-law prepared these hearty sandwiches that are filled with chicken, mushrooms and pepperoni. My husband loved them so much, he insisted I ask for the recipe.* —Tricia Buss
Sellersville, Pennsylvania

    3/4 pound boneless skinless chicken breast, cubed
      2 tablespoons olive *or* vegetable oil
      1 medium green pepper, chopped
      1 cup sliced fresh mushrooms
      1 package (3-1/2 ounces) sliced pepperoni
      1 cup spaghetti sauce
      3 pita breads (6 inches), halved and warmed
Grated Parmesan cheese, optional

In a large skillet, saute chicken in oil until no longer pink. Add the green pepper and mushrooms; cook until tender. Stir in pepperoni; heat through. Drain. Stir in spaghetti sauce; heat through. Spoon into pita bread halves. Sprinkle with Parmesan cheese if desired. **Yield:** 6 servings.

## Herbed Onion Salad Dressing

*(Pictured at left and on page 182)*

**Ready in 15 minutes or less**

*My dad is an excellent cook and this is one of his favorites. The slightly sweet dressing has plenty of onion flavor and a tasty blend of herbs.* —Nancy Fettig
Billings, Montana

    1/2 cup cider vinegar
  1-1/2 cups sugar
      1 large onion, cut into wedges
      2 teaspoons salt
      1 teaspoon celery seed
      1 teaspoon ground mustard
    1/4 teaspoon *each* dried basil, marjoram, oregano and thyme
    1/4 teaspoon dried rosemary, crushed
    1/4 teaspoon pepper
      2 cups vegetable oil

In a blender, combine the vinegar, sugar and onion; cover and process until smooth. Add the seasonings; cover and blend well. While processing, gradually add oil in a steady stream until dressing is thickened. Store in the refrigerator. **Yield:** 4 cups.

## Ham 'n' Egg Salad Subs

**Ready in 15 minutes or less**

*Friends often drop by after church, so these sandwiches are a delicious way to enjoy lunch while we're visiting.*
—Marian Aikema, Langley, British Columbia

      2 cups chopped fully cooked ham
      2 hard-cooked eggs, chopped
    1/2 cup mayonnaise
      3 tablespoons diced green onions
      2 tablespoons diced green pepper
      1 tablespoon dill pickle relish
      1 teaspoon prepared mustard
      1 teaspoon cider vinegar
    6 to 8 French *or* Italian sandwich rolls (5 to 6 inches), split
    3/4 cup shredded cheddar cheese

In a bowl, combine the first eight ingredients; mix well. Place bottom halves of rolls on a baking sheet; spread about 1/4 cup ham mixture on each. Sprinkle each with 2-3 tablespoons cheese. Broil for 1-2 minutes or until cheese is melted. Replace the roll tops. Broil 1 minute longer. **Yield:** 6-8 servings.

### No More Soggy Sandwiches

My daughter likes to take peanut butter and jelly sandwiches to school for lunch, but she doesn't like it when the bread gets soggy. So now we spread peanut butter on both slices of bread and then spread the jelly. The peanut butter doesn't allow the jelly to soak through the bread. —*Teresa Gilmore-Tedder*
*Rocky Point, North Carolina*

# Chapter 13

END YOUR DINNERS on a sweet note with one of these time-easing treats. Folks will think you fussed when you serve any of these impressive—yet easy-to-make—cakes, cookies, pies, desserts and more.

Each irresistible treat featured here looks and tastes special enough to serve weekend company. Yet they're so fast to fix you'll find yourself whipping them up for family and drop-in guests during the week.

The memorable results will have them asking for more!

**DESSERTS IN A DASH.** Clockwise from upper left: Citrus Sherbet Torte, Lime Cooler Bars and Mandarin Orange Cream Pie (all recipes on p. 205).

# Sweetheart Trifle

*(Pictured at right)*

**Plan ahead...needs to chill**

*If you're a peanut butter and chocolate lover, this fantastic trifle is for you. With luscious pudding, cake and candy layers, this tall impressive trifle is a huge hit every time I serve it.*          —*Lorie Cooper Chatham, Ontario*

- 1 package (18-1/4 ounces) chocolate cake mix
- 1 package (10 ounces) peanut butter chips
- 4-1/4 cups cold milk, *divided*
- 1/2 cup whipping cream
- 1/4 teaspoon vanilla extract
- 2 packages (5.9 ounces *each*) instant chocolate pudding mix
- 1 carton (12 ounces) frozen whipped topping, thawed
- 4 Nestle Crunch candy bars (1.55 ounces *each*), crumbled

Prepare cake mix according to package directions. Pour the batter into a greased 13-in. x 9-in. x 2-in. baking pan. Bake at 350° for 30-35 minutes or until a toothpick inserted near the center comes out clean. Cool on a wire rack.

In a heavy saucepan, combine chips, 1/4 cup milk and cream. Cook and stir over low heat until chips are melted. Remove from the heat; stir in vanilla. Cool to room temperature. Place the remaining milk in a mixing bowl; beat in pudding mixes on low speed for 2 minutes.

To assemble, crumble half of the cake into a 4-qt. trifle bowl or large bowl. Layer with half of the peanut butter sauce, pudding, whipped topping and candy bars; repeat layers. Cover and refrigerate for at least 3 hours before serving. **Yield:** 12-15 servings.

# Glazed Mint Brownies

*(Pictured at right)*

*I love taking these rich minty bars to a ladies luncheon. The women always think I've worked so hard to make these layered brownies when they're so easy!*
          —*Diana Conner, Wichita, Kansas*

- 2 squares (1 ounce *each*) unsweetened chocolate
- 1/2 cup butter (no substitutes)
- 2 eggs
- 1 cup sugar
- 1/2 cup all-purpose flour
- **FILLING:**
- 3 tablespoons butter, softened
- 1-1/2 cups confectioners' sugar
- 2 tablespoons milk
- 3/4 teaspoon peppermint extract
- 3 to 4 drops green food coloring, optional
- **GLAZE:**
- 1/2 cup semisweet chocolate chips
- 2 tablespoons butter

In a heavy saucepan or microwave oven, melt the unsweetened chocolate and butter. Cool slightly. In a mixing bowl, beat the eggs, sugar and flour. Stir in the chocolate mixture. Pour into a greased 9-in. square baking pan. Bake at 350° for 20-25 minutes or until a toothpick inserted near the center comes out clean. Cool on a wire rack.

In a mixing bowl, combine the filling ingredients; beat until creamy. Spread over brownies. For glaze, melt chocolate chips and butter; stir until smooth. Spread over filling. Refrigerate until filling and glaze are set. **Yield:** 12-16 brownies.

# Chocolate Berry Pound Cake

*(Pictured at right)*

*This moist cake topped with raspberry whipped cream is from a dear friend's vast recipe collection. It tastes like something Grandma would make and is pretty enough to serve at a special luncheon or shower.*          —*Christi Ross Guthrie, Texas*

- 1 jar (10 ounces) seedless blackberry *or* black raspberry spreadable fruit, *divided*
- 2/3 cup butter *or* margarine, softened
- 1-1/2 cups sugar
- 2 eggs
- 1 teaspoon vanilla extract
- 2 cups all-purpose flour
- 3/4 cup baking cocoa
- 1-1/2 teaspoons baking soda
- 1 teaspoon salt
- 2 cups (16 ounces) sour cream
- Confectioners' sugar, optional
- **RASPBERRY CREAM:**
- 1 package (10 ounces) frozen sweetened raspberries, thawed
- 1 carton (8 ounces) frozen whipped topping, thawed
- Fresh raspberries and blackberries, optional

Place 3/4 cup of spreadable fruit in a microwave-safe bowl. Cover and microwave on high for 40-60 seconds or until melted; set aside. In a mixing bowl, cream butter and sugar. Add eggs and vanilla; mix well. Combine the flour, cocoa, baking soda and salt. Combine sour cream and melted fruit spread; add to creamed mixture alternately with dry ingredients.

Pour into a greased and floured 10-in. fluted tube pan. Bake at 350° for 50-55 minutes or until a toothpick inserted near the center comes out clean. Cool for 10 minutes before removing from pan to a wire rack. Place remaining spreadable fruit in a microwave-safe bowl. Cover and microwave on high for 20-30 seconds or until melted. Brush over warm cake. Cool. Dust with confectioners' sugar if desired.

For raspberry cream, puree the raspberries in a blender or food processor; strain and discard seeds. Fold in the whipped topping. Serve with the cake. Garnish individual servings with fresh berries if desired. **Yield:** 10-12 servings.

**Editor's Note:** This recipe was tested in an 850-watt microwave.

On Valentine's Day

Sweetheart Trifle
Glazed Mint Brownies
Chocolate Berry Pound Cake

No-Bake Chocolate Cheesecake
Banana Macaroon Trifle
Chocolate Peanut Bars

## No-Bake Chocolate Cheesecake

*(Pictured at left and on front cover)*

**Plan ahead...needs to chill**

*Milky Way candy bars and make-ahead convenience give this sweet specialty its fantastic flair. Our children and their families love this impressive eye-appealing dessert. And I never worry about leftovers because it's gone in a flash.* —Pat Pierce
Epworth, Iowa

  1 cup milk
  1 envelope unflavored gelatin
  4 Milky Way candy bars (2.05 ounces *each*), sliced
1-1/2 cups finely crushed chocolate wafers
 1/4 cup butter *or* margarine, melted
  2 packages (8 ounces *each*) cream cheese, softened
  2 tablespoons sugar
  1 teaspoon vanilla extract
  1 cup whipping cream
Whipped topping and fresh raspberries *or* sliced strawberries

In a saucepan, combine the milk and gelatin; let stand for 1 minute. Add the candy bars; cook over medium heat for 5 minutes or until chocolate is melted and gelatin is dissolved. Cool to room temperature, about 45 minutes. Meanwhile, combine the wafer crumbs and butter. Press onto the bottom and 1 in. up the sides of a greased 9-in. springform pan; set aside.

In a mixing bowl, beat cream cheese, sugar and vanilla until smooth. Add the chocolate mixture and cream. Beat on high speed for 4 minutes. Pour into prepared crust. Cover and refrigerate for 8 hours or overnight. Carefully run a knife around edge of pan to loosen. Remove sides of pan. Garnish with whipped topping and berries. **Yield:** 8-10 servings.

## Chocolate Peanut Bars

*(Pictured at left)*

*I use common pantry items to whip up these scrumptious bars. Peanut butter combines with a cake mix for a tender crust. Then a rich layer of cream cheese is topped with chocolate chips and nuts before baking.* —Sue Ross
Casa Grande, Arizona

  1 package (18-1/4 ounces) white cake mix
  1 cup peanut butter, *divided*
  1 egg
  1 package (8 ounces) cream cheese, softened
 1/3 cup milk
 1/4 cup sugar
  1 cup (6 ounces) semisweet chocolate chips
 3/4 cup salted peanuts

In a mixing bowl, beat the cake mix, 2/3 cup peanut butter and egg until crumbly. Press into a greased 13-in. x 9-in. x 2-in. baking pan. In a mixing bowl, combine cream cheese and remaining peanut butter. Gradually beat in milk and sugar. Carefully spread over crust. Sprinkle with chocolate chips and peanuts.

Bake at 350° for 25-30 minutes or until edges are lightly browned and center is set. Cool completely before cutting. Store in the refrigerator. **Yield:** about 2-1/2 dozen.

## Banana Macaroon Trifle

*(Pictured at left)*

*A chewy homemade macaroon mixture takes the place traditionally held by cake in this trifle. Sometimes I serve the sweet treat in individual cups. No time to bake? Use store-bought macaroons instead.* —Barbara Keith
Faucett, Missouri

  2 tablespoons butter *or* margarine, softened
  1 cup sugar
  1 egg
  1 cup flaked coconut
 1/2 cup old-fashioned oats
  2 tablespoons all-purpose flour
  1 teaspoon baking powder
 1/4 cup milk
  1 teaspoon vanilla extract
  3 to 4 small firm bananas, sliced
  1 tablespoon pineapple juice
  1 carton (12 ounces) frozen whipped topping, thawed

For macaroon mixture, beat butter and sugar in a mixing bowl until well blended. Add egg; mix well. Combine coconut, oats, flour and baking powder. Combine milk and vanilla; add to the sugar mixture alternately with coconut mixture (mixture will appear curdled).

Spread in a well-greased 13-in. x 9-in. x 2-in. baking pan. Bake at 325° for 25-30 minutes or until edges are golden brown. Cool completely; crumble. Set aside 1/4 cup for topping.

Just before serving, toss bananas with pineapple juice. In a 2-1/2-qt. serving bowl, layer a third of the macaroon crumbs, whipped topping and bananas. Repeat layers twice. Sprinkle with reserved crumbs. **Yield:** 8-10 servings.

## Check an Egg's Freshness

It's a snap to determine the freshness of an uncooked egg. Simply place it in a glass of cold water. If it's not fresh, it will float to the surface. If it's fresh, it will stay on the bottom of the glass.

## Creamy Peanut Butter Pie

*(Pictured at right)*

**Plan ahead...needs to chill**

*Quartered peanut butter cups top this rich smooth pie. It's always a hit at gatherings.* —Rhonda McDaniel Rossville, Georgia

  1 package (8 ounces) cream cheese, softened
1/2 cup sugar
1/3 cup creamy peanut butter
1/3 cup whipped topping
 10 peanut butter cups
  1 chocolate crumb crust (9 inches)

In a small mixing bowl, beat the cream cheese, sugar and peanut butter until smooth. Fold in the whipped topping. Coarsely chop half of the peanut butter cups; stir into cream cheese mixture. Spoon into crust. Quarter remaining peanut butter cups; arrange over top. Refrigerate for at least 4 hours before cutting. **Yield:** 6-8 servings.

## Pineapple Cheesecake

*(Pictured at right)*

**Plan ahead...needs to chill**

*A co-worker shared the recipe for this easy elegant dessert years ago, and our family has enjoyed it many times since.* —Phoebe Carré, Mullica Hill, New Jersey

  2 packages (8 ounces *each*) cream cheese, softened
1/2 cup sugar
  1 can (20 ounces) crushed pineapple, drained
  1 carton (8 ounces) frozen whipped topping, thawed
  2 packages (3 ounces *each*) ladyfingers
  1 pint fresh strawberries, sliced

In a mixing bowl, beat cream cheese and sugar until smooth. Stir in pineapple. Fold in whipped topping. Place ladyfingers around sides and on bottom of a greased 9-in. springform pan. Pour filling into pan. Cover and refrigerate for 8 hours or overnight. Remove sides of pan. Top with strawberries. **Yield:** 8-10 servings.

## Frosted Orange Cookies

*(Pictured at right)*

*I remember my dad making a big batch of these citrus cookies when I was a child. They're moist and have a wonderful taste.* —Tammie Young, Mattoon, Illinois

  2 medium navel oranges
1/2 cup butter-flavored shortening
  1 cup sugar
1/2 cup milk
  2 cups all-purpose flour
  1 teaspoon baking powder
1/2 teaspoon baking soda
1/2 teaspoon salt
2-1/2 cups confectioners' sugar
  1 tablespoon butter *or* margarine, melted

With a sharp paring knife, score each orange into quarters; remove peel. Use knife to remove white pith from peel and fruit; discard. Quarter oranges and place in a blender. Add peel; cover and process until smooth (mixture should measure 3/4 cup).

In a mixing bowl, cream shortening and sugar. Beat in milk and 6 tablespoons orange mixture. Combine the flour, baking powder, baking soda and salt; add to creamed mixture until blended. Drop by rounded teaspoonfuls 2 in. apart onto greased baking sheets. Bake at 350° for 10-13 minutes or until set and edges are lightly browned. Remove to wire racks to cool.

For frosting, in a mixing bowl, combine confectioners' sugar, butter and enough of the remaining orange mixture to achieve spreading consistency. Frost cookies. **Yield:** about 4 dozen.

## Rhubarb Dream Bars

*Dreaming of a different way to use up garden rhubarb? Try these sweet bars. I top a tender shortbread-like crust with rhubarb, walnuts and coconut for delicious results.* —Marion Tomlinson, Madison, Wisconsin

1-1/4 cups all-purpose flour, *divided*
1/3 cup confectioners' sugar
1/2 cup cold butter *or* margarine
1-1/4 to 1-1/2 cups sugar
  2 eggs
  2 cups finely chopped rhubarb
1/2 cup chopped walnuts
1/2 cup flaked coconut

In a bowl, combine 1 cup flour and confectioners' sugar. Cut in the butter until crumbly. Pat into a lightly greased 13-in. x 9-in. x 2-in. baking dish. Bake at 350° for 13-15 minutes or until edges are lightly browned.

In a bowl, combine the sugar and remaining flour. Add eggs; mix well. Stir in rhubarb, walnuts and coconut; pour over crust. Bake 30-35 minutes longer or until set. Cool on a wire rack. Cut into bars. **Yield:** 2-1/2 to 3 dozen.

## Clean Plate Club

It's easy to frost a cake without leaving a mess around the edge of the serving plate...just use waxed paper to protect it. Before transferring the cooled cake layers to the plate, cut narrow strips of waxed paper and place them around the edge of the plate.

Then center the cake layers on the plate over the strips of waxed paper. When you're finished frosting the cake, carefully remove the waxed paper by pulling out one piece at a time from under the cake. You'll have a beautifully frosted cake and a clean serving plate.

Pineapple Cheesecake
Creamy Peanut Butter Pie
Frosted Orange Cookies

Citrus Sherbet Torte
Lime Cooler Bars
Mandarin Orange Cream Pie

## Citrus Sherbet Torte

*(Pictured at left and on page 196)*

**Plan ahead...needs to freeze**

*When my mother-in-law first served this tall torte, I thought it was the prettiest dessert I ever saw. Not only does it keep well in the freezer, but different flavors of sherbet can be used to reflect the colors of the season.* —Betty Tabb
*Mifflintown, Pennsylvania*

1 package (16 ounces) angel food cake mix
2 pints orange sherbet
2 pints lime sherbet
1 carton (12 ounces) frozen whipped topping, thawed
Assorted cake decorator sprinkles, optional

Prepare and bake cake according to package directions, using an ungreased 10-in. tube pan. Cool.

Remove cake from pan; split horizontally into three layers. Place bottom layer on a serving plate; spread with orange sherbet. Top with another cake layer; spread with lime sherbet. Top with remaining cake layer. Frost top and sides with whipped topping. Decorate with colored sprinkles if desired. Freeze until serving. **Yield:** 12-14 servings.

## Mandarin Orange Cream Pie

*(Pictured at left and on page 196)*

**Plan ahead...needs to chill**

*I never heat up my kitchen when this heavenly sensation is on the menu. That's because the pie's delightful layers of orange gelatin, creamy whipped topping and mandarin oranges rely on the refrigerator instead of the oven.*
—Gusty Crum, Dover, Ohio

1 package (3 ounces) orange *or* sparkling mandarin orange gelatin
1/2 cup boiling water
1-1/4 cups cold club soda
1 graham cracker crust (9 inches)
1/2 cup whipped topping
1 can (11 ounces) mandarin oranges, well drained

In a bowl, dissolve gelatin in boiling water. Stir in soda. Set aside 1/2 cup at room temperature. Refrigerate remaining gelatin mixture for 20 minutes or until slightly thickened; pour into crust. Refrigerate for 30 minutes or until set.

Whisk whipped topping into reserved gelatin mixture. Slowly pour into crust. Arrange orange segments over the top and press down lightly. Refrigerate for at least 3 hours or until firm. **Yield:** 6-8 servings.

## Lime Cooler Bars

*(Pictured at left and on page 197)*

*This is our family favorite that's guaranteed to get thumbs-up approval from your gang, too. Lime juice puts a tangy twist on these bars, with a burst of citrus flavor in every bite.* —Dorothy Anderson, Ottawa, Kansas

2-1/2 cups all-purpose flour, *divided*
1/2 cup confectioners' sugar
3/4 cup cold butter *or* margarine
4 eggs
2 cups sugar
1/3 cup lime juice
1/2 teaspoon lime peel
1/2 teaspoon baking powder
Additional confectioners' sugar

In a bowl, combine 2 cups flour and confectioners' sugar; cut in butter until mixture resembles coarse crumbs. Pat into a greased 13-in. x 9-in. x 2-in. baking pan. Bake at 350° for 20 minutes or until lightly browned.

In a bowl, whisk the eggs, sugar, lime juice and peel until frothy. Combine the baking powder and remaining flour; whisk in egg mixture. Pour over hot crust. Bake for 20-25 minutes or until light golden brown. Cool on a wire rack. Dust with confectioners' sugar. Cut into squares. **Yield:** 3 dozen.

## Raisin-Nut Chocolate Cake

*My husband asks for this yummy cake every year for his birthday. Dotted with raisins and walnuts, the moist treat makes a fitting finale to any meal regardless of the season. No one ever guesses it starts with a handy boxed cake mix.*
—Carol Clarke, Orem, Utah

1 cup chopped walnuts
1 cup raisins
1 cup miniature marshmallows
1 package (18-1/4 ounces) chocolate cake mix
4 eggs
1 cup mayonnaise*
1 cup water

In a bowl, combine walnuts, raisins and marshmallows; set aside. In a mixing bowl, combine cake mix, eggs, mayonnaise and water. Beat on low speed 30 seconds. Beat on medium for 2 minutes. Stir in nut mixture.

Pour into a greased and floured 10-in. fluted tube pan. Bake at 350° for 45-50 minutes or until a toothpick inserted near the center comes out clean. Cool for 10 minutes before removing from pan to a wire rack to cool completely. **Yield:** 12-16 servings.

**\*Editor's Note:** Reduced-fat or fat-free mayonnaise may not be substituted for regular mayonnaise in this recipe.

### Convenient Cutter

I used to have trouble cutting baked itmes like sheet cakes or brownies, because too much of the bakery would stick to the knife. One day, I tried using my pizza cutter instead. It rolled along smoothly and simply, cutting nice clean squares. Now I use it all the time.
—Carolyn Ouimette, Blairsville, Georgia

# Cappuccino Mousse Trifle

### (Pictured at right)

**Ready in 45 minutes or less**

*This is the easiest trifle, yet it looks like I spent so much time on it. I like to pipe whipped topping around the edge of the bowl, grate chocolate in the center and sprinkle with cinnamon.* —Tracy Bergland, Prior Lake, Minnesota

2-1/2 cups cold milk
  1/3 cup instant coffee granules
    2 packages (3.4 ounces *each*) instant vanilla pudding mix
    1 carton (16 ounces) frozen whipped topping, thawed, *divided*
    2 loaves (10-3/4 ounces *each*) frozen pound cake, thawed and cubed
    1 square (1 ounce) semisweet chocolate, grated
  1/4 teaspoon ground cinnamon

In a mixing bowl, stir the milk and coffee granules until dissolved; remove 1 cup and set aside. Add pudding mixes to the remaining milk mixture; beat on low speed for 2 minutes or until thickened. Fold in half of the whipped topping.

Place a third of the cake cubes in a 4-qt. serving or trifle bowl; layer with a third of the reserved milk mixture and pudding mixture and a fourth of the grated chocolate. Repeat layers twice. Garnish with remaining whipped topping and chocolate. Sprinkle with cinnamon. Cover and refrigerate until serving. **Yield:** 16-20 servings.

# Frost-on-the-Pumpkin Pie

### (Pictured at right)

**Plan ahead...needs to chill**

*Like the spices in traditional pumpkin pie? Then try this tasty twist. Most people make this cool fluffy version for the holidays, but I think it's wonderful any time of year.* —Tammy Covey, Huntington, Arkansas

1-1/2 cups graham cracker crumbs (about 24 squares)
    3 tablespoons sugar
  1/4 teaspoon ground nutmeg
  1/8 teaspoon ground cloves
  1/3 cup butter *or* margarine, melted
FILLING:
    1 can (16 ounces) vanilla frosting
    1 can (15 ounces) solid-pack pumpkin
    1 cup (8 ounces) sour cream
    1 to 1-1/2 teaspoons ground cinnamon
  1/2 to 1 teaspoon ground ginger
  1/4 to 1/2 teaspoon ground cloves
    1 cup whipped topping

In a small bowl, combine the first five ingredients. Set aside 1 tablespoon for topping. Press remaining crumb mixture onto the bottom and up the sides of an ungreased 9-in. pie plate. Bake at 350° for 7-9 minutes or until crust just begins to brown. Cool on a wire rack.

In a mixing bowl, combine frosting, pumpkin, sour cream, cinnamon, ginger and cloves. Fold in whipped topping. Spoon into the crust. Sprinkle with the reserved crumb mixture. Refrigerate for at least 4 hours before serving. **Yield:** 6-8 servings.

# Cranberry Crispies

### (Pictured at right)

**Ready in 1 hour or less**

*At holiday rush time, you can't go wrong with these quick simple cookies.* —LaVern Kraft, Lytton, Iowa

    1 package (15.6 ounces) cranberry quick bread mix
  1/2 cup butter *or* margarine, melted
  1/2 cup finely chopped walnuts
    1 egg
  1/2 cup dried cranberries

In a bowl, combine the bread mix, butter, walnuts and egg; mix well. Stir in cranberries. Roll into 1-1/4-in. balls. Place 3 in. apart on ungreased baking sheets. Flatten to 1/8-in. thickness with a glass dipped in sugar. Bake at 350° for 10-12 minutes or until light golden brown. Remove to wire racks to cool. **Yield:** 2-1/2 dozen.

# Zucchini Crisp

*I fix this dessert that tastes like it's made with apples but uses up a bounty of our garden zucchini. It's so good, even those who don't like vegetables enjoy it.* —Deborah Trescott, Marianna, Florida

    8 cups cubed peeled zucchini
  3/4 cup lemon juice
  1/2 to 3/4 cup sugar
    2 teaspoons ground cinnamon
    1 teaspoon ground nutmeg
TOPPING:
1-1/3 cups packed brown sugar
    1 cup old-fashioned oats
    1 cup all-purpose flour
  2/3 cup cold butter *or* margarine

In a bowl, combine the zucchini, lemon juice, sugar, cinnamon and nutmeg; mix well. Pour into a greased 13-in. x 9-in. x 2-in. baking dish.

For topping, combine brown sugar, oats and flour in a bowl; cut in butter until crumbly. Sprinkle over the zucchini mixture. Bake at 375° for 45-50 minutes or until bubbly and the zucchini is tender. **Yield:** 12-15 servings.

## Simple Slicing

Oatmeal cookies with gumdrops are a popular treat in our house. But I'm the first to admit that chopping the little spicy gumdrops with a knife can be a sticky and lengthy job.

So I came up with a faster and neater method. I simply dip my kitchen scissors in flour and snip, snip, snip the gumdrops. The process is so much quicker and cleanup's easier, too. —Mary Guyer, Albany, New York

Cappuccino Mousse Trifle
Cranberry Crispies
Frost-on-the-Pumpkin Pie

WHETHER they're luscious layered bars, crunchy cookies or super snack mixes, on-the-go goodies are always in demand for bake sales, church socials, potlucks and other gatherings.

For the benefit of time-crunched cooks, this chapter provides standout specialties that offer make-ahead convenience, travel well and feed a crowd.

Check out these pages when you need sensational snacks that are taste-tested and family approved.

One of these taste-tempting treats is sure to steal the show at your next bake sale—and sell out in seconds!

**BEST-SELLERS.** Top to bottom: Toffee Oat Cookies and Fudge-Filled Bars (both recipes on p. 213).

Meanwhile, in a saucepan, heat the caramels and condensed milk over low heat until caramels are melted. Pour over baked brownie layer. Sprinkle with remaining walnuts. Drop remaining batter by teaspoonfuls over caramel layer; carefully swirl brownie batter with a knife. Bake 35-40 minutes longer or until a toothpick inserted near the center comes out with moist crumbs. Cool on a wire rack. **Yield:** 2 dozen.

**\*Editor's Note:** This recipe was tested with Hershey caramels.

## Pretzel-Topped Sugar Cookies

### (Pictured at left)

*It's tough to beat a three-ingredient treat...especially one that's so easy and sweet! I rely on refrigerated cookie dough to make these munchable morsels. I dress up each cookie with a white fudge-covered pretzel and melted white chocolate.* —Michelle Brenneman, Orrville, Ohio

    **2 tubes (18 ounces *each*) refrigerated sugar cookie dough**
**2-1/2 cups vanilla *or* white chips, *divided***
    **1 package (7-1/2 ounces) white fudge-covered pretzels\***

Crumble cookie dough into a large bowl; stir in 1-1/2 cups chips. Drop by tablespoonfuls 2 in. apart onto ungreased baking sheets. Bake at 325° for 15-18 minutes or until lightly browned. Immediately press a pretzel into the center of each cookie. Remove to wire racks to cool.

In a microwave, heat remaining chips at 70% power for 1 minute or until melted; stir until smooth. Drizzle over cookies. **Yield:** about 4-1/2 dozen.

**\*Editor's Note:** This recipe was tested with Nestle Flipz.

## Peanut Cereal Squares

*When I need to throw together something in a hurry, I turn to these no-bake squares. And because the recipe doesn't include chocolate, you can pack them for long drives or vacations without worrying about melted-chocolate messes.* —Kathy Steffen, Fond du Lac, Wisconsin

    **4 cups Rice Chex**
    **1 cup light corn syrup**
    **1 cup sugar**
    **1 cup peanut butter**
    **1 cup salted peanuts**
    **1 teaspoon vanilla extract**

Place cereal in a greased 13-in. x 9-in. x 2-in. pan. In a saucepan, bring corn syrup and sugar to a boil; boil for 1 minute. Remove from the heat; stir in peanut butter until blended. Stir in peanuts and vanilla. Pour over cereal. Cool completely. Cut into squares. **Yield:** 2 dozen.

**Caramel Brownies**
**Pretzel-Topped Sugar Cookies**

## Caramel Brownies

### (Pictured above)

*I love to cook. My family can't possibly eat all of the sweets I whip up, so my co-workers are more than happy to sample them—particularly these rich chewy brownies that are full of gooey caramel, chocolate chips and crunchy walnuts.* —Clara Bakke, Coon Rapids, Minnesota

    **2 cups sugar**
    **3/4 cup baking cocoa**
    **1 cup vegetable oil**
    **4 eggs**
    **1/4 cup milk**
**1-1/2 cups all-purpose flour**
    **1 teaspoon salt**
    **1 teaspoon baking powder**
    **1 cup (6 ounces) semisweet chocolate chips**
    **1 cup chopped walnuts, *divided***
    **1 package (14 ounces) caramels\***
    **1 can (14 ounces) sweetened condensed milk**

In a mixing bowl, combine the sugar, cocoa, oil, eggs and milk. Combine the flour, salt and baking powder; add to the egg mixture and mix until combined. Fold in the chocolate chips and 1/2 cup walnuts. Spoon two-thirds of the batter into a greased 13-in. x 9-in. x 2-in. baking pan. Bake at 350° for 12 minutes.

## Caramel Corn Chocolate Bars

*(Pictured below)*

**Ready in 45 minutes or less**

*Five ingredients are all you'll need to make a pan of these no-bake bars. I've brought these sweet treats to bake sales and office parties for 50 years. Wrapped individually, they're perfect for after-school snacks and long car trips.*  —Jean Roczniak, Rochester, Minnesota

- 5 cups caramel corn
- 1 cup chopped pecans
- 1 package (10-1/2 ounces) miniature marshmallows, *divided*
- 1/4 cup butter *or* margarine
- 1/2 cup semisweet chocolate chips

In a large bowl, combine caramel corn, pecans and 1 cup marshmallows. In a heavy saucepan, melt butter over low heat. Add chips and remaining marshmallows; cook and stir until smooth. Pour over caramel corn mixture; toss to coat. With buttered hands, press into a greased 13-in. x 9-in. x 2-in. pan. Cool. Cut with a serrated knife. **Yield:** 2 dozen.

## Nutty Cereal Crunch

*(Pictured below)*

**Ready in 45 minutes or less**

*This is one of my favorite snacks to take to large get-togethers. Cinnamon, brown sugar and butter create a lip-smacking coating for cereal and a variety of nuts in this change-of-pace party mix. One handful simply isn't enough!*  —Grace Yaskovic, Branchville, New Jersey

- 1 cup butter *or* margarine
- 1-1/3 cups packed brown sugar
- 1/2 teaspoon ground cinnamon
- 6 cups cornflakes
- 1 cup salted peanuts
- 1 cup salted cashews
- 1/2 cup almonds *or* macadamia nuts

In a Dutch oven or large saucepan, melt butter; stir in brown sugar and cinnamon until sugar is dissolved. Remove from the heat. Combine cornflakes and nuts; add to sugar mixture and stir to coat. Spread onto two greased baking sheets. Cool; break apart. **Yield:** 10 cups.

## Orange Crispy Cookies

*A boxed cake mix brings these cookies together in a snap. Big on orange flavor but short on kitchen time, the crowd-pleasers are the solution to your bake sale needs. In fact, they're so tasty, you might have trouble getting them past your family and to the sale!* —Barbara Wentzel
*Fort Bragg, California*

- 1 package (18-1/4 ounces) white cake mix
- 1/2 cup butter *or* margarine, melted
- 1 egg, beaten
- 2 teaspoons grated orange peel
- 2 teaspoons orange extract
- 1 cup crisp rice cereal
- 1 cup chopped walnuts, optional

In a mixing bowl, combine the first five ingredients; mix well. Stir in cereal and walnuts if desired. Roll into 1-in. balls. Place 2 in. apart on ungreased baking sheets. Bake at 350° for 12-14 minutes or until lightly browned. Cool for 1 minute before removing to wire racks. **Yield:** about 4 dozen.

**Nutty Cereal Crunch**
**Caramel Corn Chocolate Bars**

## Chocolate Oatmeal Bars

*(Pictured below)*

*I made this dessert for eight ladies who recently stayed at our bed-and-breakfast, and they just raved about it. An oat crust is topped with chocolate and peanut butter, then sprinkled with crushed toffee candy bars.*
—Mary Ann Meredith, Pittsford, Michigan

- 2/3 cup butter *or* margarine, softened
- 1 cup packed brown sugar
- 1/3 cup corn syrup
- 1 teaspoon vanilla extract
- 4 cups quick-cooking oats
- 1 package (11-1/2 ounces) milk chocolate chips
- 2/3 cup chunky peanut butter
- 4 Heath candy bars (1.4 ounces *each*), crushed

In a mixing bowl, cream the butter and brown sugar. Add corn syrup and vanilla; beat well. Stir in oats; press into a greased 13-in. x 9-in. x 2-in. baking pan. Bake at 350° for 12-15 minutes or until golden brown. Cool on a wire rack.

In a microwave or heavy saucepan, melt chocolate chips and peanut butter; stir until blended. Spread over cooled bars. Sprinkle with crushed candy bars. Refrigerate until set before cutting. **Yield:** 3 dozen.

## Drop Sugar Cookies

*(Pictured below)*

*This is a recipe I've been relying on for more than 25 years. The cookies have a crisp edge, soft center and subtle lemon flavor. Choose colored sugar to tailor them to any occasion.* —Shirley Brazel, Coos Bay, Oregon

- 2 eggs
- 3/4 cup sugar
- 2/3 cup vegetable oil
- 2 teaspoons vanilla extract
- 1 teaspoon grated lemon peel
- 2 cups all-purpose flour
- 2 teaspoons baking powder
- 1/2 teaspoon salt
- Additional sugar *or* colored sugar

In a mixing bowl, beat eggs, sugar, oil, vanilla and lemon peel until blended. Combine the flour, baking powder and salt; gradually beat into egg mixture. Drop by rounded teaspoonfuls 2 in. apart onto greased baking sheets. Flatten with a glass dipped in sugar.

Bake at 350° for 8-10 minutes or until edges are lightly browned. Cool for 1-2 minutes before removing to wire racks. **Yield:** about 3-1/2 dozen.

## Sweet Chocolate Bars

*Using a refrigerated pizza crust saves time when preparing this sweet treat. Loaded with chocolate chips, coconut and nuts, the chewy bars are extra rich and tasty.*
—Linda Binger, Taylorville, Illinois

- 1 tube (10 ounces) refrigerated pizza crust
- 1-1/2 cups semisweet chocolate chips
- 1/2 cup chopped pecans
- 1/2 cup flaked coconut
- 1 can (14 ounces) sweetened condensed milk
- 1 package (7-1/2 ounces) white frosting mix*
- 1/2 cup butter *or* margarine, melted

Press pizza dough onto the bottom of a greased 13-in. x 9-in. x 2-in. baking pan. Sprinkle with chocolate chips, pecans and coconut. Drizzle with milk. Sprinkle with dry frosting mix. Drizzle with butter. Bake at 350° for 35-40 minutes or until golden brown. Cool on a wire rack for 10 minutes; run a knife around edges. Cool completely before cutting. **Yield:** 4-1/2 dozen.

**\*Editor's Note:** This recipe was tested with Jiffy dry frosting mix.

## Peanut Butter Cupcakes

*Peanut butter lovers can double their pleasure with these tender treats. I use the popular ingredient in the cupcakes as well as their creamy homemade frosting.*
—Ruth Hutson, Westfield, Indiana

- 1/3 cup butter *or* margarine, softened
- 1/2 cup peanut butter*
- 1-1/4 cups packed brown sugar
- 1 egg
- 1 teaspoon vanilla extract
- 2 cups all-purpose flour
- 2 teaspoons baking powder
- 1/2 teaspoon salt
- 1/4 teaspoon ground cinnamon
- 3/4 cup milk

FROSTING:
- 1/3 cup peanut butter*
- 2 cups confectioners' sugar

Drop Sugar Cookies
Chocolate Oatmeal Bars

2 teaspoons honey
1 teaspoon vanilla extract
3 to 4 tablespoons milk

In a mixing bowl, cream the butter, peanut butter and brown sugar. Beat in egg and vanilla. Combine the dry ingredients; add to creamed mixture alternately with milk. Fill paper-lined muffin cups two-thirds full. Bake at 350° for 26-30 minutes or until a toothpick comes out clean. Cool for 10 minutes before removing from pans to wire racks to cool completely.

For frosting, cream peanut butter and sugar in a small mixing bowl. Add the honey and vanilla. Beat in enough milk to achieve a spreading consistency. Frost cupcakes. **Yield:** about 1-1/2 dozen.

***Editor's Note:*** Reduced-fat or generic brands of peanut butter are not recommended for this recipe.

## Toffee Oat Cookies

*(Pictured above right and on page 208)*

**Ready in 1 hour or less**

*A friend shared this delicious recipe with me. The crisp yet chewy cookies are bound to satisfy big and little kids alike.* —*Jean Dandrea Burkesville, Kentucky*

Toffee Oat Cookies
Fudge-Filled Bars

3/4 cup butter (no substitutes),
    softened
1 cup packed brown sugar
3/4 cup sugar
2 eggs
3 teaspoons vanilla extract
2-1/4 cups all-purpose flour
2-1/4 cups old-fashioned oats
1 teaspoon baking soda
1 teaspoon baking powder
1/2 teaspoon salt
1 package English toffee bits (10 ounces)
    *or* almond brickle chips (7-1/2 ounces)

In a mixing bowl, cream butter and sugars. Add eggs, one at a time, beating well after each addition. Beat in vanilla. Combine the flour, oats, baking soda, baking powder and salt; gradually add to creamed mixture. Stir in toffee bits.

Drop by rounded tablespoonfuls 2 in. apart onto ungreased baking sheets. Bake at 375° for 10-12 minutes or until golden brown. Cool for 1 minute before removing from pans to wire racks. **Yield:** about 4 dozen.

## Fudge-Filled Bars

*(Pictured above right and on page 208)*

*I appreciate the ease of baking these oat bars on a busy day, and our children love their fudgy filling. With colorful candies on top, the sweet squares are sure to sell at bake sales.* —*Reneé Zimmer, Gig Harbor, Washington*

2 cups quick-cooking oats
1-1/2 cups all-purpose flour
1 cup packed brown sugar
3/4 teaspoon salt
1 cup butter *or* margarine, melted
1 cup chopped pecans
1 can (14 ounces) sweetened condensed milk
1 cup (6 ounces) semisweet chocolate chips
2 tablespoons shortening
1 cup plain M&M's

In a bowl, combine the oats, flour, brown sugar and salt. Add butter and mix until crumbly. Stir in the pecans. Set aside 1-1/2 cups for topping. Press remaining crumb mixture into a greased 13-in. x 9-in. x 2-in. baking pan.

In a saucepan, combine the milk, chocolate chips and shortening; cook and stir over low heat until chips are melted. Spread over crust; sprinkle with the reserved crumb mixture. Top with M&M's. Bake at 350° for 20-25 minutes or until edges are golden brown. **Yield:** 2-1/2 dozen.

Halloween Snack Mix
Crispy Kiss Squares

6 cups Cocoa Puffs
1/4 cup butter *or* margarine
40 large marshmallows
1 package (11-1/2 ounces) milk chocolate chips
24 striped chocolate *or* milk chocolate kisses

Place cereal in a large bowl; set aside. In a microwave-safe bowl, combine the butter and marshmallows. Microwave, uncovered, on high for 3 minutes; stir. Continue cooking until smooth, stirring every minute. Add chocolate chips and stir until melted.

Pour over cereal; stir until well-coated. Spread evenly in a greased 13-in. x 9-in. x 2-in. pan. Arrange kisses in rows over the top. Cool before cutting. **Yield:** 2 dozen.

**Editor's Note:** This recipe was tested in an 850-watt microwave.

## No-Bake Chocolate Cookies

### Plan ahead...needs to chill

*These cookies are my oldest son's favorite. When his children tried them, the cookies became their favorites, too. I like them for two reasons—they're quick and they're chocolate!*
—Connie Sackett, Glennallen, Alaska

1 can (14 ounces) sweetened condensed milk
2 cups (12 ounces) semisweet chocolate chips
3 cups crushed graham crackers (about 48 squares)
1/2 cup chopped walnuts
1 teaspoon vanilla extract
Confectioners' sugar

In a microwave-safe bowl, combine milk and chocolate chips. Microwave, uncovered, on high for 1-2 minutes or until chips are melted; stir until smooth. Stir in cracker crumbs, walnuts and vanilla. Shape into a 17-in. log; roll in sugar. Wrap in plastic wrap. Refrigerate for 1 hour or until firm. Unwrap and cut into 1/4-in. slices. **Yield:** about 5-1/2 dozen.

**Editor's Note:** This recipe was tested in an 850-watt microwave.

## Halloween Snack Mix

### (Pictured above)

### Ready in 15 minutes or less

*Here is a simple snack mix I created on the spur of the moment. With just a few ingredients, it's easy to toss together for a Halloween party or to package in individual bags for a fall bake sale. Folks seem to enjoy its festive look and flavor.*
—Barbara Roberts, Middleton, Wisconsin

6 cups caramel corn
2 cups salted cashews *or* peanuts
1-1/2 cups candy corn
1/3 cup raisins

In a large bowl, combine all ingredients; mix well. **Yield:** about 2 quarts.

## Crispy Kiss Squares

### (Pictured above)

*White or milk chocolate kisses add the fun final touch to these chocolaty treats. Since you need just four other ingredients, you can stir up a pan of the sweet squares in a jiffy.* —Chris Budd, Lewiston, Idaho

## Candy Cane Reindeer

### (Pictured at right)

*Our Test Kitchen staff had a blast creating these adorable candy cane stocking stuffers. Rudolph and his friends never looked sweeter than they do with pretzel antlers, chocolate eyes and red-hot candy noses.*

8 ounces white candy coating
12 candy canes (6 inches)
12 to 20 regular-size pretzel twists
12 red-hot candies

24 candy-coated milk chocolate balls*
  *or* miniature chocolate chips

In a microwave or heavy saucepan, melt candy coating. Stir until smooth; keep warm. Holding the curved end of a candy cane, use a spoon to drizzle coating over the straight part of cane. Gently shake off excess. Place on waxed paper to dry. Repeat with remaining candy canes. Break pretzels into pieces to resemble antlers; set aside 24 pieces.

For each reindeer nose, dab a small amount of melted candy coating onto a red-hot. Press onto the end of the curved portion of the candy cane and hold for about 10 seconds. For the eyes, dab a small amount of coating on two chocolate balls and attach to candy cane above nose.

Select two similar pretzel pieces; dab a small amount of coating onto the candy cane where antlers will be attached. Press pretzel pieces into the coating and hold for about 30 seconds. Repeat for remaining reindeer. Place in mugs or drinking glasses; let dry for about 1 hour. **Yield:** 1 dozen.

**\*Editor's Note:** This recipe was tested with Hershey's candy-coated milk chocolate balls.

## Surefire Sugar Cookies

### (Pictured below)

*You can invite kids to help make these easy treats. Sometimes I melt white coating instead of chocolate chips because it can be tinted to match the season. And for a shortcut, I purchase sugar cookies from the bakery.*
—Victoria Zmarzley-Hahn, Northampton, Pennsylvania

1 tube (18 ounces) refrigerated sugar
  cookie dough

1-1/2 cups semisweet chocolate chips
4-1/2 teaspoons shortening
Colored sprinkles, chopped nuts *or* flaked coconut

Slice and bake the sugar cookies according to package directions. Cool on wire racks.

In a microwave-safe bowl, combine the chocolate chips and shortening. Microwave on high for 1-2 minutes or until melted; stir until smooth. Dip each cookie halfway in melted chocolate. Place on waxed paper; immediately sprinkle with colored sprinkles, nuts or coconut. Let stand until chocolate is completely set. **Yield:** 2 dozen.

## Almond Bars

*This is one of my favorite recipes for last-minute school bake sales. The cake-like snacks are the first items to go...that is, if they're not grabbed by a teacher first. I also include them in Christmas cookie gift baskets.* —Sandy Kerrison
Lockport, New York

4 eggs
2 cups sugar
1 cup butter (no substitutes), melted
2 cups all-purpose flour
2-1/2 teaspoons almond extract
Confectioners' sugar

In a mixing bowl, beat the eggs and sugar until lemon-colored. Add the butter, flour and extract; mix well. Spread into a greased 13-in. x 9-in. x 2-in. baking pan. Bake at 325° for 30-35 minutes or until a toothpick inserted near the center comes out clean. Cool on a wire rack. Sprinkle with confectioners' sugar. **Yield:** 2 dozen.

Surefire Sugar Cookies
Candy Cane Reindeer

IF YOU'RE SEARCHING for fast-to-fix dishes that fit today's healthy lifestyle, then you've turned to the right chapter. The lighter fare featured here is perfect for those counting calories or trying to reduce fat, sugar or salt in their diet (and doing all this while keeping one eye on the clock).

We've pared down the fat, calories, sugar and salt but not the taste. Each rapid recipe includes a Nutritional Analysis and Diabetic Exchanges.

Anyone on a special diet—and even those who aren't—will enjoy these delicious and nutritious dishes.

(All the quick good-for-you foods in this book are flagged with a red checkmark in the indexes beginning on page 332.)

**TRIMMED-DOWN DISHES.** Top to bottom: Orange Chiffon Pie, Pepper Pea Salad and Creamy Ham Turnovers (all recipes on p. 222).

Corn Pasta Salad
Glazed Orange Roughy

crunchy corn, red onion and green pepper to give the zippy potluck pleaser plenty of color.
—Bernice Morris, Marshfield, Missouri

2 cups cooked tricolor spiral pasta
1 package (16 ounces) frozen corn, thawed
1 cup chopped celery
1 medium green pepper, chopped
1 cup chopped seeded tomatoes
1/2 cup diced pimientos
1/2 cup chopped red onion
1 cup picante sauce
2 tablespoons canola *or* vegetable oil
1 tablespoon lemon juice
1 garlic clove, minced
1 tablespoon sugar
1/2 teaspoon salt

In a large bowl, combine the first seven ingredients. In a jar with a tight-fitting lid, combine the picante sauce, oil, lemon juice, garlic, sugar and salt; shake well. Pour over pasta mixture and toss to coat. Cover and refrigerate overnight. **Yield:** 10 servings.

**Nutritional Analysis:** One serving (3/4 cup) equals 133 calories, 3 g fat (trace saturated fat), 0 cholesterol, 301 mg sodium, 24 g carbohydrate, 3 g fiber, 3 g protein. **Diabetic Exchanges:** 1 starch, 1 vegetable, 1/2 fat.

 All recipes in this chapter use less fat, sugar or salt and include Nutritional Analysis and Diabetic Exchanges.

## Glazed Orange Roughy

### (Pictured above)

### Ready in 15 minutes or less

*Dijon mustard and apricot fruit spread create a golden glaze for fish fillets in this easy entree. Guests won't believe you used only four ingredients to prepare this delightful full-flavored dinner.* —Jo Baker, Litchfield, Illinois

4 orange roughy, flounder *or* red snapper fillets (1 pound)
1/4 cup apricot spreadable fruit *or* orange marmalade
2 teaspoons stick margarine, melted
2 teaspoons Dijon mustard

Place fillets on an ungreased shallow baking pan. Broil 4-6 in. from the heat for 5-6 minutes. Combine spreadable fruit, margarine and mustard; spoon over fillets. Broil 3-4 minutes longer or until fish flakes easily with a fork (do not turn). **Yield:** 4 servings.

**Nutritional Analysis:** One serving equals 136 calories, 3 g fat (trace saturated fat), 23 mg cholesterol, 157 mg sodium, 10 g carbohydrate, trace fiber, 17 g protein. **Diabetic Exchanges:** 3 very lean meat, 1/2 fruit.

## Corn Pasta Salad

### (Pictured above)

### Plan ahead...start the night before

*After tasting this chilled salad at a family reunion, I immediately asked for the recipe. I use tricolor pasta,*

## Turkey Spinach Casserole

### Ready in 1 hour or less

*I lightened up a family recipe to come up with this turkey and rice bake. Accompanied by fresh tomato slices and hot corn bread, this quick casserole is one of my gang's favorites.* —Becca Brasfield, Burns, Tennessee

1 can (10-3/4 ounces) reduced-fat reduced-sodium condensed cream of chicken soup, undiluted
1/2 cup reduced-fat mayonnaise
1/2 cup water
2 cups cubed cooked turkey breast
1 package (10 ounces) frozen chopped spinach, thawed and squeezed dry
3/4 cup uncooked instant brown rice
1 medium yellow summer squash, cubed
1/4 cup chopped red onion
1 teaspoon ground mustard
1/2 teaspoon dried parsley flakes
1/2 teaspoon garlic powder
1/8 teaspoon pepper
1/4 cup fat-free Parmesan cheese topping
1/8 teaspoon paprika

In a large bowl, combine the soup, mayonnaise and water. Stir in the next nine ingredients. Transfer to a shallow 2-1/2-qt. baking dish coated with nonstick cooking spray. Cover and bake at 350° for 35-40 minutes or until rice is tender. Uncover; sprinkle with Parmesan topping and paprika. Bake 5 minutes longer. **Yield:** 6 servings.

**Nutritional Analysis:** One serving equals 323 calories,

13 g fat (3 g saturated fat), 54 mg cholesterol, 669 mg sodium, 28 g carbohydrate, 3 g fiber, 23 g protein. **Diabetic Exchanges:** 2 lean meat, 1-1/2 starch, 1-1/2 fat, 1 vegetable.

## Spiced Peaches

### Ready in 15 minutes or less

*Canned peaches get special attention from cinnamon and brown sugar. Served warm, these peaches offer down-home comfort. Chilled, they make a refreshing treat with frozen yogurt.* —Debbie Schrock, Jackson, Mississippi

- 1 can (15 ounces) reduced-sugar peach halves
- 2 tablespoons brown sugar
- 1 teaspoon lemon juice
- 1 teaspoon orange juice
- 2 cinnamon sticks (3-1/2 inches)

Drain peaches, reserving juice; set the peaches aside. Pour juice into a saucepan; add brown sugar and lemon and orange juices. Bring to a boil over medium heat; add cinnamon sticks. Reduce heat; simmer, uncovered, for 5 minutes. Add peach halves; heat through. Discard cinnamon sticks. Serve warm or cold. **Yield:** 4 servings.

**Nutritional Analysis:** One serving equals 74 calories, trace fat (0 saturated fat), 0 cholesterol, 7 mg sodium, 19 g carbohydrate, 1 g fiber, 1 g protein. **Diabetic Exchange:** 1 fruit.

## Angel Food Cake Roll

### (Pictured below right)

### Plan ahead...needs to freeze

*There's always room for dessert—especially when it's this eye-catching frozen fare. We like strawberry yogurt in the filling, but different flavors work well, too.* —Joan Colbert, Sigourney, Iowa

- 1 package (16 ounces) angel food cake mix
- 5 teaspoons confectioners' sugar
- 1 carton (8 ounces) reduced-fat strawberry yogurt
- 1 package (1 ounce) instant sugar-free vanilla pudding mix
- 3 drops red food coloring, optional
- 2 cups reduced-fat whipped topping

Line a 15-in. x 10-in. x 1-in. baking pan with waxed paper. Prepare cake according to package directions. Pour batter into prepared pan. Bake at 350° for 15-20 minutes or until cake springs back when lightly touched. Cool for 5 minutes. Turn cake onto a kitchen towel dusted with confectioners' sugar. Gently peel off waxed paper. Roll up jelly-roll style in the towel, starting with a short side. Cool on a wire rack.

In a bowl, whisk the yogurt, pudding mix and food coloring if desired. Fold in whipped topping. Unroll cake; spread filling evenly over cake to within 1/2 in. of edges. Roll up. Cover and freeze. Remove from freezer 30 minutes before slicing. **Yield:** 10 servings.

**Nutritional Analysis:** One slice equals 236 calories, 2 g fat (2 g saturated fat), 2 mg cholesterol, 464 mg

sodium, 49 g carbohydrate, trace fiber, 5 g protein. **Diabetic Exchange:** 3 starch.

## Sausage Egg Pitas

### Ready in 30 minutes or less

*When we were kids, my mom made these sausage and egg sandwiches for us on Sundays. Now that I'm a mom, I like to make them, too.* —Melanie Love Pittsburgh, Pennsylvania

- 1 package (7 ounces) reduced-fat brown-and-serve sausage links
- 1 cup egg substitute
- 1/2 cup chopped green onions
- 2 tablespoons fat-free milk
- 1/8 teaspoon dried oregano
- 1/8 teaspoon pepper
- 2 tablespoons fat-free mayonnaise
- 3 pita breads (6 inches), halved
- 1/3 cup chopped lettuce
- 1/3 cup chopped fresh tomato
- 2 tablespoons sliced ripe olives

In a skillet, cook the sausage until heated through; remove to a cutting board. Cut into 1/4-in. slices; keep warm.

In a small bowl, beat the egg substitute, onions, milk, oregano and pepper. Lightly coat a skillet with nonstick cooking spray. Add egg mixture; cook and stir over medium heat until eggs are set. Spread 1 teaspoon mayonnaise inside each pita half. Fill with the egg mixture, sausage, lettuce, tomato and olives. **Yield:** 6 servings.

**Nutritional Analysis:** One serving (1 filled pita half) equals 198 calories, 7 g fat (2 g saturated fat), 26 mg cholesterol, 531 mg sodium, 21 g carbohydrate, 1 g fiber, 13 g protein. **Diabetic Exchanges:** 2 lean meat, 1 starch, 1/2 fat.

Angel Food Cake Roll

## Turkey Sloppy Joes

*(Pictured below)*

**Plan ahead...uses a slow cooker**

*This tangy sandwich filling is so easy to prepare in the slow cooker, and it goes over well at large and small gatherings. I frequently take it to potlucks, and I'm always asked for my secret ingredient.* —Marylou LaRue, Freeland, Michigan

    1 pound ground turkey breast
    1 small onion, chopped
  1/2 cup chopped celery
  1/4 cup chopped green pepper
    1 can (10-3/4 ounces) reduced-fat reduced-sodium condensed tomato soup, undiluted
  1/2 cup ketchup
    1 tablespoon brown sugar
    2 tablespoons prepared mustard
  1/4 teaspoon pepper
    8 hamburger buns, split

In a large saucepan coated with nonstick cooking spray, cook the turkey, onion, celery and green pepper over medium heat until the meat is no longer pink; drain if necessary. Stir in the soup, ketchup, brown sugar, mustard and pepper. Transfer to a slow cooker. Cover and cook on low for 4 hours. Serve on buns. **Yield:** 8 servings.

    **Nutritional Analysis:** One serving equals 247 calories, 7 g fat (2 g saturated fat), 45 mg cholesterol, 553 mg sodium, 32 g carbohydrate, 2 g fiber, 14 g protein. **Diabetic Exchanges:** 2 starch, 1-1/2 lean meat.

**Turkey Sloppy Joes**
**Brown Rice Slaw**

## Brown Rice Slaw

*(Pictured below left)*

**Ready in 15 minutes or less**

*It's simple to put a refreshing salad on the menu when you follow this rapid recipe. Brown rice, coleslaw mix, apples and nuts make an appealing combination when coated with a sweet orange dressing.* —Mary McGeorge, Little Rock, Arkansas

    2 cups coleslaw mix
    2 cups cooked brown rice
    1 medium tart apple, chopped
  1/3 cup orange juice concentrate
  1/3 cup fat-free mayonnaise
    1 teaspoon sugar
  1/4 teaspoon salt
  1/4 cup chopped pecans, toasted

In a bowl, combine the coleslaw mix, rice and apple. In a small bowl, combine orange juice concentrate, mayonnaise, sugar and salt; pour over coleslaw mixture and toss to coat. Cover and refrigerate until serving. Stir in pecans. **Yield:** 8 servings.

    **Nutritional Analysis:** One 1/2-cup serving equals 109 calories, 3 g fat (trace saturated fat), 1 mg cholesterol, 159 mg sodium, 19 g carbohydrate, 3 g fiber, 2 g protein. **Diabetic Exchanges:** 1 starch, 1 vegetable.

## Three-Cheese Pasta Shells

*Sliced mushrooms and shredded carrot and zucchini add freshness to the cheesy filling in these flavorful shells. This pasta bake makes a nice company meal.* —Kara De la vega, Suisun City, California

    1 jar (16 ounces) salsa
    1 can (8 ounces) no-salt-added tomato sauce
  1/2 cup shredded carrot
  1/2 cup shredded zucchini
  1/2 cup sliced fresh mushrooms
  1/4 cup chopped green onions
    1 garlic clove, minced
    1 teaspoon canola *or* vegetable oil
    1 carton (15 ounces) reduced-fat ricotta cheese
  1/4 cup grated Parmesan cheese
  1/4 cup shredded part-skim mozzarella cheese
  1/4 cup egg substitute
    2 teaspoons dried basil
  16 jumbo pasta shells, cooked and drained

In a bowl, combine the salsa and tomato sauce; spread half in an 11-in. x 7-in. x 2-in. baking dish coated with nonstick cooking spray.

    In a skillet, saute the carrot, zucchini, mushrooms, onions and garlic in oil until crisp-tender. Remove from the heat. Stir in the cheeses, egg substitute and basil. Stuff into pasta shells; place in prepared baking dish. Top with the remaining salsa mixture. Cover and bake at 350° for 40-45 minutes or until heated through. **Yield:** 8 servings.

    **Nutritional Analysis:** One serving (2 stuffed shells) equals 203 calories, 7 g fat (4 g saturated fat), 21 mg cholesterol, 416 mg sodium, 23 g carbohydrate, 2 g fiber,

12 g protein. **Diabetic Exchanges:** 1 starch, 1 lean meat, 1 vegetable, 1 fat.

## Fruit Cup with Citrus Sauce

*(Pictured at right)*

**Plan ahead...needs to chill**

*This medley of fresh fruits is so elegant that I serve it in my prettiest crystal bowls. With its dressed-up flavor, it's perfect for a special event.*
—Edna Lee, Greeley, Colorado

3/4 cup orange juice
1/4 cup white wine *or* white grape juice
2 tablespoons lemon juice
1 tablespoon sugar
1-1/2 cups fresh *or* frozen cantaloupe balls
1 cup halved green grapes
1 cup halved fresh strawberries
Fresh mint, optional

In a small bowl, combine the orange juice, wine or grape juice, lemon juice and sugar; mix well. In a large bowl, combine the fruit; add juice mixture and toss to coat. Cover and refrigerate for 2-3 hours, stirring occasionally. Garnish with mint if desired. **Yield:** 6 servings.

**Nutritional Analysis:** One 3/4-cup serving equals 63 calories, trace fat (trace saturated fat), 0 cholesterol, 5 mg sodium, 14 g carbohydrate, 1 g fiber, 1 g protein. **Diabetic Exchange:** 1 fruit.

**Fruit Cup with Citrus Sauce**

## Curried Chicken

**Ready in 30 minutes or less**

*I season tender chicken and apples with curry powder and a dash of cinnamon. My husband and I enjoy this dish frequently because it's great-tasting and quick to prepare.* —Karen McLaughlin, Hamilton, Ontario

1/2 pound boneless skinless chicken breasts, cubed
2 medium tart apples, peeled and cubed
1 medium onion, chopped
2 garlic cloves, minced
3 tablespoons water
1 to 2 teaspoons curry powder
1/4 teaspoon ground cinnamon
1 tablespoon all-purpose flour
1 cup (8 ounces) reduced-fat sour cream
4 cups hot cooked rice

In a nonstick skillet, cook chicken until juices run clear; drain. Remove chicken and keep warm. In the same skillet, cook the apples, onion and garlic in water until tender. Return chicken to the pan; sprinkle with curry powder and cinnamon. Heat through. Combine the flour and sour cream until smooth; stir into chicken mixture. Bring to a gentle boil; cook and stir for 2 minutes. Serve over rice. **Yield:** 4 servings.

**Nutritional Analysis:** One serving (1 cup chicken mixture with 1 cup rice) equals 414 calories, 6 g fat (4 g saturated fat), 53 mg cholesterol, 80 mg sodium, 65 g carbohydrate, 4 g fiber, 22 g protein. **Diabetic Exchanges:** 3 starch, 2 lean meat, 1 fruit.

## Apple Tapioca

**Ready in 1 hour or less**

*Serve this warm spiced apple mixture over frozen yogurt or angel food cake for a delicious down-home dessert. It's tasty on a cool evening or anytime for that matter.*
—Dorothy Pritchett, Wills Point, Texas

4 medium tart apples, peeled and sliced
2 cups water
1 cup packed brown sugar
1/2 cup quick-cooking tapioca
2 tablespoons lemon juice
1/2 teaspoon salt
1/4 teaspoon ground nutmeg

Arrange the apples in a 2-qt. baking dish coated with nonstick spray. In a saucepan, combine the water, brown sugar, tapioca, lemon juice, salt and nutmeg. Let stand for 5 minutes. Bring to a boil over medium heat, stirring constantly. Pour over the apples. Cover and bake at 350° for 30-35 minutes or until apples are tender. Serve warm. **Yield:** 8 servings.

**Nutritional Analysis:** One 1/2-cup serving equals 177 calories, 0 fat (0 saturated fat), 0 cholesterol, 158 mg sodium, 47 g carbohydrate, 3 g fiber, trace protein. **Diabetic Exchange:** 3 fruit.

Orange Chiffon Pie
Pepper Pea Salad
Creamy Ham Turnovers

## Pepper Pea Salad

*(Pictured at left and on page 216)*

**Plan ahead...needs to chill**

*Take a break from pasta and potato salads with this easy-to-assemble medley. Peas are one of my favorite vegetables. They complement nearly every meal, particularly when used in this cool summer salad.* —Jan Roat
Grass Range, Montana

1 package (16 ounces) frozen peas, thawed
1 medium green pepper, julienned
1/2 cup chopped sweet onion
1/4 cup white vinegar
4 teaspoons olive *or* canola oil
1 teaspoon Italian seasoning

In a large bowl, combine the peas, green pepper and onion. In a small bowl, whisk the vinegar, oil and Italian seasoning. Pour over vegetables and toss to coat. Cover and refrigerate for at least 1 hour. **Yield:** 5 servings.
   **Nutritional Analysis:** One serving (2/3 cup) equals 114 calories, 4 g fat (1 g saturated fat), 0 cholesterol, 103 mg sodium, 16 g carbohydrate, 5 g fiber, 5 g protein. **Diabetic Exchanges:** 1 starch, 1/2 fat.

## Creamy Ham Turnovers

*(Pictured above and on page 216)*

**Ready in 30 minutes or less**

*Prepared pizza crust makes these tasty turnovers a time-saver. The golden-brown bundles look like you fussed, but they're very simple.* —Earnestine Jackson
Beaumont, Texas

4 ounces reduced-fat cream cheese
2 tablespoons fat-free milk
1 teaspoon dill weed
1 cup diced fully cooked lean ham
2 tablespoons diced onion
1 celery rib, diced
2 tablespoons diced pimientos
1 tube (10 ounces) refrigerated pizza crust
1 egg white, beaten

In a mixing bowl, beat cream cheese, milk and dill until blended. Stir in the ham, onion, celery and pimientos. Roll out pizza dough into a 12-in. x 10-in. rectangle; cut in half lengthwise and widthwise. Place on a baking sheet coated with nonstick cooking spray.
   Divide ham mixture evenly between the four rectangles. Fold opposite corners over ham mixture; pinch to seal. Brush with egg white. Bake at 400° for 20-25 minutes or until golden brown. **Yield:** 4 servings.
   **Nutritional Analysis:** One serving equals 308 calories, 9 g fat (4 g saturated fat), 27 mg cholesterol, 967 mg sodium, 37 g carbohydrate, 1 g fiber, 17 g protein. **Diabetic Exchanges:** 2-1/2 starch, 2 lean meat.

## Orange Chiffon Pie

*(Pictured above left and on page 216)*

**Plan ahead...needs to chill**

*You'll be greeted with smiles when you put this no-bake dessert on your menu. This pie is wonderfully refreshing in the summer. It's an old recipe that stands the test of time.* —Tina Dierking, Skowhegan, Maine

1 package (3 ounces) orange gelatin
1 tablespoon sugar
3/4 cup boiling water
1/2 cup orange juice
1 teaspoon grated orange peel
1 carton (8 ounces) frozen reduced-fat whipped topping, thawed
1 reduced-fat graham cracker crust (9 inches)

In a large mixing bowl, dissolve gelatin and sugar in water. Add orange juice and peel. Refrigerate for 1 hour or until thickened but not set. Beat on high speed for 3 minutes or until foamy and thickened. Fold in whipped topping until completely combined. Pour into crust. Cover and refrigerate for 4 hours or until set. **Yield:** 8 servings.
   **Nutritional Analysis:** One piece equals 223 calories, 7 g fat (5 g saturated fat), 0 cholesterol, 119 mg sodium, 36 g carbohydrate, trace fiber, 2 g protein. **Diabetic Exchanges:** 2-1/2 starch, 1 fat.

## Low-Fat Chocolate Muffins

**Ready in 1 hour or less**

*The men in my house don't like low-fat foods. But I always keep these muffins in the freezer because the guys can't seem to get enough of them.* —Mona Kruse, Milan, Illinois

1-1/2 cups all-purpose flour
3/4 cup sugar
1/4 cup baking cocoa
2 teaspoons baking powder
1 teaspoon baking soda
1/2 teaspoon salt
2/3 cup fat-free vanilla yogurt
2/3 cup fat-free milk
1/2 teaspoon vanilla extract
Confectioners' sugar, optional

In a bowl, combine the first six ingredients. Stir in yogurt, milk and vanilla just until moistened. Coat muffin cups with nonstick cooking spray; fill two-thirds full. Bake at 400° for 15-20 minutes or until a toothpick comes out clean. Cool for 5 minutes before removing from pan to a wire rack; dust with confectioners' sugar if desired. **Yield:** 1 dozen.

**Nutritional Analysis:** One muffin equals 128 calories, trace fat (trace saturated fat), 1 mg cholesterol, 258 mg sodium, 29 g carbohydrate, 1 g fiber, 3 g protein. **Diabetic Exchange:** 2 starch.

## Eggplant Pockets

**Ready in 45 minutes or less**

*I saute chopped veggies in a blend of seasonings, then stuff them into pita halves. These sandwiches are an ideal way to take advantage of homegrown harvests.* —Judy White, Hawesville, Kentucky

1 large eggplant, cubed
1 cup sweet red pepper, diced
2 celery ribs, diced
1 cup shredded carrots
1 cup chopped zucchini
1/2 cup chopped onion
1/4 cup olive or canola oil
1 cup chopped tomatoes
2 tablespoons red wine vinegar or cider vinegar
1 tablespoon lemon juice
1 garlic clove, minced
1 teaspoon salt-free seasoning blend
1/2 teaspoon salt-free lemon-pepper seasoning
1/4 teaspoon dried basil
1/8 teaspoon cayenne pepper
4 whole pita breads, halved

In a large saucepan, place 1 in. of water and the eggplant; bring to a boil. Reduce heat; cover and cook for 2-3 minutes or until tender. Drain and set aside. In a large skillet, saute the red pepper, celery, carrots, zucchini and onion in oil for 6-8 minutes until tender. Stir in the tomatoes, vinegar, lemon juice, garlic, seasonings and reserved eggplant. Cook, uncovered, for 10-15 minutes or until vegetables are tender. Spoon into pitas. **Yield:** 8 servings.

**Nutritional Analysis:** One serving (half of a filled pita) equals 176 calories, 8 g fat (1 g saturated fat), 0 cholesterol, 164 mg sodium, 25 g carbohydrate, 4 g fiber, 3 g protein. **Diabetic Exchanges:** 1-1/2 starch, 1 vegetable, 1/2 fat.

## Penne from Heaven

*(Pictured below)*

**Ready in 30 minutes or less**

*This fast, fresh-tasting side dish comes very close to a delicious treatment for pasta I enjoyed while in Italy. You can also serve it with a green salad and toasted garlic bread for a light meal.* —Dorothy Roche, Menomonee Falls, Wisconsin

6 ounces uncooked penne or other small pasta
1/2 pound fresh mushrooms, sliced
1 tablespoon olive or canola oil
1 can (14-1/2 ounces) diced tomatoes, undrained
1 tablespoon minced fresh basil or 1 teaspoon dried basil
1/4 teaspoon salt
1/3 cup crumbled feta cheese

Cook pasta according to package directions. Meanwhile, in a large skillet, saute mushrooms in oil for 5 minutes. Add the tomatoes, basil and salt; cook and stir for 5 minutes. Drain pasta and add to the skillet. Stir in cheese; heat through. **Yield:** 5 servings.

**Nutritional Analysis:** One serving equals 188 calories, 5 g fat (2 g saturated fat), 9 mg cholesterol, 335 mg sodium, 28 g carbohydrate, 3 g fiber, 7 g protein. **Diabetic Exchanges:** 2 starch, 1/2 fat.

Penne from Heaven

## Orange Pork Stir-Fry

*(Pictured below)*

**Ready in 30 minutes or less**

*My family really enjoys this colorful stovetop supper that's lower in sodium than typical stir-fries. We have it often on weekends instead of going out for Chinese food.*
—Wilma Jones, Mobile, Alabama

      1 can (8 ounces) unsweetened pineapple
         chunks
      1 tablespoon brown sugar
      2 teaspoons cornstarch
   1/4 cup chicken broth
      2 tablespoons lemon juice
      1 tablespoon reduced-sodium soy sauce
      1 teaspoon grated lemon peel
      1 pound pork tenderloin, cut into thin strips
      1 cup julienned sweet red *and/or* green pepper
      1 small onion, quartered and thinly sliced
      1 garlic clove, minced
 1-1/2 teaspoons canola *or* vegetable oil
      1 medium navel orange, peeled, sectioned and
         halved
      3 cups hot cooked rice

Drain pineapple, reserving juice; set juice and pineapple aside. In a bowl, combine brown sugar and cornstarch. Stir in the broth, lemon juice, soy sauce, lemon peel and reserved juice until blended; set aside.

In a nonstick skillet coated with nonstick cooking spray, stir-fry pork for 3-4 minutes or until meat is no longer pink; remove and keep warm. In the same skillet, stir-fry pepper, onion and garlic in oil for 3-4 minutes or until crisp-tender. Stir the broth mixture; add to vegetables. Bring to a boil; cook and stir for 2 minutes.

Return pork to the pan. Add orange pieces and pineapple; heat through. Serve over rice. **Yield:** 4 servings.

**Nutritional Analysis:** One serving (1 cup stir-fry mixture with 3/4 cup cooked rice) equals 366 calories, 6 g fat (2 g saturated fat), 74 mg cholesterol, 278 mg sodium, 49 g carbohydrate, 3 g fiber, 28 g protein. **Diabetic Exchanges:** 3 lean meat, 2 starch, 1 fruit.

## Blackberry Cake

*(Pictured below left)*

*I take advantage of boxed mixes to bake this moist berry-flavored cake. My husband and I started watching our fat and sugar intake, so I made several changes to the original recipe to come up with this lighter version. It's best prepared the day before serving, and it freezes well, too.*
—Ann Kelly, Gallatin, Tennessee

      1 package (18-1/4 ounces) reduced-fat
         yellow cake mix
      1 package (1 ounce) sugar-free instant
         vanilla pudding mix
      1 package (.3 ounce) sugar-free raspberry
         gelatin
      2 eggs
   1/3 cup egg substitute
      1 jar (10 ounces) seedless blackberry
         spreadable fruit
   1/2 cup unsweetened applesauce
   1/4 cup canola *or* vegetable oil
**ICING:**
   1/4 cup butter *or* stick margarine, softened
      3 cups confectioners' sugar
      3 tablespoons fat-free milk

In a large bowl, combine the cake mix, pudding mix and gelatin. In a small bowl, beat the eggs, egg substitute, spreadable fruit, applesauce and oil. Stir into dry ingredients just until moistened. Pour into a 15-in. x 10-in. x 1-in. baking pan coated with nonstick cooking spray. Bake at 350° for 35-40 minutes or until a toothpick inserted near the center comes out clean. Cool on a wire rack.

In a small mixing bowl, combine icing ingredients until smooth. Spread over cooled cake. **Yield:** 20 servings.

**Nutritional Analysis:** One piece equals 263 calories, 7 g fat (2 g saturated fat), 28 mg cholesterol, 266 mg sodium, 48 g carbohydrate, 1 g fiber, 2 g protein. **Diabetic Exchanges:** 2 starch, 1 fruit, 1 fat.

## Sausage Egg Puff

**Plan ahead...start the night before**

*I stir up this full-flavored brunch dish at night so it's ready to bake up light and fluffy the next morning. The recipe came from a beautiful bed-and-breakfast my husband and I stayed at several years ago.* —Tammy Lamb
Campbellsville, Kentucky

      1 pound turkey sausage links, casings removed
      1 cup reduced-fat biscuit/baking mix
      1 cup (4 ounces) shredded reduced-fat
         cheddar cheese
      1 teaspoon ground mustard

**Blackberry Cake**
**Orange Pork Stir-Fry**

1 teaspoon Italian seasoning
1 cup egg substitute
2 eggs
2 cups fat-free milk

In a large skillet, crumble sausage and cook until no longer pink; drain. In a bowl, combine the biscuit mix, cheese, mustard and Italian seasoning; add sausage. In another bowl, whisk the egg substitute, eggs and milk; stir into the sausage mixture. Transfer to a shallow 2-qt. baking dish coated with nonstick cooking spray. Cover and refrigerate overnight.

Remove from the refrigerator 30 minutes before baking. Bake, uncovered, at 350° for 50-55 minutes or until a knife inserted near the center comes out clean. **Yield:** 6 servings.

**Nutritional Analysis:** One serving equals 324 calories, 14 g fat (4 g saturated fat), 134 mg cholesterol, 1,111 mg sodium, 19 g carbohydrate, trace fiber, 30 g protein. **Diabetic Exchanges:** 4 lean meat, 1 starch, 1/2 fat.

## Veggie Macaroni Salad

*(Pictured at right)*

**Ready in 45 minutes or less**

*When I bring this super salad to church dinners, there is usually nothing to take home. Add 2 or 3 cups leftover turkey or chicken to create a filling main-dish salad. The dressing is so good that we use it on potato salads and even lettuce salads.* —Lynn Cole, Sagle, Idaho

2 cups uncooked elbow macaroni
1 large tomato, seeded and chopped
1 cup frozen peas, thawed
1/2 cup reduced-fat shredded cheddar cheese
1/2 cup chopped celery
1 hard-cooked egg, chopped
2 green onions, sliced
DRESSING:
3/4 cup low-fat mayonnaise
1 cup fat-free plain yogurt
2 tablespoons sugar
1 tablespoon prepared mustard
1/8 teaspoon celery seed

Cook macaroni according to package directions; drain and rinse in cold water. In a large bowl, combine the macaroni, tomato, peas, cheese, celery, egg and onions. In a small bowl, combine the dressing ingredients. Pour over macaroni mixture and toss to coat. Refrigerate until serving. **Yield:** 10 servings.

**Nutritional Analysis:** One 3/4-cup serving equals 234 calories, 8 g fat (2 g saturated fat), 31 mg cholesterol, 246 mg sodium, 32 g carbohydrate, 2 g fiber, 8 g protein. **Diabetic Exchanges:** 2 starch, 1-1/2 fat.

## Skillet Olé

**Ready in 30 minutes or less**

*This pleasantly spiced skillet dish gets extra zip when served with salsa. While it's cooking, I fix ranch-style beans and a green salad so the whole meal is ready in about 30 minutes.* —Lillie Glass, Dripping Springs, Texas

Veggie Macaroni Salad

1/2 pound lean ground beef
1/2 pound ground turkey breast
1 small onion, chopped
1/4 cup chopped green pepper
1 can (8 ounces) no-salt-added tomato sauce
1 cup cooked rice
1 to 1-1/2 teaspoons chili powder
3/4 cup reduced-fat shredded cheddar cheese

In a large skillet, cook beef, turkey, onion and green pepper over medium heat until meat is no longer pink; drain. Stir in tomato sauce, rice and chili powder. Cook for 10 minutes; sprinkle with the cheese. Cover and cook for 2 minutes or until cheese is melted. **Yield:** 4 servings.

**Nutritional Analysis:** One serving equals 268 calories, 8 g fat (3 g saturated fat), 43 mg cholesterol, 236 mg sodium, 16 g carbohydrate, 2 g fiber, 32 g protein. **Diabetic Exchanges:** 3 lean meat, 1 starch, 1 vegetable.

## Seeding Tomatoes

Fresh juicy tomatoes enhance all types of recipes. It's usually not necessary to remove the seeds from tomatoes before using. But for some recipes, seeding the tomatoes can improve the dish's appearance or eliminate excess moisture.

To remove the seeds from a tomato, cut it in half horizontally and remove the stem. Holding a tomato half over a bowl or sink, scrape out seeds with a small spoon or squeeze the tomato to force out the seeds. Then slice or dice as directed in the recipe.

## Vibrant Veggie Stir-Fry

*(Pictured at left)*

**Ready in 15 minutes or less**

*I like to whip up this simple side dish featuring broccoli, carrots and zucchini. Over the years, my husband and I have learned to cook with less fat and sugar so we can enjoy good health as we grow older.*
—Betty Claycomb, Alverton, Pennsylvania

  **4 cups fresh broccoli florets**
**3/4 cup fresh baby carrots, quartered lengthwise**
  **2 teaspoons canola *or* vegetable oil**
  **1 medium zucchini, halved lengthwise and sliced**
**1/2 teaspoon salt**
**1/4 teaspoon pepper**

In a nonstick skillet or wok, stir-fry broccoli and carrots in oil for 5 minutes. Add the zucchini, salt and pepper; stir-fry 4-5 minutes longer or until vegetables are crisp-tender. **Yield:** 4 servings.
  **Nutritional Analysis:** One serving (3/4 cup) equals 58 calories, 3 g fat (trace saturated fat), 0 cholesterol, 322 mg sodium, 8 g carbohydrate, 3 g fiber, 3 g protein. **Diabetic Exchange:** 2 vegetable.

**Vibrant Veggie Stir-Fry**
**Chicken Supreme**

## Chicken Supreme

*(Pictured above)*

**Ready in 45 minutes or less**

*I received this wonderful recipe from a friend at church. A light breading seals in the juices of tender chicken breasts, making them special enough to serve company. Sliced almonds top off the eye-catching entree.*
—Candace Black, Durham, North Carolina

**1/2 cup dry bread crumbs**
**1/2 cup grated Parmesan cheese**
  **2 tablespoons minced fresh parsley**
  **1 garlic clove, minced**
**1/4 teaspoon pepper**
  **3 egg whites**
  **6 boneless skinless chicken breast halves (1-1/2 pounds)**
**1/4 cup sliced almonds**
**Refrigerated butter-flavored spray***

In a shallow bowl, combine the first five ingredients. In another shallow bowl, beat the egg whites. Dip chicken in egg whites, then coat with crumb mixture. Place in a 13-in. x 9-in. x 2-in. baking dish coated with nonstick cooking spray. Sprinkle almonds over chicken. Spritz with butter-flavored spray. Bake, uncovered, at 350° for 30 minutes or until chicken juices run clear. **Yield:** 6 servings.
  **Nutritional Analysis:** One serving equals 224 calories, 6 g fat (2 g saturated fat), 71 mg cholesterol, 304 mg sodium, 8 g carbohydrate, 1 g fiber, 33 g protein. **Diabetic Exchanges:** 3-1/2 lean meat, 1/2 starch.
  ***Editor's Note:** This recipe was tested with I Can't Believe It's Not Butter Spray.

## Apple Rice Betty

**Plan ahead...needs to chill**

*This cinnamony dessert is a longtime favorite. When our six children lived at home, I made this often. When my husband became diabetic, I reduced the sugar in the recipe. He enjoys this version as much as the original.*
—Thelma Brown, Fulton, Illinois

  **2 cups apple juice**
**1-1/2 cups chopped peeled tart apples (about 2 medium)**
  **1 cup uncooked instant rice**
**1/2 cup raisins**
**1/2 teaspoon ground cinnamon**
**1/8 teaspoon salt**
**1/3 cup sugar substitute***
  **6 tablespoons reduced-fat whipped topping**

In a large saucepan, combine the first six ingredients. Bring to a boil. Reduce heat; cook and stir for 6-7 minutes or until most of the liquid is absorbed and rice is tender. Remove from the heat; stir in sugar substitute. Refrigerate for 1 hour. Garnish each serving with 1 tablespoon whipped topping. **Yield:** 6 servings.
  **Nutritional Analysis:** One serving (1/2 cup) equals 177 calories, 1 g fat (1 g saturated fat), 0 cholesterol, 56 mg sodium, 42 g carbohydrate, 3 g fiber, 2 g protein. **Diabetic Exchanges:** 2 fruit, 1/2 starch.
  ***Editor's Note:** This recipe was tested with Splenda No Calorie sweetener. Look for it in the baking aisle of your grocery store.

## Turkey Loaf

*Looking for a healthy main dish that doesn't take up a lot of kitchen time? Consider this easy-to-assemble moist loaf made with ground turkey. When I serve this, it always gets thumbs-up approval. A jar of fat-free gravy streamlines the preparation.* —Janet Crowell, San Antonio, Texas

1/2 cup quick-cooking oats
1/4 cup egg substitute
  1 teaspoon poultry seasoning
  1 teaspoon rubbed sage
1/2 teaspoon celery salt
  2 pounds ground turkey breast
  1 jar (12 ounces) fat-free turkey gravy, warmed

In a large bowl, combine the first five ingredients. Crumble turkey over mixture and mix well. Press into a 9-in. x 5-in. x 3-in. loaf pan coated with nonstick cooking spray. Cover and bake at 350° for 65-70 minutes or until juices run clear. Serve with gravy. **Yield:** 8 servings.
  **Nutritional Analysis:** One serving equals 207 calories, 10 g fat (3 g saturated fat), 90 mg cholesterol, 414 mg sodium, 6 g carbohydrate, 1 g fiber, 22 g protein. **Diabetic Exchanges:** 2 lean meat, 1 fat, 1/2 starch.

## Vegetable Bean Soup

(Pictured at right)

**Ready in 30 minutes or less**

*My family loves this vegetable soup. Chock-full of kidney beans, celery, spinach, carrots, zucchini and tomatoes, the comforting broth is ideal to serve on cool autumn days with a loaf of crusty bread or warm biscuits.*
—Lillian Palko, Napa, California

  1 can (16 ounces) kidney beans, rinsed and drained
  1 medium zucchini, cubed
  1 medium carrot, diced
  2 celery ribs, chopped
  3 green onions, sliced
1/4 cup chopped fresh spinach
  3 tablespoons quick-cooking barley
  3 cans (14-1/2 ounces *each*) low-sodium chicken broth
1/4 cup minced fresh parsley
  1 garlic clove, minced
1/2 teaspoon garlic salt
  1 can (14-1/2 ounces) Italian diced tomatoes, undrained

In a large saucepan, combine the first 11 ingredients. Bring to a boil. Reduce heat; cover and simmer for 10-12 minutes or until the barley and vegetables are tender. Add the tomatoes; heat through. **Yield:** 8 servings (2 quarts).
  **Nutritional Analysis:** One serving (1 cup) equals 103 calories, trace fat (trace saturated fat), 0 cholesterol, 939 mg sodium, 19 g carbohydrate, 4 g fiber, 7 g protein. **Diabetic Exchanges:** 1 starch, 1 vegetable.

## Layered Orange Gelatin

**Plan ahead...needs to chill**

*To come up with this treat, I reduced the calories and fat in a tangy gelatin recipe my mom gave me. The lovely molded salad forms layers as it chills. We especially enjoy it with ham.*
—Angie Philkill, Zeeland, Michigan

  2 packages (.3 ounce *each*) sugar-free orange gelatin
  2 cups boiling water
  1 can (15 ounces) mandarin oranges
  3 ounces reduced-fat cream cheese, cubed
  1 pint orange sherbet, softened
1-1/2 cups reduced-fat whipped topping

In a mixing bowl, dissolve gelatin in boiling water. Drain oranges, reserving the juice; set oranges aside. Stir juice into gelatin. Add cream cheese; beat until smooth. Stir in sherbet and whipped topping. Pour into a 6-cup ring mold coated with nonstick cooking spray. Top with oranges. Cover and refrigerate overnight. **Yield:** 10 servings.
  **Nutritional Analysis:** One serving equals 125 calories, 4 g fat (3 g saturated fat), 7 mg cholesterol, 90 mg sodium, 20 g carbohydrate, trace fiber, 2 g protein. **Diabetic Exchanges:** 1 starch, 1/2 fruit, 1/2 fat.

Vegetable Bean Soup

# Pork Chops in Tomato Sauce

*(Pictured below)*

**Ready in 30 minutes or less**

*This is a variation of a main dish that my dad always made. I now add some special touches of my own when I make it for my husband and two children. The tender chops are fast to fix on a weeknight.*
—Cindy Glancy
*Point Pleasant, New Jersey*

1/2 small onion, thinly sliced
  1 garlic clove, minced
  1 tablespoon butter *or* stick margarine
  4 bone-in pork loin chops (6 ounces *each*), trimmed
  1 can (8 ounces) tomato sauce
1/4 cup dry white wine *or* chicken broth
  1 teaspoon dried oregano
1/8 teaspoon pepper

In a large nonstick skillet, saute onion and garlic in butter until tender. Add pork chops; brown on both sides. In a small bowl, combine the tomato sauce, wine or broth, oregano and pepper; pour over chops. Bring to a boil. Reduce heat; cover and simmer for 10-15 minutes or until tender. **Yield:** 4 servings.

**Nutritional Analysis:** One serving (1 pork chop with 1/4 cup sauce) equals 216 calories, 10 g fat (4 g saturated fat), 75 mg cholesterol, 417 mg sodium, 6 g carbohydrate, 1 g fiber, 23 g protein. **Diabetic Exchanges:** 3 lean meat, 1 vegetable, 1/2 fat.

# Potato Bean Skillet

*(Pictured below left)*

**Ready in 30 minutes or less**

*This is a quick side dish for a pork chop supper. Our eight grandkids like its mild sweet-and-sour taste. However, the recipe has to be doubled or tripled when they're around for supper!* —Dixie Terry, Goreville, Illinois

  1 pound fresh *or* frozen green beans, cut into 2-inch pieces
  2 medium red potatoes, peeled and sliced
  1 small onion, chopped
  1 tablespoon olive *or* canola oil
  3 tablespoons cider vinegar
  2 tablespoons water
  2 teaspoons sugar
1/2 teaspoon ground mustard
1/2 teaspoon salt
1/8 teaspoon pepper

Place beans and potatoes in a saucepan; cover with water. Bring to a boil. Reduce heat; cover and simmer for 5 minutes; drain well.

In a large skillet, saute beans, potatoes and onion in oil until tender. In a small bowl, combine the remaining ingredients; pour over vegetables. Cook and stir over medium heat until the liquid is evaporated. **Yield:** 6 servings.

**Nutritional Analysis:** One serving (3/4 cup) equals 95 calories, 3 g fat (trace saturated fat), 0 cholesterol, 200 mg sodium, 17 g carbohydrate, 3 g fiber, 2 g protein. **Diabetic Exchanges:** 1 vegetable, 1/2 starch, 1/2 fat.

# Ham Tetrazzini

**Plan ahead...uses slow cooker**

*I modified a recipe that came with my slow cooker to reduce the fat without sacrificing the flavor. I've served this at parties, family dinners and potlucks. Everyone is pleasantly surprised to find they're eating healthy.* —Susan Blair
*Sterling, Michigan*

  1 can (10-3/4 ounces) reduced-fat reduced-sodium condensed cream of mushroom soup, undiluted
  1 cup sliced fresh mushrooms
  1 cup cubed fully cooked lean ham
1/2 cup fat-free evaporated milk
  2 tablespoons white wine *or* water
  1 teaspoon prepared horseradish
  1 package (7 ounces) spaghetti
1/2 cup shredded Parmesan cheese

In a slow cooker, combine the soup, mushrooms, ham, milk, wine or water and horseradish. Cover and cook on low for 4 hours. Cook spaghetti according to package directions; drain. Add the spaghetti and cheese to slow cooker; toss to coat. **Yield:** 6 servings.

**Nutritional Analysis:** One serving (3/4 cup) equals 231 calories, 5 g fat (2 g saturated fat), 18 mg choles-

Potato Bean Skillet
Pork Chops in Tomato Sauce

terol, 607 mg sodium, 32 g carbohydrate, 1 g fiber, 14 g protein. **Diabetic Exchanges:** 2 starch, 1 lean meat, 1/2 fat.

## Kielbasa Bean Soup

### Ready in 45 minutes or less

*This satisfying soup is full of good-for-you ingredients, such as potatoes, cabbage and carrots. Simmer up a batch on a cold winter day.*
*—LaVerne Brandmeyer, San Antonio, Texas*

  1 small onion, chopped
  2 garlic cloves, minced
  2 teaspoons stick margarine
  2 cans (14-1/2 ounces *each*) reduced-sodium chicken broth
  1 medium potato, peeled and cubed
1/2 pound fully cooked turkey kielbasa *or* smoked turkey sausage, cut into 1/4-inch slices
  3 cups shredded cabbage
  1 can (15 ounces) garbanzo beans *or* chickpeas, rinsed and drained
  1 cup sliced fresh carrots
  2 tablespoons minced fresh parsley
  1 tablespoon white wine vinegar *or* cider vinegar
1/2 teaspoon pepper

In a large saucepan, saute onion and garlic in margarine until tender. Stir in broth and potato. Bring to a boil. Reduce heat; cover and simmer for 10 minutes. Stir in the remaining ingredients. Return to a boil. Reduce heat; cover and simmer for 10 minutes. **Yield:** 8 servings (2 quarts).
  **Nutritional Analysis:** One serving (1 cup) equals 147 calories, 2 g fat (trace saturated fat), 10 mg cholesterol, 694 mg sodium, 23 g carbohydrate, 4 g fiber, 9 g protein. **Diabetic Exchanges:** 1 starch, 1 lean meat, 1 vegetable.

## Apple Cranberry Bread

### (Pictured above right)

*Cranberries lend a burst of tart flavor and bright color to this quick bread. Dotted with crunchy nuts, slices of the moist loaf are good for breakfast with a cup of coffee or as a snack any time of the day.* —*Phyllis Schmalz Kansas City, Kansas*

    2 eggs
  3/4 cup sugar
    2 tablespoons canola *or* vegetable oil
1-1/2 cups all-purpose flour
1-1/2 teaspoons baking powder
    1 teaspoon ground cinnamon
  1/2 teaspoon baking soda
  1/2 teaspoon salt
    2 cups chopped peeled tart apples
    1 cup fresh *or* frozen cranberries
  1/2 cup chopped walnuts

Apple Cranberry Bread

In a mixing bowl, beat the eggs, sugar and oil. Combine the flour, baking powder, cinnamon, baking soda and salt; add to egg mixture just until combined (batter will be very thick). Stir in the apples, cranberries and walnuts.
  Transfer to an 8-in. x 4-in. x 2-in. loaf pan coated with nonstick cooking spray. Bake at 350° for 60-65 minutes or until a toothpick inserted near the center comes out clean. Cool for 10 minutes before removing from pan to a wire rack to cool completely. **Yield:** 1 loaf (16 slices).
  **Nutritional Analysis:** One slice equals 140 calories, 5 g fat (1 g saturated fat), 27 mg cholesterol, 143 mg sodium, 22 g carbohydrate, 1 g fiber, 3 g protein. **Diabetic Exchanges:** 1 starch, 1 fat, 1/2 fruit.

## Creamy Banana Pie

### Plan ahead...needs to chill

*I tried a lot of different banana pie recipes before I found one that could be modified into a low-fat version with great results.* —*Martha Domeny, San Diego, California*

    1 package (8 ounces) reduced-fat cream cheese
Sugar substitute equivalent to 1/2 cup sugar
    1 carton (8 ounces) frozen reduced-fat whipped topping, thawed, divided
    1 reduced-fat graham cracker crust (8 inches)
    3 medium firm bananas, sliced
1-1/3 cups cold 2% milk
    1 package (1 ounce) sugar-free instant vanilla pudding mix

In a mixing bowl, beat cream cheese and sugar substitute until smooth. Fold in 1 cup whipped topping; spoon into crust. Arrange banana slices on top. In a bowl, whisk milk and pudding mix for 2 minutes. Pour over the bananas. Spread with the remaining whipped topping. Refrigerate for at least 4 hours or overnight. **Yield:** 8 servings.
  **Nutritional Analysis:** One piece equals 302 calories, 11 g fat (7 g saturated fat), 19 mg cholesterol, 347 mg sodium, 43 g carbohydrate, 1 g fiber, 6 g protein. **Diabetic Exchanges:** 2 starch, 2 fat, 1 fruit.

# Chapter 16

# Centsible Foods—Fast and Frugal

PUTTING a good meal on the table doesn't have to take hours in the kitchen, and it doesn't have to cost a lot either.

Instead of relying on convenient yet costly carryout restaurant meals and store-bought packaged foods, look here for "centsible" express-eating alternatives that are as easy on the family budget as they are appetizing.

Our test kitchen has figured the cost per serving for each delicious dish. So these fast and frugal recipes will result in prompt meals and a plumper pocketbook.

**TIMELY AND TASTY.** Zucchini Pie (recipe on p. 236).

Glazed Lemon Cake

## Glazed Lemon Cake

*(Pictured above)*

*My mother baked this light moist treat when I was growing up. I loved it as much then as my children do now. Convenient boxed cake and pudding mixes make this delightful dessert wonderfully simple.* —Missy Andrews
Rice, Washington

> 1 package (18-1/4 ounces) white cake mix
> 1 package (3.4 ounces) instant lemon pudding mix
> 3/4 cup vegetable oil
> 3 eggs
> 1 cup lemon-lime soda
> 1 cup confectioners' sugar
> 2 tablespoons lemon juice

In a mixing bowl, combine the cake mix, pudding mix, oil and eggs; beat on medium speed for 1 minute. Gradually beat in soda. Pour into a greased 13-in. x 9-in. x 2-in. baking dish. Bake at 350° for 40-45 minutes or until cake springs back when lightly touched in center.

Combine confectioners' sugar and lemon juice until smooth; carefully spread over warm cake. Cool on a wire rack. **Yield:** 12 servings (22¢ per serving).

## Hurry-Up Ham Carbonara

**Ready in 30 minutes or less**

*This pasta will satisfy your taste buds and your pocketbook. Try adding peas or mushrooms for even more flavor.*
—Ramona Parris, Marietta, Georgia

> 1 package (8 ounces) angel hair pasta
> 1 medium onion, thinly sliced
> 1/4 cup vegetable oil
> 1 cup cubed fully cooked ham
> 1/2 cup chicken broth
> 1/4 cup stick margarine, melted
> 2 egg yolks, beaten
> 1/2 cup minced fresh parsley
> 1/2 cup grated Parmesan cheese

Cook pasta according to package directions. Meanwhile, in a large skillet, saute the onion in oil. Add the ham, broth and margarine; heat through.

Drain pasta; add to ham mixture. Add egg yolks; cook until the eggs are completely set. Sprinkle with parsley and Parmesan cheese; toss to coat. **Yield:** 4 servings (96¢ per serving).

## Pork-Potato Meatballs

**Ready in 45 minutes or less**

*My family just loves these delicious meatballs. Ground pork, shredded potato, green onion and mustard combine to create this savory sensation.* —Julaine Roach
Mauston, Wisconsin

1 cup finely shredded peeled potato
1/4 cup chopped green onions
1 egg, beaten
2 tablespoons milk
1 teaspoon prepared mustard
1/2 teaspoon salt
1/8 teaspoon pepper
1 pound ground pork
1/4 cup dry bread crumbs
1-1/3 cups water, *divided*
1 teaspoon chicken bouillon granules
2 tablespoons all-purpose flour

In a bowl, combine the first seven ingredients. Crumble pork over mixture and sprinkle with bread crumbs; mix gently. Shape into 1-in. balls. In a large skillet, brown meatballs in batches over medium heat; drain. Remove and keep warm.

Add 1 cup water and bouillon to skillet; stir until bouillon is dissolved. Return meatballs to the pan; cover and cook for 20 minutes or until no longer pink. Combine flour and remaining water until smooth; gradually add to skillet. Bring to a boil; cook and stir for 2 minutes or until thickened. **Yield:** 4 servings (48¢ per serving).

## Cajun Macaroni

**Ready in 30 minutes or less**

*When I have an extra half pound of ground beef, I use it in this easy dish.* —June Ellis, Erie, Illinois

1/2 pound ground beef
1/3 cup chopped onion
1/3 cup chopped green pepper
1/3 cup chopped celery
1 can (14-1/2 ounces) diced tomatoes, undrained
1-1/2 teaspoons Cajun seasoning
1 package (7-1/4 ounces) macaroni and cheese dinner mix
2 tablespoons milk
1 tablespoon butter *or* margarine

In a large saucepan, cook the beef, onion, green pepper and celery over medium heat until meat is no longer pink and vegetables are tender; drain. Add the tomatoes and Cajun seasoning; mix well. Cook, uncovered, for 15-20 minutes, stirring occasionally.

Meanwhile, prepare macaroni and cheese, using 2 tablespoons milk and 1 tablespoon butter. Stir in beef mixture; cook for 2-3 minutes or until heated through. **Yield:** 4 servings (76¢ per serving).

## Frosty Pineapple Salad

**Plan ahead...needs to freeze**

*Serve this refreshing pineapple treat as a salad or light dessert.* —Lillian Volf, Moncks Corner, South Carolina

✓ Uses less fat, sugar or salt. Includes Nutritional Analysis and Diabetic Exchanges.

1-1/2 cups buttermilk
3/4 cup sugar

1 can (20 ounces) unsweetened crushed pineapple, drained
1 carton (8 ounces) frozen whipped topping, thawed

In a bowl, combine the buttermilk, sugar and pineapple; mix well. Fold in the whipped topping. Transfer to a 13-in. x 9-in. x 2-in. dish. Freeze for 4 hours or until firm. Remove from the freezer 20 minutes before serving. **Yield:** 12 servings (23¢ per serving).

**Nutritional Analysis:** One 1/2-cup serving (prepared with reduced-fat whipped topping) equals 135 calories, 3 g fat (3 g saturated fat), 1 mg cholesterol, 36 mg sodium, 25 g carbohydrate, trace fiber, 1 g protein. **Diabetic Exchanges:** 1-1/2 fruit, 1 fat.

## Curried Bean Salad

*(Pictured below)*

**Plan ahead...needs to chill**

*Cumin and curry powder give this chilled three-bean salad terrific zip. I get a lot of compliments on it.* —Howie Wiener, Spring Hill, Florida

1 can (16 ounces) kidney beans, rinsed and drained
1 can (15 ounces) pinto beans, rinsed and drained
1 can (15 ounces) garbanzo beans *or* chickpeas, rinsed and drained
1 can (15-1/4 ounces) whole kernel corn, drained
3 celery ribs, chopped
1/2 cup chopped green onions
1/2 cup cider vinegar
1/4 cup vegetable oil
4 garlic cloves, minced
2 teaspoons dried oregano
1 teaspoon pepper
1/2 teaspoon ground cumin
1/2 teaspoon curry powder

In a bowl, combine the beans, corn, celery and onions. In a jar with a tight-fitting lid, combine the remaining ingredients; shake well. Drizzle over bean mixture and toss gently to coat. Cover and refrigerate overnight. Serve with a slotted spoon. **Yield:** 6 servings (70¢ per serving).

**Curried Bean Salad**

## Tex-Mex Rice

**Ready in 30 minutes or less**

*My grandmother gave me the recipe for this nicely spiced rice. Or add some ground beef for a satisfying skillet meal.*
—Kat Thompson, Prineville, Oregon

  1 cup uncooked long grain rice
  1 medium onion, chopped
  2 tablespoons vegetable oil
  2 cups boiling water
  1 medium green pepper, chopped
1-1/2 teaspoons chili powder
  1 teaspoon salt
  1 can (14-1/2 ounces) diced tomatoes, drained

In a skillet, saute rice and onion in oil until rice is browned and onion is tender. Stir in the water, green pepper, chili powder and salt. Bring to a boil. Reduce heat; cover and simmer for 15 minutes or until rice is tender. Stir in tomatoes; heat through. **Yield:** 6 servings (24¢ per serving).

## Garlic Salmon Linguine

*(Pictured below)*

**Ready in 15 minutes or less**

*This garlic-seasoned main dish calls for handy pantry ingredients, including pasta and canned salmon. I serve it with asparagus, rolls and fruit.*
—Theresa Hagan, Glendale, Arizona

**Garlic Salmon Linguine**

  1 package (16 ounces) linguine
  3 garlic cloves, minced
1/3 cup olive *or* vegetable oil
  1 can (14-3/4 ounces) salmon, drained, bones and skin removed
3/4 cup chicken broth
1/4 cup minced fresh parsley
1/2 teaspoon salt
1/8 teaspoon cayenne pepper

Cook the linguine according to package directions. Meanwhile, in a large skillet, saute garlic in oil. Stir in the salmon, broth, parsley, salt and cayenne. Cook until heated through. Drain linguine; add to the salmon mixture and toss to coat. **Yield:** 6 servings (67¢ per serving).

## Mushroom Beef Patties

**Ready in 1 hour or less**

*My husband and I work full-time off the farm, so I'm always looking for quick recipes that don't need much attention. Our three girls really like this beef and gravy combination.*
—Janice Miller, Creston, Iowa

  1 egg
1-3/4 cups milk, *divided*
  2 cups crushed cornflakes
  1 medium onion, chopped
  2 pounds ground beef
  1 can (10-3/4 ounces) condensed cream of mushroom soup, undiluted

In a bowl, combine egg, 1/2 cup milk, cornflakes and onion. Crumble beef over mixture and mix well. Shape into eight patties. In a large skillet, cook patties over medium heat until meat is no longer pink; drain. Transfer to a greased 13-in. x 9-in. x 2-in. baking dish. In a bowl, combine the soup and remaining milk until blended. Pour over patties. Bake, uncovered, at 350° for 30 minutes or until hot and bubbly. **Yield:** 8 servings (70¢ per serving).

## Golden Coconut Pie

**Plan ahead...needs to chill**

*Coconut lovers will enjoy the appealing look and taste of this lovely dessert. It'll please your palate as well as your pocketbook.*
—Helen Budin, Sterling, Colorado

1/2 cup stick margarine, softened
1/2 cup sugar
1/2 cup packed brown sugar
  2 eggs
  1 cup milk
3/4 cup corn syrup
  1 teaspoon vanilla extract
3/4 cup old-fashioned oats
3/4 cup flaked coconut
  1 unbaked pastry shell (9 inches)

In a mixing bowl, cream margarine and sugars. Add eggs, one at a time, beating well after each addition. Beat in milk, corn syrup and vanilla. Stir in oats and coconut. Pour into pastry shell. Cover edges loosely with foil. Bake at

350° for 40-50 minutes or until set. Cool on a wire rack. Refrigerate for at least 2 hours before serving. **Yield:** 8 servings (35¢ per serving).

## BBQ Chicken Sandwiches

*(Pictured at right)*

**Ready in 45 minutes or less**

*With four small children at home, I need quick yet filling meals. For a spicier taste, eliminate the ketchup and increase the amount of salsa to 1 cup.* —Leticia Lewis, Kennewick, Washington

✓ Uses less fat, sugar or salt. Includes Nutritional Analysis and Diabetic Exchanges.

Lime-Thyme Potato Wedges
BBQ Chicken Sandwiches

  1/2 cup chopped onion
  1/2 cup diced celery
    1 garlic clove, minced
    1 tablespoon butter
  1/2 cup salsa
  1/2 cup ketchup
    2 tablespoons brown sugar
    2 tablespoons cider vinegar
    1 tablespoon Worcestershire sauce
  1/2 teaspoon chili powder
  1/4 teaspoon salt
  1/8 teaspoon pepper
    2 cups shredded cooked chicken
    6 hamburger buns, split and toasted

In a saucepan, saute the onion, celery and garlic in butter until tender. Stir in the salsa, ketchup, brown sugar, vinegar, Worcestershire sauce, chili powder, salt and pepper. Add chicken; stir to coat. Bring to a boil. Reduce heat; cover and simmer for 15 minutes. Serve about 1/3 cup chicken mixture on each bun. **Yield:** 6 servings (66¢ per serving).
  **Nutritional Analysis:** One sandwich equals 270 calories, 6 g fat (2 g saturated fat), 45 mg cholesterol, 764 mg sodium, 35 g carbohydrate, 2 g fiber, 19 g protein. **Diabetic Exchanges:** 2 starch, 2 lean meat.

## Lime-Thyme Potato Wedges

*(Pictured above right)*

**Ready in 30 minutes or less**

*Toss together this side dish in less than a half hour. The delightful wedges are a refreshing change from typical baked potatoes.* —Edna Hoffman, Hebron, Indiana

  1/4 cup margarine, melted
    1 tablespoon lime juice
    1 teaspoon grated lime peel
    1 teaspoon dried thyme
    3 large potatoes
  1/4 cup grated Romano cheese
  1/2 teaspoon salt
  1/4 teaspoon paprika

In a large bowl, combine the margarine, lime juice, peel and thyme. Cut each potato into eight wedges; add to lime mixture and toss to coat. Place wedges skin side down on a greased baking sheet. Combine the cheese, salt and paprika; sprinkle over potatoes. Bake at 400° for 20-25 minutes or until tender. **Yield:** 6 servings (25¢ per serving).

## Zucchini Cakes

**Ready in 15 minutes or less**

*If you like crab cakes, try this unusual version made from zucchini. Maryland is famous for its crab cakes, but this recipe can sure fool you. They're easy and economical.* —Pat Tillman, Pylesville, Maryland

2-1/2 cups shredded zucchini
    1 cup seasoned bread crumbs
    1 egg, lightly beaten
    2 tablespoons chopped onion
    1 tablespoon butter, melted
    1 teaspoon prepared mustard
  3/4 teaspoon seafood seasoning
  1/2 cup crushed butter-flavored crackers (about 13 crackers)
    2 tablespoons vegetable oil

In a bowl, combine the zucchini, bread crumbs, egg, onion, butter, mustard and seafood seasoning; mix well. Shape into five patties. Dip in cracker crumbs. Heat oil in a large skillet; fry patties for 4 minutes on each side or until golden brown. Drain on paper towels. **Yield:** 5 patties (46¢ per serving).

Zucchini Pie

## Zucchini Pie

(Pictured above and on page 230)

**Ready in 45 minutes or less**

*This fluffy savory zucchini pie is delicious, easy and inexpensive.* —Melissa Collins, South Daytona, Florida

  1 tube (8 ounces) refrigerated crescent rolls
  3 medium zucchini, thinly sliced
  1 garlic clove, minced
  2 tablespoons butter *or* margarine
  2 teaspoons minced fresh parsley
  1 teaspoon snipped fresh dill
1/4 teaspoon salt
1/4 teaspoon pepper
  1 cup (4 ounces) shredded Monterey Jack
    cheese, *divided*
  2 eggs, lightly beaten

Separate crescent dough into eight triangles; place in a greased 9-in. pie plate with points toward the center. Press onto the bottom and up the sides of plate to form a crust; seal perforations.

In a skillet, saute zucchini and garlic in butter. Add the parsley, dill, salt, pepper and 1/2 cup cheese. Spoon into the crust. Pour eggs over top; sprinkle with remaining cheese. Cover edges loosely with foil. Bake at 375° for 25-30 minutes or until a knife inserted near the center comes out clean. Let stand for 5 minutes before cutting. **Yield:** 6 servings (76¢ per serving).

## Corn Bread Veggie Bake

**Ready in 45 minutes or less**

*This hearty casserole is a great addition to any meal. It's a nice change.* —Sharon Van Ornum, Hilton, New York

  1 can (10-3/4 ounces) condensed cream of
    mushroom soup, undiluted
  1 cup milk, *divided*

1-1/2 cups frozen mixed vegetables, thawed
  1 package (8-1/2 ounces) corn
    bread/muffin mix
  1 egg, beaten
2/3 cup french-fried onions

In a bowl, combine soup, 2/3 cup milk and vegetables. Transfer to a greased 11-in. x 7-in. x 2-in. baking dish. In a bowl, combine corn bread mix, egg and remaining milk just until blended. Carefully spread over vegetable mixture.

Sprinkle with onions (pan will be full). Bake at 350° for 25-30 minutes or until lightly browned and a toothpick inserted near the center comes out clean. **Yield:** 6 servings (52¢ per serving).

## Hamburger Soup

**Ready in 1 hour or less**

*I can't wait for chilly weather just so I can make this hearty soup! I came across the recipe a few years ago, and my family loves it.* —Sandra Koch, Elyria, Ohio

1-1/2 pounds ground beef
  2 cups diced onions
  1 cup diced carrots
  1 cup diced celery
  3 garlic cloves, minced
  3 cans (14-1/2 ounces *each*) chicken broth
  1 can (15 ounces) crushed tomatoes
  2 tablespoons Worcestershire sauce
  1 teaspoon hot pepper sauce
1/4 cup stick margarine
1/2 cup all-purpose flour

In a large saucepan or soup kettle, cook the beef, onions, carrots, celery and garlic over medium heat until meat is no longer pink and vegetables are tender; drain. Stir in broth, tomatoes, Worcestershire sauce and hot pepper sauce. Bring to a boil. Reduce heat; cover and simmer for 15 minutes.

In another saucepan, melt margarine over medium-low heat. Stir in flour until smooth. Cook and stir for 6-8 minutes or until mixture turns golden brown. Carefully stir into soup. Cover and simmer for 15 minutes, stirring occasionally. **Yield:** 10 servings (2-1/2 quarts, 68¢ per serving).

## Chicken Veggie Casserole

*(Pictured below right)*

*To save time, you can substitute a package of frozen vegetables.* —Bonnie Smith
Goshen, Indiana

- 3 cups cubed cooked chicken
- 4 medium carrots, cut into chunks
- 3 medium red potatoes, cut into chunks
- 3 celery ribs, sliced
- 1 can (10-3/4 ounces) condensed cream of chicken soup, undiluted
- 2/3 cup water
- 1/2 teaspoon salt
- 1/4 teaspoon pepper

Place chicken in a greased shallow 2-qt. baking dish. Top with the carrots, potatoes and celery. Combine the soup, water, salt and pepper; pour over vegetables. Cover and bake at 350° for 60-75 minutes or until vegetables are tender. **Yield:** 5 servings (98¢ per serving).

## Sausage Vermicelli

**Ready in 45 minutes or less**

*This is a longtime family favorite. Sausage adds savory flavor to this speedy skillet supper.* —Shauna Hamman
Mesa, Arizona

- 1 pound bulk pork sausage
- 1 medium onion, chopped
- 1 cup sliced celery
- 4-1/2 cups water
- 1 cup uncooked long grain rice
- 2 packages (2.1 ounces *each*) chicken noodle soup mix

In a large skillet, cook the sausage, onion and celery over medium heat until meat is no longer pink; drain. Remove meat and vegetables with a slotted spoon and set aside.

In the same skillet, combine the water, rice and soup mixes. Bring to a boil. Reduce heat; cover and simmer for 12-15 minutes or until rice is tender. Stir in sausage mixture; heat through. **Yield:** 5 servings (63¢ per serving).

## Stroganoff in a Bun

**Ready in 30 minutes or less**

*After just one taste, my family couldn't get enough of these. They're great with deviled eggs and baked beans.* —Corrine Lingberg
Beresford, South Dakota

- 2 pounds ground beef
- 1 large onion, chopped
- 1 can (10-3/4 ounces) condensed cream of mushroom soup, undiluted
- 1 cup mayonnaise*
- 3/4 cup finely chopped celery
- 2/3 cup condensed cheddar cheese soup, undiluted
- 18 hamburger buns, split

In a large skillet, cook beef and onion over medium heat until meat is no longer pink; drain. Stir in the mushroom soup, mayonnaise, celery and cheese soup. Bring to a boil. Reduce heat; simmer, uncovered, for 10 minutes or until heated through. Serve on buns. **Yield:** 18 servings (44¢ per serving).

**\*Editor's Note:** Light or fat-free mayonnaise may not be substituted for regular mayonnaise in this recipe.

## Apple Spice Snack Cake

*Nothing could be simpler or more delicious than this moist apple cake. It's easy to create the four-ingredient treat with a spice cake mix.* —Reba Savoie
Roswell, New Mexico

- 1 package (18-1/4 ounces) spice cake mix
- 1 can (21 ounces) apple pie filling
- 2 eggs
- 2 tablespoons vegetable oil

In a mixing bowl, combine all ingredients. Beat on medium speed for 2 minutes. Pour into a greased 13-in. x 9-in. x 2-in. baking dish. Bake at 350° for 30-35 minutes or until a toothpick inserted near the center comes out clean. Cool on a wire rack. **Yield:** 15 servings (18¢ per serving).

Chicken Veggie Casserole

KIDS like to help prepare fun food almost as much as they like to eat it. They'll especially want to get involved when they see the fast, flavorful foods on the following pages.

From speedy snacks and hearty entrees to tasty side dishes and sweet desserts, younger children can mix and measure ingredients while older ones help you get a head start on dinner.

Your children or grandchildren are sure to enjoy the hands-on experience, and you'll appreciate the quality time spent together.

Best of all, the whole family will be pleased—and proud—to sit down to a delectable dinner they helped make.

**KID-FRIENDLY FOODS.** From left to right: Banana Split Smoothies and Pizza Corn Dog Snacks (both recipes on p. 242).

**Biscuit Tostadas**

## Biscuit Tostadas

*(Pictured above)*

**Ready in 30 minutes or less**

*Refrigerated biscuits and just four other ingredients make it easy for little hands to assemble these cute kid-size tostadas. They're best eaten on a plate with a fork.*
—*Terrie Stampor, Sterling Heights, Michigan*

- 1 pound ground beef
- 1 jar (16 ounces) salsa, *divided*
- 1 tube (17.3 ounces) large refrigerated biscuits
- 2 cups (8 ounces) shredded Colby-Monterey Jack cheese
- 2 cups shredded lettuce

In a skillet, cook beef over medium heat until no longer pink; drain. Add 1-1/2 cups salsa; heat through. Split each biscuit in half; flatten into 4-in. rounds on un-greased baking sheets. Bake at 350° for 10-12 minutes or until golden brown. Top with meat mixture, cheese, lettuce and remaining salsa. **Yield:** 16 servings.

## Cereal Clusters

**Ready in 45 minutes or less**

*The recipe for this sweet and salty snack is so simple, children of almost any age can help in some way, if not prepare it themselves. There is not much mess to clean up afterward, so kids can enjoy the munchable treat soon after it's prepared.* —*Peggy-Jo Thompson, Lebanon, Tennessee*

- 12 ounces white candy coating, broken into pieces

- 1-1/2 cups crisp rice cereal
- 1-1/2 cups Peanut Butter Cap'n Crunch
- 1-1/2 cups salted dry roasted peanuts
- 1-1/2 cups miniature marshmallows

In a saucepan over medium-low heat, melt candy coating; stir until smooth. In a large bowl, combine the remaining ingredients. Pour coating over cereal mixture; stir to coat. Spread onto a waxed paper-lined baking sheet. Chill until firm. Break into pieces. Store in an airtight container. **Yield:** about 1-1/2 pounds.

## Cinnamon Pancake Cubes

**Ready in 15 minutes or less**

*When I was young, my mother introduced our family to this delicious way to use up leftover buttermilk pancakes. In fact, my father urged us not to eat all the pancakes so we could have these yummy cinnamon-and-sugar squares later.*
—*Donna Bielenberg, Tabernash, Colorado*

- 1 tablespoon butter *or* margarine
- 2 to 3 pancakes (about 6 inches), cut into 1-inch pieces
- 1 tablespoon sugar
- 1/8 teaspoon ground cinnamon

In a skillet, melt butter. Add the pancakes, sugar and cinnamon. Cook over low heat until heated through, about 3 minutes. **Yield:** 2 servings.

## Ribs for Kids

**Ready in 1 hour or less**

*This is one of my standby recipes. I always have wieners on hand, so it's easy to dress them up with a tangy homemade barbecue sauce to create these "ribs" that youngsters love. They're delicious served over rice, and leftovers reheat well.*
—*Valorie Walker, Bradley, South Carolina*

- 1 medium onion, chopped
- 2 tablespoons vegetable oil
- 1 cup water
- 1 cup ketchup
- 1/2 cup cider vinegar
- 2 tablespoons sugar
- 2 tablespoons Worcestershire sauce
- 2 teaspoons ground mustard
- 2 teaspoons paprika
- 1/8 teaspoon hot pepper sauce
- 6 hot dogs
- Hot cooked rice

In a saucepan, saute onion in oil until tender. Stir in water, ketchup, vinegar, sugar, Worcestershire sauce, mustard, paprika and hot pepper sauce. Bring to a boil. Reduce heat; simmer, uncovered, for 15 minutes.

Cut hot dogs in half lengthwise and then widthwise. Place in a greased 11-in. x 7-in. x 2-in. baking dish. Top with sauce. Bake, uncovered, at 350° for 20-25 minutes or until heated through. Serve over rice. **Yield:** 4-6 servings.

# Cute Cones Are Kid-Friendly

YOUR YOUNGSTERS will be eager to get the scoop on this fun idea sent in by Edna Hoffman. When her grandchildren and great-grandchildren come to visit the Hebron, Indiana cook, she often enlists their help to put the finishing touches on a batch of crowd-pleasing Puddin' Cones.

Kids can't wait to get a lick at these sweet snacks that look just like traditional ice cream cones. But since they're filled with a thick creamy mixture of pudding and whipped topping mix, they're less messy than ice cream.

You can sprinkle them with chopped nuts, candy sprinkles or miniature baking chips. Just tailor the tongue-tickling toppings to suit the tastes of your youngsters. No matter what they choose, these treats will be hard to top!

## Puddin' Cones

**Plan ahead...needs to chill**

1-1/2 cups cold milk
   1 package (3.4 ounces) instant vanilla
     pudding mix
   3 envelopes whipped topping mix
   8 cake ice cream cones (about 3 inches)
Chopped nuts, jimmies and miniature color-coated
   baking chips *or* topping of your choice

In a mixing bowl, beat milk and pudding mix on low speed for 2 minutes. Blend in whipped topping mix; cover and refrigerate for at least 1 hour. Spoon 1/4 cup into each cone; sprinkle with toppings. **Yield:** 8 servings.

Puddin' Cones

# Banana Split Smoothies

*(Pictured below and on page 238)*

**Ready in 15 minutes or less**

*This smooth and creamy beverage tastes just like a banana split. It's easy to blend together and not too sweet, so it's great any time of day. It's also a delicious way to get kids to eat fruit.* —Darlene Markel, Salem, Oregon

> 2 medium ripe bananas
> 1 can (8 ounces) crushed pineapple, drained
> 1-1/2 cups milk
> 1/2 cup fresh *or* frozen unsweetened sliced strawberries
> 2 tablespoons honey
> 5 ice cubes
> Whipped topping, chocolate syrup and maraschino cherries

In a blender, combine the first five ingredients; cover and process until smooth. Gradually add ice, blending until slushy. Pour into chilled glasses. Garnish with whipped topping, chocolate syrup and cherries. **Yield:** 4 servings.

# Pizza Corn Dog Snacks

*(Pictured below and on page 239)*

**Ready in 30 minutes or less**

*I dress up frozen corn dogs to create these tasty bite-size treats. Just slice 'em and spread 'em with pizza sauce and other toppings for a fun snack for kids or an easy appetizer for adults.* —Linda Knopp, Camas, Washington

> 1 package (16 ounces) frozen corn dogs, thawed
> 1/2 cup pizza sauce
> 3 tablespoons chopped ripe olives
> 1 jar (4-1/2 ounces) sliced mushrooms, drained
> 1/4 cup shredded mozzarella cheese

Remove stick from each corn dog; cut into 1-in. slices. Place on an ungreased baking sheet. Spread with pizza sauce. Top with olives, mushrooms and cheese. Bake at 350° for 15-20 minutes or until the cheese is melted and corn dogs are heated through. **Yield:** 30 snacks.

**Banana Split Smoothies**
**Pizza Corn Dog Snacks**

# Bake These Blooming Snacks

WANT your children to cultivate an interest in the culinary arts? It's easy to plant the seed. Just ask them to help you create these cute Flowerpot Cupcakes ...and their enthusiasm for baking is sure to grow!

Judi Oudekerk of Buffalo, Minnesota features these sweet treats as one of a number of "cooking club" projects at the after-school child-care program she supervises at a local elementary school.

"The flower-topped cupcakes are so easy that even our kindergartners make them," she assures. A strip of fruit roll is used to wrap a chocolate cupcake and form a mini flowerpot. Giving color to each pot are easy gumdrop blossoms growing from pretzel stick stems.

"They're great for a spring or summer birthday party," Judi adds.

## Flowerpot Cupcakes

1 package (18-1/4 ounces) devil's food
   cake mix
16 pieces Fruit by the Foot
24 large green gumdrops
48 large assorted gumdrops
48 pretzel sticks

Prepare cake batter according to package directions. Fill greased muffin cups two-thirds full. Bake at 350° for 18-20 minutes or until a toothpick comes out clean. Cool for 5 minutes; remove from pans to wire racks to cool completely.

Cut three 9-in. pieces from each fruit roll piece (save small pieces for another use). With a small pastry brush, lightly brush water on one end of a fruit strip. Wrap around bottom of cupcake; press ends together. Repeat with remaining cupcakes. Lightly brush water on one side of remaining fruit strips; fold in half lengthwise. Brush one end with water; wrap around cupcake top, slightly overlapping bottom fruit strip.

Press each gumdrop into a 1-1/4-in. circle. With scissors, cut each green gumdrop into four leaf shapes; set aside. Cut one end of each remaining gumdrop into a tulip shape. Gently press a pretzel into each tulip-shaped gumdrop. Gently press gumdrop leaves onto pretzels. Press two flowers into the top of each cupcake. **Yield:** 2 dozen.

## Secrets to Successful School Bake Sales

IF YOU'RE contributing goodies to a bake sale at your child's school, you may want to consider these creative packaging ideas from Diane Watson of Pawcatuck, Connecticut.

"Place six decorated cupcakes in a new Frisbee and cover with plastic wrap. Then attach a note that says 'free Frisbee' on the package," she shares. "Or fill a new beach pail with a dozen cookies. These colorful items went first at our bake sale."

Diane says lollipop cookies also were big sellers. The "cookies on a stick" were wrapped individually in plastic wrap and tied with a ribbon. Then the sticks were poked into a piece of foam placed in the bottom of a basket to create an inviting display. "We sold each lollipop cookie for 50¢," she says.

Here are some additional hints for decorating and packaging bake sale goodies for school events:

- Decorate treats with small gumdrops, M&M's or other candies in the school's colors.
- Package a few bars or cupcakes together with the school's initials spelled out on top using chocolate chips, cinnamon red-hots or other edible treats.
- Kids of all ages think small is cute. So stir up a batch of mini muffins, bite-size cupcakes or mini loaves of bread.
- Top frosted bars, brownies or cupcakes with bite-size candy bars or colorful gummy bears, fish or other creatures. Or use animal crackers, small teddy bear shaped cookies or miniature versions of popular cookies.
- Wrap cookies in pairs—with their bottoms together—or in short stacks of four or six. Package snack mixes in individual sandwich bags.
- Decorate frosted bars, brownies or cupcakes with colored sprinkles that coordinate with the current holiday or season.
- Place homemade candies or squares of fudge in foil candy cups or decorative mini muffin liners, then sell a half dozen on a small paper plate.
- Wrap breads in colored plastic wrap and decorate with bright stickers.

# Homemade Pizza Takes the Cake

IT'S NO SECRET that kids love pizza and they love dessert. Here's an extra-special treat that combines the two. Pizza Cake looks like a pepperoni pizza but has sweet tooth-tickling taste.

"Our kids had a great time putting together this cute creation for a Cub Scout cake auction," writes Caroline Simzisko of Cordova, Tennessee. "Using a boxed cake mix made preparation of the crust fast and easy."

Canned vanilla frosting tinted with red food coloring creates the pizza sauce while grated white baking chocolate sprinkled over the top looks like mozzarella cheese. Circles cut from fruit roll strips represent the palate-pleasing pepperoni.

"The recipe makes two cakes, so we were able to enjoy one at home and take the other to the Cub Scout event," says Caroline.

"Taylor, our son-turned-pizza-chef, isn't sure which he liked better—baking the cake or eating it. I, on the other hand, certainly appreciated the quality time we spent together in the kitchen."

## Pizza Cake

1 package (18-1/4 ounces) yellow cake mix
1 cup vanilla frosting
Red liquid *or* paste food coloring
3 squares (1 ounce *each*) white baking chocolate, grated
2 strawberry Fruit Roll-Ups

Prepare cake mix according to package directions. Pour the batter into two greased and floured 9-in. round baking pans. Bake at 350° for 20 minutes or until a toothpick inserted near the center comes out clean and cake is golden brown. Cool for 10 minutes before removing from pans to wire racks to cool completely.

Place each cake on a 10-in. serving platter. Combine the frosting and food coloring; spread over the top of each cake to within 1/2 in. of edges. Sprinkle with grated chocolate for cheese. Unroll Fruit Roll-Ups; use a 1-1/2-in. round cutter to cut into circles for pepperoni. Arrange on cakes. **Yield:** 2 cakes (6-8 servings each).

Pizza Cake

# Tuna Noodle Cups

**Ready in 1 hour or less**

*Older kids can get a jump on preparing dinner by stirring up these miniature tuna casseroles. Or serve them for brunch with fresh fruit, a tossed salad and rolls.*
*—Marlene Pugh, Fort McMurray, Alberta*

    8 ounces medium egg noodles
    1 package (10 ounces) frozen peas and
       carrots, thawed
    1 small onion, finely chopped
    1 can (6-1/2 ounces) tuna, drained
    2 cups (8 ounces) shredded cheddar cheese
    3 eggs
    1 can (12 ounces) evaporated milk
    1/2 cup water

Cook noodles according to package directions; drain and place in a large bowl. Add the peas and carrots, onion, tuna and cheese. In a small bowl, combine eggs, milk and water; stir into the noodle mixture. Spoon into greased muffin cups.

Bake at 350° for 30-35 minutes or until a knife comes out clean. Cool for 5 minutes; loosen edges with a knife to remove from cups. Serve immediately. **Yield:** about 1-1/2 dozen.

# Taco Meatballs

**Ready in 1 hour or less**

*If your family likes meatballs, try these for something a little different. The moist meatballs get plenty of zippy flavor from taco seasoning mix. Plus, they're baked, so there is very little mess.   —Jackie Hannahs, Fountain, Michigan*

    1 cup biscuit/baking mix
    1 envelope taco seasoning
    1 cup (4 ounces) shredded cheddar cheese
    1/2 cup water
    1 pound lean ground beef
Salsa *or* taco sauce

In a bowl, combine the first four ingredients. Crumble beef over mixture and mix well. Shape into 1-in. balls. Place in an ungreased 15-in. x 10-in. x 1-in. baking pan. Bake, uncovered, at 350° for 15-20 minutes or until no longer pink. Serve with salsa. **Yield:** 3-1/2 dozen.

# Purple Cows

**Ready in 15 minutes or less**

*Kids will need only three ingredients to whip up this bright beverage. The sweet blend gets its purple color and refreshing flavor from grape juice concentrate.*
*—Renee Schwebach, Dumont, Minnesota*

    1-1/2 cups milk
    3/4 cup grape juice concentrate
    2 cups vanilla ice cream

In a blender, combine milk and grape juice concentrate. Add ice cream; cover and blend until smooth. Serve immediately. **Yield:** 4 servings.

# Cinnamon Syrup

**Ready in 15 minutes or less**

*It's a snap to stir together this warm blend of cinnamon, butter and store-bought syrup. It's the perfect pancake topping. With its cinnamon-sugar taste, it's terrific on French toast and waffles, too.        —Janice Nightingale*
*Cedar Rapids, Iowa*

    1/2 cup butter *or* margarine
    1/4 cup maple pancake syrup
    3/4 to 1 teaspoon ground cinnamon

In a saucepan over low heat, heat butter, syrup and cinnamon until butter is melted. Stir until smooth. Serve warm over pancakes, French toast or waffles. **Yield:** about 3/4 cup.

# Hearty Mac 'n' Cheese

**Ready in 30 minutes or less**

*I do most of the cooking for our family of eight. Here is a hearty main dish that's a family favorite. It's a breeze to fix with boxed macaroni and cheese mix, and it tastes delicious.        —Tiffanie Froese, Athena, Oregon*

    1 pound ground beef
    1 small onion, chopped
    2 packages (7-1/4 ounces *each*) macaroni and
       cheese dinner
    1 cup (4 ounces) shredded mozzarella cheese
    6 bacon strips, cooked and crumbled

In a large skillet, cook beef and onion over medium heat until the meat is no longer pink. Meanwhile, prepare macaroni and cheese according to package directions.

Drain beef mixture; stir into macaroni and cheese. Transfer to a greased shallow 2-1/2-qt. baking dish. Sprinkle with mozzarella cheese and bacon. Broil until mozzarella is melted, about 2 minutes. **Yield:** 6-8 servings.

## More Pleasant Meals

EVEN the most delicious, nutritious dinner won't do any good if children refuse to eat it. Some youngsters are naturally finicky eaters, according to the American Dietetic Association, which shares these tips to make mealtime more enjoyable for everyone:

- If your child doesn't like one group of foods, try offering a nutritional substitute. For example, if the child won't eat vegetables, try serving fruit instead. Substitute cheese or yogurt for milk.

- To boost the nutritional values of prepared dishes, combine foods in unique ways, like adding nonfat dry milk to cream soups or puddings or mixing grated zucchini and carrots into quick breads, muffins, meat loaf and lasagna.

- Cut foods into interesting shapes. Draw a smiling face on top of a casserole with cheese, vegetables or fruit strips.

- Let children help with food preparation. Helping to prepare foods makes eating it a lot more fun.

Hot Dog Soup
No-Noodle Lasagna

## No-Noodle Lasagna

*(Pictured at left)*

**Ready in 45 minutes or less**

*Here's how to get all the comforting flavors of lasagna without all the work. Seal traditional lasagna ingredients between two layers of refrigerated crescent dough for a speedy specialty that's requested time and again.*
—Mary Moore, Omaha, Nebraska

1-1/2 pounds ground beef
1/2 cup chopped onion
1 can (6 ounces) tomato paste
1 tablespoon dried parsley flakes
1/2 teaspoon dried basil
1/2 teaspoon dried oregano
1/2 teaspoon salt
1/2 teaspoon pepper
Dash garlic salt
1 egg
1-1/2 cups (12 ounces) small-curd cottage cheese
1/4 cup grated Parmesan cheese
2 tubes (8 ounces *each*) refrigerated crescent rolls
1/2 pound sliced mozzarella cheese
1 tablespoon milk
1 tablespoon sesame seeds

In a large skillet, cook beef and onion over medium heat until meat is no longer pink; drain. Add tomato paste and seasonings; mix well. In a bowl, combine the egg, cottage cheese and Parmesan.

Roll out each tube of crescent dough between waxed paper into a 15-in. x 10-in. rectangle. Transfer one rectangle to a greased 15-in. x 10-in. x 1-in. baking pan. Spread with half of the meat mixture to within 1 in. of edges; top with half of the cheese mixture. Repeat meat and cheese layers.

Top with mozzarella. Carefully place second dough rectangle on top; press edges to seal. Brush with milk; sprinkle with sesame seeds. Bake, uncovered, at 350° for 25-30 minutes or until golden brown. **Yield:** 6 servings.

## Hot Dog Soup

*(Pictured at left)*

**Ready in 1 hour or less**

*We can always count on our retired pastor for good advice and good recipes, like this thick and hearty soup. Chock-full of hot dogs and vegetables, it quickly became my children's favorite.*
—Kim Holliday
Bellefonte, Pennsylvania

4 medium carrots, cut into thin strips
2 medium potatoes, peeled and cubed
2 medium parsnips, peeled and chopped
1 medium onion, chopped
1/4 cup butter *or* margarine
2 tablespoons all-purpose flour
1 package (1 pound) hot dogs, halved lengthwise and cut into bite-size pieces
1 can (12 ounces) evaporated milk
1 can (10-3/4 ounces) condensed cream of mushroom soup, undiluted
1 cup water
1 teaspoon dried basil
1/2 teaspoon pepper

In a soup kettle or large saucepan, saute the carrots, potatoes, parsnips and onion in butter for 5 minutes. Stir in flour until blended. Add the hot dogs, milk, soup, water, basil and pepper; bring to a boil. Reduce heat; cover and simmer for 25-30 minutes or until vegetables are tender, stirring occasionally. **Yield:** 8 servings (2 quarts).

## Crunchy Peanut Butter Drops

*Four pantry items are all you'll need to whip up these no-bake nibbles. These simple treats are an ideal after-school snack.* —Tammy Lewis, Hudson, South Dakota

1 cup light corn syrup
1 cup sugar
2 cups peanut butter*
4 cups cornflakes

In a large saucepan over medium heat, cook and stir corn syrup and sugar for 7-8 minutes or until sugar is dissolved (do not boil). Remove from the heat; add peanut butter and mix well. Fold in cornflakes. Drop by rounded tablespoonfuls onto waxed paper coated with nonstick cooking spray. Let stand for 1-1/2 to 2 hours or until set. Store in a waxed paper-lined airtight container. **Yield:** about 3-1/2 dozen.

**\*Editor's Note:** Reduced-fat or generic brands of peanut butter are not recommended for this recipe.

## Cheeseburger Biscuit Bake

**Ready in 45 minutes or less**

*Refrigerated biscuits are the easy golden topping on this casserole my daughter Kate loves to make and eat. This family favorite has the fun flavor of cheeseburgers.*
—Joy Frasure, Longmont, Colorado

1 pound ground beef
1/4 cup chopped onion
1 can (8 ounces) tomato sauce
1/4 cup ketchup
Dash pepper
2 cups (8 ounces) shredded cheddar cheese, *divided*
1 tube (12 ounces) refrigerated buttermilk biscuits, separated into 10 biscuits

In a large skillet, cook beef and onion over medium heat until meat is no longer pink; drain. Stir in tomato sauce, ketchup and pepper. Spoon half into a greased 8-in. square baking dish; sprinkle with half of the cheese. Repeat layers.

Place biscuits around edges of dish. Bake, uncovered, at 400° for 18-22 minutes or until the meat mixture is bubbly and biscuits are golden brown. **Yield:** 5 servings.

Pineapple Ice Pops
Sloppy Joe Wagon Wheels

## Sloppy Joe Wagon Wheels

*(Pictured at left)*

**Ready in 30 minutes or less**

*Sloppy joe sauce gives a bit of sweetness to prepared spaghetti sauce in this meaty mixture served over pasta wheels. My family likes it and doesn't realize how easy it is to make.*
—Lou Ellen McClinton, Jacksonville, North Carolina

1 package (16 ounces) wagon wheel pasta
2 pounds ground beef
1 medium green pepper, chopped
1 medium onion, chopped
1 jar (28 ounces) meatless spaghetti sauce
1 jar (15-1/2 ounces) sloppy joe sauce

Cook pasta according to package directions. Meanwhile, in a large skillet, cook beef, green pepper and onion until meat is no longer pink; drain. Stir in the spaghetti sauce and sloppy joe sauce; heat through. Drain pasta; top with beef mixture. **Yield:** 8 servings.

## Pineapple Ice Pops

*(Pictured at far left)*

**Plan ahead...needs to freeze**

*My grandmother passed down this ice cream recipe. Our kids loved it when I made it into Popsicles. Now our grandchildren enjoy the frozen treats...the older ones can assemble their own.* —Jo Snyder, South Bend, Indiana

1 quart buttermilk
1 can (20 ounces) crushed pineapple, drained
1-1/2 cups sugar
1 teaspoon vanilla extract
1/2 teaspoon salt
18 to 20 paper cups (3 ounces *each*) and Popsicle sticks *or* 18 to 20 Popsicle molds

In a bowl, combine the buttermilk, pineapple, sugar, vanilla and salt; mix well. Pour about 1/3 cup into each cup or mold; insert sticks into cups or top molds with holders. Freeze until solid. **Yield:** 18-20 servings.

# Cucumber Canoes Make a Splash

OH, BUOY! Lunchtime is sure to be a boatload of fun when you serve cool Cucumber Canoes from Robert Gibson of Norristown, Pennsylvania.

The youngster hollows out crunchy cucumber halves and fills them with a tasty tuna mixture to create these fuss-free boats.

To complete the look, he adds cherry tomatoes to represent people and crisp carrot sticks for paddles.

"This recipe is a great light lunch or dinner," reports his mom, Celeste. "The cute canoes are fun for kids to put together using healthy vegetables. And they love eating them, because they made the meal themselves."

Slice cucumbers in half lengthwise; with a spoon, remove and discard the seeds. Cut a thin slice from bottom of each cucumber half if necessary so it sits flat. In a bowl, combine the tuna, mayonnaise, celery, onion, salt and pepper. Spoon into cucumber halves. Add tomatoes for people and carrot sticks for paddles. **Yield:** 4 servings.

## Cucumber Canoes

**Ready in 30 minutes or less**

2 medium cucumbers
2 cans (6 ounces *each*) tuna, drained
1/2 cup mayonnaise
1 celery rib, finely chopped
1 teaspoon finely chopped onion
Salt and pepper to taste
8 cherry tomatoes
1 medium carrot, cut into eight sticks

Cucumber Canoes

## Pizza Grilled Cheese

*(Pictured below)*

**Ready in 15 minutes or less**

*My son Tim created this sandwich with dipping sauce to satisfy his love for pizza. He combined two all-time lunch favorites into one with this recipe*
—Robin Kettering, Newville, Pennsylvania

1 tablespoon butter *or* margarine, softened
2 slices bread
1 slice provolone *or* mozzarella cheese
6 slices pepperoni
3 tablespoons pizza sauce
Additional pizza sauce, optional

Butter one side of each slice of bread. Place one slice in a skillet, butter side down. Top with the cheese, pepperoni, pizza sauce and second bread slice, butter side up. Cook over medium heat until golden brown, turning once. Serve with additional pizza sauce if desired. **Yield:** 1 serving.

## Cheerio Treats

*(Pictured below)*

**Ready in 30 minutes or less**

*I use peanut butter, Cheerios and candies to put a tooth-tingling spin on marshmallow-cereal bars. Whether I take them to picnics or bake sales, I'm always asked for the recipe.* —Penny Reifenrath, Wynot, Nebraska

3 tablespoons butter *or* margarine

1 package (10-1/2 ounces) miniature marshmallows
1/2 cup peanut butter
5 cups Cheerios
1 cup plain M&M's

Place the butter and marshmallows in a large microwave-safe bowl. Microwave, uncovered, on high for 2 minutes or until puffed. Stir in the peanut butter until blended. Add the cereal and M&M's; mix well. Spoon into a greased 13-in. x 9-in. x 2-in. pan; press down gently. Cool slightly before cutting. **Yield:** 15 servings.

## Cookie Dessert

**Plan ahead...needs to chill**

*This no-bake treat tastes so good that no one believes how quickly it comes together. The recipe calls for just five ingredients.* —June Smith, Byron Center, Michigan

36 crisp chocolate chip cookies*
3/4 cup milk
1 carton (12 ounces) frozen whipped topping, thawed
2 tablespoons chocolate syrup
2 tablespoons chopped pecans

Quickly dip cookies completely in milk. Place 12 of the cookies in an ungreased 8-in. square dish; top with a third of the whipped topping. Repeat layers twice. Cover and refrigerate overnight. Drizzle with chocolate syrup; sprinkle with nuts. **Yield:** 9 servings.
*Editor's Note: This recipe was tested with Chips Ahoy chocolate chip cookies.

Cheerio Treats
Pizza Grilled Cheese

# Spider Surprises Are Full of Fun

BIG and little monsters alike will love making and munching these cute creatures from Andrea Chapman of Helena, Oklahoma.

Andrea and her grandmother, Flo Burtnett of Gage, Oklahoma, created Spooky Spider Snacks for festive no-fuss nibbling.

The kooky critters feature bodies made of creamy peanut butter simply sandwiched between round butter crackers. Chow mein noodles are ideal as the crunchy legs, and plump raisins act as eyes.

The clever crawlers come together in no time and pack the peanut butter punch that kids crave. And because there is no baking involved, children can help from start to finish.

Let these silly spiders creep their way into your kitchen after pumpkin carving or trick-or-treating. You'll be amazed at the web of fun they'll spin.

## Spooky Spider Snacks

**Ready in 15 minutes or less**

1/2 cup plus 1 tablespoon
    peanut butter
48 butter-flavored crackers
1/2 cup chow mein noodles
1/4 cup raisins

Spread 1 teaspoon of peanut butter on the tops of 24 crackers. Place three noodles on each side of each cracker; top with the remaining crackers. Spread a small amount of peanut butter on each raisin; place two on each cracker for eyes. **Yield:** 2 dozen.

Spooky Spider Snacks

## Spooky Celebrations Made Simple

ARE YOU hosting a gruesome get-together for a crew of pint-size goblins? Throwing a children's Halloween party is no reason to be scared silly. Consider the following tips, and your fall festival will be as easy as pumpkin pie!

- Keep decorations simple...and have the kids pitch in. They'll have fun making tissue paper ghosts and creating paper chains out of orange and black construction paper. Complete the look with inexpensive store-bought items, such as spiderwebs, black and orange balloons and crepe paper streamers.

- Put a spooky spin on everyday foods by giving them goose bump-inspiring names. If punch is on the menu, call it "Witch's Brew". Bowls of chili might be "Creepy Cauldrons" while a sweet snack mix can be "Graveyard Goodies". Peel red or green seedless

grapes and serve them as "Monster Eyeballs".

- If you're carving pumpkins before your autumn affair, don't discard the seeds. Wash them and lightly brown in vegetable oil; drain, then place on a baking sheet. Season and bake until crisp. Store the snacks in an airtight container until the party.

- For an eerie entree, place English muffin halves on a baking sheet and top with pizza sauce and shredded cheddar cheese. Arrange chopped black olives over the cheese to make jack-o'-lantern faces. Bake until the cheese is melted.

- Let little guests turn sugar cookies or cupcakes into monster morsels. Kids can frost the treats and use gumdrops, licorice and candy corn to create the faces of comical characters. Save time by baking the goodies a day early.

high heat. Remove and keep warm.

In the same skillet, saute the onion, green pepper and pineapple until vegetables are tender and pineapple is golden brown. Stir in barbecue sauce and reserved pineapple juice. Return chicken to the pan. Cover and simmer for 15 minutes or until chicken juices run clear. Serve over rice. **Yield:** 4 servings.

## Candy Bar Pie

*(Pictured at left)*

**Plan ahead...needs to chill**

*I've made this no-bake dessert for many occasions because the recipe is so simple and easy to remember. I freeze the candy bars and use a rolling pin to make crushing them easy.* —Sharlie Hanson
*Tulsa, Oklahoma*

  1 **package (8 ounces) cream cheese, softened**
  1 **carton (8 ounces) frozen whipped topping, thawed**
  4 **Butterfinger candy bars (2.1 ounces** *each***)**
  1 **prepared graham cracker crust (9 inches)**

In a small mixing bowl, beat the cream cheese until smooth. Fold in whipped topping. Crush the candy bars; fold 1 cup into cream cheese mixture. Spoon into crust. Sprinkle with remaining candy bar crumbs. Refrigerate for 2-4 hours before slicing. **Yield:** 6-8 servings.

Candy Bar Pie
Honey Barbecue Chicken

## Honey Barbecue Chicken

*(Pictured above)*

**Ready in 30 minutes or less**

*I love the combination of chicken and pineapple, yet I wanted to try something different. So I came up with this sweet and tangy chicken entree that doesn't take long to prepare and uses only one pan.* —Carrie Price
*Uneeda, West Virginia*

    1 **can (20 ounces) pineapple chunks**
    4 **boneless skinless chicken breast halves**
    1 **teaspoon curry powder**
    1 **tablespoon vegetable oil**
1/2 **cup chopped onion**
1/2 **cup chopped green pepper**
    1 **bottle (18 ounces) honey barbecue sauce**
**Hot cooked rice**

Drain pineapple, reserving juice; set fruit and juice aside. Sprinkle chicken with curry powder. In a large skillet, brown the chicken on both sides in oil over medium-

## Crazy Corn

*This snack is great at children's parties and a fun treat on TV night. When our boys were small, they loved making and eating it. It can be sent home in snack bags as a party favor with the recipe attached to the bag.* —Lee Ann Stidman, Spirit Lake, Idaho

    3 **quarts popped popcorn**
1/2 **cup light corn syrup**
1/4 **cup butter** *or* **margarine, melted**
    3 **tablespoons assorted colored sprinkles** *or* **colored sugar**
    1 **tablespoon sugar**
1/8 **teaspoon ground cinnamon**

Place popcorn in a large bowl. In a microwave-safe bowl, combine corn syrup and butter. Cover and microwave on high for 30-45 seconds; stir. Pour over popcorn; stir to coat. Immediately add colored sprinkles, sugar and cinnamon; toss to coat.

Transfer to two greased 15-in. x 10-in. x 1-in. baking pans; let stand for 1 hour or until dry. Store in an airtight container. **Yield:** 3 quarts.

# Bake a Big Batch of Beary Cute Critters

Peanut Butter Teddies

KIDS of all ages will cuddle up to these charming teddy bears that are packed with yummy peanut butter.

"I use the recipe for Peanut Butter Teddies in my home ec foods classes at the school where I teach," says Cynthia Kolberg of Syracuse, Indiana.

"The students love to make the cookies and think they're so cute," she notes. "However, that's never stopped them from eating the adorable little treats!"

Just a few basic ingredients are needed to create the dough. Then it's easy to roll it into balls and form the plump peanut butter bears. A few mini chocolate chips quickly complete the lovable look of the creatures.

## Peanut Butter Teddies

- 1 can (14 ounces) sweetened condensed milk
- 1 cup creamy peanut butter
- 1 teaspoon vanilla extract
- 1 egg
- 2 cups all-purpose flour
- 2 teaspoons baking soda
- 1/2 teaspoon salt
- 72 miniature semisweet chocolate chips (about 2 teaspoons)

In a large mixing bowl, beat the milk, peanut butter, vanilla and egg until smooth. Combine the flour, baking soda and salt; add to peanut butter mixture and mix well.

For each bear, shape the dough into one 1-in. ball, one 3/4-in. ball, six 1/2-in. balls and one 1/4-in. ball. On an ungreased baking sheet, slightly flatten the 1-in. ball to form the body. Place the 3/4-in. ball above body for head. For ears, place two 1/2-in. balls above head. For limbs, place four 1/2-in. balls next to the body.

For nose, place the 1/4-in. ball in the center of the head. Add two chocolate chips for eyes and one chip for belly button. Bake at 350° for 6-8 minutes or until lightly browned. Cool on baking sheets. **Yield:** 2 dozen.

## Bake Up a Family Tradition

FOR MANY PARENTS, baking goodies with their kids is a wonderful holiday tradition.

While decorating cookies, kneading dough and filling pies might take a bit longer with little ones in the kitchen, the memories can last a lifetime. So keep the following tips in mind the next time your tiny baker asks, "Can I help?"

- Set aside some time to bake with children. The holidays can be hectic, so consider devoting an afternoon or evening to this fun family event.
- Decide what you're going to bake first. Stick with something simple, and remember that children are likely to be more enthusiastic if they're baking a treat they enjoy eating.
- Determine which steps in the recipe each child will carry out before calling them into the kitchen. Younger children can decorate cookies and cupcakes while school-aged kids can measure ingredients and roll out dough. Pre-teens are old enough to frost cakes and handle some supervised oven work.
- Organize and clean the work area. Put all of the ingredients, pans, baking sheets and utensils on the counter. This ensures that you have everything you need, saving time that would otherwise be spent running to the grocery story or searching cabinets.
- Baking can be messy—even for grown-ups. Make sure children are dressed appropriately or have them wear an apron. Spreading newspaper on the floor can help reduce cleanup time.
- Be sure to supervise children at all times. Don't stretch yourself by preparing dinner or baking a separate item while you're working with kids. Instead, use this time to enjoy their company. With each memory that's made, you'll be glad you did!

# Chapter 18

# Timeless Recipes with Kitchen Tools

BUSY COOKS appreciate the convenience of slow cookers, grills and microwaves to get them out of the kitchen fast when time is tight.

With just a little preparation, you can assemble all the ingredients for wonderful recipes in your slow cooker. Then simply put on the lid, switch on the pot...and go!

When it comes to putting a meal on the table in a hurry, grilling is "hot" no matter what the season.

Time-conscious cooks know the magic of a microwave. Now you can use yours for more than warming coffee and reheating leftovers.

**SLOW-COOKED AND SENSATIONAL.** Barbecued Beef Brisket and Sweet 'n' Sour Sausage (recipes on pp. 260 and 261).

# Slow-Cooked Specialties

WHEN a full schedule keeps you away from the kitchen, put your slow cooker to work making a meal you and your family will love.

## Round Steak Roll-Ups

*(Pictured below)*

*Since I'm a working mom, I like to assemble these tasty steak rolls the night before and pop them in the slow cooker the next morning before we're all out the door. They make a great meal after a long day.* —Kimberly Alonge Westfield, New York

✓ Uses less fat, sugar or salt. Includes Nutritional Analysis and Diabetic Exchanges.

  2 pounds boneless beef round steak
1/2 cup grated carrot
1/3 cup chopped zucchini
1/4 cup chopped sweet red pepper
1/4 cup chopped green pepper
1/4 cup sliced green onions
  2 tablespoons grated Parmesan cheese
  1 tablespoon minced fresh parsley
    *or* 1 teaspoon dried parsley flakes
  1 garlic clove, minced
1/4 teaspoon salt
1/4 teaspoon pepper
  2 tablespoons canola oil
  1 jar (14 ounces) meatless spaghetti sauce
Hot cooked spaghetti
Additional Parmesan cheese, optional

Cut meat into six pieces; pound to 1/4-in. thickness. Combine the vegetables, Parmesan cheese and seasonings; place 1/3 cup in the center of each piece. Roll meat up around filling; secure with toothpicks.

In a large skillet, brown roll-ups in oil over medium-high heat. Transfer to a 5-qt. slow cooker; top with spaghetti sauce. Cover and cook on low for 6 hours or until meat is tender. Discard toothpicks. Serve roll-ups and sauce over spaghetti. Sprinkle with additional Parmesan if desired. **Yield:** 6 servings.

**Nutritional Analysis:** One serving (calculated without spaghetti or additional Parmesan) equals 289 calories, 11 g fat (3 g saturated fat), 96 mg cholesterol, 500 mg sodium, 9 g carbohydrate, 2 g fiber, 38 g protein. **Diabetic Exchanges:** 4 very lean meat, 2 vegetable.

**Round Steak Roll-Ups**
**Fruit Dessert Topping**

## Fruit Dessert Topping

*(Pictured below left)*

*You'll quickly warm up to the old-fashioned taste of this fruit topping. Spoon it over vanilla ice cream or slices of pound cake.* —Doris Heath, Franklin, North Carolina

    3 medium tart apples, peeled and sliced
    3 medium pears, peeled and sliced
    1 tablespoon lemon juice
1/2 cup packed brown sugar
1/2 cup maple syrup
1/4 cup butter *or* margarine, melted
1/2 cup chopped pecans
1/4 cup raisins
    2 cinnamon sticks (3 inches)
    1 tablespoon cornstarch
    2 tablespoons cold water
Pound cake *or* ice cream

In a slow cooker, toss apples and pears with lemon juice. Combine the brown sugar, maple syrup and butter; pour over fruit. Stir in the pecans, raisins and cinnamon sticks. Cover and cook on low for 3-4 hours.

Combine cornstarch and water until smooth; gradually stir into slow cooker. Cover and cook on high for 30-40 minutes or until thickened. Discard cinnamon sticks. Serve over pound cake or ice cream. **Yield:** about 6 cups.

## Chicken in Sour Cream Sauce

*Tender chicken is deliciously dressed up in a flavorful cream sauce with fresh mushrooms. This is an excellent entree for your family or guests.* —Jane Carlovsky, Sebring, Florida

1-1/2 teaspoons salt
1/4 teaspoon pepper
1/4 teaspoon paprika
1/4 teaspoon lemon-pepper seasoning
    6 bone-in chicken breast halves, skin removed
    1 can (10-3/4 ounces) condensed cream of mushroom soup, undiluted
    1 cup (8 ounces) sour cream
1/2 cup dry white wine *or* chicken broth
1/2 pound fresh mushrooms, sliced

Combine the first four ingredients; rub over chicken. Place in a slow cooker. In a bowl, combine the soup, sour cream, and wine or broth; stir in mushrooms. Pour over chicken. Cover and cook on low for 6-8 hours or until chicken juices run clear. Thicken the sauce if desired. **Yield:** 6 servings.

## Roast Beef and Gravy

*This is by far the simplest way to make roast beef and gravy. On busy days, I can put this main dish in the slow cooker and forget about it. My family likes it with mashed potatoes and fruit salad.* —Abby Metzger, Larchwood, Iowa

    1 boneless beef chuck roast (3 pounds)
    2 cans (10-3/4 ounces *each*) condensed cream of mushroom soup, undiluted
1/3 cup sherry, wine *or* beef broth
    1 envelope onion soup mix

Cut roast in half; place in a slow cooker. In a bowl, combine the remaining ingredients; pour over roast. Cover and cook on low for 8-9 hours or until meat is tender. **Yield:** 8-10 servings.

## Slow-Cooked Pork Barbecue

*I need only five ingredients to fix this sweet and tender shredded pork for sandwiches. Feel free to adjust the sauce ingredients to suit your family's tastes.* —Connie Johnson, Springfield, Missouri

    1 boneless pork loin roast (3 to 4 pounds)
1-1/2 teaspoons seasoned salt
    1 teaspoon garlic powder
    1 cup barbecue sauce
    1 cup cola
    8 to 10 sandwich rolls, split

Cut roast in half; place in a slow cooker. Sprinkle with seasoned salt and garlic powder. Cover and cook on low for 4 hours or until meat is tender.

Remove meat; skim fat from cooking juices. Shred meat with a fork and return to the slow cooker. Combine barbecue sauce and cola; pour over meat. Cover and cook on high for 1-2 hours or until sauce is thickened. Serve on rolls. **Yield:** 8-10 servings.

## Ground Beef Stew

*I created this chunky soup when looking for something inexpensive and easy to make. The thick and hearty mixture is chock-full of ground beef, potatoes and baby carrots.* —Sandra Castillo, Sun Prairie, Wisconsin

 Uses less fat, sugar or salt. Includes Nutritional Analysis and Diabetic Exchanges.

    1 pound ground beef
    6 medium potatoes, peeled and cubed
    1 package (16 ounces) baby carrots
    3 cups water
    2 tablespoons dry onion soup mix
    1 garlic clove, minced
    1 teaspoon Italian seasoning
    1 to 1-1/2 teaspoons salt
1/4 teaspoon garlic powder
1/4 teaspoon pepper
    1 can (10-3/4 ounces) condensed tomato soup, undiluted
    1 can (6 ounces) Italian tomato paste

In a skillet, cook beef over medium heat until no longer pink; drain. In a slow cooker, combine the next nine ingredients.

Stir in the beef. Cover and cook on high for 4-5 hours. Stir in soup and tomato paste; cover and cook for 1 hour or un-til heated through. **Yield:** 12 servings.

**Nutritional Analysis:** One 1-cup serving (prepared with lean ground beef, 1 teaspoon salt and reduced-fat reduced-sodium tomato soup) equals 180 calories, 4 g fat (2 g saturated fat), 14 mg cholesterol, 434 mg sodium, 26 g carbohydrate, 3 g fiber, 10 g protein. **Diabetic Exchanges:** 1-1/2 starch, 1 lean meat, 1 vegetable.

## Red Pepper Chicken

*Chicken breasts are treated to a bevy of black beans, red peppers and tomatoes in this Southwestern supper. We love this colorful dish over rice cooked in chicken broth. —Piper Spiwak, Vienna, Virginia*

      4 boneless skinless chicken breast halves
      1 can (15 ounces) black beans, rinsed and drained
      1 jar (15 ounces) roasted red peppers, undrained
      1 can (14-1/2 ounces) Mexican stewed tomatoes, undrained
      1 large onion, chopped
  1/2 teaspoon salt
Pepper to taste
Hot cooked rice

Place the chicken in a slow cooker. In a bowl, combine the beans, red peppers, tomatoes, onion, salt and pepper. Pour over the chicken. Cover and cook on low for 6 hours or until chicken is no longer pink. Serve over rice. **Yield:** 4 servings.

## Mushroom Round Steak

*I think our family would starve if I didn't have a slow cooker—I use it twice a week. This tender beef entree is perfect with mashed potatoes. —Linda Krivanek, Oak Creek, Wisconsin*

  1/2 cup all-purpose flour
      1 teaspoon salt
  1/4 teaspoon pepper
      2 to 2-1/2 pounds boneless beef round steak (1/2 inch thick), cut into serving-size pieces
      2 tablespoons vegetable oil
      1 can (10-1/2 ounces) condensed French onion soup, undiluted
      1 can (8 ounces) mushroom stems and pieces, drained
  3/4 cup water
  1/4 cup ketchup
      1 tablespoon Worcestershire sauce
      2 tablespoons cornstarch
  1/4 cup cold water
      1 cup (8 ounces) sour cream

In a large resealable plastic bag, combine the flour, salt and pepper. Add beef, a few pieces at a time, and shake to coat. In a large skillet, brown the beef in batches in oil. Transfer meat to a slow cooker with a slotted spoon. In a bowl, combine the soup, mushrooms, water, ketchup and Worcestershire sauce. Pour over meat. Cover and cook on low for 8 hours or until meat is tender.

Remove beef with a slotted spoon; keep warm. Transfer cooking liquid to a saucepan. Combine cornstarch and cold water until smooth; gradually stir into cooking liquid. Bring to a boil; cook and stir for 1-2 minutes or until thickened. Stir a small amount of hot liquid into sour cream. Return all to the pan; cook on low until heated through. Serve over meat. **Yield:** 6 servings.

## Fruity Pork Chops

*I simmer pork chops in fruit juice seasoned with orange peel, mustard and red wine vinegar, then top them with a delightful sauce made with handy fruit cocktail. —Bonnie Baumgardner, Sylva, North Carolina*

      4 bone-in pork loin chops (1 inch thick)
  1/2 teaspoon salt
  1/4 teaspoon pepper
  1/8 teaspoon dried rosemary, crushed
  1/8 teaspoon dill weed
  1/8 teaspoon ground ginger
      2 tablespoons vegetable oil
      1 can (15 ounces) fruit cocktail
      2 tablespoons red wine vinegar *or* cider vinegar
      1 tablespoon prepared mustard
  1/4 teaspoon grated orange peel
      2 tablespoons cornstarch
      2 tablespoons cold water

Sprinkle pork chops with salt, pepper, rosemary, dill and ginger. In a skillet, brown chops on both sides in oil; transfer to a slow cooker. Drain fruit cocktail, reserving juice. Refrigerate fruit cocktail. In a bowl, combine the vinegar, mustard, orange peel and reserved fruit juice. Pour over pork. Cover and cook on low for 7-8 hours or until meat is tender.

Remove chops and keep warm. Strain the cooking liquid into a small saucepan. Combine the cornstarch and water until smooth; stir into the cooking liquid. Bring to a boil; cook and stir for 2 minutes or until thickened and bubbly. Add fruit cocktail; heat through. Serve over pork chops. **Yield:** 4 servings.

## Corny Chili

*(Pictured above right)*

*This is so delicious and simple that I had to share it. I'm sure busy moms will be just as happy as I am with the taste and time-saving convenience of this pleasant chili. —Marlene Olson, Hoople, North Dakota*

✓ Uses less fat, sugar or salt. Includes Nutritional Analysis and Diabetic Exchanges.

      1 pound ground beef
      1 small onion, chopped
      1 can (16 ounces) kidney beans, rinsed and drained
      2 cans (14-1/2 ounces *each*) diced tomatoes, undrained
      1 can (11 ounces) whole kernel corn, drained
  3/4 cup picante sauce
      1 tablespoon chili powder
  1/4 to 1/2 teaspoon garlic powder
Corn chips, sour cream and shredded cheddar cheese, optional

In a skillet, cook beef and onion over medium heat until meat is no longer pink; drain. Transfer to a slow cooker. Stir in the beans, tomatoes, corn, picante sauce, chili powder and garlic powder. Cover and cook on low for 3-4 hours or until heated through. Serve with corn chips,

Corny Chili
Bandito Chili Dogs

sour cream and cheese if desired. **Yield:** 4-6 servings.
   **Nutritional Analysis:** One 1-cup serving (prepared with lean ground beef; calculated without accompaniments) equals 408 calories, 12 g fat (4 g saturated fat), 41 mg cholesterol, 1,311 mg sodium, 45 g carbohydrate, 10 g fiber, 32 g protein. **Diabetic Exchanges:** 4 lean meat, 3 vegetable, 2 starch.

## Bandito Chili Dogs

*(Pictured above)*

*I've brought these beefy chili dogs to family functions for years. The ingredients cook while you're at a game or other activity, so the meal is ready when you get home.*
   —Marion Lowery, Medford, Oregon

   1 package (1 pound) hot dogs
   2 cans (15 ounces *each*) chili without beans
   1 can (10-3/4 ounces) condensed cheddar cheese soup, undiluted
   1 can (4 ounces) chopped green chilies
 10 hot dog buns, split
   1 medium onion, chopped
   1 to 2 cups corn chips, coarsely crushed
   1 cup (4 ounces) shredded cheddar cheese

Place hot dogs in a slow cooker. In a bowl, combine the chili, soup and green chilies; pour over hot dogs.

Cover and cook on low for 4-5 hours. Serve hot dogs in buns; top with chili mixture, onion, corn chips and cheese. **Yield:** 10 servings.

## Pizza Rigatoni

*I turn my slow cooker into a pizzeria with this zesty layered casserole. It is loaded with cheese, Italian sausage, pepperoni and pasta.* —Marilyn Cowan
North Manchester, Indiana

1-1/2 pounds bulk Italian sausage
   3 cups uncooked rigatoni *or* large tube pasta
   4 cups (16 ounces) shredded mozzarella cheese
   1 can (10-3/4 ounces) condensed cream of mushroom soup, undiluted
   1 small onion, chopped
   2 cans (one 15 ounces, one 8 ounces) pizza sauce
   1 package (3-1/2 ounces) sliced pepperoni
   1 can (6 ounces) pitted ripe olives, drained and halved

In a skillet, cook sausage until no longer pink; drain. Cook pasta according to package directions; drain. In a 5-qt. slow cooker, layer half of the sausage, pasta, cheese, soup, onion, pizza sauce, pepperoni and olives. Repeat layers. Cover and cook on low for 4 hours. **Yield:** 6-8 servings.

## Sweet 'n' Sour Sausage

*(Pictured below and on page 254)*

*Carrots, green pepper and pineapple lend gorgeous color to this slow-cooked sausage supper. Serve this combination stir-fry style over rice or chow mein noodles.*

*—Barbara Schutz, Pandora, Ohio*

☑ Uses less fat, sugar or salt. Includes Nutritional Analysis and Diabetic Exchanges.

- 1 pound fully cooked kielbasa *or* Polish sausage, sliced
- 1 can (20 ounces) unsweetened pineapple chunks, undrained
- 1-1/2 cups baby carrots, quartered lengthwise
- 1 large green pepper, cut into 1-inch pieces
- 1 medium onion, cut into chunks
- 1/3 cup packed brown sugar
- 1 tablespoon soy sauce
- 1/2 teaspoon chicken bouillon granules
- 1/4 teaspoon garlic powder
- 1/4 teaspoon ground ginger
- 2 tablespoons cornstarch
- 1/4 cup cold water
- Hot cooked rice *or* chow mein noodles

In a slow cooker, combine the first 10 ingredients. Cover and cook on low for 4-5 hours; drain. In a small saucepan, combine the cornstarch and water until smooth. Bring to a boil; cook and stir for 1 minute or until thickened. Stir into the sausage mixture. Serve over rice. **Yield:** 6 servings.

**Nutritional Analysis:** One 1-cup serving (prepared with smoked turkey sausage and reduced-sodium soy sauce; calculated without rice) equals 250 calories, 4 g fat (1 g saturated fat), 34 mg cholesterol, 869 mg sodium, 43 g carbohydrate, 1 g fiber, 10 g protein. **Diabetic Exchanges:** 2 fruit, 1 lean meat, 1 vegetable, 1/2 starch.

Barbecued Beef Brisket
Sweet 'n' Sour Sausage

## Chicken with Stuffing

*I need only five ingredients to create this comforting home-style meal of chicken topped with corn bread stuffing. I sometimes add two cans of soup so there's more sauce.* —Susan Kutz
Stillman Valley, Illinois

4 boneless skinless chicken breast halves
1 can (10-3/4 ounces) condensed cream of chicken soup, undiluted
1-1/4 cups water
1/4 cup butter *or* margarine, melted
1 package (6 ounces) corn bread stuffing mix

Place chicken in a greased slow cooker. Top with soup. In a bowl, combine the water, butter and stuffing mix; spoon over the chicken. Cover and cook on low for 4 hours or until chicken juices run clear. **Yield:** 4 servings.

## Veggie Meatball Soup

*It's a snap to put together this hearty soup before I leave for work. I just add cooked pasta when I get home, and I have a few minutes to relax before supper is ready.* —Charla Tinney, Tyrone, Oklahoma

3 cups beef broth
2 cups frozen mixed vegetables, thawed
1 can (14-1/2 ounces) stewed tomatoes
15 frozen fully cooked meatballs, thawed
3 bay leaves
1/4 teaspoon pepper
1 cup spiral pasta, cooked and drained

In a slow cooker, combine the first six ingredients. Cover and cook on low for 4-5 hours. Just before serving, stir in the pasta; heat through. Discard the bay leaves. **Yield:** 6 servings.

## Barbecued Beef Brisket

*(Pictured at left and on page 255)*

*I enjoy fixing a sit-down meal for my husband and myself every evening, so this entree is often on the menu. It's fairly inexpensive and takes little effort to prepare. The tender beef tastes wonderful. It has delicious homemade goodness without a lot of fuss.* —Anita Keppinger
Philomath, Oregon

1 teaspoon salt
1 teaspoon chili powder
1/2 teaspoon garlic powder
1/4 teaspoon onion powder
1/4 teaspoon celery seed
1/4 teaspoon pepper
1 fresh beef brisket* (2-1/2 pounds), trimmed
SAUCE:
1/2 cup ketchup
1/2 cup chili sauce
1/4 cup packed brown sugar
2 tablespoons cider vinegar
2 tablespoons Worcestershire sauce

1 to 1-1/2 teaspoons liquid smoke, optional
1/2 teaspoon ground mustard

Combine first six ingredients; rub over brisket. Place in a slow cooker. In a bowl, combine sauce ingredients. Pour half over brisket; set remaining sauce aside. Cover and cook on high for 4-5 hours or until meat is tender. Serve with the reserved sauce. **Yield:** 8 servings.

**\*Editor's Note:** This is a fresh beef brisket, not corned beef.

## Party-Pleasing Beef Dish

*I often prepare this mild spaghetti sauce-like mixture when I'm not sure how many guests are coming. It's easy to fix, easy to serve with tortilla chips and toppings and easy to clean up.* —Glee Witzke
Crete, Nebraska

1 pound ground beef
1 medium onion, chopped
3/4 cup water
1 can (8 ounces) tomato sauce
1 can (6 ounces) tomato paste
2 teaspoons sugar
1 garlic clove, minced
1 teaspoon chili powder
1 teaspoon ground cumin
1 teaspoon dried oregano
1 cup cooked rice
Tortilla chips
Toppings—shredded cheddar cheese, chopped green onions, sliced ripe olives, sour cream, chopped tomato and taco sauce

In a large skillet, cook beef and onion over medium heat until meat is no longer pink; drain. Transfer to a slow cooker. Add the next eight ingredients; mix well. Cover and cook on low for 4 hours or until heated through. Add rice; cover and cook 10 minutes longer. Serve over tortilla chips with toppings of your choice. **Yield:** 6-8 servings.

## Lemon Pork Chops

*These chops can simmer all day on low and be super-tender by dinnertime. I serve them with a crisp salad and macaroni and cheese as a side dish.* —Barbara De Frang
Hazen, North Dakota

4 bone-in pork loin chops (3/4 inch thick)
1/2 teaspoon salt
1/4 teaspoon pepper
1 medium onion, cut into 1/4-inch slices
1 medium lemon, cut into 1/4-inch slices
1/4 cup packed brown sugar
1/4 cup ketchup

Place the pork chops in a slow cooker. Sprinkle with salt and pepper. Top with onion and lemon. Sprinkle with brown sugar; drizzle with ketchup. Cover and cook on low for 6 hours or until meat juices run clear. **Yield:** 4 servings.

# Pizza Casserole

*A friend from church gave me the recipe for this satisfying casserole for the slow cooker. It's always one of the first dishes emptied at potlucks, and it can easily be adapted to personal tastes.* —Julie Sterchi, Harrisburg, Illinois

      3 pounds ground beef
  1/2 cup chopped onion
      1 jar (28 ounces) spaghetti sauce
      2 jars (4-1/2 ounces *each*) sliced mushrooms, drained
      1 teaspoon salt
  1/2 teaspoon garlic powder
  1/2 teaspoon dried oregano
Dash pepper
      1 package (16 ounces) wide egg noodles, cooked and drained
      2 packages (3-1/2 ounces *each*) sliced pepperoni
      2 cups (8 ounces) shredded cheddar cheese
      2 cups (8 ounces) shredded mozzarella cheese

In a Dutch oven, brown beef and onion over medium heat until meat is no longer pink; drain. Add spaghetti sauce, mushrooms, salt, garlic powder, oregano and pepper; heat through. Spoon 4 cups into a 5-qt. slow cooker. Top with half of the noodles, pepperoni and cheeses. Repeat layers. Cover and cook on high for 1 hour or until cheese is melted. **Yield:** 12 servings.

# Creamy Potatoes 'n' Kielbasa

*I rely on five ingredients and my slow cooker to create this hearty meal-in-one that my whole family loves. Kielbasa beefs up the hash browns and cheese in this comforting main dish.* —Beth Sine Faulkner, Maryland

      1 package (28 ounces) frozen O'Brien hash brown potatoes
      1 pound fully cooked kielbasa *or* Polish sausage, cut into 1/4-inch slices
      1 can (10-3/4 ounces) condensed cream of mushroom soup, undiluted
      1 cup (4 ounces) shredded cheddar cheese
  1/2 cup water

In a slow cooker, combine all ingredients. Cover and cook on low for 6-8 hours or until the potatoes are tender. **Yield:** 4-6 servings.

# Slow-Cooked Corn Chowder

*I combine and refrigerate the ingredients for this easy chowder the night before. In the morning, I pour the mixture into the slow cooker and turn it on before I leave for work. When I come home, a hot tasty meal awaits.* —Mary Hogue, Rochester, Pennsylvania

2-1/2 cups milk
      1 can (14-3/4 ounces) cream-style corn
      1 can (10-3/4 ounces) condensed cream of mushroom soup, undiluted

1-3/4 cups frozen corn
      1 cup frozen shredded hash brown potatoes
      1 cup cubed fully cooked ham
      1 large onion, chopped
      2 tablespoons butter *or* margarine
      2 teaspoons dried parsley flakes
Salt and pepper to taste

In a slow cooker, combine all ingredients. Cover and cook on low for 6 hours. **Yield:** 8 servings (2 quarts).

# Flavorful Beef in Gravy

*Served over noodles, this fantastic supper showcases tender chunks of savory beef stew meat. I use canned soups and onion soup mix to make the mouth-watering gravy. With a green salad and crusty bread, dinner is complete.* —Cheryl Sindergard, Plover, Iowa

  1/3 cup all-purpose flour
      3 pounds beef stew meat, cut into 1-inch cubes
      3 tablespoons vegetable oil
      2 cans (10-3/4 ounces *each*) condensed cream of mushroom soup, undiluted
      1 can (10-3/4 ounces) condensed golden mushroom soup, undiluted
      1 can (10-3/4 ounces) condensed cream of celery soup, undiluted
1-1/3 cups milk
      1 envelope onion soup mix
Hot cooked noodles *or* mashed potatoes

Place flour in a large resealable plastic bag; add beef and toss to coat. In a skillet, brown beef in oil. Transfer beef to a 5-qt. slow cooker. Stir in the soups, milk and soup mix. Cover and cook on low for 7-8 hours or until the meat is tender. Serve over noodles or potatoes. **Yield:** 10-12 servings.

# Spicy Chicken Tomato Soup

*(Pictured above right)*

*Cumin, chili powder and cayenne pepper give this slow-cooked specialty its kick. I serve bowls of it with crunchy tortilla strips that bake in no time. Leftover soup freezes well for nights I don't feel like cooking.* —Margaret Bailey, Coffeeville, Mississippi

      2 cans (14-1/2 ounces *each*) chicken broth
      3 cups cubed cooked chicken
      2 cups frozen corn
      1 can (10-3/4 ounces) tomato puree
      1 can (10 ounces) diced tomatoes and green chilies
      1 large onion, finely chopped
      2 garlic cloves, minced
      1 bay leaf
      1 to 2 teaspoons ground cumin
      1 teaspoon salt
  1/2 to 1 teaspoon chili powder
  1/8 teaspoon pepper

Spicy Chicken Tomato Soup
Chicken with Vegetables

1/8 teaspoon cayenne pepper
4 white *or* yellow corn tortillas (6 inches), cut into 1/4-inch strips

In a slow cooker, combine the first 13 ingredients. Cover and cook on low for 4 hours. Place the tortilla strips on an ungreased baking sheet. Bake at 375° for 5 minutes; turn. Bake 5 minutes longer. Discard bay leaf from soup. Serve with tortilla strips. **Yield:** 8 servings.

## Chicken with Vegetables

### (Pictured above)

*You'll be surprised at how easily this tender chicken entree comes together. It's simple, delicious and a great way to get your family to eat vegetables. —Norlene Razak, Tye, Texas*

✓ Uses less fat, sugar or salt. Includes Nutritional Analysis and Diabetic Exchanges.

1 cup sliced fresh mushrooms
4 chicken legs, skin removed
4 chicken thighs, skin removed
4 celery ribs, sliced
1 cup sliced zucchini
1 cup sliced carrots
1 medium onion, sliced
1 cup tomato juice
1/2 cup chicken broth
1 garlic clove, minced
1/4 teaspoon paprika
Pepper to taste
3 tablespoons cornstarch
3 tablespoons cold water
Hot cooked rice

Place mushrooms and chicken in a slow cooker. Add the celery, zucchini, carrots, onion, tomato juice, broth, garlic, paprika and pepper. Cover and cook on low for 5 hours or until meat juices run clear.

Remove chicken and vegetables and keep warm. Transfer cooking juices to a saucepan; skim fat. Combine the cornstarch and water until smooth; add to the juices. Bring to a boil; cook and stir for 2 minutes or until thickened. Pour over chicken and vegetables; serve over rice. **Yield:** 4 servings.

**Nutritional Analysis:** One leg and one thigh with 3/4 cup vegetable mixture (prepared with reduced-sodium tomato juice; calculated without rice) equals 315 calories, 9 g fat (2 g saturated fat), 152 mg cholesterol, 371 mg sodium, 18 g carbohydrate, 3 g fiber, 40 g protein. **Diabetic Exchanges:** 4 lean meat, 2 vegetable, 1/2 starch.

## Spicy Lemon Chicken

*(Pictured below)*

*I took a favorite recipe and modified it to work in our slow cooker. We enjoy this tender lemony chicken with rice or buttered noodles.* —Nancy Rambo, Riverside, California

✓ Uses less fat, sugar or salt. Includes Nutritional Analysis and Diabetic Exchanges.

    1 medium onion, chopped
  1/3 cup water
  1/4 cup lemon juice
    1 tablespoon vegetable *or* canola oil
  1/2 to 1 teaspoon salt
  1/2 teaspoon *each* garlic powder, chili powder
      and paprika
  1/2 teaspoon ground ginger
  1/4 teaspoon pepper
    4 boneless skinless chicken breast halves (4
      ounces *each*)
4-1/2 teaspoons cornstarch
4-1/2 teaspoons cold water
Hot cooked noodles
Chopped fresh parsley, optional

In a greased slow cooker, combine the onion, water, lemon juice, oil and seasonings. Add chicken; turn to coat. Cover and cook on low for 4-5 hours or until a meat thermometer reads 170°. Remove chicken and keep warm.

In a saucepan, combine the cornstarch and cold water until smooth. Gradually add the cooking juices. Bring to a boil; cook and stir for 2 minutes or until thickened. Serve with chicken over noodles. Sprinkle with parsley if desired. **Yield:** 4 servings.

**Nutritional Analysis:** One chicken breast with 1/4 cup sauce (prepared with 1/2 teaspoon salt; calculated without noodles) equals 190 calories, 5 g fat (1 g saturated fat), 66 mg cholesterol, 372 mg sodium, 8 g carbohydrate, 1 g fiber, 27 g protein. **Diabetic Exchanges:** 3 lean meat, 1/2 starch.

## Meatball Stew

*(Pictured below)*

*I came up with this hearty meal-in-one as another way to use frozen meatballs. It's quick to put together in the morning and ready when my husband gets home in the evening.* —Iris Schultz, Miamisburg, Ohio

Spicy Lemon Chicken
Meatball Stew

3 medium potatoes, peeled and cut into
  1/2-inch cubes
1 package (16 ounces) fresh baby carrots,
  quartered
1 large onion, chopped
3 celery ribs, sliced
1 package (12 ounces) frozen cooked
  meatballs
1 can (10-3/4 ounces) condensed tomato
  soup, undiluted
1 can (10-1/2 ounces) beef gravy
1 cup water
1 envelope onion soup mix
2 teaspoons beef bouillon granules

Place the potatoes, carrots, onion, celery and meatballs in a 5-qt. slow cooker. In a bowl, combine the remaining ingredients. Pour over meatball mixture. Cover and cook on low for 9-10 hours or until the vegetables are crisp-tender. **Yield:** 6 servings.

## Sweet Sausage 'n' Beans

*This is a slow-cooker version of a traditional French dish called cassoulet. It's sweet, saucy and chock-full of beans, smoked sausage and vegetables.* —Doris Heath
*Franklin, North Carolina*

1/2 cup thinly sliced carrots
1/2 cup chopped onion
  2 cups frozen lima beans, thawed
  2 cups frozen green beans, thawed
  1 pound fully cooked smoked sausage, cut into
    1/4-inch slices
  1 can (16 ounces) baked beans
1/2 cup ketchup
1/3 cup packed brown sugar
  1 tablespoon cider vinegar
  1 teaspoon prepared mustard

In a slow cooker, layer carrots, onion, lima beans, green beans, sausage and baked beans. Combine ketchup, brown sugar, vinegar and mustard; pour over beans. Cover and cook on high for 4 hours or until vegetables are tender. Stir before serving. **Yield:** 4-6 servings.

## Fudgy Peanut Butter Cake

*I clipped this recipe from a newspaper years ago. The house smells great while it's cooking. My husband and son enjoy this warm dessert with vanilla ice cream and nuts on top.* —Bonnie Evans, Norcross, Georgia

3/4 cup sugar, *divided*
1/2 cup all-purpose flour
3/4 teaspoon baking powder
1/3 cup milk
1/4 cup peanut butter
  1 tablespoon vegetable oil
1/2 teaspoon vanilla extract
  2 tablespoons baking cocoa
  1 cup boiling water
Vanilla ice cream

In a bowl, combine 1/4 cup sugar, flour and baking powder. In another bowl, combine the milk, peanut butter, oil and vanilla; stir into dry ingredients just until combined. Spread evenly into a slow cooker coated with nonstick cooking spray.

In a bowl, combine the cocoa and remaining sugar; stir in boiling water. Pour into slow cooker (do not stir). Cover and cook on high for 1-1/2 to 2 hours or until a toothpick inserted near the center of cake comes out clean. Serve warm with ice cream. **Yield:** 4 servings.

## Italian Pork Chops

*Tomato sauce seasoned with oregano, basil and garlic gives Italian flavor to tender chops. It's a deliciously different way to serve pork chops.* —Vickie Lowe
*Lititz, Pennsylvania*

4 bone-in pork loin chops (1 inch thick)
1/2 pound fresh mushrooms, sliced
  1 medium onion, chopped
  1 garlic clove, minced
  2 cans (8 ounces *each*) tomato sauce
  1 tablespoon lemon juice
1/2 teaspoon salt
1/2 teaspoon *each* dried oregano, basil and
    parsley flakes
1/4 cup cornstarch
1/4 cup cold water
Green pepper rings, optional

In a nonstick skillet, brown pork chops on both sides. In a slow cooker, combine the mushrooms, onion and garlic. Top with the pork chops. In a bowl, combine the tomato sauce, lemon juice, salt, oregano, basil and parsley. Pour over pork. Cover and cook on low for 6-8 hours or until meat is tender.

Remove pork and keep warm. Transfer mushroom mixture to a saucepan. In a small bowl, combine the cornstarch and water until smooth; add to sauce-pan. Bring to a boil; cook and stir for 2 minutes or until thickened. Serve over the pork chops. Garnish with green pepper rings if desired. **Yield:** 4 servings.

## Chinese Pork Ribs

*This is one of the only dishes that both of my sons love. They even come back for seconds.* —June Ross
*Landing, New Jersey*

1/3 cup soy sauce
1/3 cup orange marmalade
  3 tablespoons ketchup
  2 garlic cloves, minced
  3 to 4 pounds bone-in country-style pork ribs

In a bowl, combine the soy sauce, marmalade, ketchup and garlic. Pour half into a slow cooker. Top with ribs; drizzle with remaining sauce. Cover and cook on low for 6 hours or until tender. Thicken cooking juices if desired. **Yield:** 6-8 servings.

## Golden Peach Pork Chops

*Peach halves add a hint of sweetness to pork chops in this time-tested favorite. The flavorful sauce is nicely seasoned with cinnamon and cloves.* —Adele Durocher
Newport Beach, California

    1 can (29 ounces) peach halves
    5 bone-in pork loin chops (1 inch thick)
    1 tablespoon vegetable oil
Salt and pepper to taste
  1/4 cup packed brown sugar
  1/2 teaspoon ground cinnamon
  1/4 teaspoon ground cloves
    1 can (8 ounces) tomato sauce
  1/4 cup cider vinegar

Drain peaches, reserving 1/4 cup juice (discard remaining juice or save for another use); set fruit and juice aside. In a large skillet, brown pork chops on both sides in oil; transfer to a slow cooker. Sprinkle with salt and pepper.

In a bowl, combine the brown sugar, cinnamon and cloves; mix well. Add the tomato sauce, vinegar and reserved peach juice. Pour over the chops. Arrange peach halves on top. Cover and cook on low for 6-8 hours or until the meat is tender. **Yield:** 5 servings.

## Granola Apple Crisp

*Tender apple slices are tucked beneath a sweet crunchy topping in this comforting crisp. For variety, replace the apples with your favorite fruit.* —Barbara Schindler
Napoleon, Ohio

    8 medium tart apples, peeled and sliced
  1/4 cup lemon juice
1-1/2 teaspoons grated lemon peel
2-1/2 cups granola cereal with fruit and nuts
    1 cup sugar
    1 teaspoon ground cinnamon
  1/2 cup butter *or* margarine, melted

In a large bowl, toss apples, lemon juice and peel. Transfer to a greased slow cooker. Combine cereal, sugar and cinnamon; sprinkle over apples. Drizzle with butter. Cover and cook on low for 5-6 hours or until the apples are tender. Serve warm. **Yield:** 6-8 servings.

## French Beef Stew

*When it comes to this thick down-home stew, I let my slow cooker do the work. Then I simply toss together a green salad and dinner is ready.* —Iola Egle
Bella Vista, Arkansas

    3 medium potatoes, peeled and cut into
       1/2-inch cubes
    2 pounds beef stew meat
    4 medium carrots, sliced
    2 medium onions, sliced
    3 celery ribs, sliced
    2 cups tomato juice
    1 cup water

  1/3 cup quick-cooking tapioca
    1 tablespoon sugar
    1 tablespoon salt
    1 teaspoon dried basil
  1/2 teaspoon pepper

Place the potatoes in a greased 5-qt. slow cooker. Top with the beef, carrots, onions and celery. In a bowl, combine the remaining ingredients. Pour over the vegetables. Cover and cook on low for 9-10 hours or until vegetables and beef are tender. **Yield:** 8-10 servings.

## White Chili

*This is a specialty that's sure to warm you up on winter nights. Cilantro, green chilies and ground cumin make this a winner.* —Shari Meissner, Chester, Montana

    3 medium onions, chopped
    2 garlic cloves, minced
    1 tablespoon olive *or* vegetable oil
    4 cups cubed cooked chicken *or* turkey
    2 cans (15 ounces each) white kidney *or*
       cannellini beans, rinsed and drained
    1 can (15 ounces) garbanzo beans *or*
       chickpeas, rinsed and drained
    2 cups chicken broth
    1 can (4 ounces) chopped green chilies
    2 teaspoons ground cumin
  1/2 teaspoon dried oregano
  1/4 teaspoon salt
  1/4 teaspoon cayenne pepper
  1/4 cup minced fresh cilantro *or* parsley
Corn chips, shredded Monterey Jack cheese and
  sour cream

In a skillet, saute the onions and garlic in oil until tender. Transfer to a slow cooker. Add the chicken, beans, broth, green chilies, cumin, oregano, salt and cayenne; stir well. Cover and cook on low for 6-7 hours or until bubbly. Stir in the cilantro. Serve over corn chips; top with cheese and sour cream. **Yield:** 8 servings (2 quarts).

## Squash Stuffing Casserole

*My friends just rave about this creamy side dish. It's a snap to jazz up summer squash, zucchini and carrots with canned soup and stuffing mix.* —Pamela Thorson
Hot Springs, Arkansas

  1/4 cup all-purpose flour
    1 can (10-3/4 ounces) condensed cream of
       chicken soup, undiluted
    1 cup (8 ounces) sour cream
    2 medium yellow summer squash, cut into
       1/2-inch slices
    2 medium zucchini, cut into 1/2-inch slices
    1 small onion, chopped
    1 cup shredded carrots
    1 package (8 ounces) stuffing mix
  1/2 cup butter *or* margarine, melted

In a bowl, combine the flour, soup and sour cream until blended. Add the vegetables and gently stir to coat.

Cornish Hens with Potatoes
Reuben Spread

Combine the stuffing mix and butter; sprinkle half into a 5-qt. slow cooker. Top with vegetable mixture and remaining stuffing mixture. Cover and cook on low for 4-5 hours or until vegetables are tender. **Yield:** 8 servings.

## Cornish Hens with Potatoes

*(Pictured above)*

*For a wonderful holiday meal with only a fraction of the work, consider this savory selection. This special slow-cooked dinner is delicious. I serve it with green beans and French bread.* —Deborah Randall, Abbeville, Louisiana

    4 Cornish game hens (20 ounces *each*)
    2 tablespoons vegetable oil
    4 large red potatoes, cut into 1/8-inch slices
    4 bacon strips, cut into 1-inch pieces
Lemon-pepper seasoning and garlic powder to taste
Minced fresh parsley

In a large skillet, brown hens in oil. Place the potatoes in a 5-qt. slow cooker. Top with the hens and bacon. Sprinkle with lemon-pepper and garlic powder. Cover and cook on low for 6-8 hours or until meat juices run clear and potatoes are tender. Thicken the cooking juices if desired. Sprinkle the hens with parsley. **Yield:** 4 servings.

## Reuben Spread

*(Pictured above)*

*I received the recipe for this hearty spread from my daughter. It tastes just like a Reuben sandwich. I keep the slow cooker plugged in while serving it, so it stays warm.*
    —Rosalie Fuchs, Paynesville, Minnesota

    1 jar (16 ounces) sauerkraut, rinsed and drained
    1 package (8 ounces) cream cheese, cubed
    2 cups (8 ounces) shredded Swiss cheese
    1 package (3 ounces) deli corned beef, chopped
    3 tablespoons Thousand Island salad dressing
Snack rye bread *or* crackers

In a 1-1/2-qt. slow cooker, combine the first five ingredients. Cover and cook for 2 hours or until cheeses are melted; stir to blend. Serve warm with bread or crackers. **Yield:** 3-1/2 cups.

# Great Grilling Recipes

WANT to spend a lot less time in the kitchen? Stop outdoors any time of year and fix a meal on the grill. It's easy to cook up an entire menu at once...plus there's less mess and cleanup.

## Chicken Bundles for Two

(Pictured below)

**Ready in 45 minutes or less**

*I prepare a picture-perfect dinner for two...without a lot of work. I season chicken and vegetables with sage and dill, then wrap them in aluminum foil, so everything grills together and cleanup is a snap.* —Cheryl Landis
Honey Brook, Pennsylvania

 2 boneless skinless chicken breast halves
 2 medium red potatoes, quartered and cut into 1/2-inch slices
1/4 cup chopped onion
 1 medium carrot, cut into 1/4-inch slices
 1 celery rib, cut into 1/4-inch slices
1/2 teaspoon rubbed sage
Salt and pepper to taste
Fresh dill sprigs

Divide chicken and vegetables between two pieces of double-layered heavy-duty foil (about 18 in. square). Sprinkle with sage, salt and pepper; top with dill sprigs. Fold foil around the mixture and seal tightly. Grill, covered, over medium heat for 30 minutes or until the chicken juices run clear and vegetables are tender. **Yield:** 2 servings.

## Marinated Sirloin Steak

**Plan ahead...needs to marinate**

*This recipe was given to me by a friend who knows I like to grill. No one ever guesses that the secret ingredient is lemon-lime soda. Try the marinade with chicken, too. It's wonderful!* —Corina Flansberg
Carson City, Nevada

 1 cup lemon-lime soda
3/4 cup vegetable oil
3/4 cup soy sauce
1/4 cup lemon juice
 1 teaspoon garlic powder
 1 teaspoon prepared horseradish
 1 boneless beef sirloin steak (about 1 pound)

In a large resealable plastic bag, combine the first six ingredients. Add steak and turn to coat. Seal and refrigerate 8 hours or overnight, turning occasionally. Drain and discard marinade. Grill steaks, covered, over medium-hot heat for 3-5 minutes on each side or until meat reaches desired doneness (for rare, a meat thermometer should read 140°; medium, 160°; well-done, 170°). **Yield:** 4 servings.

Chicken Bundles for Two

## Pepper-Lime Pork Kabobs

**Plan ahead...needs to marinate**

*This is my family's favorite treatment for pork. The slices of tenderloin get a flavorful zip from a Mexican-inspired marinade. I often fix the skewers for company, because much of the prep work can be done ahead of time.*
 —Donna Godfrey, Cumming, Georgia

3/4 cup olive *or* vegetable oil
1/4 cup lime juice
1/4 cup minced fresh parsley
 2 tablespoons cider vinegar
 2 jalapeno peppers, seeded and chopped*
1/2 teaspoon *each* salt, garlic powder and ground cumin
 3 pounds pork tenderloin, thinly sliced

In a large resealable plastic bag, combine the oil, lime juice, parsley, vinegar, jalapenos and seasonings; mix well. Add pork and turn to coat. Seal and refrigerate for 24 hours, turning occasionally.

 Drain and discard marinade. Loosely thread the pork slices onto metal or soaked wooden skewers. Coat grill rack with nonstick cooking spray before starting the grill. Grill kabobs, covered, over medium heat for 7-8 minutes or until the meat juices run clear, turning once. **Yield:** 10-12 servings.

**\*Editor's Note:** When cutting or seeding hot peppers, use rubber or plastic gloves to protect your hands. Avoid touching your face.

Sausage Shrimp Kabobs

## Sausage Shrimp Kabobs

*(Pictured at right)*

### Ready in 45 minutes or less

*We love these full-flavored kabobs and fix them often, even in winter. A sweet sauce is used to baste and later serve alongside the colorful combination of sausage, bacon, shrimp, vegetables and pineapple.*
—Gloria Warczak
Cedarburg, Wisconsin

```
1 can (8 ounces) pineapple chunks
4 uncooked bacon strips
8 large fresh mushrooms
8 uncooked large shrimp, peeled and deveined
8 large cherry tomatoes
8 ounces fully cooked smoked sausage, cut
    into 1/2-inch slices
1 large sweet onion, cut into 8 wedges
1 large green pepper, cut into 1-inch pieces
1/2 cup barbecue sauce
1/3 cup corn syrup
1/4 cup ketchup
3 tablespoons soy sauce
1 tablespoon lime juice
1/2 teaspoon maple flavoring
1/4 teaspoon garlic powder
1/4 teaspoon ground ginger
1/8 teaspoon dried coriander
```

Drain pineapple, reserving juice. Cut bacon strips in half; wrap each around a mushroom. On metal or soaked wooden skewers, alternately thread the shrimp, pineapple chunks, tomatoes, sausage, bacon-wrapped mushrooms, onion and green pepper.

In a bowl, combine the barbecue sauce, corn syrup, ketchup, soy sauce, lime juice, maple flavoring, seasonings and reserved pineapple juice. Set aside 2/3 cup for serving. Grill the kabobs, covered, over medium heat for 10-15 minutes or until vegetables are tender and shrimp turn pink, turning and basting occasionally with remaining sauce. Serve with the reserved sauce. **Yield:** 4 servings.

## Zippy Pork Chops

### Plan ahead...needs to marinate

*Just four ingredients are needed to prepare this simple seasoning mix for pork. The spicy herb rub sparks the taste of these tender boneless chops that cook in no time. They're one of my favorite meats.*
—Donna Glascoe
Dayton, Ohio

```
4 teaspoons chili powder
1-1/2 teaspoons dried oregano
3/4 teaspoon ground cumin
2 garlic cloves, minced
6 boneless pork loin chops (3/4 inch thick)
```

Combine the chili powder, oregano, cumin and garlic; gently rub over both sides of pork chops. Cover and refrigerate for at least 2 hours. Grill, covered, over medium-hot heat for 5-7 minutes on each side or until a meat thermometer reads 160°. **Yield:** 6 servings.

## Salmon in Lime Juice

### Plan ahead...needs to marinate

*I marinate salmon in a pleasant lime and vegetable mixture, then tuck individual portions into foil packets. I like to serve them with grilled skewers of corn-on-the-cob rounds, mushrooms and cherry tomatoes.*
—Helen Vail
Glenside, Pennsylvania

```
1 small tomato, chopped
1 small sweet red pepper, chopped
2 green onions, thinly sliced
2/3 cup lime juice
2 tablespoons vegetable oil
1/2 teaspoon grated lime peel
1/4 to 1/2 teaspoon cayenne pepper
1 salmon fillet (1-1/2 pounds)
```

In a large resealable plastic bag, combine the first seven ingredients; mix well. Cut salmon into four pieces; place in the bag. Seal and turn to coat; refrigerate for 30 minutes.

Drain and discard marinade from fish and vegetables. Place each piece of salmon and about 1/3 cup vegetable mixture on a piece of double-layered heavy-duty foil (about 18 in. square). Fold foil around the mixture and seal tightly. Grill, covered, over medium heat for 15-20 minutes or until salmon flakes easily with a fork. **Yield:** 4 servings.

Special Grilled Veggies
Chili Sauce Chicken

## Chili Sauce Chicken

*(Pictured at left)*

**Plan ahead...needs to marinate**

*I combine chili sauce with plenty of garlic and basil to flavor these moist chicken thighs. We enjoy this tender grilled chicken not just in summertime, but throughout the year.*
—Marilyn Waltz
Idyllwild, California

  1 bottle (12 ounces) chili sauce
  1/3 cup white wine *or* chicken broth
  1/4 cup olive *or* vegetable oil
  10 to 12 garlic cloves, minced
  4-1/2 teaspoons dried basil
  1/2 teaspoon salt
  1/8 teaspoon pepper
  8 chicken thighs

In a large resealable plastic bag, combine the first seven ingredients; mix well. Remove 1/3 cup for basting; cover and refrigerate. Add chicken to bag; seal and turn to coat. Chill for at least 2 hours.

Drain and discard marinade from chicken. Grill, covered, skin side down, over medium heat for 20 minutes. Baste with some of the reserved marinade. Turn; grill 10 minutes longer or until the chicken juices run clear, basting frequently. **Yield:** 8 servings.

## Special Grilled Veggies

*(Pictured above)*

**Plan ahead...needs to marinate**

*I fixed this colorful side dish on Father's Day one year and it has been requested many times since. It goes well with any grilled meat, chicken or seafood. It's easy to prepare but looks like you spent a lot of time on it.*
—Kimberly Hennes-Skar, Minot, North Dakota

  1/2 cup red wine vinegar *or* cider vinegar
  1/4 cup olive *or* vegetable oil
  2 garlic cloves, minced
  1/2 teaspoon dried basil
  1/2 teaspoon dried thyme
  1/2 teaspoon lemon-pepper seasoning
  1 pound fresh asparagus, trimmed
  1 large red onion, sliced and separated into rings
  1 large sweet red pepper, cut into 1-inch strips
  1 large sweet yellow pepper, cut into 1-inch strips

In a large resealable plastic bag, combine the first six ingredients; mix well. Add vegetables and turn to coat. Seal and refrigerate for 1 hour or overnight, turning once.

Drain and reserve marinade. Place vegetables in a grill basket or disposable foil pan with slits cut in the bottom. Grill, uncovered, over medium-high heat for 5 minutes. Turn; baste with reserved marinade. Grill 5-8 minutes longer or until the vegetables are tender. **Yield:** 4-6 servings.

## Beef Shish Kabobs

**Plan ahead...needs to marinate**

*Bacon-wrapped water chestnuts, pineapple chunks and stew meat are basted with a simple marinade. These kabobs can be assembled ahead, so they're ideal for family get-togethers. They're a delicious alternative to hot dogs and hamburgers.*
—Gerri Layo, Massena, New York

  1 cup soy sauce
  1/2 cup red wine vinegar *or* cider vinegar
  1/2 cup water
  1/2 cup vegetable oil
  1 teaspoon dried oregano
  1/2 teaspoon onion powder
  1 to 2 garlic cloves, minced
  1 pound beef stew meat, cut into 1-1/2-inch cubes
  1 pound sliced bacon, halved widthwise
  1 can (8 ounces) sliced water chestnuts, drained
  1 can (8 ounces) pineapple chunks, drained

In a large resealable plastic bag, combine the first seven ingredients; mix well. Remove 1/3 cup for basting; cover and refrigerate. Add beef to bag; seal and turn to coat. Refrigerate overnight.

In a skillet over medium heat, partially cook the bacon. Wrap each piece around a water chestnut slice. Drain and discard marinade from beef. On metal or soaked wooden skewers, alternately thread bacon-wrapped water chestnuts, pineapple and beef. Grill, covered, over medium heat for 10-15 minutes or until meat reaches desired doneness, basting frequently with reserved marinade. **Yield:** 4 servings.

## Tacos on a Stick

### Plan ahead...needs to marinate

*Teens like assembling these creative kabobs almost as much as they like devouring them. The whole family is sure to love the sensational Southwestern flavor of this twist on beef shish kabobs.* —Dixie Terry, Goreville, Illinois

✓ Uses less fat, sugar or salt. Includes Nutritional Analysis and Diabetic Exchanges.

    1 envelope taco seasoning
    1 cup tomato juice
    2 to 4 tablespoons canola oil
    2 pounds boneless beef top sirloin, cut into
        1-inch cubes
    1 medium green pepper, cut into chunks
    1 medium sweet red pepper, cut into chunks
    1 large onion, cut into wedges
   16 cherry tomatoes

In a large resealable plastic bag, combine the taco seasoning, tomato juice and oil; mix well. Remove 1/2 cup for basting; refrigerate. Add beef to the bag; seal and turn to coat. Refrigerate for at least 5 hours.

Drain and discard marinade from beef. On metal or soaked wooden skewers, alternately thread beef, peppers, onion and tomatoes. Grill, uncovered, over medium heat for 3 minutes on each side. Baste with reserved marinade. Continue turning and basting for 8-10 minutes or until the meat reaches desired doneness. **Yield:** 6 servings.

**Nutritional Analysis:** One serving (prepared with low-sodium tomato juice and 2 tablespoons oil) equals 298 calories, 12 g fat (3 g saturated fat), 100 mg cholesterol, 386 mg sodium, 11 g carbohydrate, 2 g fiber, 35 g protein. **Diabetic Exchanges:** 5 lean meat, 2 vegetable.

## Potato Chicken Packets

### Ready in 1 hour or less

*I season chicken breasts with a delightful combination of herbs before topping each with veggies. Servings are individually wrapped in foil, so I can enjoy nature's beauty in my backyard while the packets cook on the grill.*
—Pam Hall, Elizabeth City, North Carolina

    4 boneless skinless chicken breast halves
  1/4 cup olive *or* vegetable oil
    3 teaspoons dried rosemary, crushed
    1 teaspoon dried thyme
  1/2 teaspoon dried basil
    1 garlic clove, minced
    8 to 10 small red potatoes, quartered
    2 medium yellow summer squash, cut into
        1/4-inch slices
    1 large onion, chopped
    2 tablespoons butter *or* margarine, cubed
Salt and pepper to taste

Place each chicken breast on a piece of heavy-duty foil (about 14 in. square). Combine the oil, rosemary, thyme, basil and garlic; drizzle over chicken. Top with potatoes, squash, onion, butter, salt and pepper. Fold foil over vegetables and seal tightly. Grill, covered, over medium heat for 30 minutes or until the chicken juices run clear and potatoes are tender. **Yield:** 4 servings.

## Orange Roughy Bundles

### (Pictured below)

### Ready in 30 minutes or less

*Cleanup is a breeze with this simple seafood supper. Each meal-in-one packet contains zucchini, red pepper and a flaky full-flavored fish fillet. It cooks in no time and is just as delicious with flounder or sole.* —Margaret Wilson Hemet, California

✓ Uses less fat, sugar or salt. Includes Nutritional Analysis and Diabetic Exchanges.

    4 fresh *or* frozen orange roughy fillets
        (6 ounces *each*), thawed
  1/4 cup grated Parmesan cheese
  1/8 to 1/4 teaspoon cayenne pepper
    2 medium zucchini, cut into 1/4-inch slices
    1 small sweet red pepper, julienned
  1/2 teaspoon salt

Place each fillet on a piece of heavy-duty foil (about 12 in. square). Sprinkle with Parmesan cheese and cayenne. Top with zucchini, red pepper and salt. Fold foil over vegetables and seal tightly. Grill, covered, over indirect heat for 8-10 minutes or until fish flakes easily with a fork. **Yield:** 4 servings.

**Nutritional Analysis:** One bundle equals 159 calories, 3 g fat (1 g saturated fat), 38 mg cholesterol, 497 mg sodium, 4 g carbohydrate, 2 g fiber, 28 g protein. **Diabetic Exchange:** 4-1/2 very lean meat.

Orange Roughy Bundles

# Flavorful Flank Steak

### (Pictured below)

#### Plan ahead...needs to marinate

*This is a variation of an old Southern recipe with a Texas twist. I've been making it at least once a month for the last 15 years. The overnight marinade gives the beef a wonderful taste.*
—Janice Montiverdi, Sugar Land, Texas

☑ Uses less fat, sugar or salt. Includes Nutritional Analysis and Diabetic Exchanges.

1/2 cup soy sauce
1/2 cup vegetable *or* canola oil
3 tablespoons red wine vinegar *or* cider vinegar
3 tablespoons barbecue sauce
3 tablespoons steak sauce
2 tablespoons dried minced onion
1 tablespoon liquid smoke, optional
1/2 teaspoon garlic powder
1 beef flank steak (1-1/2 pounds)

In a large resealable plastic bag, combine the first eight ingredients; mix well. Add the steak; seal bag and turn to coat. Refrigerate for 8 hours or overnight.

Drain and discard marinade. Grill steak, covered, over medium-hot heat for 6-8 minutes on each side or until meat reaches desired doneness (for rare, a meat thermometer should read 140°; medium, 160°; well-done, 170°). Slice steak across the grain. **Yield:** 6 servings.

**Nutritional Analysis:** One serving (3 ounces cooked meat, prepared with reduced-sodium soy sauce) equals 235 calories, 14 g fat (4 g saturated fat), 59 mg cholesterol, 343 mg sodium, 2 g carbohydrate, trace fiber, 24 g protein. **Diabetic Exchanges:** 3 lean meat, 1-1/2 fat.

# Skewered Shrimp

#### Plan ahead...needs to marinate

*I combine four ingredients to create a ginger mixture that's used as both a marinade and a sauce for these barbecued shrimp. Serve them with toothpicks as an appetizer or stir the shrimp into pasta for an entree.*
—Joan Morris
Lillian, Alabama

☑ Uses less fat, sugar or salt. Includes Nutritional Analysis and Diabetic Exchanges.

3 tablespoons soy sauce
2 tablespoons lemon juice
1 tablespoon chili sauce
3/4 teaspoon ground ginger *or* 1 tablespoon minced fresh gingerroot
1 pound uncooked medium shrimp, peeled and deveined

In a bowl, combine the soy sauce, lemon juice, chili sauce and ginger; mix well. Pour half into a large resealable plastic bag; add the shrimp. Seal bag and turn to coat; refrigerate for 2 hours. Cover and refrigerate remaining marinade.

Drain and discard marinade from shrimp. Thread onto metal or soaked wooden skewers. Grill, uncovered, over medium heat for 6-8 minutes or until shrimp turn pink, turning once. Serve with reserved marinade. **Yield:** 4 servings.

**Nutritional Analysis:** One serving (prepared with reduced-sodium soy sauce) equals 136 calories, 2 g fat (trace saturated fat), 172 mg cholesterol, 742 mg sodium, 4 g carbohydrate, trace fiber, 24 g protein. **Diabetic Exchange:** 3 very lean meat.

# Reuben Burgers

#### Ready in 30 minutes or less

*Put a new spin on a classic with this recipe. I use ground pork and sauerkraut in this fun alternative to traditional burgers. For true Reuben flavor, top with Thousand Island salad dressing.*
—Jeanne Fenstermaker
Kendallville, Indiana

2 pounds ground pork
2 teaspoons salt

Flavorful Flank Steak

1 teaspoon pepper
1 garlic clove, minced
1/2 cup sauerkraut, drained
8 slices Swiss cheese
8 hamburger buns, split and toasted

In a bowl, combine pork, salt, pepper and garlic; mix well. Shape into 16 patties, about 3/8 in. thick. Spoon 1 tablespoon sauerkraut in the center of eight patties; top each with a second patty and press edges to seal.

Grill the burgers, uncovered, over medium heat for 6-8 minutes on each side or until juices run clear. Top with cheese. Serve on buns. **Yield:** 8 servings.

Grilled Peppers and Zucchini
Tangy Ham Steak

## Taste-of-Summer Chicken

### Plan ahead...needs to marinate

*I rely on bottled Italian salad dressing and pineapple juice for the made-in-minutes marinade. Enjoy the summery flavors of this tender charbroiled chicken anytime of year.*
—*Beverly Saunders, Lexington, Virginia*

✓ Uses less fat, sugar or salt. Includes Nutritional Analysis and Diabetic Exchanges.

3/4 cup Italian salad dressing
3/4 cup unsweetened pineapple juice
3/4 cup white wine *or* white grape juice
6 boneless skinless chicken breast halves (1-1/2 pounds)

In a large resealable plastic bag, combine the salad dressing, pineapple juice and wine or grape juice. Add the chicken. Seal bag and turn to coat; refrigerate for 8 hours or overnight.

Drain and discard marinade. Grill chicken, covered, over medium heat for 6-7 minutes on each side or until juices run clear. **Yield:** 6 servings.

**Nutritional Analysis:** One serving (prepared with fat-free Italian dressing) equals 140 calories, 3 g fat (1 g saturated fat), 63 mg cholesterol, 151 mg sodium, 3 g carbohydrate, trace fiber, 23 g protein. **Diabetic Exchange:** 3 lean meat.

## Grilled Peppers and Zucchini

### (Pictured above right)

### Ready in 30 minutes or less

*This versatile side dish is so easy. Grilling the colorful veggies in a foil packet means one less dish to wash, but I often stir-fry the mixture on the stovetop instead.*
—*Karen Anderson, Fair Oaks, California*

1 medium green pepper, julienned
1 medium sweet red pepper, julienned
2 medium zucchini, julienned
1 tablespoon butter *or* margarine
2 teaspoons soy sauce

Place the vegetables on a double layer of heavy-duty foil (about 18 in. x 15 in.). Dot with butter; drizzle with soy sauce. Fold foil around vegetables and seal tightly. Grill, covered, over medium heat for 10-15 minutes or until vegetables are crisp-tender. **Yield:** 3-4 servings.

## Tangy Ham Steak

### (Pictured above)

### Ready in 30 minutes or less

*I need only a handful of ingredients for the lip-smacking sauce that jazzes up grilled ham. Flavored with pickle relish, the blend is used for basting and for spooning over individual servings.*
—*Evelyn Kennell, Roanoke, Illinois*

1/2 cup ketchup
1/3 cup sweet pickle relish
1 tablespoon cider vinegar
1 teaspoon brown sugar
1/8 teaspoon cayenne pepper
1 fully cooked ham steak (about 1 pound)

In a bowl, combine the ketchup, relish, vinegar, brown sugar and cayenne; set aside 1/2 cup for serving. Grill the ham steak, uncovered, over medium heat for 3 minutes on each side, basting occasionally with the remaining sauce. Serve with the reserved sauce. **Yield:** 3-4 servings.

# Microwave Magic

TRY THESE made-in-minutes recipes and you'll never again use your "zapper" just for heating up coffee or warming leftovers. This marvelous kitchen tool is wonderful for preparing main meals, side dishes, snacks, desserts and more!

**Editor's Note:** All of these recipes were tested in an 850-watt microwave.

## Sunny Chicken 'n' Rice

*(Pictured below)*

**Plan ahead...needs to marinate**

*A sweet and spicy apricot sauce gives lots of flavor to the tender chicken in this dish. It's especially fast because it's made with instant rice. —Diana Duda, Glenwood, Illinois*

✓ Uses less fat, sugar or salt. Includes Nutritional Analysis and Diabetic Exchanges.

- 1-1/2 cups orange juice
- 1 cup apricot preserves
- 1/4 teaspoon ground allspice
- 1/4 teaspoon salt
- 1/4 teaspoon pepper
- 1/8 teaspoon ground ginger
- 2 cups uncooked instant rice
- 6 boneless skinless chicken breast halves (1-1/2 pounds)

In a small microwave-safe bowl, combine the orange juice, preserves, allspice, salt, pepper and ginger. Microwave, uncovered, on high for 1 to 1-1/2 minutes or until preserves begin to melt; stir to blend.

Place the rice in a shallow 3-qt. microwave-safe dish; arrange chicken on top. Pour sauce over chicken and rice. Cover and refrigerate for 4 hours.

Cover and microwave at 80% power for 15-20 minutes or until chicken juices run clear and the rice is tender. **Yield:** 6 servings.

**Nutritional Analysis:** One chicken breast with 1 cup rice (prepared with reduced-sugar preserves) equals 323 calories, 2 g fat (trace saturated fat), 66 mg cholesterol, 173 mg sodium, 46 g carbohydrate, 1 g fiber, 29 g protein. **Diabetic Exchanges:** 3 very lean meat, 2 starch, 1 fruit.

## Omelet in a Mug

**Ready in 15 minutes or less**

*This is a great way to make a quick-and-easy breakfast for one person. I love to fix this flavorful omelet for my husband, who rarely has time for breakfast. It takes no time at all to prepare or clean up!*
—Susan Adair
Muncie, Indiana

- 2 eggs, beaten
- 2 to 3 tablespoons shredded cheddar cheese
- 2 tablespoons diced fully cooked ham
- 1 tablespoon diced green pepper
- Salt and pepper to taste

In a microwave-safe mug coated with nonstick cooking spray, combine all ingredients. Microwave, uncovered, on high for 1 minute; stir. Cook 1 to 1-1/2 minutes longer or until eggs are completely set. **Yield:** 1 serving.

## Microwave Scalloped Potatoes

**Ready in 30 minutes or less**

*These creamy potatoes taste much better than those made from a boxed mix. It's a tradition to prepare them for family gatherings. I usually double the recipe and use one can of cream of chicken soup and one can of cream of mushroom soup. —Betty Menerey, Auburn, Michigan*

- 1 can (10-3/4 ounces) condensed cream of chicken soup, undiluted
- 3/4 cup evaporated milk
- 4 medium potatoes, peeled and cut into 1/8-inch slices
- 1 cup (4 ounces) shredded cheddar cheese
- 1/4 cup chopped onion

Sunny Chicken 'n' Rice

1/2 teaspoon salt
1/8 teaspoon pepper
1 tablespoon grated Parmesan cheese, optional

In a 3-qt. microwave-safe dish, combine soup and milk until blended. Stir in the potatoes, cheddar cheese, onion, salt and pepper. Cover and microwave on high for 10 minutes; stir. Cook 10-12 minutes longer or until the potatoes are tender; stir. Sprinkle with Parmesan cheese if desired. **Yield:** 6-8 servings.

## Dilly Mushrooms

### Ready in 15 minutes or less

*I dress up fresh mushrooms with mild seasonings that let their flavor shine through. I've prepared this side dish often—mushroom lovers always come back for more.* —Kathy Rairigh
Milford, Indiana

1 pound whole fresh mushrooms
3 tablespoons butter *or* margarine, melted
1 tablespoon lemon juice
1 tablespoon snipped fresh dill *or* 1 teaspoon dill weed
1/2 teaspoon salt
1/2 teaspoon onion salt

In a 1-qt. microwave-safe dish, combine all ingredients. Cover and cook on high for 3 minutes; stir. Cook 3 minutes longer or until mushrooms are tender. Stir before serving. **Yield:** 4 servings.

## Microwave Mexican Manicotti

### (Pictured above right)

### Ready in 45 minutes or less

*This recipe is a time-saver because you don't need to cook the pasta shells first. It's easy to prepare and a delightful twist to Mexican cooking.* —Nancy Ensor
Oviedo, Florida

✓ Uses less fat, sugar or salt. Includes Nutritional Analysis and Diabetic Exchanges.

1/2 pound uncooked lean ground beef
1 cup refried beans
1 teaspoon dried oregano
1/2 teaspoon ground cumin
8 uncooked manicotti shells
1-1/4 cups water
1 cup taco *or* picante sauce
1 cup (8 ounces) sour cream
1/4 cup finely chopped green onions
1/4 cup sliced ripe olives, optional
1/2 cup shredded Monterey Jack cheese

In a bowl, combine the beef, beans, oregano and cumin; mix well. Stuff into shells; place in an ungreased 11-in. x 7-in. x 2-in. microwave-safe dish. Combine water and

**Microwave Mexican Manicotti**

taco sauce; pour over shells. Loosely cover dish; microwave on high for 5 minutes; turn shells with tongs. Microwave 5 minutes longer; turn shells again.

Cover and cook at 50% power for 17-19 minutes or until pasta is tender and meat juices run clear, turning dish a half turn once. Spoon sour cream lengthwise down center; sprinkle with onions, olives if desired and cheese. Microwave, uncovered, on high for 2-3 minutes or until cheese is melted. **Yield:** 4 servings.

**Nutritional Analysis:** One serving (two stuffed shells, prepared with fat-free refried beans, reduced-fat sour cream and reduced-fat cheese and without olives) equals 408 calories, 14 g fat (8 g saturated fat), 51 mg cholesterol, 954 mg sodium, 44 g carbohydrate, 5 g fiber, 27 g protein. **Diabetic Exchanges:** 3 starch, 3 lean meat.

## Fiesta Cheese Rice

### Ready in 30 minutes or less

*I usually serve this spicy rice side dish alongside chicken enchiladas or tacos for a great Mexican meal.* —Sarah Rodefeld
Maud, Oklahoma

3 cups uncooked instant rice
3 cups water
1 can (10 ounces) diced tomatoes with green chilies, undrained
1 tablespoon chicken bouillon granules
3/4 cup sour cream
1-1/2 cups (6 ounces) shredded cheddar cheese, *divided*

In a bowl, combine the rice, water, tomatoes and bouillon; mix well. Pour into a greased 2-qt. microwave-safe dish. Cover and microwave on high for 10 minutes. Stir in sour cream and 1/2 cup of cheese; mix well. Sprinkle with the remaining cheese. Cover and microwave for 1 minute or until cheese is melted. **Yield:** 8 servings.

Crab-Stuffed Chicken

## Crab-Stuffed Chicken

### (Pictured above)

### Ready in 30 minutes or less

*This is a luscious change from plain chicken and it's nice for company. The combination of crab, chicken, spaghetti sauce and cheese is great.* —Pat Durrie
Omaha, Nebraska

✓ Uses less fat, sugar or salt. Includes Nutritional Analysis and Diabetic Exchanges.

    4 boneless skinless chicken breast halves
    4 ounces flaked crabmeat
1/2 cup dry bread crumbs
1/4 cup grated Parmesan cheese
    1 teaspoon garlic powder
    1 teaspoon onion powder
    1 teaspoon dried basil
    2 cups meatless spaghetti sauce
1/2 cup shredded mozzarella cheese
Hot cooked pasta, optional

Flatten chicken to 1/4-in. thickness; top with crab. Roll up tightly and secure with toothpicks. In a shallow bowl, combine the bread crumbs, Parmesan cheese, garlic powder, onion powder and basil. Roll chicken in crumb mixture; set remaining mixture aside.

Place chicken in a shallow 1-1/2-qt. microwave-safe dish coated with nonstick cooking spray. Cover and microwave on high for 3 minutes. Turn the chicken; sprinkle with reserved crumb mixture. Cover and cook for 2-3 minutes.

Top with spaghetti sauce. Cover and microwave on high for 5 minutes or until heated through. Sprinkle with the mozzarella cheese; heat, uncovered, for 1-1/2 minutes or until the cheese is melted. Let stand for 5 minutes. Serve over pasta if desired. **Yield:** 4 servings.

**Nutritional Analysis:** One serving (prepared with imitation crabmeat and part-skim mozzarella; calculated without pasta) equals 328 calories, 7 g fat (3 g saturated fat), 85 mg cholesterol, 1,165 mg sodium, 26 g carbohydrate, 3 g fiber, 40 g protein. **Diabetic Exchanges:** 4 lean meat, 1-1/2 starch.

## Bacon Cheddar Quiche

### Ready in 30 minutes or less

*Whenever company comes to stay over, I make this wonderful breakfast dish. They think I've worked for hours when it only takes about 20 minutes start to finish.*
—Val Forsythe, Albert Lea, Minnesota

    14 bacon strips, cooked and crumbled
    1 cup (4 ounces) shredded cheddar cheese
    1 jar (6 ounces) sliced mushrooms, drained
    1 tablespoon dried minced onion

5 eggs
1 can (5 ounces) evaporated milk
1/4 teaspoon cayenne pepper

In a greased 9-in. microwave-safe pie plate, layer the bacon, cheese, mushrooms and onion. In a bowl, beat the eggs, milk and cayenne; pour over the onion. Microwave, uncovered, on high for 6 minutes, stirring twice. Cook 2-3 minutes longer or until a knife inserted near the center comes out clean. Let stand for 5 minutes or until set. Cut into wedges. **Yield:** 4-6 servings.

## Cajun Shrimp with Potatoes

### Ready in 45 minutes or less

*This is a quick-and-easy version of a seafood-stuffed baked potato. Not only does this recipe reduce prep time, it cuts down on cleanup, too. I buy cooked crumbled bacon to speed it along even more.*
—Angelique Schultz
Denham Springs, Louisiana

1/2 cup chopped onion
2 tablespoons vegetable oil
1/4 cup chopped green onions
1/4 cup chopped celery
6 medium potatoes, peeled and diced
1 teaspoon salt
2 teaspoons Cajun seasoning
1/2 teaspoon pepper
1 pound uncooked medium shrimp, peeled and deveined
1/4 cup cooked crumbled bacon

In a 2-1/2-qt. microwave-safe dish, combine the onion and oil. Cover and microwave on high for 3 minutes. Stir in green onions and celery; cover and cook 3 minutes longer. Add potatoes, salt, Cajun seasoning and pepper. Cover and cook for 12 minutes or until potatoes are nearly tender.

Stir in the shrimp and bacon. Cover and cook on high for 5 minutes or until shrimp is pink and potatoes are tender. **Yield:** 4 servings.

## Creamy Garlic Ham Spread

### Ready in 15 minutes or less

*This rich, creamy cracker spread is great to snack on when watching football games. You can have it ready in about 10 minutes.* —Elsie Krueger, Bloomer, Wisconsin

2 packages (8 ounces *each*) cream cheese, softened
1 small onion, chopped
1/3 cup mayonnaise*
1 teaspoon sugar
1 garlic clove, minced
Dash salt
1/2 pound diced fully cooked ham
Assorted crackers

In a mixing bowl, combine the first six ingredients; beat until blended. Stir in ham. Transfer to a 1-qt. microwave-safe dish. Cover and heat at 50% power for 5 minutes or until heated through. Serve with crackers. **Yield:** 4 cups.

**\*Editor's Note:** Reduced-fat or fat-free mayonnaise may not be substituted for regular mayonnaise in this recipe.

## Fiesta Dip

### (Pictured below)

### Ready in 15 minutes or less

*I sprinkle a warm creamy bean mixture with colorful toppings to create an effortless appetizer. This delicious dip is a favorite at get-togethers.* —Rhonda Cowden
Quincy, Illinois

2 cups (16 ounces) sour cream
1 can (16 ounces) refried beans
1 can (4 ounces) chopped green chilies *or* jalapenos
1 envelope fiesta ranch dip mix
2 cups (8 ounces) shredded Mexican cheese blend *or* cheddar cheese, *divided*
Sliced ripe olives, chopped tomatoes, sliced green onions and shredded lettuce, optional
Tortilla chips

In a shallow 1-1/2-qt. microwave-safe dish, combine the sour cream, beans, chilies and dip mix. Stir in 1 cup cheese. Cover and microwave on high for 3 minutes. Stir; rotate dish a quarter turn. Cover and microwave 2 minutes longer or until heated through. Sprinkle with remaining cheese. Top with olives, tomatoes, onions and lettuce if desired. Serve with tortilla chips. **Yield:** about 5 cups.

Fiesta Dip

# Christmas Meatballs

*(Pictured below)*

**Ready in 30 minutes or less**

*Cranberry sauce and brown sugar create a tangy glaze for moist meatballs that are good as an appetizer or as a main dish over rice. We love them so much, I prepare them year-round.* —Joyce Bentley Redlands, California

    2 eggs
    1 envelope onion soup mix
  1/2 cup seasoned bread crumbs
  1/4 cup chopped dried cranberries
    2 tablespoons minced fresh parsley
1-1/2 pounds lean ground beef
SAUCE:
    1 can (16 ounces) whole-berry cranberry sauce
  3/4 cup ketchup
  1/2 cup beef broth
    3 tablespoons brown sugar
    3 tablespoons finely chopped onion
    2 teaspoons cider vinegar

In a bowl, combine eggs, soup mix, bread crumbs, cranberries and parsley. Crumble beef over mixture and mix well. Shape into 1-in. balls; place 12 to 14 balls on a microwave-safe plate. Cover with waxed paper; microwave on high for 3-4 minutes or until no longer pink. Remove to paper towels to drain. Repeat with remaining meatballs.

In a 2-qt. microwave-safe dish, combine sauce ingredients. Cover and microwave on high for 3-4 minutes or until heated through, rotating once. Gently stir in meatballs. Cover and cook on high for 1-2 minutes or until heated through. **Yield:** about 3 dozen.

# Caramel Apple Crisp

**Christmas Meatballs**

**Ready in 45 minutes or less**

*You can't beat this combination of tender apples, gooey caramel sauce and sweet oat topping. My husband and I are retired and love to cook and bake.* —Alta Looney Howard, Ohio

    6 cups sliced peeled tart apples
      (about 5 medium)
    1 tablespoon lemon juice
  28 caramels*
    2 tablespoons water
    6 tablespoons butter *or* margarine
  3/4 cup packed brown sugar
  3/4 cup quick-cooking oats
  1/2 cup all-purpose flour
    1 teaspoon ground cinnamon

Place apples in a 2-qt. microwave-safe dish. Sprinkle with lemon juice; toss to coat and set aside. Place caramels and water in another microwave-safe dish. Cover and microwave on high for 2 to 2-1/2 minutes or until melted; stir until blended. Pour over apples.

Place butter in a microwave-safe dish; cover and heat on high for 45-60 seconds or until melted. Stir in brown sugar, oats, flour and cinnamon until crumbly. Sprinkle over caramel mixture. Microwave, uncovered, on high for 14-15 minutes until apples are tender, turning a half turn once. **Yield:** 6-8 servings.

**\*Editor's Note:** This recipe was tested with Hershey caramels.

# Hollandaise Sauce

**Ready in 15 minutes or less**

*I drizzle this rich sauce over veggies or eggs Benedict. It cooks in the microwave while you poach the eggs. Add muffins and fruit, and it beats breakfast at a fancy restaurant.*
—Linda Oelrich, Plainfield, Illinois

    4 tablespoons butter (no
      substitutes), *divided*
    3 tablespoons all-purpose flour
    1 cup milk
    2 egg yolks
    2 tablespoons lemon juice
  1/2 teaspoon salt

In a 1-qt. microwave-safe dish, heat 2 table-spoons butter, uncovered, on high for 30 seconds or until melted. Whisk in flour until smooth. Gradually add the milk. Microwave, uncovered, on high for 1 minute; whisk lightly. Heat 1 minute longer or until thickened. Whisk in the remaining butter until melted.

In a small bowl, beat egg yolks; add a small amount of hot milk mixture. Return all to the 1-qt. dish, stirring constantly. Whisk in the lemon juice and salt until combined. Microwave, uncovered, on high for 1-2 minutes or until a thermometer reads 160°. Refrigerate leftovers. **Yield:** 1-1/4 cups.

## Herbed Veggie Platter

### (Pictured at right)

#### Ready in 30 minutes or less

*This eye-appealing combination is an interesting twist on mixed vegetables. Topped with herb butter and Parmesan cheese, the crowd-pleaser is an ideal addition to buffets. Divide the ingredients between two plates if your microwave can't accommodate one large platter.*
—*Patricia Vandiver, Tucson, Arizona*

Herbed Veggie Platter

- 1 small head cauliflower, broken into florets
- 1 medium bunch broccoli, cut into florets
- 2 medium zucchini, cut into 1/4-inch slices
- 1/2 cup butter *or* margarine, cubed
- 3/4 teaspoon dried thyme
- 3/4 teaspoon dried parsley flakes
- 1/2 teaspoon onion salt
- 2 medium tomatoes, cut into wedges
- 1/3 cup grated Parmesan cheese

On a large round microwave-safe platter, arrange the cauliflower, broccoli and zucchini. Cover and microwave on high for 7 minutes or until crisp-tender, rotating a half turn three times; drain.

In a small microwave-safe bowl, combine the butter, thyme, parsley and onion salt. Cover and microwave on high for 1 minute or until the butter is melted. Arrange tomatoes on platter. Drizzle butter mixture over vegetables; sprinkle with Parmesan cheese. Cook, uncovered, on high for 1-2 minutes or until heated through. **Yield:** 8-10 servings.

## Banana Cream Pie

### Plan ahead...needs to chill

*I fix this creamy dessert whenever I need a no-fuss treat. Friends are surprised to hear that it's made in the microwave because the soft banana filling and thick buttery crust taste like I slaved over the stove for hours.*
—*Anne Schroeder, Yarrow, British Columbia*

- 1/3 cup butter *or* margarine
- 1-1/4 cups graham cracker crumbs

- 3 tablespoons sugar

FILLING:
- 1/2 cup sugar
- 2 tablespoons all-purpose flour
- 2 tablespoons cornstarch
- 2-1/4 cups milk
- 3 egg yolks, lightly beaten
- 2 tablespoons butter *or* margarine
- 1 teaspoon vanilla extract
- 1/4 teaspoon salt
- 1 to 2 medium firm bananas, cut into 1/4-inch slices

Whipped topping and additional banana slices, optional

Place butter in a greased 9-in. microwave-safe pie plate. Heat, uncovered, on high for 1 minute or until melted, turning once. Stir in crumbs and sugar; mix well. Press onto the bottom and up the sides of plate. Cook, uncovered, on high for 1-1/2 to 2 minutes or until crust is firm and holds together. Cool completely.

For filling, in a 2-qt. microwave-safe bowl, combine sugar, flour and cornstarch. Gradually whisk in milk until smooth. Microwave, uncovered, on high for 9-10 minutes or until thickened, stirring every 2 minutes. Stir a small amount of hot liquid into egg yolks. Gradually return to the bowl, stirring constantly. Cook 1 to 1-1/2 minutes longer or until bubbly, stirring every 30 seconds. Stir in butter, vanilla and salt until butter is melted. Cool for 20 minutes, stirring several times.

Arrange bananas in crust. Top with filling. Cover and chill 8 hours or overnight. Top with whipped topping and additional bananas if desired. **Yield:** 6-8 servings.

Mustard Chicken Breasts

## Custard Cups

**Ready in 30 minutes or less**

*Enjoy homemade custard without the fuss. This is one of my favorite desserts. You can serve it warm or chilled and top it with berries, other fruit or whipped cream.* —Ruth Andrewson, Peck, Idaho

1-3/4 cups milk
1/4 cup sugar
3 eggs, beaten
1/4 teaspoon salt
1/2 teaspoon vanilla extract
Ground cinnamon

In a 1-qt. microwave-safe dish, heat the milk, uncovered, on high for 3 minutes or until hot (do not boil). With an electric mixer, beat in sugar, eggs, salt and vanilla.

Pour into six ungreased 4-oz. microwave-safe custard cups. Sprinkle with cinnamon. Microwave, uncovered, on high for 5 to 5-1/2 minutes or until a knife inserted near the center comes out clean. Let stand for 5 minutes before serving. Refrigerate leftovers. **Yield:** 6 servings.

## Mustard Chicken Breasts

*(Pictured above)*

**Ready in 30 minutes or less**

*Curry powder, lemon juice, honey and mustard make a lip-smacking sauce for paprika-sprinkled chicken that is cooked in the microwave. The made-in-minutes main dish is a favorite with my family, and I'm sure it will be with yours, too.* —Tina Footen, Nampa, Idaho

✓ Uses less fat, sugar or salt. Includes Nutritional Analysis and Diabetic Exchanges.

4 bone-in chicken breast halves (6 ounces each), skin removed
1 teaspoon paprika
1 medium lemon, thinly sliced
1/3 cup spicy brown *or* horseradish mustard
1/3 cup honey
1 teaspoon dried minced onion
1/2 teaspoon curry powder
1/2 teaspoon lemon juice

Arrange chicken in a 9- or 10-in. microwave-safe pie plate, with the thickest side toward the outside of the plate. Sprinkle with paprika; top with lemon slices. Cover with waxed paper. Microwave on high for 8-10 minutes, rotating dish a half turn once.

In a small microwave-safe bowl, combine the remaining ingredients. Microwave, uncovered, on high for 1-1/2 to 2 minutes or until heated through; stir. Drain chicken; top with sauce. Cover and cook on high for 2 minutes or until meat juices run clear. **Yield:** 4 servings.

**Nutritional Analysis:** One serving equals 232 calories, 3 g fat (1 g saturated fat), 63 mg cholesterol, 332 mg sodium, 28 g carbohydrate, 2 g fiber, 27 g protein. **Diabetic Exchanges:** 2-1/2 lean meat, 1-1/2 fruit.

## Beef 'n' Bean Enchiladas

**Ready in 30 minutes or less**

*After cooking ground beef in the microwave, I combine it with cans of bean dip and green chilies to fill flour tortillas. Cheddar cheese and black olives jazz up the prepared enchilada sauce that tops this swift Mexican specialty.* —Linda Lundmark, Martinton, Illinois

3 tablespoons all-purpose flour
1 teaspoon salt, *divided*
1/4 teaspoon paprika
1-1/2 cups milk
1 can (10 ounces) enchilada sauce
1 cup (4 ounces) shredded cheddar cheese
1 can (2-1/4 ounces) sliced ripe olives, drained
3/4 pound ground beef
1 medium onion, chopped
1 can (9 ounces) bean dip
1 can (4 ounces) chopped green chilies
1/8 teaspoon pepper
1 large tomato, seeded and diced
9 white *or* yellow corn tortillas (6 inches), warmed

In a 1-qt. microwave-safe bowl, combine the flour, 1/2 teaspoon salt, paprika, milk and enchilada sauce until smooth. Microwave, uncovered, on high for 2 minutes; stir. Cook 4-5 minutes longer or until thickened, stirring every minute. Stir in cheese and olives; set aside.

Place beef and onion in a microwave-safe dish. Cover and microwave on high for 5 minutes or until meat is no longer pink; drain. Stir in the bean dip, chilies, pepper and remaining salt. Spoon about 1/3 cup meat mixture and 1 tablespoon of diced tomato down the center of each tortilla; roll up tightly.

Place enchiladas seam side down in an ungreased 11-in. x 7-in. x 2-in. microwave-safe dish. Top with sauce.

Microwave, uncovered, on high for 10 minutes or until bubbly around the edges, rotating dish twice. **Yield:** 4 servings.

## Creamy Swiss Spinach Dip

**Ready in 15 minutes or less**

*A few items and a microwave oven are all you need to throw together this warm cheesy dip. It's always gone at the party's end. My favorite way to serve the dip is in a bread bowl with bread cubes.* —Heather Millican
Fort Myers, Florida

  1 package (8 ounces) cream cheese, softened
  1 teaspoon garlic powder
  1 package (9 ounces) frozen creamed spinach, thawed
  2 cups diced Swiss cheese
  2 unsliced round loaves (1 pound *each*) Italian *or* French bread

In a small microwave-safe mixing bowl, beat cream cheese and garlic powder until smooth. Stir in spinach and Swiss cheese. Cover and microwave on high for 5-8 minutes or until cheese is melted, stirring occasionally.

Meanwhile, cut a 4-in. circle in the center of one loaf of bread. Remove bread, leaving 1 in. at bottom of loaf. Cut removed bread and the second loaf into 1-1/2-in. cubes. Spoon hot spinach dip into bread shell. Serve with bread cubes. **Yield:** 3-1/2 cups.

## Cran-Apple Ham Slice

**Ready in 30 minutes or less**

*Cranberries, apple and a little brown sugar blend into a chunky accompaniment to ham. The not-too-sweet sauce gets its pretty pink color from cranberry juice. When cranberries are in season, I freeze some specifically for this down-home dinner.* —Jena Coffey, Rock Hill, Missouri

  1 tablespoon brown sugar
  2 teaspoons cornstarch
Dash ground allspice
  1/2 cup cranberry juice
  1 small apple, peeled and chopped
  1/2 cup fresh *or* frozen cranberries
  1 fully cooked center-cut ham slice (about 1 pound)

In a microwave-safe bowl, combine the brown sugar, cornstarch and allspice. Stir in cranberry juice until smooth. Add apple and cranberries; mix well. Mi-

crowave, uncovered, on high for 3-5 minutes or until thickened, stirring every minute. Keep warm.

Place ham slice in a shallow 3-qt. microwave-safe dish. Cover and microwave at 70% power for 4-6 minutes or until heated through. Top with fruit mixture. **Yield:** 4 servings.

## Cashew Chicken Toss

*(Pictured below)*

**Ready in 45 minutes or less**

*As a home economics teacher, I gave presentations on cooking with microwave ovens when they first became popular. Back then, I shared this pretty salad and warm citrus dressing with my students. It remains one of my favorites today.* —Pamela Martin, Huntsville, Texas

  2 cans (8 ounces *each*) pineapple chunks
  3 tablespoons sugar
  2 teaspoons cornstarch
  2 teaspoons grated orange peel
  1/4 to 1/2 teaspoon dried basil
Dash pepper
  1 pound boneless skinless chicken breasts
  4 cups ready-to-serve salad greens
  1 can (11 ounces) mandarin oranges, drained
  1/3 cup cashews

Drain pineapple, reserving juice; set pineapple aside. In a microwave-safe bowl, combine the sugar, cornstarch, orange peel, basil and pepper. Gradually whisk in pineapple juice until blended. Microwave, uncovered, on high for 2 to 2-1/2 minutes or until mixture boils and is thickened, stirring every 30 seconds. Set aside; stir occasionally.

Place chicken in a greased 8-in. square microwave-safe dish. Cover and microwave on high for 5-7 minutes or until juices run clear, turning every 2 minutes. Let stand, covered, for 10 minutes. Cut into thin strips.

Arrange the salad greens, chicken, oranges and reserved pineapple on individual plates. Drizzle with warm dressing. Sprinkle with cashews. **Yield:** 4 servings.

Cashew Chicken Toss

## Save a Step

When I set the table for a meal, I take clean plates, glasses and flatware right out of the dishwasher instead of taking them out of the cupboards. It saves me the step of putting away some of the items when I empty the dishwasher. —*Jonene Bernhardt, Portland, Oregon*

Broccoli Ham Quiche

1 medium onion, chopped
1 celery rib, chopped
2 tablespoons butter *or* margarine
2 cups milk
1-1/4 cups uncooked instant rice
2 cups diced cooked turkey
1 can (10-3/4 ounces) condensed cream of mushroom soup, undiluted
1 cup seasoned stuffing croutons
1 can (4 ounces) chopped green chilies, drained
1 cup (4 ounces) shredded cheddar cheese, *divided*

In a 2-qt. microwave-safe dish, combine the onion, celery and butter. Cover and microwave on high for 2-3 minutes or until butter is melted. Stir in milk. Cover and cook on high for 4-6 minutes or until milk is steaming (do not boil). Stir in rice. Cover and let stand for 2 minutes.

Add the turkey, soup, croutons, chilies and 1/2 cup cheese. Cover and microwave on high for 5-7 minutes or until heated through, stirring once. Sprinkle with remaining cheese. Cover and let stand for 5 minutes. **Yield:** 6-8 servings.

## Broccoli Ham Quiche

*(Pictured above)*

**Ready in 30 minutes or less**

*This is a great way for overnight guests to start the day. Chock-full of cheese, ham and broccoli, the quiche features an easy crust made of frozen hash browns. And because it cooks in the microwave oven, it doesn't heat up the kitchen.* —Sue Armstrong, Norman, Oklahoma

2 cups frozen shredded hash browns
1 cup (4 ounces) shredded cheddar cheese
1 cup diced fully cooked ham
1/2 cup chopped fresh broccoli
4 eggs
1/2 cup milk
1 teaspoon dried minced onion
1/2 teaspoon garlic powder
1/2 teaspoon salt
1/2 teaspoon pepper

Place hash browns in a greased 9-in. microwave-safe pie plate. Microwave, uncovered, on high for 4 minutes or until thawed. Press onto the bottom and halfway up the sides of the plate. Microwave, uncovered, on high for 3 minutes. Sprinkle with cheese, ham and broccoli.

In a bowl, beat the eggs, milk and seasonings; pour over ham mixture. Cover with waxed paper. Microwave at 70% power for 10-12 minutes or until set. Let stand for 5 minutes before cutting. **Yield:** 4-6 servings.

## Turkey Rice Casserole

**Ready in 45 minutes or less**

*The recipe for this creamy and comforting casserole came from my aunt as a way to use leftover turkey. I love it so much, however, that I don't wait for leftovers to make it. The green chilies provide the memorable flavor.* —Tamy Baker, Kearney, Nebraska

## Sausage Chicken Soup

*(Pictured below)*

**Ready in 30 minutes or less**

*I've been making this satisfying soup for years, but my husband still is thrilled whenever I put it on the table. It's loaded with slices of smoked sausage, chunks of chicken, fresh peppers and hearty potatoes. Spice it up or tone it down with your family's favorite picante sauce.* —Helen MacDonald, Lazo, British Columbia

 Uses less fat, sugar or salt. Includes Nutritional Analysis and Diabetic Exchanges.

**Sausage Chicken Soup**

3/4 pound boneless skinless chicken breasts
2 medium potatoes, peeled and cut into
    1/4-inch cubes
1 can (14-1/2 ounces) chicken broth
1 medium onion, diced
1 medium sweet red pepper, diced
1 medium green pepper, diced
1 garlic clove, minced
3/4 cup picante sauce
3 tablespoons all-purpose flour
3 tablespoons water
1/2 pound fully cooked smoked sausage, diced
Sliced habanero peppers, optional

Place chicken in a greased microwave-safe dish. Cover and microwave on high for 5-7 minutes or until juices run clear, turning every 2 minutes. Cut into cubes; set aside. Place potatoes and broth in a 2-1/2-qt. microwave-safe bowl. Cover and microwave on high for 5 minutes; add the onion, peppers and garlic. Cover and cook on high for 5 minutes or until potatoes are tender. Stir in the picante sauce.

In a small bowl, combine the flour and water until smooth. Add to the potato mixture. Cover and cook on high for 3 minutes or until thickened. Add chicken and sausage. Cover and microwave for 1-2 minutes until heated through. Garnish with habaneros if desired. **Yield:** 6 servings.

**Nutritional Analysis:** One 1-cup serving (prepared with turkey sausage) equals 212 calories, 6 g fat (2 g saturated fat), 57 mg cholesterol, 877 mg sodium, 20 g carbohydrate, 3 g fiber, 20 g protein. **Diabetic Exchanges:** 2 lean meat, 1 starch, 1 vegetable.

## Saucy Orange Roughy

### Ready in 15 minutes or less

*Both the seafood and citrus lovers in your home will request this entree time and again. Not only are the orange roughy fillets tender and the sauce delicious, but the dish is ready in moments. I haven't found anyone who didn't think it was wonderful!* —Bette Hunn
Orosi, California

✓ Uses less fat, sugar or salt. Includes Nutritional Analysis and Diabetic Exchanges.

1 tablespoon sugar
2 teaspoons cornstarch
1/2 teaspoon chicken bouillon granules
Dash pepper
1/2 cup orange juice
1 teaspoon lemon juice
1/4 teaspoon grated orange peel
1/8 teaspoon dried tarragon
1 pound orange roughy fillets
1/2 teaspoon salt
Orange slices and fresh tarragon, optional

In a small microwave-safe dish, combine the first six ingredients until smooth. Microwave, uncovered, on high for 1 minute; stir. Cook 1 minute longer or until thickened. Stir in orange peel and tarragon; set aside.

Place fish in an ungreased 11-in. x 7-in. x 2-in. mi-

**Dressed-Up Meatballs**

crowave-safe dish, with the thickest side toward the outside of the dish. Sprinkle with salt. Cover and microwave on high for 4 minutes. Top with orange sauce. Microwave, uncovered, on high for 45-60 seconds or until fish flakes easily with a fork. Garnish with orange slices and fresh tarragon if desired. **Yield:** 4 servings.

**Nutritional Analysis:** One serving equals 111 calories, 1 g fat (trace saturated fat), 23 mg cholesterol, 475 mg sodium, 8 g carbohydrate, trace fiber, 17 g protein. **Diabetic Exchanges:** 2-1/2 very lean meat, 1/2 fruit.

## Dressed-Up Meatballs

### (Pictured above)

### Ready in 30 minutes or less

*Frozen meatballs and a jar of sweet-and-sour sauce make this microwave meal a last-minute lifesaver when racing against the clock. The flavorful sauce is dressed up with a hint of garlic and nicely coats the colorful mixture of meatballs, carrots, green pepper and onion.* —Ivy Eresmas, Dade City, Florida

2 pounds frozen fully cooked meatballs,
    thawed
1 small onion, sliced
2 medium carrots, julienned
1 small green pepper, julienned
1 garlic clove, minced
1 jar (10 ounces) sweet-and-sour sauce
4-1/2 teaspoons soy sauce
Hot cooked rice

Place the meatballs in a 3-qt. microwave-safe dish; top with the onion, carrots, green pepper and garlic. Combine the sauces; pour over meatballs. Cover and microwave on high for 8-10 minutes or until vegetables are tender and meatballs are heated through, stirring twice. Serve over rice. **Yield:** 8 servings.

# Chapter 19

HERE'S a collection of theme-related recipes that taste great and are real time-savers, too.

For "berry" delicious dishes, raspberries add lovely color and a sweet fruity flavor.

Cabbage, cauliflower and broccoli are versatile vegetables that enhance soups, salads, side dishes and entrees.

There's no pressure on you to get dinner done when a pressure cooker prepares a tempting recipe in mere minutes.

Savor Southwestern flavor with sensational salsas and quick-to-fix quesadillas.

Even a speedy meal can include dessert of cupcakes, pound cakes and other treats.

And if recipes that feed a crowd don't suit your smaller household, check out the rapid recipes here that are perfectly portioned to serve one or two.

**BERRY TASTY.** Fresh Raspberry Pie and Raspberry Chicken (both recipes on p. 290).

Cabbage Sausage Soup
Cabbage Sloppy Joes

# Crunchy Cabbage

NO LONGER content to star in salads or play second fiddle to corned beef, cabbage is proving itself an invaluable addition to a variety of rapid recipes.

## Cabbage Sausage Soup

*(Pictured above)*

**Ready in 45 minutes or less**

*This hearty autumn soup features smoked sausage. My mother made it when we had garden cabbage.*
—Nancy Allman, Derry, Pennsylvania

- 4 cups chicken broth
- 1 small cabbage, chopped (about 10 cups)
- 1 medium onion, chopped
- 1/2 pound fully cooked smoked sausage, halved lengthwise and sliced
- 1/2 cup all-purpose flour
- 1-1/2 teaspoons salt
- 1/4 teaspoon pepper
- 1 cup milk

In a Dutch oven, bring broth, cabbage and onion to a boil. Reduce heat; cover and simmer for 10-15 minutes or until cabbage is tender. Add sausage; heat through. In a bowl, combine the flour, salt and pepper. Gradually add milk, stirring until smooth. Gradually stir into soup. Bring to a boil; cook and stir for 2 minutes or until thickened. **Yield:** 8 servings (about 2 quarts).

## Cabbage Sloppy Joes

*(Pictured above)*

**Ready in 45 minutes or less**

*Many friends don't realize these tangy sandwiches include cabbage.*
—Darlene Markel, Salem, Oregon

- 1 pound ground beef
- 1-1/2 cups finely shredded cabbage
- 1 medium onion, chopped
- 1 celery rib, chopped
- 1/4 cup chopped green pepper
- 1 cup ketchup
- 3 tablespoons brown sugar
- 2 tablespoons lemon juice
- 1 tablespoon white vinegar
- 1 tablespoon Worcestershire sauce
- 1 tablespoon prepared mustard
- 1 teaspoon salt
- Dash pepper
- 8 sandwich rolls, split

In a large skillet, cook the beef, cabbage, onion, celery and green pepper over medium heat until meat is no longer pink and vegetables are crisp-tender; drain. Stir in the ketchup, brown sugar, lemon juice, vinegar, Worcestershire sauce, mustard, salt and pepper. Cover and simmer for 10 minutes or until cabbage is tender. Spoon 1/2 cup onto each roll. **Yield:** 8 servings.

## Cabbage Wedges with Beef

**Ready in 45 minutes or less**

*This skillet dinner is always a hit. I love preparing it for my family.* —Sue VanDlac, Everett, Washington

- 1-1/2 pounds ground beef
- 1/2 cup *each* chopped onion, celery and green pepper
- 1 can (15 ounces) tomato sauce
- 3 tablespoons cider vinegar
- 3 tablespoons brown sugar
- 1-1/4 teaspoons salt
- 3 tablespoons quick-cooking oats
- 2 tablespoons minced fresh parsley
- 1/2 teaspoon garlic powder
- 1/8 teaspoon pepper
- 1 medium cabbage

In a large skillet, cook the beef, onion, celery and green pepper over medium heat until meat is no longer pink; drain. In a bowl, combine tomato sauce, vinegar, brown sugar and salt; add to skillet. Stir in the oats, parsley, garlic powder and pepper.

Core the cabbage and cut into six wedges; arrange over meat mixture. Cover and simmer for 15-20 minutes or until cabbage is tender. **Yield:** 6 servings.

## Red Cabbage Slaw

**Ready in 15 minutes or less**

*This is a colorful alternative to traditional coleslaw. We love the dressing.* —Gladys De Boer, Castleford, Idaho

- 3/4 cup vegetable oil
- 1/2 cup white vinegar
- 1/4 cup honey
- 1/2 teaspoon salt
- 1/2 teaspoon ground mustard
- 8 cups shredded red cabbage

In a jar with a tight-fitting lid, combine the oil, vinegar, honey, salt and mustard; shake well. Place cabbage in a large bowl; add dressing and toss to coat. Refrigerate until serving. **Yield:** 10 servings.

# Flavorful Florets

ANYTIME is the right time for broccoli. This bright green good-for-you vegetable is available year-round to add flavor and freshness to soups, salads and skillet dishes. Showcase this versatile veggie in one of the following fast-to-fix recipes.

## Broccoli Crab Bisque

**Ready in 30 minutes or less**

*For a casual meal, I serve this creamy soup along with ham sandwiches. Sometimes we leave the bay leaf in the soup as a sign of good luck for the person who gets it in their bowl. —Karen Balistrieri, Oconomowoc, Wisconsin*

- 1 cup sliced leeks (white portion only)
- 1 cup sliced fresh mushrooms
- 1 cup chopped fresh broccoli florets
- 1 garlic clove, minced
- 1/4 cup butter *or* margarine
- 1/4 cup all-purpose flour
- 1/4 to 1/2 teaspoon dried thyme
- 1/8 teaspoon pepper
- 1 bay leaf
- 3 cups chicken broth
- 1 cup half-and-half cream
- 1 cup (4 ounces) shredded Swiss cheese
- 1 can (6 ounces) crabmeat, drained, flaked and cartilage removed

In a large saucepan, saute leeks, mushrooms, broccoli and garlic in butter until tender. Add flour, thyme, pepper and bay leaf; mix well. Stir in the broth and cream. Bring to a boil; cook and stir for 2 minutes or until thickened.

Add the cheese and crab; stir until cheese is melted and soup is heated through. Discard bay leaf before serving. **Yield:** 8 servings (2 quarts).

## Ranch Floret Salad

**Ready in 30 minutes or less**

*Ranch dressing mix seasons the tasty mixture that coats crunchy cauliflower and broccoli florets in this salad. It's good at a gathering, for guests or to enjoy with your family.* —*Pam May, Auburn, Alabama*

- 6 bacon strips, diced
- 1 medium head cauliflower, cut into small florets
- 1 medium bunch broccoli, cut into small florets
- 1 envelope ranch salad dressing mix
- 3/4 to 1 cup mayonnaise
- 3/4 to 1 cup sour cream

In a skillet, cook bacon over medium heat until crisp. Remove to paper towels to drain. In a large bowl, combine cauliflower and broccoli. In a small bowl, combine salad dressing mix, mayonnaise and sour cream. Pour over vegetables and toss to coat. Cover and refrigerate until serving. Stir in bacon. **Yield:** 8 servings.

## Broccoli Sausage Simmer

*(Pictured below)*

**Ready in 30 minutes or less**

*I created this meal-in-one-dish when trying to use up a large head of broccoli. It's requested at least once a week in our home, which is handy for me since it's easy to prepare and we always have the ingredients.*
—*Lisa Montgomery, Elmira, Ontario*

✓ Uses less fat, sugar or salt. Includes Nutritional Analysis and Diabetic Exchanges.

- 1 pound fully cooked kielbasa *or* Polish sausage, cut into 1/4-inch slices
- 1 medium bunch broccoli, cut into florets
- 1/2 cup sliced red onion
- 1 can (14-1/2 ounces) diced tomatoes, undrained
- 1 tablespoon minced fresh basil *or* 1 teaspoon dried basil
- 1 tablespoon minced fresh parsley *or* 1 teaspoon dried parsley flakes
- 1 teaspoon sugar
- 3 cups cooked spiral pasta

In a large skillet, saute sausage, broccoli and onion for 5-6 minutes or until broccoli is crisp-tender. Add the tomatoes, basil, parsley and sugar. Cover and simmer for 10 minutes. Add pasta and heat through. **Yield:** 8 servings.

**Nutritional Analysis:** One 1-cup serving (prepared with reduced-fat turkey Italian sausage) equals 183 calories, 6 g fat (2 g saturated fat), 30 mg cholesterol, 418 mg sodium, 20 g carbohydrate, 2 g fiber, 13 g protein. **Diabetic Exchanges:** 2 lean meat, 1 starch.

Broccoli Sausage Simmer

# Sensational Salsa

WHETHER you like it on the hot and spicy side or prefer the cool and refreshing variety, nothing beats homemade salsa for snacking.

## Cucumber Salsa

*(Pictured below)*

**Plan ahead...needs to chill**

*Zippy jalapeno, tart lime juice and garden-fresh cucumbers take center stage in this chunky salsa.  —Sandy Lee Choctaw, Oklahoma*

✓ Uses less fat, sugar or salt. Includes Nutritional Analysis and Diabetic Exchanges.

   2 medium cucumbers, peeled, seeded and chopped
   2 medium tomatoes, chopped
1/2 cup chopped green pepper
   1 jalapeno pepper, seeded and chopped*
   1 small onion, chopped
   1 garlic clove, minced
   2 tablespoons lime juice
   1 teaspoon minced fresh parsley
   2 teaspoons minced fresh cilantro *or* parsley
1/2 teaspoon dill weed
1/2 teaspoon salt
Tortilla chips

In a bowl, combine the first 11 ingredients. Cover and refrigerate for 1 hour. Serve with chips. **Yield:** 4 cups.

   **Nutritional Analysis:** One serving (1/4 cup salsa) equals 11 calories, trace fat (trace saturated fat), 0 cholesterol, 76 mg sodium, 2 g carbohydrate, 1 g fiber, trace protein. **Diabetic Exchange:** Free food.

   **\*Editor's Note:** When cutting or seeding hot peppers, use rubber or plastic gloves to protect your hands. Avoid touching your face.

## Garden Salsa

*(Pictured below left)*

**Ready in 30 minutes or less**

*Everyone loves this fresh-tasting salsa. It has a wonderful crunch.  —Tammy Mahlke, La Crescent, Minnesota*

 Uses less fat, sugar or salt. Includes Nutritional Analysis and Diabetic Exchanges.

   1 medium green pepper, chopped
   2 celery ribs, chopped
   1 medium tomato, diced
   1 small onion, chopped
   1 medium carrot, chopped
1/4 cup minced fresh cilantro *or* parsley
   1 can (14-1/2 ounces) diced tomatoes, drained
1/2 cup water
1/2 cup tomato sauce
1/3 cup tomato paste
   3 garlic cloves, minced
   1 tablespoon lemon juice
1/4 teaspoon pepper
Tortilla chips

In a bowl, combine first seven ingredients. In another bowl, combine water, tomato sauce, tomato paste, garlic, lemon juice and pepper; stir into vegetable mixture. Serve with chips. Refrigerate leftovers. **Yield:** about 3 cups.

   **Nutritional Analysis:** One serving (1/4 cup salsa) equals 29 calories, trace fat (trace saturated fat), 0 cholesterol, 122 mg sodium, 7 g carbohydrate, 2 g fiber, 1 g protein. **Diabetic Exchange:** 1 vegetable.

## California Avocado Salsa

**Ready in 30 minutes or less**

*This spicy salsa's festive green and red colors always bring a bit of cheer.  —Mary Vosika, Magalia, California*

   3 large ripe avocados, peeled and cubed
   3 medium tomatoes, seeded and chopped
1-1/2 cups chopped sweet red pepper
   1 small onion, chopped
   1 to 2 jalapeno peppers, seeded and chopped*
   3 tablespoons minced fresh cilantro *or* parsley
1/4 cup lime juice
Salt to taste
Tortilla chips

In a bowl, combine the first eight ingredients; mix well. Serve immediately with chips. **Yield:** 5 cups.

   **\*Editor's Note:** When cutting or seeding hot peppers, use rubber or plastic gloves to protect your hands. Avoid touching your face.

## No More Tears

Chop onions without tears using your blender! Quarter the onions, place them in the blender and cover with water. Put the top back on the blender and process on high speed for a second or two or until chopped. Pour into a colander to drain. —*Shirley Marshall, Alvin, Texas*

Cucumber Salsa
Garden Salsa

Baked Chicken Quesadillas

# Quick-to-Fix Quesadillas

MAKE WAY, tacos! A new fiesta of flavors is coming to town. It's the quesadilla—a simple dish that sandwiches savory fillings between tasty time-saving tortillas.

This south-of-the-border specialty stands out for its streamlined specifics. Not only does it come together in a flash, but it's versatile enough to suit individual tastes. So try one of these recipes and make quesadillas a swift standby in your home.

## Baked Chicken Quesadillas

*(Pictured above)*

**Ready in 15 minutes or less**

*I created these after ordering something similar at a local restaurant. My husband loves the crispy tortillas and spicy filling.*
*—Deborah Hord*
*Concord, North Carolina*

    4 flour tortillas (7 inches)
    1 package (6 ounces) fully cooked
       Southwestern chicken breast strips
    1 can (10 ounces) diced tomatoes and green
       chilies, well drained
    1 cup (4 ounces) shredded Mexican cheese
       blend
Shredded lettuce, sliced ripe olives and chopped
    tomatoes, optional

Coat one side of two tortillas with nonstick cooking spray; place coated side down on an ungreased baking sheet. Top each with chicken, tomatoes and cheese. Cover with remaining tortillas; spritz tops with nonstick cooking spray.

Bake at 450° for 10 minutes or until golden brown. Cut into wedges. Garnish with lettuce, olives and tomatoes if desired. **Yield: 2-4 servings.**

## Smoked Salmon Quesadillas

**Ready in 30 minutes or less**

*I serve these golden tortilla wedges filled with a rich combination of smoked salmon, cream cheese, Swiss cheese, garlic and dill. They're a snap to whip up for the salmon lovers in your family.*
*—Becky Applebee, Chiniak, Alaska*

    4 ounces cream cheese, softened
    2 tablespoons sour cream
    1 teaspoon dill weed
    1 garlic clove, minced
    2 tablespoons butter *or* margarine,
       softened
    6 flour tortillas (7 inches)
    4 ounces smoked salmon, diced
    2 cups (8 ounces) shredded
       Swiss *or* cheddar cheese

In a small mixing bowl, combine the cream cheese, sour cream, dill and garlic. Spread butter over one side of each tortilla. Place three tortillas, buttered side down, on a griddle or large skillet. Spread with cream cheese mixture; sprinkle with salmon and cheese. Cover with remaining tortillas, buttered side up.

Cook over low heat for 2-3 minutes or until golden brown. Turn and cook 2-3 minutes longer or until cheese is melted. Cut into wedges. **Yield: 3 servings.**

## Bacon Avocado Quesadillas

**Ready in 30 minutes or less**

*Chock-full of bacon, mushrooms, tomato, cheese and avocado, these must-try mainstays are terrific topped with salsa and sour cream.* *—Janet Lipner, Chicago, Illinois*

    8 bacon strips, diced
    1/2 pound fresh mushrooms, sliced
    1 to 2 tablespoons butter *or* margarine,
       softened
    4 flour tortillas (7 inches)
    2 cups (8 ounces) shredded Colby-Monterey
       Jack cheese
    1 medium tomato, chopped
    1 ripe avocado, peeled and sliced
Sour cream and salsa, optional

In a large skillet, cook the bacon over medium heat until crisp. Remove to paper towels. Drain, reserving 1 tablespoon drippings. Saute mushrooms in the drippings.

Spread butter over one side of each tortilla. Place two tortillas, buttered side down, on a griddle or skillet. Top with bacon, mushrooms, cheese, tomato and avocado. Cover with remaining tortillas, buttered side up.

Cook over low heat for 1-2 minutes or until golden brown. Turn and cook 1-2 minutes longer or until the cheese is melted. Cut into wedges. Serve with sour cream and salsa if desired. **Yield: 2-4 servings.**

# Relish Refreshing Raspberries

RELAX! You can enjoy the luscious flavor of fresh raspberries without spending hours in the kitchen.

Simply gather sun-warmed berries from your backyard patch or purchase pints from your local grocer. Then use the ripe ruby-red fruit in one of these recipes. You're sure to receive rave reviews.

## Raspberry Chicken

*(Pictured below right and on page 284)*

**Ready in 45 minutes or less**

*This is one of my favorite ways to serve chicken. My wife and I garnish it with fresh raspberries and sprigs of thyme from our garden.* —Robert Jost, Manitowoc, Wisconsin

```
2-1/4 cups fresh raspberries
    4 teaspoons sugar
  1/4 cup apple juice
    2 tablespoons red wine vinegar or
        cider vinegar
    1 tablespoon soy sauce
    1 garlic clove, minced
  1/2 teaspoon snipped fresh thyme or 1/8
        teaspoon dried thyme
    1 tablespoon cornstarch
    1 tablespoon water
    4 boneless skinless chicken breast halves
    1 tablespoon vegetable oil
    1 tablespoon butter or margarine
Salt and pepper to taste
```

Place raspberries in a bowl; sprinkle with sugar and mash. Let stand for 15 minutes; mash again. Strain, reserving juice; discard pulp and seeds. In a saucepan, combine the raspberry juice, apple juice, vinegar, soy sauce, garlic and thyme. Simmer, uncovered, for 5 minutes. In a bowl, combine cornstarch and water; stir into raspberry juice mixture until smooth. Bring to a boil; cook and stir for 1 minute or until thickened. Keep warm.

Flatten chicken to 1/4-in. thickness. In a large skillet, heat oil and butter over medium-high heat. Add the chicken; cook until juices run clear. Sprinkle with salt and pepper. Serve with raspberry sauce. **Yield:** 4 servings.

## Fresh Raspberry Pie

*(Pictured at right and on page 284)*

**Plan ahead...needs to chill**

*I pile fresh berries in a pastry crust, then dress them up with an easy glaze and whipped cream. It's the best fresh fruit pie I have ever tasted.* —Ruth Andersson
Richmond, British Columbia

```
    4 cups fresh raspberries, divided
  1/3 cup water
  3/4 cup sugar
7-1/2 teaspoons cornstarch
Dash salt
    1 pastry shell (9 inches), baked
Whipped cream, optional
```

In a saucepan, crush 1 cup of berries. Add water; simmer for 3 minutes. Strain, reserving juice; discard pulp and seeds. Add enough water to juice to measure 1 cup liquid. In a saucepan, combine sugar, cornstarch and salt. Slowly stir in raspberry liquid. Bring to a boil; cook and stir for 2 minutes or until thickened. Remove from the heat; cool slightly.

Place remaining raspberries in pastry shell; pour glaze over top. Refrigerate for 2-3 hours or until set. Serve with whipped cream if desired. **Yield:** 6-8 servings.

## Berries 'n' Cream Dessert

**Ready in 1 hour or less**

*For a refreshing end to a summer meal, try this cool combination. This rich dessert has a satiny texture and not-too-sweet taste.* —Rita Farmer, Greendale, Wisconsin

```
  3/4 cup sour cream
  1/3 cup packed brown sugar
    1 cup vanilla ice cream
  3/4 cup whipping cream
    1 tablespoon sugar
  1/2 teaspoon vanilla extract
    3 cups fresh raspberries
```

In a bowl, whisk the sour cream and brown sugar. Stir in ice cream. Refrigerate. In a chilled mixing bowl, beat whipping cream until it begins to thicken. Add sugar and vanilla; beat until stiff peaks form and sugar is dissolved. Fold in sour cream mixture and berries. Pour into serving dishes. Serve immediately or refrigerate. **Yield:** 8-10 servings.

Fresh Raspberry Pie
Raspberry Chicken

# Pressure Cooking

German Potato Salad
Swiss Steak

UNDER PRESSURE to get dinner on the table in a hurry? Try the speedy solution that's been a favorite of busy cooks for years—the pressure cooker.

## Swiss Steak

*(Pictured at right)*

**Ready in 1 hour or less**

*I rely on my pressure cooker to fix this tender round steak in a saucy vegetable mixture. It's delicious over rice.*
—Susan Kelly, Englewood, New Jersey

  1-1/2 pounds boneless beef round steak
     (1/2 inch thick)
    2 tablespoons all-purpose flour
  1/2 teaspoon salt
  1/4 teaspoon pepper
    2 tablespoons vegetable oil
    2 medium carrots, chopped
    1 medium onion, chopped
    1 cup chopped green pepper
  3/4 cup chopped celery
    1 teaspoon cornstarch
  1/2 cup cold water
    1 can (10-3/4 ounces) condensed tomato
     soup, undiluted
    1 teaspoon prepared horseradish

Cut steak into serving-size pieces. Combine flour, salt and pepper; sprinkle over both sides of steak. In a pressure cooker, brown steak on both sides in oil; drain. Add carrots, onion, green pepper and celery. In a bowl, combine cornstarch and water until smooth; add soup and horseradish. Pour over vegetables.

Close cover securely; place pressure regulator on vent pipe. Bring cooker to full pressure over high heat. Reduce heat to medium and cook for 12 minutes. (Pressure regulator should maintain a slow steady rocking motion or release of steam; adjust heat if needed.) Remove from the heat. Immediately cool according to manufacturer's directions until pressure is completely reduced. **Yield:** 4-6 servings.

## German Potato Salad

*(Pictured above right)*

**Ready in 30 minutes or less**

*Just fill the pressure cooker, put the lid on, cook for a short time and this wonderful potato salad is done.*
—Diane Wilson, Charlotte, North Carolina

    6 bacon strips, diced
    7 unpeeled medium red potatoes, cubed
    2 medium onions, thinly sliced

  1/3 cup cider vinegar
  1/3 cup water
    2 tablespoons sugar
    3 tablespoons minced fresh parsley, *divided*
    1 to 2 teaspoons salt
    1 teaspoon prepared mustard
  1/4 teaspoon pepper

In a pressure cooker, cook bacon over medium heat until crisp; drain. Add potatoes and onions. In a bowl, combine the vinegar, water, sugar, 2 tablespoons parsley, salt, mustard and pepper; pour over potatoes.

Close cover securely; place pressure regulator on vent pipe. Bring cooker to full pressure over high heat. Reduce heat to medium and cook for 5 minutes. (Pressure regulator should maintain a slow steady rocking motion or release of steam; adjust heat if needed.) Remove from the heat. Immediately cool according to manufacturer's directions until pressure is completely reduced. Just before serving, sprinkle with remaining parsley. **Yield:** 8 servings.

## Pork Chop 'n' Kraut Dinner

**Ready in 45 minutes or less**

*This dish is practically a meal. Add a salad or veggie and dinner's ready.*    —Leota Hall, Lincoln, Nebraska

    6 bone-in pork loin chops (1/2 inch thick)
    2 tablespoons vegetable oil
  1/2 teaspoon salt
  1/4 teaspoon pepper
    2 cans (14 ounces *each*) Bavarian sauerkraut,
     drained
    2 tablespoons brown sugar
    6 medium potatoes, peeled
  1-1/2 cups water

In a pressure cooker, cook pork chops in oil until lightly browned on each side; drain. Remove chops; sprinkle with salt and pepper. Add sauerkraut to cooker; sprinkle with brown sugar. Place pork chops and potatoes over sauerkraut; add water.

Close cover securely; place pressure regulator on vent pipe. Bring cooker to full pressure over high heat. Reduce heat to medium and cook for 15 minutes. (Pressure regulator should maintain a slow steady rocking motion or release of steam; adjust heat if needed.) Remove from the heat. Immediately cool according to manufacturer's directions until pressure is completely reduced. **Yield:** 6 servings.

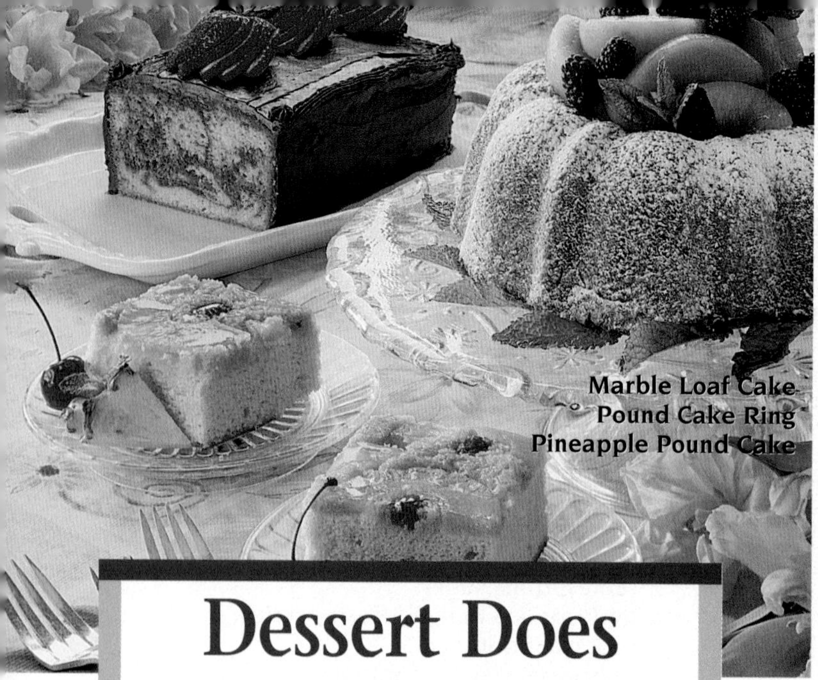

325°; bake 45 minutes longer or until a toothpick inserted near the center comes out clean. Cool for 10 minutes before inverting onto a wire rack to cool completely. If desired, dust with confectioners' sugar and garnish with fruit and mint. **Yield:** 2 cakes (9 cups batter).

**Editor's Note:** Recipe can be halved.

## Pineapple Pound Cake

*(Pictured at left)*

*Jazz up the basic batter with pineapple, red cherries and pecan halves to create this lovely upside-down dessert.*

>     1 can (20 ounces) sliced pineapple
>   2/3 cup packed brown sugar
>   1/4 cup butter *or* margarine
>     9 maraschino cherries, halved
> Pecan halves, optional
> 4-1/2 cups pound cake batter (from Pound
>       Cake Ring recipe on this page)

Drain pineapple, reserving 1 tablespoon juice; set aside (discard remaining juice or save for another use). In a saucepan over low heat, cook and stir brown sugar and butter until sugar is dissolved; add the reserved pineapple juice. Pour into an ungreased 13-in. x 9-in. x 2-in. baking dish.

Cut pineapple slices in half. Arrange in a single layer in three lengthwise rows, alternating the direction of each row. Place a cherry, cut side up, between each pineapple slice. If desired, place pecan halves around the sides of the dish. Carefully spoon batter over the top and spread gently.

Bake at 350° for 15 minutes. Reduce heat to 325°; bake 40 minutes longer or until a toothpick inserted into cake near the center comes out clean. Immediately invert onto a serving platter. Cool. **Yield:** 12 servings.

## Marble Loaf Cake

*(Pictured above left)*

*Joan sometimes adds chocolate syrup to the basic batter to produce the lovely swirls in this moist marbled loaf.*

> 4-1/2 cups pound cake batter (from Pound Cake
>       Ring recipe on this page), *divided*
>     3 tablespoons chocolate syrup
>     1 can (16 ounces) chocolate frosting
> Fresh strawberries, optional

In a small bowl, combine 1/2 cup batter and chocolate syrup. Pour the remaining batter into a greased and floured 9-in. x 5-in. x 3-in. loaf pan. Spoon chocolate batter over the top; gently cut through batter with a knife to swirl.

Bake at 350° for 15 minutes. Reduce heat to 325°; bake 40 minutes longer or until a toothpick inserted near the center comes out clean. Cool for 10 minutes before removing from pan to a wire rack to cool completely. Frost top and sides of cake. Garnish with strawberries if desired. **Yield:** 8-10 servings.

Marble Loaf Cake
Pound Cake Ring
Pineapple Pound Cake

## Dessert Does Double Duty

IN A HURRY? Need to serve sweets to a crowd? Time-crunched cooks will find this feature twice as nice for potlucks and large gatherings.

The basic Pound Cake Ring recipe sent in by Joan Piotrowski of Chicago, Illinois produces enough batter to make two of the three crowd-pleasing desserts shared here, so the results are doubly delicious.

## Pound Cake Ring

*(Pictured above)*

*Use half of the batter from this recipe to bake pound cake sprinkled with powdered sugar. The other half can be used in one of the terrific treatments that follow.*

>     1 pound butter (no substitutes), softened
>     3 cups sugar
>     6 eggs
>   1/2 cup plus 1 tablespoon milk
>     1 tablespoon lemon juice
> 1-1/2 teaspoons vanilla extract
>     1 teaspoon grated lemon peel
>   1/2 teaspoon lemon extract
>     4 cups cake flour
>   1/2 teaspoon salt
>   1/2 teaspoon baking soda
> Confectioners' sugar, fresh peaches, blackberries
>       and mint, optional

In a mixing bowl, cream butter and sugar until light and fluffy, about 5 minutes. Add eggs, one at a time, beating well after each addition. Combine the milk, lemon juice, vanilla, lemon peel and extract. Combine the flour, salt and baking soda; add to creamed mixture alternately with milk mixture and mix well.

Pour 4-1/2 cups of batter into a greased and floured 10-in. fluted tube pan. (Use the remaining batter to prepare a second pound cake or one of the other cakes on this page.) Bake at 350° for 15 minutes. Reduce heat to

# Sweet Treats

FORGET FLOWERS. When it's time to express your affection, try a tempting homemade treat. Your valentine is sure to fall head over heels for one of the easy and irresistible ideas shared below. And you'll be fond of how fast you can fix these dazzling desserts!

## Heart's Delight Torte

*Pie filling dresses up homemade chocolate cake layers in this yummy dessert. It has become our traditional birthday cake.* —Nancy Heesch, Sioux Falls, South Dakota

```
1/3 cup shortening
  1 cup sugar
  1 egg
3/4 cup buttermilk
  1 teaspoon vanilla extract
  1 cup plus 2 tablespoons all-purpose flour
1/3 cup baking cocoa
1/2 teaspoon baking soda
1/2 teaspoon salt
  2 cans (21 ounces each) cherry pie filling
  1 cup whipped topping
  2 tablespoons semisweet chocolate chips
```

In a mixing bowl, cream shortening and sugar. Add the egg, buttermilk and vanilla. Combine the dry ingredients; gradually add to creamed mixture. Pour into a greased 9-in. heart-shaped or round baking pan. Bake at 350° for 30-35 minutes or until a toothpick inserted near the center comes out clean. Cool for 10 minutes before removing from pan to a wire rack to cool completely.

Split cake in half; place one layer on a serving plate. Spread with one can of pie filling; top with second cake layer. Pipe whipped topping around edge; garnish with chocolate chips. Spoon cherries from the second can of pie filling onto the top of the cake (refrigerate any remaining filling for another use). **Yield:** 10-12 servings.

## White Chocolate Pie

### Plan ahead...needs to chill

*For Valentine's Day, tint whipped topping pink to cover this creamy dessert. Garnish each slice with an Oreo cookie for a fast finishing touch.* —Sue Brown, Hanover, Indiana

```
  1 package (8 ounces) cream cheese, softened
3/4 cup confectioners' sugar
  1 carton (8 ounces) frozen whipped topping,
    thawed, divided
  1 chocolate crumb crust (8 inches)
1-1/4 cups cold milk
  1 package (3.3 ounces) instant white chocolate
    pudding mix
Red food coloring
```

In a mixing bowl, beat cream cheese, confectioners' sugar and 1/4 cup whipped topping until light and fluffy. Spread over crust. In a mixing bowl, beat milk and pudding mix on low speed for 2 minutes. Pour over cream cheese mixture. Refrigerate for 2 hours or until firm.

Tint remaining whipped topping pink with red food coloring. Spread over pie just before serving. Refrigerate leftovers. **Yield:** 6-8 servings.

## For-My-Love Sugar Cookies

### Plan ahead...needs to chill

*Cut the dough for these crisp cookies into heart shapes...or form into letters to spell out sweet nothings to your honey. These are our favorite sugar cookies. They're one of the homemade treats I love to bake for friends and neighbors.* —Marilyn Wheeler, Ellijay, Georgia

```
3/4 cup shortening
1-1/2 cups sugar
  2 eggs
  3 cups self-rising flour*
  1 teaspoon orange extract
Colored sugar, optional
```

In a mixing bowl, cream shortening and sugar. Add the eggs, flour and extract; mix well. Cover and refrigerate for 1 hour or until easy to handle.

On floured surface, roll out dough to 1/4-in. thickness. Cut with 2-in. cookie cutters dipped in flour. Sprinkle with colored sugar if desired. Place 1 in. apart on ungreased baking sheets. Bake at 375° for 6-8 minutes or until lightly browned. Remove to wire racks to cool. **Yield:** about 5-1/2 dozen.

***Editor's Note:** As a substitute for each cup of self-rising flour, place 1-1/2 teaspoons baking powder and 1/2 teaspoon salt in a measuring cup. Add all-purpose flour to measure 1 cup.

**Heart's Delight Torte**
**White Chocolate Pie**
**For-My-Love Sugar Cookies**

## Chocolate Caramel Cupcakes

*(Pictured at left)*

*A few baking staples are all you need to throw together these chewy delights. Boxed cake mix and a can of frosting make them fast, but caramel, walnuts and chocolate chips tucked inside make them memorable. We like them with ice cream.*

—Bev Spain, Bellville, Ohio

> 1 package (18-1/4 ounces) chocolate cake mix
> 24 caramels
> 3/4 cup semisweet chocolate chips
> 1 cup chopped walnuts
> Chocolate frosting
> Additional walnuts, optional

Prepare cake batter according to package directions. Fill 24 greased or paper-lined muffin cups one-third full; set remaining batter aside. Bake at 350° for 7-8 minutes or until top of cupcake appears set.

Gently press a caramel into each cupcake; sprinkle with chocolate chips and walnuts. Top with remaining batter. Bake 15-20 minutes longer or until a toothpick inserted near the center of cake comes out clean. Cool for 5 minutes; remove from pans to wire racks to cool completely. Frost with chocolate frosting. Sprinkle with additional nuts if desired. **Yield:** 2 dozen.

**Editor's Note:** This recipe was tested with Betty Crocker cake mix and Hershey caramels.

Surprise Cupcakes
Chocolate Caramel Cupcakes

# Cupcakes–Yum!

PERFECT for birthday treats, bake sales, morning coffee breaks or late-night snack attacks, cupcakes satisfy the sweet tooth in kids of all ages. So the next time you need to whip up a tasty handheld tidbit, consider one of these recipes. Each has delicious flavor you'll gladly savor.

## Surprise Cupcakes

*(Pictured above)*

*My mother taught me this simple way to fill cupcakes with fruit jelly. Take these tender treats to your next get-together and watch faces light up after just one bite.*

—Edith Holliday, Flushing, Michigan

> 1 cup shortening
> 2 cups sugar
> 2 eggs
> 2 teaspoons vanilla extract
> 3-1/2 cups all-purpose flour
> 5 teaspoons baking powder
> 1 teaspoon salt
> 1-1/2 cups milk
> 3/4 cup strawberry *or* grape jelly
> Vanilla frosting
> Colored sprinkles, optional

In a mixing bowl, cream shortening and sugar. Add eggs, one at a time, beating well after each addition. Beat in vanilla. Combine the flour, baking powder and salt; add to creamed mixture alternately with milk. Fill 36 greased or paper-lined muffin cups half full. Spoon 1 teaspoon jelly in the center of each.

Bake at 375° for 15-20 minutes or until a toothpick inserted 1 in. from the edge comes out clean. Cool for 5 minutes; remove from pans to wire racks to cool completely. Frost and decorate with sprinkles if desired. **Yield:** 3 dozen.

## Banana Cupcakes

*This recipe was given to me by my mother, and I've since handed it down to my daughters. The moist cupcakes are topped with a frosting that comes together in no time. And if you'd like even more banana taste, stir some mashed banana into it.* —Wanda Thole, Leonard, Minnesota

> 1/2 cup shortening
> 1-1/2 cups sugar
> 2 eggs
> 1 teaspoon vanilla extract
> 1 cup mashed ripe bananas (about 2 medium)
> 1/4 cup buttermilk
> 2 cups all-purpose flour
> 1 teaspoon baking powder
> 3/4 teaspoon baking soda
> 1/2 teaspoon salt
> FROSTING:
> 1/2 cup butter *or* margarine, softened
> 2-1/2 cups confectioners' sugar
> 3 to 4 tablespoons milk

In a mixing bowl, cream shortening and sugar. Add the eggs, vanilla, bananas and buttermilk. Combine the flour, baking powder, baking soda and salt; add to banana mixture. Fill 18 paper-lined muffin cups two-thirds full.

Bake at 350° for 15-20 minutes or until a toothpick comes out clean. Remove to wire racks to cool completely. In a small mixing bowl, cream the butter, sugar and enough milk to achieve desired spreading consistency. Frost cupcakes. **Yield:** 1-1/2 dozen.

# Dinner Duets

**Salmon with Chive Mayonnaise**

SPEEDY SUPPERS that feed a crowd can hit the right note for large households, family get-togethers and church potlucks. But for some folks, like Kathy Agnew from Chattanooga, Tennessee, those meals are not always in harmony with their lifestyle.

"I am a single professional," she says. "While I enjoy cooking, many of the recipes make so much that a lot of food ends up going to waste. It would be helpful if some recipes served just enough for one or two people."

For Kathy and folks like her, our Test Kitchen came up with six recipes that serve two people. (These recipes are great for singles...just refrigerate the extras to enjoy a day or two later.)

## Breaded Chicken with Avocado

*(Pictured below)*

**Ready in 30 minutes or less**

*A tasty topping of sour cream, avocado and cheese adds richness to this crunchy coated chicken. To round out the meal, fix steamed broccoli and cubed red potatoes as shown in the photo below. Or prepare frozen stir-fry vegetables and warm up bakery breadsticks.*

    3 tablespoons cornmeal
    1 tablespoon cornstarch
  1/2 teaspoon garlic salt
  1/2 teaspoon ground cumin
    1 egg

**Breaded Chicken with Avocado**

    1 tablespoon water
    2 boneless skinless chicken breast halves
    4 teaspoons vegetable oil
  1/2 cup shredded Monterey Jack cheese
    6 slices ripe avocado
  1/4 cup sour cream
    2 tablespoons sliced green onion

In a large resealable plastic bag, combine the cornmeal, cornstarch, garlic salt and cumin. In a shallow bowl, beat the egg and water. Flatten chicken to 1/4-in. thickness; dip into egg mixture, then place in the bag and shake to coat.

In a large skillet, heat oil. Cook chicken for 4 minutes on each side. Top with cheese and avocado; cover and cook until chicken juices run clear and cheese is melted. Garnish with sour cream and onion. **Yield:** 2 servings.

## Salmon with Chive Mayonnaise

*(Pictured above)*

**Ready in 30 minutes or less**

*It's easy to stir together this thick sauce to dress up broiled salmon steaks. The steaks seem special but are really no fuss to prepare. Serve with crisp deli coleslaw and store-bought lemon cake for dessert...or try a Caesar salad and frozen key lime pie.*

  1/2 cup mayonnaise
    3 tablespoons white wine *or* chicken broth
  1/4 cup minced chives
    1 tablespoon minced fresh thyme
    1 tablespoon snipped fresh dill *or* 1 teaspoon
       dill weed
  1/8 teaspoon pepper
    2 salmon steaks (3/4 inch thick)

In a bowl, combine the first six ingredients; set aside 1/3 cup for serving. Place salmon steaks on a broiler rack. Broil 4 in. from the heat for 9 minutes. Brush with remaining mayonnaise mixture. Turn salmon over; broil 9 minutes longer or until fish flakes easily with a fork. Serve with reserved mayonnaise mixture. **Yield:** 2 servings.

Flank Steak Stir-Fry

# Flank Steak Stir-Fry

*(Pictured at left)*

**Ready in 30 minutes or less**

*Tender strips of flank steak share the stage with julienned carrot and red pepper, fresh mushrooms and broccoli florets in this full-flavored feast for two. For traditional accompaniments to a stir-fry, consider hot tea and fortune cookies. Or serve with fresh cubed fruit and orange sherbet for dessert.*

    2 teaspoons cornstarch
 1/3 cup beef broth
    1 tablespoon soy sauce
 1/8 teaspoon pepper
 1/2 pound beef flank steak, cut into 1/4-inch strips
 3/4 cup fresh *or* frozen broccoli florets
 1/2 cup sliced fresh mushrooms
 1/4 cup julienned sweet red pepper
 1/4 cup julienned carrot
 1/8 teaspoon ground ginger
    1 tablespoon vegetable oil
Hot cooked rice

In a small bowl, combine the cornstarch, broth, soy sauce and pepper until smooth; set aside. In a skillet, stir-fry the beef, broccoli, mushrooms, red pepper, carrot and ginger in oil until meat is no longer pink and vegetables are crisp-tender. Stir broth mixture; add to the skillet. Bring to a boil; cook and stir for 2 minutes or until thickened. Serve over rice. **Yield:** 2 servings.

# Basil Pasta Sauce

*(Pictured below right)*

**Ready in 30 minutes or less**

*Nothing beats the aroma of this speedy simmered pasta sauce...except its wonderful taste. To round out the meal, toss together a green salad and pop some garlic bread in the oven as shown in the photo at right. Or, steam asparagus for a swift side dish and pick up a chocolate cream pie from the supermarket.*

 1/4 cup sliced fresh mushrooms
 1/4 cup sliced green onions
    2 garlic cloves, minced
    1 tablespoon olive *or* vegetable oil
    1 can (14-1/2 ounces) diced tomatoes with garlic, undrained
    2 tablespoons white wine *or* chicken broth
    1 tablespoon minced fresh basil
 1/8 teaspoon salt
 1/4 pound bulk Italian sausage, cooked and drained
    3 tablespoons tomato paste
Hot cooked fettuccine *or* pasta of your choice

In a saucepan, saute the mushrooms, onions and garlic in oil. Add the tomatoes, wine or broth, basil and salt. Bring to a boil; simmer, uncovered, for 5 minutes. Stir in the sausage and tomato paste; heat through. Serve over pasta. **Yield:** 2 servings.

Basil Pasta Sauce

Ham 'n' Swiss Soup

## Turkey Lattice Pie

*(Pictured below right)*

**Ready in 45 minutes or less**

*After tasting this savory sensation, you'll find yourself turning to the recipe time and again. Prepared crescent roll dough makes the lattice crust a snap. Enjoy it with a side dish of cranberry relish and mint brownies for dessert…or whip up an apple Waldorf salad and round out the menu with raspberry sherbet.*

```
      1 cup water
    1/2 cup frozen mixed vegetables
      2 teaspoons chicken bouillon granules
      2 tablespoons plus 1/2 teaspoon cornstarch
      1 cup milk
      1 cup cubed cooked turkey
    1/2 cup shredded cheddar cheese
      2 teaspoons minced fresh parsley
    1/4 teaspoon salt
    1/8 teaspoon pepper
      1 tube (4 ounces) refrigerated crescent rolls
```

In a saucepan, bring the water, vegetables and bouillon to a boil. Reduce heat; simmer, uncovered, for 3-5 minutes or until vegetables are tender. In a small bowl, combine cornstarch and milk until smooth; add to the vegetable mixture. Bring to a boil; cook and stir for 1-2 minutes or until thickened. Add the turkey, cheese, parsley, salt and pepper. Pour into a greased 8-in. square baking dish.

Unroll crescent roll dough; separate into two rectangles. Seal seams and perforations. Place long sides together to form a square; pinch edges together to seal. Cut into eight strips; make a lattice crust over hot turkey mixture. Bake at 375° for 25-30 minutes or until top is golden brown. **Yield: 2 servings.**

## Ham 'n' Swiss Soup

*(Pictured at left)*

**Ready in 30 minutes or less**

*Chock-full of ham and broccoli, this flavorful soup is sure to warm spirits on a cool day. Add buttermilk biscuits and a simple spinach salad topped with bottled Italian dressing. Or, bake up golden corn bread muffins and open a can of fruit cocktail to complete this memorable meal.*

```
4-1/2 teaspoons butter or margarine
4-1/2 teaspoons all-purpose flour
      1 can (14-1/2 ounces) reduced-
        sodium chicken broth
      1 cup chopped broccoli
      2 tablespoons chopped onion
      1 cup cubed fully cooked ham
    1/2 cup whipping cream
    1/8 teaspoon dried thyme
    3/4 cup shredded Swiss cheese
```

In a saucepan, melt butter; whisk in flour until smooth. Gradually add broth. Bring to a boil; cook and stir for 2 minutes or until thickened. Add the broccoli and onion; cook and stir until crisp-tender. Add the ham, cream and thyme; heat through. Stir in the cheese until melted. **Yield: 2 servings.**

Turkey Lattice Pie

# Chapter 20

# ⏱ *Company's Coming!*

YOU DO have time to entertain! An impressive meal can have time-saving elements that make hosting a get-together a snap—and a lot of fun—for the hostess.

Here, fellow busy cooks share an assortment of favorite, fast-to-fix recipes they like to prepare for company.

Our test kitchen combined some of these timely dishes to create six complete menus that will keep your kitchen time to a minimum and will easily impress family and friends.

Plus, you'll see how to add special touches to your table with easy and inexpensive garnishes and table decorations.

**ENTERTAIN WITH EASE.** Apple Kielbasa Coins, Mocha Morning Drink, Fruit with Marshmallow Dip and Florentine Crepe Cups (all recipes on p. 304).

NO TIME for company? Think again! Here we share step-shaving dishes and timely tips that will have you feeling like a guest at your own party. (Turn to page 312 for quick tips on creating the lovely lemon swans that garnish individual plates as well as other helpful hints for dressing up your dinner table.)

## Hot Artichoke Spread

### Ready in 30 minutes or less

*Green chilies add a bit of zip to this rich cracker spread. I serve this appetizer often because it's tasty, quick to make and looks so pretty with the red tomatoes and green onions on top.*
*—Victoria Casey*
*Coeur d'Alene, Idaho*

  1 can (14 ounces) water-packed artichoke
     hearts, drained and chopped
  1 cup mayonnaise*
  1 cup grated Parmesan cheese
  1 can (4 ounces) chopped green chilies,
     drained
  1 garlic clove, minced
  1 cup chopped fresh tomatoes
  3 green onions, thinly sliced
Crackers *or* pita bread

In a bowl, combine the first five ingredients. Spread into a 1-qt. baking dish or 9-in. pie plate. Bake, uncovered, at 350° for 20-25 minutes or until top is lightly browned. Sprinkle with tomatoes and onions. Serve with crackers or pita bread. **Yield:** 4-1/2 cups.

***Editor's Note:** Reduced-fat or fat-free mayonnaise may not be substituted for regular mayonnaise.

## Pineapple-Onion Pork Chops

### Ready in 45 minutes or less

*I prepared these tender pork chops for my teenage grandson's birthday meal. Brown sugar and pineapple juice provide this onion-topped entree with its sweetness.*
*—Marjorie Bruner, Parchment, Michigan*

1/4 cup all-purpose flour
1/2 teaspoon salt
1/4 teaspoon pepper
  6 boneless pork loin chops (3/4 inch thick)
  3 tablespoons butter *or* margarine
1/2 cup water
  1 medium onion, sliced
1-1/2 cups pineapple juice
  2 tablespoons brown sugar
  2 tablespoons honey mustard*

In a large resealable plastic bag, combine the flour, salt and pepper. Add pork chops and shake to coat. In a skillet, brown the chops on both sides in butter. Transfer to a greased 13-in. x 9-in. x 2-in. baking dish. Add water to dish. Place onion over chops. Cover and bake at 350° for 20 minutes.

Meanwhile, in a saucepan, combine the pineapple juice, brown sugar and mustard. Bring to a boil. Reduce heat; simmer, uncovered, for 10 minutes. Pour over pork. Bake, uncovered, for 5-10 minutes or until meat juices run clear. **Yield:** 6 servings.

***Editor's Note:** As a substitute for honey mustard, combine 1 tablespoon Dijon mustard and 1 tablespoon honey.

## Lemon-Butter Red Potatoes

### Ready in 30 minutes or less

*I need just a handful of herbs and spices to season the lemony glaze that coats the red potatoes.*
*—Jane Walker*
*Dewey, Arizona*

 10 medium red potatoes, quartered
1/3 cup butter (no substitutes)
  2 tablespoons olive *or* vegetable oil
1/3 cup lemon juice
  3 tablespoons minced chives
  2 tablespoons minced parsley
  1 tablespoon grated lemon peel
  1 teaspoon salt
1/4 teaspoon pepper
1/4 teaspoon ground nutmeg

Place potatoes in a large saucepan and cover with water. Cover and bring to a boil. Cook for 15-20 minutes or until tender. In a small saucepan, heat butter over medium heat for 2-3 minutes or until lightly browned. Remove from the heat; stir in the remaining ingredients. Drain potatoes; top with lemon butter. **Yield:** 6 servings.

## Mountainous Mandarin Pie

### Plan ahead...needs to chill

*As a chocolate lover, I created this creamy chocolate and orange pie to satisfy my cravings. When I served it to friends, they immediately polished off one piece and asked for seconds.*  *—Shelly Platten, Amherst, Wisconsin*

  1 package (8 ounces) cream cheese, softened
  1 can (14 ounces) sweetened condensed milk
1/2 cup orange juice concentrate
1/2 cup sour cream
  2 drops yellow food coloring, optional
  1 drop red food coloring, optional
  1 carton (8 ounces) frozen whipped topping,
     thawed
  1 chocolate crumb crust (9 inches)
  1 can (15 ounces) mandarin oranges, drained
  1 square (1 ounce) unsweetened chocolate
  1 teaspoon shortening

In a mixing bowl, beat cream cheese until fluffy. Add the milk, orange juice concentrate, sour cream and food coloring if desired; beat until smooth. Fold in the whipped topping. Spoon half into crust. Set eight mandarin orange segments aside. Arrange remaining oranges over filling. Top with remaining filling and reserved oranges.

In a microwave, melt chocolate and shortening. Stir until smooth; cool slightly. Drizzle over pie. Chill for at least 4 hours before slicing. **Yield:** 6-8 servings.

# Easy Dinner Seems Fancy

# Special Meal Welcomes Spring

WELCOME SPRING or celebrate Easter with this easy exquisite meal. (Turn to page 313 for table decorating ideas.)

## Veggie Tortilla Pinwheels

### Plan ahead...needs to chill

*These bite-size snacks are delicious any time of the day.*
—Doris Ann Yoder, Arthur, Illinois

   1 package (8 ounces) cream cheese, softened
   4 teaspoons ranch salad dressing mix
   1 package (2-1/4 ounces) dried beef, chopped
1/2 cup chopped broccoli
1/2 cup chopped cauliflower
1/4 cup chopped green onions
1/4 cup chopped stuffed olives
   5 flour tortillas (8 inches)
Salsa, optional

In a mixing bowl, combine cream cheese and dressing mix. Stir in the beef, broccoli, cauliflower, onions and olives. Spread over tortillas. Roll up tightly; wrap in plastic wrap. Chill for at least 2 hours. Unwrap and cut into 1/2-in. slices. Serve with salsa if desired. **Yield:** about 5 dozen.

## Beef Wellington Bundles

*Guests love this succulent steak topped with pesto and mushrooms.* —Penny Walton, Westerville, Ohio

   5 tablespoons olive *or* vegetable oil, *divided*
1/2 cup *each* tightly packed fresh basil leaves
     and fresh parsley leaves
1/4 cup grated Parmesan cheese
1/8 teaspoon salt
   6 beef tenderloin steaks (6 ounces *each*)
   4 tablespoons butter *or* margarine, *divided*
1/2 pound fresh mushrooms, chopped
   6 sheets refrigerated pie pastry
   1 egg, beaten
   3 tablespoons all-purpose flour
1-1/4 cups beef broth
1/4 cup dry red wine *or* additional beef broth
1/4 cup water
1/2 teaspoon browning sauce, optional

For pesto, combine 3 tablespoons oil, basil, parsley, Parmesan cheese and salt in a food processor. Cover and process until smooth; set aside. In a large skillet, brown steaks in 2 tablespoons butter and remaining oil for 5-6 minutes on each side. Remove and keep warm. In the skillet, saute mushrooms until liquid is absorbed.

Cut each pastry sheet into an 8-in. square (discard scraps). Place a steak on each square. Spread steak with about 1 tablespoon of pesto; top with mushrooms. Bring opposite corners of pastry over steak and pinch seams to seal tightly. Place in a greased 15-in. x 10-in. x 1-in. baking pan. Brush egg over pastry. Bake at 450° for 18-20 minutes or until golden brown. Let stand for 10 minutes before serving.

For gravy, melt remaining butter in the same skillet; stir in flour until smooth. Gradually stir in the remaining ingredients. Bring to a boil; cook and stir for 2 min-

utes or until thickened. Serve with the beef bundles. **Yield:** 6 servings.

## Snow Pea Medley

### Ready in 30 minutes or less

*A hint of soy sauce adds a tasty twist to this side dish.*
—Kathleen Higginbotham, Grass Valley, California

✓ Uses less fat, sugar or salt. Includes Nutritional Analysis and Diabetic Exchanges.

   4 cups fresh snow peas
   1 cup sliced carrots
   1 cup sliced water chestnuts
   2 teaspoons olive *or* canola oil
   2 teaspoons cornstarch
   1 cup chicken broth
   2 teaspoons soy sauce

In a skillet, saute the peas, carrots and water chestnuts in oil. In a bowl, combine the cornstarch, broth and soy sauce until smooth; add to the pea mixture. Bring to a boil; cook and stir for 1-2 minutes or until thickened. **Yield:** 6 servings.

**Nutritional Analysis:** One 1/2-cup serving (prepared with reduced-sodium soy sauce) equals 56 calories, 2 g fat (trace saturated fat), 0 cholesterol, 182 mg sodium, 9 g carbohydrate, 3 g fiber, 2 g protein. **Diabetic Exchanges:** 1 vegetable, 1/2 fat.

## Cappuccino Chocolate Pie

### Plan ahead...needs to chill

*This rich dessert looks impressive but comes together in no time.* —Gail Moineau, Murphy, North Carolina

   1 cup (6 ounces) semisweet chocolate chips
1/3 cup whipping cream
   1 tablespoon light corn syrup
1/2 teaspoon vanilla extract
Dash salt
   1 graham cracker crust (10 inches)
   1 cup chopped pecans
   4 ounces cream cheese, softened
1-1/2 cups milk
   2 tablespoons brewed coffee
   2 packages (3.4 ounces *each*) instant vanilla
     pudding mix
   2 tablespoons instant coffee granules
   1 carton (8 ounces) frozen whipped topping,
     thawed, *divided*
Chocolate leaves (see page 313)

In a saucepan, melt chocolate chips, cream, corn syrup, vanilla and salt over low heat; stir until smooth. Spoon into the crust. Sprinkle with pecans.

In a mixing bowl, beat cream cheese until smooth. Gradually add milk and brewed coffee; mix well. Add pudding mixes and instant coffee; beat until smooth. Fold in 1-1/2 cups whipped topping. Spoon over pecans. Spread remaining whipped topping over filling. Refrigerate for at least 3 hours before serving. Garnish with chocolate leaves. **Yield:** 6-8 servings.

TOYING with the idea of hosting a weekend brunch for Father's Day or Grandpa's birthday? It's child's play when you follow this menu of reader recipes compiled by our Test Kitchen.

The appealing breakfast dishes and bright table trimmings were chosen so that kids can lend a hand. (Turn to page 314 for tips on creating the green onion garnish as well as ways your children can help decorate the table.)

## Florentine Crepe Cups

*(Also pictured on page 298)*

*Easy homemade crepes form the quick crust for these tempting brunch cups. The flavorful filling includes spinach, mushrooms and bacon.*  —Kaye Whiteman
*Charleston, West Virginia*

2/3 cup all-purpose flour
1/2 teaspoon salt
3 eggs
1 cup milk
FILLING:
1-1/2 cups (6 ounces) shredded cheddar cheese
3 tablespoons all-purpose flour
1 package (10 ounces) frozen chopped spinach, thawed and squeezed dry
1 can (4 ounces) mushroom stems and pieces, drained
2/3 cup mayonnaise
3 eggs, lightly beaten
6 bacon strips, cooked and crumbled
1/2 teaspoon salt
Pepper to taste

In a bowl, whisk the flour, salt, eggs and milk until smooth. Heat a lightly greased 8-in. nonstick skillet; add 3 tablespoons of batter. Lift and tilt pan to evenly coat bottom. Cook for 1-2 minutes or until top appears dry. Place in a greased muffin cup. Repeat with the remaining batter.

In a bowl, combine the filling ingredients. Place 1/4 cup in each crepe cup. Bake, uncovered, at 350° for 30 minutes or until eggs are completely set. **Yield:** 6 servings (12 crepe cups).

## Fruit with Marshmallow Dip

*(Also pictured on page 299)*

**Ready in 30 minutes or less**

*Our family loves this recipe. It's truly a time-saver. I can assemble the kabobs and dip in minutes, yet they taste like I fussed all day.*  —Joan Hallford
*North Richland Hills, Texas*

1 can (20 ounces) pineapple chunks
1 jar (7 ounces) marshmallow creme
3 tablespoons mayonnaise
1/4 teaspoon vanilla extract
3 medium firm bananas, cut into 3/4-inch chunks
3 to 4 tablespoons orange juice concentrate
1 to 1-1/4 cups flaked coconut, toasted

1 jar (6 ounces) maraschino cherries, drained
1 cup seedless grapes

Drain pineapple, reserving 4 teaspoons juice (discard remaining juice or save for another use); set pineapple aside. In a bowl, combine marshmallow creme, mayonnaise, vanilla and the reserved pineapple juice until blended.

Roll banana chunks in orange juice concentrate, then in coconut. Thread bananas, pineapple, cherries and grapes on skewers. Serve with dip. **Yield:** 6 servings (about 1 cup dip).

## Apple Kielbasa Coins

*(Also pictured on page 298)*

**Ready in 30 minutes or less**

*Apple juice, jelly and syrup add sweetness to sliced sausage in this stovetop sensation. My grown children look forward to this breakfast dish on special occasions.*
—JoAnn Lee, Kerhonkson, New York

✓ Uses less fat, sugar or salt. Includes Nutritional Analysis and Diabetic Exchanges.

1-1/2 pounds fully cooked kielbasa *or* Polish sausage, cut into 1/4-inch slices
1/4 cup apple juice
1/4 cup apple jelly
2 tablespoons maple syrup

In a large skillet, bring sausage and apple juice to a boil. Cover and cook for 5 minutes. Uncover and cook 5 minutes longer. Drain. Add jelly and syrup; cook and stir until jelly is melted and sausage is coated. **Yield:** 6 servings.

**Nutritional Analysis:** One 4-ounce serving (prepared with smoked turkey sausage) equals 224 calories, 5 g fat (2 g saturated fat), 51 mg cholesterol, 980 mg sodium, 27 g carbohydrate, trace fiber, 14 g protein. **Diabetic Exchanges:** 2 lean meat, 2 fruit.

## Mocha Morning Drink

*(Also pictured on page 299)*

**Ready in 15 minutes or less**

*When I'm sipping this delicious coffee, I almost feel like I've been to my favorite coffeehouse.*  —Jill Rodriguez
*Gonzales, Louisiana*

6 cups hot brewed coffee
3/4 cup half-and-half cream
6 tablespoons chocolate syrup
7 teaspoons sugar
6 cinnamon sticks (3 inches)
Whipped cream in a can, optional

In a saucepan, combine the coffee, cream, chocolate syrup and sugar. Cook and stir over medium heat until sugar is dissolved and mixture is heated through. Ladle into six large mugs. Stir with a cinnamon stick. Garnish with whipped cream if desired. **Yield:** 6 servings.

# Feed Dad Like a King

# Speedy Sensations Make Star-Spangled Supper

SALUTE the red, white and blue and celebrate summer with a mouth-watering menu that's as special as it is speedy.

This colorful meal compiled by our food editors is perfect for a backyard barbecue, Independence Day dinner or picnic on the patio.

Get a jump start on things by marinating the chicken breasts the night before. Then all that's left to do is brown them and pop them in the oven.

Jazzing up bottled salad dressing not only puts a zesty spin on spinach leaves, tomatoes and blue cheese, but it requires less time in the kitchen so there's more time with guests.

And by brewing iced tea earlier in the day, you can beat the clock with a colorful beverage that complements your meal. (See page 315 for tips on creating flavored ice cubes as well as ways to give your table festive flair.)

The finale? You're sure to end the meal with a bang when you serve a luscious layered dessert. The no-bake treat relies on frozen pound cake, canned pie fillings and whipped topping to keep prep work at a minimum.

## Garlic Lime Chicken

### Plan ahead...needs to marinate

*I love cooking with garlic. This golden-brown chicken with its fragrant spices and citrus tang is an excellent way to showcase its popular flavor.* —Dorothy Smith
El Dorado, Arkansas

    1/2 cup lime juice
    1/4 cup cider vinegar
      6 garlic cloves, minced
      2 tablespoons minced fresh oregano
        *or* 2 teaspoons dried oregano
      1 tablespoon dried coriander
      2 teaspoons pepper
      1 teaspoon salt
      1 teaspoon paprika
      8 bone-in chicken breast halves
    1/4 cup vegetable oil

In a large resealable plastic bag, combine the first eight ingredients; add chicken. Seal bag and turn to coat; refrigerate for 8 hours or overnight.

Discard marinade. In a skillet, brown chicken in oil on all sides. Transfer to a greased 15-in. x 10-in. x 1-in. baking pan. Bake, uncovered, at 375° for 30-35 minutes or until the juices run clear. **Yield:** 8 servings.

## Bacon-Tomato Spinach Salad

### Ready in 30 minutes or less

*To dress up this swift spinach salad, I blend bottled Catalina dressing with warm bacon drippings and mustard. It's a tasty addition to summer menus. I'm sure your family will enjoy this salad as much as mine.*
—Wendy Barnwell, Fortuna, California

    1/2 pound sliced bacon, diced
    1/3 cup Catalina salad dressing

    1/2 teaspoon prepared mustard
    1/4 teaspoon salt
    1/8 teaspoon pepper
      8 cups baby spinach *or* torn fresh spinach
      2 medium tomatoes, cut into wedges
    1/2 cup crumbled blue *or* feta cheese

In a large skillet, cook bacon over medium heat until crisp; remove to paper towels. Drain, reserving 2 tablespoons of drippings. Add the salad dressing, mustard, salt and pepper to the drippings; cook and stir over low heat until heated through.

In a large salad bowl, combine the spinach, tomatoes, cheese and bacon. Drizzle with warm dressing; toss gently to coat. **Yield:** 8 servings.

## Raspberry Iced Tea

### Ready in 45 minutes or less

*I treasure this recipe because of the make-ahead convenience it offers. A few common ingredients are all I need to serve this refreshing beverage. My guests enjoy the appealing rosy color and fruity flavor of this tea.*
—Lois McGrady
Hillsville, Virginia

      4 quarts water
    1-1/2 cups sugar
      1 package (12 ounces) frozen unsweetened raspberries
     10 individual tea bags
    1/4 cup lemon juice
    Raspberry ice cubes (see page 315)

In a Dutch oven, bring water to a boil. Remove from the heat; stir in the sugar until dissolved. Add the raspberries, tea bags and lemon juice. Cover and steep for 3 minutes. Strain; discard berries and tea bags. Cool. Serve over ice. **Yield:** 16 servings (4 quarts).

## Red, White 'n' Blue Torte

*Folks practically see fireworks when I serve this patriotic pleaser, which I create using frozen pound cake and pie filling. I assemble the tempting torte early in the day, then store it in the refrigerator until it's time for dessert.* —Margery Bryan
Royal City, Washington

      1 loaf (10-3/4 ounces) frozen pound cake, thawed
    1/2 cup blueberry pie filling
    1/2 cup strawberry *or* raspberry pie filling
    1-3/4 cups whipped topping

Split cake horizontally into three layers. Place bottom layer on a serving platter; spread with blueberry filling. Top with middle cake layer; spread with strawberry filling. Replace top of cake. Frost top and sides with whipped topping. Refrigerate for several hours before slicing. **Yield:** 8 servings.

EVEN an elaborate meal can have time-saving elements that make entertaining easier. Citrus accents this delightful ham dinner that's easy and elegant. It's a superb supper that's sure to satisfy. (Turn to page 316 for a speedy way to core the pears...and for hints to dress up your dinner table.)

## Ham with Citrus Sauce

*If ham is included at our holiday family gatherings, everyone requests that it's served with this tasty orange sauce. It is equally good served hot or cold.*
—*Shelly Eckholm, Wing, North Dakota*

  1 fully cooked boneless ham (3 pounds)
  1 cup sugar
  2 tablespoons plus 1-1/2 teaspoons cornstarch
1/4 teaspoon salt
1-1/4 cups orange juice
1/2 cup water
1/4 cup lemon juice
  1 tablespoon butter *or* margarine
1/2 teaspoon grated orange peel
1/2 teaspoon grated lemon peel

Place ham on a greased rack in a shallow roasting pan. Bake, uncovered, at 325° for 50-60 minutes.

In a saucepan, combine the sugar, cornstarch and salt. Add the orange juice, water, lemon juice and butter. Bring to a boil; cook and stir for 1-2 minutes or until thickened. Add the orange and lemon peel. Brush about 3 tablespoons of sauce over ham. Bake 10-15 minutes longer or until a meat thermometer reads 140° and ham is heated through. Serve remaining sauce with ham. **Yield:** 8-10 servings.

## Cheddar Mashed Potatoes

**Ready in 1 hour or less**

*This new twist on an old favorite is great for company because it makes plenty. The original recipe called for baked potatoes, but boiling them is quicker.*
—*Debra Francis, Nathalie, Virginia*

  8 medium potatoes, peeled and cubed
1/2 cup sour cream
1/3 cup butter *or* margarine, softened
  1 teaspoon salt
1/4 teaspoon pepper
  1 cup (4 ounces) shredded cheddar cheese
  2 bacon strips, cooked and crumbled
  1 teaspoon minced chives, optional

Place potatoes in a saucepan and cover with water; cover and bring to a boil over medium-high heat. Cook for 15-20 minutes or until tender. Drain and mash. Add sour cream, butter, salt and pepper; beat until smooth and fluffy.

Transfer to a greased 2-1/2-qt. baking dish. Sprinkle with cheese, bacon and chives if desired. Bake, uncovered, at 325° for 20 minutes or until heated through and cheese is melted. **Yield:** 8-10 servings.

## Mushroom Green Beans

**Ready in 30 minutes or less**

*I spark the fresh taste of the veggies with lemon juice and Dijon mustard.*          —*Mary Buhl, Duluth, Georgia*

✓ Uses less fat, sugar or salt. Includes Nutritional Analysis and Diabetic Exchanges.

1-1/4 pounds fresh green beans
1/2 pound fresh mushrooms, sliced
  2 tablespoons olive *or* canola oil
  5 teaspoons lemon juice
  2 teaspoons Dijon mustard
1/2 teaspoon salt
1/4 teaspoon pepper

Place beans in a steamer basket. Place in a saucepan over 1 in. of water; bring to a boil. Cover and steam for 7-8 minutes or until crisp-tender. Meanwhile, in a skillet, saute mushrooms in oil for 5-7 minutes or until tender.

Drain beans; add mushrooms. In a small bowl, combine the lemon juice, mustard, salt and pepper. Drizzle over vegetables and toss to coat. **Yield:** 8 servings.
**Nutritional Analysis:** One 3/4-cup serving equals 61 calories, 4 g fat (trace saturated fat), 0 cholesterol, 179 mg sodium, 6 g carbohydrate, 3 g fiber, 2 g protein. **Diabetic Exchanges:** 1 vegetable, 1 fat.

## Orange Poached Pears

**Ready in 1 hour or less**

*Drizzling a chocolate sauce over orange-flavored pears brings a formal dinner to an elegant conclusion.*
—*Jacquie Ogden, Dawson Creek, British Columbia*

  8 whole pears
1/2 cup orange juice
1/3 cup water
1/3 cup packed brown sugar
  2 tablespoons butter (no substitutes)
1/2 teaspoon grated orange peel
CHOCOLATE SAUCE:
  1 package (4 ounces) German sweet chocolate, coarsely chopped
1/4 cup half-and-half cream
  1 tablespoon butter
Orange peel strips, optional

With an apple corer or sharp knife, carefully remove core from bottom of pears to within 1 in. of stem, leaving pears whole with stem (see page 316). Peel the pears.

In a Dutch oven, combine the orange juice, water, brown sugar, butter and orange peel. Bring to a boil; add pears. Reduce heat; cover and simmer for 10-15 minutes or until pears are tender, turning several times. Remove pears and set aside. Simmer cooking juices, uncovered, for 5 minutes or until thickened to a syrup consistency.

For chocolate sauce, in a heavy saucepan over low heat, heat the chocolate, cream and butter until chocolate is melted; stir until smooth. Spoon pear syrup into dessert dishes; place a pear in each dish and drizzle with chocolate sauce. Garnish with orange peel if desired. **Yield:** 8 servings.

# Tangy Citrus Adds To Elegant Dinner

# Fast Festive Fare Suits the Season

WONDERING how to fix a festive feast without spending forever in the kitchen? The swift specialties featured here make entertaining easy, so you have plenty of time to enjoy the season. (Turn to page 317 for a quick way to stuff a pork roast...and tips on dressing up your table.)

## Berry Pretty Pork Roast

*Berries add such wonderful flavor to recipes. This moist roast is perfect for special dinners. Slices are particularly tasty when served with the cooking juices.*
—Paula Marchesi
*Lenhartsville, Pennsylvania*

    1 whole boneless pork loin roast (about 2-1/2 pounds)
1/2 cup chopped dried plums
1/3 cup each fresh *or* frozen blueberries, raspberries and sliced strawberries
    2 garlic cloves, cut into slivers
1/4 cup butter *or* margarine, melted
1/2 teaspoon dried oregano
1/4 teaspoon salt
1/4 teaspoon pepper
1/2 cup red wine *or* chicken broth
    1 tablespoon brown sugar
    1 tablespoon seedless raspberry jam

Cut a horizontal slit through the center of the pork roast to within 1/2 in. of the opposite side; open roast so it lies flat (see page 317). Combine the fruit; place on one side of roast. Fold other side of meat over filling; tie securely with kitchen string. Cut slits in roast; insert garlic slivers. Place in an ungreased shallow baking pan. Drizzle with butter; sprinkle with oregano, salt and pepper.

In a small bowl, combine the wine or broth, brown sugar and jam. Drizzle over roast. Bake, uncovered, at 350° for 75-80 minutes or until a meat thermometer reaches 160°. Let stand for 10 minutes before slicing. **Yield:** 8-10 servings.

## Lemon Almond Asparagus

### Ready in 15 minutes or less

*This is a time-easing way to dress up fresh asparagus. I drizzle butter and lemon juice over the spears before topping them with almonds and lemon peel.* —Linda Barry
*Yakima, Washington*

    2 pounds fresh asparagus, trimmed
1/4 cup butter *or* margarine
    5 teaspoons lemon juice
1/3 cup slivered almonds, toasted
Lemon peel strips, optional

In a large skillet, bring asparagus and 1/2 in. of water to a boil. Reduce heat; cover and simmer for 3-5 minutes or until crisp-tender. Meanwhile, melt butter; stir in lemon juice. Drain asparagus; top with butter mixture, almonds and lemon peel if desired. **Yield:** 8-10 servings.

## Holiday Wild Rice

### Ready in 45 minutes or less

*Wild rice mix gets a boost of seasonal color from red pepper and green onions in this side dish. It's my husband's favorite.* —Diane Dalovisio, Charles, Louisiana

✓ Uses less fat, sugar or salt. Includes Nutritional Analysis and Diabetic Exchanges.

    3 tablespoons chopped onion
    3 tablespoons chopped sweet red pepper
    2 green onions, thinly sliced
    2 to 3 tablespoons olive *or* canola oil
    2 packages (6 ounces *each*) long grain and wild rice mix
2-1/3 cups water
    1 can (14-1/2 ounces) beef broth
Dash cayenne pepper

In a large saucepan, saute the onion, red pepper and green onions in oil until tender. Stir in the rice mixes with contents of seasoning packets, water, broth and cayenne. Bring to a boil. Reduce heat; cover and simmer for 20-25 minutes or until rice is tender and liquid is absorbed. **Yield:** 10 servings.

**Nutritional Analysis:** One 3/4-cup serving (prepared with 2 tablespoons olive oil and reduced-sodium beef broth) equals 148 calories, 3 g fat (1 g saturated fat), 0 cholesterol, 585 mg sodium, 26 g carbohydrate, 1 g fiber, 4 g protein. **Diabetic Exchanges:** 1-1/2 starch, 1/2 fat.

## Cranberry Layer Cake

*Cranberries, walnuts and homemade frosting make this dessert taste so delicious that you'd never guess it starts with a cake mix.* —Sandy Burkett, Galena, Ohio

    1 package (18-1/4 ounces) white cake mix
1-1/3 cups water
1/3 cup vegetable oil
    3 eggs
    1 tablespoon grated orange peel
    1 cup fresh *or* frozen cranberries, thawed and coarsely chopped
    1 cup finely chopped walnuts
CREAM CHEESE FROSTING:
    1 package (8 ounces) cream cheese, softened
1/2 cup butter *or* margarine, softened
    1 teaspoon vanilla extract
1/2 teaspoon grated orange peel
3-1/2 cups confectioners' sugar
1/4 cup finely chopped walnuts

In a large mixing bowl, combine the first five ingredients; mix well. Stir in the cranberries and walnuts. Pour into two greased 9-in. round baking pans. Bake at 350° for 30-35 minutes or until a toothpick inserted near the center comes out clean. Cool for 10 minutes before removing from pans to wire racks to cool completely.

For frosting, in a small mixing bowl, beat cream cheese, butter, vanilla and orange peel until blended. Gradually beat in confectioners' sugar. Spread between layers and over top and sides of cake. Sprinkle with walnuts. **Yield:** 12 servings.

# Table Toppers

ADDING no-fuss finishing touches to your dinner table can make any occasion special. Whether it's a quick-to-fold cracker holder, stenciled place mat or lemon garnish, table toppers like these take mere minutes. Best of all, each idea is easy and inexpensive, too.

## Fold Napkin into Cute Cracker Holder

CAN'T FIND a basket to hold the crackers that accompany an appetizer? You can whip up a decorative holder in no time. It's as simple as folding a square cloth napkin.

1. Place the napkin on a flat surface. Fold one edge over about 3/4 of an inch; repeat fold about five more times. Do the same with the opposite edge until folded edges meet in the center.

2. Tuck one short end about 4 inches underneath the folded napkin. Fold the other end under so the ends meet in the middle.

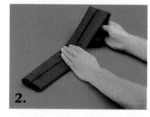

3. Separate the folds to create an opening for the crackers and place them inside.

You can use this in-a-hurry cracker holder to accompany Hot Artichoke Spread (recipe on page 300) or to serve slices of cocktail rye, breadsticks, mini muffins or drop biscuits.

## Stenciled Snowflake Trims Place Mats

IT'S EASY to perk up plain place mats with a wintry design. Simply create snowflake stencils to paint pretty patterns onto fabric place mats.

You'll need some white paper, scissors, a small piece of cellulose sponge, a disposable plate, acrylic fabric paint (available at craft stores) and plain place mats.

To start, cut paper into 4-1/4-inch squares. For each stencil, fold the square into quarters, then fold once more.

Cut out small shapes from both folded edges. Do not cut along the open edge. It will become the outside edge of the stencil and will provide a border to hold onto when you paint.

Pour a small amount of paint onto a plate. Dampen the sponge with water to soften it, then squeeze out any extra moisture.

Dip the damp sponge into the paint, blotting off excess on the plate. Don't use too much or it will seep under the stencil and blur the design.

Now place the snowflake stencil on the corner of the place mat and smooth it flat. Holding it in place, press the paint-dipped sponge over the holes in the stencil to transfer the design.

Gently peel the stencil away. Allow to dry before topping your table with these lovely linens.

## Slice a Lemon into Graceful Garnishes

YOU CAN TURN an ordinary lemon into a group of citrus swans in just a few simple steps.

To begin, cut a lemon into 1/8-inch slices and then cut the slices in half.

1. With kitchen shears, cut a lemon slice between the peel and pulp to within 1/4 inch of opposite end, leaving a small section uncut. Be sure to leave some of the white part of the peel attached to the pulp so it doesn't fall apart.

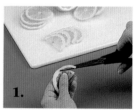

2. Curl the lemon peel strip under and position it against the pulp to form the head of the swan.

Repeat steps with remaining lemon slices.

Use these garnishes to dress up an individual serving of Lemon-Butter Red Potatoes and Pineapple-Onion Pork Chops (recipes on page 300).

## Chocolate Leaves Top a Tasteful Treat

IT ONLY TAKES a few steps to prepare chocolate leaves that are as delicious as they are delicate.

To create the garnishes, wash mint, lemon or rose leaves and set them aside to dry. In a microwave-safe bowl, melt 1/4 cup semisweet chocolate chips and 1 teaspoon shortening; stir until smooth.

1. With a small new paintbrush, apply a thin even coat of melted chocolate to the underside of each leaf. Place leaves chocolate side up on waxed paper and refrigerate for 10 minutes or until set. Brush on a second layer of chocolate and chill until set.

2. Gently peel the green leaves away from the chocolate. Cover and refrigerate the chocolate leaves until ready to use.

When it's time for dessert, arrange the garnishes on slices of Cappuccino Chocolate Pie (recipe on page 303), or use with a favorite sweet-to-eat treat.

## Cute Eggcups Hold Dainty Flowers

LET GUESTS know how special they are by placing individual flower arrangements at their place settings. Eggcups make the perfect holders for small bunches of spring flowers.

To begin, fill an eggcup halfway with water. Then gather small blooms, such as violet buds or forget-me-nots, and delicate greenery. (We used white wax flowers and trailing vines of baby's tears cut from a small potted plant.) (See photo at top.)

Snip the stems of the flowers to an appropriate length to fit in the eggcup and arrange them in a pleasing fashion.

If the flowers won't stay in the cup, gently gather the stems into a bunch and wrap them with a small rubber band. Then place the bunch in the eggcup and adjust the arrangement as necessary.

Or, you may find it easier to bundle the greens together first, then poke the stems of the flowers into the greenery to make an attractive arrangement.

## Tidy Turf Is Ideal Nest for Easter Eggs

ADD A SPLASH of color to your table with an inviting grass centerpiece you can grow from seed.

This little patch of lush lawn looks lovely on its own but is simply irresistible when it acts as a nest for bright Easter eggs. Although it requires a little planning, this spot of turf is easy to cultivate.

About 3 weeks beforehand, gather your supplies. You will need a shallow dish or plastic plant saucer without drainage holes, a small bag of grass seed (we used perennial ryegrass), some potting soil, a plant sprayer and plastic wrap. Most of these items can be found year-round at garden centers.

1. Start by spreading the potting soil evenly in the saucer to cover the bottom. The soil should measure about 1/2 inch deep. Next, cover the soil with a thick layer of grass seed.

2. Water the seeds gently but thoroughly. We used a spray bottle to mist them.

3. Tightly wrap a sheet of clear plastic wrap over the saucer to seal in the moisture. Place the saucer in an area in your home that receives plenty of sunlight.

We found it worked best to leave the saucer untouched for the first 2 days. Then discard the plastic wrap and water again.

Keep the saucer in a sunny spot and mist daily. Be sure the soil stays moist.

The seeds should sprout within a few days. The grass may look patchy at first; be patient—it should fill out nicely.

As the grass grows, you may need to increase the amount of water you use.

The day of your event, trim the grass with scissors for an even look. Place colored hard-cooked eggs in the grass (see photo at top left) and your home-grown centerpiece is ready.

## Centerpiece Spells Out Good Wishes

A SET of children's wooden alphabet blocks is all you need to build this cute centerpiece that greets the guest of honor.

Since you can easily change the greeting to fit the occasion, it's wonderful for Mother's Day or Father's Day, baby showers, graduation celebrations or kids' birthday parties.

Simply stack the blocks to spell out the appropriate message such as "Happy Father's Day", "Welcome Baby", "Congratulations" or "Happy Birthday".

Use the picture side of blocks to act as spaces between the words and to add color (see photo at top).

You'll want to place the centerpiece so it faces the guest of honor. Or use it to decorate a buffet, dessert or gift table.

If you have plenty of blocks, use them to create place markers at each person's place setting. Spell out each guest's name by stacking the blocks vertically (see photo below).

## Give Place Mats a Hand-Painted Look

KIDS will be eager to "lend a hand" setting the table when they get to create these painted paper place mats. They're easy to make ahead of time with the help of an adult.

To start, you'll need 12-inch by 18-inch finger paint paper, washable finger paints, wooden craft sticks to stir the paints and disposable plastic or paper plates to hold the paint.

Since this activity can get messy, you may want to cover your work surface with newspaper first.

1. Spread one color of finger paint in a thin layer on a plate. Press child's palm and fingers into the paint to coat them evenly.

2. Firmly press child's coated hand onto a sheet of finger paint paper, making sure the palm and fingers come in full contact with the paper.

Lift the hand, cover it with more paint if needed, and repeat on another area of the paper.

You may want to make handprints in the same color on all of the place mats you're creating, then allow them to dry a few minutes before continuing.

Wash child's hand and repeat process using a different color of paint.

Feel free to border the place mat with the handprints to create a frame for the dinner plate or overlap them in a random design for a different effect.

Allow the paint to dry completely before placing place mats on the table. Then top each place mat with a plate and silverware (see photo at top).

## Curly Onion Greens Garnish Dishes

IT'S EASY to dress up a serving dish or platter when you slice green onions into quick curly garnishes.

For best results, choose fresh, crisp green onions. The greens should be 5 to 8 inches long, securely joined to the white portion of the onion and free of cracks, bends or bruises.

For each onion garnish, remove all of the outer greens except the center one and one on each side.

Use a paring knife to split the greens lengthwise to within an inch or two of the white portion. Make a V-shaped cut at the top of each of the greens about 1 inch deep.

Now, fringe the greens by making cuts on one side along the length of each green. Start near the white portion and make a 2-inch cut from the center to the outer edge. Repeat cuts, starting each cut where the previous one ended.

When all of the greens are cut, soak onions in cold water until they curl, about 10 minutes.

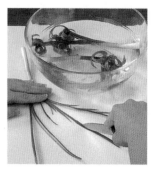

When it's time to serve brunch, arrange a few of these festive garnishes in the serving bowl of Apple Kielbasa Coins (photo and recipe on pages 304-305), or use them to top a savory entree or side dish.

## Neckerchief Napkin Dresses Up Dinner

BRING a touch of cowboy country to your table with this neat napkin fold. It looks like a cross between a ranch hand's neckerchief and a bolo tie, and it's easy to create using the classic cloths and napkin rings with a star design.

**1.** To start, place a new, washed and ironed bandanna flat on your work surface with one corner pointing toward you. Fold that corner about 2 inches toward the center of the bandanna. Starting at that fold, begin rolling the bandanna toward the center.

Continue rolling the bandanna until the entire cloth has been rolled into a long strip.

**2.** Fold the strip in half. Slip the bandanna ends through a napkin ring, sliding the ring halfway up.

Gently tuck under and smooth out any prominent folds. Then place the nifty napkin on a plate to add color to each place setting (see photo below right).

## Candle Centerpiece Is "Berry" Patriotic

FEW THINGS mark special occasions like candlelight. So on nights when the sky is full of fireworks, why not bring a little of that glow to the table, too?

The only materials you need for this pretty project are a heat-proof plate or dish, a pillar candle and an assortment of colorful berries or small fruits.

We selected a star-shaped dish to coordinate with our Independence Day theme, but your dish can be any shape.

Don't be concerned if it has a colorful pattern on it...you won't see it. The berries conveniently hide the holiday design that's on our star plate.

To begin, place the candle in the center of your plate. Then simply arrange the fruit around the base of the candle. We piled raspberries, blueberries and strawberries around a white candle to fit the red, white and blue color scheme of our table (see photo at right).

The amount of berries you'll need will vary with the size of your dish and how full you make your arrangement.

## Fruity Cubes Keep Drinks Frosty

LOOKING for an easy way to keep your cool and add pizzazz to your summer drinks? Why not freeze a few fresh berries inside your ice cubes? Although it takes a little planning, the materials are inexpensive, the process is simple and the results are refreshing!

Begin by deciding which berries best complement your beverage. For example, ice cubes with raspberries are an ideal accompaniment to Raspberry Iced Tea (recipe and photo on pages 306-307).

To make raspberry ice cubes, gently rinse the fresh berries. Then place two or three berries in each section of an ice cube tray. Keep in mind the number of berries you'll need depends on the size of the berries and the number of ice trays you fill. We found that one pint of raspberries is enough for two trays.

Once the berries are placed in the tray, carefully fill each section of the tray with water. Or, to keep your beverages cold without watering them down, fill the tray with the beverage you plan to serve, like we did with Raspberry Iced Tea.

If you do this, you may need to increase your beverage recipe, so you have plenty to serve guests.

Freeze the trays several hours or overnight. When it's time to pour drinks, simply pop the raspberry ice cubes out of the tray and add a few to each glass.

## Savor Fragrance of Citrus Centerpiece

GREET GUESTS with the citrusy scent of freshly zested oranges when this sunny arrangement takes center stage at your dinner party. It's simple to assemble with colorful fruit from the produce section of your grocery store.

We used a kitchen tool called a citrus zester to create simple designs on a few oranges, but you can use this technique to decorate limes and lemons, too.

1. To create a spiral design, start at one end of an orange. Use the zester to create a circular path around the fruit, removing peel until you get to the opposite end of the orange. Feel free to remove the peel in one long strip or in shorter strips if that's easier for you.

For a different design, try removing evenly spaced strips of peel from one end of the orange to the other.

Or try your hand at making other simple but lovely patterns.

But be sure to save the orange peel that you remove. Use it to garnish Orange Poached Pears (photo and recipe on pages 308-309).

Extra peel can also be stored in the refrigerator to use in other recipes or to garnish refreshing summer drinks.

2. Now, arrange the zested oranges and other colorful fruit in a footed bowl. In addition to lemons and limes, we filled out the arrangement with green and red pears to tie in with our homemade place markers and menu.

For a finishing touch, tuck some greenery between the pieces of fruit and around the edge of the bowl (see photo at top) for a festive and fragrant centerpiece.

## Pear Place Marker Is Fast Yet Fancy

FOR formal affairs, place markers not only let guests know where to be seated, they can add an elegant element to most any table setting.

To tie in with the distinctive dinner that includes eye-catching poached pears for dessert (see pages 308-309), we turned fresh pears into place markers.

We chose red pears for extra color, but green ones would also work.

When shopping for pears, look for nicely shaped ones that stand upright. (Otherwise you may need to trim the bottoms of the pears to make them sit flat.)

We used a gold paint pen to write each guest's name on the side of a pear. But you can also use a metallic calligraphy pen or gold leafing pen available at craft or stationery stores.

That's it! Just place each pear on a plate for place markers that add instant elegance (see photo above).

## Cored Pear Ensures Pretty Presentation

SERVING gorgeous Orange Poached Pears (photo on page 309) to cap off dinner is a surefire way to impress your company. But to make this distinguished dessert easy for your guests to eat, the fresh pears should have their cores removed before cooking. This takes just seconds.

To core a fresh pear, insert an apple corer into the bottom of the pear to within 1 inch of its top. Twist the corer to cut around the core, then slowly pull the corer out of the pear to remove the core.

This procedure is very simple, yet it allows the pears to retain their lovely shape.

If you don't have an apple corer, use a sharp knife to carefully cut out the core from the bottom of the pear.

Then continue the recipe as directed on page 308.

## Nifty Napkin Rings Add Fabulous Flair

DRESS UP your table with fast, fun napkin rings that conveniently coordinate with the peppermint stick vase featured on this page.

All you need are red and white 12-inch x 6-millimeter pipe cleaners (chenille stems) available at craft stores or in the craft area of most discount stores.

One red pipe cleaner and one white pipe cleaner will make two napkin rings, so figure the total number of pipe cleaners you'll need. If you're making eight napkin rings, for example, you'll need four red and four white pipe cleaners.

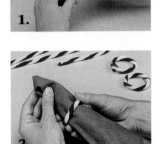

1. To begin, twist one red and one white pipe cleaner together, being certain to evenly space the colors as you twist them. When they're twisted into one piece, use a wire cutters or utility scissors to cut them in half.

2. Shape each half into a circle and twist the ends together to form a ring. Slip a napkin through each ring, reshaping the ring if necessary. Repeat with additional pipe cleaners until you've made a napkin ring for each guest at your table.

## Savory Stuffed Roast Is Sure to Impress

IT TAKES only a few steps to give an eye-appealing look to a special-occasion entree, such as Berry Pretty Pork Roast (see photo and recipe on pages 310-311). Stuffing the roast pays off when it's sliced and served to reveal the colorful filling.

1. On a cutting board, slice the pork loin lengthwise three-quarters of the way through the meat. Open the slices to lie flat and spoon the filling onto one side. Fold the other side of the roast over the filling.

2. Cut several 10-inch pieces of kitchen string and place them beneath the pork loin, spacing them evenly. Tie the ends of each string into a knot and trim away the excess string with a kitchen scissors. When each string has been tied and trimmed, continue with the recipe as directed.

## Candy Sticks Circle Sweet Centerpiece

EVERYONE will be so taken with the colorful holiday vase holding your arrangement of fresh flowers that they won't believe how simple it is to make.

You will need a clean empty aluminum can, individually wrapped peppermint sticks, a rubber band and decorative ribbon.

We used a 28-ounce bean can and 27 peppermint sticks (7-1/4 inches long). The number of candy sticks you'll need will depend on the variety you use and the size of the can. Any can will work as long as it's shorter than the sticks.

We kept the wrappers on the candy to avoid sticky fingers. But we trimmed off the bottoms of the wrappers so the ends of the sticks sit flat on the table.

1. Place the rubber band around the can. Tuck peppermint sticks behind the band, keeping the bottoms of the sticks flush with the bottom of the can. Continue to add them around the can until it is hidden.

If you're having trouble keeping the peppermint sticks in place, use two rubber bands. Place one a few inches from the top of the can and the other a few inches from the bottom. Then tuck the sticks beneath both bands. Remove one rubber band and center the other on the can before continuing to the next step.

2. Hide the rubber band with a ribbon that coordinates with your table decorations. Our red ribbon was 1-1/2 inches wide.

Fill the can with water. (Be sure not to get the peppermint sticks wet or you'll end up with a sticky mess on your table.) To complete the merry centerpiece, just add fresh flowers, like the red and white carnations shown below.

# Chapter 21

# ⏱ *Back to the Basics*

ON WEEKDAYS, many people hardly have an extra moment to sit and relax, much less spend time cooking.

But on those more leisurely weekends, when you do have a few minutes to spare, why not head to the kitchen for a refresher on common cooking techniques or for a chance to tackle a little more challenging recipes?

Whether you need to review the basics for making bread in the bread machine, mixing up an old-fashioned meat loaf and preparing various types of seafood, or you'd like to learn how to pack the perfect picnic, make homemade pizza and bake terrific Christmas cookies, these easy-to-follow recipes and helpful hints will sharpen your culinary skills.

**QUALITY KITCHEN TIME.** Left to right: Sugar Cookies, Jelly Sandwich Cookies, Chocolate Mallow Cookies and Cherry Surprise Cookies (all recipes on p. 331).

# Sensational Seafood

WHETHER you serve spicy shrimp, savory salmon or succulent scallops, you'll find that seafood is a swift way to reel in your family's taste buds.

Saltwater fish and other ocean-fresh items stand on their own as easy entrees and make tasty additions to pasta dishes, casseroles and salads. They are a good source of protein, and many types are naturally low in calories and fat.

Plus, they're a boon to busy families because they cook quickly and can be prepared with many of the same cooking methods that are used for beef, pork and chicken.

If you're in the mood for seafood, you have plenty of choices. There are countless species available today from finned fish to shellfish. We'll talk about selecting and preparing a few of the most common types.

Whether you shop at the grocery store or a fish market, you'll find fresh and frozen fish presented in a variety of ways. You can choose from whole fish to thick steaks to boneless fillets. (See glossary on the opposite page for descriptions of common cuts and their preferred cooking methods.)

No matter the type of fish or cut you prefer, it's important to check the freshness before you buy it. Since its enzymes are accustomed to working in cold water, fish perishes more quickly than meat and poultry.

Fresh fish should have a sea-breeze aroma, not a heavy fishy odor. When buying whole fish, check that it has a rigid body with shiny scales lying close to the skin. Its gills should be moist and bright red. Make sure the eyes are shiny, clear and fill the eye socket.

## Snappy Substitutions

USE THIS CHART when you'd like to make substitutions in seafood recipes. For example, if a recipe calls for flounder, you can easily substitute halibut, sole, turbot or even another mild-flavored fish with similar results.

**Mild-Flavored Fish**
  **Sea Bass:** grouper, sea bass and ocean perch
  **Cod Type:** cod, haddock and pollack
  **Flatfish:** flounder, halibut, sole and turbot
  **Miscellaneous:** orange roughy and red snapper
**Full-Flavored Fish**
  Mackerel, tuna, swordfish, salmon and arctic char
**Shellfish**
  Shrimp, lobster, crab and scallops

Fish fillets and steaks should be moist with no dryness or browning around the edges. The flesh should be firm and spring back when pressed.

Take particular care when storing fresh fish, because the temperature in your refrigerator alone cannot slow down the rate at which it spoils. Place fresh fish in an airtight container and store in the refrigerator for a day or two.

If you put the fish in a resealable plastic bag covered with ice in your refrigerator, you can extend the storage time to about 4 days.

To prevent freezer burn from the ice, keep the fish from making direct contact with it. Don't allow the fish to lie in the water from the melted ice either. Drain and add ice as needed.

Frozen fish, if vacuum-packed or deep-frozen, can offer much the same quality as fresh fish. Choose fish that is free of freezer burn and ice crystals.

Packages should be tightly sealed and labeled with the date of freezing. Check this date to determine if the fish has exceeded its shelf life. Lean mild-flavored fish can be frozen for up to 6 months. Full-flavored fish, which is often more fatty, should be frozen no longer than 3 months.

To thaw, place frozen fish in a bowl of cold water or in the refrigerator. Don't run it under warm water or thaw it at room temperature. Once frozen fish has thawed, it shouldn't be returned to the freezer.

Fish and seafood are great for on-the-go folks because these items cook quickly and often can be interchanged in recipes.

If a recipe calls for a type of fish not available locally, you can often substitute a similar type of fish or shellfish with equally delicious results. (See the Snappy Substitutions chart below left.)

Plus, many cuts of fish are adaptable to a variety of traditional cooking methods, including baking, broiling, grilling, poaching, sauteing and steaming. No matter how you prepare it, be sure not to overcook it. If not checked regularly, fish can be cooked too long and become tough, dry and tasteless.

Fish is properly cooked when it becomes opaque, its juices are milky white and it reaches an internal temperature of 145°.

To check a fillet or steak for doneness, insert a fork at an angle into the fish's thickest portion, gently parting the flesh. The fish is completely cooked if it flakes.

Dressed fish are done when the flesh is easily pulled from the bones.

Like fish, shellfish are available in an assortment of ways. Shrimp comes in a variety of sizes and is offered fresh, frozen or canned, uncooked or cooked, and peeled or in the shell.

When purchasing fresh shrimp, choose those with firm textures and mild aromas. They should be eaten the day you buy them, but can be held for 24 hours if they're refrigerated on ice and covered with moist paper towels to prevent them from drying out.

Nearly all cooking methods are suitable for shrimp. No matter which one you use, keep in mind that shrimp cooks quickly, turning from translucent to pink in mere minutes.

## A Fin-Filled Glossary

THERE'S no need to feel like a fish out of water when it comes to seafood specialties. Keep the following terms in mind when purchasing and preparing fish, and you're sure to whip up dinner swimmingly:

- **Dressed:** A whole fish whose internal organs have been removed. It is best baked.
- **Pan-dressed:** A whole fish whose internal organs, head and tail are removed. It's ideal for grilling, steaming, poaching or pan-frying.
- **Steak:** A thick single-serving cut, usually from a large fish. It is a good candidate for baking, broiling, grilling, poaching, sauteing or steaming.
- **Fillet:** A boneless piece of fish. This versatile cut can be baked, broiled, grilled, pan-fried, poached, sauteed or steamed.
- **Butterflied:** Two fish fillets connected by the uncut belly skin.

Scallops also come in different sizes and are usually sold shucked (without their shells), either fresh or frozen.

Buy fresh scallops that are shiny, white and moist with a sweet smell. Fresh scallops should be kept refrigerated and used within a day or two of purchasing.

Like shrimp, scallops benefit from a short cooking time. Small ones can cook in just 3-4 minutes or until opaque, depending on the cooking method.

Now that you know a little more about seafood, why not try one of the recipes here? We guarantee that your family will fall for them—hook, line and sinker!

## Tangy Shrimp and Scallops

*(Pictured at right)*

**Plan ahead...needs to marinate**

*Shrimp and scallops together make this a special dish for company. I serve these appealing kabobs over pasta with a green salad and garlic bread.*
—Lauren Llewellyn, Raleigh, North Carolina

```
28 large shrimp (about 1-1/2 pounds),
   peeled and deveined
28 sea scallops (about 1/2 pound)
1/2 cup butter or margarine
 7 tablespoons lemon juice
 5 tablespoons Worcestershire sauce
 1 to 2 teaspoons garlic powder
 1 teaspoon paprika
```

Place shrimp and scallops in a large resealable plastic bag. In a microwave-safe bowl, combine the butter, lemon juice, Worcestershire sauce, garlic powder and paprika. Microwave at 50% power for 1-1/2 minutes or until butter is melted. Stir to blend; set aside 1/3 cup for basting. Pour remaining marinade over shrimp and scallops. Seal bag and turn to coat; refrigerate for 1 hour, turning occasionally.

Drain and discard marinade. Alternately thread shrimp and scallops on metal or soaked wooden skewers. Grill, uncovered, over medium-hot heat for 6 minutes, turning once. Brush with reserved marinade. Grill 8-10 minutes longer or until shrimp turn pink and scallops are opaque. **Yield:** 4 servings.

## Herbed Salmon Steaks

*(Pictured below)*

**Ready in 45 minutes or less**

*This is one of my husband's favorites. We prepare these delightful yet simple steaks with salmon that we catch ourselves.*
—Karyn Schlamp
Vanderhoof, British Columbia

```
1/4 cup butter or margarine, melted
2/3 cup crushed saltines (about 20 crackers)
1/4 cup grated Parmesan cheese
1/2 teaspoon salt
1/2 teaspoon dried basil
1/2 teaspoon dried oregano
1/4 teaspoon garlic powder
  4 salmon steaks (6 to 8 ounces each)
```

Place butter in a shallow dish. In another dish, combine the cracker crumbs, Parmesan cheese, salt, basil, oregano and garlic powder. Dip salmon into butter, then coat both sides with crumb mixture. Place in a greased 13-in. x 9-in. x 2-in. baking dish. Bake, uncovered, at 350° for 30-35 minutes or until fish flakes easily with a fork. **Yield:** 4 servings.

Herbed Salmon Steaks
Tangy Shrimp and Scallops

Cranberry Oat Knots
Herbed Bread ◄

# Bread Machines

BY TAKING ADVANTAGE of your bread machine, you can enjoy the old-fashioned goodness of homemade breads and rolls without a lot of work.

Here we explore some bread maker basics. But remember, since machines differ depending on the manufacturer, the instruction manual that came with your machine is your best reference.

First, become familiar with your bread machine by reading your manual and by using the recipes the manufacturer has supplied.

Once you're comfortable using your machine, you're ready to try the terrific recipes here or from other sources.

Before trying any new recipe, check to see the size loaf your bread maker can accommodate. Loaves are usually given in yields of 1 pound (8 slices), 1-1/2 pounds (12 slices) or 2 pounds (16 slices).

These sizes are determined by the amount of flour and other dry ingredients, such as oats and cornmeal, called for in the recipe. A 1-pound loaf typically has 2 cups flour; a 1-1/2-pound loaf has 3 cups flour; and a 2-pound loaf has 4 cups flour.

A bread machine should be able to handle any size loaf up to its largest capacity. It's crucial to stay within the limits of the maximum flour amounts listed in the recipes in your instruction manual.

Use the proper ingredients, measure them accurately and place them in the bread machine pan according to the manufacturer's instructions.

Generally, liquids and fat go in the pan first. Wet ingredients (including water, milk, juice, applesauce, yogurt, sour cream, eggs, etc.) should be at 70° to 80° to properly activate the yeast. Fats (butter, oil, shortening, etc.) should also be at room temperature.

The sweetener (sugar, honey, molasses, etc.) and salt usually are added next. Salt not only flavors the bread but controls the activity of the yeast. It should be put in before the flour to keep it separate from the yeast. Not enough salt (or no salt) can result in a coarse, uneven texture and poor taste.

Flour, dry ingredients and seasonings are commonly added next. Most bread machine recipes call for bread flour rather than all-purpose flour. Bread flour has a higher content of gluten, which is needed to form the structure of the bread.

Bread made with all whole wheat or rye flour will produce a shorter, heavier loaf than one made with bread flour because these flours contain less gluten.

The yeast is usually sprinkled over the flour to keep it separate from wet ingredients and the salt. Our bread machine recipes are tested with traditional active dry yeast.

You can use bread machine yeast—a form of quick-rise yeast—instead, but you'll need to reduce the amount. Use 1/2 teaspoon bread machine yeast per cup of flour when 3/4 teaspoon active dry yeast per cup of flour is called for.

Loaves that don't rise may be due to outdated yeast or yeast coming in contact with the liquids or salt.

Extra items like cereal, nuts, raisins, dried fruit and coconut are often added before the final kneading.

Now it's time to select the correct settings (such as bread type and crust color). Also, some machines have a time-delayed bake feature. This allows ingredients to be added early but the machine to turn on at a later predetermined time. Do not use this feature if your recipe calls for perishable ingredients, such as eggs and dairy products.

Since the bread maker does the mixing and kneading for you, you must learn to judge the bread with your eyes and ears to decide whether a recipe is right for your machine or needs adjusting.

Listen to your machine as it kneads the dough. If it sounds labored, the dough might be too dry. In the first 5 minutes of mixing, look at the dough. It should be forming a smooth satiny ball.

If the dough looks dry or cracked, add 1 tablespoon of water. If the dough is flat and wet looking, add 1 tablespoon of flour. Continue adding 1 tablespoon of water or flour at a time until the dough looks the right consistency.

Once that's achieved, leave your bread maker to handle the rising and baking...and soon you'll be enjoying hot home-baked bread!

**Editor's Note:** All the bread machine recipes in this book have been tested in a Regal brand bread machine and in a Black & Decker or West Bend bread machine.

## Herbed Bread

*(Pictured far left)*

*The original recipe for this bread was printed in the cookbook that came with my bread machine. I liked it so much, I added some seasonings to produce a loaf similar in flavor to a focaccia bread I like.* —Florence Lowe
Zanesville, Ohio

    1-1/2 cups water (70° to 80°)
        1 tablespoon butter *or* margarine, softened
        2 tablespoons dried minced onion
        2 tablespoons mashed potato flakes
    1-1/2 teaspoons sugar
    1-1/2 teaspoons salt
        3/4 teaspoon dried rosemary, crushed
        3/4 teaspoon dried basil
        1/2 teaspoon dried thyme
    3-1/2 cups bread flour
    2-1/4 teaspoons active dry yeast

In bread machine pan, place all ingredients in order suggested by manufacturer. Select basic bread setting. Choose crust color and loaf size if available. Bake according to bread machine directions (check dough after 5 minutes of mixing; add 1 to 2 tablespoons of water or flour if needed). **Yield:** 1 loaf (about 1-1/2 pounds).

## Cranberry Oat Knots

*(Pictured above left)*

*I use the dough setting on my bread machine to help prepare these golden rolls. The orange flavor and dried cranberries give the tender treats a special taste for the holidays or anytime.* —Rosann Knox, Andrew, Iowa

✓ Uses less fat, sugar or salt. Includes Nutritional Analysis and Diabetic Exchanges.

        1 cup plus 2 tablespoons water (70° to 80°)
    1/4 cup warm orange juice (70° to 80°)
        2 tablespoons butter *or* stick margarine, softened
    1/2 teaspoon orange extract
        1 teaspoon salt
    3/4 cup quick-cooking oats
        2 tablespoons brown sugar
        2 teaspoons grated orange peel
        3 cups bread flour
        3 teaspoons active dry yeast
        1 cup dried cranberries
Additional butter *or* margarine, melted

In bread machine pan, place the first 11 ingredients in the order suggested by manufacturer. Select dough setting (check dough after 5 minutes of mixing; add 1 to 2 tablespoons of water or flour if needed). When cycle is completed, turn dough onto a lightly floured surface. Let rest for 15 minutes.

On a lightly floured surface, roll dough into an 18-in. x 10-in. rectangle; cut into eighteen 1-in. strips. Tie each strip into a knot. Place on greased baking sheets. Cover and let rise until doubled, about 1 hour. Bake at 350° for 10-15 minutes or until browned. Brush with melted butter. **Yield:** 1-1/2 dozen.

**Nutritional Analysis:** One roll equals 134 calories, 2 g fat (1 g saturated fat), 3 mg cholesterol, 144 mg sodium, 25 g carbohydrate, 2 g fiber, 4 g protein. **Diabetic Exchanges:** 1 starch, 1/2 fruit, 1/2 fat.

## Coffee Raisin Bread

*(Pictured below)*

*This bread brings back memories of Easter mornings when I was a child and enjoyed toasted hot cross buns.* —Lois Head, Portland, Oregon

    3/4 cup raisins
        1 tablespoon plus 3 cups bread flour, *divided*
        1 cup strong brewed coffee (70° to 80°)
        3 tablespoons vegetable oil
        1 egg, lightly beaten
    1-1/2 teaspoons salt
        3 tablespoons sugar
        1 teaspoon ground cinnamon
    1/4 teaspoon ground allspice
    1/4 teaspoon ground cloves
    2-1/2 teaspoons active dry yeast

Toss raisins with 1 tablespoon flour; set aside. In bread machine pan, place the coffee, oil, egg, salt, sugar, spices, yeast and remaining flour in order suggested by the manufacturer. Select basic bread setting. Choose crust color and loaf size if available. Bake according to bread machine directions (check dough after 5 minutes of mixing; add 1 to 2 tablespoons of water or flour if needed).

Just before the final kneading (your machine may audibly signal this), add the raisins. **Yield:** 1 loaf (about 1-1/2 pounds).

**Editor's Note:** If your bread machine has a time-delay feature, we recommend you do not use it for this recipe.

Coffee Raisin Bread

# Easy Meat Loaf

FEW FOODS stir up childhood memories of cozy nights around the dinner table like mouth-watering meat loaf. After all, this comforting classic has been a suppertime standby for decades.

Meat loaf is possibly one of the easiest, heartiest and most versatile main dishes to prepare.

It comes together in a snap, its ingredients can be adjusted to suit household tastes and it doesn't put a burden on food budgets.

Plus, it can be assembled ahead of time and frozen for later use. Meat loaves can be frozen after baking and reheated on busy nights. Uncooked loaves can also be frozen as long as they're baked within a month.

Making meat loaf is little more than mixing, shaping and baking. Review the basics and you'll soon be making meat loaves just like Mom's.

To start, consider the main ingredients in the recipe you're preparing. Meat loaf recipes most commonly call for ground beef; however, ground sausage, veal, pork, ham and poultry also can be used.

On their own, ground sausage, veal and pork tend to be greasy while ground turkey and chicken can dry out. To help ensure a nicely textured loaf, recipes that require one of these meats usually call for some ground beef as well.

Binding ingredients—the items that hold the meat together and keep it firm but soft—are another component to any meat loaf recipe. Traditional meat loaf uses soft or dry bread crumbs, but many feature oatmeal or other grains, crushed crackers, crisp cereals or cooked rice instead.

Eggs are also added to hold the ingredients together and enrich flavor. A liquid such as milk, tomato or Worcestershire sauce, broth or condensed soup may be included to keep the loaf moist while baking.

Almost any herb or spice can be used to season meat loaf, so feel free to get creative when experimenting with a recipe. Try a little cayenne pepper to spice things up, or add some nutmeg and allspice.

When mixing, it's best to stir together all of the ingredients except the meat. Crumble the meat over the combination of eggs, bindings and seasonings, then use your hands to gently mix them. Be sure not to overwork the mixture, because that can produce a tough meat loaf.

After everything is combined, you can shape the meat loaf in a shallow baking pan. If you're having trouble shaping it, moisten your hands with cold water to prevent the mixture from sticking.

Or you can press the meat mixture into a mold or loaf pan. While molds and loaf pans usually yield juicier results, loaves cooked in baking pans brown on three sides rather than just the top. Also,

fat runs off hand-shaped loaves, since it isn't trapped between the meat mixture and the mold or pan.

Some loaves are baked with a filling such as cheese or rice. In these cases, half of the meat mixture is shaped in a baking pan or pressed into a mold. It is then topped with the filling and the remaining meat and is ready for baking.

When baking a meat loaf, follow the recipe's instructions carefully, being certain not to overcook.

If you're in a hurry, reduce the baking time by shaping the meat mixture into several smaller individual-sized loaves, like the Spicy Meat Loaves recipe at right. If you try this with your favorite recipe, remember to check for doneness early.

To determine if a meat loaf is fully baked, insert an instant-read thermometer in its center. If the thermometer reads 160°, the loaf should be done.

Many meat loaves benefit from the addition of a sauce, typically added toward the end of baking. Simply top with a little ketchup or chili sauce, or combine these ingredients with brown sugar, mustard and seasonings for a more flavorful sauce.

After baking, drain the drippings and let the meat loaf stand for 5 to 10 minutes. Then remove it from the pan and you're ready to tempt the taste buds of family and friends.

## Easy Meat Loaf

*My mother-in-law invented this recipe by mistake, but it was so well received, it became the most popular way for her to make meat loaf.* —Pat Jensen, Oak Harbor, Ohio

> 1 egg, lightly beaten
> 1 can (10-1/2 ounces) condensed French onion soup, undiluted
> 1-1/3 cups crushed butter-flavored crackers (about 33 crackers)

Spicy Meat Loaves
Reuben Meat Loaf

1 pound lean ground beef
1 can (10-3/4 ounces) condensed golden
   mushroom soup, undiluted

In a bowl, combine the egg, onion soup and cracker crumbs. Crumble beef over mixture and mix well. Shape into a loaf. Place in a greased 11-in. x 7-in. x 2-in. baking dish. Bake, uncovered, at 350° for 30 minutes.

Pour mushroom soup over loaf. Bake 1 hour longer or until meat is no longer pink and a meat thermometer reads 160°; drain. Let stand for 10 minutes before slicing. **Yield:** 4 servings.

## Spicy Meat Loaves

*(Pictured below left)*

**Ready in 1 hour or less**

*I put a fun spin on meat loaf with this Southwestern specialty. I top the taco-flavored single-serving loaves with zesty tomato sauce and shredded cheese. —Melanie Ellis Marion, North Carolina*

  2 eggs, lightly beaten
1/2 cup seasoned bread crumbs
  2 tablespoons taco seasoning
  2 tablespoons onion-mushroom soup mix
  1 tablespoon Italian seasoning
  1 tablespoon Worcestershire sauce
1/2 teaspoon pepper
  1 can (15 ounces) Italian tomato sauce, *divided*
  2 pounds lean ground beef
1/2 cup shredded Colby-Monterey Jack cheese

In a large bowl, combine the first seven ingredients. Stir in 3/4 cup tomato sauce. Crumble beef over mixture and mix well. Shape into six loaves. Place in an ungreased 13-in. x 9-in. x 2-in. baking dish. Top each with 1 tablespoon of tomato sauce (save remaining sauce for another use). Sprinkle with cheese.

Bake, uncovered, at 350° for 35-40 minutes or until meat is no longer pink and a meat thermometer reads 160°; drain. Let stand for 5 minutes before serving. **Yield:** 6 servings.

## Reuben Meat Loaf

*(Pictured at left)*

*This loaf is sure to become a favorite with sauerkraut lovers. —Mary Alice Taylor, Downingtown, Pennsylvania*

  1 egg, lightly beaten
  1 medium onion, chopped
1/4 cup sweet pickle relish
  1 tablespoon Worcestershire sauce
  1 cup soft rye bread crumbs
1/2 teaspoon salt
1/4 teaspoon pepper
  2 pounds lean ground beef
1/4 cup Thousand Island salad dressing
  1 can (8 ounces) sauerkraut, rinsed and
     drained
  1 cup (4 ounces) shredded Swiss cheese,
     *divided*

**String Cheese Meat Loaf**

In a large bowl, combine the first seven ingredients. Crumble beef over mixture and mix well. On a piece of heavy-duty aluminum foil, pat meat mixture into a 14-in. x 10-in. rectangle. Spread with salad dressing; top with sauerkraut and 1/2 cup Swiss cheese. Roll up, starting with a long side and peeling foil away while rolling; seal seams and ends.

Place in a greased 15-in. x 10-in. x 1-in. baking pan. Bake, uncovered, at 350° for 50-55 minutes or until meat is no longer pink and a meat thermometer reads 160°; drain. Sprinkle with remaining cheese. Bake 2 minutes longer or until cheese is melted. Let stand 10 minutes before slicing. **Yield:** 8 servings.

## String Cheese Meat Loaf

*(Pictured above)*

*My daughter likes the cheese stuffed into this flavorful meat loaf made with a blend of ground beef and Italian sausage. Served with a salad and sourdough bread, the meal is special enough for company. —Laura Lawrence Salinas, California*

  1 cup meatless spaghetti sauce, *divided*
  1 egg, lightly beaten
  1 cup seasoned bread crumbs
  2 garlic cloves, minced
1-1/2 teaspoons dried rosemary, crushed
  1 pound lean ground beef
  8 ounces bulk Italian sausage
  3 pieces string cheese*

In a bowl, combine 1/2 cup spaghetti sauce, egg, bread crumbs, garlic and rosemary. Crumble meat over mixture and mix well. Press half into a greased 8-in. x 4-in. x 2-in. loaf pan. Place two pieces of cheese, side by side, near one end of loaf. Cut the remaining piece of cheese in half; place side by side on opposite end of loaf. Top with remaining meat mixture; press down firmly to seal.

Bake, uncovered, at 350° for 1-1/4 to 1-1/2 hours or until meat is no longer pink and a meat thermometer reads 160°; drain. Drizzle with the remaining spaghetti sauce; bake 10 minutes longer. Let stand for 10 minutes before slicing. **Yield:** 6 servings.

**\*Editor's Note:** 3 ounces of mozzarella cheese, cut into 4- x 1/2-inch sticks, may be substituted for the string cheese.

**Citrus Cookies**
**Picnic Salad Skewers**
**Turkey Dill Subs**

tablecloth on top. (See box at far right for a complete list of items you may want to consider packing.)

- If you're feeding a lot of people, bring two coolers. Since frequent opening of a cooler allows the cool air to escape, use one for frequently used items such as beverages. Use the second cooler for perishable foods like meats and salads.
- Closely estimate how much food your group will eat to avoid leftovers. Unless they can be kept very cold or very hot, leftovers of perishable items should be thrown away.
- Bring along plastic bags to cart home dirty dishes and silverware, and for garbage in case there are no trash barrels at the picnic site.

Cold sandwiches, chilled salads and icy beverages really hit the spot on warm days. To ensure these items stay cool—and safe to eat—remember these rules:

- Cold foods should be kept at 40° or colder.
- When packing a cooler, it should be about 25% ice and 75% food. Place ice on the bottom and along the sides of the cooler. Then place the heaviest and most perishable foods on top of the ice. Fill in with lighter items.
- Transfer chilled foods directly from the refrigerator to the cooler. Don't use the cooler to chill warm or room temperature items.
- A full cooler will stay colder longer than one that is partially empty, so choose an appropriate sized cooler. If food doesn't completely fill your cooler, add more ice.
- Large pieces of ice melt more slowly than ice cubes. If you plan to be gone awhile, use chunks of ice instead of ice cubes. Simply fill clean empty milk cartons with water and freeze.
- To protect your cooler from the sun's rays, place it in the shade as soon as you arrive at your picnic spot.
- When setting out chilled salads or other cold foods, consider placing the serving containers in a larger pan filled with ice to keep them cold.

# Perfect Picnic

THE LAZY DAYS of summer call for cuisine that's carefree, too. So it's no surprise that picnics are a popular choice when the weather warms.

The mobile meals require little planning and can be as simple or as elegant as you'd like. For outdoor dining in a dash, choose cold deli chicken, crusty bread, fresh fruit and a wedge of cheese.

If you have a few minutes to spare, assemble a lunch of savory turkey subs, chilled salad skewers and sweet home-baked treats (photo above and recipes on opposite page).

Or, if you prefer flame-broiled fare, tote along the items you'll need to fix your favorites on the grill.

Whether your outing is for two or 20, you're sure to have a good time if you keep these picnic pointers in mind:

- Consider packing two containers—a picnic basket for tableware and nonperishable items and a cooler for cold food and beverages.
- To make it easy to get at the items you need when you arrive at your picnic site, pack your basket in reverse order. Place nonperishable food on the bottom, then serving items and tableware, and finally the

While subs and other sandwiches are common alfresco fare, grilled foods are popular, too. If you plan to cook meats such as chicken, steak, hamburgers or hot dogs at your picnic site, heed these helpful hints:

- Wrap raw meat, poultry or fish separately from cooked foods in airtight plastic containers or resealable plastic bags.
- Freeze meats before packing so they remain cold longer. This is especially important if you must travel a long distance to the picnic location or if the foods won't be grilled immediately upon arrival.
- Do not partially cook foods at home to speed up cooking at the picnic site; bacteria grows faster in partially cooked foods.
- Hot foods should be kept at 140° or hotter and should be eaten within 2 hours of being cooked.

Equipped with these tips and a packed picnic basket, you're ready to go. All that's left is choosing a place to spread out your portable feast. Consider the banks of a nearby lake or stream, a local park or a shady spot in your own backyard. Then sit back, relax and enjoy a picture-perfect picnic.

## Turkey Dill Subs

*(Pictured at left)*

**Ready in 30 minutes or less**

*For a change of pace from usual sandwiches, try these dill-seasoned subs. You can use salmon or pickled herring tidbits instead of turkey to make them like a Swedish hero.* —Violet Beard Marshall, Illinois

1/2 cup butter *or* margarine, softened
4 tablespoons snipped fresh dill *or* 4 teaspoons dill weed
8 submarine sandwich buns (about 8 inches *each*), split
Lettuce leaves
12 radishes, thinly sliced
2 cups thinly sliced zucchini *or* cucumber
2 to 3 teaspoons cider vinegar, optional
2 to 3 pounds thinly sliced deli smoked turkey

In a small bowl, combine butter and dill; spread on sub buns. Layer the lettuce, radishes and zucchini on bottom of buns. Sprinkle with vinegar if desired. Top with turkey; replace bun tops. **Yield:** 8 servings.

## Picnic Salad Skewers

*(Pictured at left)*

**Plan ahead...needs to marinate**

*These make-ahead kabobs are a fun way to serve a chilled salad. A homemade vinaigrette complements the tender potatoes, crisp peppers, cherry tomatoes and sliced zucchini.* —Iola Egle, Bella Vista, Arkansas

8 unpeeled small red potatoes
8 fresh pearl onions
1 tablespoon water
1 medium sweet red pepper, cut into 1-inch pieces
1 medium green pepper, cut into 1-inch pieces
16 cherry tomatoes
1 small zucchini, cut into 1/4-inch slices
VINAIGRETTE:
2/3 cup olive *or* vegetable oil
1/3 cup red wine vinegar *or* cider vinegar
2 garlic cloves, minced
1 tablespoon dried oregano
1 teaspoon salt
1/4 teaspoon pepper
4 ounces crumbled feta cheese, optional

Place potatoes in a saucepan and cover with water; bring to a boil. Cook for 15-20 minutes or until tender; drain. Place onions and water in a microwave-safe bowl. Cover and microwave on high for 1-2 minutes or until crisp-tender; drain.

On metal or wooden skewers, alternately thread potatoes, onions, peppers, tomatoes and zucchini. Place in a large shallow plastic container or large resealable plastic bag.

In a bowl, whisk together the oil, vinegar, garlic, oregano, salt and pepper. Pour over vegetable skewers. Marinate for at least 1 hour, turning frequently. Sprinkle with feta cheese if desired. **Yield:** 8 servings.

## Citrus Cookies

*(Pictured at far left)*

**Plan ahead...needs to chill**

*Our Test Kitchen dressed up convenient refrigerated cookie dough to create these sweet summery treats. They taste like the sunny citrus slices they resemble.*

1 tube (18 ounces) refrigerated sugar cookie dough
2 teaspoons grated orange peel
2 teaspoons orange extract
Orange and yellow paste food coloring
2 teaspoons grated lemon peel
2 teaspoons lemon extract
Granulated sugar
1/2 cup vanilla frosting
Orange and yellow colored sugar

Divide cookie dough in half. Place one half in a bowl. Add the orange peel, orange extract and orange food coloring; mix well. Add lemon peel, lemon extract and yellow food coloring to the remaining dough; mix well. Cover and refrigerate for 2 hours or until firm.

Roll the dough into 1-in. balls. Place 2 in. apart on ungreased baking sheets. Coat the bottom of a glass with nonstick cooking spray, then dip in granulated sugar. Flatten the dough balls, redipping glass in sugar as needed. Bake at 375° for 8-10 minutes or until edges are golden brown. Remove to wire racks to cool completely.

Cut a small hole in the corner of a small plastic bag; add frosting. Pipe circle of frosting on cookie tops; dip in colored sugar. Pipe lines of frosting for citrus sections. **Yield:** about 2 dozen.

## Picnic Provisions

PREVENT picnic pitfalls by reviewing this list of items you may want to bring along as you grab your picnic basket and head out the door:

- ❑ tablecloth or blanket
- ❑ plates
- ❑ cups
- ❑ flatware
- ❑ napkins
- ❑ serving utensils
- ❑ salt and pepper
- ❑ condiments
- ❑ paring knife
- ❑ cutting board
- ❑ bottle opener
- ❑ paper towels or moistened hand wipes
- ❑ plastic bags for dirty dishes
- ❑ garbage bags
- ❑ insect repellent
- ❑ sunscreen
- ❑ charcoal and lighter fluid
- ❑ matches

# Popular Pizza

NO MATTER HOW you slice it, serving a streamlined supper the whole gang looks forward to is as easy as pie—pizza pie, that is!

Homemade pizzas can be a snap to prepare. So forget your grocer's frozen food aisle, bypass pizza chains and turn your kitchen into a family-pleasing pizzeria.

One of the keys to a perfect pizza is a good crust. Making pizza dough with traditional yeast can be a lengthy process, but you can move things along with your bread machine. Or try a recipe that relies on quick-rise yeast. It produces tasty results in a fraction of the time traditional yeast dough requires.

If possible, prepare homemade dough ahead of time. It can be kept in the refrigerator for up to 2 days. Punch the dough down after the first hour or so and repeat every 24 hours. To use, punch the dough down again and let it rest for a final rising. When the dough has reached room temperature, roll it out or shape it onto a pizza pan.

You can also store dough in the freezer for up to 4 weeks. After kneading, divide the dough into appropriate portions and place each in a freezer storage bag. When ready to use, thaw the dough to room temperature, punch it down and shape it onto a pizza pan.

For fuss-free crusts, use convenience items like boxed mixes. Follow the directions on the package.

Refrigerated dough is another way to beat the clock. Just follow the directions and you're on your way. Frozen bread dough works great, too. Thaw and knead in a few herbs. Roll the dough to the desired thickness, transfer it to a pan and bake it before adding your toppings.

Prebaked bread shells are another effortless option. They can usually be found in the bread, pasta or pizza ingredient area of most supermarkets.

You don't have to go the homemade route for a sensational pizza sauce. Prepared pizza or pasta sauces work well, and you can easily dress them up with extra herbs and seasonings.

Remember that traditional pizza sauce isn't your only option. Top your crust with creamy Alfredo, tangy barbecue, zippy salsa or flavorful pesto.

Ladle the sauce onto the center of the crust, using the back of the ladle to spread it outward. Keep in mind that too much sauce can make the crust soggy. Complete your pizza with favorite toppings.

Italian sausage, taco meat, barbecued chicken, spicy shrimp or any other meat should be completely cooked before it's sprinkled over the pizza.

Cheese should be one of the last items added so that when it melts, it holds the other toppings to the crust.

Here are a few more ideas to ensure that your pizza-making experience is as promising as possible:

- For crispy from-scratch crusts, experiment with using less yeast than the recipe suggests. For thicker crusts, add more yeast and allow the crust ample time to rise before baking.
- Roll out or thinly press packaged dough onto the pizza pan for crispier crusts. Purchased dough can be rolled thicker for a chewy crust.
- The temperature of the oven is extremely important in pizza baking, so always be sure to preheat the oven to the proper temperature.
- Pizzas often call for baking the crust before the sauce and toppings are added. This helps keep the crust firm.

Once your pizza is in the oven, simply toss together a salad and you're ready to serve a meal with guaranteed appeal.

## Personal Pepperoni Pizza

### (Pictured at left)

#### Plan ahead...uses bread machine

*Let your bread machine do the work mixing the dough for these single-serving sensations.* —Ann Tino
Winside, Nebraska

```
3/4 cup water (70° to 80°)
   2 tablespoons olive or vegetable oil
   1 teaspoon sugar
1/2 teaspoon salt
1/2 teaspoon garlic powder
1/4 cup shredded Parmesan cheese
2-1/2 cups all-purpose flour
2-1/4 teaspoons active dry yeast
   1 can (8 ounces) pizza sauce
   2 cups (8 ounces) shredded pizza cheese blend
  24 slices pepperoni
```

In bread machine pan, place the first eight ingredients in order suggested by manufacturer. Select dough setting (check dough after 5 minutes of mixing; add 1 to 2 tablespoons of water or flour if needed).

Personal Pepperoni Pizza

When cycle is completed, turn dough onto a lightly floured surface. Punch down; cover and let rest for 10 minutes. Divide dough into fourths. Roll each portion into a 7-in. circle. Place on greased baking sheets. Top with pizza sauce, cheese and pepperoni. Bake at 400° for 14-16 minutes or until golden brown. **Yield:** 4 servings.

BLT Pizza
Garlic Chicken Pizza

## BLT Pizza

*(Pictured at right)*

**Ready in 30 minutes or less**

*I use a prebaked crust and fixings from the much-loved BLT sandwich to create this fun variation.*
—Marilyn Ruggles, Lees Summit, Missouri

  1 prebaked Italian bread shell crust (16 ounces)
1/2 cup mayonnaise *or* salad dressing*
  2 teaspoons dried basil
1/2 teaspoon garlic powder
1/8 teaspoon onion powder
 12 bacon strips, cooked and crumbled
3/4 cup shredded cheddar cheese
3/4 cup shredded mozzarella cheese
1-1/2 cups shredded lettuce
  2 medium tomatoes, thinly sliced

Place the crust on an ungreased 12-in. pizza pan. In a bowl, combine the mayonnaise, basil, garlic powder and onion powder; spread over crust. Set aside 1/4 cup bacon. Sprinkle cheeses and remaining bacon over crust. Bake at 425° for 8-12 minutes or until cheese is melted. Top with lettuce, tomatoes and reserved bacon. Cut into wedges. Serve immediately. **Yield:** 4-6 servings.

**\*Editor's Note:** Reduced-fat or fat-free mayonnaise may not be substituted for regular mayonnaise.

## Garlic Chicken Pizza

*(Pictured above right)*

**Ready in 1 hour or less**

*We like this pizza's garlic sauce, crust, chicken and red pepper.* —Sam and Millie Lawrence, Stockton, California

**CRUST:**
  3 to 3-1/2 cups all-purpose flour
  2 tablespoons sugar
  3 teaspoons quick-rise yeast
  1 teaspoon salt
  1 cup buttermilk
1/4 cup olive *or* vegetable oil
  1 tablespoon butter *or* margarine
  1 tablespoon honey
  1 tablespoon cider vinegar
  1 egg yolk
  1 teaspoon vanilla extract
**GARLIC SAUCE/TOPPINGS:**
  6 garlic cloves, minced
  2 tablespoons olive *or* vegetable oil
  1 cup whipping cream
Salt and pepper to taste
  2 cups cubed cooked chicken

  1 cup julienned sweet red pepper
  2 cups (12 ounces) shredded pizza cheese blend

In a large mixing bowl, combine 3 cups flour, sugar, yeast and salt. In a saucepan, heat buttermilk, oil, butter, honey and vinegar to 120°-130°. Add to dry ingredients; beat just until moistened. Add egg yolk and vanilla; beat until smooth. Stir in enough remaining flour to form a soft dough. Cover and let rest for 10 minutes.

Press dough into a greased 15-in. x 10-in. x 1-in. baking pan. Prick with a fork. Bake at 400° for 10-12 minutes or until lightly browned.

Meanwhile, in a saucepan, saute garlic in oil. Add the cream, salt and pepper. Bring to a boil; reduce heat. Simmer, uncovered, until reduced to 2/3 cup, about 10 minutes. Spread over crust. Sprinkle with chicken, red pepper and cheese. Bake 10-15 minutes longer or until the cheese is melted. **Yield:** 8-10 servings.

## Pesto Pizza

**Ready in 45 minutes or less**

*Our Test Kitchen kneaded basil, oregano and Parmesan cheese into packaged bread dough for this crust. Purchased pesto sauce makes this pizza tasty and convenient.*

  1 loaf (1 pound) frozen bread dough, thawed
1/2 cup shredded Parmesan cheese, *divided*
1/2 teaspoon dried basil
1/2 teaspoon dried oregano
1/4 cup prepared pesto sauce
  1 cup sliced fresh mushrooms
  1 cup (4 ounces) shredded mozzarella cheese

Place dough on a lightly floured surface; let rest 10 minutes. Knead in 1/4 cup Parmesan cheese, basil and oregano. Roll into a 12-in. circle; place on greased 12-in. pizza pan. Prick with a fork. Bake at 425° for 10 minutes.

Spread pesto sauce over the crust. Sprinkle with mushrooms, mozzarella cheese and the remaining Parmesan cheese. Bake 8-10 minutes longer or until golden brown. **Yield:** 6-8 servings.

Crumb-Topped Date Bars

cookies right away, then pop the extra dough in the freezer for later. —Gloria McBride, Payson, Utah

2-1/2 cups butter (no substitutes), softened
2 cups sugar
2 eggs
1/4 cup milk
2 teaspoons vanilla extract
8 cups all-purpose flour
4 teaspoons baking powder
1 teaspoon salt

In a large mixing bowl, cream butter and sugar. Add the eggs, milk and vanilla; mix well. Combine the flour, baking powder and salt; gradually add to creamed mixture, beating just until combined. Divide dough into four 2-cup portions. Cover and refrigerate. **Yield:** 8 cups.

# Holiday Baking

WHEN it comes to holiday baking, clever cooks come up with lots of time-saving methods to cut down on the hustle and bustle of the season. While some start their cookie baking early, others turn to tried-and-true recipes that offer plenty of versatility.

For example, Gloria McBride of Payson, Utah relies on one recipe for a basic cookie dough, then transforms it into a variety of sweet treats for ladies luncheons, special occasions and holidays.

"I use this recipe in a deli where I'm the baker and cook," she says. "It's easy to stir up one batch that will make four or five different kinds of cookies. I know everyone loves them, because we always sell out. And no one even suspects that one basic dough makes all the cookies."

For best results with Gloria's recipe and most other cookie recipes, keep these baking tips in mind:

• Use either butter or regular margarine in recipes, not whipped or reduced-fat margarine or spread. These products contain water, which will change the taste and texture of cookies.

• Preheat the oven for 10-15 minutes before baking cookies.

• Place dough on cooled cookie sheets. Using pans that are hot from the oven can cause dough to spread and lose its shape before baking.

• Leave at least 2 inches around the sides of the baking sheet in the oven. If time allows, bake only one sheet of cookies at a time on the middle rack.

With these tips, the following recipes and the helpful pointers for storing your baked goods listed on the opposite page, you're well on your way to stress-free baking this holiday season!

## Basic Cookie Dough

*I turn everyday ingredients into a versatile dough that's the basis for five sensational sweets. You can bake some*

## Crumb-Topped Date Bars

*(Pictured above left)*

*The basic dough doubles as a shortbread-like crust and crumbly topping for these sweet date bars Gloria shares.*

1 package (8 ounces) chopped dates
1/2 cup sugar
1/2 cup water
1 tablespoon lemon juice
2 cups Basic Cookie Dough (recipe above)

In a saucepan, bring dates, sugar, water and lemon juice to a boil. Reduce heat; simmer, uncovered, for 5 minutes, stirring occasionally. Remove from heat; cool.

Press half of the cookie dough into a greased 9-in. square baking pan. Spread with date mixture. Crumble remaining dough over filling. Bake at 375° for 25-30 minutes or until top is golden brown. Cool on a wire rack. Cut into bars. **Yield:** about 2 dozen.

Sugar Cookies
Jelly Sandwich Cookies
Chocolate Mallow Cookies
Cherry Surprise Cookies

## Sugar Cookies

*(Pictured below left and on page 318)*

*Use cookie cutters to cut seasonal shapes from a few cups of Gloria's dough. Prepared frosting and colored sugar make it a snap to decorate these classic Christmas cookies.*

**2 cups Basic Cookie Dough (recipe on opposite page)**
**Colored sugar and frosting of your choice**

On a lightly floured surface, roll out dough to 1/4-in. thickness. Using 2-1/2-in. cookie cutters, cut out desired shapes. Place 2 in. apart on ungreased baking sheets. Leave plain or sprinkle with colored sugar. Bake at 375° for 8-10 minutes or until the edges are golden brown. Remove to wire racks to cool. Frost plain cookies; sprinkle with colored sugar if desired. **Yield:** about 3 dozen.

## Jelly Sandwich Cookies

*(Pictured below left and on page 318)*

*Sandwiching jelly between two layers of the basic dough creates these stained glass-like creations. Your favorite raisin filling is excellent in these cookies, too.*

**2 cups Basic Cookie Dough (recipe on opposite page)**
**Assorted jellies *or* jams**

On a lightly floured surface, roll out dough to 1/8-in. thickness. Cut with a 2-1/2-in. round cookie cutter. Using a 1-1/2-in. cookie cutter of your choice, cut out the center of half of the cookies (discard centers).

Place whole cookies 2 in. apart on greased baking sheets. Spread with 1 teaspoon jelly or jam; top with cutout cookies. Pinch edges with a fork to seal. Bake at 375° for 10-12 minutes or until edges are golden brown. Remove to wire racks to cool. **Yield:** about 2 dozen.

## Chocolate Mallow Cookies

*(Pictured at left and on page 319)*

*Cocoa, marshmallows and ready-made frosting transform the basic dough into these delightful treats. Top each with a pecan half.*

**2 cups Basic Cookie Dough (recipe on opposite page)**
**1/2 cup sugar**
**1/2 cup baking cocoa**
**1 egg**
**1/4 cup milk**
**1/2 cup chopped pecans**
**20 large marshmallows, halved**
**1 can (16 ounces) chocolate frosting**

In a mixing bowl, combine the cookie dough, sugar, cocoa, egg and milk; mix well. Stir in the pecans. Drop by tablespoonfuls 2 in. apart onto ungreased baking sheets. Bake at 375° for 8 minutes. Press a marshmallow half onto the top of each cookie. Bake 2 minutes longer or until marshmallow is puffed. Remove to wire racks to cool.

---

## Keeping Your Goodies Fresh

MANY holiday baked goods, including cookies, can be made ahead of time and stored until you're ready to send them or serve to friends and family. If you start your baking early, keep these tips in mind:

**Short-Term Storage**
- Cool cookies completely before storing.
- Store different kinds of cookies in separate containers.
- Store soft cookies in a container with a tight-fitting lid. To prevent cookies from sticking together, place waxed paper between the layers of cookies. Frosted or filled cookies should be stored in a single layer.
- Keep crisp cookies in a storage container with a loose-fitting lid.
- Some cookies, such as those containing cream cheese or sour cream in the fillings, may need to be refrigerated. Check individual recipes for storage suggestions.

**Fresh from the Freezer**
- For longer storage, place baked goods in heavy-duty foil, freezer bags or plastic containers with tight-fitting lids before freezing.
- Label the container with cookie name and date.
- Cookies can be frozen for up to 3 months. Thaw them in the container at room temperature. If cookies should be crisp when eaten, remove from the container before thawing.

**Mailing Cookies**
- Choose cookies that can withstand the trip. Drop cookies, soft moist cookies and bars travel well.
- Pack cookies snugly in a cardboard box or metal tin. Line the container with plastic wrap, waxed paper or foil to preserve flavors, then use crumpled waxed paper between cookies and layers for cushion.
- Wrap the cookie container in bubble wrap or crumpled newspaper, then place it in a sturdy shipping box that's slightly larger than the container.
- Mark the box "perishable" to encourage careful handling.

Cut a hole in the corner of a pastry or plastic bag; insert a medium star tip. Fill bag with frosting. Pipe a star onto each cookie. **Yield:** 40 cookies.

## Cherry Surprise Cookies

*(Pictured at left and on page 319)*

*Gloria tucks a rich chocolate surprise into each of these cute bites. Candied cherries add a colorful finishing touch.*

**2 cups Basic Cookie Dough (recipe on opposite page)**
**36-40 chocolate stars *or* chocolate kisses**
**36-40 candied cherry halves**

Drop cookie dough by heaping teaspoonfuls 2 in. apart onto greased baking sheets. Top each with a chocolate star and wrap dough around it. Top each with a candied cherry half. Bake at 375° for 10-12 minutes or until bottoms are lightly browned. Remove to wire racks to cool. **Yield:** 36-40 cookies.

# General Recipe Index

*This handy index lists every recipe by food category, major ingredient and/or cooking method, so you can easily locate recipes to suit your needs.*

**APPETIZERS & SNACKS**

**Cold Appetizers**
Ladybug Appetizers, 43
Noisemaker Appetizers, 47
Simple Guacamole, 69
Taco Pinwheels, 105
Veggie Tortilla Pinwheels, 303

**Dips**
Cheesy Chili Dip, 100
Cinnamon 'n' Spice Dip, 70
Creamy Swiss Spinach
    Dip, 281
Fiesta Dip, 277
Fruit with Marshmallow
    Dip, 304
Strawberry Dip, 55
Taco Dip Dragon, 37

**Hot Appetizers**
Christmas Meatballs, 278
Pizza Corn Dog Snacks, 242
Taco Meatballs, 245

**Snacks**
Candy Cane Reindeer, 214
Cereal Clusters, 240
Crazy Corn, 252
Crunchy Peanut Butter
    Drops, 247
Dragon Dippers, 37
Halloween Snack Mix, 214
Nutty Cereal Crunch, 211
Peppermint Pretzel
    Dippers, 61
Spooky Spider Snacks, 251

**Spreads**
Creamy Chicken Spread, 76
Creamy Garlic Ham
    Spread, 277
Hot Artichoke Spread, 300
Pineapple Ham Spread, 59
Reuben Spread, 267
Zippy Sausage Spread, 56

**APPLES**
✓Apple Cranberry Bread, 229
Apple-Glazed Pork Chops, 45
✓Apple Kielbasa Coins, 304
Apple-Nut Coffee Cake, 165
✓Apple Rice Betty, 226
Apple Spice Cupcakes, 45
Apple Spice Snack Cake, 237
Apple Streusel Muffins, 172
✓Apple Tapioca, 221
Apple Walnut Crescents, 129
Caramel Apple Crisp, 278
Chunky Apple Bread, 162
Cinnamon Apple Pizza, 85
Cran-Apple Ham Slice, 281
✓Creamy Waldorf Salad, 73
Fruit Dessert Topping, 257
Fruity Apple Salad, 45
Glazed Apples and Sausage, 139
Granola Apple Crisp, 266
Harvest Apple Cider, 45
Maple Apple Topping, 140
Meaty Apple Skillet, 141
Pork Chops with Apples, 157
Raisin-Nut Baked Apples, 17

**APRICOTS**
Apricot Muffins, 166
Apricot Pecan Sauce, 31

**ASPARAGUS**
Asparagus Omelet, 134
Asparagus Soup, 188
Chicken Asparagus Bake, 80
Feta-Topped Asparagus, 29
Lemon Almond Asparagus, 311
✓Roasted Tarragon
    Asparagus, 24

**AVOCADOS**
Bacon Avocado Quesadillas, 289
Breaded Chicken with
    Avocado, 295
California Avocado Salsa, 288
✓Jalapeno Avocado Salad, 33
Simple Guacamole, 69

**BACON**
Amish Breakfast Casserole, 130
Bacon Avocado Quesadillas, 289
Bacon Cheddar Pinwheels, 169
Bacon Cheddar Quiche, 276
Bacon Cheese Biscuits, 162
Bacon-Feta Stuffed Chicken, 30
Bacon Quiche Tarts, 133
Bacon Swiss Squares, 140
Bacon Tater Bake, 59
Bacon-Tomato Spinach
    Salad, 307
Bacon-Wrapped Corn, 28
Beef Shish Kabobs, 270
BLT Pizza, 329
Breakfast Burritos, 122
Breakfast Pie, 139
Florentine Crepe Cups, 304
Green Beans with Bacon, 27
Pasta Carbonara, 151
Tomato Bacon Pie, 56

**BANANAS**
Banana Bran Muffins, 175
✓Banana Chip Muffins, 163
Banana Cream Brownie
    Dessert, 91
Banana Cream Pie, 279
Banana Cupcakes, 294
Banana Macaroon Trifle, 201
Banana Nut Bread, 59
Banana Split Smoothies, 242
✓Creamy Banana Pie, 229
Frozen Banana Pineapple
    Cups, 141
✓Fruity Gelatin Salad, 59
Orange Banana Tapioca, 81

**BARLEY** *(see Rice & Barley)*

**BARS & BROWNIES**

**Bars**
Almond Bars, 215
Caramel Chip Bars, 91
Caramel Corn Chocolate
    Bars, 211
Caramel Oat Bar Mix, 94

*✓ Recipe includes Nutritional Analysis and Diabetic Exchanges*

Caramel Pecan Bars, 51
Cheerio Treats, 250
Chocolate Oatmeal Bars, 212
Chocolate Peanut Bars, 201
Crispy Kiss Squares, 214
Crumb-Topped Date
    Bars, 330
Fudge-Filled Bars, 213
Lime Cooler Bars, 205
Oatmeal Breakfast Bars, 23
Peanut Cereal Squares, 210
Peanut Mallow Bars, 90
Rhubarb Dream Bars, 202
Sweet Chocolate Bars, 212
  **Brownies**
Brownie Mix, 95
Caramel Brownies, 210
Double Frosted Brownies, 80
Glazed Mint Brownies, 198
Walnut Brownies, 95

## BEANS
**Dried and Canned**
Baked Bean Chili, 106
Bean and Ham Pasta, 152
Beef 'n' Bean Chili, 115
Beef 'n' Bean Enchiladas, 280
Beef 'n' Bean Starter, 114
Beef 'n' Bean Tortellini
    Soup, 114
Cajun Hot Dish, 154
Chili Mac Skillet, 22
✓Colorful Black Bean
    Salad, 191
✓Corny Chili, 258
Curried Bean Salad, 233
Fiesta Dip, 277
Four-Bean Taco Chili, 100
Ground Beef Baked
    Beans, 125
Hearty Burritos, 115
✓Kielbasa Bean Soup, 229
Pork Chops with Baked
    Beans, 106
Red Pepper Chicken, 258
✓Vegetable Bean Soup, 227
White Chili, 266
  **Green and Yellow**
French Bean Salad, 66
Green Beans with a Twist, 50
Green Beans with Bacon, 27
✓Mushroom Green
    Beans, 308

✓Potato Bean Skillet, 228
Seasoned Green Beans, 32
Sweet Sausage 'n' Beans, 265

## BEEF (also see Ground Beef)
**Appetizers and Snacks**
Reuben Spread, 267
Veggie Tortilla Pinwheels, 303
**Main Dishes**
Barbecued Beef Brisket, 261
Beef 'n' Bean Starter, 114
Beef Shish Kabobs, 270
Beef Wellington Bundles, 303
Cranberry Beef Brisket, 111
Flank Steak Stir-Fry, 296
Flavorful Beef in Gravy, 262
✓Flavorful Flank Steak, 272
Grilled Rib Eye Steaks, 106
✓Hearty Fajitas, 151
Marinated Sirloin Steak, 268
✓Microwave Stroganoff, 31
Mushroom Beef Skillet, 111
Mushroom Round Steak, 258
New Year's Surf 'n' Turf, 47
✓Pepper Steak with
    Potatoes, 10
✓Round Steak Roll-Ups, 256
Summer Steak Kabobs, 14
Swiss Steak, 291
**Sandwiches**
Italian Steak Sandwiches, 68
Pepper Steak Salad, 106
Pepper Steak Sandwiches, 192
Steak Tortillas, 107
**Soups, Stews & Chili**
Beef 'n' Bean Chili, 115
Beef 'n' Bean Tortellini
    Soup, 114
French Beef Stew, 266
Tomato and Beef Soup, 111

## BEVERAGES
Banana Split Smoothies, 242
Beetle Juice, 43
Cherry Berry Smoothies, 139
✓Creamy Orange Drink, 133
Frosty Mocha Drink, 140
Harvest Apple Cider, 45
Hot Drink Mix, 97
✓Lemonade Slush, 28
Mocha Morning Drink, 304

✓Pineapple Strawberry
    Punch, 60
Purple Cows, 245
Raspberry Iced Tea, 307
Strawberry Yogurt Shakes, 23
Sunset Cooler, 39

## BISCUITS & SCONES
Bacon Cheese Biscuits, 162
Blueberry Scones, 168
Chive Cheese Biscuits, 169
Cinnamon Fruit Biscuits, 164
Currant Scone Mix, 97
Golden Biscuits, 96
Jam Biscuits, 136
Pepperoni Drop Biscuits, 165
Pineapple Biscuits, 166
Poppy Seed Biscuit Ring, 84
Ranch Eggs 'n' Biscuits, 133

## BLACKBERRIES
✓Blackberry Cake, 224
Chocolate Berry Pound
    Cake, 198

## BLUEBERRIES
Berry Pleasing Muffins, 175
Berry Pretty Pork Roast, 311
Blueberry Cream Muffins, 171
Blueberry Pear Cobbler, 56
Blueberry Scones, 168
Red, White 'n' Blue Torte, 307
Triple Berry Muffins, 173

## BREAD MACHINE RECIPES
Bread Bowls, 180
Carrot Raisin Bread, 176
Coffee Raisin Bread, 323
Cornmeal Molasses Bread, 180
✓Cranberry Oat Knots, 323
Date-Nut Yeast Bread, 179
Family-Favorite Bread, 176
Gingered White Bread, 181
Granola Wheat Bread, 181
Hawaiian Dinner Rolls, 178
Herbed Bread, 323
✓Nutty Wheat Bread, 179
Parmesan Herb Bread, 179
Personal Pepperoni Pizza, 328

*✓ Recipe includes Nutritional Analysis and Diabetic Exchanges*

**BREAD MACHINE RECIPES**
*(continued)*
Pineapple Bread, 176
Pizza Bread, 181
Poppy Seed Lemon Bread, 177
Raisin Bran Bread, 180
Veggie Pull-Apart Bread, 15
White Rice Bread, 179
Wild Rice Bread, 108

**BREADS** *(also see Biscuits &
Scones; Bread Machine Recipes;
Coffee Cakes; Corn Bread &
Cornmeal; Muffins; Rolls; Waffles,
Pancakes & French Toast)*
✓Apple Cranberry Bread, 229
Apple Walnut Crescents, 129
Bacon Cheddar Pinwheels, 169
Banana Nut Bread, 59
Chunky Apple Bread, 162
Coconut Loaf, 164
Garlic-Cheese Flat Bread, 170
✓Granola Peach Bread, 169
Herbed Focaccia, 17
Honey Spice Bread, 167
Monterey Ranch Bread, 51
No-Knead Casserole Bread, 163
Pineapple Date Bread, 170
Quick Baking Mix, 96
Quick Onion Bread, 165
Savory Sausage Bread, 166
Sweet Potato Bread, 170

**BROCCOLI**
Broccoli Corn Casserole, 51
Broccoli Crab Bisque, 287
Broccoli Ham Quiche, 282
✓Broccoli Sausage Simmer, 287
Broccoli Shrimp Alfredo, 155
Cheesy Floret Soup, 191
Chicken Broccoli Shells, 83
Creamy Chicken and
    Broccoli, 158
Open-Faced Sandwich
    Supreme, 76
Ranch Floret Salad, 287
Turkey Broccoli
    Hollandaise, 148

**BUNS** *(see Rolls)*

**BURRITOS, TACOS,
ENCHILADAS, TOSTADAS &
QUESADILLAS**
Bacon Avocado Quesadillas, 289
Baked Chicken Quesadillas, 289
Beef 'n' Bean Enchiladas, 280
Biscuit Tostada, 240
Breakfast Burritos, 122
Cheesy Crab Burritos, 51
Hearty Burritos, 115
Jalapeno Chicken
    Enchiladas, 120
Make-Ahead Burritos, 124
Seasoned Taco Meat, 104
Smoked Salmon
    Quesadillas, 289
Two-Cheese Quesadillas, 72

**CABBAGE & SAUERKRAUT**
Cabbage Sausage Soup, 286
Cabbage Sloppy Joes, 286
Cabbage Wedges with Beef, 286
Pork Chop 'n' Kraut Dinner, 291
Pork Chops and Kraut, 151
Red Cabbage Slaw, 286
Reuben Burgers, 272
Reuben Meat Loaf, 325
Reuben Spread, 267
✓Turkey Cabbage Stew, 16
✓Unstuffed Cabbage, 149

**CAKES & TORTES** *(also see
Cheesecakes; Coffee Cakes;
Cupcakes)*
✓Angel Food Cake Roll, 219
Apple Spice Snack Cake, 237
Basic Cake Mix, 93
✓Blackberry Cake, 224
Breakfast Upside-Down
    Cake, 141
Brownie Snack Cake, 95
Castle Cakes, 37
Caterpillar Cake, 43
✓Cherry Dream Cake, 87
Chocolate Berry Pound
    Cake, 198
Chocolate Cherry Angel Cake, 9
Citrus Sherbet Torte, 205

Countdown Cheesecake, 47
Cranberry Layered Cake, 311
Fudgy Peanut Butter Cake, 265
Gingerbread Cake, 110
Glazed Lemon Cake, 232
Hawaiian Sunset Cake, 88
Heart's Delight Torte, 293
Marble Loaf Cake, 292
Mayonnaise Chocolate Cake, 11
Peach-Glazed Cake, 52
Pecan Chip Tube Cake, 91
Pineapple Pound Cake, 292
Pizza Cake, 244
Pound Cake Ring, 292
Raisin-Nut Chocolate Cake, 205
Red, White 'n' Blue Torte, 307

**CARAMEL**
Caramel Apple Crisp, 278
Caramel Brownies, 210
Caramel Chip Bars, 91
Caramel Corn Chocolate
    Bars, 211
Caramel Oat Bar Mix, 94
Caramel Pecan Bars, 51
Chocolate Caramel
    Cupcakes, 294
Chocolate Caramel Fondue, 66

**CARROTS**
Carrot Pancakes, 134
Carrot Raisin Bread, 176
Cheesy Carrots, 55

**CASSEROLES** *(also see Meat
Pies & Pizzas; Microwave
Recipes; Oven Entrees; Slow
Cooker Recipes)*
**Main Dishes**
    Amish Breakfast
        Casserole, 130
    Baked Spaghetti, 147
    Cheeseburger Biscuit
        Bake, 247
    Cheesy Beef Macaroni, 144
    Chicken Asparagus Bake, 80
    Chicken Veggie Casserole, 237

*✓ Recipe includes Nutritional Analysis and Diabetic Exchanges*

Chili Manicotti, 101
Colorful Pasta with Ham, 146
Comforting Chicken, 147
Fiesta Macaroni, 55
French Toast Bake, 133
Golden Tuna Casserole, 144
Ground Beef Baked
    Beans, 125
Ham and Rice Bake, 56
Hawaiian Ham Bake, 144
Home-Style Mac 'n'
    Cheese, 100
Jalapeno Chicken
    Enchiladas, 120
Onion-Chicken Stuffing
    Bake, 146
Pizza Macaroni Bake, 84
Popular Potluck Casserole, 145
Pork Chop Casserole, 51
Ribs for Kids, 240
✓Sausage Egg Puff, 224
Sausage Hash Brown
    Bake, 129
✓Sausage Spaghetti
    Spirals, 50
✓Sausage with Corn
    Stuffing, 149
Savory Pork Roast, 108
Southwest Sausage Bake, 135
Spaghetti Ham Bake, 116
Swiss Macaroni, 148
Tater Taco Casserole, 81
✓Thanksgiving in a Pan, 87
✓Three-Cheese Pasta
    Shells, 220
Tuna Noodle Cups, 245
Tuna Noodle Supreme, 148
Turkey Broccoli
    Hollandaise, 148
✓Turkey Spinach
    Casserole, 218
✓Unstuffed Cabbage, 149
Side Dishes
Bacon Tater Bake, 59
Broccoli Corn Casserole, 51
Cheddar Mashed
    Potatoes, 308
Cheesy Carrots, 55
Cheesy Vegetable
    Medley, 147
Corn Bread Veggie Bake, 236
Golden Corn Casserole, 85
Mixed Vegetable Bake, 145

CAULIFLOWER
Cauliflower Romaine Salad, 192
Cheesy Floret Soup, 191
Ranch Floret Salad, 287
Tangy Cauliflower Salad, 68


CHEESE
Appetizers and Snacks
    Cheesy Chili Dip, 100
    Creamy Swiss Spinach
        Dip, 281
    Fiesta Dip, 277
    Veggie Tortilla Pinwheels, 303
Breads
    Bacon Cheddar
        Pinwheels, 169
    Bacon Cheese Biscuits, 162
    Cheeseburger Mini
        Muffins, 173
    Chive Cheese Biscuits, 169
    Cranberry Cream Cheese
        Muffins, 172
    Garlic-Cheese Flat Bread, 170
    Monterey Ranch Bread, 51
    Parmesan Herb Bread, 179
    Sausage Swiss Muffins, 174
Desserts
    Countdown Cheesecake, 47
    No-Bake Chocolate
        Cheesecake, 201
    Pineapple Cheesecake, 202
Main Dishes
    Amish Breakfast
        Casserole, 130
    Bacon Cheddar Quiche, 276
    Bacon-Feta Stuffed
        Chicken, 30
    Bacon Swiss Squares, 140
    ✓Blintz Pancakes, 134
    Breakfast Pie, 139
    Cajun Macaroni, 233
    Cheddar Chicken Pie, 145
    Cheesy Beef Macaroni, 144
    Cheesy Crab Burritos, 51
    Cheesy Egg Puffs, 135
    Chicken Pasta Primavera, 150
    Denver Omelet Pie, 136
    Ham 'n' Cheese Egg Loaf, 130
    Hearty Mac 'n' Cheese, 245
    Home-Style Mac 'n'
        Cheese, 100

    Omelet with Cheese
        Sauce, 129
    Pasta Carbonara, 151
    ✓Pepper Jack Meat Loaf, 8
    Pizza Casserole, 262
    Pizza Rigatoni, 259
    Reuben Meat Loaf, 325
    String Cheese Meat Loaf, 325
    Swiss Macaroni, 148
    ✓Three-Cheese Pasta
        Shells, 220
    Two-Cheese Quesadillas, 72
Salads
    Cottage Cheese Veggie
        Salad, 25
    Creamy Pea Salad, 9
Sandwiches
    Beef Stroganoff Melt, 25
    Pizza Grilled Cheese, 250
Sides Dishes
    Blue Cheese Potatoes, 52
    Cheddar Cheese Sauce, 100
    Cheddar Mashed
        Potatoes, 308
    Cheddar Stuffing Puff, 79
    Cheesy Carrots, 55
    Cheesy Vegetable
        Medley, 147
    Feta-Topped Asparagus, 29
    Fiesta Cheese Rice, 275
Soups
    Cheddar Vegetable Soup, 100
    Cheesy Floret Soup, 191
    Cheesy Vegetable Soup, 125
    Ham 'n' Swiss Soup, 297
    Parmesan Corn Chowder, 192


CHEESECAKES
Countdown Cheesecake, 47
No-Bake Chocolate
    Cheesecake, 201
Pineapple Cheesecake, 202


CHERRIES
Cherry Berry Smoothies, 139
✓Cherry Dream Cake, 87
Cherry Mousse, 29
Cherry Surprise Cookies, 331
Chocolate Cherry Angel Cake, 9
Easy Cherry Tarts, 55
Heart's Delight Torte, 293
✓Moist Ham Loaf, 18

✓ *Recipe includes Nutritional Analysis and Diabetic Exchanges*

## CHICKEN

**Appetizer**
Creamy Chicken Spread, 76
**Main Dishes**
Artichoke Chicken, 56
Bacon-Feta Stuffed
Chicken, 30
Baked Chicken
Quesadillas, 289
Breaded Chicken with
Avocado, 295
Cashew Chicken Toss, 281
Cheddar Chicken Pie, 145
Chicken Asparagus Bake, 80
Chicken Broccoli Shells, 83
Chicken Bundles for Two, 268
Chicken in Sour Cream
Sauce, 257
Chicken Pasta Primavera, 150
Chicken Spaghetti Toss, 24
✓Chicken Supreme, 226
Chicken Veggie Casserole, 237
Chicken with Peach
Stuffing, 32
Chicken with Stuffing, 261
✓Chicken with
Vegetables, 263
Chili Sauce Chicken, 270
Comforting Chicken, 147
✓Crab-Stuffed Chicken, 276
Creamy Chicken and
Broccoli, 158
✓Curried Chicken, 221
Fried Chicken Coating, 93
Fried Chicken Nuggets, 55
Fruited Chicken Curry, 159
Garlic Chicken Pizza, 329
Garlic Lime Chicken, 307
✓Hearty Fajitas, 151
Honey Barbecue Chicken, 252
Italian Pineapple Chicken, 29
Jalapeno Chicken
Enchiladas, 120
Make-Ahead Burritos, 124
✓Maple Barbecued
Chicken, 53
✓Mustard Chicken
Breasts, 280
Onion-Chicken Stuffing
Bake, 146
✓Orange Cashew
Chicken, 153
Orange Chicken Supper, 79

✓Pineapple Chicken Lo
Mein, 157
Potato Chicken Packets, 271
Raspberry Chicken, 290
Red Pepper Chicken, 258
✓Rosemary Chicken, 65
✓Sesame Chicken, 12
Smothered Chicken, 73
✓Spicy Lemon Chicken, 264
✓Sunny Chicken and
Rice, 274
Taco Chicken Rolls, 58
✓Taste-of-Summer
Chicken, 273
**Salad**
✓Chicken Salad in Melon
Rings, 188
**Sandwiches**
✓BBQ Chicken
Sandwiches, 235
Butterfly Sandwiches, 43
Chicken Salad Clubs 71
Italian Chicken Pockets, 195
Luau Chicken Sandwiches, 39
**Soups and Chili**
Chicken Wild Rice Soup, 76
Enchilada Chicken Soup, 68
✓Sausage Chicken Soup, 282
Spicy Chicken Tomato
Soup, 262
White Chili, 266
Zippy Chicken Soup, 64


## CHILI

Baked Bean Chili, 106
Beef 'n' Bean Chili, 115
✓Corny Chili, 258
Four-Bean Taco Chili, 100
White Chili, 266


## CHOCOLATE

**Bars and Brownies**
Brownie Mix, 95
Caramel Brownies, 210
Caramel Chip Bars, 91
Caramel Corn Chocolate
Bars, 211
Cheerio Treats, 250
Chocolate Oatmeal Bars, 212
Chocolate Peanut Bars, 201
Crispy Kiss Squares, 214

Double Frosted Brownies, 80
Fudge-Filled Bars, 213
Glazed Mint Brownies, 198
Sweet Chocolate Bars, 212
Walnut Brownies, 95
**Cakes and Cupcakes**
Brownie Snack Cake, 95
Chocolate Berry Pound
Cake, 198
Chocolate Caramel
Cupcakes, 294
Chocolate Cherry Angel
Cake, 9
Flowerpot Cupcakes, 243
Fudgy Peanut Butter
Cake, 265
Heart's Delight Torte, 293
Marble Loaf Cake, 292
Mayonnaise Chocolate
Cake, 11
Potato Chocolate Cake, 105
Raisin-Nut Chocolate
Cake, 205
**Cookies**
Brownie Crinkles, 95
Cherry Surprise Cookies, 331
Chocolate Mallow
Cookies, 331
Mint Sandwich Cookies, 89
No-Bake Chocolate
Cookies, 214
Surefire Sugar Cookies, 215
Toffee Oat Cookies, 213
**Desserts**
Banana Cream Brownie
Dessert, 91
Cappuccino Mousse
Trifle, 206
Chocolate Caramel
Fondue, 66
Chocolate Peanut Sundaes, 24
Cookie Dessert, 250
Fudge Sauce, 95
No-Bake Chocolate
Cheesecake, 201
Orange Poached Pears, 308
Peanut Butter Chocolate
Dessert, 88
Peanut Ice Cream
Squares, 121
Rocky Road Pudding, 22
✓S'more Parfaits, 57
Sweetheart Trifle, 198

*✓ Recipe includes Nutritional Analysis and Diabetic Exchanges*

Toasted Coconut Pudding, 26
Toffee Brownie Trifle, 90
**Muffins**
Banana Bran Muffins, 175
✓Banana Chip Muffins, 163
✓Low-Fat Chocolate
    Muffins, 223
**Pies**
Candy Bar Pie, 252
Cappuccino Chocolate
    Pie, 303
Creamy Peanut Butter
    Pie, 202
Frosty Chocolate Pie, 123
Mountainous Mandarin
    Pie, 300
White Chocolate Pie, 293
**Snacks**
Peppermint Pretzel
    Dippers, 61

**CHOWDER**
Celery Potato Chowder, 105
Haddock Clam Chowder, 103
Salmon Chowder, 72
Slow-Cooked Corn
    Chowder, 262

**CINNAMON**
Cinnamon Pancake Cubes, 240
Cinnamon Syrup, 245

**COCONUT**
Banana Macaroon Trifle, 201
Coconut Angel Squares, 89
Coconut Cream Pie, 25
Coconut Loaf, 164
Coconut Muffins, 166
Coconut Oat Cookies, 85
Coconut Peach Pie, 59
Coconut Pecan Rolls, 162
Hawaiian Dinner Rolls, 178
Toasted Coconut Pudding, 26
Tropical Muffins, 165

**COFFEE CAKES**
Apple-Nut Coffee Cake, 165
Cinnamon Coffee Cake, 96
Coffee Cake Mix, 92

Lemon Coffee Cake, 166
Walnut-Rippled Coffee Cake, 78

**COLESLAW**
✓Brown Rice Slaw, 220
Red Cabbage Slaw, 286

**CONDIMENTS** (also see Salads
& Dressings; Salsas)
Apricot Pecan Sauce, 31
Cajun Seasoning Mix, 92
Cheddar Cheese Sauce, 100
Cinnamon Syrup, 245
Fudge Sauce, 95
Hollandaise Sauce, 278
Maple Apple Topping, 140
Sweet Pineapple Sauce, 64

**COOKIES** (also see Bars &
Brownies)
**Cutout**
For-My-Love Sugar
    Cookies, 293
Sugar Cookies, 331
**Drop**
Brownie Crinkles, 95
Chocolate Mallow
    Cookies, 331
Drop Sugar Cookies, 212
Frosted Orange Cookies, 202
Toffee Oat Cookies, 213
**Shaped**
Buttery Almond Cookies, 52
Citrus Cookies, 327
Coconut Oat Cookies, 85
Cranberry Crispies, 206
No-Bake Chocolate
    Cookies, 214
Orange Crispy Cookies, 211
Peanut Butter Chip
    Cookies, 13
**Specialty**
Checkered Flag Cookies, 41
Cherry Surprise Cookies, 331
Cookie Lei, 39
Jelly Sandwich Cookies, 331
Mint Sandwich Cookies, 89
Peanut Butter Teddies, 253
Pretzel-Topped Sugar
    Cookies, 210
Surefire Sugar Cookies, 215

**CORN**
Bacon-Wrapped Corn, 28
Broccoli Corn Casserole, 51
✓Corn Pasta Salad, 218
✓Corny Chili, 258
Creamy Corn, 52
Golden Corn Casserole, 85
Parmesan Corn Chowder, 192
Shoepeg Corn Salad, 191
Slow-Cooked Corn
    Chowder, 262
✓Smoky Corn Muffins, 82

**CORN BREAD & CORNMEAL**
Corn Bread Veggie Bake, 236
Cornmeal Molasses Bread, 180
Cornmeal Muffins, 93
Country Corn Bread, 96
Green Chili Corn Bread, 22
Raspberry Corn Bread
    Muffins, 173
✓Sausage with Corn
    Stuffing, 149
✓Smoky Corn Muffins, 82

**CRANBERRIES**
✓Apple Cranberry Bread, 229
Berry Pleasing Muffins, 175
Cran-Apple Ham Slice, 281
Cranberry Beef Brisket, 111
Cranberry Cream Cheese
    Muffins, 172
✓Cranberry Cream Delight, 122
Cranberry Crispies, 206
Cranberry Layered Cake, 311
✓Cranberry Oat Knots, 323
✓Creamy Cranberry Gelatin, 86

**CUCUMBERS**
Cucumber Canoes, 249
✓Cucumber Salsa, 288
Cucumber Shell Salad, 54

**CUPCAKES**
Apple Spice Cupcakes, 45
Banana Cupcakes, 294

*✓ Recipe includes Nutritional Analysis and Diabetic Exchanges*

**CUPCAKES** (continued)
Chocolate Caramel
    Cupcakes, 294
Flowerpot Cupcakes, 243
Peanut Butter Cupcakes, 212
Surprise Cupcakes, 294


**DATES** (see Raisins & Dates)


**DESSERTS** (also see specific kinds)
✓Apple Rice Betty, 226
✓Apple Tapioca, 221
Apricot Pecan Sauce, 31
Banana Cream Brownie
    Dessert, 91
Banana Macaroon Trifle, 201
Berries 'n' Cream Dessert, 290
Blueberry Pear Cobbler, 56
Cappuccino Mousse Trifle, 206
Caramel Apple Crisp, 278
Cherry Mousse, 29
Chocolate Caramel Fondue, 66
Cinnamon Apple Pizza, 85
Cinnamon Graham Sundaes, 33
Coconut Angel Squares, 89
Cookie Dessert, 250
✓Cranberry Cream Delight, 122
Creamy Fruit Fluff, 116
Custard Cups, 280
Easy Cherry Tarts, 55
Easy Tiramisu, 19
Frozen Fruit Fluff, 121
Fruity Sherbet, 125
Fudge Sauce, 95
Gingerbread Men, 110
Gingerbread Trifle, 111
Granola Apple Crisp, 266
Gumdrop Fudge, 61
✓Heavenly Strawberry Tarts, 27
Homemade Ladyfingers, 119
Miniature Castle Cakes, 37
Orange Poached Pears, 308
Peanut Butter Chocolate
    Dessert, 88
Pineapple Ice Pops, 249
Raisin-Nut Baked Apples, 17
Raspberry Icebox Dessert, 89
✓S'more Parfaits, 57
✓Spiced Peaches, 219
Strawberry Cheesecake Trifle, 82

Sweetheart Trifle, 198
Toffee Brownie Trifle, 90
Winner's Trophy Dessert, 41
Zucchini Crisp, 206


**DIPS**
Cheesy Chili Dip, 100
✓Cinnamon 'n' Spice Dip, 70
Creamy Swiss Spinach Dip, 281
Fiesta Dip, 277
Fruit with Marshmallow
    Dip, 304
✓Strawberry Dip, 55
Taco Dip Dragon, 37


**DRESSING** (see Stuffing & Dressing)


**EGGS** (also see Quiche)
Amish Breakfast Casserole, 130
Asparagus Omelet, 134
Bacon Cheddar Quiche, 276
Bacon Swiss Squares, 140
Baked Eggs with Basil
    Sauce, 130
✓Blintz Pancakes, 134
Breakfast Burritos, 122
Breakfast Pie, 139
Cheesy Egg Puffs, 135
Creamy Egg Salad, 102
Custard Cups, 280
Denver Omelet Pie, 136
Eggs Bravo, 136
Florentine Crepe Cups, 304
Ham 'n' Cheese Egg Loaf, 130
Ham and Egg Pizza, 23
Ham 'n' Egg Salad Subs, 195
Ham 'n' Egg Sandwich, 135
Hollandaise Sauce, 278
Hot Ham 'n' Egg
    Sandwiches, 184
Layered Veggie Egg Salad, 103
Omelet in a Mug, 274
Omelet with Cheese Sauce, 129
Pasta Crab Egg Salad, 102
Ranch Eggs 'n' Biscuits, 133
✓Sausage Egg Pitas, 219
✓Sausage Egg Puff, 224
Southwest Sausage Bake, 135
Spinach Wild Rice Quiche, 108

**FISH & SEAFOOD**
**Appetizers**
    Noisemaker Appetizers, 47
**Main Dishes**
    Almond Sole Fillets, 67
    Angel Hair Tuna, 153
    Baked Haddock, 103
    Broccoli Shrimp Alfredo, 155
    Cajun Shrimp with
        Potatoes, 277
    Cheesy Crab Burritos, 51
    Crabby Alfredo, 67
    ✓Crab-Stuffed Chicken, 276
    Creamy Shrimp Linguine, 152
    Curried Shrimp, 154
    Fish with Florentine Rice, 86
    Garlic Salmon Linguine, 234
    ✓Glazed Orange Roughy, 218
    Golden Tuna Casserole, 144
    ✓Hearty Fajitas, 151
    Herbed Salmon Steaks, 321
    Mushroom Haddock Loaf, 103
    New Year's Surf 'n' Turf, 47
    ✓Orange Roughy
        Bundles, 271
    Salmon in Lime Sauce, 269
    Salmon with Chive
        Mayonnaise, 295
    ✓Saucy Orange Roughy, 283
    Sausage Shrimp Kabobs, 269
    Shrimp Jambalaya, 157
    ✓Skewered Shrimp, 272
    Smoked Salmon
        Quesadillas, 289
    Tangy Shrimp and
        Scallops, 321
    ✓Tuna Delight, 67
    Tuna Noodle Cups, 245
    Tuna Noodle Supreme, 148
**Salads**
    Pasta Crab Egg Salad, 102
    Warm Shrimp Salad, 70
**Sandwiches**
    Triple-Decker Salmon
        Club, 188
**Soup and Chowder**
    Broccoli Crab Bisque, 287
    Haddock Clam Chowder, 103
    Salmon Chowder, 72


**FRUIT** (also see specific kinds)
Chicken Salad in Melon
    Rings, 188

*✓ Recipe includes Nutritional Analysis and Diabetic Exchanges*

Cinnamon Fruit Biscuits, 164
✓Cream-Topped Grapes, 129
Creamy Fruit Fluff, 116
Frozen Fruit Fluff, 121
✓Fruit Cup with Citrus
    Sauce, 221
Fruit with Marshmallow
    Dip, 304
✓Fruit Yogurt Medley, 66
Fruited Chicken Curry, 159
Fruity Apple Salad, 45
✓Fruity Gelatin Salad, 59
Fruity Pork Chops, 258
Fruity Sherbet, 125
Hawaiian Fruit Salad, 39
Mallow Fruit Salad, 79
Rhubarb Dream Bars, 202
✓Tropical Fruit Salad, 130
Warm Fruit Compote, 136


**GAME**
Cornish Hens with Potatoes, 267


**GARLIC**
Creamy Garlic Ham Spread, 277
Garlic-Cheese Flat Bread, 170
Garlic Chicken Pizza, 329
Garlic Lime Chicken, 307
Garlic Salmon Linguine, 234
Pesto Pizza, 329


**GRILLED & BROILED**
**Appetizers**
    Cheeseburger Mini
        Muffins, 173
**Main Dishes**
    Beef Shish Kabobs, 270
    Chicken Bundles for Two, 268
    Chili Sauce Chicken, 270
    Dilly Pork Chops, 68
    ✓Flavorful Flank Steak, 272
    ✓Glazed Orange Roughy, 218
    Grilled Rib Eye Steaks, 106
    ✓Herbed Pork Medallions, 26
    ✓Maple Barbecued
        Chicken, 53
    Marinated Sirloin Steak, 268
    ✓Orange Roughy
        Bundles, 271
    Pepper-Lime Pork
        Kabobs, 268

Potato Chicken Packets, 271
Salmon in Lime Sauce, 269
Salmon with Chive
    Mayonnaise, 295
Sausage Shrimp Kabobs, 269
✓Sesame Chicken, 12
✓Skewered Shrimp, 272
Summer Steak Kabobs, 14
✓Tacos on a Stick, 271
Tangy Ham Steak, 273
Tangy Shrimp and
    Scallops, 321
✓Taste-of-Summer
    Chicken, 273
Zippy Pork Chops, 269
**Sandwiches**
    Beef 'n' Pork Burgers, 28
    Ham 'n' Egg Salad Subs, 195
    Luau Chicken Sandwiches, 39
    Reuben Burgers, 272
**Side Dishes**
    Grilled Peppers and
        Zucchini, 273
    Special Grilled Veggies, 270


**GROUND BEEF**
**Appetizers and Snacks**
    Cheesy Chili Dip, 100
    Christmas Meatballs, 278
    Taco Meatballs, 245
    Taco Pinwheels, 105
**Main Dishes**
    Baked Spaghetti, 147
    Basic Beef Starter, 118
    Beef 'n' Bean Enchiladas, 280
    Beef-Stuffed Peppers, 118
    Biscuit Tostadas, 240
    Cabbage Wedges with
        Beef, 286
    Cajun Macaroni, 233
    Cheeseburger Biscuit
        Bake, 247
    Cheesy Beef Macaroni, 144
    Chili Mac Skillet, 22
    Chili Manicotti, 101
    Easy Meat Loaf, 324
    Fiesta Macaroni, 55
    Ground Beef 'n' Rice Pie, 146
    Ground Beef Baked
        Beans, 125
    Ground Beef Shepherd's
        Pie, 149

✓Hamburger Skillet
    Supper, 52
Hearty Burritos, 115
Hearty Mac 'n' Cheese, 245
✓Microwave Mexican
    Manicotti, 275
Mini Meat Loaves, 116
Mushroom Beef Patties, 234
No-Noodle Lasagna, 247
Party-Pleasing Beef Dish, 261
Pizza Casserole, 262
Pizza Macaroni Bake, 84
Pizza Meat Loaf Cups, 125
Popular Potluck Casserole, 145
Quick 'n' Easy Lasagna, 61
Reuben Meat Loaf, 325
Santa Fe Supper, 158
Seasoned Taco Meat, 104
✓Skillet Olé, 225
Sloppy Joe Wagon
    Wheels, 249
✓Southwestern Spaghetti, 154
Speedy Beef Hash, 77
Spicy Meat Loaves, 325
Start-Ahead Stroganoff, 119
String Cheese Meat Loaf, 325
Taco Pizza Squares, 105
Taco Skillet, 156
✓Tacos on a Stick, 271
Tater Taco Casserole, 81
✓Unstuffed Cabbage, 149
**Sandwiches**
    Beef 'n' Pork Burgers, 28
    Beef Stroganoff Melt, 25
    Cabbage Sloppy Joes, 286
    Oven-Baked Burgers, 54
    Stroganoff in a Bun, 237
**Soups, Stews and Chili**
    Beef Barley Soup, 116
    ✓Beefy Tomato Pasta
        Soup, 187
    Chili Macaroni Soup, 82
    ✓Corny Chili, 258
    Four-Bean Taco Chili, 100
    ✓Ground Beef Stew, 257
    Hamburger Soup, 236
    Taco Soup, 33


**HAM**
**Appetizers and Snacks**
    Creamy Garlic Ham
        Spread, 277

*✓ Recipe includes Nutritional Analysis and Diabetic Exchanges*

## HAM

**Appetizers and Snacks** (continued)
Pineapple Ham Spread, 59
**Main Dishes**
Bean and Ham Pasta, 152
Broccoli Ham Quiche, 282
Colorful Pasta with Ham, 146
Cran-Apple Ham Slice, 281
Denver Omelet Pie, 136
Eggs Bravo, 136
Ham 'n' Cheese Egg Loaf, 130
Ham and Egg Pizza, 23
Ham and Rice Bake, 56
✓Ham Tetrazzini, 228
Ham with Citrus Sauce, 308
Hawaiian Ham Bake, 144
Hurry-Up Ham
Carbonara, 232
Moist Ham Loaf, 18
Omelet in a Mug, 274
One-Pot Ham Dinner, 153
Potato Ham Skillet, 70
Spaghetti Ham Bake, 116
Tangy Ham Steak, 273
Tortellini Alfredo, 78
Veggies and Ham, 150
**Salads**
✓Catalina Rice Salad, 188
Ham 'n' Egg Salad Subs, 195
**Sandwiches**
Baked Ham Sandwiches, 119
✓Creamy Ham Turnovers, 222
Ham 'n' Egg Sandwich, 135
Hot Ham 'n' Egg
Sandwiches, 184
Hot Ham and Pineapple
Sub, 187
Italian Subs, 184
Open-Faced Sandwich
Supreme, 76
Spiral Stromboli, 191
**Soup & Chowder**
Ham 'n' Swiss Soup, 297
Slow-Cooked Corn
Chowder, 262

## HOT DOGS
Bandito Chili Dogs, 259
Hot Dog Race Cars, 41
Hot Dog Soup, 247
Pizza Corn Dog Snacks, 242
Ribs for Kids, 240

## ICE CREAM
Chocolate Peanut Sundaes, 24
Cinnamon Graham Sundaes, 33
Citrus Sherbet Torte, 205
Peanut Ice Cream Squares, 121
Pineapple Ice Cream, 119
Purple Cows, 245

## LEMON & LIME
Citrus Cookies, 327
Citrus Sherbet Torte, 205
Garlic Lime Chicken, 307
Glazed Lemon Cake, 232
Ham with Citrus Sauce, 308
Lemon Almond Asparagus, 311
Lemon-Butter Red
Potatoes, 300
Lemon Coffee Cake, 166
Lemon Pork Chops, 261
✓Lemonade Slush, 28
Lime Cooler Bars, 205
Lime-Thyme Potato
Wedges, 235
Pepper-Lime Pork Kabobs, 268
Pineapple Lime Molds, 83
Poppy Seed Lemon Bread, 177
Poppy Seed Lemonade
Muffins, 168
Salmon in Lime Sauce, 269
✓Spicy Lemon Chicken, 264

## MARSHMALLOWS
Caramel Corn Chocolate
Bars, 211
Cereal Clusters, 240
Cheerio Treats, 250
Chocolate Mallow Cookies, 331
Fruit with Marshmallow
Dip, 304
Peanut Mallow Bars, 90

## MEAT LOAVES & MEATBALLS
Christmas Meatballs, 278
Dressed-Up Meatballs, 283
Easy Meat Loaf, 324
Mini Meat Loaves, 116
Mushroom Haddock Loaf, 103
Pizza Meat Loaf Cups, 125
Pork-Potato Meatballs, 232
Reuben Meat Loaf, 325
Spicy Meat Loaves, 325
String Cheese Meat Loaf, 325
✓Turkey Loaf, 226

## MEAT PIES & PIZZAS
BLT Pizza, 329
Breakfast Pie, 139
Cheddar Chicken Pie, 145
Denver Omelet Pie, 136
Garlic Chicken Pizza, 329
Ground Beef 'n' Rice Pie, 146
Ground Beef Shepherd's
Pie, 149
Ham and Egg Pizza, 23
Mini Sausage Pizzas, 121
Personal Pepperoni Pizza, 328
Pesto Pizza, 329
Taco Pizza Squares, 105
Tomato Bacon Pie, 56
Turkey Lattice Pie, 297

## MICROWAVE RECIPES
**Appetizers and Snacks**
Christmas Meatballs, 278
Creamy Garlic Ham
Spread, 277
Creamy Swiss Spinach
Dip, 281
Fiesta Dip, 277
**Desserts**
Banana Cream Pie, 279
Caramel Apple Crisp, 278
Chocolate Berry Pound
Cake, 198
Crispy Kiss Squares, 214
Custard Cups, 280
No-Bake Chocolate
Cookies, 214
**Main Dishes**
Almond Sole Fillets, 67
Bacon Cheddar Quiche, 276
Beef 'n' Bean Enchiladas, 280
Broccoli Ham Quiche, 282
Cajun Shrimp with
Potatoes, 277
✓Crab-Stuffed Chicken, 276
Cran-Apple Ham Slice, 281
Dressed-Up Meatballs, 283
Garden Squash Ravioli, 65
✓Microwave Mexican
Manicotti, 275
✓Microwave Stroganoff, 31

*✓ Recipe includes Nutritional Analysis and Diabetic Exchanges*

✓Mustard Chicken
    Breasts, 280
Omelet in a Mug, 274
✓Saucy Orange Roughy, 283
✓Sunny Chicken and
    Rice, 274
Turkey Rice Casserole, 282
**Salad and Soup**
    Cashew Chicken Toss, 281
    ✓Sausage Chicken Soup, 282
**Sauce**
    Hollandaise Sauce, 278
**Side Dishes**
    Dilly Mushrooms, 275
    Fiesta Cheese Rice, 275
    Herbed Veggie Platter, 279
    Microwave Scalloped
        Potatoes, 274
    Twice-Baked Ranch
        Potatoes, 121

**MUFFINS**
Apple Streusel Muffins, 172
Apricot Muffins, 166
Banana Bran Muffins, 175
✓Banana Chip Muffins, 163
Berry Pleasing Muffins, 175
Blueberry Cream Muffins, 171
Brown Sugar Muffins, 162
Butterscotch Muffins, 77
Cheeseburger Mini Muffins, 173
Coconut Muffins, 166
Coffee Cake Muffins, 174
Cornmeal Muffins, 93
Cranberry Cream Cheese
    Muffins, 172
Herb Muffin Mix, 94
Honey Oat Muffins, 169
Jumbo Onion Cheese
    Muffins, 172
✓Low-Fat Chocolate
    Muffins, 223
Peanut Butter 'n' Jelly Mini
    Muffins, 174
Pecan Pear Muffins, 174
Poppy Seed Lemonade
    Muffins, 168
Raspberry Corn Bread
    Muffins, 173
Sausage Swiss Muffins, 174
✓Smoky Corn Muffins, 82
Triple Berry Muffins, 173

Tropical Muffins, 165
Turkey Dinner Muffins, 170

**MUSHROOMS**
Dilly Mushrooms, 275
Mushroom Beef Patties, 234
Mushroom Beef Skillet, 111
✓Mushroom Green Beans, 308
Mushroom Haddock Loaf, 103
Mushroom Meatball Soup, 72
✓Mushroom Rice Pilaf, 72
Mushroom Round Steak, 258
Spinach Mushroom Salad, 184

**MUSTARD**
Honey Mustard Dressing, 187
✓Mustard Chicken Breasts, 280

**NUTS** (also see Peanut Butter)
**Breads, Rolls and Muffins**
    Apple-Nut Coffee Cake, 165
    Banana Bran Muffins, 175
    Banana Nut Bread, 59
    Berry Pleasing Muffins, 175
    Chunky Apple Bread, 162
    Coconut Pecan Rolls, 162
    Date-Nut Yeast Bread, 179
    ✓Nutty Wheat Bread, 179
    Pecan Pear Muffins, 174
    Tropical Muffins, 165
    Walnut Cinnamon Rolls, 170
**Desserts**
    Almond Bars, 215
    Apple Walnut Crescents, 129
    Apricot Pecan Sauce, 31
    Buttery Almond Cookies, 52
    Caramel Pecan Bars, 51
    Chocolate Peanut Bars, 201
    Chocolate Peanut Sundaes, 24
    Peanut Cereal Squares, 210
    Peanut Ice Cream
        Squares, 121
    Peanut Mallow Bars, 90
    Pecan Chip Tube Cake, 91
    Raisin-Nut Baked Apples, 17
    Raisin-Nut Chocolate
        Cake, 205
    Walnut Brownies, 95
    Walnut-Rippled Coffee
        Cake, 78
**Main Dishes**
    Almond Sole Fillets, 67

Cashew Chicken Toss, 281
✓Orange Cashew
    Chicken, 153
**Side Dishes**
    Almond Rice Seasoning
        Mix, 97
    Lemon Almond
        Asparagus, 311
**Snacks**
    Cereal Clusters, 240

**OATS**
Caramel Oat Bar Mix, 94
Chocolate Oatmeal Bars, 212
Coconut Oat Cookies, 85
Crispy Baked Oatmeal, 139
Fudge-Filled Bars, 213
Honey Oat Muffins, 169
Oatmeal Breakfast Bars, 23
Toffee Oat Cookies, 213

**ONIONS**
Herbed Onion Salad
    Dressing, 195
Onion-Chicken Stuffing
    Bake, 146
Pineapple-Onion Pork
    Chops, 300
Quick Onion Bread, 165

**ORANGE**
Citrus Cookies, 327
Citrus Sherbet Torte, 205
✓Creamy Orange Drink, 133
Frosted Orange Cookies, 202
✓Fruit Cup with Citrus
    Sauce, 221
Ham with Citrus Sauce, 308
✓Layered Orange Gelatin, 227
Mandarin Orange Cream
    Pie, 205
Mountainous Mandarin Pie, 300
Orange Banana Tapioca, 81
✓Orange Cashew Chicken, 153
Orange Chicken Supper, 79
✓Orange Chiffon Pie, 222
Orange Crispy Cookies, 211
Orange Poached Pears, 308
✓Orange Pork Stir-Fry, 224
Orange Swirl Yogurt Pie, 115
Tossed Salad with Oranges, 13

*✓ Recipe includes Nutritional Analysis and Diabetic Exchanges*

**OVEN ENTREES** (*also see Casseroles; Meat Pies & Pizza; Microwave Recipes*)

**Beef and Ground Beef**
Beef Wellington Bundles, 303
Cranberry Beef Brisket, 111
Easy Meat Loaf, 324
Mushroom Beef Patties, 234
Oven-Baked Burgers, 54
✓Pepper Jack Meat Loaf, 8
Pizza Meat Loaf Cups, 125
Reuben Meat Loaf, 325
Spicy Meat Loaves, 325
String Cheese Meat Loaf, 325

**Chicken and Turkey**
Baked Chicken Quesadillas, 289
✓Chicken Supreme, 226
Garlic Lime Chicken, 307
Taco Chicken Rolls, 58
✓Turkey Loaf, 226

**Fish and Seafood**
Baked Haddock, 103
Herbed Salmon Steaks, 321

**Meatless**
Baked Eggs with Basil Sauce, 130

**Pork, Ham and Bacon**
Berry Pretty Pork Roast, 311
Florentine Crepe Cups, 304
Ham 'n' Cheese Egg Loaf, 130
Ham with Citrus Sauce, 308
Pineapple-Onion Pork Chops, 300

**PASTA & NOODLES**
**Main Dishes**
Angel Hair Tuna, 153
Baked Spaghetti, 147
Basil Pasta Sauce, 296
Bean and Ham Pasta, 152
Cajun Macaroni, 233
Cheesy Beef Macaroni, 144
Chicken Broccoli Shells, 83
Chicken Pasta Primavera, 150
Chicken Spaghetti Toss, 24
Chili Mac Skillet, 22
Chili Manicotti, 101
Colorful Pasta with Ham, 146
Crabby Alfredo, 67
Creamy Shrimp Linguine, 152
Fiesta Macaroni, 55
Garden Squash Ravioli, 65

Garlic Salmon Linguine, 234
✓Ham Tetrazzini, 228
Hearty Mac 'n' Cheese, 245
Home-Style Mac 'n' Cheese, 100
Hurry-Up Ham Carbonara, 232
Meat Sauce for Pasta, 122
✓Microwave Mexican Manicotti, 275
Pasta Carbonara, 151
✓Penne from Heaven, 223
Pesto Pasta, 69
Pizza Casserole, 262
Pizza Macaroni Bake, 84
Pizza Rigatoni, 259
Popular Potluck Casserole, 145
Quick 'n' Easy Lasagna, 61
✓Round Steak Roll-Ups, 256
✓Sausage Spaghetti Spirals, 50
Sausage Vermicelli, 237
Sloppy Joe Wagon Wheels, 249
✓Southwestern Spaghetti, 154
Spaghetti Ham Bake, 116
Swiss Macaroni, 148
✓Three-Cheese Pasta Shells, 220
Tortellini Alfredo, 78
Tuna Noodle Cups, 245
Tuna Noodle Supreme, 148
✓Vegetarian Linguine, 158

**Salads**
Antipasto Pasta Salad, 192
✓Corn Pasta Salad, 218
✓Cucumber Shell Salad, 54
Kielbasa Pasta Salad, 80
Pasta Crab Egg Salad, 102
Pepperoni Angel Hair, 71
✓Veggie Macaroni Salad, 225

**Soups**
Beef 'n' Bean Tortellini Soup, 114
✓Beefy Tomato Pasta Soup, 187
Chili Macaroni Soup, 82

**PEACHES**
Chicken with Peach Stuffing, 32
Coconut Peach Pie, 59
Golden Peach Pork Chops, 266
✓Granola Peach Bread, 169

Peach-Glazed Cake, 52
Peachy Cream Pie, 90
✓Spiced Peaches, 219

**PEANUT BUTTER**
Cheerio Treats, 250
Chocolate Oatmeal Bars, 212
Chocolate Peanut Bars, 201
Chocolate Peanut Sundaes, 24
Creamy Peanut Butter Pie, 202
Crunchy Peanut Butter Drops, 247
Fudgy Peanut Butter Cake, 265
Peanut Butter 'n' Jelly Mini Muffins, 174
Peanut Butter Chip Cookies, 13
Peanut Butter Chocolate Dessert, 88
Peanut Butter Cupcakes, 212
Peanut Butter Teddies, 253
Peanut Cereal Squares, 210
Spooky Spider Snacks, 251
Sweetheart Trifle, 198

**PEARS**
Blueberry Pear Cobbler, 56
Fruit Dessert Topping, 257
Orange Poached Pears, 308
Pecan Pear Muffins, 174
Pork Chops with Pears, 61

**PEAS**
Black-Eyed Pea Sausage Stew, 159
Black-Eyed Pea Soup, 184
Creamy Pea Salad, 9
✓Pepper Pea Salad, 222
✓Snow Pea Medley, 303
Turkey Pea Skillet, 152

**PEPPERONI**
Antipasto Pasta Salad, 192
Pepperoni Angel Hair, 71
Pepperoni Drop Biscuits, 165
Personal Pepperoni Pizza, 328
Pizza Bread, 181
Pizza Casserole, 262
Pizza Rigatoni, 259

**PEPPERS**
Beef-Stuffed Peppers, 118

*✓ Recipe includes Nutritional Analysis and Diabetic Exchanges*

Green Chili Corn Bread, 22
Grilled Peppers and
    Zucchini, 273
✓Jalapeno Avocado Salad, 33
Jalapeno Chicken
    Enchiladas, 120
Pepper-Lime Pork Kabobs, 268
✓Pepper Pea Salad, 222
Pepper Steak Salad, 106
Pepper Steak Sandwiches, 192
✓Pepper Steak with
    Potatoes, 10
Red Pepper Chicken, 258
Savory Sausage and
    Peppers, 156

**PIES**
Banana Cream Pie, 279
Candy Bar Pie, 252
Cappuccino Chocolate Pie, 303
Coconut Cream Pie, 25
Coconut Peach Pie, 59
✓Creamy Banana Pie, 229
Creamy Peanut Butter Pie, 202
Crustless Pineapple Pie, 15
Fresh Raspberry Pie, 290
Frost-on-the-Pumpkin Pie, 206
Frosty Chocolate Pie, 123
Fudge Berry Pie, 60
Mandarin Orange Cream
    Pie, 205
Mocha Pie, 88
Mountainous Mandarin Pie, 300
✓Orange Chiffon Pie, 222
Orange Swirl Yogurt Pie, 115
Peachy Cream Pie, 90
✓Raspberry Yogurt Pie, 32
White Chocolate Pie, 293

**PINEAPPLE**
Crustless Pineapple Pie, 15
✓Frosty Pineapple Salad, 233
Frozen Banana Pineapple
    Cups, 141
✓Fruity Gelatin Salad, 59
Hawaiian Dinner Rolls, 178
Hawaiian Fruit Salad, 39
Hot Ham and Pineapple
    Sub, 187
Italian Pineapple Chicken, 29
Pineapple Biscuits, 166
Pineapple Bread, 176

Pineapple Cheesecake, 202
✓Pineapple Chicken Lo
    Mein, 157
Pineapple Date Bread, 170
Pineapple Ham Spread, 59
Pineapple Ice Cream, 119
Pineapple Ice Pops, 249
Pineapple Lime Molds, 83
Pineapple Pound Cake, 292
✓Pineapple Strawberry
    Punch, 60
Pineapple-Onion Pork
    Chops, 300
Red-Hot Candy Fluff, 51
✓Sweet 'n' Sour Sausage, 260
Sweet Pineapple Sauce, 64
Tropical Muffins, 165

**POPCORN**
Caramel Corn Chocolate
    Bars, 211
Crazy Corn, 252
Halloween Snack Mix, 214

**PORK** (also see Bacon; Ham;
Sausage)
Apple-Glazed Pork Chops, 45
Beef 'n' Pork Burgers, 28
Chinese Pork Ribs, 265
Dilly Pork Chops, 68
Fruity Pork Chops, 258
✓Ginger Pork Stir-Fry, 155
Golden Peach Pork Chops, 266
✓Herbed Pork Medallions, 26
Italian Pork Chops, 265
Italian Pork Hoagies, 109
Lemon Pork Chops, 261
✓Orange Pork Stir-Fry, 224
Pepper-Lime Pork Kabobs, 268
Pineapple-Onion Pork
    Chops, 300
Pork Chop 'n' Kraut Dinner, 291
Pork Chop Casserole, 51
Pork Chops and Kraut, 151
✓Pork Chops in Tomato
    Sauce, 228
Pork Chops with Apples, 157
Pork Chops with Baked
    Beans, 106
Pork Chops with Pears, 61
Pork Fried Rice, 108
Pork-Potato Meatballs, 232

Reuben Burgers, 272
Saucy Spareribs, 61
Savory Pork Roast, 108
Slow-Cooked Pork
    Barbecue, 257
Zippy Pork Chops, 269

**POTATOES**
**Dessert**
    Potato Chocolate Cake, 105
**Main Dishes**
    Amish Breakfast
        Casserole, 130
    Breakfast Pie, 139
    Cajun Shrimp with
        Potatoes, 277
    Chicken Bundles for Two, 268
    Cornish Hens with
        Potatoes, 267
    Creamy Potatoes 'n'
        Kielbasa, 262
    Ground Beef Shepherd's
        Pie, 149
    ✓Pepper Steak with
        Potatoes, 10
    Pork-Potato Meatballs, 232
    Potato Chicken Packets, 271
    Potato Ham Skillet, 70
    Sausage Hash Brown
        Bake, 129
    Speedy Beef Hash, 77
    Tater Taco Casserole, 81
**Salad and Soup**
    Celery Potato Chowder, 105
    German Potato Salad, 291
**Side Dishes**
    Bacon Tater Bake, 59
    Blue Cheese Potatoes, 52
    Cheddar Mashed
        Potatoes, 308
    Lemon-Butter Red
        Potatoes, 300
    Lime-Thyme Potato
        Wedges, 235
    Mashed Potatoes, 105
    Microwave Scalloped
        Potatoes, 274
    Midnight Mashed
        Potatoes, 47
    ✓Potato Bean Skillet, 228
    Potato Chip Potatoes, 8
    Potato Pancakes, 122

*✓ Recipe includes Nutritional Analysis and Diabetic Exchanges*

**POTATOES**
**Side Dishes** (continued)
Potato Rosettes, 117
Twice-Baked Ranch
Potatoes, 121

**PRESSURE COOKER RECIPES**
German Potato Salad, 291
Pork Chop 'n' Kraut Dinner, 291
Swiss Steak, 291

**PRETZELS**
Candy Cane Reindeer, 214
Pretzel-Topped Sugar
Cookies, 210

**PUDDING**
Orange Banana Tapioca, 81
Puddin' Cones, 241
Rocky Road Pudding, 22
Toasted Coconut Pudding, 26

**PUMPKIN**
Frost-on-the-Pumpkin Pie, 206
Pumpkin Pancakes, 139

**QUICHE**
Bacon Cheddar Quiche, 276
Bacon Quiche Tarts, 133
Broccoli Ham Quiche, 282
Savory Pork Roast, 108
Spinach Wild Rice Quiche, 108
Zucchini Pie, 236

**RAISINS & DATES**
Carrot Raisin Bread, 176
Chunky Apple Bread, 162
Coffee Raisin Bread, 323
Crumb-Topped Date Bars, 330
Date-Nut Yeast Bread, 179
Pineapple Date Bread, 170
Raisin Bran Bread, 180
Raisin-Nut Baked Apples, 17
Raisin-Nut Chocolate Cake, 205

**RASPBERRIES**
Berries 'n' Cream Dessert, 290
Berry Pretty Pork Roast, 311
Cherry Berry Smoothies, 139
Chocolate Berry Pound
Cake, 198

Fresh Raspberry Pie, 290
Fudge Berry Pie, 60
No-Bake Chocolate
Cheesecake, 201
Raspberry Chicken, 290
Raspberry Corn Bread
Muffins, 173
Raspberry Icebox Dessert, 89
Raspberry Iced Tea, 307
✓Raspberry Yogurt Pie, 32
Red, White 'n' Blue Torte, 307
Triple Berry Muffins, 173

**RICE & BARLEY**
Almond Rice Seasoning Mix, 97
✓Apple Rice Betty, 226
Beef Barley Soup, 116
✓Brown Rice Slaw, 220
Cajun Hot Dish, 154
✓Catalina Rice Salad, 188
Chicken Wild Rice Soup, 76
Comforting Chicken, 147
Fiesta Cheese Rice, 275
Ground Beef 'n' Rice Pie, 146
Ham and Rice Bake, 56
✓Holiday Wild Rice, 311
Mexican Rice Mix, 92
✓Mushroom Rice Pilaf, 72
Party-Pleasing Beef Dish, 261
Pork Fried Rice, 108
✓Salsa Rice, 58
Santa Fe Supper, 158
✓Sausage Rice Skillet, 150
Sausage Vermicelli, 237
Spinach Wild Rice Quiche, 108
✓Sunny Chicken and Rice, 274
Tex-Mex Rice, 234
Turkey Rice Casserole, 282
Vegetable Wild Rice, 108
White Rice Bread, 179
Wild Rice Bread, 108

**ROLLS**
Coconut Pecan Rolls, 162
✓Cranberry Oat Knots, 323
Walnut Cinnamon Rolls, 170

**SALADS & DRESSINGS** (also
see Coleslaw)
**Bean Salads**
✓Colorful Black Bean
Salad, 191

Curried Bean Salad, 233
French Bean Salad, 66
**Dressings**
Herbed Onion Salad
Dressing, 195
Honey Mustard Dressing, 187
**Fruit and Gelatin Salads**
✓Cranberry Cream
Delight, 122
✓Cream-Topped Grapes, 129
✓Creamy Cranberry
Gelatin, 86
✓Creamy Waldorf Salad, 73
✓Frosty Pineapple Salad, 233
✓Fruit Cup with Citrus
Sauce, 221
Fruity Apple Salad, 45
✓Fruity Gelatin Salad, 59
Hawaiian Fruit Salad, 39
✓Layered Orange
Gelatin, 227
Mallow Fruit Salad, 79
Pineapple Lime Molds, 83
Red-Hot Candy Fluff, 51
✓Tropical Fruit Salad, 130
**Green Salads**
Antipasto Salad, 187
Bacon-Tomato Spinach
Salad, 307
Cauliflower Romaine
Salad, 192
Greek Tossed Salad, 30
✓Jalapeno Avocado Salad, 33
Layered Veggie Egg
Salad, 103
Mock Caesar Salad, 56
Speedy Southwest Salad, 66
Spinach Mushroom Salad, 184
Start-Your-Engine Salad, 41
Sweet Sesame Salad, 11
Tossed Salad with Oranges, 13
Wilted Lettuce Salad, 31
**Main-Dish Salads**
Cashew Chicken Toss, 281
✓Chicken Salad in Melon
Rings, 188
Pepper Steak Salad, 106
Warm Shrimp Salad, 70
**Pasta and Rice Salads**
Antipasto Pasta Salad, 192
✓Catalina Rice Salad, 188
✓Corn Pasta Salad, 218
✓Cucumber Shell Salad, 54

✓ *Recipe includes Nutritional Analysis and Diabetic Exchanges*

Kielbasa Pasta Salad, 80
Pasta Crab Egg Salad, 102
Pepperoni Angel Hair, 71
✓Veggie Macaroni Salad, 225
**Potato Salad**
German Potato Salad, 291
**Vegetable Salads**
Cottage Cheese Veggie
    Salad, 25
Creamy Pea Salad, 9
Cucumber Canoes, 249
✓Hungarian Salad, 64
✓Marinated Artichoke
    Salad, 52
✓Pepper Pea Salad, 222
Picnic Salad Skewers, 327
Ranch Floret Salad, 287
Shoepeg Corn Salad, 191
Tangy Cauliflower Salad, 68


**SALSAS**
California Avocado Salsa, 288
✓Cucumber Salsa, 288
✓Garden Salsa, 288


**SANDWICHES**
**Cold Sandwiches**
Butterfly Sandwiches, 43
Chicken Salad Clubs 71
Creamy Egg Salad, 102
Italian Subs, 184
Triple-Decker Salmon
    Club, 188
Turkey Dill Subs, 327
**Hot Sandwiches**
Baked Ham Sandwiches, 119
✓BBQ Chicken
    Sandwiches, 235
Beef 'n' Pork Burgers, 28
Beef Stroganoff Melt, 25
Cabbage Sloppy Joes, 286
✓Creamy Ham Turnovers, 222
✓Eggplant Pockets, 223
Ham 'n' Egg Salad Subs, 195
Ham 'n' Egg Sandwich, 135
Hot Dog Race Cars, 41
Hot Ham 'n' Egg
    Sandwiches, 184
Hot Ham and Pineapple
    Sub, 187
Italian Chicken Pockets, 195
Italian Pork Hoagies, 109

Italian Steak Sandwiches, 68
Luau Chicken Sandwiches, 39
Open-Faced Sandwich
    Supreme, 76
Oven-Baked Burgers, 54
Pepper Steak Sandwiches, 192
Pizza Grilled Cheese, 250
Reuben Burgers, 272
✓Sausage Egg Pitas, 219
Slow-Cooked Pork
    Barbecue, 257
Spiral Stromboli, 191
Steak Tortillas, 107
Stroganoff in a Bun, 237
✓Turkey Crescents, 86
✓Turkey Sloppy Joes, 220


**SAUSAGE** (also see Hot Dogs;
Pepperoni)
**Appetizer**
Zippy Sausage Spread, 56
**Breads**
Sausage Swiss Muffins, 174
Savory Sausage Bread, 166
**Main Dishes**
✓Apple Kielbasa Coins, 304
Baked Spaghetti, 147
Basil Pasta Sauce, 296
Black-Eyed Pea Sausage
    Stew, 159
✓Broccoli Sausage
    Simmer, 287
Cajun Hot Dish, 154
Creamy Potatoes 'n'
    Kielbasa, 262
Meat Sauce for Pasta, 122
Meaty Apple Skillet, 141
Mini Sausage Pizzas, 121
Pizza Rigatoni, 259
✓Sausage Egg Puff, 224
Sausage Hash Brown
    Bake, 129
✓Sausage Rice Skillet, 150
Sausage Shrimp Kabobs, 269
✓Sausage Spaghetti Spirals, 50
Sausage Vermicelli, 237
✓Sausage with Corn
    Stuffing, 149
Savory Sausage and
    Peppers, 156
Southwest Sausage Bake, 135
String Cheese Meat Loaf, 325

✓Sweet 'n' Sour Sausage, 260
Sweet Sausage 'n' Beans, 265
**Salads and Side Dish**
Antipasto Pasta Salad, 192
Antipasto Salad, 187
Glazed Apples and
    Sausage, 139
Kielbasa Pasta Salad, 80
**Sandwiches**
Italian Subs, 184
✓Sausage Egg Pitas, 219
Spiral Stromboli, 191
**Soups**
Cabbage Sausage Soup, 286
✓Sausage Chicken Soup, 282
✓Sausage Tomato Soup, 195


**SEAFOOD** (see Fish & Seafood)


**SESAME SEED**
Sesame Chicken, 12
Sweet Sesame Salad, 11


**SIDE DISHES** (also see
Casseroles)
**Miscellaneous**
Squash Stuffing Casserole, 266
Stovetop Baked Beans, 106
Warm Fruit Compote, 136
**Potatoes**
Lemon-Butter Red
    Potatoes, 300
Lime-Thyme Potato
    Wedges, 235
Mashed Potatoes, 105
Midnight Mashed Potatoes, 47
Potato Chip Potatoes, 8
Potato Pancakes, 122
Potato Rosettes, 117
Twice-Baked Ranch
    Potatoes, 121
**Rice**
Almond Rice Seasoning
    Mix, 97
✓Holiday Wild Rice, 311
Mexican Rice Mix, 92
✓Mushroom Rice Pilaf, 72
✓Salsa Rice, 58
Tex-Mex Rice, 234
Vegetable Wild Rice, 108
**Vegetables**
Feta-Topped Asparagus, 29

✓ *Recipe includes Nutritional Analysis and Diabetic Exchanges*

**SIDE DISHES**
**Vegetables** *(continued)*
  Lemon Almond
    Asparagus, 311
  ✓Mushroom Green Beans, 308
  ✓Potato Bean Skillet, 228
  ✓Roasted Tarragon
    Asparagus, 24
  ✓Snow Pea Medley, 303
  ✓Vibrant Veggie Stir-Fry, 226
  ✓Vinaigrette Vegetables, 26
  Winter Vegetable Medley, 19
  Zucchini Cakes, 235

**SKILLET & STOVETOP**
**SUPPERS**
**Beef and Ground Beef**
  Cabbage Wedges with
    Beef, 286
  Cajun Macaroni, 233
  Chili Mac Skillet, 22
  Flank Steak Stir-Fry, 296
  ✓Hamburger Skillet Supper, 52
  ✓Hearty Fajitas, 151
  Hearty Mac 'n' Cheese, 245
  Mushroom Beef Skillet, 111
  ✓Pepper Steak with
    Potatoes, 10
  Santa Fe Supper, 158
  ✓Skillet Olé, 225
  Sloppy Joe Wagon
    Wheels, 249
  ✓Southwestern Spaghetti, 154
  Speedy Beef Hash, 77
  Start-Ahead Stroganoff, 119
  Steak Tortillas, 107
  Taco Skillet, 156
**Chicken**
  Breaded Chicken with
    Avocado, 295
  Chicken Pasta Primavera, 150
  Chicken Spaghetti Toss, 24
  Creamy Chicken and
    Broccoli, 158
  ✓Curried Chicken, 221
  Fruited Chicken Curry, 159
  ✓Hearty Fajitas, 151
  Honey Barbecue Chicken, 252
  ✓Orange Cashew
    Chicken, 153
  Orange Chicken Supper, 79
  ✓Pineapple Chicken Lo
    Mein, 157
  Raspberry Chicken, 290
  ✓Rosemary Chicken, 65

  Smothered Chicken, 73
**Fish and Seafood**
  Angel Hair Tuna, 153
  Broccoli Shrimp Alfredo, 155
  Crabby Alfredo, 67
  Creamy Shrimp Linguine, 152
  Curried Shrimp, 154
  Fish with Florentine Rice, 86
  Garlic Salmon Linguine, 234
  ✓Hearty Fajitas, 151
  Shrimp Jambalaya, 157
  Smoked Salmon
    Quesadillas, 289
  ✓Tuna Delight, 67
**Ham and Bacon**
  Asparagus Omelet, 134
  Bacon Avocado
    Quesadillas, 289
  Bean and Ham Pasta, 152
  Hurry-Up Ham
    Carbonara, 232
  One-Pot Ham Dinner, 153
  Pasta Carbonara, 151
  Potato Ham Skillet, 70
  Ranch Eggs 'n' Biscuits, 133
  Veggies and Ham, 150
**Meatless**
  Omelet with Cheese
    Sauce, 129
  ✓Vegetarian Linguine, 158
**Pork**
  ✓Ginger Pork Stir-Fry, 155
  ✓Orange Pork Stir-Fry, 224
  Pork Chops and Kraut, 151
  ✓Pork Chops in Tomato
    Sauce, 228
  Pork Chops with Apples, 157
  Pork Fried Rice, 108
  Saucy Spareribs, 61
**Sausage**
  ✓Apple Kielbasa Coins, 304
  Black-Eyed Pea Sausage
    Stew, 159
  ✓Broccoli Sausage
    Simmer, 287
  Cajun Hot Dish, 154
  Meat Sauce for Pasta, 122
  Meaty Apple Skillet, 141
  ✓Sausage Rice Skillet, 150
  Sausage Vermicelli, 237
  Savory Sausage and
    Peppers, 156
**Turkey**
  ✓Skillet Olé, 225
  Turkey Pea Skillet, 152

**SLOW COOKER RECIPES**
**Appetizer and Beverage**
  Harvest Apple Cider, 45
  Reuben Spread, 267
**Desserts**
  Fruit Dessert Topping, 257
  Fudgy Peanut Butter
    Cake, 265
  Granola Apple Crisp, 266
**Main Dishes**
  Barbecued Beef Brisket, 261
  Beef 'n' Bean Starter, 114
  Chicken in Sour Cream
    Sauce, 257
  Chicken with Stuffing, 261
  ✓Chicken with Vegetables, 263
  Chinese Pork Ribs, 265
  Cornish Hens with
    Potatoes, 267
  Creamy Potatoes 'n'
    Kielbasa, 262
  Flavorful Beef in Gravy, 262
  Fruity Pork Chops, 258
  Golden Peach Pork
    Chops, 266
  ✓Ham Tetrazzini, 228
  Italian Pork Chops, 265
  King-Size Drumsticks, 37
  Lemon Pork Chops, 261
  Mushroom Round Steak, 258
  Party-Pleasing Beef Dish, 261
  Pizza Casserole, 262
  Pizza Rigatoni, 259
  Red Pepper Chicken, 258
  Roast Beef and Gravy, 257
  ✓Round Steak Roll-Ups, 256
  ✓Spicy Lemon Chicken, 264
  ✓Sweet 'n' Sour Sausage, 260
  Sweet Sausage 'n' Beans, 265
**Sandwiches**
  Bandito Chili Dogs, 259
  Slow-Cooked Pork
    Barbecue, 257
  ✓Turkey Sloppy Joes, 220
**Side Dish**
  Squash Stuffing Casserole, 266
**Soups, Stews and Chili**
  ✓Corny Chili, 258
  French Beef Stew, 266
  ✓Ground Beef Stew, 257
  Meatball Stew, 264
  Slow-Cooked Corn
    Chowder, 262
  Spicy Chicken Tomato
    Soup, 262

*✓ Recipe includes Nutritional Analysis and Diabetic Exchanges*

Veggie Meatball Soup, 261
White Chili, 266

**SOUPS** (also see Chili; Chowder)
Asparagus Soup, 188
✓Beefy Tomato Pasta Soup, 187
Black-Eyed Pea Soup, 184
Broccoli Crab Bisque, 287
Cabbage Sausage Soup, 286
Cheddar Vegetable Soup, 100
Cheesy Floret Soup, 191
Cheesy Vegetable Soup, 125
Chicken Wild Rice Soup, 76
Chili Macaroni Soup, 82
Enchilada Chicken Soup, 68
Ham 'n' Swiss Soup, 297
Hamburger Soup, 236
Hot Dog Soup, 247
✓Kielbasa Bean Soup, 229
Mushroom Meatball Soup, 72
Parmesan Corn Chowder, 192
✓Sausage Chicken Soup, 282
✓Sausage Tomato Soup, 195
Spicy Chicken Tomato
    Soup, 262
Taco Soup, 33
✓Vegetable Bean Soup, 227
Veggie Meatball Soup, 261
Zippy Chicken Soup, 64

**SPINACH**
Bacon-Tomato Spinach
    Salad, 307
Creamy Swiss Spinach Dip, 281
Florentine Crepe Cups, 304
Spinach Mushroom Salad, 184
Spinach Wild Rice Quiche, 108
✓Turkey Spinach Casserole, 218

**SPREADS**
Creamy Chicken Spread, 76
Creamy Garlic Ham Spread, 277
Hot Artichoke Spread, 300
Pineapple Ham Spread, 59
Reuben Spread, 267
Zippy Sausage Spread, 56

**SQUASH & ZUCCHINI**
Garden Squash Ravioli, 65
Grilled Peppers and
    Zucchini, 273
✓Southwestern Spaghetti, 154
Squash Stuffing Casserole, 266
Zucchini Cakes, 235
Zucchini Crisp, 206
Zucchini Pie, 236

**STEWS**
Black-Eyed Pea Sausage
    Stew, 159
French Beef Stew, 266
Meatball Stew, 264
✓Turkey Cabbage Stew, 16

**STRAWBERRIES**
✓Angel Food Cake Roll, 219
Berry Pretty Pork Roast, 311
Countdown Cheesecake, 47
✓Fruity Gelatin Salad, 59
Fudge Berry Pie, 60
✓Heavenly Strawberry Tarts, 27
No-Bake Chocolate
    Cheesecake, 201
Pineapple Cheesecake, 202
✓Pineapple Strawberry
    Punch, 60
Red, White 'n' Blue Torte, 307
Strawberry Cheesecake Trifle, 82
✓Strawberry Dip, 55
Strawberry Yogurt Shakes, 23
Triple Berry Muffins, 173

**STUFFING & DRESSING**
Broccoli Corn Casserole, 51
Cheddar Stuffing Puff, 79
Chicken with Peach Stuffing, 32
Chicken with Stuffing, 261
Onion-Chicken Stuffing
    Bake, 146
Squash Stuffing Casserole, 266
✓Thanksgiving in a Pan, 87

**TOMATOES**
Bacon-Tomato Spinach
    Salad, 307
✓Beefy Tomato Pasta Soup, 187
BLT Pizza, 329
✓Pork Chops in Tomato
    Sauce, 228
✓Sausage Tomato Soup, 195
Spicy Chicken Tomato
    Soup, 262
Tomato and Beef Soup, 111
Tomato Bacon Pie, 56

**TURKEY & TURKEY SAUSAGE**
Breaded Turkey Slices, 27
✓Kielbasa Bean Soup, 229
King-Size Drumsticks, 37
✓Moist Ham Loaf, 18
Open-Faced Sandwich
    Supreme, 76
✓Skillet Olé, 225

✓Thanksgiving in a Pan, 87
Turkey Broccoli Hollandaise, 148
✓Turkey Cabbage Stew, 16
✓Turkey Crescents, 86
Turkey Dill Subs, 327
Turkey Dinner Muffins, 170
Turkey Lattice Pie, 297
✓Turkey Loaf, 226
Turkey Pea Skillet, 152
Turkey Rice Casserole, 282
✓Turkey Sloppy Joes, 220
✓Turkey Spinach Casserole, 218

**VEGETABLES** (also see specific
kinds)
Cheddar Vegetable Soup, 100
Cheesy Vegetable Medley, 147
Cheesy Vegetable Soup, 125
Chicken Veggie Casserole, 237
✓Chicken with Vegetables, 263
Corn Bread Veggie Bake, 236
Cottage Cheese Veggie Salad, 25
✓Eggplant Pockets, 223
✓Garden Salsa, 288
Herbed Veggie Platter, 279
Hot Artichoke Spread, 300
Layered Veggie Egg Salad, 103
Picnic Salad Skewers, 327
Special Grilled Veggies, 270
Sweet Potato Bread, 170
✓Vegetable Bean Soup, 227
Vegetable Wild Rice, 108
✓Vegetarian Linguine, 158
✓Veggie Macaroni Salad, 225
Veggie Meatball Soup, 261
Veggie Pull-Apart Bread, 15
Veggie Tortilla Pinwheels, 303
Veggies and Ham, 150
✓Vibrant Veggie Stir-Fry, 226
✓Vinaigrette Vegetables, 26
Winter Vegetable Medley, 19

**WAFFLES, PANCAKES &
FRENCH TOAST**
✓Blintz Pancakes, 134
Carrot Pancakes, 134
French Toast Bake, 133
Pumpkin Pancakes, 139
Whole-Grain Waffle Mix, 94

**YOGURT**
✓Fruit Yogurt Medley, 66
Orange Swirl Yogurt Pie, 115
✓Raspberry Yogurt Pie, 32
Strawberry Yogurt Shakes, 23

✓ *Recipe includes Nutritional Analysis and Diabetic Exchanges*

# Alphabetical Index

*This handy index lists every recipe in alphabetical order so you can easily find your favorite recipes.*

## A

Almond Bars, 215
Almond Rice Seasoning Mix, 97
Almond Sole Fillets, 67
Amish Breakfast Casserole, 130
✓Angel Food Cake Roll, 219
Angel Hair Tuna, 153
Antipasto Pasta Salad, 192
Antipasto Salad, 187
✓Apple Cranberry Bread, 229
Apple-Glazed Pork Chops, 45
✓Apple Kielbasa Coins, 304
Apple-Nut Coffee Cake, 165
✓Apple Rice Betty, 226
Apple Spice Cupcakes, 45
Apple Spice Snack Cake, 237
Apple Streusel Muffins, 172
✓Apple Tapioca, 221
Apple Walnut Crescents, 129
Apricot Muffins, 166
Apricot Pecan Sauce, 31
Artichoke Chicken, 56
Asparagus Omelet, 134
Asparagus Soup, 188

## B

Bacon Avocado Quesadillas, 289
Bacon Cheddar Pinwheels, 169
Bacon Cheddar Quiche, 276
Bacon Cheese Biscuits, 162
Bacon-Feta Stuffed Chicken, 30
Bacon Quiche Tarts, 133
Bacon Swiss Squares, 140
Bacon Tater Bake, 59
Bacon-Tomato Spinach Salad, 307
Bacon-Wrapped Corn, 28
Baked Bean Chili, 106
Baked Chicken Quesadillas, 289
Baked Eggs with Basil Sauce, 130
Baked Haddock, 103
Baked Ham Sandwiches, 119
Baked Spaghetti, 147
Banana Bran Muffins, 175
✓Banana Chip Muffins, 163
Banana Cream Brownie Dessert, 91
Banana Cream Pie, 279
Banana Cupcakes, 294

Banana Macaroon Trifle, 201
Banana Nut Bread, 59
Banana Split Smoothies, 242
Bandito Chili Dogs, 259
Barbecued Beef Brisket, 261
Basic Beef Starter, 118
Basic Cake Mix, 93
Basic Cookie Dough, 330
Basil Pasta Sauce, 296
✓BBQ Chicken Sandwiches, 235
Bean and Ham Pasta, 152
Beef 'n' Bean Chili, 115
Beef 'n' Bean Enchiladas, 280
Beef 'n' Bean Starter, 114
Beef 'n' Bean Tortellini Soup, 114
Beef 'n' Pork Burgers, 28
Beef Barley Soup, 116
Beef Shish Kabobs, 270
Beef Stroganoff Melt, 25
Beef-Stuffed Peppers, 118
Beef Wellington Bundles, 303
✓Beefy Tomato Pasta Soup, 187
Beetle Juice, 43
Berries 'n' Cream Dessert, 290
Berry Pleasing Muffins, 175
Berry Pretty Pork Roast, 311
Biscuit Tostadas, 240
✓Blackberry Cake, 224
Black-Eyed Pea Sausage Stew, 159
Black-Eyed Pea Soup, 184
✓Blintz Pancakes, 134
BLT Pizza, 329
Blue Cheese Potatoes, 52
Blueberry Cream Muffins, 171
Blueberry Pear Cobbler, 56
Blueberry Scones, 168
Bread Bowls, 180
Breaded Chicken with
   Avocado, 295
Breaded Turkey Slices, 27
Breakfast Burritos, 122
Breakfast Pie, 139
Breakfast Upside Down Cake, 141
Broccoli Corn Casserole, 51
Broccoli Crab Bisque, 287
Broccoli Ham Quiche, 282
✓Broccoli Sausage Simmer, 287
Broccoli Shrimp Alfredo, 155

✓Brown Rice Slaw, 220
Brown Sugar Muffins, 162
Brownie Crinkles, 95
Brownie Mix, 95
Brownie Snack Cake, 95
Butterfly Sandwiches, 43
Butterscotch Muffins, 77
Buttery Almond Cookies, 52

## C

Cabbage Sausage Soup, 286
Cabbage Sloppy Joes, 286
Cabbage Wedges with Beef, 286
Cajun Hot Dish, 154
Cajun Macaroni, 233
Cajun Seasoning Mix, 92
Cajun Shrimp with Potatoes, 277
California Avocado Salsa, 288
Candy Bar Pie, 252
Candy Cane Reindeer, 214
Cappuccino Chocolate Pie, 303
Cappuccino Mousse Trifle, 206
Caramel Apple Crisp, 278
Caramel Brownies, 210
Caramel Chip Bars, 91
Caramel Corn Chocolate Bars, 211
Caramel Oat Bar Mix, 94
Caramel Pecan Bars, 51
Carrot Pancakes, 134
Carrot Raisin Bread, 176
Cashew Chicken Toss, 281
✓Catalina Rice Salad, 188
Caterpillar Cake, 43
Cauliflower Romaine Salad, 192
Celery Potato Chowder, 105
Cereal Clusters, 240
Checkered Flag Cookies, 41
Cheddar Cheese Sauce, 100
Cheddar Chicken Pie, 145
Cheddar Mashed Potatoes, 308
Cheddar Stuffing Puff, 79
Cheddar Vegetable Soup, 100
Cheerio Treats, 250
Cheeseburger Biscuit Bake, 247
Cheeseburger Mini Muffins, 173
Cheesy Beef Macaroni, 144
Cheesy Carrots, 55
Cheesy Chili Dip, 100

*✓ Recipe includes Nutritional Analysis and Diabetic Exchanges*

Cheesy Crab Burritos, 51
Cheesy Egg Puffs, 135
Cheesy Floret Soup, 191
Cheesy Vegetable Medley, 147
Cheesy Vegetable Soup, 125
Cherry Berry Smoothies, 139
✓Cherry Dream Cake, 87
Cherry Mousse, 29
Cherry Surprise Cookies, 331
Chicken Asparagus Bake, 80
Chicken Broccoli Shells, 83
Chicken Bundles for Two, 268
Chicken in Sour Cream Sauce, 257
Chicken Pasta Primavera, 150
Chicken Salad Clubs, 71
✓Chicken Salad in Melon Rings, 188
Chicken Spaghetti Toss, 24
✓Chicken Supreme, 226
Chicken Veggie Casserole, 237
Chicken Wild Rice Soup, 76
Chicken with Peach Stuffing, 32
Chicken with Stuffing, 261
✓Chicken with Vegetables, 263
Chili Mac Skillet, 22
Chili Macaroni Soup, 82
Chili Manicotti, 101
Chili Sauce Chicken, 270
Chinese Pork Ribs, 265
Chive Cheese Biscuits, 169
Chocolate Berry Pound Cake, 198
Chocolate Caramel Cupcakes, 294
Chocolate Caramel Fondue, 66
Chocolate Cherry Angel Cake, 9
Chocolate Mallow Cookies, 331
Chocolate Oatmeal Bars, 212
Chocolate Peanut Bars, 201
Chocolate Peanut Sundaes, 24
Christmas Meatballs, 278
Chunky Apple Bread, 162
✓Cinnamon 'n' Spice Dip, 70
Cinnamon Apple Pizza, 85
Cinnamon Coffee Cake, 96
Cinnamon Fruit Biscuits, 164
Cinnamon Graham Sundaes, 33
Cinnamon Pancake Cubes, 240
Cinnamon Syrup, 245
Citrus Cookies, 327
Citrus Sherbet Torte, 205
Coconut Angel Squares, 89
Coconut Cream Pie, 25
Coconut Loaf, 164
Coconut Muffins, 166
Coconut Oat Cookies, 85
Coconut Peach Pie, 59

Coconut Pecan Rolls, 162
Coffee Cake Mix, 92
Coffee Cake Muffins, 174
Coffee Raisin Bread, 323
✓Colorful Black Bean Salad, 191
Colorful Pasta with Ham, 146
Comforting Chicken, 147
Cookie Dessert, 250
Cookie Lei, 39
Corn Bread Veggie Bake, 236
✓Corn Pasta Salad, 218
Cornish Hens with Potatoes, 267
Cornmeal Molasses Bread, 180
Cornmeal Muffins, 93
✓Corny Chili, 258
Cottage Cheese Veggie Salad, 25
Countdown Cheesecake, 47
Country Corn Bread, 96
Crabby Alfredo, 67
✓Crab-Stuffed Chicken, 276
Cran-Apple Ham Slice, 281
Cranberry Beef Brisket, 111
Cranberry Cream Cheese
    Muffins, 172
✓Cranberry Cream Delight, 122
Cranberry Crispies, 206
Cranberry Layer Cake, 311
✓Cranberry Oat Knots, 323
Crazy Corn, 252
✓Cream-Topped Grapes, 129
✓Creamy Banana Pie, 229
Creamy Chicken and Broccoli, 158
Creamy Chicken Spread, 76
Creamy Corn, 52
✓Creamy Cranberry Gelatin, 86
Creamy Egg Salad, 102
Creamy Fruit Fluff, 116
Creamy Garlic Ham Spread, 277
✓Creamy Ham Turnovers, 222
✓Creamy Orange Drink, 133
Creamy Pea Salad, 9
Creamy Peanut Butter Pie, 202
Creamy Potatoes 'n' Kielbasa, 262
Creamy Shrimp Linguine, 152
Creamy Swiss Spinach Dip, 281
✓Creamy Waldorf Salad, 73
Crispy Baked Oatmeal, 139
Crispy Kiss Squares, 214
Crumb-Topped Date Bars, 330
Crunchy Peanut Butter Drops, 247
Crustless Pineapple Pie, 15
Cucumber Canoes, 249
✓Cucumber Salsa, 288
✓Cucumber Shell Salad, 54

Currant Scone Mix, 97
Curried Bean Salad, 233
✓Curried Chicken, 221
Curried Shrimp, 154
Custard Cups, 280

## D

Date-Nut Yeast Bread, 179
Denver Omelet Pie, 136
Dilly Mushrooms, 275
Dilly Pork Chops, 68
Double Frosted Brownies, 80
Dragon Dippers, 37
Dressed-Up Meatballs, 283
Drop Sugar Cookies, 212

## E

Easy Cherry Tarts, 55
Easy Meat Loaf, 324
Easy Tiramisu, 19
✓Eggplant Pockets, 223
Eggs Bravo, 136
Enchilada Chicken Soup, 68

## F

Family-Favorite Bread, 176
Feta-Topped Asparagus, 29
Fiesta Cheese Rice, 275
Fiesta Dip, 277
Fiesta Macaroni, 55
Fish with Florentine Rice, 86
Flank Steak Stir-Fry, 296
Flavorful Beef in Gravy, 262
✓Flavorful Flank Steak, 272
Florentine Crepe Cups, 304
Flowerpot Cupcakes, 243
For-My-Love Sugar Cookies, 293
Four-Bean Taco Chili, 100
French Bean Salad, 66
French Beef Stew, 266
French Toast Bake, 133
Fresh Raspberry Pie, 290
Fried Chicken Coating, 93
Fried Chicken Nuggets, 55
Frost-on-the-Pumpkin Pie, 206
Frosted Orange Cookies, 202
Frosty Chocolate Pie, 123
Frosty Mocha Drink, 140
✓Frosty Pineapple Salad, 233
Frozen Banana Pineapple Cups, 141
Frozen Fruit Fluff, 121
✓Fruit Cup with Citrus Sauce, 221
Fruit Dessert Topping, 257

*✓ Recipe includes Nutritional Analysis and Diabetic Exchanges*

Fruit with Marshmallow Dip, 304
✓Fruit Yogurt Medley, 66
Fruited Chicken Curry, 159
Fruity Apple Salad, 45
✓Fruity Gelatin Salad, 59
Fruity Pork Chops, 258
Fruity Sherbet, 125
Fudge Berry Pie, 60
Fudge-Filled Bars, 213
Fudge Sauce, 95
Fudgy Peanut Butter Cake, 265

## G

✓Garden Salsa, 288
Garden Squash Ravioli, 65
Garlic-Cheese Flat Bread, 170
Garlic Chicken Pizza, 329
Garlic Lime Chicken, 307
Garlic Salmon Linguine, 234
German Potato Salad, 291
✓Ginger Pork Stir-Fry, 155
Gingerbread Cake, 110
Gingerbread Men, 110
Gingerbread Trifle, 111
Gingered White Bread, 181
Glazed Apples and Sausage, 139
Glazed Lemon Cake, 232
Glazed Mint Brownies, 198
✓Glazed Orange Roughy, 218
Golden Biscuits, 96
Golden Coconut Pie, 234
Golden Corn Casserole, 85
Golden Peach Pork Chops, 266
Golden Tuna Casserole, 144
Granola Apple Crisp, 266
✓Granola Peach Bread, 169
Granola Wheat Bread, 181
Greek Tossed Salad, 30
Green Beans with a Twist, 50
Green Beans with Bacon, 27
Green Chili Corn Bread, 22
Grilled Peppers and Zucchini, 273
Grilled Rib Eye Steaks, 106
Ground Beef 'n' Rice Pie, 146
Ground Beef Baked Beans, 125
Ground Beef Shepherd's Pie, 149
✓Ground Beef Stew, 257
Gumdrop Fudge, 61

## H

Haddock Clam Chowder, 103
Halloween Snack Mix, 214
Ham 'n' Cheese Egg Loaf, 130

Ham and Egg Pizza, 23
Ham 'n' Egg Salad Subs, 195
Ham 'n' Egg Sandwich, 135
Ham and Rice Bake, 56
Ham 'n' Swiss Soup, 297
✓Ham Tetrazzini, 228
Ham with Citrus Sauce, 308
✓Hamburger Skillet Supper, 52
Hamburger Soup, 236
Harvest Apple Cider, 45
Hawaiian Dinner Rolls, 178
Hawaiian Fruit Salad, 39
Hawaiian Ham Bake, 144
Hawaiian Sunset Cake, 88
Heart's Delight Torte, 293
Hearty Burritos, 115
✓Hearty Fajitas, 151
Hearty Mac 'n' Cheese, 245
✓Heavenly Strawberry Tarts, 27
Herb Muffin Mix, 94
Herbed Bread, 323
Herbed Focaccia, 17
Herbed Onion Salad Dressing, 195
✓Herbed Pork Medallions, 26
Herbed Salmon Steaks, 321
Herbed Veggie Platter, 279
✓Holiday Wild Rice, 311
Hollandaise Sauce, 278
Homemade Ladyfingers, 119
Home-Style Mac 'n' Cheese, 100
Honey Barbecue Chicken, 252
Honey Mustard Dressing, 187
Honey Oat Muffins, 169
Honey Spice Bread, 167
Hot Artichoke Spread, 300
Hot Dog Race Cars, 41
Hot Dog Soup, 247
Hot Drink Mix, 97
Hot Ham 'n' Egg Sandwiches, 184
Hot Ham and Pineapple Sub, 187
✓Hungarian Salad, 64
Hurry-Up Ham Carbonara, 232

## I

Italian Chicken Pockets, 195
Italian Pineapple Chicken, 29
Italian Pork Chops, 265
Italian Pork Hoagies, 109
Italian Steak Sandwiches, 68
Italian Subs, 184

## J

✓Jalapeno Avocado Salad, 33
Jalapeno Chicken Enchiladas, 120

Jam Biscuits, 136
Jelly Sandwich Cookies, 331
Jumbo Onion Cheese Muffins, 172

## K

✓Kielbasa Bean Soup, 229
Kielbasa Pasta Salad, 80
King-Size Drumsticks, 37

## L

Ladybug Appetizers, 43
✓Layered Orange Gelatin, 227
Layered Veggie Egg Salad, 103
Lemon Almond Asparagus, 311
Lemon-Butter Red Potatoes, 300
Lemon Coffee Cake, 166
Lemon Pork Chops, 261
✓Lemonade Slush, 28
Lime Cooler Bars, 205
Lime-Thyme Potato Wedges, 235
✓Low-Fat Chocolate Muffins, 223
Luau Chicken Sandwiches, 39

## M

Make-Ahead Burritos, 124
Mallow Fruit Salad, 79
Mandarin Orange Cream Pie, 205
Maple Apple Topping, 140
✓Maple Barbecued Chicken, 53
Marble Loaf Cake, 292
✓Marinated Artichoke Salad, 52
Marinated Sirloin Steak, 268
Mashed Potatoes, 105
Mayonnaise Chocolate Cake, 11
Meat Sauce for Pasta, 122
Meatball Stew, 264
Meaty Apple Skillet, 141
Mexican Rice Mix, 92
✓Microwave Mexican
  Manicotti, 275
Microwave Scalloped Potatoes, 274
✓Microwave Stroganoff, 31
Midnight Mashed Potatoes, 47
Mini Meat Loaves, 116
Mini Sausage Pizzas, 121
Miniature Castle Cakes, 37
Mint Sandwich Cookies, 89
Mixed Vegetable Bake, 145
Mocha Morning Drink, 304
Mocha Pie, 88
Mock Caesar Salad, 56
✓Moist Ham Loaf, 18
Monterey Ranch Bread, 51

*✓ Recipe includes Nutritional Analysis and Diabetic Exchanges*

Mountainous Mandarin Pie, 300
Mushroom Beef Patties, 234
Mushroom Beef Skillet, 111
✓Mushroom Green Beans, 308
Mushroom Haddock Loaf, 103
Mushroom Meatball Soup, 72
✓Mushroom Rice Pilaf, 72
Mushroom Round Steak, 258
✓Mustard Chicken Breasts, 280

## N

New Year's Surf 'n' Turf, 47
No-Bake Chocolate Cheesecake, 201
No-Bake Chocolate Cookies, 214
Noisemaker Appetizers, 47
No-Knead Casserole Bread, 163
No-Noodle Lasagna, 247
Nutty Cereal Crunch, 211
✓Nutty Wheat Bread, 179

## O

Oatmeal Breakfast Bars, 23
Omelet in a Mug, 274
Omelet with Cheese Sauce, 129
One-Pot Ham Dinner, 153
Onion-Chicken Stuffing Bake, 146
Open-Faced Sandwich Supreme, 76
Orange Banana Tapioca, 81
✓Orange Cashew Chicken, 153
Orange Chicken Supper, 79
✓Orange Chiffon Pie, 222
Orange Crispy Cookies, 211
Orange Poached Pears, 308
✓Orange Pork Stir-Fry, 224
✓Orange Roughy Bundles, 271
Orange Swirl Yogurt Pie, 115
Oven-Baked Burgers, 54

## P

Parmesan Corn Chowder, 192
Parmesan Herb Bread, 179
Party-Pleasing Beef Dish, 261
Pasta Carbonara, 151
Pasta Crab Egg Salad, 102
Peach-Glazed Cake, 52
Peachy Cream Pie, 90
Peanut Butter 'n' Jelly Mini
    Muffins, 174
Peanut Butter Chip Cookies, 13
Peanut Butter Chocolate Dessert, 88
Peanut Butter Cupcakes, 212
Peanut Butter Teddies, 253
Peanut Cereal Squares, 210

Peanut Ice Cream Squares, 121
Peanut Mallow Bars, 90
Pecan Chip Tube Cake, 91
Pecan Pear Muffins, 174
✓Penne from Heaven, 223
✓Pepper Jack Meat Loaf, 8
Pepper-Lime Pork Kabobs, 268
✓Pepper Pea Salad, 222
Pepper Steak Salad, 106
Pepper Steak Sandwiches, 192
✓Pepper Steak with Potatoes, 10
Peppermint Pretzel Dippers, 61
Pepperoni Angel Hair, 71
Pepperoni Drop Biscuits, 165
Personal Pepperoni Pizza, 328
Pesto Pasta, 69
Pesto Pizza, 329
Picnic Salad Skewers, 327
Pineapple Biscuits, 166
Pineapple Bread, 176
Pineapple Cheesecake, 202
✓Pineapple Chicken Lo Mein, 157
Pineapple Date Bread, 170
Pineapple Ham Spread, 59
Pineapple Ice Cream, 119
Pineapple Ice Pops, 249
Pineapple Lime Molds, 83
Pineapple-Onion Pork Chops, 300
Pineapple Pound Cake, 292
✓Pineapple Strawberry Punch, 60
Pizza Bread, 181
Pizza Cake, 244
Pizza Casserole, 262
Pizza Corn Dog Snacks, 242
Pizza Grilled Cheese, 250
Pizza Macaroni Bake, 84
Pizza Meat Loaf Cups, 125
Pizza Rigatoni, 259
Poppy Seed Biscuit Ring, 84
Poppy Seed Lemon Bread, 177
Poppy Seed Lemonade Muffins, 168
Popular Potluck Casserole, 145
Pork Chop 'n' Kraut Dinner, 291
Pork Chop Casserole, 51
Pork Chops and Kraut, 151
✓Pork Chops in Tomato Sauce, 228
Pork Chops with Apples, 157
Pork Chops with Baked Beans, 106
Pork Chops with Pears, 61
Pork Fried Rice, 108
Pork-Potato Meatballs, 232
✓Potato Bean Skillet, 228
Potato Chicken Packets, 271
Potato Chip Potatoes, 8

Potato Chocolate Cake, 105
Potato Ham Skillet, 70
Potato Pancakes, 122
Potato Rosettes, 117
Pound Cake Ring, 292
Pretzel-Topped Sugar Cookies, 210
Puddin' Cones, 241
Pumpkin Pancakes, 139
Purple Cows, 245

## Q

Quick 'n' Easy Lasagna, 61
Quick Baking Mix, 96
Quick Onion Bread, 165

## R

Raisin Bran Bread, 180
Raisin-Nut Baked Apples, 17
Raisin-Nut Chocolate Cake, 205
Ranch Eggs 'n' Biscuits, 133
Ranch Floret Salad, 287
Raspberry Chicken, 290
Raspberry Corn Bread Muffins, 173
Raspberry Icebox Dessert, 89
Raspberry Iced Tea, 307
✓Raspberry Yogurt Pie, 32
Red Cabbage Slaw, 286
Red-Hot Candy Fluff, 51
Red Pepper Chicken, 258
Red, White 'n' Blue Torte, 307
Reuben Burgers, 272
Reuben Meat Loaf, 325
Reuben Spread, 267
Rhubarb Dream Bars, 202
Ribs for Kids, 240
Roast Beef and Gravy, 257
Roasted Tarragon Asparagus, 24
Rocky Road Pudding, 22
✓Rosemary Chicken, 65
✓Round Steak Roll-Ups, 256

## S

✓S'more Parfaits, 57
Salmon Chowder, 72
Salmon in Lime Sauce, 269
Salmon with Chive
    Mayonnaise, 295
✓Salsa Rice, 58
Santa Fe Supper, 158
✓Saucy Orange Roughy, 283
Saucy Spareribs, 61
✓Sausage Chicken Soup, 282
✓Sausage Egg Pitas, 219

*✓ Recipe includes Nutritional Analysis and Diabetic Exchanges*

✓Sausage Egg Puff, 224
Sausage Hash Brown Bake, 129
✓Sausage Rice Skillet, 150
Sausage Shrimp Kabobs, 269
✓Sausage Spaghetti Spirals, 50
Sausage Swiss Muffins, 174
✓Sausage Tomato Soup, 195
Sausage Vermicelli, 237
✓Sausage with Corn Stuffing, 149
Savory Pork Roast, 108
Savory Sausage and Peppers, 156
Savory Sausage Bread, 166
Seasoned Green Beans, 32
Seasoned Taco Meat, 104
✓Sesame Chicken, 12
Shoepeg Corn Salad, 191
Shrimp Jambalaya, 157
Simple Guacamole, 69
✓Skewered Shrimp, 272
✓Skillet Olé, 225
Sloppy Joe Wagon Wheels, 249
Slow-Cooked Corn Chowder, 262
Slow-Cooked Pork Barbecue, 257
Smoked Salmon Quesadillas, 289
✓Smoky Corn Muffins, 82
Smothered Chicken, 73
✓Snow Pea Medley, 303
Southwest Sausage Bake, 135
✓Southwestern Spaghetti, 154
Spaghetti Ham Bake, 116
Special Grilled Veggies, 270
Speedy Beef Hash, 77
Speedy Southwest Salad, 66
✓Spiced Peaches, 219
Spicy Chicken Tomato Soup, 262
✓Spicy Lemon Chicken, 264
Spicy Meat Loaves, 325
Spinach Mushroom Salad, 184
Spinach Wild Rice Quiche, 108
Spiral Stromboli, 191
Spooky Spider Snacks, 251
Squash Stuffing Casserole, 266
Start-Ahead Stroganoff, 119
Start-Your-Engine Salad, 41
Steak Tortillas, 107
Stovetop Baked Beans, 106
Strawberry Cheesecake Trifle, 82
✓Strawberry Dip, 55
Strawberry Yogurt Shakes, 23
String Cheese Meat Loaf, 325

Stroganoff in a Bun, 237
Sugar Cookies, 331
Summer Steak Kabobs, 14
✓Sunny Chicken and Rice, 274
Sunset Cooler, 39
Surefire Sugar Cookies, 215
Surprise Cupcakes, 294
✓Sweet 'n' Sour Sausage, 260
Sweet Chocolate Bars, 212
Sweet Pineapple Sauce, 64
Sweet Potato Bread, 170
Sweet Sausage 'n' Beans, 265
Sweet Sesame Salad, 11
Sweetheart Trifle, 198
Swiss Macaroni, 148
Swiss Steak, 291

**T**

Taco Chicken Rolls, 58
Taco Dip Dragon, 37
Taco Meatballs, 245
Taco Pinwheels, 105
Taco Pizza Squares, 105
Taco Skillet, 156
Taco Soup, 33
✓Tacos on a Stick, 271
Tangy Cauliflower Salad, 68
Tangy Ham Steak, 273
Tangy Shrimp and Scallops, 321
✓Taste-of-Summer Chicken, 273
Tater Taco Casserole, 81
Tex-Mex Rice, 234
✓Thanksgiving in a Pan, 87
✓Three-Cheese Pasta Shells, 220
Toasted Coconut Pudding, 26
Toffee Brownie Trifle, 90
Toffee Oat Cookies, 213
Tomato and Beef Soup, 111
Tomato Bacon Pie, 56
Tortellini Alfredo, 78
Tossed Salad with Oranges, 13
Triple Berry Muffins, 173
Triple-Decker Salmon Club, 188
✓Tropical Fruit Salad, 130
Tropical Muffins, 165
✓Tuna Delight, 67
Tuna Noodle Cups, 245
Tuna Noodle Supreme, 148
Turkey Broccoli Hollandaise, 148
✓Turkey Cabbage Stew, 16

✓Turkey Crescents, 86
Turkey Dill Subs, 327
Turkey Dinner Muffins, 170
Turkey Lattice Pie, 297
✓Turkey Loaf, 226
Turkey Pea Skillet, 152
Turkey Rice Casserole, 282
✓Turkey Sloppy Joes, 220
✓Turkey Spinach Casserole, 218
Twice-Baked Ranch Potatoes, 121
Two-Cheese Quesadillas, 72

**U**

✓Unstuffed Cabbage, 149

**V**

✓Vegetable Bean Soup, 227
Vegetable Wild Rice, 108
✓Vegetarian Linguine, 158
✓Veggie Macaroni Salad, 225
Veggie Meatball Soup, 261
Veggie Pull-Apart Bread, 15
Veggie Tortilla Pinwheels, 303
Veggies and Ham, 150
✓Vibrant Veggie Stir-Fry, 226
✓Vinaigrette Vegetables, 26

**W**

Walnut Brownies, 95
Walnut Cinnamon Rolls, 170
Walnut-Rippled Coffee Cake, 78
Warm Fruit Compote, 136
Warm Shrimp Salad, 70
White Chili, 266
White Chocolate Pie, 293
White Rice Bread, 179
Whole-Grain Waffle Mix, 94
Wild Rice Bread, 108
Wilted Lettuce Salad, 31
Winner's Trophy Dessert, 41
Winter Vegetable Medley, 19

**Z**

Zippy Chicken Soup, 64
Zippy Pork Chops, 269
Zippy Sausage Spread, 56
Zucchini Cakes, 235
Zucchini Crisp, 206
Zucchini Pie, 236

*✓ Recipe includes Nutritional Analysis and Diabetic Exchanges*